Seventeenth Edition

World Politics
Trend and Transformation

Shannon Lindsey Blanton
University of Alabama at Birmingham

Charles William Kegley
Carnegie Council for Ethics in International Affairs

 CENGAGE

Australia • Brazil • Canada • Mexico • Singapore • United Kingdom • United States

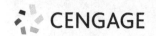

World Politics: Trend and Transformation,
Seventeenth Edition
Shannon Lindsey Blanton and Charles William Kegley

Product Director: Laura Ross

Associate Product Manager: Lauren Gerrish

Product Assistant: Haley Gaudreau

Marketing Director: Neena Bali

Senior Marketing Manager: Valerie Hartman

Senior Content Manager: Claire Branman

Learning Designer: Erika Hayden

Senior Subject Matter Expert: Emily Hickey

IP Analyst: Deanna Ettinger

IP Project Manager: Kelli Bessi

Production Service & Compositor: SPi Global

Senior Designer: Sarah Cole

Text and Cover Designer: Red Hangar Design

Cover Image: iStockPhoto.com/vladystock

For product information and technology assistance, contact us at Cengage **Customer & Sales Support, 1-800-354-9706** or **support.cengage.com**.

For permission to use material from this text or product, submit all requests online at **www.cengage.com/permissions**.

Library of Congress Control Number: 2019919326

Student Edition:
ISBN: 978-0-357-14180-9

Loose-leaf Edition:
ISBN: 978-0-357-14187-8

Cengage
200 Pier 4 Boulevard
Boston, MA 02210
USA

Cengage is a leading provider of customized learning solutions with employees residing in nearly 40 different countries and sales in more than 125 countries around the world. Find your local representative at **www.cengage.com**.

To learn more about Cengage platforms and services, register or access your online learning solution, or purchase materials for your course, visit **www.cengage.com**.

Printed at CLDPC, USA, 02-21

Brief Contents

Contents

PART I Trend and Transformation in World Politics

CHAPTER 1 Discovering World Politics 2

CHAPTER 2 Interpreting World Politics Through the Lens of Theory 22

CHAPTER 3 Theories of International Decision Making 54

Letter to Instructors

Dear International Relations Instructor:

Understanding world politics requires up-to-date information and analysis. In a constantly changing world, it is imperative for our students to develop the intellectual skills to be better global citizens and to analyze effectively key events and issues in international affairs. By presenting the leading ideas and the latest information available, *World Politics: Trend and Transformation* provides the tools necessary for understanding world affairs, for anticipating probable developments, and for thinking critically about the potential long-term impact of those developments on institutions, countries, and individuals across the globe.

World Politics aims to put both change and continuity into perspective. **It provides a picture of the evolving relations among all transnational actors, the historical developments that affect those actors' relationships, and the salient contemporary global trends that those interactions produce**. The key theories for understanding international relations—realism, liberalism, constructivism, as well as feminist and Marxist interpretations—frame the investigation. At the same time, this book presents all the complexities of world politics, as well as the necessary analytic tools to make sense of a wide range of substantive issues, from war to global finance to human rights. To foster critical thinking skills, the text provides evidence-based assessments and intentionally presents contending views—throughout the chapters, but especially in our **A Closer Look** and **Controversy** features—so that students have a chance to critically evaluate opposed positions and construct their own judgments about key issues. Moreover, our **enhanced video resource program**, provided in partnership with the Carnegie Council for Ethics in International Affairs (CCEIA), further highlights current international trends and transformations by applying *World Politics'* **key terms** and concepts in real-world applications.

New to this Edition

To keep you abreast of the latest developments, *World Politics: Trend and Transformation* continues to change in response to unfolding events around our world. Since publication of the 2016–2017 edition, numerous changes have taken place in international relations. To provide students with the most current information, we have revised the entire text of this seventeenth edition to incorporate the latest global events and scholarly research. Major changes include:

- Each chapter highlights Learning Objectives that serve as a guide to key concepts—at the start of the chapter, at the beginning of each corresponding section, and at the end of the chapter.

- A brand new Summary tied to the learning objectives is included at the end of each chapter to help students collect their thoughts about key concepts and issues, trend and transformation.

- Vibrant and engaging illustrations—thirty-seven new and updated maps, fifty-four new and updated figures, and a host of photos of real-world events—to provoke student interest and enable them to visualize central global developments through the most recently available data. Brand new to this edition are critical thinking questions following each map throughout the text.

- New and revised **A Closer Look** and **Controversy** features highlight real-world events and feature essential debates.

- New key terms—such as **counterterrorism**, **biodiversity hotspots**, and **transnational advocacy networks**, with definitions that appear in the text and the glossary—help students understand key concepts in the study of world politics.

- Expanded discussions of theories for understanding world politics, including enhanced discussions of a constructivist emphasis on affective sources of behavior, feminist perspectives of international relations, and hegemonic stability theory.

- Updated discussions of conflict and cooperation around the world, including the prospect of a resurgent Russia and an increasingly powerful China, terrorist groups such as the Islamic State, and international bodies such as the United Nations, International Court of Justice, and the International Criminal Court.

- Discussion of global trends, such as the challenge of fragile states, the consequences of youth bulges and aging populations, international crime and human trafficking, increased migration and the quest for human security, advances in global communications, and technological innovation.

- Discussion of the latest advances in military technology, including developments in artificial intelligence and autonomous weapons systems, growing prevalence of drones and the threat of information warfare, as well as a look at the changing nuclear environment in Iran and North Korea, the diffusion of civil war, and the role of peacekeeping in containing conflict.

- Updated discussions of the global political economy, including new coverage of cryptocurrencies, dilemmas in the wake of the 2008 global financial crisis, implications of the globalization of labor and increase in protectionist tendencies, the vision for the BRICS New Development Bank and the Asia Infrastructure Investment Bank, illicit financial flows, and the prospect of trade wars.

- Enhanced discussion of countering the spread of global diseases such as Ebola, the challenge of protecting human rights, implications of the global trend toward urbanization and megacities, the threat of identity politics and disinformation campaigns, climate change and environmental degradation, and the record number of forcibly displaced persons.

- New suggested resources for further investigation of world politics at the close of each chapter.

MindTap™

As an instructor, MindTap™ is here to simplify your workload, organize and immediately grade your students' assignments, and enable you to customize your course as you see fit. Through deep-seated integration with your Learning Management System, grades are easily exported and analytics are pulled with just the click of a button. MindTap™ provides you with a platform to easily add current events videos and article links from national or local news sources.

We thank you for using this book to help introduce your students to world politics. Our hope is that it helps students to critically analyze and understand global affairs—and to better assess the possibilities for the global future and its potential impact on their own lives.

Sincerely,

Shannon L. Blanton & Charles W. Kegley

Letter to Students

Dear Student:

In a constantly changing world, it is important to be able to analyze effectively key events and issues in international affairs, and to assess critically different viewpoints concerning these issues. By providing you with the leading ideas and the latest information available, *World Politics: Trend and Transformation* offers the tools necessary for understanding world affairs, for anticipating probable developments, and for thinking critically about the potential long-term impact of those developments on institutions, countries, and individuals across the globe. In essence, *World Politics* strives to help you become an informed global citizen and establish a foundation for life-long learning about international affairs.

World Politics aims to put both change and continuity into perspective. It provides a picture of the evolving relations among all transnational actors, the historical developments that affect those actors' relationships, and the salient contemporary global trends that those interactions produce. You will learn about key theories and worldviews for understanding international relations, and examine some of the most prominent issues in global politics, including war, terrorism, world trade, global finance, demographic trends, environmental degradation, and human rights. To facilitate your understanding, *World Politics* incorporates a number of features to clarify complex ideas and arguments:

- An **Atlas** with detailed political maps of each continent opens the book.

- **Learning Objectives** open each chapter, serving as a road map to the book's key concepts and helping you assess your understanding.

- **Controversy** features examine rival viewpoints on major international relations issues and encourage you to think critically and develop your own opinions.

- **A Closer Look** features address contemporary issues, pose critical thinking questions, and feature relevant videos through the Carnegie Council for Ethics in International Affairs (CCEIA).

- Each chapter includes key terms, their definitions, and pertinent videos through the Carnegie Council.

- Each chapter ends with a **Summary** of the learning objectives and a list of **Suggested Readings**, **Videos**, and **Web Resources** to help you prepare for your papers and essays.

As a student, the benefits of using MindTap with this book are endless. With automatically graded practice quizzes and activities, an easily navigated learning path, and an interactive eBook, you will be able to test yourself in and out of the classroom with ease. The accessibility of current events coupled with interactive media makes the content fun and engaging. On your computer, phone, or tablet, MindTap is there when you need it, giving you easy access to flashcards, quizzes, readings, and assignments.

We trust that you will find *World Politics: Trend and Transformation* to be an invaluable resource as you seek to learn more about global affairs. Whether the study of world politics is one among many interests that you are exploring as you earn your degree or a keen passion that may lead you to play an active role in shaping our world, this book is designed to provide you a comprehensive coverage of the trends and transformations that characterize international relations. It is our hope that as you conclude reading *World Politics* you will be as fascinated as we are with the complex dynamics of global interactions, and feel compelled to continue to observe, critically analyze, and address the challenges and opportunities that we share as members of a global community.

Sincerely,
Shannon L. Blanton & Charles W. Kegley

Resources for Students and Instructors

Students

Cengage Unlimited

Cengage Unlimited is the first-of-its-kind digital subscription that empowers students to learn more for less. One student subscription includes total access to every Cengage online textbook, platform, career and college success centers, and more—in one place. Learn across courses and disciplines with confidence that you won't pay more to access more. Available now in bookstores and online. Details at www.cengage.com/unlimited.

Access your World Politics, Seventeenth Edition *resources via www.cengage.com/login.*

If you purchased MindTap™ access with your book, click on "Register a Product" and then enter your access code.

Instructors

Access your World Politics, Seventeenth Edition *resources via www.cengage.com/login.*

Log in using your Cengage Learning single sign-on user name and password, or create a new instructor account by clicking on "New Faculty User" and following the instructions.

CENGAGE | MINDTAP

MindTap™ for *World Politics*, Seventeenth Edition

ISBN for Instant Access Code: 9780357141830
ISBN for Printed Access Code: 9780357141847

MindTap™ for *World Politics, Seventeenth Edition* is a highly personalized, fully online learning experience built on Cengage content correlated to a core set of learning outcomes. MindTap™ guides students through the course curriculum via an innovative Learning Path Navigator where they will complete reading assignments, challenge themselves with focus activities, and engage with interactive quizzes. Through a variety of gradable activities, MindTap™ provides students with opportunities to check themselves for where they need extra help, as well as allowing faculty to measure and assess student progress. Integration with platforms like YouTube and Google Drive enables instructors to add and remove content of their choosing with ease. The product can be used fully online with its interactive eBook for *World Politics, Seventeenth Edition*, or in conjunction with the printed text.

MindTap™ Resource Center

Thousands of primary and secondary sources at your fingertips! Access to Gale's authoritative library reference content is now available in every Political Science MindTap™. Gale, part of Cengage, has been providing research and education resources for libraries for over 60 years.

As an instructor, you have the option to choose from thousands of primary and secondary sources, images, and videos to enhance your MindTap™ course with the click of a button. This capability can replace a separate reader and conveniently keeps all course materials in one place. The selections are curated by experts, designed specifically for introductory courses, and can be accessed through the MindTap™ Activity Builder feature.

Instructor Companion Website for *World Politics, Seventeenth Edition*—for Instructors Only

ISBN: 9780357141816

This Instructor Companion Website is an all-in-one multimedia online resource for class preparation, presentation, and testing. Accessible through Cengage.com/login with your faculty account, you will find available for download: book-specific Microsoft® PowerPoint® presentations; a Test Bank compatible with multiple learning management systems (LMSs); and an Instructor's Manual.

The Test Bank, offered in Blackboard, Moodle, Desire2Learn, Canvas, and Angel formats, contains Learning Objective–specific multiple-choice and essay questions for each chapter. Import the Test Bank into your LMS to edit and manage questions and to create tests.

The Instructor's Manual contains chapter-specific Learning Objectives, an outline, key terms with definitions, and a chapter summary. Additionally, the Instructor's Manual features a critical thinking question, lecture-launching suggestion, and an in-class activity for each Learning Objective.

The Microsoft® PowerPoint® presentations are ready-to-use, visual outlines of each chapter. These presentations are easily customized for your lectures. Access the Instructor Companion Website at www.cengage.com/login.

Cognero for *World Politics, Seventeenth Edition*

ISBN: 9780357141861

Cengage Testing Powered by Cognero is a flexible, online system that allows you to author, edit, and manage Test Bank content from multiple Cengage solutions; create multiple test versions in an instant; and deliver tests from your LMS, your classroom, or wherever you want. The Test Bank for *World Politics, Seventeenth Edition*, contains learning objective–specific multiple-choice and essay questions for each chapter.

Acknowledgments

Many people—in fact, too many to identify and thank individually—have contributed to the development of this leading textbook in international relations. We are thankful for the constructive comments, advice, and data provided by an array of scholars and colleagues.

Reviewers for this Edition

Daniel S. Geller, Wayne State University
Nicholas Giordano, Suffolk County Community College
Walter Hill, St. Mary's College of Maryland
Mir Husain, University of South Alabama
Baris Kesgin, Elon University
Anip Uppal, Central New Mexico Community College

Past Reviewers and Other Contributors

Duane Adamson, Brigham Young University–Idaho
Daniel Allen, Anderson University
Ruchi Anand, American Graduate School in Paris
Osmo Apunen, University of Tampere
Bossman Asare, Graceland University
Chad Atkinson, University of Illinois
Andrew J. Bacevich, Boston University
Yan Bai, Grand Rapids Community College
Katherine Barbieri, University of South Carolina
George Belzer, Johnson County Community College
John Boehrer, University of Washington
Pamela Blackmon, Penn State Altoona
Austin Blanton, Auburn University
Cullen M. Blanton, Hoover High School
Robert G. Blanton, University of Alabama at Birmingham
Linda P. Brady, University of North Carolina at Greensboro
Leann Brown, University of Florida
Dan Caldwell, Pepperdine University
John H. Calhoun, Palm Beach Atlantic University
John Candido, La Trobe University
Colin S. Cavell, Bluefield State College
Roger A. Coate, Georgia College & State University
Jonathan E. Colby, Carlyle Group, Washington, D.C.
Phyllis D. Collins, Keswick Management Inc., New York City
Christopher R. Cook, University of Pittsburgh at Johnstown
Reverend George Crow, Northeast Presbyterian Church

Rebecca Cruise, University of Oklahoma
Jonathan Davidson, European Commission
Philippe Dennery, J-Net Ecology Communication Company, Paris
Drew Dickson, Atlantic Council of the United States
Agber Dimah, Chicago State University
Gregory Domin, Mercer University
Thomas Donaldson, Wharton School of the University of Pennsylvania
Nicole Detraz, University of Memphis
Zach Dorfman, Carnegie Council for Ethics in International Affairs
Ayman I. El-Dessouki and Kamal El-Menoufi, Cairo University
Sid Ellington, University of Oklahoma
Robert Fatton, University of Virginia
Matthias Finger, Columbia University
John Freeman, University of Minnesota–Minneapolis
Eytan Gilboa, Bar-Ilan University in Israel
Giovanna Gismondi, University of Oklahoma
Srdjan Gligorijevic, Defense and Security Studies Centre, G-17 Plus Institute, Belgrade, Serbia
Richard F. Grimmett, Congressional Research Office
Ted Robert Gurr, University of Maryland
Aref N. Hassan, St. Cloud State University
Russell Hardin, New York University
James E. Harf, Maryville University
Cristian A. Harris, North Georgia College and State University
Charles Hermann, Texas A&M University
Margaret G. Hermann, Syracuse University
Stephen D. Hibbard, Shearman & Sterling, LLP
Steven W. Hook, Kent State University
Jack Hurd, Nature Conservatory
Ashley Brooke Huddleston, University of Memphis
Lisa Huffstetler, University of Memphis
Patrick James, University of Southern California
Loch Johnson, University of Georgia
Christopher M. Jones, Northern Illinois University

Christopher Joyner, Georgetown University
Boris Khan, American Military University
Michael D. Kanner, University of Colorado
Mahmoud Karem, Egyptian Foreign Service
Deborah J. Kegley, Kegley International, Inc.
Mary V. Kegley, Kegley Books, Wytheville, Virginia
Susan Kegley, University of California–Berkeley
Julia Kennedy, Carnegie Council for Ethics in
    International Affairs
Lidija Kos-Stanišic, University of Zagreb
Matthias Kranke, University of Trier
Barbara Kyker, University of Memphis
Imtiaz T. Ladak, Projects International, Washington, D.C.
Jack Levy, Rutgers University
Carol Li, Taipei Economic and Cultural Office, New York
Alexis Lincoln, University of Alabama at Birmingham
Urs Luterbacher, Graduate Institute of International and
    Development Studies, Geneva
Gen. Jeffrey D. McCausland, U.S. Army War College
James McCormick, Iowa University
Kelly A. McCready, Maria College
Karen Ann Mingst, University of Kentucky
James A. Mitchell, California State University
Shea Mize, Georgia Highlands College
Mahmood Monshipouri, San Francisco State University
Robert Morin, Western Nevada College
Donald Munton, University of Northern British Columbia
Todd Myers, Grossmont College
Ahmad Noor, Youth Parliament Pakistan
Evan O'Neil, Carnegie Council for Ethics in International
    Affairs
Anthony Perry, Henry Ford Community College
Jeffrey Pickering, Kansas State University
Desley Sant Parker, United States Information Agency
Albert C. Pierce, U.S. Naval Academy
Alex Platt, Carnegie Council for Ethics in International
    Affairs
Ignacio de la Rasilla, Université de Genève
James Ray, Vanderbilt University
Gregory A. Raymond, Boise State University
Andreas Rekdal, Carnegie Council for Ethics in
    International Affairs

Neil R. Richardson, University of Wisconsin
Peter Riddick, Berkhamsted School
Jeff Ringer, Brigham Young University
James N. Rosenau, George Washington University
Joel Rosenthal, Carnegie Council for Ethics in
    International Affairs
Thomas E. Rotnem, Southern Polytechnic State
    University
Tapani Ruokanen, Suomen Kuvalehti, Finland
Alpo M. Rusi, Finnish Ambassador to Switzerland
Jan Aart Scholte, University of Warwick, UK
Rebecca R. Sharitz, International Association for
    Ecology
Shalendra D. Sharma, University of San Francisco
Richard H. Shultz, Fletcher School of Law and
    Diplomacy, Tufts University
Dragan R. Simić, Centre for the Study of the United
    States, University of Belgrade
Michael J. Siler, University of California
Christopher Sprecher, Texas A&M University
Jelena Subotic, Georgia State University
Bengt Sundelius, National Defense College, Stockholm
David Sylvan, Graduate Institute of International and
    Development Studies, Geneva
William R. Thompson, Indiana University
Clayton L. Thyne, University of Kentucky
Rodney Tomlinson, U.S. Naval Academy
Deborah Tompsett-Makin, Riverside Community
    College, Norco Campus
John Tuman, University of Nevada, Las Vegas
Denise Vaughan, Bellevue Community College
Rob Verhofstad, Radboud University
William C. Vocke, Jr., Carnegie Council for Ethics in
    International Affairs
William Wagstaff, USAF Center for Strategy and
    Technology
Seth Weinberger, University of Puget Sound
Robert Weiner, University of Massachusetts–Boston
Jonathan Wilkenfeld, University of Maryland
Alex Woodson, Carnegie Council for Ethics in
    International Affairs
Samuel A. Worthington, InterAction

Also helpful was the input provided by Honors undergraduate student Lyndsey Shelton at the University of Alabama at Birmingham, who provided invaluable research assistance. The always helpful and accommodating Project Manager Phil Scott with SPi Global, and Photo Researcher Sujatha Selvakumar with Lumina Datamatics, made valuable contributions to this book. In addition, our highly skilled, dedicated, and helpful editors at Cengage deserve special gratitude: Lauren Gerrish, Associate Product Manager, and Claire Branman, Senior Content Manager, exercised extraordinary professionalism in guiding the process that brought this edition into print. Gratitude is also expressed to the always instructive advice of Valerie Hartman, Cengage's skilled Political Science Senior Marketing Manager.

About the Authors

Courtesy of Shannon L. Blanton and Charles W. Kegley.

SHANNON LINDSEY BLANTON is a Professor in the Department of Political Science & Public Administration at the University of Alabama at Birmingham, where she is also the inaugural Dean of the UAB Honors College. Dr. Blanton is a past vice provost for undergraduate programs, department chair, and undergraduate coordinator and has served nationally as a facilitator for leadership development in higher education. A graduate of Georgia College (BA), the University of Georgia (MA), and the University of South Carolina (PhD), Dr. Blanton has received numerous research awards and professional recognitions. She has served on a number of editorial boards, including those for five of the discipline's foremost journals: *International Studies Quarterly, Foreign Policy Analysis, International Interactions, International Studies Perspectives,* and *International Studies Review.* Dr. Blanton has published articles on U.S. foreign policy decision making, with a particular focus on the determinants and consequences of U.S. arms transfers and foreign aid. Her work has also examined the significance of human rights concerns in global political and economic interactions.

CHARLES WILLIAM KEGLEY is a past president of the International Studies Association and has been serving the past two decades on the Board of Trustees of the Carnegie Council for Ethics in International Affairs. Dr. Kegley holds the title of Pearce Distinguished Professor of International Relations Emeritus at the University of South Carolina. A graduate of American University (BA) and Syracuse University (PhD) and a Pew Faculty Fellow at Harvard University, Kegley previously served on the faculty at Georgetown University, and has held visiting professorships at the University of Texas, Rutgers University, the People's University of China, and the Institute Universitaire de Hautes Études Internationales Et du Développement in Geneva, Switzerland. He is also a recipient of the Distinguished Scholar Award of the Foreign Policy Analysis Section of the International Studies Association. A founding partner of Kegley International, Inc., a publishing, research, and consulting foundation, Dr. Kegley has authored more than fifty scholarly books and more than one hundred articles in journals.

Professors Blanton and Kegley have individually published extensively in leading scholarly journals, including *Alternatives, American Journal of Political Science, Armed Forces and Society, Asian Forum, The Brown Journal of International Affairs, Business and Society, Comparative Political Studies, Conflict Management and Peace Science, Conflict Quarterly, Cooperation and Conflict, Ethics and International Affairs, Feminist Economics, Politics and Gender, The Fletcher Forum of World Affairs, Foreign Policy Analysis, Futures Research Quarterly, Harvard International Review, International Interactions, International Organization, International Politics, International Studies Quarterly, Jerusalem Journal of International Relations, Journal of Conflict Resolution, Journal of Peace Research, Journal of Politics, Journal of Political and Military Sociology, Journal of Third World Studies, Korean Journal of International Studies, Leadership, Orbis, Political Research Quarterly, Social Science Journal, Sociological Forum,* and *Western Political Quarterly.*

Together Blanton and Kegley have coauthored publications appearing in the *Brown Journal of World Affairs, Futures Research Quarterly, Mediterranean Quarterly,* and *Rethinking the Cold War,* as well as multiple editions of *World Politics* (since the twelfth edition's 2009-2010 update).

Dedication

To my husband Rob and our sons Austin and Cullen,
in deep appreciation of their love and support
—*Shannon Lindsey Blanton*

To my loving wife Debbie
And to the Carnegie Council for Ethics in International Affairs,
in appreciation for its invaluable contribution to building through
education a more just and secure world
—*Charles William Kegley*

WORLD

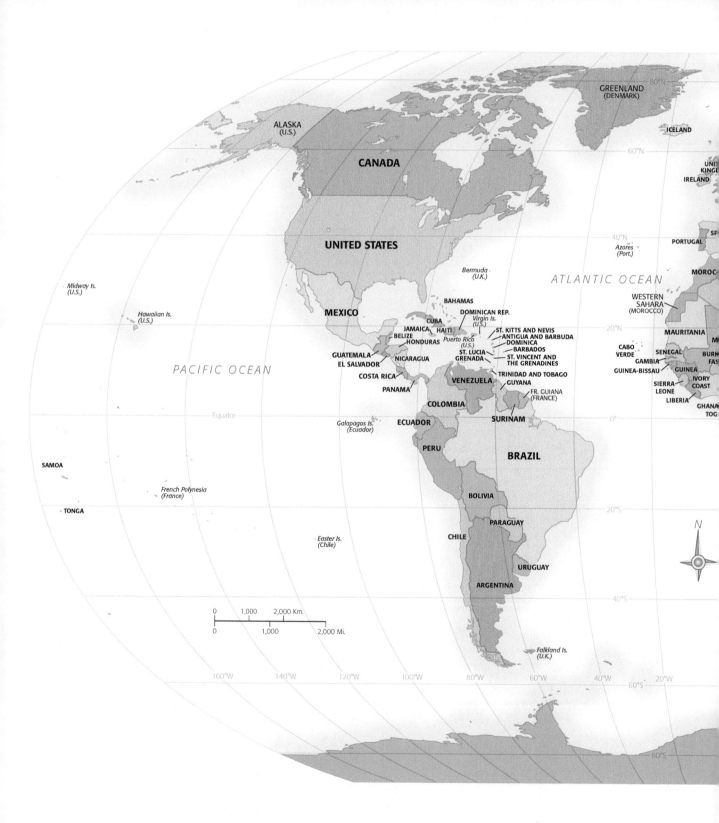

ALASKA
(U.S.)

GREENLAND
(DENMARK)

ICELAND

CANADA

60°N

UNITED
KINGDOM

IRELAND

40°N

UNITED STATES

Azores
(Port.)

PORTUGAL

SP

Bermuda
(U.K.)

ATLANTIC OCEAN

MOROC

Midway Is.
(U.S.)

WESTERN
SAHARA
(MOROCCO)

Hawaiian Is.
(U.S.)

MEXICO

BAHAMAS

DOMINICAN REP.

CUBA

Virgin Is.
(U.S.)

20°N

MAURITANIA

JAMAICA

HAITI

ST. KITTS AND NEVIS

CABO
VERDE

SENEGAL

BELIZE

Puerto Rico
(U.S.)

ANTIGUA AND BARBUDA

BURK
FAS

HONDURAS

DOMINICA

GAMBIA

GUATEMALA

ST. LUCIA

BARBADOS

GUINEA-BISSAU

GUINEA

EL SALVADOR

NICARAGUA

GRENADA

ST. VINCENT AND

SIERRA
LEONE

IVORY
COAST

PACIFIC OCEAN

THE GRENADINES

COSTA RICA

TRINIDAD AND TOBAGO

LIBERIA

GHANA

PANAMA

VENEZUELA

GUYANA

TOG

COLOMBIA

FR. GUIANA
(FRANCE)

SURINAM

0°

Equator

Galapagos Is.
(Ecuador)

ECUADOR

SAMOA

PERU

BRAZIL

French Polynesia
(France)

BOLIVIA

20°S

TONGA

PARAGUAY

Easter Is.
(Chile)

CHILE

URUGUAY

ARGENTINA

40°S

0   1,000   2,000 Km.

0   1,000   2,000 Mi.

Falkland Is.
(U.K.)

N

60°S

160°W   140°W   120°W   100°W   80°W   60°W   40°W   20°W

80°S

ARCTIC OCEAN

NORWAY
SWEDEN FINLAND
ESTONIA
DEN.
LATVIA
LITHUANIA
GERMANY POLAND BELARUS
LUX.
CZ.
SLK.
AUS. HUNG. UKRAINE
SLN.CR. ROMANIA MOLDOVA
B. H.
SE.
ITALY MO. BULGARIA
ALBANIA K. NMAC.
GREECE
TUNISIA MALTA
CYPRUS

RUSSIA

KAZAKHSTAN

MONGOLIA

N. KOREA

PACIFIC OCEAN

S. KOREA JAPAN

NIGERIA LIBYA EGYPT

NIGER CHAD SUDAN

BENIN
NIGERIA

CAMEROON

EQ.
NEA

GABON

SÃO TOMÉ
PRÍNCIPE

CENTRAL
AFRICAN REP.

REP. OF
CONGO

RWANDA
DEM. REP.
OF CONGO

BURUNDI

ANGOLA

NAMIBIA

BOTSWANA

ZAMBIA

ZIMBABWE

SOUTH
AFRICA

LESOTHO

ESWATINI

MOZAMBIQUE

UGANDA KENYA

TANZANIA

MALAWI

MADAGASCAR

COMOROS

SEYCHELLES

MAURITIUS

ERITREA

DJIBOUTI

ETHIOPIA

SOMALIA

YEMEN

TURKEY ARMENIA
AZERBAIJAN
SYRIA
LEBANON
ISRAEL IRAQ
JORDAN
KUWAIT
BAHRAIN
QATAR
SAUDI
ARABIA
UNITED
ARAB EMIRATES OMAN

GEORGIA

TURKMENISTAN

UZBEKISTAN

KYRGYZSTAN

TAJIKISTAN

AFGHANISTAN

IRAN

PAKISTAN

NEPAL

INDIA

BHUTAN

PEOPLE'S REPUBLIC OF CHINA

Taiwan

BANGLADESH

MYANMAR
(BURMA)

LAOS

THAILAND

CAMBODIA
(KAMPUCHEA)

VIETNAM

PHILIPPINES

SRI LANKA

MALDIVES

BRUNEI
DARUSSALAM

MALAYSIA

PALAU

SINGAPORE

INDIAN OCEAN

INDONESIA

TIMOR LESTE

PAPUA
NEW
GUINEA

Mariana
Islands
(U.S.)

Guam
(U.S.)

FEDERATED STATES
OF MICRONESIA

Wake I.
(U.S.)

MARSHALL
ISLANDS

KIRIBATI

NAURU

SOLOMON IS.

TUVALU

VANUATU

FIJI

New Caledonia
(France)

AUSTRALIA

NEW
ZEALAND

ABBREVIATIONS	
AUS.	AUSTRIA
BEL.	BELGIUM
B. H.	BOSNIA AND HERZEGOVINA
CR.	CROATIA
CZ.	CZECHIA
DEN.	DENMARK
EQ. GUINEA	EQUATORIAL GUINEA
HUNG.	HUNGARY
K.	KOSOVO
LUX.	LUXEMBOURG
NMAC.	NORTH MACEDONIA
MO.	MONTENEGRO
NETH.	NETHERLANDS
SE.	SERBIA
SLK.	SLOVAKIA
SLN.	SLOVENIA
SWITZ.	SWITZERLAND

20°E   40°E   60°E   80°E   100°E   120°E   140°E   160°E

NORTH AMERICA

RUSSIA

ARCTIC
OCEAN

ICELAND

Qaanaaq
(Thule)

GREENLAND
(Denmark)

Barrow

Nome

Prudhoe
Bay

Illulissat
(Jakobshavn)

Tasiilaq

ALASKA
(U.S.)

Resolute

Pond Inlet

Sisimiut
(Holsteinsborg)

Bethel

Fairbanks

Inuvik

Cambridge
Bay

Nuuk
(Godthåb)

Qaqortoq
(Julianehåb)

Anchorage
Valdez

Dawson

Gjoa
Haven

Whitehorse

Iqaluit

Juneau

Rankin
Inlet

Kuujjuaq

Fort Nelson

Arviat

Hudson
Bay

Happy Valley-
Goose Bay

St. John's

Prince
George

Fort
McMurray

Churchill

Chisasibi

Edmonton

CANADA

Sydney

Saskatoon

Moosonee

Chicoutimi
(Saguenay)

Charlottetown

Vancouver

Calgary

Regina

Winnipeg

Thunder
Bay

Québec

Fredericton

Moncton

Victoria

Great
Lakes

Montréal

Halifax
St. John

Seattle

Missouri R.

Ottawa

Portland

Fargo

ROCKY MOUNTAINS

Toronto

Buffalo

Boston
Providence
Hartford
New York

Boise

Minneapolis

Milwaukee

Detroit

Pittsburgh

Philadelphia

UNITED STATES

Chicago

Cleveland

Baltimore

Salt Lake
City

Omaha

Columbus

Cincinnati

Washington, D.C.

San Francisco

Sacramento
San Jose

Denver

Kansas City

Indianapolis

Ohio

APPALACHIAN MTS.

Virginia Beach

Fresno

Colorado

St. Louis

Louisville

Arkansas R.

Charlotte

Las Vegas

Oklahoma
City

Nashville

Los Angeles

Albuquerque

Memphis

ATLANTIC
OCEAN

San Diego

Phoenix

Birmingham

Atlanta

PACIFIC
OCEAN

Tijuana

Mexicali

Tucson

Dallas

El Paso

Jacksonville

Ciudad
Juárez

Austin

Houston

New Orleans

Orlando

Hermosillo

San
Antonio

Tampa

Chihuahua

Rio Grande

Miami

Tropic of Cancer

Torreón

Monterrey

Gulf of
Mexico

La Paz

Culiacán

MEXICO

Matamoros

CUBA

San Luis Potosí

HAITI

Aguascalientes

León

Tampico

Cancun

Guadalajara

Querétaro

Mérida

JAMAICA

DOMINICAN
REPUBLIC

Morelia

Veracruz

Toluca

México

Caribbean Sea

Acapulco

Oaxaca

BELIZE

GUATEMALA HONDURAS
EL SALVADOR

140°W

120°W

100°W

80°W

60°W

40°W

20°N

40°N

60°N

Arctic
Circle

Columbia R.

Mississippi R.

N

0   300   600 Km.

0   300   600 Mi.

ATLANTIC OCEAN

N

UNITED STATES

Houston

New Orleans

Monterrey

MEXICO

Miami

BAHAMAS

Gulf of Mexico

Havana

CUBA

HAITI

DOMINICAN REP.

Mexico City

Veracruz

Guantánamo

Port-au-Prince

20°N

Acapulco

BELIZE

HONDURAS

JAMAICA

Santo Domingo

Puerto Rico (U.S.)

Guadeloupe (Fr.)

GUATEMALA

NICARAGUA

Managua

Caribbean Sea

Martinique (Fr.)

EL SALVADOR

Panama City

ST. VINCENT

BARBADOS

GRENADA

COSTA RICA

TRINIDAD & TOBAGO

100°W

PANAMA

Caracas

VENEZUELA

GUYANA

Georgetown

Panama Canal

Paramaribo

FRENCH GUIANA (Fr.)

Bogotá

COLOMBIA

SURINAME

Galápagos Islands (Ec.)

Quito

ECUADOR

Negro R.

Equator 0°

Manaus

Amazon R.

BRAZIL

Madeira R.

Recife

PACIFIC OCEAN

PERU

Lima

Lake Titicaca

Brasília

La Paz

BOLIVIA

20°S

PARAGUAY

Rio de Janeiro

CHILE

Asunción

São Paulo

Paraná R.

URUGUAY

Santiago

Montevideo

ARGENTINA

Buenos Aires

0   500   1000 Km.

0   500   1000 Mi.

Falkland Islands (Gr. Br.)

Cape Horn

80°W   60°W   40°W

AFRICA

EUROPE

Madeira Is.
(Portugal)

Black Sea

Mediterranean Sea

TURKEY

⊛Rabat   ⊛Algiers   Tunis
MOROCCO   TUNISIA   •Tripoli

CYPRUS   SYRIA
LEBANON   ⊛Baghdad   I R A N
ISRAEL   IRAQ   KUWAIT
Alexandria•   JORDAN

Canary Is.
(Spain)

WESTERN
SAHARA
(MOROCCO)

ALGERIA   LIBYA

EGYPT
⊛Cairo

BAHRAIN
SAUDI   QATAR
ARABIA

OMAN

Tropic of Cancer

UNITED
ARAB
EMIRATES

20°N

OMAN

CABO
VERDE

MAURITANIA

MALI

NIGER   CHAD

SUDAN
⊛Khartoum

ERITREA   YEMEN

Dakar⊛
THE GAMBIA   SENEGAL
Bamako⊛
GUINEA-BISSAU   GUINEA   BURKINA
FASO
Freetown⊛   CÔTE
SIERRA LEONE   D'IVOIRE
Monrovia⊛   GHANA
LIBERIA   Abidjan⊛ ⊛Accra

NIGERIA
⊛N'Djamena
Lagos•
BENIN
TOGO
Benue R.

CENTRAL
AFRICAN
REPUBLIC

SOUTH
SUDAN
⊛Juba

DJIBOUTI

Addis
Ababa⊛

ETHIOPIA

SOMALIA

CAMEROON

Uele R.
Congo R.

UGANDA
Kampala⊛

⊛Mogadishu

0° Equator

EQUATORIAL GUINEA
SÃO TOMÉ &
PRÍNCIPE

GABON   REP. CONGO

DEM. REP.
CONGO

RWANDA
BURUNDI

KENYA
⊛Nairobi

SEYCHELLES

Brazzaville⊛
Kinshasa⊛

Lake
Tanganyika

Lake
Victoria

TANZANIA

Zanzibar (Gr. Br.)
⊛Dar es Salaam

(ANGOLA)

Luanda⊛

ATLANTIC
OCEAN

COMOROS

ANGOLA

ZAMBIA
Lusaka⊛

Lake
Malawi

MALAWI

MADAGASCAR

⊛Antananarivo

Zambezi R.
Harare⊛
ZIMBABWE   MOZAMBIQUE

MAURITIUS
Tropic of Capricorn

20°S

NAMIBIA

BOTSWANA

Pretoria⊛
Johannesburg⊛   ⊛Maputo
ESWATINI

INDIAN
OCEAN

N

SOUTH
AFRICA
Cape Town⊛
Cape of
Good Hope

•Durban
LESOTHO

0   400   800 Km.

0   400   800 Mi.

ATLANTIC OCEAN

ICELAND
Reykjavik

Faroe Islands (Den.)
Shetland Islands (U.K.)

North Sea

Glasgow
UNITED KINGDOM
London
NORTHERN IRELAND
IRELAND
Dublin

NORWAY
Oslo

SWEDEN
Stockholm

FINLAND
Helsinki

Arctic Circle

RUSSIA
Moscow
St. Petersburg
Lake Ladoga
Volga R.
Don R.
Kharkov
Donetsk

KAZAKHSTAN
Aral Sea

UZBEKISTAN

TURKMENISTAN

Caspian Sea
Baku
AZERBAIJAN
AZER.
ARMENIA
Yerevan
GEORGIA
Tbilisi

IRAN
IRAQ
KUWAIT
SAUDI ARABIA

SYRIA
LEBANON
ISRAEL
WEST BANK
GAZA
JORDAN
Nicosia
CYPRUS

TURKEY
Ankara
Istanbul

EGYPT

Black Sea

Tallinn
ESTONIA
Riga
LATVIA
LITHUANIA
Vilnius
(RUSSIA)

Minsk
BELARUS

Kiev
UKRAINE
Dnieper R.
Dnepropetrovsk
Odessa
Chisinau
MOLDOVA

ROMANIA
Bucharest
Danube R.

BULGARIA
Sofia

Athens
GREECE
Crete (Gr.)

Copenhagen
DENMARK
Hamburg
Elbe R.
Baltic Sea
Gdansk
POLAND
Warsaw
Vistula R.

Berlin
GERMANY
Bonn
Leipzig
Frankfurt
Amsterdam
NETHERLANDS
Brussels
BELGIUM
LUX.
Luxembourg
Paris
Seine R.

Prague
CZECHIA
Munich
Stuttgart
Vienna
AUSTRIA
SLOVAKIA
Bratislava
Budapest
HUNGARY
LIECH.
Vaduz
SWITZ.
Zurich
Bern
Geneva
Ljubljana
SLOVENIA
Zagreb
CROATIA

Milan
Po R.
Turin
Lyons
Loire R.
FRANCE

Rhone R.

MONACO
Monaco
Corsica (Fr.)

San Marino
SAN MARINO
Rome
ITALY
VATICAN CITY
Naples
Sardinia (It.)

Sicily (It.)

Mediterranean Sea

Valletta MALTA

BOSNIA & HERZEGOVINA
Sarajevo
SERBIA
Belgrade
MONT.
Podgorica
KOSOVO
Pristina
ALBANIA
Tiranë
NORTH MACEDONIA
Skopje

ANDORRA
Andorra la Vella
Barcelona
Balearic Islands (Sp.)

SPAIN
Madrid
Tagus R.
Gibraltar (U.K.)

PORTUGAL
Porto
Lisbon

MOROCCO
ALGERIA
TUNISIA
LIBYA

N

60N
50N
70N
40N

80E
70E
60E
50E
40E
30E
20E
10E
0
10W
20W
30W

0 200 400 Km.
0 200 400 Mi.

ASIA

PACIFIC OCEAN

KAMCHATKA PENINSULA

Sea of Okhotsk

Sakhalin

Sea of Japan (East Sea)

NORTH KOREA

Pyongyang

SOUTH KOREA

Seoul

JAPAN

Tokyo
Nagoya
Osaka
Kitakyushu

Harbin

Shenyang

Yellow Sea

Beijing
Tianjin

Nanjing

Shanghai
Hangzhou
Suzhou

East China Sea

Taiwan

CHINA

Xi'an

Wuhan

Chengdu

Chongqing

Guangzhou Dongguan
Foshan Shenzhen
Hong Kong

Hainan

South China Sea

East China Sea

Manila

PHILIPPINES

INDONESIA

TIMOR-LESTE

Dili

Bandar Seri Begawan

BRUNEI

MALAYSIA

Kuala Lumpur

Singapore

Borneo

Sumatra

Jakarta

Java

VIETNAM

Ho Chi Minh City

LAOS

Vientiane

THAILAND

Bangkok

CAMBODIA

Phnom Penh

MYANMAR

Naypyidaw

Yangon

MONGOLIA

Ulaanbaatar

GOBI

Lake Baikal

SIBERIA

RUSSIA

Moscow

URAL MTS.

KAZAKHSTAN

Nur-Sultan

Bishkek

KYRGYZSTAN

Tashkent

UZBEKISTAN

Dushanbe

TAJIKISTAN

TURKMENISTAN

Ashgabat

Aral Sea

Caspian Sea

Tehran

IRAN

AFGHANISTAN

Kabul

PAKISTAN

Islamabad

Lahore

Delhi
New Delhi

Karachi

INDIA

Ahmadabad

Surat

Mumbai

Pune

Hyderabad

Bangalore

Chennai

Arabian Sea

BHUTAN

Thimphu

NEPAL

Kathmandu

HIMALAYA MTS.

BANGLADESH

Dhaka

Kolkata

Bay of Bengal

SRI LANKA

Colombo

MALDIVES

Male

INDIAN OCEAN

OMAN

Muscat

Abu Dhabi

UNITED ARAB EMIRATES

Doha

QATAR

Manama

BAHRAIN

Riyadh

SAUDI ARABIA

Kuwait

KUWAIT

Baghdad

IRAQ

YEMEN

Sanaa

Red Sea

Black Sea

Ankara

TURKEY

Nicosia

CYPRUS

Beirut

LEBANON

Damascus

SYRIA

Jerusalem

ISRAEL

Amman

JORDAN

GEORGIA

Tbilisi

ARMENIA

Yerevan

Baku

AZERBAIJAN

N

Equator

0°

40°N

60°N

20°N

0°

140°E

120°E

100°E

80°E

60°E

1000 Mi.

1000 Km.

500

500

0

0

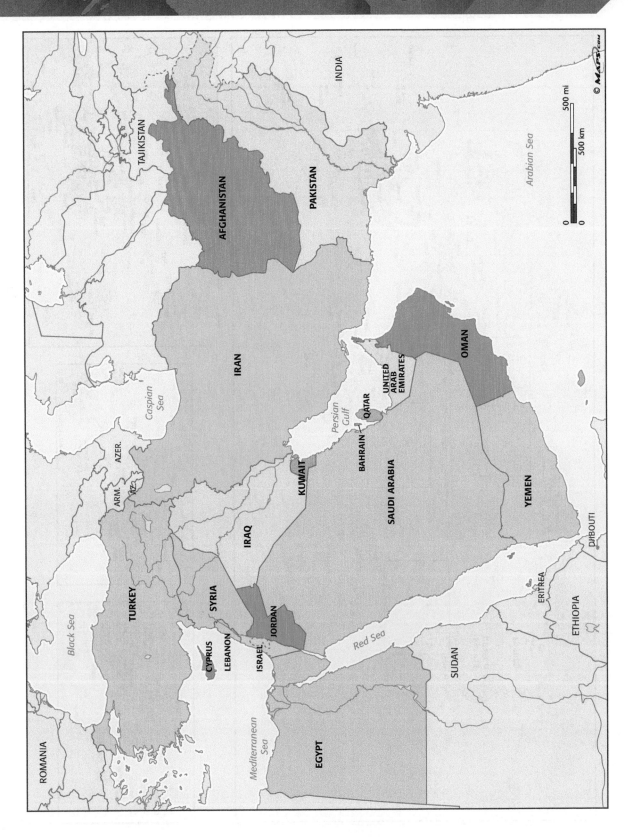

© MAPS.com

500 mi

500 km

INDIA

Arabian Sea

TAJIKISTAN

AFGHANISTAN

PAKISTAN

IRAN

OMAN

UNITED ARAB EMIRATES

Caspian Sea

QATAR

AZER.

Persian Gulf

BAHRAIN

KUWAIT

ARM.

SAUDI ARABIA

YEMEN

IRAQ

DJIBOUTI

TURKEY

SYRIA

JORDAN

ERITREA

ETHIOPIA

Black Sea

CYPRUS

LEBANON

ISRAEL

Red Sea

SUDAN

ROMANIA

Mediterranean Sea

EGYPT

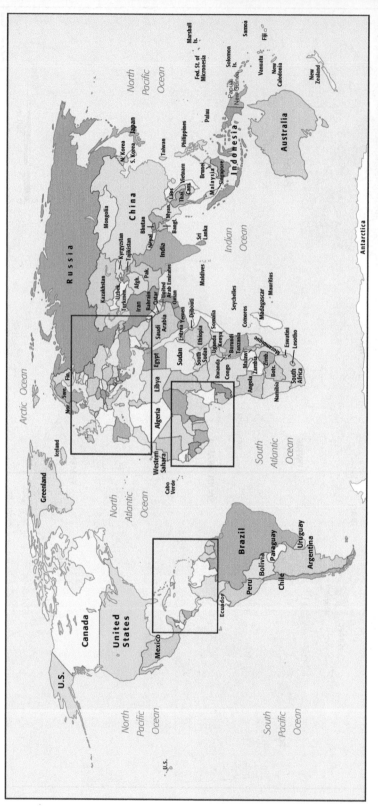

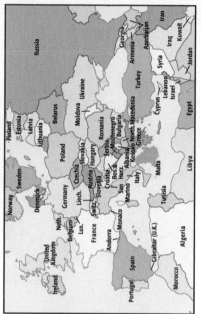

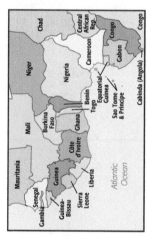

Part 1
Trend and Transformation in World Politics

These are turbulent times, inspiring both anxiety and hope. What lies ahead for the world? What are we to think about the global future? Part 1 of this book introduces you to the study of world politics in a period of rapid change. It opens a window on the many unfolding trends, some of them moving in contrary directions. Chapter 1 looks at our perceptions of global events and realities, explains how they can lead to distorted understandings, and suggests ways to move beyond the limited scope of those views. Chapter 2 continues with an overview of the realist, liberal, and constructivist theoretical traditions that scholars and policy makers use most often to interpret world politics, and also considers the feminist and Marxist critiques of these mainstream traditions. Chapter 3 further strengthens your understanding of world politics by introducing three ways of looking at international decision-making processes by transnational actors.

NASA Images

A World Without Borders

Reflecting on his space shuttle experience, astronaut Sultan bin Salman Al-Saud remarked that "the first day or so we all pointed to our countries. The third or fourth day we were pointing to our continents. By the fifth day, we were aware of only one Earth." As viewed from outer space, planet Earth looks as if it has continents without borders. As viewed from newspaper headlines, however, world politics looks much different.

Chapter 1

Discovering World Politics

IMAGE 1.1 What Future for Humankind? Many global trends are sweeping across a transforming planet. Environmental issues often transcend state boundaries and call for a global response. Shown here, thousands of youth demonstrate in Parliament Square in central London in 2019 to object to the government's lack of action regarding climate change. How might you influence the future of world politics?

Learning Objectives

LO 1-1 Describe the core difficulty of investigating human phenomena such as international relations.

LO 1-2 Explain different ways in which we perceive reality, and how these perceptions can influence international politics.

LO 1-3 Identify foundational concepts and units of analysis used to assess world politics.

The glorious thing about the human race is that it does change the world—constantly. It is the human being's capacity for struggling against being overwhelmed which is remarkable and exhilarating."

—LORRAINE HANSBERRY, AMERICAN AUTHOR

Imagine yourself returning home from a two-week vacation on a tropical island where you were completely "off the grid," with no access to the news. The trip gave you a well-deserved break before starting a new school term, but now you are curious about what has happened while you were away. Checking your newsfeed, the headlines catch your eye. The civil war in Syria, which has displaced almost a fourth of the entire country and created a massive refugee crisis, seems to be grinding to a halt, though a report reveals the government committed human rights atrocities in putting down its opposition. You read that elsewhere in the Middle East, an intense famine will have lasting effects in Yemen, as emphasized by a United Nations report that half of the children under the age of five will have stunted growth due to the lack of food. The deadly Ebola virus is resurfacing in the Congo, with over one thousand deaths thus far. A series of church bombings took place in Sri Lanka. These attacks, which killed almost 300 people, were apparently the responsibility of ISIS, which is still a threat despite losing its home territory.

Listening to NPR reports on your drive home, you hear coverage of several economic crises around the world. The situation in Venezuela is particularly dire; the rate of inflation over the past year was an astounding 10 million percent, which has rendered their currency essentially worthless and left many people at the brink of starvation. Despite this, it appears that their president will survive the latest round of protests against his rule. Puerto Rico, which was already facing a massive debt crisis, continues to struggle to rebuild from a hurricane that devastated the island in 2017. Across the Atlantic, the United Kingdom continues to wrestle with how to implement the "Brexit" plan that will formally separate it from the rest of the European Union. In addition to the economic uncertainties and disruptions that could result from this move, the report indicates that Brexit could potentially reignite tensions between the United Kingdom and Northern Ireland. You wonder if this will interfere with your plans to spend a month in Europe after your graduation next year. You hear about the ongoing "trade war" between the United States and China. As these conflicts will result in higher prices on a wide variety of products, you worry about how much the conflict will affect the cost of the new laptop you need to purchase for the upcoming semester. On a global scale, a recent forecast by the International Monetary Fund points out that this trade conflict, as well as trade problems between the United States and the European Union, could contribute to a further slowing of the world economy as a whole. You hope that conditions improve before you graduate and enter the job market.

Shortly after arriving home, you get a news alert that social media companies are coming under fire in the United States as well as Europe, as these platforms are connected with politically-related misinformation campaigns that influenced several elections around the world. You also hear that relations between the United States and Cuba are deteriorating, with the U.S. government seeking to strengthen existing sanctions on the neighboring country and further limit travel. You wonder if this will affect the study abroad that your roommate plans to take during the upcoming semester.

After such a depressing series of news items, you decide to seek out some more positive stories, and find a couple of interesting podcasts to listen to while you unpack. You learn about the Event Horizon Telescope Project, whose work has resulted in the first actual pictures of a black hole, something that scientists have long known existed but never actually seen before. You are encouraged by how hundreds of scientists from twenty countries were able to cooperate in this massive project. The energy and enthusiasm of Katie Bouman, the 29-year-old computer scientist who played a lead role in the project, is particularly impressive to you. Next you hear about the various school strikes for climate that are taking place throughout the world, in which elementary through high school students are demonstrating to demand action in response to climate change. You listen to an interesting interview with one of the leaders of the group, Greta Thunberg, a 16-year-old student who has been successful in pushing for climate-friendly policies in her home country of Sweden, and recently addressed the United Nations on the topic. With all of the conflict and hardship in the world, you find it encouraging that people can work together to advance human knowledge and to confront global challenges.

The scenario just described is not hypothetical. The events identified record what actually occurred during the month of May 2019. Undoubtedly, many individuals experienced fear and confusion during this period. However, it is, uncomfortably, not so different from other eras. Putting this information about unfolding events together, you cannot help but be reminded that international affairs matter and events around the world powerfully affect your circumstances and future. The "news" you received is not truly new, because it echoes many old stories from the past about the growing sea of turmoil sweeping the contemporary world. Nevertheless, the temptation to wish that this depressing, chaotic world would just go away is overwhelming. If only the unstable world would be still long enough for a sense of predictability and order to prevail . . . . Alas, that does not appear likely. You cannot escape the world or control its turbulence, and you cannot single-handedly alter its character.

We are all a part of this world. If we are to live adaptively amid the fierce winds of global change, then we must face the challenge of discovering the dynamic properties of **world politics**. Because world events increasingly influence every person, all can benefit from investigating how the global system works, how the decisions and behavior of individuals, states, and transnational actors influence the global condition, and how changes in world politics are remaking our political and economic lives. Only by doing so, can we address what former U.S. President Bill Clinton defined as "the question of our time—whether we can make change our friend and not our enemy."

world politics
The study of how global actors' activities entail the exercise of influence to achieve and defend their goals and ideals, and how it affects the world at large.

> *The whole purpose of education is to turn mirrors into windows.*
>
> **—SYDNEY J. HARRIS, AMERICAN POLITICAL JOURNALIST**

The Challenge of Investigating International Relations

LO 1-1 Describe the core difficulty of investigating human phenomena such as international relations.

To understand the political convulsions that confront the world's almost 8 billion people, it is critical that we perceive our times accurately. Yet interpreting the world in which we now live and anticipating what lies ahead for the globe's future—and yours—presents formidable challenges. Indeed, it could be the most difficult task you will ever face. Why? In part, it is because the study of international relations requires taking into account every factor that influences human behavior. This is a task that seminal scientist Albert Einstein believed is extremely challenging. He once hinted at how big the challenge of explaining world politics was when he was asked, "Why is it that when the mind of man has stretched so far as to discover the structure of the atom we have been unable to devise the political means to keep the atom from destroying us?" He replied, "This is simple, my friend; it is because politics is more difficult than physics."

Another part of the challenge stems from our constant bombardment with a bewildering amount of new information and new developments, and the tendency of people to resist new information and ideas that undermine their habitual ways of thinking about world affairs. We know from repeated studies that people do not want to accept ideas that do not conform to their prior beliefs. A purpose of this book is to help you question your preexisting beliefs about global affairs and about the world stage's many actors. To that end, we ask you to evaluate rival perspectives on global issues, even if they differ from your current images. Indeed, we expose you to prevailing schools of thought that you may find unconvincing, and possibly offensive.

Why are they included? Many other people make these views the bedrock of their interpretations of the world around them, and these viewpoints accordingly enjoy a popular following. For this reason, the text describes some visions of world politics with which even your authors may not agree so that you may weigh the wisdom or foolishness of contending perspectives. The interpretive challenge is to observe unfolding global realities objectively in order to describe and explain them accurately.

To appreciate how our images of reality shape our expectations, we begin with a brief introduction to the role that subjective images play in understanding world politics. We then present a set of analytic tools that this book uses to help you overcome perceptual obstacles to understanding world politics and to empower you to more capably interpret the forces of change and continuity that affect our world.

How Do Perceptions Influence Images of Global Reality?

LO 1-2   Explain different ways in which we perceive reality, and how these perceptions can influence international politics.

Although you may not have attempted to define explicitly your perceptions about the world in your subconscious, we all hold mental images of world politics. Whatever our level of self-awareness, these images perform the same function: they simplify "reality" by exaggerating some features of the real world while ignoring others. Thus, we live in a world defined by our images.

Many of our images of the world's political realities are shaped by illusions and misconceptions. Our images cannot fully capture the complexity and configurations of even physical objects, such as the globe itself (see "Controversy: Should We Believe What We See?"). Even images that are currently accurate can easily become outdated if we fail to recognize changes in the world. Indeed, the world's future will be determined not only by changes in the "objective" facts of world politics but also by the meaning that people ascribe to those facts, the assumptions

Controversy

SHOULD WE BELIEVE WHAT WE SEE?

Without questioning whether the ways they have organized their perceptions are accurate, many people simply assume seeing is believing. But is there more to seeing than meets the eye? Students of perceptual psychology think so. They maintain that seeing is not a strictly passive act: what we observe is influenced by our preexisting values and expectations (and by the visual habits reinforced by the constructions society has inculcated in us about how to view objects). Students of perception argue that what you see is what you get, and that two observers looking at the same object might easily see different realities.

This principle has great importance for the investigation of international relations, where, depending on one's perspective, people can vary greatly on how they view international events, actors, and issues. Intense disagreements often arise from competing images.

To appreciate the controversies that can result when different people (with different perspectives) see different realities, even though they are looking at the same thing, consider something as basic as objectively viewing the location and size of the world's continents. All maps of the globe are distorted because it is impossible to represent perfectly the three-dimensional globe on a two-dimensional piece of paper. The difficulty cartographers face can be appreciated by trying to flatten an orange peel. You can only flatten it by separating pieces of the peel that were joined when it was spherical.

Cartographers who try to flatten the globe on paper, without ripping it into separate pieces, face the same problem. Although there are a variety of ways

to represent three-dimensional objects on paper, all of them involve some kind of distortion. Thus, cartographers must choose among the imperfect ways of representing the globe by selecting those aspects of the world's geography they consider most important to describe accurately, while adjusting other parts.

There exists a long-standing controversy among cartographers about the "right" way to map the globe; that is, how to make an accurate projection. Consider these four maps (Maps 1.1, 1.2, 1.3, and 1.4). Cartographers' ideas of what is most important in world geography have varied according to their own global perspectives. Each depicts the distribution of the Earth's land surfaces and territory but portrays a different image. In turn, the accuracy of their rival maps matters politically because they shape how people view what is important.

What Do You Think?

1. What are some of the policy implications associated with the image of the world as depicted in each of the respective projections?

2. Why are some features of the map distorted? Consider the role that politics, history, culture, and racism, among others, might play. Can you think of any ways modern cartographers might modify any of these world projections?

3. In thinking about images and the important role they play in foreign policy, should a consensus be reached as to the map that is distorted the least? Would it be better for everyone to use one map or to use many different types of projections? Why?

(Continued)

MAP 1.1 **Mercator Projection** Named for the Flemish cartographer Gerard Mercator, this Mercator projection was popular in sixteenth-century Europe and presents a classic Eurocentric view of the world. It mapped the Earth without distorting direction, making it useful for navigators. However, distances were deceptive, placing Europe at the center of the world and exaggerating the continent's importance relative to other landmasses.

MAP 1.2 **Peter's Projection** In the Peter's projection, each landmass appears in correct proportion in relation to all others, but it distorts the shape and position of the Earth's landmasses. In contrast to most geographic representations, it draws attention to the less developed countries of the Global South, where more than three-quarters of the world's population lives today.

MAP 1.3 **Orthographic Projection** The orthographic projection, centering on the mid-Atlantic, conveys some sense of the curvature of the Earth by using rounded edges. The sizes and shapes of continents toward the outer edges of the circle are distorted to give a sense of spherical perspective.

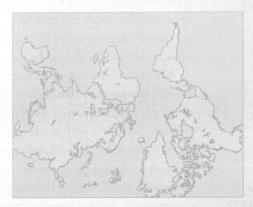

MAP 1.4 **"Upside-Down" Projection** This projection gives a different perspective on the world by depicting it upside down, with the Global South positioned above the Global North. The map challenges the modern "Eurocentric" conceptualization of the positions of the globe's countries and peoples by putting the Global South "on top."

on which they base their interpretations, and the actions that flow from these assumptions and interpretations—however accurate or inaccurate they might be.

The Nature and Sources of Images

The effort to simplify one's view of the world is inevitable and even necessary. Just as cartographers' projections simplify complex geophysical space so that we can better understand the world, each of us inevitably creates a "mental map"—a habitual way of organizing information—to make sense of a confusing abundance of information. These mental maps are neither inherently right nor wrong, and they are important because we tend to react according to the way the world appears to us rather than to the way it is.

How we perceive the world (not what it is really like) determines our attitudes, our beliefs, and our behavior. Most of us—political leaders included—look for information that reinforces our preexisting beliefs about the world, assimilate new data into familiar images, mistakenly equate what we believe with what we know, and ignore information that contradicts our expectations. We also rely on our intuition without thinking and emotionally make snap judgments (Ariely, 2012; Walker et al., 2011).

In addition, we rely on learned habits for viewing new information and making judgments, because these "schema" guide our perceptions and help us organize information. Research in cognitive psychology shows that human beings are "categorizers" who match what they see with images in their memories of prototypical events. People attempting to understand the world also use **schematic reasoning**. The absentminded professor, the shady lawyer, and the kindly grandmother are examples of "stock" images that many of us have created about certain types of people. Although the professors, lawyers, and grandmothers that we meet may bear only a superficial resemblance to these stereotypical images, when we know little about someone, our expectations will be shaped by presumed similarities to these characters.

Many factors shape our images, including how we were socialized as children, traumatic events we experience that shape our personality and psychological needs, exposure to the ideas of people whose expertise we respect, and the opinions about world affairs expressed by our frequent associates such as close friends and coworkers. Once we have acquired an image, it seems self-evident. Accordingly, we try to keep that image consistent with other beliefs, and through a psychological process known as **cognitive dissonance** we reject information that contradicts that image of the world. In short, our minds select, screen, and filter information; consequently, our perceptions depend not only on what happens in daily life but also on how we interpret and internalize those events.

The Impact of Perceptions on World Politics

We must be careful not to assume automatically that what applies to individuals applies to entire countries, and we should not equate the beliefs of leaders, such as heads of state, with the beliefs of the people under their authority. Still, leaders have extraordinary influence, and their images of historical circumstances often predispose them to behave in particular ways toward others, regardless of "objective" facts. For instance, the loss of 26 million Soviet lives in the "Great Patriotic War" (as the Russians refer to World War II) reinforced a longstanding fear of

schematic reasoning
The process of reasoning by which new information is interpreted according to a memory structure, called a schema, which contains a network of generic scripts, metaphors, and simplified characterizations of observed objects and phenomena.

cognitive dissonance
The general psychological tendency to deny discrepancies between one's preexisting beliefs (cognitions) and new information.

foreign invasion, which caused a generation of Soviet policy makers to perceive U.S. defensive moves with suspicion and often alarm.

Similarly, the founders of the United States viewed eighteenth-century European power politics and its repetitive wars as corrupt, contributing to two seemingly contradictory tendencies later evident in U.S. foreign policy. The first is America's impulse to isolate itself (its disposition to withdraw from world affairs), and the other is its determination to reform the world in its own image whenever global circumstances become highly threatening. The former led the country to reject membership in the League of Nations after World War I; the latter gave rise to the U.S. globalist foreign policy following World War II, which committed the country to active involvement nearly everywhere on nearly every issue. Many Americans, thinking of their country as virtuous, have difficulty understanding why others sometimes regard such far-reaching international activism as arrogant or threatening; instead, they see only good intentions in active U.S. interventionism.

Because leaders and citizens are prone to ignore or reinterpret information that runs counter to their beliefs and values, mutual misperceptions often fuel discord in world politics, especially when relations between countries are hostile. Distrust and suspicion arise as conflicting parties view each other in the same negative light—that is, as **mirror images** develop. This occurred in Moscow and Washington during the Cold War. Each side saw its own actions as constructive but its adversary's responses as hostile, and both sides erroneously assumed that their counterpart would clearly interpret the intentions of their own policy initiatives. When psychologist Urie Bronfenbrenner (1961) traveled to Moscow, for example, he was amazed to hear Russians describing the United States in terms that were strikingly similar to the way Americans described the Soviet Union: each side saw itself as virtuous and peace-loving, whereas the other was seen as untrustworthy, aggressive, and ruled by a corrupt government.

mirror images
The tendency of states and people in competitive interaction to perceive each other similarly—to see others the same hostile way others see them.

Mirror-imaging is a property of nearly all **enduring rivalries**—long-lasting contests between opposing groups. For example, in rivalries such as Christianity with Islam during the Crusades in the Middle Ages, Israel and Palestine since the birth of the sovereign state of Israel in 1948, and India and Pakistan since decolonization in 1947, both sides demonize the image of their adversary while perceiving themselves as virtuous. Self-righteousness often leads one party to view its own actions as constructive but its adversary's responses as negative and hostile.

enduring rivalries
Prolonged competition fueled by deep-seated mutual hatred that leads opposed actors to feud and fight over a long period of time without resolution of their conflict.

When this occurs, conflict resolution is extraordinarily difficult. Not only do the opposing sides have different preferences for certain outcomes over others, but they do not see the underlying issues in the same light. Further complicating matters, the mirror images held by rivals tend to be self-confirming. When one side expects the other to be hostile, it may treat its opponent in a manner that leads the opponent to take counteractions that confirm the original expectation, therein creating a vicious circle of deepening hostilities that reduce the prospects for peace (Sen, 2006). Clearing up mutual misperceptions can facilitate negotiations between the parties, but fostering peace is not simply a matter of expanding trade and other forms of transnational contact, or even of bringing political leaders together in international summits. Rather, it is a matter of changing deeply entrenched beliefs.

Although our constructed images of world politics are resistant to change, change is possible. Overcoming old thinking habits sometimes occurs when we experience punishment or discomfort as a result of clinging to false assumptions. As Benjamin Franklin once observed,

"The things that hurt, instruct." Dramatic events in particular can alter international images, sometimes drastically. The Vietnam War caused many Americans to reject their previous images about using military force in world politics. The defeat of the Third Reich and revelations of Nazi atrocities committed before and during World War II caused the German people to confront their past as they prepared for a democratic future imposed by the victorious Allies. More recently, the human and financial costs of the prolonged U.S. wars in Iraq and Afghanistan led many policy makers and political commentators to reexamine their assumptions about the meaning of "victory" and the potential implications as U.S. engagement moved beyond initial combat to address issues of governance and stability.

Often, such jolting experiences encourage us to construct new mental maps, perceptual filters, and criteria through which we interpret later events and define situations. As we shape and reshape our images of world politics and its future, we need to think critically about the foundations on which our perceptions rest (see "A Closer Look: A Clash of Civilizations? Freedom, Security, and Values"). Are they accurate? Are they informed? Do they inhibit our ability to gain greater understanding of others? Questioning our images is one of the major challenges we all face in confronting contemporary world politics.

Key Concepts and Terms for Understanding World Politics

LO 1-3   Identify foundational concepts and units of analysis used to assess world politics.

If we exaggerate the accuracy of our perceptions and seek information that confirms what we believe, how can we escape the biases created by our preconceptions? How can we avoid overlooking or dismissing evidence that runs counter to our intuition?

There are no sure-fire solutions to ensure accurate observations, no ways to guarantee that we have constructed an impartial view of international relations. However, a number of tools can improve our ability to interpret world politics. As you undertake an intellectual journey of discovery, a set of intellectual roadmaps provides guidance for your interpretation and understanding of past, present, and future world politics. To arm you for your quest, *World Politics: Trend and Transformation* advances four keys to aid you in your inquiry.

> *The belief that one's own view of reality is the only reality is the most dangerous of all delusions.*
>
> **—PAUL WATZLAWICK, AUSTRIAN PSYCHOLOGIST**

Introducing Terminology

A primary goal of this text is to introduce you to the vocabulary used by scholars, policy makers, and the "attentive public" who routinely observe international affairs. You need to be literate and informed about the shared meaning of common words used worldwide to discuss and debate world politics and foreign policy. Some of this language has been in use

A Closer Look

A CLASH OF CIVILIZATIONS? FREEDOM, SECURITY, AND VALUES

Islamic head coverings that obscure the face, such as the niqab and burqa, have become a contentious political issue in many societies around the world. In 2018, Denmark became the fifth European country to enact a national ban on full-facial veils in public places, and others including Muslim-majority Turkey have some limitations on where they may be worn. Widespread demand for such legislation began in France in 2011, with French President Nicolas Sarkozy declaring, "the burqa is not welcome in France. In our country, we can't accept women prisoners behind a screen, cut off from all social life, deprived of all identity. That's not our idea of freedom." The European Court of Human Rights supported arguments that such laws do not prevent the free exercise of religion in a place of worship, the face plays an important role in social interaction within secular society, and hidden identity creates a potential security risk. In 2017, it further ruled that Belgium's ban on veils does not violate the European Convention on Human Rights.

Europe is not alone in its resistance to full-face veils. The African countries of Chad, Cameroon, and Niger have also restricted head-coverings, citing terrorism concerns. However in Canada, a federal court took a different approach in February 2015 when it ruled in favor of a native Pakistani woman who challenged the Canadian prohibition against wearing clothing that obscures the face during citizenship ceremonies. Touching off a firestorm of debate within that country, the finding supported her argument that wearing a veil is an expression of her Muslim faith and cultural values.

Perceptions clearly vary on whether such coverings are repressive or liberating, and whether legislation banning the clothing is a victory for democracy or a blow for individual freedom. Some women say they

choose to wear the concealing garments to protect their femininity and express their devotion to God. Some argue that such coverings enable them to move about in public anonymously, shielded from sexual pressure, and so actually allow considerable personal freedom. Others decry the practice and point to cases where women are forced to wear such garments or face violent repercussions such as disfigurement, beatings, or death. In this context, the practice induces fearful obedience, denies individual choice, and silences the voices of women. Such was evident in February 2015 when Al Khansa, an all-female policing unit of the Islamic State, poured acid on the faces of fifteen Iraqi women because they were not properly covered. As explained by Saed Mamuzini, an official from the Kurdistan Democratic Party in Mosul, "they have implemented this punishment so that other women in the city will never consider removing or not wearing the niqab" (Constante, 2015).

Watch the Carnegie Council Video:

"Who Cares What You Wear on Your Head?"

You Decide:

1. How do our perceptions shape how we view the burqa or niqab? How is clothing an expression of a society's collective awareness?

2. Does wearing the burqa inhibit or promote women's freedom and dignity?

3. Would you support a similar ban in your country? Why?

since antiquity, and some of it has only recently become part of the terminology employed in diplomatic circles, scholarly research, and the media. These words are the kind of vocabulary you are likely to encounter long after your formal collegiate education (and the course in which you are reading *World Politics*) has ended, and your future employers and educated neighbors will expect you to know. Some of these words are already likely to be part of your working vocabulary, but others may look new, esoteric, pedantic, and overly sophisticated. Nonetheless, you need to know their meaning to engage in effective analysis and well-informed debate with other scholars, practitioners, and attentive observers of world politics. So take advantage of this "high definition" feature of *World Politics*. Learn these words and use them for the rest of your life—not to impress others, but to understand and communicate intelligently.

To guide you in identifying these terms, as you may already have noticed, we present certain words in **boldface** in the text and provide a broad definition in the margin. When we use a key term again in a different chapter, we will highlight it at least once in *italics*, although the marginal definition will not be repeated. In all cases, the definition will appear in the Glossary at the end of the book with a notation of the chapter in which it first appeared.

Distinguishing the Primary Transnational Actors

actor
An individual, group, state, or organization that plays a major role in world politics.

power
The factors that enable one actor to change another actor's behavior against its preferences.

state sovereignty
A state's supreme authority to manage internal affairs and foreign relations.

state
An independent legal entity with a government exercising exclusive control over the territory and population it governs.

nation
A collectivity whose people see themselves as members of the same group because they share the same ethnicity, culture, or language.

ethnic groups
People whose identity is primarily defined by their sense of sharing a common ancestral nationality, language, cultural heritage, and kinship.

The world is a stage and in the drama there are many players. It is important to identify and classify the major categories of actors (sometimes called agents) who take part in international engagements. The actions of each transnational **actor**—individually, collectively, and with various degrees of influence—shape the trends that are transforming world politics. So how do scholars conventionally categorize the types of actors and structure analysis of them as players in international affairs?

The essential building-block units, of course, are individual people—almost 8 billion of us. Every day, whether each of us chooses to litter, purchase something made abroad, or parent a child, we affect some small measure of how trends in the world will unfold. People, however, also join and participate in various groups. All of these groups combine people and their choices in various collectivities and thereby aggregate the **power** of each group. Such groups often compete with one another because they frequently have divergent interests and goals.

For most periods of world history, the prime actors were groupings of religions, tribes whose members shared ethnic origins, and empires or expansionist centers of power. When they came into contact, they sometimes collaborated with each other for mutual benefit; more often, they competed for and fought over valued resources. The more than 8000 years of recorded international relations history between and among these groups provided the precedent for the formation of today's system of interactions.

As a network of relationships among independent territorial units, the modern state system was not born until the Peace of Westphalia in 1648, which ended the Thirty Years' War (1618–1648) in Europe. Thereafter, rulers refused to recognize the secular authority of the Roman Catholic Church, replacing the system of papal governance in the Middle Ages with geographically and politically separate states that recognized no superior authority. The newly independent states all gave to rulers the same legal rights: territory under their sole control, unrestricted control of their domestic affairs, and the freedom to conduct foreign relations and negotiate treaties with other states. The concept of **state sovereignty**—that no other actor is above the state—still captures these legal rights and identifies the state as the primary actor today.

The Westphalian system continues to color every dimension of world politics and provides the terminology used to describe the primary units in international affairs. Although the term nation-state is often used interchangeably with state and nation, technically the three are different. A **state** is a legal entity that enjoys a permanent population, a well-defined territory, and a government capable of exercising sovereignty. A **nation** is a collection of people who, on the basis of ethnic, linguistic, or cultural commonality, construct their reality to primarily perceive themselves to be members of the same group, which defines their identity. Thus, the term *nation-state* implies a convergence between territorial states and the psychological identification of people within them (Stewart, Gvosdev, and Andelman, 2008).

However, in employing this familiar terminology, we should exercise caution because this condition is relatively rare; there are few independent states comprising a single nationality. Most states today encompass many nations, and some nations are not states. "Nonstate nations" are **ethnic groups**—such as Native Americans in the United States, Sikhs in India, Basques in Spain, or Kurds in Iraq, Turkey, Iran, and Syria—composed of people without sovereign power over the territory in which they live.

The history of world politics since 1648 has largely been a chronicle of interactions among states, which remain the dominant political organizations in the world. However, in recent years nonstate actors have significantly challenged the supremacy of the state. Increasingly, intergovernmental organizations and nongovernmental organizations influence global affairs (see Figure 1.1).

Intergovernmental organizations (IGOs), which transcend national boundaries and whose members are states, carry out independent foreign policies and therefore can be considered global actors in their own right. Purposively created by states to solve shared problems, IGOs include global organizations such as the United Nations (UN) and the North Atlantic Treaty Organization (NATO), and derive their authority from the will of their membership. IGOs are characterized by permanence and institutional organization, and they vary widely in their size and purpose.

Nongovernmental organizations (NGOs), whose members are private individuals and groups, are another principal type of nonstate actor. NGOs are diverse in scope and purpose

intergovernmental organizations (IGOs) Institutions created and joined by states' governments, which give them authority to make collective decisions to manage particular problems on the global agenda.

nongovernmental organizations (NGOs) Transnational organizations of private citizens maintaining consultative status with the UN; they include professional associations, foundations, multinational corporations, or simply internationally active groups in different states joined together to work toward common interests.

States	Intergovernmental Organizations (IGOs)	Nongovernmental Organizations (NGOs)
Afghanistan	African Union	Amnesty International
Bangladesh	Association of Southeast Asian Nations	BRAC
Brazil	Community of Latin American and Caribbean States	CARE International
Canada	Economic Community of West African States	Catholic Relief Services
Ethiopia	European Union	Cure Violence
France	International Chamber of Commerce	Danish Refugee Council
Haiti	International Monetary Fund	Doctors without Borders
Iraq	Interpol	Freedom House
Japan	Organization of American States	Greenpeace
Kuwait	Organization of Petroleum Exporting Countries	Heifer International
Mexico	United Nations	Human Rights Watch
Peru	World Bank	Mercy Corp
Poland	World Health Organization	National Endowment for Democracy
Saudi Arabia	World Trade Organization	Oxfam International
Turkey		The Wikimedia Foundation
United States		World Vision International

FIGURE 1.1 Three Categories of Transnational Actors Shown here in three prominent categories of transnational actors are specific examples of states, intergovernmental organizations, and nongovernmental organizations. As you embark upon your discovery of world politics, it is useful to distinguish between various types of actors and begin to think about how they influence issues and outcomes around the world.

levels of analysis
The different aspects of and agents in international affairs that may be stressed in interpreting and explaining global phenomena, depending on whether the analyst chooses to focus on "wholes" (the complete global system and large collectivities) or on "parts" (individual states or people).

and seek to push their own agendas and exert global influence on an array of issues, such as environmental protection, disarmament, and human rights. For example, Amnesty International and Doctors Without Borders are NGOs that work to bring about change in the world and influence international decision making. Yet although many NGOs are seen in a positive light, others, such as terrorist groups and international drug cartels, are seen as ominous nonstate actors.

In thinking about world politics and its future, we will probe all of these "units" or categories of actors. The emphasis and coverage will vary, depending on the topics under examination in each chapter. But you should keep in mind that all actors (individuals, states, and nonstate organizations) are simultaneously active today, and their importance and power depend on the trend or issue under consideration. So continuously ask yourself the question, now and in the future: which actors are most active, most influential, on which issues, and under what conditions? Doing this will help you think like an international relations scholar.

Distinguishing Levels of Analysis

When we describe international phenomena, we answer a "what" question—What is happening? What is changing? When we move from description to explanation, we face the more difficult task of answering a "why" question—Why did a particular event occur? Why is global warming happening? Why is the gap between rich and poor widening?

One useful key for addressing such puzzles is to visualize an event or trend as the result of some unknown process. This encourages us to think about the causes that might have produced the phenomenon we are trying to explain. Most events and developments in world politics are influenced simultaneously by many determinants, each connected to the rest in a complex web of causal linkages.

World Politics provides an analytic set of categories to help make interpretive sense of the multiple causes that explain why international events and circumstances occur. This analytic distinction conforms to a widespread scholarly consensus that international events or developments can best be analyzed and understood by first separating the multiple pieces of the puzzle into different categories or levels. Following the influential work of Kenneth Waltz (1959) that examined the causes of war according to three "images," investigators conventionally focus on one (or more) of three levels. Known as **levels of analysis**, as shown in Figure 1.2, this classification distinguishes between individual influences, state or internal influences, and structural systemic influences for understanding and explaining world politics.

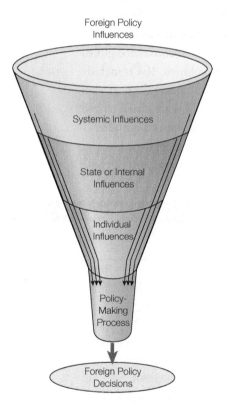

FIGURE 1.2 Three Levels of Influence: Analyzing Factors That Shape International Relations We can group the factors that affect states' foreign policies and the decisions of all other global actors into three basic categories. At the systemic level are structural features of the international system, at the state level are internal or domestic influences, and at the individual level are the characteristics of leaders. All three levels simultaneously influence decisions, but their relative weight usually depends on the issues and circumstances at the time of decision.

To predict which forces will dominate the future, we also must recognize that many influences are operating at the same time. No trend stands alone; all interact simultaneously. The future is influenced by many determinants, each connected to the rest in a complex web of linkages. Collectively, these may produce stability by limiting the impact of any single disruptive force. If interacting forces converge, however, their combined effects can accelerate the pace of change in world politics, moving it in directions otherwise not possible.

The **individual level of analysis** refers to the personal characteristics of human beings, including those responsible for making important decisions on behalf of state and nonstate actors, as well as ordinary citizens whose behavior has important political consequences. At this level, for example, we may properly locate the impact of individuals' perceptions on their political attitudes, beliefs, and behavior. We may also explore the questions of why each person is a crucial part of the global drama and why the study of world politics is relevant to our lives and future.

The **state level of analysis** consists of the authoritative decision-making units that govern states' foreign policy processes and the internal attributes of those states (e.g., type of government, level of economic development, public opinion of its citizens, and strength of military power), which both shape and constrain leaders' foreign policy choices. The processes by which states make decisions regarding war and peace and their capabilities for carrying out those decisions, for instance, fall within the state level of analysis.

The **systemic level of analysis** refers to the interactions of states and nonstate actors on the global stage whose behaviors ultimately shape the international political system and the levels of conflict and cooperation that characterize world politics. The capacity of rich states to dictate the choices of poor states falls properly within the systemic level of analysis. So does the capacity (or incapacity) of the UN to maintain peace.

Examples abound of the diverse ways in which global trends and issues are the product of influences at each level of analysis. Protectionist trade policies by an importing country increase the costs to consumers of clothing and cars and reduce the standard of living of citizens in the manufacturing states. Such policies are initiated by a state government (state level), but they diminish the quality of life of people living both within the protectionist country and those living abroad (individual level) and reduce the level of global trade while threatening to precipitate retaliatory trade wars (systemic level).

Of course, for some developments and issues, factors and forces emanating primarily from one or two particular levels provide more analytical leverage than do those from the other level(s). Accordingly, as we confront specific global issues in subsequent chapters, we emphasize those levels of analysis that provide the most informative lens for viewing them.

Distinguishing Change, Continuities, and Cycles

After having identified factors from different levels of analysis that may combine to produce some outcome, it is useful to place them in a chronological sequence. Anyone who owns a combination lock knows that the correct numbers must be entered in their proper order to open the lock. Similarly, to explain why something happened in world politics, we must determine how various factors at the individual, state, and global systemic levels fit together in a configuration that unfolds over time.

individual level of analysis
An analytical approach that emphasizes the psychological and perceptual variables motivating people, such as those who make foreign policy decisions on behalf of states and other global actors.

state level of analysis
An analytical approach that emphasizes how the internal attributes of states influence their foreign policy behaviors.

systemic level of analysis
An analytical approach that emphasizes the impact of worldwide conditions on foreign policy behavior and human welfare.

One key to anticipating probable human destiny is to look beyond the confines of our immediate time. It is important to appreciate the impact of previous ideas and events on current realities. As philosopher George Santayana cautioned, "Those who cannot remember the past are condemned to repeat it." Similarly, former British Prime Minister Winston Churchill advised, "The farther backward you look, the farther forward you are likely to see." Thus, to understand the dramatic changes in world politics today and to predict how they will shape the future, it is important to view them in the context of a long-term perspective that examines how transnational patterns of interaction have changed and how some of their fundamental characteristics have resisted change.

What do evolving diplomatic practices suggest about the current state of world politics? Are the episodic shock waves throughout the world clearing the way for a truly new twenty-first-century world order? Or will many of today's dramatic disruptions ultimately prove temporary, mere spikes on the seismograph of history? We invite you to explore these questions with us. To begin our search, we discuss how the differences between continuities, changes, and cycles in world history can help you orient your interpretation.

Every historical period is marked to some extent by change. Now, however, the pace of change seems more rapid and its consequences more profound than ever. To many observers, the cascade of events today implies a revolutionary restructuring of world politics. Numerous integrative trends point to that possibility. The countries of the world are drawing closer together in communications and trade, producing a globalized market. Yet at the same time, disintegrative trends paint a less promising picture. Weapons proliferation, global environmental deterioration, and the resurgence of ethnic conflict all portend a restructuring fraught with disorder.

To predict which forces will dominate the future, we must recognize that no trend stands alone, and that different trends may produce stability by limiting the impact of any one disruptive force. It is also possible for converging trends to accelerate the pace of change, moving world politics in directions not possible otherwise. The opposing forces of integration and disintegration point toward the probable advent on the horizon of a **transformation**, but distinguishing true historical watersheds from temporary change is difficult. The moment of transformation from one system to another is not immediately obvious. Nevertheless, another useful key for students of world politics is to recognize that certain times are especially likely candidates.

In the past, major turning points in world politics usually have occurred at the conclusion of wars with many participants, which typically disrupt or destroy preexisting international arrangements. In the twentieth century, World Wars I and II and the Cold War caused fundamental breaks with the past and set in motion major transformations, providing countries with incentives to rethink the premises underlying their interests, purposes, and priorities. Similarly, many people concluded that the terrorist attacks on September 11, 2001, (9/11) produced a fundamental transformation in world affairs. Indeed, 9/11 seemed to change everything: in former U.S. President George W. Bush's words, "Night fell on a different world."

Yet it is equally important to look for the possibility of continuity amidst apparent transformation. Consider how, despite all that may appear radically different since the 9/11 terrorist attacks, much also may remain the same. As journalist William Dobson (2006) wrote on the eve of the fifth anniversary of 9/11, "What is remarkable is how little the world has changed." Similarly, historian Juan Cole notes that "[t]he massive forces of international trade and globalization

transformation
A change in the characteristic pattern of interaction among the most active participants in world politics of such magnitude that it appears that one "global system" has replaced another.

were largely unaffected by the attacks" (2006, p. 26). Decades-old flash points also persist, including the conflicts between India and Pakistan, North Korea and the United States, and Israel and militants in southern Lebanon and the Palestinian territories. "For all their visibility and drama," concludes Cole (2006, p. 26), "the 9/11 attacks left untouched many of the underlying forces and persistent tensions that shape international politics."

We often expect the future to bring changes automatically, and later are surprised to discover that certain patterns from the past have reappeared. Headlines are not trend lines, and a trend does not necessarily signal transformation. Given the enduring continuities that persist even alongside rapid changes, it is dangerous to assume that a major transformation in world politics is under way.

So, what criteria can help determine when an existing pattern of relationships gives way to a completely new global system? Stanley Hoffmann (1961) argues that we can identify a new **global system** when we have a new answer to one of the following three questions. Following this line of argument, there is some evidence that a new system has now emerged.

IMAGE 1.2 Was 9/11 A Global Transforming Event? The terrorist attack on the World Trade Center's Twin Towers on 9/11 is widely regarded as a revolutionary date in world history, producing a sea of change in world politics. Time will tell whether this event will rank alongside the birth of the nuclear age on August 6, 1945, when the United States bombed Hiroshima, or the November 1989 dismantling of the Berlin Wall, which signaled the end of the Cold War, as events that truly changed the world. Alternatively, a rising China may pose a new challenge that will displace 9/11 as a transformative phenomenon in world politics.

global system
The predominant patterns of behaviors and beliefs that prevail internationally to define the major worldwide conditions that heavily influence human and national activities.

- **What are the system's basic units for global governance?** Although states remain a fixture of the international system, supranational institutions and nongovernmental actors are prominent. In the realm of international trade, the World Trade Organization (WTO) has been adjudicating trade disputes since 1995 and wields substantial influence over the policies of many individual states. The United Nations (UN) plays a prominent role in conflict resolution throughout the world, with peacekeepers engaged in sixteen ongoing operations as of July 2015. Transnational terrorist movements, such as the Islamic extremist group Boko Haram, commit widespread human rights atrocities. At the same time, in its role as the first permanent treaty-based global court, the International Criminal Court (ICC) has successfully prosecuted political leaders for human rights violations.

- **What are the predominant foreign policy goals that these units seek with respect to one another?** Although geopolitical struggles remain in many areas, territorial conquest is no longer a states' predominant foreign policy goal. Rather, many key issues on the global agenda, including environmental, health, and financial crises, are transnational threats that require a collective response from countries and other global actors. As the 2008 Global Financial Crisis spread (see Chapter 10), the G-20—a grouping of the world's twenty largest economies—called for international dialogue and common efforts to promote financial stability. Epidemics, such as Ebola, underscore the critical need for timely and well-coordinated international responses to major threats to global health on the part of international organizations, nongovernmental organizations, and states.

- **What can these units do to one another with their military and economic capabilities?** The proliferation of weapons technology has profoundly altered the damage enemies can inflict on one another. **Great powers** alone no longer control the world's most lethal weapons. Increasingly, however, the great powers' prosperity depends on economic circumstances throughout the globe, reducing their ability to engineer growth.

great powers
The most powerful countries, militarily and economically, in the global system.

The profound changes in recent years of the types of actors (units), goals, and capabilities have dramatically altered the hierarchical power ranking of states, but the hierarchies themselves endure. The economic hierarchy that divides the rich from the poor, the political hierarchy that separates the rulers from the ruled, the resource hierarchy that makes some suppliers and others dependents, and the military asymmetries that pit the strong against the weak—all still shape the relations among states, as they have in the past. Similarly, the perpetuation of international **anarchy**, in the absence of institutions to govern the globe, and continuing national insecurity still encourage preparations for war and the use of force without international mandate. Thus, change and continuity coexist, with both forces simultaneously shaping contemporary world politics.

anarchy
A condition in which the units in the global system are subjected to few, if any, overarching institutions to regulate their conduct.

The interaction of constancy and change will determine future relations among global actors. This perhaps explains why **cycles**, periodic sequences of events that resemble patterns in earlier periods, so often appear to characterize world politics: because the emergent global system shares many characteristics with earlier periods, historically minded observers may experience déjà vu—the illusion of having already experienced something actually being experienced for the first time.

cycles
The periodic reemergence of conditions similar to those that existed previously.

Preparing for Your Intellectual Journey

Because world politics is complex and our images of it are often dissimilar, scholars differ in their approach to understanding world politics. Some view the world through a macro political lens, meaning they look at international affairs from a "bird's eye view" and explain the behavior of world actors based on their relative position within the global system. Other scholars adopt a micro political perspective that looks at world politics from the "ground up," meaning the individual is the unit of analysis from which aggregate behavior is extrapolated.

Both approaches make important contributions to understanding world politics: the former reveals how the global environment sets limits on political choice, the latter draws attention to how every transnational actor's preferences, capabilities, and strategic calculations influence global conditions. By looking at world politics from a macro political perspective, we can see why actors that are similarly situated within the system may behave alike, despite their internal differences. By taking a micro political perspective, we can appreciate why some actors are very different or behave differently, despite their similar placement within the global system (see Waltz, 2000).

From this analytic point of departure, *World Politics* will inspect:

- The values, interests, and capabilities of the individual actors affected by these global trends;

- The ways these actors interact in their individual and collective efforts to modify existing global circumstances, and how these interactions shape the ultimate trajectories of global trends;

- The major macro trends in world politics that set the boundaries for action.

This analytic approach looks at the dynamic interplay of actors and their environment as well as how the actors respond and seek to influence each other's behavior. It can open a window for you not only to understand contemporary world politics but also to predict the likely global future. This approach has the advantage of taking into account the interplay of proximate and remote explanatory factors at the individual, state, and global levels of analysis while avoiding dwelling on particular countries, individuals, or transitory events whose long-term significance is likely to decrease. Instead, *World Politics* attempts to identify behaviors that cohere into general patterns that measurably affect global living conditions. Thus, we explore the nature of world politics from a perspective that places historical and contemporary events into a larger, lasting theoretical context to provide you with the conceptual tools that will enable you to interpret subsequent developments later in your lifetime.

> *The world is at a critical juncture, and so are you . . . Go ahead and make your plans . . . and don't stop learning. But be open to the detours that lead to new discoveries.*
>
> **—KOFI ANNAN, FORMER UN SECRETARY-GENERAL**

Courtesy of Shannon Lindsey Blanton

IMAGE 1.3 It's a Small World As you begin your journey of discovery to extend your knowledge of world politics, it is important to be aware of the images that you hold and be open to new experiences and interpretations of the world around you. Take full advantage of all of your opportunities to study and learn about the global community. Shown here in May 2017 are U.S. students from the University of Alabama at Birmingham learning about different perspectives and issues during their study abroad program in Cuba.

Study. Apply. Analyze.

Chapter Summary

1-1 Describe the core difficulty of investigating human phenomena such as international relations. The study of international relations is challenging because of the complexity of taking into account all the factors that shape human behavior and the tendency of people to resist change in how they think about world politics.

1-2 Explain different ways in which we perceive reality, and how these perceptions can influence international politics. We all hold images and perceptions of the world around us that simplify reality by emphasizing some aspects and ignoring others. Research in cognitive psychology shows that we are "categorizers" who use "schema" to help organize information. Our perceptions, which are resistant to change, influence the way we understand and react to world politics and

predispose us to act in particular ways regardless of the objective facts.

1-3 Identify foundational concepts and units of analysis used to assess world politics. Throughout the book, you will learn terminology to help you identify core concepts important for understanding world politics. One useful analytical tool is to distinguish between different types of actors – from individuals to states to nonstate actors – that influence international relations. Another is to consider factors at different levels of analysis that may combine to produce a particular outcome. It will also be important to determine how various actors and factors at the individual, state, and systemic level reflect continuity or change in how they influence global affairs. By doing so, you enhance your ability to investigate systematically the various determinants of world politics.

Key Terms

actor	global system	mirror images	state
anarchy	great powers	nation	state level of analysis
cognitive dissonance	individual level of analysis	nongovernmental	state sovereignty
cycles	intergovernmental	organizations (NGOs)	systemic level of analysis
enduring rivalries	organizations (IGOs)	power	transformation
ethnic groups	levels of analysis	schematic reasoning	world politics

Suggested Readings and Resources

Acharya, Amitav. (2014). "Global International Relations and Regional Worlds," *International Studies Quarterly* 58 (December): 647–659.

Brown, Warner. (2015). "This Map Shows China's Hilarious Stereotypes of Europe," *Foreign Policy*, foreignpolicy.com/2015/08/20/this-map-shows-chinas-hilarious-and-racist-stereotypes-of-europe/

Carnegie Council for Ethics in International Affairs: carnegiecouncil.org. A website dedicated to all affairs international with a focus on ethics.

Duck of Minerva: duckofminerva.com/. An international studies blog.

Ellis, David C. (2009). "On the Possibility of 'International Community,'" *The International Studies Review* 11 (March):1–26.

European Council on Foreign Relations: www.ecfr.eu. A website that covers various international affairs from around the globe.

Friedman, George. (2011). *The Next Decade: Where We've Been. . . and Where We're Going*. New York: Doubleday, Random House.

Jervis, Robert. (2008). "Unipolarity: A Structural Perspective," *World Politics* 61:188–213.

Relations International: relationsinternational.com. An international studies blog with an emphasis on global relations.

Carnegie Council Videos

Key Term Videos

- World Politics
- Enduring Rivalries
- Actor

- Power
- State
- Nongovernmental Organizations

- Global System
- Great Powers
- Anarchy

Additional Videos

- Kupchan, Charles, "How Enemies Become Friends: The Sources of Stable Peace."

Chapter 2

Interpreting World Politics Through the Lens of Theory

IMAGE 2.1 **Theoretical challenges** We live in a world of ever-changing conditions. Many trends are unfolding, some in contrary directions, and obstacles exist to understanding world politics accurately. As you begin your study of trend and transformation in world politics, your challenge is to interpret theoretically the meaning of a changing world.

Learning Objectives

LO 2-1   Identify how theories are defined and articulate why they are important in world politics.

LO 2-2   Summarize the realist worldview, including its key concepts, evolution, and potential limitations.

LO 2-3   Summarize the liberal worldview, including its key concepts, evolution, and potential limitations.

LO 2-4   Summarize the constructivist worldview, including its key concepts, evolution, and potential limitations.

LO 2-5   Discuss the tenets of feminist and Marxist perspectives, and illustrate how they diverge from those of realism, liberalism, and constructivism.

LO 2-6   Understand the need for multiple theories and worldviews in developing a comprehensive understanding of world politics.

" *He who loves practice without theory is like the sailor who boards ship without a rudder and compass and never knows where he may cast.*"

—LEONARDO DA VINCI, ARTIST

Imagine yourself the newly elected president of the United States. You are delivering the State of the Union address on your views of the current global situation and your foreign policy to deal with it. You face the task of both defining the aspects of international affairs most worthy of attention and explaining the reasons for their priority. To convince citizens that these issues are important, you must present them as part of a larger picture of the world. Therefore, based on your perceptions of world politics, you must think theoretically. You must be careful because your interpretations will necessarily depend on your assumptions about international realities that your citizens might find questionable. The effort to explain the world, predict new global problems, and persuade others to support a policy to deal with them is bound to result in controversy because even reasonable people often see reality differently.

When leaders face these kinds of intellectual challenges, they can benefit from drawing on various theories of world politics. A **theory** is a set of conclusions derived from assumptions and evidence about some phenomenon, including its character, causes, probable consequences, and ethical implications. Theories provide a map, or frame of reference, that makes the complex, puzzling world around us intelligible.

theory
A set of hypotheses postulating the relationship between variables or conditions advanced to describe, explain, or predict phenomena and make prescriptions about how to pursue particular goals and follow ethical principles.

Theories and Change in World Politics

LO 2-1   Identify how theories are defined and articulate why they are important in world politics.

Theories of international relations specify the conditions under which relationships between two or more factors exist, and explain the reasons for such linkages. As political scientists Bruce Jentleson and Ely Ratner (2011, p. 9) explain, "Theory deepens understanding of patterns of causality within any particular case by penetrating beyond the situational and particularistic to get at factors with broader applicability." Choosing which theory to use is an important task, because each one rests on different assumptions about the nature of international politics, advances different claims about causes, and offers a different set of foreign policy recommendations.

Indeed, the menu of theories from which to choose is large. Rival theories of world politics abound, and there is no agreement about which one is most useful. The reason is primarily that the world is constantly changing, and no single theory has proven capable of making international events understandable for every global circumstance. There are fads and fashions in the popularity of international theories; they rise and fall over time in popularity and perceived usefulness, depending on the global conditions that prevail in any historical period.

The history of the world is the history of changes in the theoretical interpretation of international relations. In any given era, a **paradigm**, or dominant way of looking at a particular subject such as international relations, influences judgments regarding which characteristics of the subject are most important, what puzzles need to be solved, and what analytical criteria

paradigm
Derived from the Greek paradeigma, meaning an example, a model, or an essential pattern; a paradigm structures thought about an area of inquiry.

should govern investigation. Over time, paradigms are modified or abandoned as their assertions fail to mirror the prevailing patterns of international behavior. These paradigms, or "a set of assumptions, concepts, values, and practices that comprise a view of reality" (Harrison, 2006, p. 17), eventually tend to be revised in order to explain new developments.

Yet theories are not merely passive agents for explaining historical events. As they inform the worldviews of policy leaders, theoretical perspectives can play a key role in influencing policy choices. For policy makers, theory has three important applications (Jentleson and Ratner, 2011):

- **Diagnostic value.** Helps policy makers assess issues they face by facilitating their ability to discern patterns and focus on important causal factors.

- **Prescriptive value.** Provides a framework for conceptualizing strategies and policy responses.

- **Lesson-drawing value.** Facilitates critical assessment so that policy makers reach accurate conclusions about the successes and failures of a policy.

For example, the insights of realist theory (discussed later in this chapter), particularly the importance of balance of power, drove U.S. President Nixon's decision to establish diplomatic relations with China in 1971. Along realist lines, Nixon overlooked his profound ideological differences with China's government and sought to establish relations based on common strategic interests, particularly, countering the power of the Soviet Union. More recently, liberal ideas about the spread of democracy, combined with a realist emphasis on military power and

neoconservative
A political movement in the United States calling for the use of military and economic power in foreign policy to bring freedom and democracy to other countries.

disdain for international institutions, shaped the **neoconservative** approach to foreign policy and were pivotal in the U.S. decision to go to war against Iraq in 2003.

As British economist John Maynard Keynes (1936, p. 241) famously argued, "The ideas of economists and political philosophers, both when they are right and when they are wrong, are more powerful than is commonly understood. Indeed, the world is ruled by little else. Practical men, who believe themselves to be quite exempt from any intellectual influences, are usually the slaves of some defunct economist."

Simply put, the relationship between theory and historical events is interactive—theories both influence and are influenced by events and behaviors in world politics. The purpose of this chapter is to compare the assumptions, causal claims, and policy prescriptions of realism, liberalism, and constructivism—the most common theoretical perspectives policy makers and scholars use to interpret international relations. Moreover, the chapter broadens coverage of the range of contemporary international theorizing by also introducing you to the feminist and Marxist critiques of world politics and the theoretical lens that each provides for understanding international interactions.

> *Critical reflection on practice is a requirement of the relationship between theory and practice. Otherwise theory becomes simply "blah, blah, blah," and practice, pure activism.*
>
> **—PAULO FREIRE, BRAZILIAN PEDAGOGICAL THEORIST**

Realism

LO 2-2	Summarize the realist worldview, including its key concepts, evolution, and potential limitations.

Realism is the oldest of the prevailing schools of thought and has a long and distinguished history dating back to Thucydides's writings about the Peloponnesian War in ancient Greece. Other influential figures who contributed to realist thought include sixteenth-century Italian philosopher Niccolò Machiavelli and seventeenth-century English philosopher Thomas Hobbes. Realism deserves careful examination because its worldview continues to guide much understanding of international politics.

realism
A paradigm based on the premise that world politics is essentially and unchangeably a struggle among self-interested states for power and position under anarchy, with each competing state pursuing its own national interests.

What Is the Realist Worldview?

Realism, as applied to contemporary international politics, views the state as the most important actor on the world stage because it answers to no higher political authority. States are sovereign: they have supreme *power* over their territory and populace, and no other actor stands above them to wield legitimacy and coercive capability and govern the global system. Emphasizing the absence of a higher authority to which states can turn for protection and resolve disputes, realists depict world politics as a ceaseless, repetitive struggle for power where the strong dominate the weak. Because each state is ultimately responsible for its own survival and feels uncertain about its neighbors' intentions, realism claims that prudent political leaders build strong armies and allies to enhance national security. In other words, international anarchy leads even well-intentioned leaders to practice **self-help**, increase their own military strength, and opportunistically align with others to deter potential enemies.

Realist theory, however, does not preclude the possibility that rival powers will cooperate on arms control or on other security issues of common interest. Rather, it simply asserts cooperation will be rare because states worry about the unequal distribution of **relative gains**, or the unequal distribution of benefits from cooperation, and the possibility that the other side will cheat on agreements. Leaders should never entrust the task of self-protection to international security organizations or international law and should resist efforts to regulate international behavior through global governance.

At the risk of oversimplification, realism's message can be summarized by the following assumptions and related propositions:

self-help
The principle that, because in international anarchy all global actors are independent, they must rely on themselves to provide for their security and well-being.

relative gains
Conditions in which some participants in cooperative interactions benefit more than others.

- People are by nature selfish and are driven to compete with others for domination and self-advantage. "The focus on gain and greed is one reason why morality cannot be expected to play a role in relations among states" (Rathbun, 2012, p. 611) or people. Machiavelli captures the realist view of human nature in his work *The Prince* (1532, p. 120), arguing that people in general "are ungrateful, fickle, and deceitful, eager to avoid dangers, and avid for gain, and while you are useful to them they are all with you, offering you their blood, their property, and their sons so long as danger is remote, but when it approaches they turn on you."

national interest
The goals that states pursue to maximize what they perceive to be selfishly best for their country.

- By extension, the primary obligation of every state—the goal to which all other national objectives should be subordinated—is to acquire power in order to promote the **national interest**. Power is the "most important currency in international politics both to take from others and to prevent the inevitable effort by others to steal" (Rathbun, 2012, p. 622). "Might makes right," and a state's philosophical or ethical preferences are neither good nor bad. What matters is whether they serve its self-interest. As Thucydides put it, "The standard of justice depends on the equality of power to compel . . . the strong do what they have the power to do and the weak accept what they have to accept."

- World politics is a struggle for *power*—in the words of Thomas Hobbes, "a war of all against all"—and the possibility of eradicating the instinct for power is a hopeless utopian aspiration. In the pursuit of power, states must acquire sufficient military capabilities to deter attack by potential enemies and to exercise influence over others; hence, states "prepare for war to keep peace." Economic growth is important primarily as a means of acquiring and expanding state power and prestige and is less relevant to national security than is military might.

security dilemma
The tendency of states to view the defensive arming of adversaries as threatening, causing them to arm in response so that all states' security declines.

- International anarchy and a lack of trust perpetuate the principle of self-help and can give rise to the **security dilemma**. As a state builds up its power to protect itself, others inevitably become threatened and are likely to respond in kind. An arms race is seen as a manifestation of the security dilemma, for even if a state is truly arming only for defensive purposes, it is rational in a self-help system for opponents to assume the worst and keep pace in any arms buildup.

balance of power
The theory that peace and stability are most likely to be maintained when military power is distributed to prevent a single superpower hegemon or bloc from controlling the world.

- If all states seek to maximize power, stability results from a **balance of power**, facilitated by shifts in alliances that counter another state's growing power or expansionist behavior. Thus, allies might be sought to increase a state's ability to defend itself, but their loyalty and reliability should not be assumed, and commitments to allies should be repudiated if it is no longer in a state's national interests to honor them (see Chapter 8 for further discussion).

With their emphasis on the ruthless nature of international life, realists often question letting ethical considerations enter foreign policy deliberations. As they see it, some policies are driven by strategic imperatives that may require national leaders to disregard moral norms. Embedded in this "philosophy of necessity" is a distinction between private morality, which guides the behavior of ordinary people in their daily lives, and raison d'état (reason of state), which governs the conduct of leaders responsible for the security and survival of the state. Actions that are dictated by national interest must be carried out no matter how repugnant in the light of private morality. Reflecting upon his decision in 2009 to send additional U.S. troops to Afghanistan, in his acceptance speech for the Nobel Peace Prize then-President Obama noted, "I face the world as it is, and cannot stand idle in the face of threats to the American people."

The Evolution of Realism

We have seen how the intellectual roots of realism reach back to ancient Greece. They also extend beyond the Western world to India and China. Discussions of "power politics" abound in the *Arthashastra*, an Indian treatise on statecraft written during the fourth century BCE by Kautilya, as well as in works written by Han Fei and Shang Yang in ancient China.

Modern realism emerged on the eve of World War II, when the prevailing belief in a natural harmony of interests among states came under attack. Just a decade earlier, this belief had led numerous countries to sign the 1928 **Kellogg-Briand Pact**, which renounced war as an instrument of national policy. Yet Nazi Germany, fascist Italy, and Imperial Japan all violated the treaty. In retrospect, British historian and diplomat E. H. Carr (1939) complained that the assumption of a universal interest in peace had allowed too many people to "evade the unpalatable fact of a fundamental divergence of interest between nations desirous of maintaining the status quo and nations desirous of changing it."

In an effort to counter what they saw as a utopian, legalistic approach to foreign affairs, Reinhold Niebuhr (1947), Hans J. Morgenthau (1948), and other realists painted a pessimistic view of human nature. Echoing seventeenth-century philosopher Baruch Spinoza, many of them pointed to an innate conflict between passion and reason; furthermore, in the tradition of St. Augustine, they stressed that material appetites enabled passion to overwhelm reason. For them, the human condition was such that the forces of light and darkness would perpetually combat for control.

The realists' picture of international life appeared particularly persuasive after World War II. The onset of rivalry between the United States and the Soviet Union, the expansion of the Cold

Kellogg-Briand Pact
A multilateral treaty negotiated in 1928 that outlawed war as a method for settling interstate conflicts.

IMAGE 2.2A AND IMAGE 2.2B **Realist Pioneers of Power Politics** In *The Prince* (1532) and *The Leviathan* (1651), Niccolò Machiavelli (left) and Thomas Hobbes (right), respectively, argued for basing international decisions on self-interest, prudence, power, and expediency above all other considerations. This formed the foundation of what became a growing body of modern realist thinking that accepts the drive for power over others as necessary and wise statecraft.

neorealism
A theoretical account of states' behavior that explains it as determined by differences in their relative power within the global hierarchy, defined primarily by the distribution of military power, instead of by other factors such as their values, types of government, or domestic circumstances.

agency
The capacity of an actor to make choices and achieve objectives.

defensive realism
A variant of realist theory that emphasizes the preservation of power, as opposed to the expansion of power, as an actor's primary security objective.

offensive realism
A variant of realist theory that stresses that, in an anarchical international system, states should always look for opportunities to gain more power.

War into a wider struggle between East and West, and the periodic crises that threatened to erupt into global violence all supported the realists' emphasis on the inevitability of conflict, the poor prospects for cooperation, and the divergence of national interests among incorrigibly selfish, power-seeking states.

Whereas these so-called classical realists sought to explain state behavior by examining assumptions about people's motives at the individual level of analysis, the next wave of realist theorizing emphasized the systemic level of analysis. **Neorealism** (often called "structural realism") understands human identity, motivation, and behavior as driven by the environment in which actors are situated. It is "based on a belief in the shaping power of conditions over **agency**" (Harknett and Yalcin, 2012, p. 500). In other words, neorealism treats "the state as a metaphorical black box and underplay(s) different internal compositions" (Foulon 2015: 647).

Kenneth Waltz (2013; 1979), the leading proponent of neorealism, proposed that international anarchy—not some allegedly evil side of human nature—explained why states were locked in fierce competition with one another. The absence of a central arbiter was the defining structural feature of international politics. Vulnerable and insecure, states behaved defensively by forming alliances against looming threats. According to Waltz, balances of power form automatically in anarchic environments. Even when disrupted, they soon reemerge.

Although there are common themes throughout realist thought, different variants of realism emphasize certain features. As shown in Table 2.1, classical realism focuses primarily on "the sources and uses of national power . . . and the problems that leaders encounter in conducting foreign policy" (Taliaferro et al., 2009, p. 16). Structural realism, as envisioned by Kenneth Waltz, is also called defensive realism to distinguish it from the more recent variant, offensive realism. Although both are structural realist theories, the two perspectives differ with regard to the underlying motivation for state behavior and conflict. **Defensive realism** sees states as focused on maintaining security by balancing others and essentially preserving the status quo, whereas **offensive realism** sees states as seeking to ensure security by aggressively maximizing their power (Harknett and Yalcin, 2012). According to offensive realism, states are locked in perpetual struggle and must be "primed for offense, because they can never be sure how much military capacity they will need in order to survive over the long run" (Kaplan, 2012; Mearsheimer, 2001). Neoclassical realism draws on both classical realism and structural

TABLE 2.1   Comparing Various Strands of Realist Theory

Variant	View of International System	Systemic Pressure	Primary State Objective
Classical realism	Somewhat important	Either defensive or offensive	Varies (e.g., security, power, or glory)
Defensive realism	Very important	Power buildup to deter potential aggressors	Survival
Offensive realism	Very important	Emphasis on extensive accumulation of power	Survival
Neoclassical realism	Important	Either defensive or offensive	Varies (e.g., security, power, or glory)

Source: Based on Taliaferro et al., 2009; Rynning and Ringsmose, 2008.

realism to provide a multi-level explanation for state behavior. **Neoclassical realism** posits that systemic-level factors significantly influence but do not absolutely determine state behavior. Decision makers' perceptions and "domestic politics affect how the government devises foreign policy in response to binding structural incentives" (Foulon 2015, p. 637).

The Limitations of Realist Thought

However persuasive the realists' image of the essential properties of international politics, their policy recommendations suffered from a lack of precision in the way they used such key terms as *power* and *national interest*. Thus, once analysis moved beyond the assertion that national leaders should acquire power to serve the national interest, important questions remained: What were the key elements of national power? What uses of power best served the national interest? Did arms furnish protection or provoke costly arms races? Did alliances enhance one's defenses or encourage threatening counter-alliances?

From the perspective of realism's critics, seeking security by amassing power was self-defeating. The quest for absolute security by one state would be perceived as creating absolute insecurity for other members of the system, with the result that everyone would become locked in an upward spiral of countermeasures jeopardizing the security of all (Glaser, 2011).

Realism offered no criteria for determining what historical data were significant in evaluating its claims and what epistemological rules to follow when interpreting relevant information (Vasquez and Elman, 2003). Even the policy recommendations that purportedly flowed from its logic were often conflicting. Realists themselves, for example, were sharply divided as to whether U.S. intervention in Vietnam served American national interests and whether nuclear weapons contributed to international security. Similarly, although some observers used realism to explain the rationale for the 2003 U.S. invasion of Iraq (Gvosdev, 2005), others drew on realist arguments to criticize the invasion (Mansfield and Snyder, 2005a; Mearsheimer and Walt, 2003).

A growing number of critics also pointed out that realism did not account for significant new developments in world politics. For instance, it could not explain the creation of new commercial and political institutions in Western Europe in the 1950s and 1960s, where the cooperative pursuit of mutual advantage led Europeans away from the unbridled power politics that had brought them incessant warfare since the birth of the nation-state some three centuries earlier. Similarly, critics challenged that "the end of the Cold War, the expansion of democracy, and the increasing importance of global trade and international organizations . . . demand scholarly explanation that realist theory is unable to provide" (Walker and Morton, 2005, p. 353). Others began to worry about realism's tendency to disregard ethical principles and the material and social costs some of its policy prescriptions imposed, such as hindered economic growth resulting from unrestrained military expenditures.

Despite realism's shortcomings, many people continue to think about world politics in the language constructed by realists, especially in times of global tension. This can be seen in Israel's Prime Minister Benjamin Netanyahu's declaration in March 2013 that Israel has "both the right and the capability" to defend itself (Yellin and Cohen, 2013). Placing great emphasis on military security and national self-interest, his statement comes amid speculation about the possibility of a unilateral Israeli military strike in response to Iran's continuing pursuit of a nuclear program.

neoclassical realism
A variant of realist theory that explains state behavior in terms of the constraints of binding systemic-level structure and the influence of domestic politics and perceptions of state policy makers.

Liberalism

LO 2-3	Summarize the liberal worldview, including its key concepts, evolution, and potential limitations.

liberalism
A paradigm predicated on the hope that the application of reason and universal ethics to international relations can lead to a more orderly, just, and cooperative world; liberalism assumes that anarchy and war can be policed by institutional reforms that empower international organization and law.

Liberalism is widely viewed as the strongest theoretical challenger to realism, and it is even argued that "there is ample evidence that liberal theory surpassed realism some time ago and now occupies the 'best in the show' position" (Sterling-Folker, 2015, p. 44). Like realism, it has a distinguished pedigree, with philosophical roots extending back to the political thought of John Locke, Immanuel Kant, and Adam Smith. Liberalism warrants our attention because it speaks to issues realism largely disregards, including the impact of domestic politics on state behavior, the implications of economic interdependence, and the role of global norms and institutions in promoting international cooperation.

What Is Liberalism's Worldview?

There are several distinct schools of thought within the liberal tradition, and drawing broad conclusions from such a diverse body of theory runs the risk of misrepresenting the position of any single author. Nevertheless, there are sufficient commonalities to abstract some general themes.

Liberals differ from realists in several important ways. At the core of liberalism is a belief in reason and the possibility of progress. Liberals view the individual as the seat of moral value and assert that human beings should be treated as ends rather than means. Whereas realists counsel decision makers to seek the lesser evil rather than the absolute good, liberals emphasize ethical principle over the pursuit of power, and institutions over military capabilities (see Ikenberry, 2011; Wilkinson, 2011). Realism anticipates competition and conflict over power and resources, whereas liberalism expects "increasing or potentially greater cooperation and progress in international affairs, generally defined in terms of increased peace and prosperity" (Rathbun, 2012, p. 612). Politics at the global level then becomes more a struggle for consensus and mutual gain than a struggle for power and prestige.

Several corollary ideas give definition to liberal theory. These include:

- An emphasis on the unity of humankind rather than parochial national loyalties to independent sovereign states.

- The importance of individuals—their essential dignity and fundamental equality—and the analogous need to place the protection and promotion of human rights and freedom ahead of national interests and state autonomy.

- The use of the power of ideas through education to arouse world public opinion against warfare.

- The conditions under which people live, rather than an inherent lust for power, as an underlying source of international conflict. Reforming those conditions, liberals argue, will enhance the prospects for peace.

Another element common to various strands of liberal thought is an emphasis on undertaking political reforms to establish stable democracies. Based on tolerance, compromise, and civil liberties, democratic political cultures are said to shun lethal force as a means of settling disagreements. Woodrow Wilson, for example, proclaimed that "democratic government will make wars less likely." Franklin Roosevelt later agreed, asserting "the continued maintenance and improvement of democracy constitute the most important guarantee of international peace."

In place of force, **diplomacy** provides a means for achieving mutually acceptable solutions to a common problem, and enables leaders to negotiate and compromise with each other in a peaceful manner. Politics is not seen as a **zero-sum** game as the use of persuasion rather than coercion, and a reliance on judicial methods to settle rival claims, is the primary means of dealing with conflict. As Executive Director of the Washington International Diplomatic Academy Nicholas Kralev (2018) notes, "In the toolbox of foreign policy, in the implementation of it, diplomacy is one of those tools. Hopefully it is the first one we use, the default we use, as the military should be the last resort."

According to liberal theory, conflict-resolution practices used at home can also be used when dealing with international disputes. Leaders socialized within democratic cultures share a common outlook. Viewing international politics as an extension of domestic politics, they generalize about the applicability of norms to regulate international competition. Disputes between democratic governments rarely escalate to war because each side accepts the other's legitimacy and expects it to rely on peaceful means of conflict resolution. The transparent nature of democracies reinforces these expectations. Anyone can scrutinize the inner workings of open polities; hence, it is difficult to demonize democratically ruled states as scheming adversaries.

A second command strand in liberal theorizing is an emphasis on free trade. The idea that commerce can reduce conflict has roots in the work of Immanuel Kant, Charles de Secondat Montesquieu, Adam Smith, Jean-Jacque Rousseau, and various Enlightenment thinkers. "Nothing is more favourable to the rise of politeness and learning," noted liberal philosopher David Hume (1817), "than a number of neighboring and independent states, connected by commerce." This view was later embraced by the Manchester School of political economy and formed the basis for Norman Angell's (1910) famous rebuttal of the assertion that military conquest produces economic prosperity.

Today, some studies contend that economic interconnectedness is an even more important factor than democracy in fostering peace (Mousseau, 2013). The doctrine that unfettered trade helps prevent disputes from escalating to wars rests on several propositions:

- Commercial intercourse creates a material incentive to resolve disputes peacefully: war reduces profits by interrupting vital economic exchanges.

- Cosmopolitan business elites who benefit most from these exchanges comprise a powerful transnational interest group with a stake in promoting amicable solutions to festering disagreements.

- The web of trade between countries increases communication, erodes national selfishness, and encourages both sides to avoid ruinous clashes.

diplomacy
Communication and negotiation between global actors that is not dependent upon the use of force and seeks a cooperative solution.

zero-sum
An exchange in a purely conflictual relationship in which what is gained by one competitor is lost by the other.

In the words of Richard Cobden, an opponent of the protectionist Corn Laws that once regulated British international grain trade: "Free Trade! What is it? Why, breaking down the barriers that separate nations; those barriers, behind which nestle the feelings of pride, revenge, hatred, and jealousy, which every now and then burst their bounds, and deluge whole countries with blood."

Finally, the third commonality in liberalism is an advocacy of global institutions. Liberals recommend replacing cutthroat, balance-of-power politics with organizations based on the principle that a threat to peace anywhere is a common threat to everyone. They see foreign policy as unfolding in a nascent global society populated by actors who recognize the cost of conflict, share significant interests, and can realize those interests by using institutions to mediate disputes whenever misconceptions, wounded sensibilities, or aroused national passions threaten peaceful relations. Realists counter, however, "neither globalization nor international institutions impose genuine constraints on great powers, simply because states have sufficient power to interpret sovereignty" (Ziegler, 2012, p. 402) and participate in global institutions only to the extent that it suits their own national interest.

collective security
A security regime agreed to by the great powers that sets rules for keeping peace, guided by the principle that an act of aggression by any state will be met by a collective response from the rest.

adjudication
A conflict-resolution procedure in which a third party makes a binding decision about a dispute in an institutional tribunal.

The Evolution of Liberalism

In the wake of World War I, contemporary liberal theory rose to prominence. Not only had the war involved more participants over a wider geographic area than any previous war, but modern science and technology made it a war of machinery. Old weapons were improved and produced in greater quantities; new and far more deadly weapons were rapidly developed and deployed. By the time the carnage was over, nearly 20 million people were dead.

For liberals such as U.S. President Woodrow Wilson, World War I was "the war to end all wars." Believing that another horrific war would erupt if states resumed practicing power politics, liberals set out to reform the global system. These "idealists," as they were sometimes called by realists, generally fell into one of three groups (Herz, 1951). The first group advocated creating global institutions to contain the raw struggle for power between self-serving, mutually suspicious states. The League of Nations was the embodiment of this strain of liberal thought. Its founders hoped to prevent future wars by organizing a system of **collective security** that would mobilize the entire international community against would-be aggressors. The League's founders declared that peace was indivisible: an attack on one member of the League would be considered an attack on all. Because no state was more powerful than the combination of all other states, aggressors would be deterred and war averted.

A second group called for the use of legal procedures to adjudicate disputes before they escalated to armed conflict. **Adjudication** is a judicial procedure for resolving conflicts by referring them to a standing court for a binding decision. Immediately after the war, several governments drafted a statute to establish a Permanent Court

The Granger Collection

IMAGE 2.3 Pioneer in the Liberal Quest for World Order Influenced by David Hume and Jean-Jacques Rousseau, Immanuel Kant, in *Perpetual Peace* (1795), helped to redefine modern liberal theory by advocating global (not state) citizenship, free trade, and a federation of democracies as a means to peace.

of International Justice (PCIJ). Hailed by Bernard C. J. Loder, the court's first president, as the harbinger of a new era of civilization, the PCIJ held its inaugural public meeting in early 1922 and rendered its first judgment on a contentious case the following year. Liberal champions of the court insisted that the PCIJ would replace military retaliation with a judicial body capable of bringing the facts of a dispute to light and issuing a just verdict.

A third group of liberal thinkers followed the biblical ideal that states should beat their swords into plowshares and sought disarmament as a means of avoiding war. Their efforts were illustrated between 1921 and 1922 by the Washington Naval Conference, which tried to curtail maritime competition among the United States, Great Britain, Japan, France, and Italy by placing limits on battleships. The ultimate goal of this group was to reduce international tensions by promoting general disarmament, which led them to convene the 1932 Geneva Disarmament Conference.

Although a tone of idealism dominated policy rhetoric and academic discussions during the interwar period, little of the liberal reform program was ever seriously attempted, and even less of it was achieved. The League of Nations failed to prevent the Japanese invasion of Manchuria (1931) or the Italian invasion of Ethiopia (1935); major disputes were rarely submitted to the PCIJ; and the 1932 Geneva Disarmament Conference ended in failure. When the threat of war began gathering over Europe and Asia in the late 1930s, enthusiasm for liberal idealism receded.

The next surge in liberal theorizing arose decades later in response to realism's neglect of **transnational relations**. Although realists continued to focus on the state, the events surrounding the 1973 oil crisis revealed that nonstate actors could affect the course of international events and occasionally compete with states. This insight led to the realization that **complex interdependence** (Keohane and Nye, 2013) sometimes offered a better description of world politics than realism, especially on international economic and environmental matters.

Rather than contacts between countries being limited to high-level governmental officials, multiple communication channels connect societies. Instead of security dominating foreign policy considerations, issues on national agendas do not always have a fixed priority, and although military force often serves as the primary instrument of statecraft, other means frequently are more effective when bargaining occurs between economically interconnected countries. In short, the realist preoccupation with government-to-government relations ignored the complex network of public and private exchanges crisscrossing state boundaries. States were becoming increasingly interdependent; that is, they were mutually dependent on, sensitive about, and vulnerable to one another in ways not captured by realist theory.

Although interdependence was not new, its growth during the last quarter of the twentieth century led many liberal theorists to challenge the realist conception of anarchy. Although they agreed that the global system was anarchic, they also argued that it was more properly conceptualized as an "ordered" anarchy because most states followed commonly acknowledged normative standards, even in the absence of hierarchical enforcement. When a body of norms fosters shared expectations that guide a regularized pattern of cooperation on a specific issue, we call it an **international regime**. Various types of regimes govern behavior in trade and monetary affairs, as well as manage access to common resources such as fisheries and river water. By the turn of the century, as pressing economic and environmental issues crowded national agendas,

transnational relations
Interactions across state boundaries that involve at least one actor that is not the agent of a government or intergovernmental organization.

complex interdependence
A model of world politics based on the assumptions that states are not the only important actors, security is not the dominant national goal, and military force is not the only significant instrument of foreign policy; this theory stresses crosscutting ways in which the growing ties among transnational actors make them vulnerable to each other's actions and sensitive to each other's needs.

international regime
Embodies the norms, principles, rules, and institutions around which global expectations unite regarding a specific international problem.

a large body of liberal "institutionalist" scholarship explored how regimes developed and what led states to comply with their injunctions.

neoliberalism
The "new" liberal theoretical perspective that accounts for the way international institutions promote global change, cooperation, peace, and prosperity through collective programs for reforms.

Fueled by the recent history suggesting that international relations can change and that increased interdependence can lead to higher levels of cooperation, **neoliberalism** emerged in the last decade of the twentieth century to challenge realism and neorealism. This new departure goes by several labels, including "neoliberal institutionalism" (Grieco, 1995), "neoidealism" (Kegley, 1993), and "neo-Wilsonian idealism" (Fukuyama, 1992).

Like realism and neorealism, neoliberalism does not represent a consistent intellectual movement or school of thought. Whatever the differences that divide them, however, all neoliberals share an interest in probing the conditions under which the convergent and overlapping interests among otherwise independent transnational actors may result in cooperation.

Neoliberalism departs from neorealism on many assumptions. In particular, neoliberalism focuses on the ways in which factors such as democratic governance, liberal commercial enterprise, international law and organization, collective security, and ethically inspired statecraft can improve life on our planet. Because they perceive change in global conditions as progressing over time through cooperative efforts, neoliberal theorists maintain that the ideas and ideals of the liberal legacy could describe, explain, predict, and prescribe international conduct in ways that they could not during the conflict-ridden Cold War.

The Limitations of Liberalism

Liberal theorists share an interest in probing the conditions under which similar interests among actors may lead to cooperation. Taking heart in the international prohibition, through community consensus, of such previously entrenched practices as slavery, piracy, dueling, and colonialism, they emphasize the prospects for progress through institutional reform. Studies of European integration during the 1950s and 1960s paved the way for the liberal institutionalist theories that emerged in the 1990s. The expansion of trade, communication, information, technology, and migrant labor led Europeans to sacrifice portions of their sovereign independence to create a new political and economic union out of previously separate units. These developments were outside of realism's worldview, creating conditions that made the call for a theory grounded in the liberal tradition more convincing. In the words of former U.S. President Bill Clinton, "In a world where freedom, not tyranny, is on the march, the cynical calculus of pure power politics simply does not compute. It is ill-suited to the new era."

Yet, as compelling as contemporary liberal institutionalism may seem at the onset of the twenty-first century, many realists complain that it has not transcended its idealist heritage. They charge that just like the League of Nations, institutions today exert minimal influence on state behavior. International organizations cannot stop states from behaving according to balance-of-power logic, calculating how each strategic move affects their relative position in a world of relentless competition.

Critics of liberalism further contend that most studies supportive of international institutions appear in the arena of commercial, financial, and environmental affairs, not in the arena of national defense. Although it may be difficult to draw a clear line between economic and security issues, some scholars note that "different institutional arrangements" exist in each realm, with the prospects for cooperation among self-interested states greater in the former than the latter (Lipson,

1984). National survival hinges on the effective management of security issues, realists insist. Collective security organizations naïvely assume that all members perceive threats in the same way and that they are willing to run the same risks and pay the same costs of countering those threats. Because power-lusting states are unlikely to always see their vital interests in this light, global institutions cannot provide timely, muscular responses to aggression. On security issues, conclude realists, states will trust in their own power, not in the promises of supranational institutions.

A final complaint lodged against liberalism is an alleged tendency to turn foreign policy into a moral crusade. Whereas realists claim that strategic necessities drive state decision making, many liberals believe moral imperatives can guide and constrain leaders. Consider the 1999 war in Kosovo, which pitted the North Atlantic Treaty Organization (NATO) against the Federal Republic of Yugoslavia. Pointing to Yugoslav leader Slobodan Milosevic's repression of ethnic Albanians living in the province of Kosovo, NATO Secretary General Javier Solana, British Prime Minister Tony Blair, and U.S. President Bill Clinton all argued that humanitarian intervention was a moral necessity. Although nonintervention into the internal affairs of other states has long been a cardinal principle of international law, they saw military action against Yugoslavia as a duty because human rights are an international entitlement and governments that violate them forfeit the protection of international law.

Sovereignty, according to many liberal thinkers, is not sacrosanct. The international community has a **responsibility to protect (RtoP, R2P)** vulnerable populations and an obligation to use armed force to stop flagrant violations of human rights. In accounting for U.S. military intervention in Libya in March 2011, these sentiments were reflected in then-President Barack Obama's declaration that the United States had a responsibility and moral obligation to respond to the violence perpetuated by Muammar al-Qaddafi's troops. "Some nations may be able to turn a blind eye to atrocities in other countries," proclaimed Obama. "The United States of America is different. And as president, I refused to wait for the images of slaughter and mass graves before taking action."

To sum up, realists remain skeptical about liberal claims of moral necessity and contend that "internal abuses by states—including the slaughter of civilians—do not automatically qualify as 'international' threats" (Doyle, 2011). On one hand, they deny the universal applicability of any single moral standard in a culturally pluralist world. On the other hand, they worry that adopting such a standard will breed a self-righteous, messianic foreign policy. Realists embrace **consequentialism**. If there are no universal standards covering the many situations in which moral choice must occur, then policy decisions can be judged only in terms of their consequences in particular circumstances. Prudent leaders recognize that competing moral values may be at stake in any given situation, and they must weigh the trade-offs among these values, as well as how pursuing them might impinge on national security and other important interests. As former U.S. diplomat and celebrated realist scholar George Kennan (1985) once put it, the primary obligation of government "is to the interests of the national society it represents, not to the moral impulses that individual elements of that society may experience."

responsibility to protect (RtoP, R2P)
Unanimously adopted in a resolution by the UN General Assembly in 2005, this principle holds that the international community must help protect populations from war crimes, ethnic cleansing, genocide, and crimes against humanity.

consequentialism
An approach to evaluating moral choices on the basis of the results of the action taken.

> *It's important that we take a hard clear look . . . not at some simple world, either of universal goodwill or universal hostility, but the complex, changing, and sometimes dangerous world that really exists.*
>
> **—JIMMY CARTER, FORMER U.S. PRESIDENT**

Constructivism

LO 2-4	Summarize the constructivist worldview, including its key concepts, evolution, and potential limitations.

constructivism
A paradigm based on the premise that world politics is a function of the ways that states construct and then accept images of reality and later respond to the meanings given to power politics; as consensual definitions change, it is possible for either conflictual or cooperative practices to evolve.

Constructivism is rapidly growing in influence as an approach for studying world politics. With intellectual roots in the twentieth-century Frankfurt School of critical social theory, contemporary scholars who have influenced the theoretical development of this perspective include Alexander Wendt, Friedrich Kratochwil, and Nicholas Onuf. Constructivism merits careful consideration because awareness of how our understandings of the world are individually and socially constructed, and of how prevailing ideas mold our beliefs about what is unchangeable and what can be reformed, enables us to see international relations in a new and critical light.

What Is the Constructivist Worldview?

Constructivism posits that world politics is best understood through the prism of intersubjective human action and the socially constructed nature of political life (DeBardeleben, 2012; Rathbun, 2012). Along these lines, a complete understanding of international relations requires knowledge of the social context underlying these relations—the identities of the actors, their norms of behavior, and their social interactions within the international system.

As discussed in the previous chapter, our images and understandings of the world define and shape reality. Though constructivists do not limit their analysis to the individual level, they view ideas, norms, and individual speech acts as shaping the global structure (Simão, 2012) and stress the intersubjective quality of images—how prevailing attitudes shape perception. For constructivists, this underscores the potential for *agency* as actors can reflect on their environment and seek change. Ideas define identities, which in turn impart meaning to material capabilities and behavior.

In the years following the Cold War, new norms about sovereignty emerged, particularly with regard to the acceptability of intervention in cases of gross human rights violations. Constructivism, like liberalism, recognizes the evolution of shared ideas as underpinning the growing legitimacy of the *responsibility to protect* concept, even though in practice it entails a violation of Westphalian sovereignty. From a constructivist perspective, this illustrates that "key elements of sovereignty, including territory, national identity and authority are not constants, but will change and evolve depending on society" (Ziegler, 2012, p. 404).

Similarly, the meaning of a concept such as "anarchy" depends on underlying shared knowledge. As Wendt (2013, p. 214) expressed, "anarchy is what states make of it." Anarchy among allies, for instance, holds a different meaning than anarchy among bitter rivals. Thus, British nuclear weapons are less threatening to the United States than the same weapons in North Korean hands, because shared Anglo-American expectations about one another differ from those between Washington and Pyongyang. The nature of an anarchic international system, therefore, is not a given. Anarchy and other socially constructed concepts, such as "sovereignty" and "power," are simply what we make of them (Wendt, 2013).

Moreover, because the social structure underlying these relationships is malleable, the ideas and interests of actors may change as the nature of their interactions, and the way they understand the other actors, changes. Thus, states with a history of rivalry can change the fundamental nature of their relationships if they are able to establish patterns of peaceful interactions and cooperation over time. A prominent example of this is the European Union, which is made up of many states that fought against each other in both World War I and World War II but subsequently have been able to develop a common identity or "we-feeling," in the latter half of the twentieth century. Key concepts of international relations, such as the institutions of war and slavery, may likewise change over time as the normative consensus surrounding them evolves.

Table 2.2 shows how constructivists differ from realists and liberals. As opposed to realism and liberalism, which assume that the fundamental structures of world politics are material and emphasize how objective factors such as military power and economic wealth affect international relations, constructivism sees the fundamental structures as social. Whereas realism and liberalism assume that an actor's preferences are given and fixed—with realism focusing on power, and liberalism on peace and prosperity—constructivism rejects rationalism and asserts that social structures shape behavior, as well as an actor's identity and interests. In other words, realism and liberalism "portray a world occupied by undifferentiated rational actors (i.e., self-interested states), whose relations are structured by the balance of material power. In contrast, constructivism . . . locate(s) actors in a social structure that both constitutes those actors and is constituted by their interaction" (Farrell, 2002, p. 50). Realism and liberalism take interests and identities as given, whereas these concepts are the central concern for constructivism.

TABLE 2.2   A Comparison of Realist, Liberal, and Constructivist Theories

Feature	Realism	Liberalism	Constructivism
Core concern	War and security: how vulnerable, self-interested states survive in an environment where they are uncertain about the intentions and capabilities of others	Institutionalized peace and prosperity: how self-serving actors learn to see benefits to coordinating behavior through rules and organizations to achieve collective gains	Social groups' shared meanings and images: how ideas, images, and identities develop, change, and shape world politics
Key actors	States	States, international institutions, global corporations	Individuals, nongovernmental organizations, transnational networks
Central concepts	Anarchy, self-help, national interest, relative gains, balance of power	Collective security, reciprocity, international regimes, complex interdependence, transnational relations	Ideas, images, shared knowledge, identities, discourses, and persuasion leading to new understandings and normative change
Approach to peace	Protect sovereign autonomy and deter rivals through military preparedness and alliances	Institutional reform through democratization, open markets, and international law and organization	Activists who promote progressive ideas and encourage states to adhere to norms for appropriate behavior
Global outlook	Pessimistic: great powers locked in relentless security competition	Optimistic: cooperative view of human nature and a belief in progress	Agnostic: global prospect hinges on the content of prevailing ideas and values

The Evolution of Constructivist Thought

The unraveling of the Warsaw Pact, the subsequent disintegration of the Soviet Union, the rise of religious fundamentalism, and the growth of micro-nationalism through the 1990s stimulated scholarly interest in constructivist interpretations of world politics. As political scientist Barry Buzan (2004, p. 1) observed, "after a long period of neglect, the social (or societal) dimension of the international system is being brought back into fashion within International Relations by the upsurge of interest in constructivism." Neither realism nor liberalism foresaw the peaceful end to the Cold War, and both theories had difficulty explaining why it occurred when it did (see Table 4.2 in Chapter 4). Constructivists attributed this to the material and individualist orientation of realism and liberalism, and argued that an explanation addressing the role of changing ideas and identities provided superior explanations for this systemic change.

social constructivism
A variant of constructivism that emphasizes the role of social discourse in the development of ideas and identities.

Like realism and liberalism, within the constructivist perspective there are several strands of thought. One of the most prominent is **social constructivism**, which emphasizes collective identity formation. Alexander Wendt, who is widely credited with the contemporary application of social constructivism to world politics, challenges the material and individualist foundations of realism and liberalism. For social constructivists, ideational construction of the self and the other are crucial: "It is through reciprocal interaction . . . that we create and instantiate the relatively enduring social structures in terms of which we define our identities and our interests" (Wendt, 2013). They see the structure of the international system in terms of the distribution of shared ideas, whereas neorealists view systemic structure within the context of the distribution of material capabilities and neoliberals see it as the distribution of capabilities within an institutional superstructure (see "Controversy: How Might Countries Respond to a Zombie Outbreak?"). According to social constructivism, all of us are influenced by collective conceptions of world politics that are reinforced by social pressures from the reference groups to which we belong.

There is, however, concern that social constructivism overemphasizes the role of social structures at the expense of the purposeful agents—such as a state's or organization's political leaders—whose practices help create and change these structures. Social constructivism tends to reify states by picturing them like individuals whose decisions become the authors of international life, and constructivism says little about the "practices that produce states as producers" (Weber, 2005, p. 76). A second strand of constructivism, **agent-oriented constructivism**, addresses this weakness with its emphasis on individual influences on identities.

agent-oriented constructivism
A variant of constructivism that sees ideas and identities as influenced in part by independent actors.

According to agent-oriented constructivism, independent actors in world politics may differ in their internal ideas or identities. Moreover, an actor can hold both domestic and international identities, which are shaped by respective dialogue at home and within the international community. Whereas social constructivists attribute the development of these identities to repeated social practices and view most identity as a shared or collective understanding, agent-oriented constructivists suggest identities need not be universally shared and allow for individual or autonomous identity within the collectivity. They credit the development of ideas in part to individual actors with the capacity for independent and critical thinking, making it far easier for new ideas to (re)construct and change the international system.

Controversy

HOW MIGHT COUNTRIES RESPOND TO A ZOMBIE OUTBREAK?

A popular phenomenon in pop culture, the emergence of zombies is commonly "related to social upheaval or historical events involving war, and appear[s] to be linked to fundamental human fears of death or infectious diseases" (Horn et al., 2015, p. 1). Viewing a zombie outbreak as a hypothetical strategic threat, and assessing the relative usefulness and applicability of different international relations theories, offers students a fun and unique way to explore the extent to which various international relations theories are able to explain state and individual responses to cataclysmic systemic change (Blanton, 2012).

Consider these questions: In a world suffering from a zombie outbreak, what effects would different systemic international relations theories predict? Would the outcomes be of little consequence, or would they result in the demise of human society as we know it?

- **Structural realism**. Due to an uneven distribution of capabilities, structural realism anticipates that some countries are better able than others to ward off zombies. Balance-of-power politics could ensue, with human states aligning with other human states to counter the global spread of zombieism. Or, as political analyst Daniel Drezner (2010, p. 37) suggests, "states could also exploit the threat from the living dead to acquire new territory, squelch irredentist movements, settle old scores, or subdue enduring rivals."

- **Liberal institutionalism**. As a strand of liberalism, liberal institutionalism sees a zombie outbreak as a problem that transcends national borders and threatens the global community writ large. Therefore, prudent states seek to cooperate with one another and coordinate efforts to contain and squash the zombie threat. Both global and regional regimes and institutions could serve as

important means for facilitating communication and directing the human response. For example, a World Zombie Organization (WZO) could be helpful in codifying international rules and procedures for responding to the zombie outbreak (see Drezner, 2011a).

- **Social constructivism**. With its emphasis on the development of norms and ideas, social constructivism anticipates that "the zombie problem is what we make of it" (Horn et al., 2015, p. 3). On one hand, relations between humans and zombies might best be reflected by the Hobbesian "kill or be killed" norm. Alternatively, a Kantian pluralistic antizombie community could emerge "that bands together and breaks down nationalist divides in an effort to establish a world state" (Drezner, 2009). Hostilities between humans and zombies might also strengthen group identity, where humans who have not been infected identify with one another as opposed to zombies, who seem to recognize each other as fellow "brain-eaters."

What Do You Think?

1. If you were the leader of your country, which theoretical orientation do you think would best help you address a zombie outbreak? Why?

2. Reflect upon the "real" global challenges facing us today, from the threat of terrorism to global warming to the worldwide economic downturn. Which concerns have the greatest impact upon our security, and how do realism, liberalism, and constructivism deal with these threats?

3. Should a country work toward international cooperation or international dominance? Draw on realism, liberalism, or constructivism to frame your response.

Accordingly, agent-oriented constructivists point to the challenge that Mikhail Gorbachev's "new thinking" posed to traditional Russian ideas about national security. Shifting from belief in irreconcilable conflict between capitalism and communism to the possibility of a foreign policy rooted in shared moral and ethical principles, Gorbachev's new thinking was reflected

norms
Generalized
standards of
behavior that,
once accepted,
shape collective
expectations about
appropriate conduct.

in a greater emphasis on political influence, diplomatic relations, and economic cooperation rather than intimidation and posturing through military power. Agent-oriented constructivism suggests that Gorbachev's new thinking led to the rise of new **norms** governing the relations between Moscow and Washington. Consensual understandings of interests, self-identities, and images of the world—how people think of themselves, who they are, and what others in the world are like—demonstrably can alter the world when these constructions of international realities change (Finnemore, 2013; Barnett, 2005).

A third strand of constructivism has more recently emerged that emphasizes the sentimental or affective sources of intersubjective instability, and addresses what some see as insufficient attention by earlier constructivist efforts to the role of psychology and emotion in shaping ideas and practices used by individual actors to promote change. Emotions are an essential element of political reasoning, shaping cognitive appraisals and value-laden perceptions, and are intrinsic to the processes of persuasion and argument (Graham, 2014; Dolan, 2016). Along these lines, constructivists have argued that "two of the most important policy failures" of the early twenty-first century—the U.S. invasion of Iraq and the Global Financial Crisis—cannot be understood without considering the psychological excesses of policy makers because "neo-conservative foreign policymakers and neoliberal economists respectively repressed unwanted information regarding weapons of mass destruction and predatory lending" (Widmaier and Park, 2012, p. 124).

The Limitations of Constructivism

Although constructivists have offered "path-breaking perspectives in the study of international politics" (Palan, 2000, p. 576) that share certain distinctive themes, some argue that constructivism is not a theory as such, but rather a general social scientific framework or "meta-approach." Whereas theoretical paradigms embrace a set of assumptions about how politics work, "constructivism is a set of assumptions about how to study politics," and hence is compatible with a variety of paradigms (Barkin, 2003, p. 338; Rathbun, 2012). Along this line of argument, constructivism supplements rather than supplants realism and liberalism.

Realists criticize constructivism for its emphasis on norms and values, and suggest that norms are simply manifestations of state or individual interests and can be superficially adopted for strategic reasons. Liberals, likewise, challenge that although many constructivists point to norms and values in explaining world politics, constructivism is agnostic and does not provide core notions about what should be right or ethical in international affairs (see Hoffmann, 2009). Although constructivism seeks to explain change, critics charge that constructivists remain unclear about what factors cause particular ideas to become dominant while others fall by the wayside. "What is crucial," asserts Robert Jervis (2005, p. 18), "is not people's thinking, but the factors that drive it." Constructivists, he continues, have excessive faith in the ability of ideas that seem self-evident today to replicate and sustain themselves; however, future generations who live under different circumstances and who may think differently could easily reject these ideas.

Although constructivism has often been portrayed as the opposite of realism due to differences in terms of realism's objective material emphasis and constructivism's intersubjective

Alexander Wendt/The Ohio State University

Martha Finnemore/The Elliott School of International Affairs

IMAGE 2.4A AND IMAGE 2.4B Pioneering Influences on Constructivist Thought Since the late 1980s, constructivism has become one of the leading schools of thought for explaining world politics. One of the most influential scholars, Alexander Wendt (left), challenged the materialism of neorealism and neoliberalism and argued that key concepts such as anarchy and power politics are socially constructed. Another, Martha Finnemore (right), emphasized the global diffusion of norms and the role of non-state actors.

ideational focus—and the liberal normative disposition of many constructivist scholars—it is now more commonly thought that realism and constructivism are not implacably opposed (Solomon, 2012b). Although constructivists recognize that shared ideas are not predetermined and can change over time, they claim a blending of constructivism with the realist and liberal paradigms could lead to greater understanding of change in the international system. Realist constructivism, for example, could look at the manner in which power structures shape patterns of normative change (Barkin, 2003).

Although scholars increasingly view constructivism as a vital perspective for understanding world politics, it is still criticized for its limited attention to methodological issues. According to Amir Lupovici (2009, p. 197), "scholars have tended to neglect the methodological dimension, providing little guidance on how to conduct a constructivist study." In an effort to address this deficiency, scholars have begun to call for a more systematic and unified framework that combines a number of existing methods so as to enable us to "examine the mutual influences of constitutive effects upon causal effects and vice versa" (Lupovici, 2009, p. 200). In other words, such a pluralistic methodology would help us to consider both the material and ideational factors that shape world politics.

Despite these criticisms, constructivism is a very popular theoretical approach in world politics. By highlighting the influence that socially constructed images of the world have on your interpretations of international events, and by making you aware of their inherent subjectivity, constructivism can remind you of the contingent nature of all knowledge and the inability of any theory of world politics to fully capture global complexities.

> *When I was working in Washington and helping formulate American foreign policies, I found myself borrowing from all three types of thinking: realism, liberalism, and constructivism. I found them all helpful, though in different ways and in different circumstances.*
>
> **—JOSEPH S. NYE, INTERNATIONAL RELATIONS SCHOLAR AND U.S. POLICY MAKER**

Other Theoretical Perspectives: Feminist and Marxist Critiques

LO 2-5   Discuss the tenets of feminist and Marxist perspectives, and illustrate how they diverge from those of realism, liberalism, and constructivism.

Although realism, liberalism, and constructivism dominate thinking about international relations in today's academic and policy communities, alternative perspectives challenge these schools of thought. Two of the most significant are feminism and Marxism.

The Feminist Critique

Beginning in the late 1980s, feminism began challenging conventional international relations theory. Cast as a "critical theory," contemporary feminist scholars "claim that we cannot fully understand international politics or the workings of the global economy without a gender analysis" (Tickner 2019, p. 153). In particular, **feminist theory** is concerned with the gender bias inherent in both mainstream theory and the practice of international affairs, and seeks to demonstrate how gendered perspectives pervade world politics. As feminist theory evolved over time, it moved away from focusing on a history of discrimination and began to explore how gender identity shapes foreign policy decision making and how gendered hierarchies reinforce practices that perpetuate inequalities between men and women (see Tickner, 2019; Peterson and Runyan, 2010; Ackerly and True, 2008; Enloe, 2004).

feminist theory Body of scholarship that emphasizes gender in the study of world politics.

According to the feminist critique, the mainstream literature on world politics dismisses the plight and contributions of women and treats differences in men's and women's status, beliefs, and behaviors as unimportant. Similar to social constructivism, the feminist critique emphasizes the role of identity in the construction of knowledge—but focuses specifically on gender identity and contends that the study of international relations draws heavily on male experiences to explain international affairs, largely dismissing the feminine dimension.

Critiquing realism, feminist scholar J. Ann Tickner (2013, p. 280) contends, "While realists claim that their theories are 'objective' and of universal validity, the assumptions they use when analyzing states and explaining their behavior in the international system are heavily dependent on characteristics that we, in the West, have come to associate with masculinity . . . it is therefore a worldview that offers us only a partial view of reality." Consider Morgenthau's classical realist depiction of states in an anarchical environment engaged in a persistent pursuit of power to further their own self-interest. Feminist scholars argue that realists overvalue the role of the state and deemphasize the individual and, when this occurs, there is even less acknowledgement of the female individual. Feminists also contend that while realism views key concepts such as national interest and security in terms of military power and protecting the state from other states, such concepts should encompass the well-being of individual citizens and safety for women against acts such as rape and violence as well. If gender considerations are not included in the discussion of security, characteristics deemed as feminine in quality may be dismissed and policy making may occur that is exclusive of and detrimental to women (Ruiz 2003).

Though liberalism considers the role of individuals, feminist critiques focus on gendered aspects of other key concepts in liberalism such as free trade and international institutions. Feminist theorists emphasize that economic inequalities disproportionately affect women and view the capitalist structure, embraced by liberalism and critiqued by Marxism, as patriarchal and prone to marginalize the work of women. Furthermore, according to feminist scholars, institutions such as the IMF and non-state actors such as multinational corporations tend to adopt elements of free trade that negatively affect women such as weakening of labor rights and reduction of public social funds (Ruiz 2003).

Feminism thus challenges the fundamentals of traditional international relations theory in four primary ways:

- **Fundamental gender bias.** A masculine tradition of thought heavily colors the basic assumptions of the mainstream theoretical literature, as well as the practice of foreign

IMAGE 2.5 Pioneering Influence on Feminist Thought Feminists challenge mainstream political thought and stress the importance of gender in studying international relations. In her path breaking book, *Bananas, Beaches and Bases: Making Feminist Sense of International Politics* (1989), Cynthia Enloe demonstrated the often invisible but important roles that women perform that influence foreign policy, diplomacy, trade, and processes of militarization.

policy. Rationality, independence, strength, protector, and public are characteristics that are considered to be masculine in nature, whereas emotionality, relational, weakness, protected, and private are associated with femininity (Tickner and Sjoberg, 2006). Whether characterizing individuals or states, these traits are seen as unequal. "To be a soldier is to be a man, not a woman; more than any other social institution, the military separates men from women. Soldiering is a role into which boys are socialized in school and on the playing fields. A soldier must be a protector; he must show courage, strength, and responsibility and repress feelings of fear, vulnerability, and compassion. Such feelings are womanly traits, which are liabilities in time of war" (Tickner, 2013, p. 283).

- **Incorporation of the female perspective.** Historically, the role of women has been marginalized in most societies. To understand how unequal gender relations have excluded women from foreign policy, perpetuated injustice and oppression, and shaped state interests and behavior, we must examine the female experience. Christine Sylvester's (2002) examination of women's cooperatives in Zimbabwe and women's peace activism at Greenham Common reflects a feminist commitment to a more flexible understanding of security that expands upon the traditional state-centric conceptualization as protection from external aggressors to include threats to economic and family concerns as well.

- **Reformulation of core concepts.** Feminists call for a closer examination of key concepts in world politics—such as state, power, interest, and security—and ask whether a "masculine" conceptualization of these ideas shapes the conduct of foreign policy. Realism, for instance, attributes to the state masculine characteristics of sovereignty that emphasize a hierarchical leader, the capacity to wage war, desirability of wealth and reputation, and the conduct of international affairs as separate from the domestic concerns of its populace. Feminist scholars such as Cynthia Enloe (2007), however, argue that gender influences power relations in ways that shape practices of war and diplomacy, and that alternative formulations of key concepts allow for the relevance of a wide range of other issues and structures, including social and economic ones, in world politics.

- **The scientific study of world politics.** As we have previously discussed, traditional international relations theory—particularly neorealism—has influenced the scientific study of world politics, which attempts to explain the behavior of states in the international system by universal, objective laws. Yet feminism questions the true objectivity of these approaches. Spike Petersen, a prominent feminist theorist, notes that there was an explicit masculine bias in the scientific revolution of the seventeenth century, with science/reasoning attributed as a "male" trait and emotion/intuition as a "female" one. Feminism does not embrace a sole methodological approach, and the "idea that theorizing is 'objective'" is rejected by many feminists in favor "of a perspectival approach, which links the possibility of insight to specific standpoints and political agendas" (Hutchings, 2008, p. 100).

IMAGE 2.6 **Protesting For Peace** Between 1981 and 2000, tens of thousands of British women mobilized to protest against nuclear proliferation and the stationing of U.S. nuclear air missiles at the Greenham Common Airbase in Berkshire, England by creating a 14-mile chain around the airbase with their bodies. They saw peace as a feminist issue, viewing nuclear weapons not only as a direct threat to themselves and their children, but also protesting the trillions spent on weapons of mass destruction while so many around the world suffered from a lack of food and water, inadequate health care, and underfunded schools.

While various feminist scholars focus on different elements of gender and international relations, the importance of gender emancipation in the practice of world politics is another common theme. Feminist theory sees key actors in world politics, such as policy makers, heads of state, and diplomats, as typically having been males who embody and perpetuate patriarchal social and political hierarchies. Over the past several decades, awareness and concern about the marginalization and exclusion of women in international affairs has increased. Women are just as skilled and competent as are men, and should have an equal opportunity to participate in world politics. Whether in positions of political, economic, or military leadership, excluding women squanders talent and means that state and organizational capabilities fall short of their full potential. Feminists call for the removal of legal and societal barriers that prevent women from full participation, and hence see the state and the international community as a possible ally (or in some cases, opponent) for overcoming the oppression of women.

Some critics of feminism are skeptical of its historical and interpretative approach to investigating research questions. They argue that there is a greater need for feminist scholars to develop scientifically testable hypotheses (Keohane, 1998); this would make it easier to assess competing claims and increase the validity of feminist research. Other critics argue that feminism has an inherent normative bias and active political agenda, and are skeptical about objectivity in feminist scholarship. Still others charge that feminism errs when it treats women as a homogenous category (Mohanty, 1988). Not all women are the same or share similar life experiences and factors such as race, culture, and social class may condition important differences.

The feminist critique continues to expand across a range of issues, from foreign policy to humanitarian intervention to terrorism, and a variety of actors, from states to nongovernmental organizations. "Women have never been absent in world politics," writes Franke Wilmer (2000), though they have largely remained "invisible within the discourse conducted by men." To counter this marginalization of women, "We must search deeper to find ways in which gender hierarchies serve to reinforce these socially constructed boundaries which perpetuate inequalities between women and men" (Tickner, 2010, p. 38).

socialism
Body of scholarship that emphasizes public ownership and control of property and resources.

capitalism
An economic system characterized by private ownership of the means of production and distribution.

The Marxist Critique

For much of the twentieth century, socialism was the primary radical alternative to mainstream international relations theorizing. Whereas realists emphasize state security, liberals accentuate individual freedom, and constructivists highlight ideas and identities, socialists focus on class conflict and the material interests of each class. Socialism envisions society as optimally characterized by public ownership and control of property and resources, to the benefit of individuals living in concert with one another. This is in contrast to capitalism, which is premised on the private ownership of the means of production and permits individual choice through a free market to determine the distribution of goods and services.

There are many strands of socialist thought, and they diverge over the extent to which society should own or control property and whether society should exercise its control through a central authority or at the local level of the people. Karl Marx, however, is widely viewed as the most prominent theorist of socialism. He, along with his coauthor Friedrich Engels (1820–1895), argued that socialism emerges through the clash of social classes as opposed to the establishment of harmonious communities. "The history of all hitherto existing society," proclaimed Marx and Engels in the *Communist Manifesto*, "is the history of class struggles."

Though Marx saw capitalism as a historically progressive force for economic development that made possible the industrial revolution, he argued that it was also highly exploitative and gave rise to two antagonistic classes: a ruling class (bourgeoisie) that owns the means of production and a subordinate class (proletariat) that sells its labor for only a token compensation. The working class is estranged from, and lacks authority over, the

INTERFOTO/Alamy Stock Photo

IMAGE 2.7 Karl Marx Challenges International Theoretical Orthodoxy Pictured here is the German philosopher Karl Marx (1818–1883). His revolutionary theory of the economic determinants of world history inspired the spread of communism to overcome the class struggles so pronounced in most countries. The target of his critique was the compulsion of the wealthy great powers to subjugate foreign people by military force and to create colonies for purposes of financial exploitation. Imperial conquest of colonial peoples could only be prevented, Marx warned, by humanity's shift from a capitalist to a socialist economy and society.

products of their labor. Instead, **Marxism** holds that the ruling class controls and benefits disproportionately from the **surplus value** generated by the subordinate working class's labor. Through the labor of workers, raw materials are transformed into products of greater value. Yet workers lack bargaining power and tend to receive a fixed wage for their labor irrespective of the value added, while the owners of companies unfairly reap a greater portion of surplus value as realized through increased profits. Marxism anticipates that class struggle will result, sometimes through violent rebellion, wherein the oppressed working class seeks power and a greater share of wealth. Marxism has had considerable influence in countries in the Global South where there is pronounced inequality and workers endure harsh labor conditions and low wages.

Although Marx's theory of economic exploitation focused on domestic class struggle, the antagonistic relationship between classes plays a key role in determining the characteristics of international relations. In Marxism, human nature per se is not treated as a given or as a primary determinant of international relations, but is rather seen as "shaped by interaction with others and with the environment" (Brown, 2012, p. 650). This interaction creates a predatory international system with the core states benefiting from the subjugation of peripheral states. According to Marx and Engels, "The need of a constantly expanding market for its products chases the bourgeoisie over the whole surface of the globe." By expanding worldwide, the bourgeoisie give "a cosmopolitan character to production and consumption in every country."

Building on these ideas, Vladimir Ilyich Lenin (1870–1924) in the Soviet Union extended Marx's analysis to the study of **imperialism**, which he interpreted as a stage in the development of capitalism when monopolies overtake free-market competition. Drawing from the work of British economist John Hobson (1858–1940), Lenin maintained that advanced capitalist states eventually face the twin problems of overproduction and under consumption. They respond by waging wars to divide the world into spheres of influence, forcing these new foreign markets to consume the surplus goods and capital. European colonization of the Global South also was seen as a means for the capitalist ruling class to placate their own domestic working class by sharing some of the profits accrued through exploitation of laborers in the colonies. Although Lenin's assertions have been heavily criticized on conceptual and empirical grounds, the socialist attention to social classes and uneven development stimulated several new waves of theorizing about capitalism as a global phenomenon.

One prominent example is **dependency theory**. As expressed in the writings of André Gunder Frank (1969), Amir Samin (1976), and others (see Chapter 4), dependency theorists claimed that much of the poverty in Asia, Africa, and Latin America stemmed from the exploitative capitalist world economy. As they saw it, the economies of less developed countries had become dependent on exporting inexpensive raw materials and agricultural commodities to advanced industrial states, while simultaneously importing expensive manufactured goods from them. Theotonio Dos Santos (1971, p. 158), a prominent dependency scholar, described dependency as a "historical condition which shapes a certain structure of the world economy such that it favors some countries to the detriment of others." Dependency theory was criticized for recommending withdrawal from the world economy (Shannon, 1989), and eventually theoretical efforts arose to trace the economic ascent and decline of individual countries as part of long-term, system-wide change (Clark, 2008).

Marxism
A theoretical critique of the capitalist status quo that views the ruling class as benefiting unfairly through the exploitation of the subordinate working class.

surplus value
From a Marxist perspective, the difference between the value of the raw materials and the value of the final product as enhanced through workers' labor.

imperialism
The policy of expanding state power through the conquest and/or military domination of foreign territory.

dependency theory
A theory hypothesizing that less developed countries are exploited because global capitalism makes them dependent on the rich countries that create exploitative rules for trade and production.

Jay Directo/AFP/Getty Images

IMAGE 2.8 Haves and Have-Nots This photo of Makati in the Philippines captures the dramatic inequalities that exist in many, if not all, cities across the globe. Some enjoy rising prosperity while some live in desperate squalor. Marxists see both domestic and international relations as shaped by class struggle between the wealthy and the poor.

world-system theory
A body of theory that treats the capitalistic world economy originating in the sixteenth century as an interconnected unit of analysis encompassing the entire globe, with an international division of labor and multiple political centers and cultures whose rules constrain and share the behavior of all transnational actors.

World-system theory, which was influenced by both Marxist and dependency theorists, interprets world politics in terms of an integrated division of labor within an overarching capitalist world economy (Wallerstein, 1988, 2005). World-system theory views the capitalist world economy, which emerged in sixteenth-century Europe and ultimately expanded to encompass the entire globe, as hierarchical in structure. Within this hierarchy, states occupy one of three positions: core (strong, well-integrated states with diversified economic activities centered on possession and use of capital), periphery (areas lacking strong state machinery and engaged in producing relatively few unfinished goods by unskilled, low-wage labor), or semi-periphery (states embodying elements of both core and peripheral production). Within the world economy as a whole, the continual accumulation of capital within the core from the periphery and semi-periphery perpetuates the advantages held by core states. A core state may gain economic primacy by achieving productive, commercial, and financial superiority over its rivals. Yet primacy is difficult to sustain. The diffusion of technological innovations and the flow of capital to competitors, plus the massive costs of maintaining global order, all erode the dominant state's economic advantage. Thus, in addition to underscoring the exploitation of the periphery by the core, world-system theory calls attention to the cyclical rise and fall of hegemonic superpowers at the top of the core hierarchy.

With the end of the Cold War, and the concomitant failures of the Soviet regime, there are fewer advocates today for organizing society along Marxist principles. Yet these various radical challenges to mainstream theorizing continue to enhance our understanding of world politics

TABLE 2.3   Additional Theoretical Perspectives: The Feminist and Marxist Critiques

Feature	Feminist Critique	Marxist Critique
Core concern	Gendered identity and bias in mainstream theory and the practice of world politics; inequality between men and women	Detrimental effects of capitalism on the world stage that result in economic and political inequality between classes
Key actors	States, individuals, women	Classes, states, owners, workers
Central concepts	Gender bias, masculine conceptualization of world politics	Inequality, exploitation of labor, imperialism, capitalism, dependency
Approach to peace	Broaden conceptualization of security to include threats to personal security; recognize peaceful externalities of respect for women's rights; and potential for cooperation	Global cooperation disproportionately benefits the wealthy; seek to transform, through political violence if necessary, an inherently unfair economic structure
Global outlook	Mixed: unequal relations between sexes and gendered power structures perpetuate injustice and oppression, though increased equality can provide sweeping benefits	Pessimistic: the rich benefit from the subjugation of the poor and this antagonistic relationship between classes leads to conflict

by highlighting the roles played by corporations, transnational religious movements, and other nonstate actors. Furthermore, they help to push mainstream theorists to identify, question, and clarify their own assumptions and theoretical propensities (see Table 2.3). Yet they overemphasize economic interpretations of international events and consequently omit other potentially important explanatory factors. Some critics of Marxism have also accused it of partaking in the theoretical simplification that it had sought to overcome and leaving key political ideas, such as revolutionary social change, ambiguous. In fact, international relations scholar Andrew Davenport (2013) goes so far as to suggest that this is one of the major deficiencies of Marxist theorizing today.

International Theory and the Global Future

LO 2-6   Understand the need for multiple theories and worldviews in developing a comprehensive understanding of world politics.

To understand our changing world and to make reasonable prognoses about the future, we must begin by arming ourselves with an array of information and conceptual tools, entertain rival interpretations of world politics in the global marketplace of ideas, and question the assumptions on which these contending worldviews rest. Because there are a great (and growing) number of alternative, and sometimes incompatible, ways of organizing theoretical inquiry about world politics, the challenge of capturing the world's political problems cannot be reduced to any one simple, yet compelling account (Chernoff, 2008). Each paradigmatic effort to do so in the past has ultimately lost advocates as developments in world affairs eroded its continuing relevance.

As you seek to understand changing global conditions, it is important to be humble in recognizing the limitations of our understandings of world politics and, at the same time, be inquisitive about its character. The task of interpretation is complicated because the world is complex. Political scientist Donald Puchala framed the challenge in 2008 by observing:

> Conceptually speaking, world affairs today can be likened to a disassembled jigsaw puzzle scattered on a table before us. Each piece shows a fragment of a broad picture that as yet remains indiscernible. Some pieces depict resurgent nationalism; others show spreading democracy; some picture genocide; others portray prosperity through trade and investment; some picture nuclear disarmament; others picture nuclear proliferation; some indicate a reinvigorated United Nations; others show the UN still enfeebled and ineffective; some describe cultural globalization; others predict clashing civilizations.
>
> How do these pieces fit together, and what picture do they exhibit when they are appropriately fitted?

Theories can guide us in fitting the pieces together to form an accurate picture. Whereas theories like realism, liberalism, constructivism, feminism, and Marxism "do not provide case-specific knowledge or recommendations, they provide general roadmaps, conceptualization of world affairs, and also have a symbolic function, legitimating or challenging established policy paradigms" (Eriksson, 2014, p. 94). However, in evaluating the usefulness of any theory to

A Closer Look

COMPETING VALUES AND INTERESTS: THE CASE OF BREXIT

Created after World War II to encourage peace through cross-border commerce and cooperation, the European Union (EU) created a "single market" that allows free movement of goods and people across state borders as well as a supranational parliament that sets rules for EU members in a number of areas such as consumer rights, the environment, and transport (see Chapter 6). The United Kingdom has long had an uneasy relationship with the EU. For example, Britain's wariness about the EU led the UK to negotiate a reduced contribution to the EU budget and opt-out of some economic policies, most notably the common EU currency (see Chapter 10).

These tensions between British sovereignty and this powerful international institution came to a head on June 23, 2016, when the UK held a referendum on whether to leave the EU, with 51.9% voting in favor of leaving. No full member has ever left the EU, and there is no precedent for the complex negotiations over the terms of the UK's exit.

"Advocates of a British exit, or Brexit, from the union argued that by reclaiming national sovereignty, the UK would be better able to manage immigration, free itself from onerous regulations, and spark more dynamic growth" (McBride 2019). Fears over mass migration, coupled with tragic terrorist attacks in Europe, fueled this perspective. With more than 300,000 people migrating to the UK in 2015, former Prime Minister David Cameron lamented, "It was never envisaged that free movement would trigger quite such vast numbers of people moving across our continent."

Opponents argue that membership in the EU has never jeopardized the sovereignty of the UK, immigration from the EU fueled growth, and the Commonwealth stands to lose preferential access to its largest trading partner. The economic costs could be prohibitive. The Bank of England estimates that a "no-deal Brexit" – a worst-case scenario in which the UK leaves without negotiating any terms for its exit – "could precipitate an 8 percent drop in gross domestic product (GDP), a 3.4 percent rise in unemployment, and a tripling of the inflation rate" (Chatzky, 2019). There are also worries that Brexit will hinder the mobility and status of millions of UK citizens living in the EU and non-UK EU citizens living in the UK, as well as damage European security and defense cooperation (Keohane, 2016).

Ultimately, many feel that Brexit undermines the liberal project of European integration, which was a model of peaceful economic growth through expanded interdependence. Others feel that Brexit was a victory for British sovereignty, which would allow the UK to focus more clearly on its own national interests, as it would no longer have to answer to a powerful international institution. Given these deep divides, the nature of UK-EU relations post-Brexit remains uncertain.

Watch the Carnegie Council Video:
"A. C. Grayling: Arguing Against the Brexit 'Leave' Vote"

You Decide:
1. What insights do realism and liberalism provide on Brexit? Do other theoretical perspectives provide additional insights about the issue?
2. Which arguments about Brexit do you find most persuasive? Why?
3. Will Brexit weaken the EU as an institution?

interpret global conditions, the historical overview in this chapter suggests that it would be wrong to oversimplify or to assume that a particular theory will remain useful in the future. Nonetheless, as American poet Robert Frost observed, any belief we cling to long enough is likely to be true again someday because "most of the change we think we see in life is due to truths being in and out of favor." So in our theoretical exploration of world politics, we must critically assess the accuracy of our impressions, avoiding the temptation to embrace one world-view and abandon another without any assurance that their relative worth is permanently fixed.

Although realism, liberalism, and constructivism are the dominant ways of thinking about world politics today, none of these theories is completely satisfactory. Recall that realism is criticized for relying on ambiguous concepts, liberalism is often derided for making naïve policy recommendations based on idealistic assumptions, and constructivism is charged with being a social scientific framework rather than a "real" theory. Moreover, as the challenges mounted by feminism and the Marxist critique suggest, these three mainstream theories overlook seemingly important aspects of world politics, which limits their explanatory power. Despite these drawbacks, each has strengths for interpreting certain kinds of international events and foreign policy behaviors and "theoretical pluralism exposes analytical and circumstantial differences that matter for understanding" (Sterling-Folker, 2015, p. 40).

Because we lack a single overarching theory able to account for all facets of world politics, we draw on realist, liberal, and constructivist thought in subsequent chapters. Moreover, we supplement them with insights from feminist and the Marxist critiques when these theoretical traditions can best help to interpret the topic covered.

> *Whenever a theory appears to you as the only possible one, take this as a sign that you have neither understood the theory nor the problem which it was intended to solve.*
>
> **— KARL POPPER, PHILOSOPHER**

Study. Apply. Analyze.

Chapter Summary

2-1 Identify how theories are defined and articulate why they are important in world politics. Theories specify conditions under which relationships between factors exist and provide reasons for those linkages. Theories have diagnostic, prescriptive, and lesson-drawing value, and the relationship between theory and world politics is interactive.

2-2 Summarize the realist worldview, including its key concepts, evolution, and potential limitations. The intellectual roots of realism reach back to ancient Greece, with modern realism emerging with the onset of World War II. There are different variants of realism,

though common threads highlight self-interested leaders and sovereign states that differ from each other in their national interests and seek advantage and power in an anarchical international system. Critics point to a lack of precision in key realist concepts, historical data, and epistemological rules. They also contend that realism has not accounted for significant new developments in world politics, such as the end of the Cold War.

2-3 Summarize the liberal worldview, including its key concepts, evolution, and potential limitations. Liberalism has roots in the Enlightenment, with contemporary liberal theory rising to prominence following World War I. Within liberalism, several distinct strands exist that vary in their emphasis on the importance of political reforms, free trade, and global institutions. Liberalism embodies a belief in human reason and the possibility of progress, with world politics a struggle for cooperation and mutual gain. Critics are skeptical of liberal claims of moral necessity. They also charge that application of liberal theory is weak in the realm of national defense and can lead to a messianic foreign policy.

2-4 Summarize the constructivist worldview, including its key concepts, evolution, and potential limitations. With intellectual roots in the twentieth-century Frankfurt School of critical theory, constructivism increased in prominence following the Cold War. It posits that we can best understand world politics in terms of intersubjective human action and the socially constructed nature of political life. Critics charge that constructivism is more of a philosophically informed perspective than a full-fledged general theory and pays limited attention to methodological issues. Some take issue with its emphasis on norms and values, and contend that it is unclear about what factors cause particular ideas to dominate.

2-5 Discuss the tenets of feminist and Marxist perspectives, and illustrate how they diverge from those of realism, liberalism, and constructivism.

Feminism and Marxism are two challengers to mainstream international relations theory. The feminist critique argues that we must pay greater attention to the plights and contributions of women, and demonstrates how gendered perspectives pervade world politics. Whereas realists claim objectivity and universal validity, liberalism focuses on individuals and values, and constructivism emphasizes ideas and identity, the feminist critique contends that mainstream theory draws heavily on male experiences to explain world politics and largely dismisses the feminine dimension. The Marxist critique sees socialism as a response to a clash of social classes, and views capitalism as a highly exploitative system wherein the ruling class controls and benefits unfairly from the labor of workers. Whereas realists emphasize state security, liberals accentuate individual freedom, and constructivists highlight ideas and identities, the Marxist critique focuses on class conflict and the material interests of each class.

2-6 Understand the need for multiple theories and worldviews in developing a comprehensive understanding of world politics. To understand world politics, you must be able to draw on an array of conceptual tools and be able to consider rival interpretations. Given the alternative ways of organizing theoretical inquiry and the challenge of simplifying the world's political phenomena, it is important to engage in a critical and complex analysis of the world around you.

Key Terms

agency	diplomacy	neorealism	social constructivism
agent-oriented constructivism	feminist theory	norms	socialism
balance of power	imperialism	offensive realism	surplus value
capitalism	international regime	paradigm	theory
collective security	Kellogg-Briand Pact	realism	transnational relations
complex interdependence	liberalism	relative gains	world-system theory
consequentialism	Marxism	responsibility to protect	zero-sum
constructivism	national interest	(RtoP, R2P)	
defensive realism	neoconservative	security dilemma	
dependency theory	neoliberalism	self-help	

Suggested Readings and Resources

Constructivism: International Relations Theory in Brief: www.bukisa.com/ articles/335688_constructivism-international-relations-theory-in-brief. A website offering a thorough insight to constructivism.

Guilhot, Nicolas. (2017). *After the Enlightenment: Political Realism and International Relations in the Mid-Twentieth Century*, Cambridge: Cambridge University Press.

International Relations Marxism: internationalrelationsonline.com/ international-relations-marxism/. A website offering an overview of Marxism.

International Relations Theories: internationalrelationsonline.com/

international-relations-theories/. A website that focuses on international relations theories.

Political Realism in International Relations: plato.stanford.edu/entries/ realism-intl-relations/. An essay on realist theory.

Srivastava, Swati. (2019), "Varieties of Social Construction," *International Studies Review* 0: 1–22.

Sterling-Folker, Jennifer. (2015). "All Hail to the Chief: Liberal IR Theory in the New World Order." *International Studies Perspectives* 16: 40–49.

Theory Talks: www.theory-talks.org. An interactive forum for discussion of

debates in world politics with an emphasis of theoretical issues.

Tickner J. Ann. (2019) "Gender Research in International Relations." In: Sawer M., Baker K. (eds). *Gender Innovation in Political Science: New Norms, New Knowledge.* Palgrave Macmillan: 153–171.

Understanding Society: understandingsociety.blogspot.com/. A blog that focuses on social agency and structure.

Walt, Stephen: foreignpolicy.com/ author/stephen-m-walt/. A blog by an international relations realist scholar.

Carnegie Council Videos

Key Term Videos

- Realism
- Liberalism
- Diplomacy

- Zero-sum
- Collective Security
- International Regime

- Neoliberalism
- Social Constructivism
- Norms

Additional Videos

- Betts, Richard. "The World Ahead: Conflict or Cooperation?"
- Nye, Joseph, Jr. "The Future of Power."
- Kegley, Charles, Jr. "East Asian Security and Democracy: The Place of Taiwan."
- Slaughter, Anne-Marie, and Joanne Myers. "The Crisis of American Foreign Policy: Wilsonianism in the Twenty-First Century."
- Wright, Robin. "Dreams and Shadows: The Future of the Middle East."

Chapter 3

Theories of International Decision Making

IMAGE 3.1 **The Determinants of Foreign Policy** Policy makers face an array of constraints and opportunities both within and outside their borders. While individual perceptions and group dynamics often play a key role in decision making, in smaller countries external factors can have a particularly profound impact upon policy options. Ukraine provides an example of such constraints, being caught between the competing interests of NATO, the EU, and Russia. Shown here, President Petro Poroshenko meets with the Ukrainian parliament in November 2018 to discuss prospects for Ukraine's integration with NATO and the EU.

Learning Objectives

LO 3-1 Use a level-of-analysis approach to identify the major influences on foreign policy decision making.

LO 3-2 Summarize and compare the rational choice, individual-based, and bureaucratic politics models of foreign policy.

LO 3-3 Describe the key ways in which state characteristics, including military capabilities, economic conditions, and regime type, influence foreign policy.

LO 3-4 Explain how power polarity and geopolitics influence foreign policy making.

> *Decisions and actions in the international arena can be understood, predicted, and manipulated only insofar as the factors influencing the decision can be identified and isolated."*
>
> **—ARNOLD WOLFERS, POLITICAL SCIENTIST**

Y ou have completed your higher education degrees in international studies and have now embarked on your career. Your employment allows you to apply your acquired knowledge to help make the world a better place. As a result of wise and efficient use of your analytic capabilities in your work with the World Health Organization (WHO), you now find that you have earned a very important appointment: to head and lead an established nongovernmental organization (NGO) in your area of expertise. In that role, you will construct your NGO's *foreign policy*. Your challenge is to make decisions, based on your organization's values, about the foreign policy goals your NGO should pursue as well as the means by which those international goals might best be realized.

Congratulations! You have decision-making power. Now your task is to make critical choices that are destined to determine whether your foreign policies will succeed. How will you, as a governing authority of a transnational *actor* on the world stage, make decisions that will best serve your organization's interest and the world at large?

There is no sure path as to how to make foreign policy decisions that are workable, moral, and successful—and your approach will partly depend on your preferences and priorities. You will face many obstacles and constraints on your ability to make informed choices. As former U.S. Secretary of State Henry Kissinger warns, foreign policy decisions are rarely made by people who have all the facts; the policy maker "has to act in the fog of incomplete knowledge without the information that will be available later to the analyst." In addition, any choice you might make is certain to carry costs that compromise some values you hold dear and undermine some of the other goals you would like to pursue. Therefore, you now face the kind of challenge that has befuddled every decision maker who has had the power to make foreign policy decisions on behalf of the transnational actor he or she led.

Foreign Policy Making in International Affairs

LO 3-1	Use a level-of-analysis approach to identify the major influences on foreign policy decision making.

This chapter, which is based on historical experience and theories of international relations, looks at patterns of international decision making by all transnational actors—the individuals, groups, states, and organizations that play a role in world politics. Thus, it not only covers the decision-making practices of countries but also those of international organizations such as the World Bank; nongovernmental organizations (NGOs) such as Amnesty International; multinational corporations such as Royal Dutch Shell; indigenous nationalities such as Kurds in Iran, Iraq, and Turkey; and terrorist networks such as Al Qaeda or ISIS.

In addition, it is important to reflect on how each of us—all individual people—are part of the equation. We are all, in a sense, transnational actors capable of making free choices that contribute to the direction of trends in world politics. When mobilized and inspired by a sense of purpose, individuals can make a difference in the course of world history; indeed, the decisions that we make every day and the groups that we join are reflections of our own personal "foreign policies," whether or not we are aware of the consequences of our daily choices. Every person matters. As American anthropologist Margaret Mead advised, "Never doubt that a small group of thoughtful, committed citizens can change the world. Indeed, it is the only thing that ever has."

Transnational Actors and Decision Processes

This chapter opens a window to rival ways of describing and analyzing international decision making by transnational actors. You will be introduced to some of the lessons that theory and history provide about the relative strengths and weaknesses of these approaches, and develop the tools to critically assess decision-making outcomes and processes.

The major theoretical schools of thought (see Chapter 2) provide some insights into international decision making. *Neorealism* eschews the explanatory importance of the individual level of analysis in favor of systemic explanations, whereas neoclassical realism allows for the dominance of the international system and relative material capabilities to be filtered through the state. "State responses are affected by a wide range of domestic political and decision-making factors including perceptions, states' motives, political traditions and identities, domestic institutions and coalition building, and perceived lessons of the past" (Kaarbo, 2015, p. 15). Thus, although system-level factors account for enduring trends, neoclassical realists look to internal and individual dynamics to explain particular foreign policies (Foulon, 2015).

Variants of *liberalism* largely assume that individuals and nonstate actors are major players in world politics and that they "pay more attention to domestic structures and individual differences than do realists" (Doyle, 2012, p. 66). Explanations for foreign policy—such as the democratic peace thesis about why democracies are less likely to go to war with one another—emphasize the role of public opinion, cultural values and norms, and institutions (Dafoe, Oneal, and Russett, 2013).

Strands of *constructivism* also address international decision making. While some constructivists focus on shared norms at the systemic level, others focus on such forces inside the decision-making unit. "Constructivist concepts of culture, identity, ideas, discourse, and roles, for example, have been used to explain why the foreign policies of some states defy realist and liberal expectations" (Kaarbo, 2015, p. 11).

Theories of international relations offer important insights, but they are critiqued as not going far enough in developing conceptions of agency and incorporating internal factors. There are, however, explanations drawn from these theories that emphasize the pivotal role of the decision-making units and provide a rich foundation for understanding policy making. These approaches enable us to move beyond the generalities of international relations theories to better understand foreign policy decisions in specific cases.

To stimulate your thinking about international decision making by all types of transnational actors, *World Politics* provides a framework for analyzing and explaining the processes by which foreign policies are made.

Influences on Making Foreign Policy Decisions

To structure theoretical thinking about international decision making, it is useful to consider the factors that influence the ways in which all transnational actors make foreign policy decisions. It is important to recognize that no single category of causation can fully explain foreign policy decisions; rather, a number of influences converge to codetermine the decisions that produce foreign policy "outputs."

Speaking on the making of American foreign policy decisions, former U.S. Secretary of State Henry Kissinger pointed out, "One of the most unsettling things for foreigners is the impression that our foreign policy can be changed by any new president on the basis of the president's personal preference." Yet, although a president's personal inclinations may influence policy decisions, all leaders are constrained by various circumstances that restrict free choice. As former U.S. presidential adviser Joseph A. Califano observed, "a president is a prisoner of historical forces that will demand his attention whatever his preference in policy objectives." Thus, to get to the essence of how international decision making takes place, we must go beyond a single-factor explanation and think in terms of multiple causes.

For that, it is useful to identify the various clusters of variables that affect the choices all types of transnational actors make when they formulate a foreign policy. Similar to the *level-of-analysis* distinction introduced in Chapter 1 (see Figure 1.1), we can construct a framework of the determinants of decision making in the foreign policy-making process by referencing three major sets of causal variables at the individual, internal, and global levels of analyses:

- **Individual decision makers.** The personal characteristics of the leaders heading international actors assume great importance in making international decisions as their individual values, personalities, beliefs, intelligence, and prior experiences predispose them to take certain kinds of positions on global issues. As political scientist Arnold Wolfers (1962, p. 50) explained, leaders are influential because:

  factors external to the actor can become determinants only as they affect the mind, the heart, and the will of the decision maker. A human decision to act in a specific way necessarily represents the last link in the chain of antecedents of any act of policy. A geographical set of conditions, for instance, can affect the behavior of a nation only as specific persons perceive and interpret these conditions.

  Although changes in global conditions and actors' collective internal characteristics may influence the costs and benefits of particular foreign policy options and stimulate the need for choice, these are mediated by leaders' perceptions. As constructivist theory argues, leaders' ideas and expectations are the intellectual filters through which they interpret objective realities. Therefore, to explain why any international decision is made, it is imperative to take into account how leaders' ideas and images influence the choices taken.

- **Internal influences.** Every actor on the global stage is defined by its own attributes, which also act to determine the actor's foreign policy choices. As important as the individual decision maker is, it would be a mistake to think foreign policy leaders alone are the sole source driving international decision making. Internal characteristics—such as wealth, military might, and public opinion—of the transnational actor making the decision heavily shape the range of choices open to the individual decision maker.

All international actors organized to take action abroad are composed of a collection of individuals. How these group actors are governed, and the processes and procedures they follow to reach foreign policy decisions, are forces of their own that structure and determine the decisions that are reached. The size of the organization, its power relative to the other actors with which it interacts, the financial resources, and the distribution of opinion within the actor all affect its capacity to make foreign policy choices in response to changes in global circumstances.

- **Global factors.** Global conditions provide constraints and opportunities for international decision making and color the degree to which both an actor's internal attributes and individual leader preferences can account for the choices made. The changing state of the world—everything that occurs beyond the actor—affects the decisions of international actors. The prevailing global circumstances define the decisional situation, provoking the need to make decisions and restricting policy options available to the actor. As John Quincy Adams noted while U.S. secretary of state, "I know of no change in policy, only of circumstances."

  Take any global trend highlighted in *World Politics*, and we can easily visualize how changes in the state of the world condition the issues on the global agenda: global warming, nuclear proliferation, international trade, international terrorism, and civil unrest—you name it. All shifts in global circumstances have an important impact upon decisions by international actors. The view that changes of global circumstances serve as a catalyst for international decision making was captured by former U.S. President Richard Nixon when he declared, "The world has changed. Our foreign policy must change with it."

This three-part framework encourages you to think in causal terms about categories of phenomena that explain why particular decisions are made. Each category encompasses a large number of factors, which, together with the influences grouped in the other two categories, tell you what to observe when you construct an explanation for why a particular decision by a particular international actor was made. Factors in the three categories serve as "inputs" that shape the policy-making process. They ultimately lead to foreign policy decisions and outcomes, or foreign policy "outputs," which in turn provide "feedback" that may subsequently affect the inputs themselves (see Figure 3.1).

This organization for interpretation is explanatory. The framework provides clues as to where to look when asking "why" a foreign policy decision has been reached. We can view each policy decision as the result of multiple prior causal events taking place in the funnel. Thus, the model stipulates the conditions that precede and promote policy decisions (bearing in mind that it is frequently difficult to distinguish decision making itself from its prior conditions).

Observe as well that our framework implies that a passage of time occurs during the transition from inputs to outputs in the foreign policy-making process. That is, changes in the determinants of foreign policy occurring at time t produce decisions at a later time $(t + 1)$, which lead to policy outcomes that affect all of the causal factors at a still later time $(t + 2)$. Moreover, these policy outcomes have consequences for the input factors themselves at a later

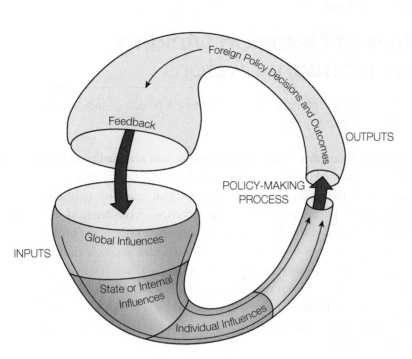

FIGURE 3.1 International Decision Making and a "Funnel of Causality" The determinants or factors that influence the foreign policy choices of transnational actors are shown here as a "funnel of causality." This construction classifies three categories of influence in the foreign policy-making process, whereby policy "inputs" shape the decisions that produce policy "outputs."

time ($t + 3$) because they exert "feedback" on these causal factors as the foreign policy decisions alter the conditions that influence subsequent ($t + 4$) decisions. For example, a cluster of factors at some point in time (t) led the United States to make the decision in March 2003 ($t + 1$) to invade Iraq ($t + 2$). This decision, furthermore, exerted a painfully negative "feedback" influence on public opinion within the United States and abroad when that invasion increased the level of international terrorism it was originally designed to end. This reaction, in turn, later ($t + 3$) transformed global conditions as well as attitudes within American society, which began to galvanize revisions ($t + 4$) of the original policy decision.

Thus, the model advanced here is dynamic. It can account for past policy decisions and behaviors as well as for the effects of those outcomes on later policy decisions. This way of tracing the determinants and consequences of international decisions provides you, the analyst, with a lens through which to view and explain the foreign policy of transnational actors in historical perspective because the model is not tied analytically to any one time period or actor.

> *In the episodic and visual comprehension of our foreign policy, there is serious danger that the larger significance of developments will be lost in a kaleidoscope of unrelated events. Continuities will be obscured, causal factors unidentified.*
>
> **—GEORGE W. BALL, FORMER U.S. UNDERSECRETARY OF STATE**

Models of Decision Making by Transnational Actors

LO 3-2   Summarize and compare the rational choice, individual-based, and bureaucratic politics models of foreign policy.

With the "funnel of causality" framework in mind, you are intellectually prepared to probe international decision making in greater depth. Drawing on the insights and responding to the shortcomings of the major theories of international relations, two schools of thought—rational choice and cognitive psychological approaches—have emerged that emphasize individual decision makers and the factors that shape foreign policy. Rational choice approaches generally address preferences and outcomes, and cognitive psychological approaches tend to focus on the role of process and how framing, beliefs, and information processing influence decision making. To better inform your analyses of the causes of international decision making, let us survey models of decision making formulated by scholars adhering to these schools of thought, looking closely at rational choice, the political psychology of leaders and leadership, and bureaucratic politics.

Decision Making as Rational Choice

Realism assumes that foreign policy making consists primarily of an international actor adjusting to the pressures of an anarchical global system whose essential properties are constant. Accordingly, it presumes that all decision makers are essentially alike in their approach to foreign policy making:

unitary actor
A transnational actor (usually a sovereign state) assumed to be internally united so that changes in its domestic opinion do not influence its foreign policy as much as do the decisions that actor's leaders make to cope with changes in its global environment.

> If they follow the [decision] rules, we need know nothing more about them. In essence, if the decision maker behaves rationally, the observer, knowing the rules of rationality, can rehearse the decisional process in his own mind, and, if he knows the decision maker's goals, can both predict the decision and understand why that particular decision was made (Verba, 1969, p. 225).

Because realists believe that every leader's goals and corresponding approach to making foreign policy choices are the same, the decision-making processes of each actor can be studied as though each were a **unitary actor**—a homogeneous or monolithic unit with few or no important internal differences that affect its choices. From this assumption follows the expectation that international actors can and do make decisions by rational calculations of the costs and benefits of different choices.

rational choice
Decision-making procedures guided by careful definition of situations, weighing of goals, consideration of all alternatives, and selection of the options most likely to achieve the highest goals.

We define rationality, or **rational choice**, as purposeful, goal-directed behavior exhibited when decision makers consider "all possible costs and benefits from a self-interested perspective and then make a thoughtful … decision" (WDR, 2015, p. 3). Scholars describe rationality as a sequence of decision-making activities involving the following intellectual steps:

- **Problem recognition and definition.** The need to decide begins when policy makers perceive an external problem and attempt to define objectively its distinguishing characteristics. Objectivity requires full information about the actions, motivations, and capabilities of other actors as well as the character of the global environment and trends within it. Ideally, the search for information will be exhaustive and decision makers will gather all the facts relevant to the problem.

- **Goal selection.** Next, those responsible for making foreign policy choices must determine what they want to accomplish. This disarmingly simple requirement is often difficult. It requires the identification and ranking of *all* values (such as security and economic prosperity) in a hierarchy from most to least preferred.

- **Identification of alternatives.** Rationality also requires the compilation of an exhaustive list of *all* available policy options and an estimate of the costs associated with each alternative.

- **Choice.** Finally, rationality requires selecting the single alternative with the best chance of achieving the desired goal(s). For this purpose, policy makers must conduct a rigorous cost–benefit analysis guided by an accurate prediction of the probable success of each option.

Policy makers often describe their own behavior as resulting from a rational decision-making process designed to reach the "best" decision possible. The quest for rational decision making was illuminated, for example, in the debate about what level of involvement the United States should maintain in Afghanistan following the death of Osama bin Laden on May 2, 2011. Those who sought a withdrawal of U.S. troops and a clear exit strategy argued that bin Laden's death should force a reevaluation of the war. Because a small special operations force in Pakistan found the terrorist leader rather than the 100,000 ground troops in Afghanistan, some brought into question whether the large commitment of U.S. resources, with the risk to the lives of American soldiers, was the most effective way to combat the terrorist threat. Furthermore, according to critics, with bin Laden's death the Afghans themselves should be able to take more responsibility for their own security. As Richard Lugar, a former chair of the Senate Foreign Relations Committee, argued, "it is exceedingly difficult to conclude that our vast expenditures in Afghanistan represent a rational allocation of our military and financial assets." The message reflected the language of deliberate rational choice to convince skeptics that policy makers had carefully weighed the costs and benefits of all options.

However, like beauty, rationality often lies in the eye of the beholder, and reasonable, clear-thinking people can and often do disagree about the facts and wisdom of foreign policy goals. House Speaker John Boehner reproached calls from fellow Republican legislators for the reduction of U.S. involvement in Afghanistan, instead viewing the killing of bin Laden as evidence that the country should recommit to the U.S. counterinsurgency strategy in Afghanistan and continue to press its advantage (Fahrenthold and Kane, 2011). "This war on terrorism is critical to the safety and security of the American people," said Boehner. "We still face a complex and dangerous terrorist threat. And it's important that we remain vigilant."

Despite the apparent application of rationality in these crises, rational choice is often more an idealized standard than an accurate description of real-world behavior. Theodore Sorenson—one of President Kennedy's closest advisers and a participant in the Cuban Missile Crisis deliberations—has written not only about the steps that policy makers in the Kennedy administration followed as they tried to adhere to rational choice but also about how actual

Charles Kegley, Jr.

IMAGE 3.2 **"How are Foreign Policy Decisions Reached?"** That was the question put to former U.S. Secretary of State Henry A. Kissinger in an interview with one of your text's authors, Charles Kegley. Kissinger has observed that "[m]uch of the anguish of foreign policy results from the need to establish priorities among competing, sometimes conflicting, necessities."

decision making often departed from it. He described an eight-step process for policy making that is consistent with the rational model we have described: (1) agreeing on the facts, (2) agreeing on the overall policy objective, (3) precisely defining the problems, (4) canvassing all possible solutions, (5) listing the consequences that flow from each solution, (6) recommending one option, (7) communicating the option selected, and (8) providing for its execution. However, he explained how difficult it is to follow these steps because:

> Each step cannot be taken in order. The facts may be in doubt or dispute. Several policies, all good, may conflict. Several means, all bad, may be all that are open. Value judgments may differ. Stated goals may be imprecise. There may be many interpretations of what is right, what is possible, and what is in the national interest (Sorensen, 1963, pp. 19–20).

Despite the virtues rational choice promises, the impediments to its realization in foreign policy making are substantial. Decision makers are limited in their ability to gather full information and process it thoroughly in a short amount of time, particularly when operating under pressure. In fact, **bounded rationality** is more common, as decision makers typically only approximate rational decision making due to the many constraints that arise (Kahneman, 2011; Simon, 1997). "Furthermore, people exhibit all sorts of cognitive deficiencies that impair their perceptions of a situation and rational responses to it" (Eder, 2019, p. 24). Though rationality is a decision-making goal to which all transnational actors aspire, it is difficult to determine when they have met the criteria for rational choice or what those rational choices look like in practice. This raises the question: what barriers to rational decision making do alternative models address?

bounded rationality
The concept that a decision maker's capacity to choose the best option is often constrained by many human and organizational obstacles.

> *A phenomenon noticeable throughout history regardless of place or period is the pursuit by governments of policies contrary to their own interests.*
>
> **—BARBARA TUCHMAN, DIPLOMATIC HISTORIAN**

Cognitive Psychological Models of Decision Making

The rational choice approach "can be powerful and useful, but in a number of contexts, it also has a liability: it ignores the psychological and social influences on behavior" (WDR, 2015, p. 3). Some of the barriers that make errors in foreign policy decisions so common are human, deriving from deficiencies in the intelligence, capability, and psychological needs and aspirations of foreign policy decision makers. Others are organizational because most decisions require group agreement about the actor's best interests and the wisest course of action. Reaching agreement is not easy, however, because reasonable people with different values often disagree about goals, preferences, and the probable results of alternative options. Thus, the impediments to rational policy making are not to be underestimated.

Scrutiny of the actual process of decision making reveals other hindrances. Available information is often insufficient to recognize emergent problems accurately, resulting in decisions made on the basis of partial information and vague memories. As General David Petraeus, U.S. commander in the Iraq and Afghanistan wars, quoted Charles W. Kegley and Eugene Wittkopf (1982) in his 1987 Princeton University PhD dissertation, "Faced with incomplete information about the immediate problem at hand, it is not surprising that decision makers turn to the past for guidance" and rely on historical analogies. Moreover, the available information is often inaccurate because the bureaucratic organizations that political leaders depend on for advice often screen, sort, and rearrange it.

Compounding the problem is decision makers' susceptibility to *cognitive dissonance*—they are psychologically prone to block out dissonant, or inconsistent, information and perceptions about their preferred choice and to look instead for information that conforms to their preexisting beliefs to justify their choice. Moreover, they are prone to make decisions on the basis of "first impressions, or intuition, or that amorphous blending of 'what is' with 'what could be' that we call imagination [even though] there is a great body of data suggesting that formal statistical analysis is a much better way of predicting everything … than the intuition even of experts" (Brooks, 2005). Leaders are prone to place faith in their prior prejudices and to draw false analogies with prior events (Brunk, 2008). Leaders may even make decisions based on emotion (McDermott, 2013). Indeed **affective intelligence theory** contends "different emotions have distinct effects on cognition, perception, and memory," such as anxiety likely leading to belief change and frustration associated with resistance to new information (Dolan, 2016, p. 571). Moreover, as **game theory** shows (Mintz, 2007), leaders are limited in their capacity to process information and avoid biases; preoccupied with preventing losses, leaders are also prone to "wishful thinking" and "shooting from the hip," which frequently results in irrational decisions. These intellectual propensities explain why policy makers sometimes pay little heed to warnings, overlook information about dangers, and repeat their past intellectual mistakes.

There seldom exists a confident basis for making foreign policy decisions. Decision making often revolves around the difficult task of choosing among values, so that the choice of one option means the sacrifice of others. Indeed, many decisions tend to produce unintended consequences—what economists call **externalities**. Especially in the realm of foreign policy, where risk is high and there is much uncertainty, decision makers' inability to rapidly gather and digest large quantities of information constrains their capacity to make informed choices.

Because policy makers work with an overloaded **policy agenda** and short deadlines, the search for policy options is seldom exhaustive. "There is little time for leaders to reflect," observed Henry Kissinger (1979). "They are locked in an endless battle in which the urgent constantly gains on the important. The public life of every political figure is a continual struggle

affective intelligence theory
A theory of how emotions shape beliefs, attitudes, and decisions.

game theory
Mathematical model of strategic interaction where outcomes are determined not only by a single actor's preferences but also by the choices of all actors involved.

externalities
The unintended side effects resulting from choices, such as inflation from runaway government spending, that are not taken into account at the time of the decision.

policy agenda
The changing list of problems or issues to which governments pay special attention at any given moment.

IMAGE 3.3 **Road-Trip Diplomacy** A willingness to engage in dialogue with leaders of other countries is a key component of diplomacy. Pictured here on February 27, 2019, are President Donald J. Trump and Chairman Kim Jong Un. The first U.S. president to meet with a leader of North Korea, Trump expressed confidence in the prospects for successful negotiation, saying that he and the North Korean communist dictator "fell in love" because of Kim's "beautiful letters."

to rescue an element of choice from the pressure of circumstance." In the choice phase, then, decision makers rarely make value-maximizing decisions.

Integrating rational and cognitive approaches to foreign policy decision making, and integrating domestic and international levels of analysis, **poliheuristic theory** envisions a two-stage noncompensatory process whereby individuals and groups make decisions (Greene, 2019; Mintz and DeRouen, 2010). In the first stage, leaders use cognitive heuristics, or mental short-cuts, to simplify the decision and eliminate some options. In the second stage, they then assess the remaining alternatives through analytic calculation as depicted by the rational choice school of decision making.

poliheuristic theory
A decision-making theory that accounts for process and outcome of decisions through a two-stage analytic model that incorporates cognitive approaches with rational choice expectations.

In the first stage of the decision-making process, poliheuristic theory anticipates that individuals will outright discard those choices that pose a potential major political risk to them. This loss-avoidance is called the noncompensatory principle, and losses and gains are weighed in terms of domestic political considerations. Decision makers then evaluate the policy choices that remain through rational calculations and select the alternative that has the strongest net gain.

Consider the landmark policy decision by the Labour Party government under British Prime Minister Tony Blair regarding the common European currency. Despite a strong commitment in principle to make Great Britain a leading partner in the European Union, the Blair government ruled out rapid entry to the single currency and set up a series of economic tests that essentially provided cover to put off indefinitely a decision to join the Euro. Poliheuristic theory indicates that because of substantial domestic opposition to joining the single currency, the Blair government quickly discarded the "early membership" option and subsequently only evaluated the "economic test" or "ruling-out membership" options (Oppermann, 2014).

Although this theoretical perspective allows for mediating influences that compromise rationality, poliheuristic theory nonetheless sees individuals as having the capacity to make decisions via a rational choice process within certain parameters. Constructivism challenges this fundamental premise, positing that human subjectivity and intentionality are conditioned by constantly changing contexts of meaning and thus there is necessarily ambiguity in decision making. Others point to what is seen as an overemphasis on domestic politics, with structural realism seeing the international system as more important and classical realism expecting a leader to apply reason to the national interest. Still others argue that factors particular to specific individual decision makers - such as personality, leadership style, operational code, and perception - may overshadow the significance of domestic politics on decision making (Greene, 2019). Nonetheless, poliheuristic theory challenges the idea that decision makers behave rationally and advances the notion that rather than making optimal policy choices, leaders instead tend to opt for "satisficing" alternatives.

Prospect theory similarly challenges the idea of rational choice in decision making. Prospect theory looks at how people perceive and misperceive risks when making choices under conditions of uncertainty, and posits that there are consistent and predictable biases in the way that people depart from rational decision making. People perceive alternatives in terms of their sense of potential gains and losses—"those faced with gains tend to be risk averse, while those confronting losses become much more risk seeking" (McDermott et al., 2008, p. 335). Indeed, "evidence suggests that individuals value losses twice as much as they value gains" (Elms, 2008, p. 245).

One implication for decision making is that people tend to gravitate toward the "status quo" (Grunwald, 2009). Like people everywhere, leaders tend to overvalue certainty and "peace of mind," even to their detriment. They do not calculate the consequence of choices and are more concerned with the potential losses that may result from a change than with the potential gains. This problematic outcome is compounded by another common decision-making error—the tendency to myopically frame decisions by focusing on short-term choices rather than long-term ones (Elms, 2008). U.S. leaders, for example, are often more concerned with the loss of sovereignty and power that would result from greater authority of international organizations such as the United Nations or the International Criminal Court than they are with the gains that could be had from greater global integration and shared governance.

Another implication of prospect theory is that when leaders take risks to initiate bold new foreign policy directions, they will have great difficulty admitting and correcting those choices if they later prove mistaken. As critics lament of George W. Bush's refusal to acknowledge decision-making failures regarding the Iraq War (Draper, 2008; Goldsmith, 2008), leaders are prone to cling to failed policies long after their deficiencies have become apparent. Similar criticisms were also made regarding both the Johnson and Nixon administrations' decisions to keep the United States mired in the unpopular war in Vietnam (Polsky, 2010).

The dilemma that prospect theory presents, of course, is that "if people can't be trusted to make the right choices for themselves, how can they possibly be trusted to make the right decisions for the rest of us?" (Kolbert, 2008). Yet while decision making that departs from

prospect theory
A social-psychological theory explaining decision making under conditions of uncertainty and risk that looks at the relationship between individual risk propensity and the perceived prospects for avoiding losses and realizing big gains.

rationality can be problematic, irrationality can still produce "good" decisions. Along these lines, experimental literature indicates that people tend to incorporate a sense of fairness into their decision making even if it is contrary to their own rational self-interest. As economic behaviorist Dan Ariely's (2008) work demonstrates, "People, it turns out, want to be generous and they want to retain their dignity—even when it doesn't really make sense" (Kolbert, 2008, p. 79).

Despite the image that policy makers seek to project, rational foreign policy making is more an ideal than a reality. Yet we can still assume that policy makers aspire to rational decision-making behavior, which they may occasionally approximate. Indeed, as a working proposition, it is useful to accept rationality as a picture of how the decision process *should* work as well as a description of key elements of how it *does* work (see Table 3.1).

The Leverage and Impact of Leaders

Political elites shape the course of history. Leaders and the style of leadership they employ shape the way in which foreign policies are made and the resulting behavior of the actors in world politics. "There is properly no history, only biography" is how Ralph Waldo Emerson encapsulated the view that individual leaders move history.

history-making individuals model
An interpretation of world politics that sees foreign policy decisions that affect the course of history as products of strong-willed leaders acting on their personal convictions.

This **history-making individuals model** of policy decision making perceives world leaders as the people who create global changes. A leader may "respond to an international situation based on his or her own interpretation, rooted in preexisting beliefs, frameworks, or stereotypes, which may not be shared by his or her colleagues or the public" (Greene, 2019, p. 48). History abounds with examples of the seminal importance of political leaders who emerge in different times and places and under different circumstances to play critical roles in shaping world history. Mikhail Gorbachev dramatically illustrates an individual's capacity to change the course of history. Many experts believe that the Cold War could not have been brought to an end, nor Communist Party rule in Moscow terminated and the Soviet state set on a path toward democracy and free enterprise, had it not been for Gorbachev's vision, courage, and commitment to engineering these revolutionary, system-transforming changes.

TABLE 3.1   Foreign Policy Decision Making in Theory and Practice

Ideal Rational Process	Actual Common Practice
Accurate, comprehensive information	Distorted, incomplete information
Clear definition of national interests	Personal motivations and organizational interests shape choices about national goals
Exhaustive analysis of all options	Limited number of options considered; none thoroughly analyzed
Selection of optimal course of action for producing desired results	Courses of action selected by political bargaining and compromise
Effective statement of decision and its rationale to mobilize domestic support	Confusing and contradictory statements of decision, often framed for media consumption
Careful monitoring of the decision's implementation by foreign affairs bureaucracies	Neglect of the tedious task of managing the decision's implementation by foreign affairs bureaucracies
Instantaneous evaluation of consequences followed by correction of errors	Superficial policy evaluation, uncertain responsibility, poor follow-through, and delayed correction

We expect leaders to lead, and we assume new leaders will make a difference. We reinforce this image when we routinely attach the names of leaders to policies—as though the leaders were synonymous with major international developments—as well as when we ascribe most successes and failures in foreign affairs to the leaders in charge at the time they occurred. Equating U.S. foreign policy with the **Bush Doctrine** in the 2000s is a recent example.

Citizens are not alone in thinking that leaders are the decisive determinants of states' foreign policies and, by extension, world history. Leaders themselves seek to create impressions of their own self-importance while attributing extraordinary powers to other leaders. The assumptions they make about the personalities of their counterparts, consciously or unconsciously, in turn influence their own behavior.

Moreover, leaders react differently to the positions they occupy. All are influenced by the **roles** or expectations that by law and tradition steer the decision maker to behave in conformity with prevailing expectations about how the role is to be performed. Most people submissively act in accordance with the customary rules that define the positions they hold, behaving as their predecessors tended to behave when they held the same position. Others, however, are by personality or preference more bold and ambitious and they seek to decisively escape the confines of their new role by redefining how it will be performed.

In seeking a more rigorous understanding of the role of personality, there is an emerging consensus that personality traits can be grouped in five broad categories: extraversion, agreeableness, conscientiousness, emotional stability, and openness. While subsuming thousands of individual personality attributes, the categories in what is known as the Big Five Model (see Figure 3.2) are consistent across gender, culture, ethnicity, and time. They provide insights into leaders' motivations and can be used to predict behavior (Gallagher and Allen, 2013; Mondak and Halperin, 2013).

In world politics, "all leaders face decision making under uncertainty. The personality of a particular leader can tell us a great deal about how he or she will choose to deal with that uncertainty" (Gallagher and Allen, 2013, p. 7). For instance, high levels of extraversion and openness, and low levels of conscientiousness, are associated with a greater likelihood of risk-acceptance (Kam and Simas, 2010). This has implications for understanding the sources of conflict as leaders who are risk-acceptant are more likely to engage in brinksmanship and the use of force.

One of the challenges illuminated by leader-driven explanations of international decision making is that history's movers and shakers often pursue

Bush Doctrine
The unilateral policies of the George W. Bush administration proclaiming that the United States will make decisions to meet America's perceived national interests, not to concede to other countries' complaints or to gain their acceptance.

roles
The constraints written into law or custom that predispose decision makers in a particular governmental position to act in a manner and style that is consistent with expectations about how the role is normally performed.

Extraversion
• Assertiveness
• Gregariousness
• Excitement-Seeking
• Warmth
• Optimism
• Energetic

Agreeableness
• Altruism
• Trust
• Compliance
• Modesty
• Directness
• Compassion

Conscientiousness
• Self-Discipline
• Deliberation
• Order
• Competence
• Sense of Duty
• Ambition

Emotional Stability
• Impulsiveness
• Vulnerability
• Self-Consciousness
• Anxiety
• Hostility
• Depression

Openness
• To Ideas
• To Values
• To Feelings
• To Aesthetics
• To Fantasy

FIGURE 3.2 The Big Five Personality Markers The Big Five personality factors represent broad dimensions. People who are highly extraverted are outgoing and enjoy the company of others. Those who are very conscientious prefer planned behavior, and high levels of openness reflect creativity and intellectual curiosity. Emotional stability is linked to one's tolerance for stress and ability to regulate emotions. Those who score high on the agreeableness factor tend to be cooperative and empathetic (see Gallagher and Allen, 2013; McCrae and Costa, 2003).

decidedly irrational policies. Personality likely plays a role as it affects a rational actor's opti-
mization process by influencing the options seen as acceptable in a particular situation. For
example, "while risk-acceptant leaders may perceive the use of force as an alternative option for
carrying out their foreign policies, leaders who are risk-averse will not seriously consider such
actions" (Gallagher and Allen, 2013, p. 2). A classic example is Adolf Hitler, whose ruthless
determination to seek military conquest proved disastrous for Germany. More recently, Tony
Blair's personality and **political efficacy**—his high belief in his ability to control events, low
conceptual complexity, and high need for power—are seen as key to his decision as Prime
Minister for the British to join the United States in attacking Iraq in 2003 (Dyson, 2006).

How do we square this kind of behavior with the logic of realism? Realism discounts
leaders by assuming that "individual leaders remain significantly constrained in ways that
assure that regardless of whether individual differences might exist, political outcomes will
emerge indistinguishable precisely because environmental pressures exert decisive influence"
(McDermott, 2013, p. 1). Realism says that survival is the paramount goal of all states and
that all leaders engage in rational calculations to advance their countries' self-advantage. But
realism cannot account for the times when leaders' choices ultimately prove counterproductive. Even defects in states' foreign policy-making processes cannot easily explain such wide
divergences between the decisions leaders sometimes make and what cold cost–benefit calculations would predict.

Having said that the history-making individuals model may be compelling, we must be
cautious and remember that leaders are not all-powerful determinants of states' foreign policy
behavior. Emmet John Hughes (1972), an adviser to President Dwight D. Eisenhower, concluded that "all of [America's presidents] from the most venturesome to the most reticent have
shared one disconcerting experience: the discovery of the limits and restraints—decreed by law,
by history, and by circumstances—that sometimes can blur their clearest designs or dull their
sharpest purposes."

Personal influence varies with the context, and often the context is more influential than the
leader (see "Controversy: Do Leaders Make a Difference?"). The "great person" versus **zeitgeist**
("spirit of the times") debate is pertinent here, as constructivist theorists like to observe. At the
core of this enduring controversy is the question of whether certain times are conducive to the
emergence of leaders or whether famous leaders would have an impact whenever and wherever
they lived. That question may be unanswerable, but at least it reminds us that multiple factors
affect states' foreign policy decisions. The history-making individuals model alone appears too
simple an explanation of how transnational actors react to external challenges.

The question is not whether political elites lead or whether they can make a difference. They
clearly do both, but leaders are not in complete control, and their influence is severely constrained. "Although leaders are quick to take credit for foreign policy successes and the public
is often quick to blame them for failures, leaders rarely make foreign policy alone" (Breuning,
2007, p. 9). As former Secretary of State Henry Kissinger cautioned, we must not place too
much reliance on personalities and personal political preferences:

> [There is] a profound American temptation to believe that foreign policy is a subdivision of
> psychiatry and that relations among nations are like relations among people. But the problem [of

political efficacy
The extent to which policy makers' self-confidence instills in them the belief that they can effectively make rational choices.

zeitgeist
The "spirit of the times," or the dominant cultural norms assumed to influence the behavior of people living in particular periods.

easing protracted conflicts] is not so simple. Tensions … must have some objective causes, and unless we can remove these causes, no personal relationship can possibly deal with them. We are [not] doing … ourselves a favor by reducing the issues to a contest of personalities (University of South Carolina Commencement Address, 1985).

The relevant question, then, is not whether leaders' personal characteristics make a difference, but rather under what conditions their characteristics are influential. The impact of leaders is modified by at least six factors:

(1) what their world view is, (2) what their political style is like, (3) what motivates them to have the position they do, (4) whether they are interested in and have any training in foreign affairs, (5) what the foreign policy climate was like when the leader was starting out his or her political career, and (6) how the leader was socialized into his or her present position. World view, political style, and motivation tell us something about the leader's personality; the other characteristics give information about the leader's previous experiences and background (Hermann, 1988, p. 268).

The impact of leaders' personal characteristics on foreign policy decisions generally increases when their authority and legitimacy are widely accepted or when leaders are protected from broad public criticism. Moreover, certain circumstances enhance individuals' potential influence. Among them are new situations that free leaders from conventional approaches to defining the situation, complex situations involving many different factors, and situations without social sanctions, which permit freedom of choice because norms defining the range of permissible options are unclear.

A leader's gender may also influence their decision making. *Feminism* suggests that men and women tend to see issues such as war, peace, security, and the use of military force in different ways, and this may influence the way in which they make decisions and interact with the world around them. Similarly, *social constructivism* considers the existence of different values and views between women and men as a product of distinct socialization experiences. "Because women tend to define themselves more through their relationships than do men, their actions and rhetoric … may be more oriented toward maintaining and protecting these relationships. In contrast, men tend to focus on end gains, making the achievement of personal preferences and goals" central to their decision making (Boyer et al., 2009, p. 27). It is likely, therefore, that gender influences the decision-making process, even if it does not make a difference in terms of the final decision outcome.

Other factors undoubtedly influence how much leaders can shape their states' choices. For instance, the timing of a leader's assumption of power is significant. When an individual first assumes a leadership position, the formal requirements of that role are least likely to restrict what he or she can do. That is especially true during the "honeymoon" period routinely afforded to newly elected leaders, during which time they are relatively free of criticism and excessive pressure. Moreover, when a leader assumes office following a dramatic event (a landslide election, for example, or the assassination of a predecessor), he or she can institute policies almost with a free hand, as "constituency criticism is held in abeyance during this time" (Hermann, 1976). During a national crisis, decision making is typically centralized and handled exclusively by the top leadership. Crucial information is often unavailable, and leaders see themselves as

Controversy

DO LEADERS MAKE A DIFFERENCE?

Some theorists, such as proponents of realism, embrace the assumption of rationality and assume that any leader will respond to a choice in the same way: the situation structures the reaction to the existing costs and benefits of any choice. But does this assumption square with the facts? What do we know about the

impact of people's perceptions and values on the way they view choices? Political psychology and constructivism tell us that the same option is likely to have different value to different leaders. Does this mean that different leaders would respond differently to similar situations?

Consider the example of Richard Nixon. In 1971, Americans took to the streets outside the White House to protest the immorality of Nixon's massive bombing of Vietnam. His reaction to this perceived threat was to shield himself from the voice of the people, without success, as it happened. Nixon complained that "nobody can know what it means for a president to be sitting in that White House working late at night and to have hundreds of thousands of demonstrators charging through the streets. Not even earplugs could block the noise."

Earlier, on a rainy afternoon in 1962, John F. Kennedy faced a similar citizen protest. Americans had gathered in front of the White House for a "Ban the Bomb" demonstration. His response was to send out urns of coffee and doughnuts and invite the leaders of the protest to come inside to state their case, believing that a democracy should encourage dissent and debate.

Nixon saw protesters as a threat; Kennedy saw them as an opportunity. This comparison suggests that the type of leader can make a difference in determining the kinds of choices likely to be made in response to similar situations (see Gallagher and Allen, 2013). More important

than each president's treatment of the protesters, however, was whether he actually changed his policy decisions based on the protests. Although Kennedy was hospitable to protesters, he did not ban nuclear weapons; in fact, military spending under Kennedy grew to consume half of the federal budget. Many would protest that Kennedy alone could not be expected to eliminate nuclear weapons—that the zeitgeist was dominated by fear of the Soviet Union and intense concern for national security. The protesters in 1971, however, were more in keeping with the spirit of the times. Although they alone may not have persuaded Nixon to alter his policies in Vietnam, widespread protest and discontentment with the war, as well as America's inability to win, eventually prompted Nixon to order the gradual withdrawal of U.S. troops, ending American participation in the Vietnam War. These outcomes suggest that leaders are captive to zeitgeist, or larger forces that drive international relations in their times.

What Do You Think?

1. Did Kennedy and Nixon choose courses of action that reflected who they were as individuals? Or would any president in their respective eras have made similar choices?

2. How would rational choice theorists understand the behavior of Nixon? Of Kennedy?

3. What are limitations of the rational choice approach for explaining their decisions?

4. Thinking ahead, what are some other factors, domestic or international, that could have affected Kennedy's and Nixon's decisions regarding their respective military engagements, beyond zeitgeist?

responsible for outcomes. Not surprisingly, great leaders (e.g., Napoleon Bonaparte, Winston Churchill, and Franklin D. Roosevelt) customarily emerge during periods of extreme tumult. A crisis can liberate a leader from the constraints that normally would inhibit his or her capacity to control events or engineer foreign policy change.

Nothing comes to my desk that is perfectly solvable. Any given decision you make you'll wind up with a 30 to 40 percent chance that it isn't going to work. You have to own that and feel comfortable with the way you made the decision.

—BARACK OBAMA, FORMER U.S. PRESIDENT

The Bureaucratic Politics of Foreign Policy Decision Making

To make the right choices, leaders must seek information and advice, and must see that others implement their decisions properly. Who can assist in these tasks?

In today's world, leaders seldom make decisions without the advice and assistance of many individuals and administrative agencies to cope with changing global circumstances. **Bureaucracy**, according to the theoretical work of the German social scientist Max Weber, is widely believed to increase efficiency and rationality by assigning responsibility for different tasks to different people. It defines rules and standard operating procedures that specify how to perform tasks, relies on record systems to gather and store information, divides authority among different organizations to avoid duplication of effort, and often leads to meritocracies by hiring and promoting the most capable individuals.

Bureaucracy also facilitates forward planning to determine long-term needs and the means to attain them. Unlike leaders, whose roles require attention to the crisis of the moment, bureaucrats are able to consider the future as well as the present. The presence of several organizations also can result in multiple advocacy of rival choices, thus improving the chance that all possible policy options will be considered.

However, before jumping to the conclusion that bureaucratic decision making is an ideal policy-making process, we should emphasize that the foregoing propositions tell us how bureaucratic decision making *should* occur; not how it *does* occur. The actual practice and the foreign policy choices that result show that bureaucracy produces burdens as well as benefits.

Consider the 1962 Cuban Missile Crisis, arguably the single most threatening crisis in the post–World War II era. The method U.S. policy makers used in orchestrating a response is often viewed as having nearly approximated the ideal of rational choice. From another decision-making perspective, however, the missile crisis reveals how decision making by and within organizational contexts sometimes compromises rather than facilitates rational choice.

In Graham Allison's well-known book on the missile crisis, *Essence of Decision* (1971; see also Allison and Zelikow, 1999), he advanced what is widely known as the **bureaucratic politics model**. This model of decision making highlights the constraints that organizations in **policy networks** place on decision makers' choices and the "pulling and hauling" that occurs among the key participants and **caucuses** of aligned bureaucracies in the decision process.

The bureaucratic politics model emphasizes how large-scale bureaucratic organizations contribute to the policy-making process by devising **standard operating procedures (SOPs)**—established methods to be followed in the performance of designated tasks. Not surprisingly, participants in the deliberations that lead to policy choices also often define issues and favor policy alternatives that serve their organization's needs. "Where you stand depends on where you sit" is a favorite aphorism reflecting these bureaucratic imperatives. Consider why professional

bureaucracy
The agencies and departments that conduct the functions of a central government or of a nonstate transnational actor.

bureaucratic politics model
A description of decision making that sees foreign policy choices as based on bargaining and compromises among competing government agencies.

policy networks
Leaders and organized interests (such as lobbies) that form temporary alliances to influence a particular foreign policy decision.

caucuses
Informal groups that individuals in governments and other groups join to promote their common interests.

standard operating procedures (SOPs)
Rules for reaching decisions about particular types of situations.

diplomats typically favor diplomatic approaches to policy problems, whereas military officers routinely favor military solutions.

The consequence is that "different groups pulling in different directions produce a result, or better a resultant—a mixture of conflicting preferences and unequal power of various individuals—distinct from what any person or group intended" (Allison, 1971, p. 145). Rather than being a value-maximizing process, then, policy making is itself an intensely competitive game of why "it is necessary to identify the games and players, to display the coalitions, bargains, and compromises, and to convey some feel for the confusion" (Allison, 1971, p. 146).

Fighting among insiders and the formation of factions to carry on battles over the direction of foreign policy decisions are chronic in nearly every transnational actor's administration (but especially in democratic actors' accepting of participation by many people in the policy-making process). Consider the United States. Splits among key advisers over important foreign policy choices have been frequent. For example, under Presidents Nixon and Ford, Secretary of State Henry Kissinger fought often with James Schlesinger and Donald Rumsfeld, who headed the Department of Defense, over strategy regarding the Vietnam War. Jimmy Carter's national security adviser, Zbigniew Brzezinski, repeatedly engaged in conflicts with Secretary of State Cyrus Vance over the Iran hostage crisis. Under Ronald Reagan, Caspar Weinberger at Defense and George Shultz at State were famous for butting heads on most policy issues.

Such conflicts are not necessarily bad because they force each side to explain better its viewpoint, and this gives heads of state the opportunity to weigh their competing advice before making decisions. However, battles among advisers can lead to paralysis or to rash decisions that produce poor results. That possibility became evident in the fall of 2002, when serious divisions within George W. Bush's administration developed over the "how and why" surrounding the president's goal to wage war against Saddam Hussein in Iraq. Fissures became apparent as key officials publicly debated the wisdom of diplomacy versus invasion, and then how best to conduct the invasion. Similarly, such tension is evident in former U.S. Under Secretary of State George W. Ball's warning that the nature of the institutional machinery produced the decisions that led to America's failed war in Vietnam: "The process was the author of the policy."

In addition to their influence on the policy choices of political leaders, bureaucratic organizations possess several other characteristics that affect decision making. One view proposes that bureaucratic agencies are driven to enlarge their prerogatives and expand the conception of their mission, seeking to take on other units' responsibilities and powers. Far from being neutral or impartial managers, desiring only to carry out orders from the leaders, bureaucratic organizations frequently take policy positions designed to increase their own influence relative to that of other agencies. Moreover, in contrast to rational choice theory, which sees decisions made by a unitary actor, bureaucratic agencies and their staff may not agree with the leader's values and priorities. As former National Security Adviser Zbigniew Brzezinski (2010, p. 18) cautions, an actor's foreign policy priorities may become diluted or delayed by unsympathetic bureaucrats, as "officials who are not in sympathy with advocated policies rarely make good executors."

The tragic surprise terrorist attack on September 11, 2001, provides a telling example of these ascribed characteristics of bureaucratic politics. Many regarded the attacks on 9/11 as the worst intelligence failure since Pearl Harbor. Alarmed U.S. citizens asked why, with an enormous army of agencies gathering intelligence, were not the multitude of messages and warnings about the attack on the World Trade Center and the Pentagon translated in time to prevent the disaster? Why weren't those dots connected? Why were the warnings ignored?

The answer at first accepted by most analysts was that America's chaotic system of intelligence was paralyzed by the morass of cross-cutting bureaucracies. They engaged in turf battles with one another and did not share the vital information that arguably could have identified and prevented the Al Qaeda plot. The problem was miscommunication and noncommunication; the signals about the attack were not forwarded to the executive branch in time. Why? Morton Abramowitz (2002), a former assistant secretary of state in the Reagan administration, voiced his explanation when he wrote, "Three features pervade the making of foreign policy in Washington today: massive over-load, internal warfare, and the short term driving out the long term." These problems exist in every administration, but are particularly problematic when intense ideological perspectives are in play.

As the horror of 9/11 persisted, so did interest and concern about who did what to disrupt the Al Qaeda terrorist network operation prior to September 11, 2001. A bipartisan congressional commission was created to investigate what had gone wrong, in order to make needed corrections in the way the U.S. government makes decisions for national security and counterterrorism. The 9/11 Commission (2004) produced a new set of explanations for why so many opportunities to head off the 9/11 disaster were missed.

The commission did not center blame on the inadequacies and infighting of the country's "alphabet soup" intelligence agencies, such as the Central Intelligence Agency (CIA) and Federal Bureau of Investigation (FBI). Instead, the commission pointed its criticism at the growing complaints about the White House's inaction and pre-9/11 downplaying or ignoring of the loud and clear warnings submitted by U.S. intelligence bureaucracies of the true, imminent dangers of a likely terrorist attack (Woodward, 2006). In this case, the failure of the U.S. government to protect its citizens might have been more due to the unwillingness of American leadership to listen to the warnings of its national security bureaucracies than to the crippling effects of bureaucratic struggles.

Still, consider the problems faced by every U.S. president who must seek to manage hundreds of competing agencies and subagencies, each of which is habitually loath to share information with one another for fear of compromising "sources and methods." Each agency competes with its rivals and engages in finger-pointing and scapegoating as a blood sport. Moreover, as FBI Special Agent Coleen Rowley testified, "There's a mutual-protection pact in bureaucracies. Mid-level managers avoid decisions out of fear a mistake will sidetrack their careers while a rigid hierarchy discourages agents from challenging superiors. There is a saying: 'Big cases, big problems; little cases, little problems; no cases, no problems.' The idea that inaction is the key to success manifests itself repeatedly" (Toner, 2002).

We can discern still another property of bureaucratic politics: the natural inclination of professionals who work in large organizations is to adapt their outlook and beliefs to those prevailing where they work. As constructivist theory explains, every bureaucracy develops a shared mind-set, or dominant way of looking at reality, akin to the **groupthink** characteristic that small groups often manifest (Janis, 1982). Groupthink is a process governing policy decision making that "finds its expression in the overestimation of the group, a closed-mindedness among its members, and a pressure towards uniformity through self-censorship, the illusion of unanimity, or silencing dissenters" (Eder, 2019, p. 25). Under these conditions, the group is less likely to conduct a thorough and unbiased search for information and completely assess all objectives and possible alternatives.

This, in turn, leads to riskier choices and more extreme policies than individuals without the pressures in peer groups would have made. An institutional mind-set, or socially constructed consensus, also discourages creativity, dissent, and independent thinking: it encourages reliance on standard operating procedures and deference to precedent rather than the exploration of

groupthink
The propensity for members of a group to accept and agree with the group's prevailing attitudes rather than speaking out for what they believe.

new options to meet new challenges. Arguably, these tendencies influenced the decision-making process of U.S. leaders in the run-up to the 2003 invasion of Iraq:

> In the first phase, President Bush and his inner circle built the decision to invade Iraq on a homogeneous and undisputed threat-perception induced by the terrorist attacks of September 11, 2001. This phase featured three signs of groupthink (Janis 1982): a cohesive decision group, a lack of norms and impartial leadership to guarantee an unbiased discussion, and a provocative situation context. In the second phase, given this perception and a dysfunctional group structure, a military policy discourse incrementally replaced the diplomacy-favoring discourse in 2002, a process that inevitably let to war (Eder, 2019, p. 23).

Yet research shows that debate and criticism stimulate, rather than inhibit, ideas. "There's this Pollyannaish notion that the most important thing to do when working together is stay positive and get along, to not hurt anyone's feelings," explains psychology professor Charlan Nemeth. "Well, that's just wrong. Maybe debate is going to be less pleasant, but it will always be more productive" (Lehrer, 2012, p. 24).

In your future employment, you are likely to observe directly the efforts of your employer to make rational decisions. You also are bound to notice firsthand within your organization both the advantages of bureaucratic administration and its liabilities. Many students, before they entered the workforce, found that the payoffs of rational choice and the pitfalls of bureaucratic politics surrounding actual practice described here were *not* figments of scholars' imagination. Rather, these properties and propensities of decision making speak to the real experiences of professionals who have entered into policy-making positions.

In classifying the determinants of international actors' foreign policies, the levels-of-analysis framework introduced in Chapter 1 (see Figure 1.1) helps to describe the multiple influences

IMAGE 3.4 Collective Decision Making Leaders often make policy decisions in small groups. Pictured here in Beijing, Chinese President Xi Jinping, who is also general secretary of the Communist Party of China (CPC) Central Committee, meets with members of the Political Bureau of the CPC Central Committee.

on the decision-making process. Recall that in addition to the level of the individual decision maker, the internal and global levels of analysis also influence foreign policy decisions. To place decision making into proper perspective, this chapter will next consider insights from the comparative study of foreign policy to help us better appreciate how foreign policy decision making is shaped.

The Domestic Determinants of Foreign Policy Decisions

LO 3-3   Describe the key ways in which state characteristics, including military capabilities, economic conditions, and regime type, influence foreign policy.

Internal, or "domestic," influences are those that exist at the level of the international actor, not the global system. Although nonstate actors have internal attributes that shape their policy decisions, here we focus on states as they are the most powerful player on the world stage, their foreign policy decisions are the most consequential, and the factors that influence their capacity to make decisions are arguably different from many of those that influence other international actors' decisions.

The proposition that domestic stimuli, and not simply international events, are a source of foreign policy is not novel. In ancient Greece, for instance, the realist historian Thucydides observed that what happened within the Greek city-states often did more to shape their external behavior than did the interactions between the states. He added that Greek leaders frequently concentrated their efforts on influencing the political climate within their own polities. Similarly, leaders today sometimes make foreign policy decisions for domestic political purposes—as, for example, when bold or aggressive acts abroad are intended to divert public attention from economic woes, improve public opinion of their leader's policy making, or influence election outcomes at home. This is sometimes called the "scapegoat" phenomenon, or the **diversionary theory of war** (Gallagher and Allen, 2013; DeRouen and Sprecher, 2006).

To better capture the way most leaders make policy decisions, Robert Putnam coined the phrase **two-level games**. Challenging the assumptions of realism, he asserted that leaders formulate policies simultaneously in both the international and domestic arenas and make choices in accordance with the rules dictated by the "game":

> At the national level, domestic groups pursue their interests by pressuring the government to adopt favorable policies, and politicians seek power by constructing coalitions among these groups. At the international level, national governments seek to maximize their own ability to satisfy domestic pressures, while minimizing the adverse consequences of foreign developments. (Putnam, 1988, p. 434).

Most leaders must meet incompatible demands of internal politics and external diplomacy, and it is seldom possible to make policy decisions that respond rationally to both sets of goals. Policies at home often have many consequences abroad. Foreign activities commonly heavily influence an actor's internal condition. This is why many leaders are likely to fuse the

diversionary theory of war
The hypothesis that leaders sometimes initiate conflict abroad as a way of increasing national cohesion at home by diverting national public attention away from controversial domestic issues and internal problems.

two-level games
A concept referring to the growing need for national policy makers to make decisions that will meet both domestic and foreign goals.

two sectors when contemplating policy decisions. Of the two, however, domestic politics are typically the top priority for leaders because they can only influence policies if they remain in power. Thus, leaders tend to seek and support international outcomes that are "both acceptable to their domestic supporters and within the bounds of their personal political preferences" (Simon, 2019, p. 120).

Yet critics suggest that the two-level game model does not go far enough and could be improved by incorporating insights from *constructivism*. These critics argue that two-level games still rely too heavily on rationalism in assuming "that international negotiators have clear self-interests, represent certain domestic and state interests, and seek to maximize these interests; how these interests are constituted is left unexplored" (Deets, 2009, p. 39).

States are administered by individuals with varying beliefs, values, preferences, and psychological needs, and such differences generate disagreements about goals and alternatives that are seldom resolved through orderly, rational processes. Moreover, these individuals are influenced by the socially accepted shared understandings within their own policy-making community and culture (O'Reilly, 2013). To more fully understand international decision making, it is important to consider not only domestic interests and identities but also the "interactive processes among domestic and international actors through which interests and identities are created and changed" (Deets, 2009, p. 39).

To further illustrate the impact of internal factors, let us now consider how variations in states' attributes—such as differences in military capabilities, level of economic development, and type of government—may influence different countries' foreign policy choices.

Military Capabilities

The realist proposition that states' internal capabilities shape their foreign policy priorities is supported by the fact that states' preparations for war strongly influence their later use of force (Levy, 2001). Although most states may seek similar goals, their ability to realize them will vary according to their military capabilities.

Because military capabilities limit a state's range of prudent policy choices, they act as a mediating factor on leaders' national security decisions. For instance, in the 1980s, Libyan leader Muammar al-Qaddafi repeatedly provoked the United States through anti-American and anti-Israeli rhetoric and by supporting various terrorist activities. Qaddafi was able to act as he did largely because neither bureaucratic organizations nor a mobilized public existed in Libya to constrain his personal whims. However, Qaddafi was doubtlessly more highly constrained by the outside world than were the leaders in the more militarily capable countries toward whom he directed his anger. Limited military muscle compared with the United States precluded the kinds of belligerent behaviors he threatened to use.

Conversely, Saddam Hussein made strenuous efforts to build Iraq's military might and by 1990 had built the world's fourth-largest army. Thus, invading Kuwait to seize its oil fields became a feasible foreign policy option. In the end, however, even Iraq's impressive military power proved ineffective against a vastly superior coalition of military forces, headed by the United States. The 1991 Persian Gulf War forced Saddam Hussein to capitulate and withdraw from the conquered territory. Twelve years later, the United States invaded Iraq and finally ousted Saddam Hussein from office. The lesson: what states believe about their own military capabilities and those of their adversaries (and their enemies' intentions) guide their decisions about war and peace.

Economic Conditions

The level of economic and industrial development a state enjoys also affects the foreign policy goals it can pursue. Generally, the more economically developed a state, the more likely it is to play an activist role in the global political economy. Rich states have interests that extend far beyond their borders and typically possess the means to pursue and protect them. Not coincidentally, states that enjoy industrial capabilities and extensive involvement in international trade also tend to be militarily powerful—in part because a robust economy is, generally speaking, a prerequisite for military might.

Although economically advanced states are more active globally, this does not mean that their privileged circumstances dictate adventuresome policies. Rich states are often "satisfied" states that have much to lose from revolutionary change and global instability (Wolfers, 1962). As a result, they usually perceive the status quo as serving their interests and often forge international economic policies to protect and expand their envied position at the pinnacle of the global hierarchy.

Levels of productivity and prosperity also affect the foreign policies of the poor states at the bottom of the global hierarchy. Some economically weak states respond to their situation by complying subserviently with the wishes of the rich on whom they depend. Others rebel defiantly, sometimes succeeding (despite their disadvantaged bargaining position) in resisting the efforts by great powers and powerful international organizations to control their behavior.

Generalizations about the economic foundations of states' international political behavior often prove inaccurate. Although levels of economic development vary widely among states in the global system, they alone do not determine foreign policies. Instead, leaders' perceptions of the opportunities and constraints that their states' economic resources provide may have a larger influence on their foreign policy choices.

Type of Government

A third important attribute affecting states' international behavior is their type of political system. Although realism predicts that all states will act similarly to protect their interests, a state's type of government demonstrably constrains important choices, including whether threats to use military force are carried out. Here the important distinction is between **constitutional democracy** (representative government) at one end of the spectrum and **autocratic rule** (authoritarian or totalitarian) at the other.

In neither democratic (sometimes called "open") nor autocratic ("closed") political systems can political leaders survive long without the support of organized domestic political interests, and sometimes the mass citizenry. But in democratic systems, those interests are likely to spread beyond the government itself. Public opinion, interest groups, and the mass media are a more visible part of the policy-making process in democratic systems. Similarly, the electoral processes in democratic societies more meaningfully frame choices than the processes in authoritarian

constitutional democracy
Government processes that allow people, through their elected representatives, to exercise power and influence the state's policies.

autocratic rule
A system of authoritarian or totalitarian government in which unlimited power is concentrated in a single leader.

IMAGE 3.5 **Choice and Consequence** The choices that leaders make, and the decisions that they reach, can have far-reaching consequences—both purposeful and unintended—on their country and the world around them. Pictured here in the streets of Quito, Ecuador in 2015, demonstrators march in protest of the social, economic, and labor policies of then-President Rafael Correa. He was succeeded in 2017 by Lenín Moreno, who is credited with reverting the authoritarian turn led by Correa and bringing about "recovered democracy" for the country (Stuenkel, 2019).

regimes, where the real choices are made by a few elites behind closed doors. In a democracy, public opinion and preferences may matter, and therefore differences in who is allowed to participate and how much they exercise their right to participate are critical determinants of foreign policy choices.

Some see the intrusion of domestic politics into foreign policy making as a disadvantage of democratic political systems that undermines their ability to deal decisively with crises or to bargain effectively with less democratic adversaries and allies (see "A Closer Look: Democratic Governance—A Foreign Policy Handicap?"). Democracies are subject to inertia. They move slowly on issues because so many disparate elements are involved in decision making. Furthermore, as liberalism depicts, officials in democracies are accountable to public opinion and must respond to pressure from a variety of domestic interest groups (groups mobilized to exercise influence over the future direction of their country's foreign policies, especially on issues highly important to them).

A crisis sufficient to rouse the attention and activity of a large proportion of the population may need to erupt in order for large changes in policy to come about. As French political sociologist Alexis de Tocqueville argued in 1835, democracies may be inclined to "impulse rather than prudence" because they overreact to perceived external dangers once they recognize them. "There are two things that a democratic people will always find difficult," de Tocqueville mused, "to start a war and to end it."

In contrast, authoritarian governments can "make decisions more rapidly, ensure domestic compliance with their decisions, and perhaps be more consistent in their foreign policy" (Jensen, 1982). But there is a cost: these governments "often are less effective in developing an innovative foreign policy because of subordinates' pervasive fear of raising questions." In short, the concentration of power and the suppression of public opposition can be both advantageous and disadvantageous.

Global Influences on Foreign Policy

LO 3-4   Explain how power polarity and geopolitics influence foreign policy making.

States' internal attributes influence their foreign policies. However, the global environment within which states operate also shapes opportunities for action, setting an ecological context that limits some foreign policy choices but facilitates others (Starr and Most, 1978; Sprout and Sprout, 1965). Global or "external" influences on foreign policy include all activities occurring beyond a state's borders that affect the choices its officials and the people they govern make. Such factors as military alliances and levels of international trade sometime profoundly affect the choices of decision makers. To recognize the influence of external factors, here we comment briefly on how two other aspects of the international environment—the global distribution of power and geostrategic position—affect international decision making.

Global Distribution of Power

Power can be distributed in many ways. It can be concentrated in the hands of a single state, as in the ancient Mediterranean world at the zenith of the Roman Empire, or it may be diffused among several rival states, as it was at the birth of the state system in 1648 following the Thirty Years' War, when a handful of great power rivals possessed approximately equal strength. Scholars use the term **polarity** to describe the distribution of power among members of the global system. As will be explained further in Chapter 4, unipolar systems have one dominant power center, bipolar systems contain two centers of power, and multipolar systems possess three or more such centers.

Closely related to the distribution of power is the pattern of alignments among states. **Polarization** refers to the degree to which states cluster around the powerful. For instance, a highly bipolarized system is one in which small and medium-sized states form alliances with one of the two dominant powers. The network of alliances around the United States and Soviet Union during the Cold War exemplified such a system. Today, the "nature of the international system … will have to be rethought as new powers rise, old ones continue to fade, and attention shifts from the Atlantic to the Pacific" (Mead, 2010, p. 64). The growing prominence of China as an active player in world politics, and the United States' attentiveness to developments in Asia, reflects a shift in political power across the globe.

polarity
The degree to which military and economic capabilities are concentrated in the global system that determines the number of centers of power, or "poles."

polarization
The formation of competing coalitions or blocs composed of allies that align with one of the major competing poles, or centers, of power.

A Closer Look

DEMOCRATIC GOVERNANCE—A FOREIGN POLICY HANDICAP?

Realism anticipates that in order to protect their national interests, states should ideally conduct their foreign policies free of ideological and domestic political constraints. Along those lines, democracies may be seen as comparatively "weak" in that they rely on public support and their political power is less centralized. Liberal theorists counter that these very constraints may be conducive to peace, as they hinder leaders from making impulsive foreign policy choices.

This tension between democratic governance and effective foreign policy making was seen within the United States in the aftermath of the U.S.-led assault on Libya on March 19, 2011. As part of a coalition effort that was authorized by the United Nations (UN) Security Council, U.S. military forces participated in a series of air strikes against Libyan air defenses and government forces. Though confronting the threat to peace and security posed by Libyan leader Muammar al-Qaddafi's regime was endorsed by many in the U.S. Congress— indeed on March 1 the Senate unanimously approved a resolution that called for the UN to impose a no-fly zone over Libya—then-President Obama faced a firestorm of criticism from members of both political parties who expressed outrage that he did not first seek congressional approval before committing U.S. military forces to the mission. They argued that Obama had exceeded his constitutional authority, and that "the merits of the operation" are "separate from the domestic legal question of whom—the president or Congress—has the authority to decide whether the United States will take part in combat" (Savage, 2011, p. A14).

For his part, Obama countered that not only were his actions in the national interest but as chief executive and commander in chief of the U.S. military, he had the power to authorize the strikes. Obama's decision was among the latest in a long line of presidential authorizations of military action without prior congressional approval, which include Harry Truman's entrance into the Korean War and Bill Clinton's bombing of Kosovo in 1999. Nonetheless, Obama later sought a resolution of support from Congress for continued U.S. military involvement in Libya, saying "it has always been my view that it is better to take military action … with congressional engagement, consultation and support."

Watch the Carnegie Council Video:

"Democracy and Waging War"

You Decide:

1. Does the nature of democratic rule help or hinder those governments' capacity to achieve their foreign policy goals?

2. What arguments and evidence can you provide to support your general conclusion?

3. Do you think that authoritarian governments are better able to conduct effective foreign policy? Why or why not?

Polarity and alliance polarization influence foreign policy by affecting the decision latitude possessed by states. For example, as discussed in Chapters 4 and 8, when power is concentrated in the hands of a single state in a unipolar system, it can more easily choose to use military force and intervene in the affairs of others than it would in a system characterized by a distribution of shared power, where rivals might obstruct its actions. However, when alliances are tight military blocs, the small state members of each alliance will tend to feel compelled to conform to the dictates of the alliance's leader.

Conversely, when alliances are loosely shifting with fluid membership, smaller states can more readily choose to craft foreign policies that are independent of the wishes of the powerful. Of course, you could think of other examples to show how the structural properties of the global system affect decision latitude. What they would show is that the foreign policy impact of polarity and polarization hinges on the geostrategic position of a given state.

Geopolitical Factors

Some of the most important influences on a state's foreign policy behavior stem from its location vis-à-vis other states in the international system, and the geostrategic advantages that this conveys. The presence of natural frontiers, for example, may profoundly guide policy makers' choices (see Map 3.1). Consider the United States, which was secure throughout most of its early history because vast oceans separated it from potential threats in Europe and Asia. The advantage of having oceans as barriers to foreign intervention, combined with the absence of militarily powerful neighbors, permitted the United States to develop into an industrial giant and to safely practice an isolationist foreign policy for more than 150 years. Consider also mountainous Switzerland, whose easily defended topography has made neutrality a viable foreign policy option.

Similarly, maintaining autonomy from continental politics has been an enduring theme in the foreign policy of Great Britain, an island country whose physical detachment from Europe long served as a buffer separating it from entanglement in major power disputes on the Continent. Preserving this protective shield has long been a priority for Britain, and it helps to explain why London was so hesitant in the past twenty years to accept full integration in the European Union (EU).

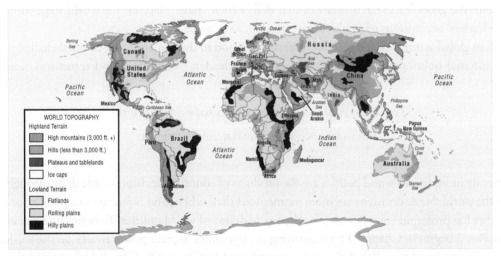

MAP 3.1 Geographic Influences on Foreign Policy According to the geopolitics approach to world politics, the number of neighboring states and the protection afforded by natural barriers shape how countries interact with one another. This map suggests how, until recently, the separation of the United States from Eurasia encouraged an isolationist policy during many periods in U.S. history.

 Think It Through How might topography, location, and other geopolitical factors have influenced the foreign policy priorities of Great Britain, Germany, China, Switzerland, and states in South America?

Most countries are not insular, however; they have many states on their borders, denying them the option of noninvolvement in world affairs. Germany, which sits in the geographic center of Europe, historically has found its domestic political system and foreign policy preferences shaped by its geostrategic position. In the twentieth century, for example, Germany struggled through no less than six major radical changes in governing institutions, each of which pursued very different foreign policies: (1) the empire of Kaiser Wilhelm II; (2) the Weimar Republic; (3) Adolf Hitler's dictatorship; its two post–World War II successors, (4) the capitalist Federal Republic in West Germany and (5) the communist German Democratic Republic in East Germany; and, finally, (6) a reunited Germany after the end of the Cold War, now committed to liberal democracy and full integration in the EU. Each of these governments was preoccupied with its relations with neighbors but responded to the opportunities and challenges presented by Germany's position in the middle of the European continent with very different foreign policy goals. In no case, however, was isolationistic withdrawal from involvement in continental affairs a practical geostrategic option.

geopolitics
The theoretical postulate that states' foreign policies are determined by their location, natural resources, and physical environment.

History is replete with other examples of geography's influence on states' foreign policy goals. This is why geopolitical theories are valuable. The **geopolitics** school of realist thought, and political geography generally, stresses the influence of geographic factors on state power and international conduct (Kissinger, 2014). Illustrative of early geopolitical thinking is Alfred Thayer Mahan's *The Influence of Sea Power in History* (1890), which maintains that control of the seas shaped national power and foreign policy. States with extensive coastlines and ports enjoyed a competitive advantage. Later geopoliticians, such as Sir Halford Mackinder (1919) and Nicholas Spykman (1944), argued that topography, size (territory and population), climate, and distance between states, in addition to location, are powerful determinants of individual countries' foreign policies. The underlying principle behind the geopolitical perspective is self-evident: the geopolitical circumstances that define their states' place on the world stage influence leaders' perceptions of available foreign policy options.

Can global actors, whether state or nonstate, respond to the demands that external challenges and internal politics simultaneously place on their leaders? The trends and transformations

> *I have not controlled events, events have controlled me.*
>
> **—ABRAHAM LINCOLN, FORMER U.S. PRESIDENT**

currently unfolding in world politics are the products of countless decisions made daily throughout the world. Some decisions are more momentous than others, and how actors respond to one another has profound consequences for the entire drama of world politics. To better understand this, Part 2 begins in Chapter 4 by examining the dynamics of great power rivalry on the world stage. Countries of the Global South are investigated in Chapter 5, followed by examination of nonstate actors in Chapter 6.

Study. Apply. Analyze.

Chapter Summary

3-1 Use a level-of-analysis approach to identify the major influences on foreign policy decision making. No single category of causation fully explains foreign policy decisions. Instead, a number of factors codetermine the decisions that produce foreign policy "outputs." Leaders' personal preferences and decision-making processes may influence foreign policy. Yet all policy makers are constrained by various circumstances, including internal attributes of their own countries as well as international conditions, which shape foreign policy as well.

3-2 Summarize and compare the rational choice, individual-based, and bureaucratic politics models of foreign policy. Some theories of international decision making focus on the individual decision maker. Rational choice approaches address preferences and outcomes, and rest on the logic of consequentialism. Yet many argue that in reality there are barriers to rationality, and that we must consider psychological and social influences. Errors in foreign policy decisions are common due to deficiencies in information processing, comprehension, and psychological needs and aspirations of foreign policy decision makers. Others are organizational and stem from the impact of group dynamics on decision making.

3-3 Describe the key ways in which state characteristics, including military capabilities, economic conditions, and regime type, influence foreign policy. Internal attributes exist at the level of the international actor. What leaders believe about their own military capabilities and those of their allies and adversaries can shape their decisions about war and peace. Levels of prosperity, as well as leaders' perceptions of the opportunities and constraints that their states' economic resources provide, may influence foreign policy choices. A state's type of government can also affect foreign policy, both in terms of the options available to policy makers and the process through which they make decisions.

3-4 Explain how power polarity and geopolitics influence foreign policy making. The global environment within which transnational actors operate facilitates some foreign policy choices but limits others. The structure of the international system, as reflected in the distribution of power among its members, affects the decision latitude of policy makers. An actor's location in relation to other members of the system, and the geostrategic advantages that this conveys, also influence foreign policy behavior.

Key Terms

affective intelligence theory
autocratic rule
bounded rationality
bureaucracy
bureaucratic politics model
Bush Doctrine
caucuses
constitutional democracy

diversionary theory of war
externalities
game theory
geopolitics
groupthink
history-making individuals model
multiple advocacy

polarity
polarization
policy agenda
policy networks
poliheuristic theory
political efficacy
prospect theory
rational choice

roles
standard operating procedures (SOPs)
two-level games
unitary actor
zeitgeist

Suggested Readings and Resources

Berry, Max: www.nationstates.net/. A web-based game that allows you to simulate running your own country and making policy decisions.

The Brookings Institution and Council on Foreign Relations (CFR): brookings.edu/blogs, cfr.org/publication/blogs.html. Blogs that provide current insights into how leading analysts view developments in the area of foreign policy.

Brummer, Klaus, and Valerie M. Hudson, eds. (2015). *Foreign Policy Analysis: Beyond North America*. Boulder, CO: Lynne Rienner.

Cyber Nations: cybernations.net/. A web-based game that allows you to simulate running your own country and making policy decisions.

The Foreign Policy Association: foreignpolicyblogs.com/. Offers a diverse group of foreign policy viewpoints from a variety of areas, including academics, activists, policy analysts, and business leaders.

Foreign Policy: foreignpolicy.com/channel/passport/. Offers a rich array of blog posts from all over the world, as well as daily news feeds.

Gallagher, Maryann E., and Susan H. Allen. (2013). "Presidential Personality: Not Just a Nuisance," *Foreign Policy Analysis* (Feb): 1–21.

Kahneman, Daniel. (2011). *Thinking, Fast and Slow*. New York: Farrar, Straus, and Giroux.

Kaarbo, Juliet. (2015). "A Foreign Policy Analysis Perspective on the Domestic Politics Turn in IR Theory," *International Studies Review* (June): 189–216.

Mintz, Alex, and Karl DeRouen. (2010). *Understanding Foreign Policy Decision Making*. New York: Cambridge University Press.

Wittkopf, Eugene R., Christopher Jones, and Charles W. Kegley Jr. (2007). *American Foreign Policy: Pattern and Process*, 7th ed. Belmont, CA: Thomson Wadsworth.

Carnegie Council Videos

Key Term Videos

- Rational Choice
- Externalities
- Policy Agenda
- Bush Doctrine
- Roles
- Political Efficacy
- Multiple Advocacy
- Policy Networks
- Autocratic Rule
- Geopolitics

Additional Videos

- Dallek, Robert. "The Lost Peace: Leadership in a Time of Horror and Hope, 1945–1953."
- Freedman, Sir Lawrence. "A Choice of Enemies: America Confronts the Middle East."
- Goldstein, Gordon M. "Lessons in Leadership from JFK and LBJ for America's Next Commander-in-Chief."
- Nye Jr., Joseph S. "The Power to Lead."
- Vocke, William. "Secrecy in Foreign Policy."
- Vocke, William. "Tunisia: The Jasmine Revolution and Western Foreign Policy."
- Stephanie Sy. "The U.S. Foreign Service and the Importance of Professional Diplomacy, with Nicholas Kralev."
- Myers, Joanne. "The Korean Peninsula: One of America's Greatest Foreign Policy Challenges, with Christopher R. Hill."

Part 2
The World's Actors and Their Relationships

Shakespeare wrote that "All the world's a stage, and all the men and women merely players." When it comes to world politics, not just people but also organizations, groups, and countries have a variety of roles to play on the global stage. Part 2 identifies the major actors in world politics today and describes the roles they perform, the policies they pursue, and the predicaments they face.

The three chapters in Part 2 each focus on a prominent type of global actor. Chapter 4 opens by giving you an overview of the great powers—the actors with the greatest military and economic capabilities. Chapter 5 compares the great powers with the weaker, economically less developed countries now known as the Global South, whose fates are powerfully shaped by others.

Chapter 6 examines the role of intergovernmental organizations, such as the United Nations and the European Union, and nongovernmental organizations, such as Greenpeace and Amnesty International, whose members actively work for global change. A window is opened for you to also explore the activities of other nonstate global actors, including multinational corporations, ethnic groups, and religious movements.

CARL DE SOUZA/AFP/Getty Images

Marching for Change

People, like states and international organizations, are transnational actors. Mobilized publics often use demonstrations to express their dissent and to draw global attention to their cause. Shown here in Burundi, protestors question the veracity of the electoral process and the decision by incumbent President Pierre Nkurunziza to seek a third term in 2015—in violation, according to critics, of the peace accord that ended the 1993–2003 civil war. During his controversial presidency, the "unrest has forced more than 400,000 people to flee their homes, with a United Nations commission of inquiry accusing the authorities of crimes including extrajudicial executions, torture and enforced disappearances" (Nimubona, 2018).

Chapter 4

Great Power Relations and Rivalries

Courtesy of the Franklin D. Roosevelt Library, Hyde Park, New York

IMAGE 4.1 Allies or New Rivals? The "Big Three" (Winston Churchill, Franklin Roosevelt, and Joseph Stalin) meet at Yalta as victorious great power allies to establish rules for all states to follow in the post–World War II global order, but that cooperation would soon be replaced by bitter competition.

Learning Objectives

LO 4-1	Discuss the cyclical nature of history as portrayed by long-cycle theory.
LO 4-2	Explain the causes and consequences of World War I.
LO 4-3	Explain the causes and consequences of World War II.
LO 4-4	Identify the causes and key phases of the Cold War.
LO 4-5	Evaluate shifts in polarity that have occurred since the end of the Cold War.
LO 4-6	Assess potential futures of great-power relations.

By virtue of the great resources they command, Great Powers, and, even more, superpowers, have special rights and special responsibilities . . . even though their great power may tempt them to overreach and neglect their duties."

—ROBERT JERVIS, POLITICAL SCIENTIST

Who is number one? Who is gaining on the leader? What does it mean for the future if the strongest faces serious competition for the predominant position? These are the kinds of questions sports fans often ask when the preceding week's competition results in shifts in the rankings of the top teams. Likewise, many people throughout the world habitually make comparisons of countries, asking which states are the biggest, strongest, wealthiest, and most militarily powerful and evaluating which states are rising or falling relative to one another. This reflects an attitude also held by world leaders that former U.S. Secretary of State Dean Rusk called a "football stadium approach to diplomacy."

When leaders attribute importance to such rankings, they are looking at world politics through the lens of *realism*. They see an international system of competitors, with winners and losers in an ancient contest for supremacy, and they look most closely at the shifting rankings at the very top of the international hierarchy of power—at the rivalry and struggle among the "great powers." Moreover, they picture this conflict as perpetual. As Arnold J. Toynbee's (1954) famous cyclical theory of history explains: "The most emphatic punctuation in a uniform series of events recurring in one repetitive cycle after another is the outbreak of a great war in which one power that has forged ahead of all its rivals makes so formidable a bid for world domination that it evokes an opposing coalition of all the other powers."

Toynbee's conclusion lies at the center of realism. The starting point for understanding world politics, as leading post–World War II realist theorist Hans J. Morgenthau (1985) elaborates, is to recognize that "all history shows that nations active in international politics are continuously preparing for, actively involved in, or recovering from organized violence in the form of war." Cycles of war and peace colored twentieth-century world politics, with three global wars breaking out. World Wars I and II were fought with fire and blood; the Cold War was fought without the same magnitude of destruction but with equal intensity. Each of these wars triggered major transformations in world politics.

This chapter explores the causes and consequences of great power rivalries. By understanding the origins and impact of these three struggles over world leadership, you will be better equipped to anticipate whether the great powers will be able to avoid yet another global war in the twenty-first century.

Good leadership in this century may or may not be transformational, but it will most certainly require a careful understanding of the context of change.

—JOSEPH S. NYE, INTERNATIONAL RELATIONS SCHOLAR AND U.S. POLICY MAKER

The Quest for World Leadership

LO 4-1   Discuss the cyclical nature of history as portrayed by long-cycle theory.

long-cycle theory
A theory that focuses on the rise and fall of the leading global power as the central political process of the modern world system.

Rivalry between great powers has long characterized world politics. As Toynbee suggested, there is a strong probability that this historical pattern is cyclical. **Long-cycle theory** elaborates on this understanding of world politics and provides a framework for our analysis of evolving great power rivalries. According to long-cycle theory (see Chapter 7 for further discussion), transitions in world leadership unfold through a series of distinct phases where periods of global war are followed by relatively stable periods of international rule making and institution building (see Table 4.1). Shifts in the cycle have occurred alongside changes in the major states' relative power, changing their relations with one another (see Chase-Dunn and Anderson, 2005).

TABLE 4.1   The Evolution of Great Power Rivalry for World Leadership, 1495–2035

Dates	Preponderant State(s) Seeking Hegemony	Other Powers Resisting Domination	Global War	New Order after Global War
1495–1540	Portugal	Spain, Valois, France, Burgundy, England	War of Italy and the Indian Ocean, 1494–1517	Treaty of Tordesillas, 1517
1560–1609	Spain	The Netherlands, France, England	Spanish-Dutch Wars, 1580–1608	Truce of 1608; Evangelical Union and the Catholic League formed
1610–1648	Holy Roman Empire (Hapsburg dynasty in Spain and Austria-Hungary)	Shifting ad hoc coalitions of mostly Protestant states (Sweden, Holland) and German principalities as well as Catholic France against remnants of papal rule	Thirty Years' War, 1618–1648	Peace of Westphalia, 1648
1650–1713	France (Louis XIV)	The United Provinces, England, the Hapsburg Empire, Spain, major German states, Russia	War of the Grand Alliance, 1688–1713	Treaty of Utrecht, 1713
1792–1815	France (Napoleon)	Great Britain, Prussia, Austria, Russia	Napoleonic Wars, 1792–1815	Congress of Vienna and Concert of Europe, 1815
1871–1914	Germany, Turkey, Austria-Hungary	Great Britain, France, Russia, United States	World War I, 1914–1918	Treaty of Versailles creating the League of Nations, 1919
1933–1945	Germany, Japan, Italy	Great Britain, France, Soviet Union, United States	World War II, 1939–1945	Bretton Woods, 1944; United Nations, Potsdam, 1945
1945–1991	United States, Soviet Union	Great Britain, France, China, Japan	Cold War, 1945–1991	NATO/Partnerships for Peace, 1995; World Trade Organization, 1995
1991–2035?	United States	China, European Union, Russia, India	A cold peace or hegemonic war, 2020–2035?	A new security regime to preserve world order?

Over the past five centuries, each global war has led to the emergence of a **hegemon**. With its unrivaled power, the hegemon has reshaped the rules and institutions of the global system to preserve its preeminent position.

Hegemony always imposes an extraordinary burden on the world leader. A hegemon must bear the costs of maintaining political and economic order while protecting its position and upholding its dominion. Over time, as the weight of global engagement takes its toll, every previous hegemon has overextended itself. As challengers have arisen, the security agreements so carefully crafted after the last global war have come under attack. Historically, this struggle for power has set the stage for another global war, the demise of one hegemon and the ascent of another. Realism contends that, from "the perspective of any one great power, all other great powers are potential enemies. . . . The basis of this fear is that in a world where great powers have the capability to attack each other and might have the motive to do so, any state bent on survival must be at least suspicious of other states and reluctant to trust them" (Mearsheimer, 2001, p. 32). Table 4.1 summarizes 500 years of the cyclical rise and fall of great powers, their global wars, and their subsequent efforts to restore order.

Critics note that long-cycle theorists disagree on whether economic, military, or domestic factors produce these cycles. They also take issue with the deterministic tone of the theory, which to them implies that global destiny is beyond any policy maker's control. Must great powers rise and fall as if by the law of gravity—what goes up must come down?

hegemon
A preponderant state capable of dominating the conduct of international political and economic relations.

IMAGE 4.2 Might Makes Fright Shown here is one example of resistance to U.S. global preeminence: Pakistanis burn a U.S. flag in an anti-American rally in protest of drone attacks in Pakistan's tribal regions. The U.S. government has defended drone attacks, claiming that airstrikes for targeted killings protect lives and prevent potential terror attacks. Others, however, charge that innocent people are killed. According to Zeke Johnson, senior director of programs for Amnesty International USA, "By its own admission, the U.S. government's use of drones has meant the deaths of civilians and there has been insufficient accountability" (Dilanian and Kube, 2017).

Still, long-cycle theory suggests you should consider how shifts in the relative strength of great powers affect world politics. In terms of our sports metaphor, who is the champion? Does the champion have any challengers on the global playing field? It draws attention to hegemonic transitions, the rise and fall of leading states in the global system, and in so doing provokes questions about whether this long cycle can be broken. To underscore the importance of struggles over world leadership and their impact on trends and transformations in world politics, this chapter accordingly asks you to inspect the three great power wars of the twentieth century, as well as the lessons these clashes suggest for the twenty-first century.

World War I

| **LO 4-2** | Explain the causes and consequences of World War I. |

World War I erupted when a Serbian nationalist seeking to free his ethnic group from Austrian rule assassinated Archduke Ferdinand, heir to the Hapsburg throne of the Austrian-Hungarian Empire, at Sarajevo in June 1914. This assassination sparked a series of great power actions and reactions in the five weeks that followed, shattering world peace. The war involved most of the European states and drew in allies in North America, Asia, and the Near East to become one of the most destructive wars in history (Cashman and Robinson, 2007). By the time the first major European war of the twentieth century had ended, nearly 10 million people had died, three empires had crumbled, new states had been born, seven decades of communist rule in Russia had begun, and the world geopolitical map had been redrawn in ways that paved the way for the rise of Adolf Hitler in Nazi Germany.

The Causes of World War I

How can we explain such a catastrophic war? Multiple answers are possible. Most popular are structural realist explanations, which hold that World War I was inadvertent, not the result of any master plan. Neorealists believe that it was a war bred by circumstances beyond the control of those involved, one that people neither wanted nor expected. Revisionist historians, however, have argued that the war was the result of deliberate choices—"a tragic and unnecessary conflict . . . because the train of events that led to its outbreak might have been broken at any point during the five weeks of crisis that preceded the first clash of arms, had prudence or common goodwill found a voice" (Keegan, 1999, p. 3).

structuralism
The neorealist proposition that states' behavior is shaped primarily by changes in the properties of the global system, such as shifts in the balance of power, instead of by individual heads of states or by changes in states' internal characteristics.

Systemic Level of Analysis   **Structuralism** postulates that the changing distribution of power within the anarchical global system is the primary factor that determines state behavior. Looking at the circumstances on the eve of World War I, many historians hypothesize that the way in which the great powers aligned against one another created an environment conducive to an armed conflict. The great powers' prior rearmament efforts, as well as their alliances and resulting counter-alliances, created a momentum that, along with the pressures created by the mobilization of armies and arms races, dragged European statesmen toward war.

This structural explanation concentrates attention on the nineteenth century, when Britain dominated world politics. Britain was an island country isolated from continental affairs by temperament, tradition, and geography. Britain's sea power gave it command of the world's shipping lanes and control over a vast empire stretching from the Mediterranean to Southeast Asia. This dominance helped to deter aggression. Germany, however, presented a challenge to British power.

After becoming a unified country in 1871, Germany prospered and used its growing wealth to create a formidable army and navy. This strength resulted in greater ambition and resentment of British preeminence. As the predominant military and industrial power on the European continent, Germany sought to compete for international position and status. As Kaiser Wilhelm II proclaimed in 1898, Germany had "great tasks outside the narrow boundaries of old Europe." Germany's rising power and global aspirations altered the European geopolitical landscape.

Furthermore, Germany was not the only new emergent power at the turn of the century. Russia was also expanding and becoming a threat to Germany. The decline of the Austrian-Hungarian Empire, Germany's only ally, heightened Germany's fear of Russia, which can be seen in Germany's strong reaction to the assassination of Archduke Ferdinand. Fearing that a long war might result in an unfavorable shift in the balance of power, Germany sought a short, localized war with a more favorable outcome. Germany thus supported Austria-Hungary's unrestrained assault on Serbia.

Although the logic behind Germany's calculation was clear—a victorious war would bolster Austria-Hungary and hamper Russian influence—it turned out to be a serious miscalculation. France and Russia joined forces to defend Serbia, and Britain soon joined them in an effort to oppose Germany and defend Belgian neutrality. In April 1917, the war became truly global in scope when the United States, reacting to German submarine warfare, entered the conflict.

Here we observe, again at the systemic level of analysis, the dynamics of shifts in the *balance of power* as a causal factor: the historic tendency for opposed coalitions to form so that the distribution of military power is "balanced" to prevent any single power or bloc from seriously threatening others. That is what happened in the decade prior to Archduke Ferdinand's assassination when European military alignments become polarized, pitting the Triple Alliance of Germany, Austria-Hungary, and the Ottoman Empire against the Triple Entente of Britain, France, and Russia. According to this structural interpretation, after Russia mobilized its armies in response to Austria's attack on Serbia, crosscutting alliance commitments pulled one European great power after another into the war.

State Level of Analysis As an alternative interpretation of the origins of World War I at the *state level of analysis*, many historians view the growth of **nationalism**, especially in southeastern Europe, as having created a climate of opinion that made war likely. Groups that glorified the distinctiveness of their national heritage began championing their own country above all others (Woodwell, 2008). Long-suppressed ethnic prejudices soon emerged, even among leaders. Russian foreign minister Sergei Sazonov, for example, claimed to "despise" Austria, and Kaiser Wilhelm II of Germany proclaimed, "I hate the Slavs" (Tuchman, 1962).

Domestic unrest inflamed these passions, making it hard to see things from another point of view. Believing that they were upholding their national honor, the Austrians could not comprehend why Russians labeled them the aggressors. German insensitivity to others' feelings prevented them from understanding "the strength of the Russians' pride, their fear of humiliation if

nationalism
A mind-set glorifying a particular state and the nationality group living in it, which sees the state's interest as a supreme value.

they allowed the Germans and Austrians to destroy their little protégé, Serbia, and the intensity of Russian anger" (White, 1990, p. 228). With each side belittling the national character and ethnic attributes of the other, diplomatic alternatives to war become untenable.

Individual Level of Analysis   Decision making theories offer a third interpretation of the causes of World War I. Recall from Chapter 3 that *rational choice theory* emphasizes that leaders make decisions in the interests of themselves and their states based on careful evaluation of the relative usefulness of alternative options. World War I's outbreak was a result of the German elites' preference for a war with France and Russia in order to consolidate Germany's position on the continent, confirm its status as a world power, and divert domestic attention from its internal troubles (Kaiser, 1990). The rational choice model of decision making suggests that World War I is best seen as a consequence of the purposive goal of rival great powers to compete against one another for global power. *Prospect theory* provides insights as well, as it stresses that leaders are likely to accept risk to prevent losses. Under this interpretation, the people gathered at the Imperial Palace in Berlin pushed Europe over the brink in "an attempt by Germany to secure its position before an increasingly powerful Russia had achieved a position of equality with Germany (which the latter expected to happen by 1917)" (Levy, 1998).

There are also questions about the rationality of decision making leading up to the start of World War I, and the *history-making individuals model* (see Chapter 3) points to the role of the German kaiser who was responsible for many critical decisions in 1914. Kaiser Wilhelm II had a grandiose vision of himself and often ignored the counsel of his cabinet ministers. When he made decisions, "they were often the result of vanity and personal feelings rather than rational calculation. The kaiser also had a tremendous capacity to see the world the way he wanted to see it; he literally had a propensity for swearing that black was white" (Cashman and Robinson, 2007, p. 77).

As these rival interpretations suggest, the causes of World War I remain in dispute. Structural explanations emphasize the global distribution of power, domestic interpretations look at causal factors *within* states, and decision-making explanations direct attention to the calculations and goals of particular leaders. All partially help us to understand the sequences that produced the world's first truly global war.

The Consequences of World War I

World War I changed the face of Europe (see Maps 4.1A and 4.1B). In its wake, three multi-ethnic empires—the Austrian-Hungarian, Russian, and Ottoman (Turkish)—collapsed, and the independent states of Poland, Czechoslovakia, and Yugoslavia emerged in their place. In addition, the countries of Finland, Estonia, Latvia, and Lithuania were born. The war also contributed to the independence of the Republic of Ireland from Britain in 1920 and the over-throw of the Russian czar in 1917 by the Bolsheviks. The emergence of communism under the leadership of Vladimir Lenin produced a change in government and ideology that would have geopolitical consequences for another seventy years.

Despite its costs, the coalition consisting of Britain, France, Russia, and (later) the United States and Italy defeated the threat of domination posed by the Central powers (Germany, Austria-Hungary, Turkey, and their allies). Moreover, the war set the stage for a determined

Europe in 1914

Europe in 1920

MAPS 4.1A AND 4.1B Territorial Changes in Europe Following World War I The map on the left shows state boundaries on the eve of war in 1914, as well as the members of the two major opposing coalitions that formed. The map on the right shows the new borders in 1920, with the nine new states that emerged from the war.

Think It Through How do you think the redefining of borders within Europe influenced individuals' national identities?

effort to build a new global system that could prevent another war. There was a pronounced distaste for war and theories of realism that justified great power competition, armaments, secret alliances, and balance-of-power politics. The staggering human and material costs of the previous four years led many of the delegates to the 1919 peace conference convened at Versailles, outside Paris, to reevaluate their convictions about statecraft. The time was ripe for a new approach to building world order. Disillusioned with realism, many turned to *liberalism* for guidance on how to manage the global future.

The decade following World War I was the high point of liberal idealism. Woodrow Wilson's ideas about world order, as expressed in his January 1917 "Fourteen Points" speech, reflected a belief that by reordering the global system according to liberal principles, the "Great War" (as World War I was then called) would be "the war to end all wars." Wilson's chief proposal was to construct a League of Nations that allegedly would guarantee the independence and territorial integrity of all states. His other recommendations included strengthening international law, settling territorial claims on the basis of self-determination, and promoting democracy, disarmament, and free trade.

However, once the peace conference began, parochial national interests resurfaced and undermined Wilson's proposals as the pontificating American president had offended many European leaders. "God was content with Ten Commandments," growled Georges Clemenceau, the cynical realist French prime minister. "Wilson must have fourteen."

As negotiations at the conference proceeded, hard-boiled power politics prevailed. Ultimately, the delegates were only willing to support those elements in the Fourteen Points that served their national interests. After considerable wrangling, Wilson's League of Nations was written into the peace treaty with Germany as the first of 440 articles. The rest of the treaty was punitive, aimed at stripping Germany of its great power status. Similar treaties were later forced on Austria-Hungary and Germany's other wartime allies.

The Treaty of Versailles grew out of a desire for retribution. In brief, Germany's military was drastically cut; it was forbidden to possess heavy artillery, military aircraft, or submarines, and its forces were banned from the Rhineland. Germany also lost territory in the west to France and Belgium, in the south to the new state of Czechoslovakia, and in the east to the new states of Poland and Lithuania. Overseas, Germany lost all of its colonies. Finally, in the most humiliating clause of the treaty, Germany was assigned responsibility for the war and charged with paying heavy financial reparations for the damages. On learning of the treaty's harsh provisions, the exiled German kaiser is said to have declared, "the war to end wars has resulted in a peace to end peace."

World War II

LO 4-3   Explain the causes and consequences of World War II.

Germany's defeat in World War I and its humiliation under the Treaty of Versailles did not extinguish its hegemonic aspirations. On the contrary, they intensified. Thus conditions were ripe for the second great power war of the twentieth century, which pitted the Axis trio of Germany, Japan, and Italy against an unlikely "grand alliance" of four great powers, who united despite their incompatible ideologies—communism in the case of the Soviet Union and democratic capitalism in the case of Britain, France, and the United States.

The world's fate depended upon the outcome of this massive effort to defeat the Axis threat. The Allied powers achieved success, but at a terrible cost: 23,000 lives were lost each day, and at least 53 million people died during six years of fighting. To understand the origins of this devastating conflict, we once again examine causal factors operating at different levels of analysis.

The Causes of World War II

Following Germany's capitulation in 1918, a constituent assembly meeting in the city of Weimar produced a draft of a democratic constitution. Yet many Germans had little enthusiasm for the Weimar Republic. In their minds, not only was the new government linked to the humiliating Versailles Treaty, but it also suffered from the 1923 French occupation of the industrial Ruhr district, various political rebellions, and the ruinous economic collapse of 1929. By the parliamentary elections of 1932, over half of the electorate supported extremist parties that disdained democratic governance. The largest of these was the Nazi, or National Socialist German Workers, Party. Thus began the long and tragic path toward World War II.

Proximate Causes of War   On January 30, 1933, the Nazi leader, Adolf Hitler, was appointed chancellor of Germany. Less than a month later, the Reichstag (Parliament) building burned down under mysterious circumstances. Hitler used the fire to justify an emergency edict allowing him to suspend civil liberties and repress communists and other political adversaries. Once all meaningful parliamentary opposition was eliminated, Nazi legislators passed an enabling act that suspended the constitution and granted Hitler dictatorial power.

In his 1924 book *Mein Kampf* ("My Struggle"), Hitler urged Germany to recover territories taken by the Treaty of Versailles, absorb Germans living in neighboring lands, and colonize Eastern Europe. During his first year in power, however, he cultivated a pacifist image, signing a nonaggression pact with Poland in 1934. The following year, the goals originally outlined in *Mein Kampf* climbed to the top of Hitler's foreign policy agenda. He thoroughly ignored the *Kellogg-Briand Pact*, which prohibited the use of military force as a means for resolving interstate conflicts. In 1935, he repudiated the military clauses of the Versailles Treaty; in 1936, he ordered troops into the demilitarized Rhineland; in March 1938, he annexed Austria; and in September 1938, he demanded control over the Sudetenland, a region of Czechoslovakia containing ethnic Germans. To address the Sudeten German question, a conference was convened in Munich. Hitler, British Prime Minister Neville Chamberlain, and leaders of France and Italy (ironically, Czechoslovakia was not invited) all attended. Convinced that **appeasement** would halt further German expansionism, Chamberlain and the others agreed to Hitler's demands.

appeasement
A strategy of making concessions to another state in the hope that, satisfied, it will not make additional claims.

Rather than satisfying Germany, appeasement whetted its appetite and that of its newly formed fascist coalition with Italy and Japan, which aimed to overthrow the international status quo. In the Eastern Hemisphere, Japan had grown disillusioned with Western liberalism and the Paris settlements, and it was suffering from the economic devastation of the Great Depression. Like Germany, Japan embraced militarism as key to its global expansion. In the might-makes-right climate that Germany's imperialistic quest for national aggrandizement helped create, Japanese nationalists led their country on the path to imperialism and **colonialism**. Japan's invasions of Manchuria in 1931 and further forays into China in 1937 were paralleled by Italy's absorption of Abyssinia (modern-day Ethiopia) in 1935 and Albania in 1939. Further, both Germany and Italy intervened in the 1936–1939 Spanish civil war on the side of the fascists, headed by General Francisco Franco, whereas the Soviet Union supported antifascist forces.

colonialism
The rule of a region by an external sovereign power.

After Germany occupied the rest of Czechoslovakia in March 1939, Britain and France formed an alliance to protect the next likely victim, Poland. They also opened negotiations with Moscow in hopes of enticing the Soviet Union to join the alliance, but the negotiations failed. Then, on August 23, 1939, Hitler, a fascist, and the Soviet dictator, Joseph Stalin, a communist, stunned the world with the news that they had signed a nonaggression pact, promising not to attack one another. Now confident that Britain and France would not intervene, Hitler invaded Poland. However, Britain and France honored their pledge to defend Poland, and two days later declared war on Germany. World War II had begun.

The war expanded rapidly. Hitler next turned his forces to the Balkans, North Africa, and westward, as the mechanized German troops invaded Norway and marched through Denmark, Belgium, Luxembourg, and the Netherlands. The German army swept around the

Maginot line, the defensive barrier on the eastern frontier that France boasted could not be breached. The quick and nearly bloodless German victory forced the British to evacuate a nearly 340,000-strong expeditionary force from the French beaches at Dunkirk. Paris itself fell in June 1940. Within six weeks France surrendered, even though Germany's forces were numerically inferior to those of France and its allies. In the months that followed, the German air force, the Luftwaffe, pounded Britain in an attempt to force it into submission as well. Instead of invading Britain, however, the Nazi troops launched a surprise attack on the Soviet Union, Hitler's supposed ally, in June 1941. Such a move would later prove to be a great strategic blunder.

Meanwhile, in the East, tensions were growing. The United States, Great Britain, and France viewed Japan's imperial expansion as a threat to their own interests in the region. In an effort to hamper Japan's ability to carry out its global ambitions, the United States embargoed the sale of strategic raw materials, such as scrap iron, steel, and oil.

Poor in natural resources, Japan saw the United States as a serious threat to its national security. In September 1940 Japan forged the Tripartite Pact with Germany and Italy that pledged the three Axis powers to come to one another's aid if attacked by another great power, such as the United States. Japan continued its aggressive expansion, and in July 1941 moved into southern Indochina (region in Southeast Asia that encompasses the present-day countries of Laos, Vietnam, and Cambodia). In response, the United States froze Japanese assets in the United States and issued demands for Japanese withdrawal. Deciding that the eviction of the United States from the Pacific was critical to its national interest, on December 7th of that same year, Japan launched a surprise assault on the United States at Pearl Harbor. Following this attack, Germany quickly declared war on the United States. The Japanese assault and the German challenge ended U.S. aloofness and **isolationism**, enabling President Franklin Roosevelt to forge a coalition with Britain and the Soviet Union to oppose the fascists.

Underlying Causes at Three Analytic Levels   Structural realism emphasizes polarity as a defining feature of the international system and, at the systemic level of analysis, regards the reemergence of **multipolarity** in global power distribution as a key factor in the onset of World War II. The post–World War I global system was precarious because the number of sovereign states increased at the same time as the number of great powers declined. In 1914, Europe had only twenty-two key states, but by 1921, the number had nearly doubled. When combined with resentment over the Versailles treaty, the Russian Revolution, and the rise of fascism, the increased number of states and the resurgence of nationalistic revolts and crises made "the interwar years the most violent period in international relations since the Thirty Years' War and the wars of the French Revolution and Napoleon" (K. Holsti 1991, p. 216).

The 1930s collapse of the global economic system also contributed to the war. Great Britain found itself unequal to the leadership and regulatory roles it had performed in the global **political economy** before World War I. Although the United States was the logical successor, its refusal to exercise leadership hastened the war. The 1929–1931 depression was followed in 1933 "by a world Monetary and Economic Conference whose failures—engineered by the United States—deepened the gloom, accelerated protectionist barriers to foreign trade such as tariffs and quotas, and spawned revolution" (Calvocoressi, Wint, and Pritchard, 1989, p. 6). In this depressed global environment, heightened by deteriorating economic circumstances at home, Germany and Japan sought solutions abroad through *imperialism*.

isolationism
A policy of withdrawing from active participation with other actors in world affairs and instead concentrating state efforts on managing internal affairs.

multipolarity
The distribution of global power into three or more great power centers, with most other states allied with one of the rivals.

political economy
A field of study that focuses on the intersection of politics and economics in international relations.

irredentism
A movement by an ethnic national group to recover control of lost territory by force so that the new state boundaries will no longer divide the group.

At the state level of analysis, collective psychological forces also led to World War II. These included "the domination of civilian discourse by military propaganda that primed the world for war," the "great wave of hypernationalism [that] swept over Europe [as] each state taught itself a mythical history while denigrating that of others," and the demise of democratic governance (Van Evera, 1990–1991, pp. 18, 23). During the Nuremberg Trials after World War II, when Nazi officials were prosecuted for war crimes committed during the Holocaust, senior Nazi Hermann Goering reflected on the Nazi propaganda success. "Why of course the people don't want war," he said, but "it is always a simple matter to drag the people along, whether it is a democracy, or a fascist dictatorship, or a parliament, or a communist dictatorship. . . . All you have to do is to tell them they are being attacked, and denounce the pacifists for lack of patriotism and exposing the country to danger."

Domestically, German nationalism inflamed latent **irredentism** and rationalized the expansion of German borders both to regain provinces previously lost in wars to others and to absorb Germans living in Austria, Czechoslovakia, and Poland. The rise of **fascism**—the Nazi regime's **ideology** championing the flag, the fatherland, nationalism, imperialism, and anti-Semitism—animated this renewed imperialistic push and preached an extreme version of realism that stressed power politics to justify the forceful expansion of the German state and other Axis powers that were aligned with Germany. "Everything for the state, nothing outside the state, nothing above the state" was the way Italy's dictator, Benito Mussolini, constructed his understanding of the fascist political philosophy, in a definition that embraced the extreme realist proposition that the state was entitled to rule every dimension of human life by force.

The importance of leaders at the individual level of analysis stands out. The war would not have been possible without Adolf Hitler and his plans to conquer the world. World War II arose primarily from German aggression. Professing the superiority of Germans as a "master race" along with virulent anti-Semitism and anticommunism, Hitler chose to wage war to create an empire that he believed could resolve conclusively the historic competition and precarious coexistence of the great powers in Europe by eliminating Germany's rivals:

> The broad vision of the Thousand-Year Reich was . . . of a vastly expanded—and continually expanding—German core, extending deep into Russia, with a number of vassal states and regions, including France, the Low Countries, Scandinavia, central Europe, and the Balkans, that would provide resources and labor for the core. There was to be no civilizing mission in German imperialism. On the contrary, the lesser peoples were to be taught only to do menial labor or, as Hitler once joked, educated sufficiently to read the road signs so they wouldn't get run over by German automobile traffic. The lowest of the low, the Poles and Jews, were to be exterminated. . . . To Hitler . . . the purpose of policy was to destroy the system and to reconstitute it on racial lines, with a vastly expanded Germany running a distinctly hierarchical and exploitative order (Holsti 1991, pp. 224–225).

fascism
A far-right ideology that promotes extreme nationalism and the establishment of an authoritarian society built around a single party with dictatorial leadership.

ideology
A set of core philosophical principles that leaders and citizens collectively construct about politics, the interests of political actors, and the ways people ought to behave.

The Print Collector/Alamy Stock Photo

IMAGE 4.3 The Rise of Hitler and German Nationalism Constructivism emphasizes the role of ideas and identities in shaping world politics. Adolf Hitler persuaded the German people of the need to persecute the Jews and expand German borders through armament and aggression. He constructed and cultivated a widespread perception in Germany that, in his words, "an evil exists that threatens every man, woman and child of this great nation. We must take steps to ensure our domestic security and protect our homeland." Pictured here on April 20, 1941, Hitler (far right) confers with senior Nazi leaders.

The Consequences of World War II

Having faced ruinous losses in Russia and a massive Allied bombing campaign at home, Germany's Thousand-Year Reich lay in ruins by May 1945. By August of that same year, the U.S. atomic bombing of Hiroshima and Nagasaki forced Japan to end its war of conquest. The Allied victory over the Axis redistributed power and reordered borders, resulting in a new geopolitical terrain.

The Soviet Union absorbed nearly 600,000 square kilometers of territory from the Baltic states of Estonia, Latvia, and Lithuania, and from Finland, Czechoslovakia, Poland, and Romania—recovering what Russia had lost in the 1918 Treaty of Brest-Litovsk after World War I. Poland, a victim of Soviet expansionism, was compensated with land taken from Germany. Germany itself was divided into occupation zones that eventually provided the basis for its partition into Cold War–era East and West Germany. Finally, pro-Soviet regimes assumed power throughout Eastern Europe (see Maps 4.2A and 4.2B). In the Far East, the Soviet Union took the four Kurile Islands from Japan—or the "Northern Territories," as Japan calls them—and Korea was divided into Soviet and U.S. occupation zones at the Thirty-Eighth Parallel.

Based on Europe in 1945 from Strategic Atlas, Comparative Geopolitics of the World's Powers, revised edition, by Gerard Chaliand and Jean-Pierre Rageau. Copyright 1990 by Gerard Chaliand and Jean-Pierre Rageau.

MAPS 4.2A AND 4.2B **World War II Redraws the Map of Europe** The map on the left shows the height of German expansion in 1943, when it occupied Europe from the Atlantic Ocean and the Baltic Sea to the gates of Moscow in the Soviet Union. The map on the right shows the new configuration of Europe after the "Grand Coalition" of Allied forces—Great Britain, the United States, and the Soviet Union—defeated the Axis's bid for supremacy.

Think It Through How could the post-World War II division of territory lead to future conflicts between the great powers?

With the defeat of the Axis, one global system ended but the defining characteristics of the new system had not yet become clear. Although the United Nations replaced the old, discredited League of Nations, the management of world affairs still rested in the hands of the victors. Yet victory only magnified their distrust of one another.

The "Big Three" leaders—Winston Churchill, Franklin Roosevelt, and Joseph Stalin—met at the **Yalta Conference** in February 1945 to design a new world order. But the vague compromises they reached concealed the differences percolating below the surface. Following Germany's unconditional surrender in May, the Big Three (with the United States now represented by Harry Truman) met again in July 1945 at Potsdam. The meeting ended without agreement, and the facade of Allied unity began to disintegrate.

In the aftermath of the war, the United States and the Soviet Union were the only two great powers that were still strong and had the capacity to impose their will. The other major-power victors, especially Great Britain, had exhausted themselves and slipped from the apex of the world-power hierarchy. The vanquished axis powers also fell from the great power ranks. Thus, as Alexis de Tocqueville had foreseen in 1835, the Americans and Russians now held in their hands the destinies of half of humankind. In comparison, all other states were dwarfs.

In this atmosphere, ideological debate arose about whether the twentieth century would become "the American century" or "the Russian century." Thus, perhaps the most important product of World War II was the *transformation* it caused, after a short interlude, in the distribution of global power from *multipolarity* to **bipolarity**. In what, after 1949, became known as the **Cold War**, Washington and Moscow used the fledgling United Nations to pursue their competition with each other rather than to keep the peace. As the third and last hegemonic struggle of the twentieth century, the Cold War and its lessons still cast dark shadows over today's geostrategic landscape.

Yalta Conference
The 1945 summit meeting of the Allied victors to resolve postwar territorial issues and voting procedures in the United Nations to collectively manage world order.

bipolarity
A condition in which power is concentrated in two competing centers so that the rest of the states define their allegiances in terms of their relationships with both rival great power superstates, or "poles."

Cold War
The forty-four-year (1947–1991) rivalry between the United States and the Soviet Union, as well as their competing coalitions, which sought to contain each other's expansion and win worldwide predominance.

> *The United States should take the lead in running the world in the way that the world ought to be run.*
>
> **—HARRY S. TRUMAN, FORMER U.S. PRESIDENT**

The Cold War

LO 4-4   Identify the causes and key phases of the Cold War.

The second great war of the twentieth century, without parallel in the number of participants and destruction, brought about a global system dominated by two superpowers whose nuclear weapons radically changed the role that threats of warfare would play in world politics. The competition between the United States and the Soviet Union for hegemonic leadership grew out of these circumstances.

The Causes and Evolutionary Course of the Cold War

The origins of the twentieth century's third hegemonic battle for domination are debated because the historical evidence lends itself to different interpretations (see Leffler and Westad, 2009). Several postulated causes stand out. At the systematic level of analysis, the first is advanced by realism: The Cold War resulted from a transition in power and leadership that propelled the United States and the Soviet Union to the top of the international hierarchy and made their rivalry inescapable. "As both sides searched beyond their core alliances for strategic advantage, the Cold War began to affect the trajectories of states and political movements across the globe" (Freedman, 2010, p. 137). Circumstances gave each superpower reasons to fear and to struggle against the other's potential global leadership, and encouraged both competitors to carve out and establish a wide sphere of influence.

A second interpretation, at the state level of analysis, holds that the Cold War was simply an extension of the superpowers' mutual disdain for each other's professed beliefs about politics and economics. U.S. animosity toward the Soviet Union was stimulated by the 1917 Bolshevik Revolution, which brought to power a government that embraced the radical Marxist critique of capitalistic imperialism (see Chapter 2). American fears of Marxism stimulated the emergence of anticommunism as an opposing ideology. Everywhere, communism became synonymous with treasonous, un-American activity. Moreover, according to the **domino theory**, which suggested that communism was inherently driven to knock over one country after another, Soviet communism was inherently expansionistic. Accordingly, the United States embarked on a missionary crusade of its own to contain and ultimately remove the atheistic communist menace from the face of the Earth.

domino theory
A metaphor popular during the Cold War that predicted that if one state fell to communism, its neighbors would also fall in a chain reaction, like a row of falling dominoes.

Similarly, Soviet policy was fueled by the belief that capitalism could not coexist with communism. The purpose of Soviet policy, therefore, was to push the pace of the historical process in which communism eventually would prevail. However, Soviet planners did not believe that this historical outcome was guaranteed. They felt that the capitalist states, led by the United States, sought to encircle the Soviet Union and smother communism in its cradle, and that resistance by the Soviets was obligatory. As a result, ideological incompatibility may have ruled out compromise as an option. Communist theoretician Vladimir Lenin described the predicament that he perceived, saying, "[a]s long as capitalism and socialism exist, we cannot live in peace; in the end, either one or the other will triumph—a funeral dirge will be sung either over the Soviet Republic or over world capitalism."

A third explanation, rooted in decision making at the individual level of analysis, sees the Cold War as being fueled by the superpowers' misperceptions of each other's motives. From this constructivist perspective, conflicting interests were secondary to misunderstandings and ideologies. Mistrustful actors are prone to see only virtue in their own actions and only malice in those of their adversaries. This tendency to see one's opponent as the complete opposite, or *mirror image*, of oneself makes hostility virtually inevitable. Moreover, when perceptions of an adversary's evil intentions are socially constructed and become accepted as truth, a self-fulfilling prophecy can develop and the future can be affected by the way it is anticipated. Thus, viewing each other suspiciously, each rival giant acted in hostile ways that encouraged the very behavior that was suspected.

Additional factors, beyond those rooted in divergent interests, ideologies, and images, undoubtedly combined to produce this explosive Soviet–American hegemonic rivalry. To sort out the relative causal influence of the various factors, we must evaluate how, once it erupted after the 1945–1948 gestation period, the Cold War changed over its forty-four-year duration. The character of the Cold War shifted in three phases over its long history (see Figure 4.1), and several distinct patterns emerged that not only provide insights into the impetus behind the Cold War but also illustrate the properties of other great power rivalries.

Confrontation, 1947–1962   Though a brief period of wary Soviet–American cordiality prevailed in the immediate aftermath of World War II, this goodwill rapidly vanished as the two giants' vital interests collided. At this critical juncture, George F. Kennan, then a diplomat in the American embassy in Moscow, sent Washington his famous "long telegram" assessing the sources of Soviet conduct. Published in 1947 by the influential *Foreign Affairs* journal, and signed as "X" to conceal his identity, Kennan argued that Soviet leaders would forever feel insecure about their political ability to maintain power against forces both within Soviet society and in the outside world. Their insecurity would lead to an active—and perhaps aggressive—Soviet foreign policy. However, the United States had the power to increase the strains under which the Soviet leadership would have to operate, which could lead to a gradual mellowing or final end of Soviet power. Kennan (1947) concluded: "In these circumstances it is clear that the main element of any United States policy toward the Soviet Union must be that of a long-term, patient but firm and vigilant containment of Russian expansive tendencies."

Soon thereafter, President Harry S. Truman made Kennan's assessment the cornerstone of American postwar foreign policy. Provoked in part by violence in Turkey and Greece, which Truman and others believed to be communist inspired, Truman declared that he believed, "it must be the policy of the United States to support free peoples who are resisting attempted subjugation by armed minorities or by outside pressures." Eventually known as the **Truman Doctrine**, this statement defined the strategy the United States would pursue for the next forty years, over Kennan's objections. This strategy, called **containment**, sought to prevent the expansion of Soviet influence by encircling the Soviet Union and intimidating it with the threat of a military attack.

A seemingly endless series of Cold War crises soon followed. They included the communist coup d'état in Czechoslovakia in 1948, the Soviet blockade of West Berlin in June of that year, the communist rise to power on the Chinese mainland in 1949, the outbreak of the Korean War in 1950, the Chinese invasion of Tibet in 1950, and the on-again, off-again Taiwan Strait crises. The Soviets finally broke the U.S. atomic monopoly in 1949. Thereafter, the risks of massive destruction necessitated restraint and changed the terms of the great powers' rivalry.

Because the Soviet Union remained strategically inferior to the United States, Nikita Khrushchev (who, upon Stalin's death in 1953, succeeded him) pursued a policy of **peaceful coexistence** with capitalism. Even so, the Soviet Union sought, however cautiously, to increase its power in places where opportunities appeared to exist. As a result, the period following Stalin's death saw many Cold War confrontations, with Hungary, Cuba, Egypt, and Berlin serving as flash points.

Truman Doctrine
The declaration by President Harry S. Truman that U.S. foreign policy would use intervention to support peoples who allied with the United States against communist external subjugation.

containment
A strategy of confronting attempts of a power rival to expand its sphere of influence, with either force or the threat of force, thereby preventing it from altering the balance of power.

peaceful coexistence
Soviet leader Nikita Khrushchev's 1956 doctrine that war between capitalist and communist states is not inevitable and that inter-bloc competition could be peaceful.

In 1962, the surreptitious placement of Soviet missiles in Cuba set the stage for the greatest test of the superpowers' capacity to manage their disputes—the Cuban Missile Crisis. The superpowers stood eyeball to eyeball. Fortunately, one (the Soviet Union) blinked, and the crisis ended. This painful learning experience both reduced enthusiasm for waging the Cold War by military means and expanded awareness of the suicidal consequences of a nuclear war.

From Coexistence to Détente, 1963–1978   The growing threat of mutual destruction, in conjunction with the approaching parity of American and Soviet military capabilities, made coexistence or nonexistence appear to be the only alternatives. At the American University commencement exercises in 1963, U.S. President John F. Kennedy warned that

> Should total war ever break out again—no matter how—our two countries would become the primary targets. It is an ironical but accurate fact that the two strongest powers are the two in the most danger of devastation. . . . We are both caught up in a vicious and dangerous cycle in which suspicion on one side breeds suspicion on the other and new weapons beget counter-weapons. In short, both the United States and its allies, and the Soviet Union and its allies, have a mutually deep interest in a just and genuine peace and in halting the arms race. . . .
>
> So let us not be blind to our differences, but let us also direct attention to our common interests and to the means by which those differences can be resolved. And if we cannot end now our differences, at least we can help make the world safe for diversity.

Kennedy signaled a shift in how the United States hoped thereafter to bargain with its adversary, and the Soviet Union reciprocally expressed its interest in more cooperative relations. That movement took another step forward following Richard Nixon's election in 1968. Coached by his national security adviser, Henry A. Kissinger, President Nixon initiated a new approach to Soviet relations that in 1969 he officially labeled **détente**. As Kissinger explained, détente was a foreign policy strategy that sought to create "an environment in which competitors can regulate and restrain their differences and ultimately move from competition to cooperation." Along these lines, the objective of the U.S. **linkage strategy** was to shape superpower relations and lessen incentives for war through the continuation of mutually rewarding exchanges. Cooperative interaction became more commonplace than hostile relations (see Figure 4.1). Visits, cultural exchanges, trade agreements, arms control talks, and joint technological ventures replaced threats, warnings, and confrontations.

From Renewed Confrontation to Rapprochement, 1979–1991   Despite the careful nurturing of détente, its spirit did not endure. When the Soviet invasion of Afghanistan in 1979 led to détente's demise, President Jimmy Carter defined the situation as "the most serious strategic challenge since the Cold War began." In retaliation, he declared America's willingness to use military force to protect its access to oil supplies from the Persian Gulf, suspended U.S. grain exports to the Soviet Union, and attempted to organize a worldwide boycott of the 1980 Moscow Olympics.

Relations deteriorated dramatically thereafter. President Ronald Reagan and his Soviet counterparts (first Yuri Andropov and then Konstantin Chernenko) exchanged a barrage of confrontational rhetoric. Reagan asserted that the Soviet Union "underlies all the unrest that is going on" and described the Soviet Union as "the focus of evil in the modern world." As talk of war increased, preparations for it escalated. The arms race resumed feverishly, often at the expense

détente
In general, a strategy of seeking to relax tensions between adversaries to reduce the possibility of war.

linkage strategy
A set of assertions claiming that leaders should take into account another country's overall behavior when deciding whether to reach agreement on any one specific issue so as to link cooperation to rewards.

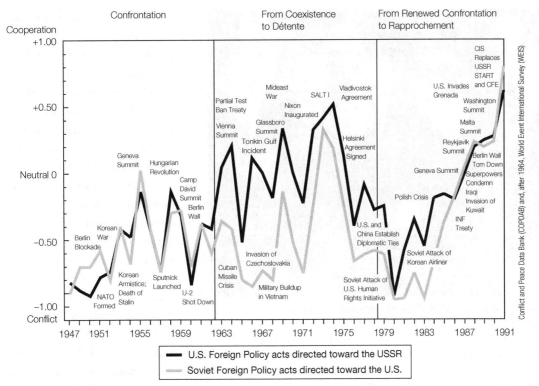

Cooperation
+1.00

| Confrontation | From Coexistence to Détente | From Renewed Confrontation to Rapprochement |

+0.50

Neutral 0

−0.50

−1.00
Conflict

1947 1951 1955 1959 1963 1967 1971 1975 1979 1983 1987 1991

Conflict and Peace Data Bank (COPDAB) and, after 1964, World Event International Survey (WEIS)

━━ U.S. Foreign Policy acts directed toward the USSR
━━ Soviet Foreign Policy acts directed toward the U.S.

Note: index is the net ratio of cooperative to conflictive acts

FIGURE 4.1 Key Events in the Cold War Evolution of the U.S.–Soviet Relationship, 1947–1991
The evolution of U.S.–Soviet relations during the Cold War displays a series of shifts between periods of conflict and cooperation. As this figure shows, each superpower's behavior toward the other tended to be reciprocal, and, for most periods before 1983, confrontation prevailed over cooperation.

of addressing domestic economic problems. The superpowers also extended the confrontation to new territory, such as Central America, and renewed their public diplomacy (propaganda) efforts to extol the virtues of their respective systems throughout the world.

Reagan pledged U.S. support for anticommunist insurgents who sought to overthrow Soviet-supported governments in Afghanistan, Angola, and Nicaragua. In addition, American leaders spoke loosely about the "winability" of a nuclear war through a "prevailing" military strategy that included the threat of a "first use" of nuclear weapons in the event of conventional war. Relations deteriorated as these moves and countermoves took their toll. The new Soviet leader, Mikhail Gorbachev, summarized the alarming state of superpower relations in 1985 by fretting that "[t]he situation is very complex, very tense. I would even go so far as to say it is explosive."

However, the situation did not explode. Instead, prospects for a more constructive phase improved greatly following Gorbachev's advocacy of "new thinking" in order to achieve **rapprochement**, or reconciliation, of the rival states' interests. He sought to settle the Soviet Union's differences with the capitalist West in order to halt the deterioration of his country's economic and international position.

rapprochement
In diplomacy, a policy seeking to reestablish normal cordial relations between enemies.

IMAGE 4.4 Easing Tensions: U.S.–Soviet Détente Pictured here, President Richard Nixon, one of the architects of the U.S. linkage strategy along with Secretary of State Henry Kissinger, shakes hands with Soviet General Secretary Leonid Brezhnev after signing the first Strategic Arms Limitations Talks (SALT) treaty.

As cornerstones of this new thinking, Gorbachev promoted "glasnost" and "perestroika." The former signifies greater openness and individual freedom, and the latter refers to the restructuring of political and economic systems. Embracing these principles, Gorbachev embarked on domestic reforms to promote democratization and the transition to a market economy, and proclaimed his desire to end the Cold War competition. "We realize that we are divided by profound historical, ideological, socioeconomic, and cultural differences," he noted during his first visit in 1987 to the United States. "But the wisdom of politics today lies in not using those differences as a pretext for confrontation, enmity, and the arms race." Soviet spokesperson Georgi Arbatov elaborated, informing the United States that "we are going to do a terrible thing to you—we are going to deprive you of an enemy."

Surprisingly, to many adherents of realism who see great power contests for supremacy as inevitable and strategic surrender or acceptance of defeat as impossible, the Soviets did what they promised: they began to act like an ally instead of an enemy. The Soviet Union agreed to end its aid to and support of the Castro regime in Cuba, withdrew from Afghanistan, and announced unilateral reductions in military spending. Gorbachev also agreed to two new disarmament agreements: the START (Strategic Arms Reduction Treaty) for deep cuts in strategic arsenals and the Conventional Forces in Europe (CFE) treaty to reduce the Soviet presence in Europe.

In 1989, the Berlin Wall came down, and by 1991 the Cold War had truly ended when the Soviet Union dissolved, accepted capitalist free-market principles, and initiated democratic reforms. To nearly everyone's astonishment, the Soviet Union acquiesced in the defeat of communism, the reunification of Germany, and the disintegration of its east European bloc of allies, the Warsaw Pact. The conclusion of the enduring rivalry between East and West, and with it the end of the seventy-year ideological dispute, was a history-transforming event in which liberalism seemed to triumph. The "sustained efforts to build a far-flung system of multilateral institutions, alliances, trade agreements, and political partnerships . . . helped draw countries into the United States' orbit. It helped strengthen global norms and rules that undercut the legitimacy of nineteenth-century-style spheres of influence, bids for regional domination, and territorial grabs" (Ikenberry, 2014, p. 2).

The Consequences of the Cold War

Despite maintaining a decades-long rivalry, the United States and the Soviet Union avoided a fatal showdown as Russian leaders made perhaps the most dramatic peaceful retreat from power in history. The collapse of the Cold War thus suggested something quite different from the lesson of the twentieth century's two world wars, which had implied that great power rivalries are necessarily doomed to end in armed conflict. Indeed, the unanticipated outcome undermined confidence in the adequacy of conventional realist theories that argued that no great power would ever accept the loss of position to another hegemonic rival without a fight. The Cold War was different; a combination of factors contributed at various stages in the Cold War's evolution to transform a global rivalry into a stable, even cooperative, relationship (see Table 4.2). This suggests that it is sometimes possible for great power rivals to reconcile their competitive differences without warfare.

TABLE 4.2   Contending Interpretations of the Causes of the Cold War's End

Level of Analysis	Theoretical Perspective		
	Realism	Liberalism	Constructivism
Individual	**Power Politics**	**Leaders as Movers of History**	**External Influences on Leadership**
	"The people who argued for nuclear deterrence and serious military capabilities contributed mightily to the position of strength that eventually led the Soviet leadership to choose a less bellicose, less menacing approach to international politics." — Richard Perle, U.S. presidential adviser	"[The end of the Cold War was possible] primarily because of one man — Mikhail Gorbachev. The transformations . . . would not have begun were it not for him." — James A. Baker III, U.S. secretary of state	"Reagan's 'tough' policy and intensified arms race [did not persuade] communists to 'give up.' [This is] sheer nonsense. Quite the contrary, this policy made the life for reformers, for all who yearned for democratic changes in their life, much more difficult. . . . The [communist hard-line] conservatives and reactionaries were given predominant influence." — Georgi Arbatov, director of the USSR's Institute for the USA and Canada Studies
State	**Economic Mismanagement**	**Grassroots Movements**	**Ideas and Ideals**
	"Soviet militarism, in harness with communism, destroyed the Soviet economy and thus hastened the self-destruction of the Soviet empire." — Fred Charles Iklé, U.S. deputy secretary of defense	"It was man who ended the Cold War in case you didn't notice. It wasn't weaponry, or technology, or armies or campaigns. It was just man. Not even Western man either, as it happened, but our sworn enemy in the East, who went into the streets, faced the bullets and the batons and said: we've had enough." — John Le Carré, author	"The root of the conflict was a clash of social systems and of ideological preferences for ordering the world. Mutual security in those circumstances was largely unachievable. A true end to the Cold War was impossible until fundamental changes occurred in Soviet foreign policy." — Robert Jervis, political scientist
Global	**Containment**	**International Public Opinion**	**Cross-Border Contagion Effects**
	"The strategy of containment that won the Cold War was the brain-child of realists. . . . Containment focused first and foremost on preventing Moscow from seizing the key centers of industrial power that lay near its borders, while eschewing attempts to 'roll back' Communism with military force." — Stephan Walt, political scientist	"The changes wrought by thousands of people serving in the trenches [throughout the world] were at least partially responsible [for ending the Cold War]." — David Cortright, political scientist	"The acute phase of the fall of communism started outside of the Soviet Union and spread to the Soviet Union itself. By 1987, Gorbachev made it clear that he would not interfere with internal experiments in Soviet bloc countries. . . . Once communism fell in Eastern Europe, the alternative in the Soviet Union became civil war or dissolution." — Daniel Klenbort, political journalist

Yet the Cold War altered the face of world politics in profound and diverse ways. One outcome was the growth of the United States' power, particularly in comparison to other developed countries, and the breadth of its involvement in international affairs. The United States exerted its influence in nearly every region of the world and achieved tremendous advances in not only its military strength, but also its economy, education levels, and technology. In fact, though conventional wisdom views the Cold War in terms of a bipolar balance of power between American and Soviet forces, in reality "Soviet economic activity never came close to U.S. levels, its political system quickly ossified, and its cultural influence was minimal. The 'superpower rivalry,' if one actually existed, was limited primarily to nuclear weapons and strategy" (Hook, 2012, p. 46).

Indeed, the proliferation of nuclear weapons and the evolution of warfare were among the most significant consequences of the Cold War. Though there was ideological competition, persistent hostilities and proxy wars, and the two opponents engaged in a protracted arms race, the United States and the Soviet Union came to view the actual use of nuclear weapons as suicidal. As Cold War historian, John Lewis Gaddis, observed:

> The Cold War may well be remembered, then, as the point at which military strength, a defining characteristic of 'power' itself for the past five centuries, ceased to be that. The Soviet Union collapsed, after all, with its military forces, even its nuclear capabilities, fully intact. The advance of technology, together with a culture of caution that transcended ideology, caused the nature of power itself to shift between 1945 and 1991: by the time the Cold War ended, the capacity to fight wars no longer guaranteed the influence of states, or even their continued existence, within the international system (Gaddis, 2005, p. 263).

At the same time, the heightened readiness for war expanded military budgets and elevated the role of the U.S. military as an instrument of a global U.S. foreign policy.

Other outcomes of the Cold War included the discrediting of dictatorships, perceived failure of communism, and the globalization of democratization. Not only did capitalism fail to instigate a global revolt of the working class, the Communist Party and the authoritarian state did not deliver political and social justice. At the same time, the number of democracies quintupled during the Cold War. Standards of living in those countries increased, with ordinary people becoming more informed and less willing for others to control their lives (Gaddis, 2005). Some thus believe that the end of the Cold War "validated Western values of individual freedom, representative government, and the rule of law—a perspective that leads them to conclude that the United States is obliged in the post-Cold War era to promote democracy and freedom in the contemporary world" (Schulzinger, 2012, p. 44).

With the dissolution of the Soviet Union in 1991, no immediate great power challenger confronted American hegemonic leadership. However, a host of new security threats emerged, ranging from aspiring nuclear powers such as North Korea and Iran to terrorist networks such as Al Qaeda and ISIS. As the turbulent twentieth century wound down, the simple Cold War world of clearly defined adversaries gave way to a shadowy world of elusive foes.

The Post–Cold War Era

LO 4-5   Evaluate shifts in polarity that have occurred since the end of the Cold War.

Rapid, unanticipated changes in world politics create uncertainty about the global future. To optimists, the swift transformations following the collapse of communism "ushered in a generation of relative political stability" (Zakaria, 2009) and signaled "the universalization of Western liberal democracy as the final form of government" (Fukuyama, 1989). To pessimists, these sea changes suggested not history's end but the resumption of contests for hegemonic domination and opposition over contested ideas and ideologies.

Both groups recognized that, in the years immediately following the end of the Cold War, bipolarity was superseded by **unipolarity**—a hegemonic configuration of power with only one predominant superstate. As time passed, however, other great powers began to vie for increased influence and visibility in world politics. This renewed contest has fueled debate as to whether *multipolarity* better describes the emerging distribution of power today. Of interest is what this might mean for relations among the great powers in meeting the new and difficult challenges in world politics in the post–Cold War era.

America's "Unipolar Moment"

Unipolarity refers to the concentration of power in a single preponderant state. At the end of the Cold War, the United States stood alone at the summit of the international hierarchy. While this "unipolar moment" may be waning, in many respects the United States retains several characteristics of a hegemon. It remains the only country with the military, economic, and cultural assets to be a decisive player in any part of the world. Its military is not just the strongest in the world, it is essentially stronger than the rest of the world, with defense expenditures in 2018 almost as much as the next eight largest-spending countries combined (SIPRI, 2019).

Complementing America's military might is its tremendous economic strength. With less than 5 percent of the global population, the United States accounts for over a fifth of global income and almost one-fourth of the entire world's combined spending on research and development (R&D Magazine, 2019). Further, because it is the hub of global communications and popular culture through which its values spread all over the world (Nye, 2015), America continues to wield enormous **soft power**. This rare confluence of military, economic, and cultural power gives the United States an extraordinary ability to shape the global future. This is why America's unique position atop the global pyramid of power seemingly allows it to act independently of worries about resistance from weaker powers. Rather than working in concert with others, a strong and dominant hegemon can sometimes address international problems without reliance on global organizations and can "go it alone," even in the face of strident foreign criticism.

Such **unilateralism** can involve a wide range of strategies, including isolationism, attempting to exert hegemonic leadership, a more nuanced strategy of **selective engagement**, or playing the role of a "balancer" in disputes involving other powers. However, unilateralism has its costs. Acting alone may appear expedient, but it can erode international support on issues such as combating terrorism or climate change that require strong cooperation from others. At the extreme, unilateralism can lead others to perceive the global leader as an international bully seeking to run the world. Dominating power can thus provoke counter-balancing. Indeed, Henry Kissinger (2001, p. 287) notes that domination "evokes nearly automatically a quest by other societies to achieve a greater voice . . . and to reduce the relative position of the strongest."

The status of being a superpower, the single "pole" or center of power, without a real challenger, has fated the United States with heavy and grave responsibilities that have come with considerable expense. Indeed, every previous leading great power has been vulnerable to

unipolarity
A condition in which the global system has a single dominant power or hegemony.

soft power
The capacity to co-opt through such intangible factors as the popularity of a state's values and institutions, as opposed to the "hard power" to coerce through military might.

unilateralism
An approach to foreign policy that relies on independent, self-help strategies in foreign policy.

selective engagement
A great power grand strategy using economic and military power to influence only important particular situations, countries, or global issues by striking a balance between a highly interventionist "global policeman" and an uninvolved isolationist.

imperial overstretch
The historic tendency for hegemons to sap their own strength through costly imperial pursuits and military spending that weaken their economies in relation to the economies of their rivals.

Global War on Terror (GWOT)
Popularized by U.S. President George W. Bush, this term refers to the era since September 11, 2001 when the struggle by the United States and its allies against radical Islamist movements and their terrorist tactics is a defining feature of world politics.

imperial overstretch, the gap between internal resources and external commitments (Kennedy, 1987). Throughout history, hegemons repeatedly have defined their security interests more broadly than other states, only to slip from the pinnacle of power by reaching beyond their grasp.

The **Global War on Terror (GWOT)** is an example of a campaign in which the United States' hegemonic leadership stems from its own security interests but has broad impact upon countries around the world. It also shows the limits that even superpowers face in reaching their strategic goals. The term refers specifically to the ongoing conflict between the United States and its allies versus Al Qaeda and other radical Islamist movements. It also refers to the post-9/11 era in general in that a focus on terrorism significantly characterizes contemporary international relations (Katz, 2017).

In the immediate aftermath of the terrorist attacks on the United States on September 11, 2001, then-President George W. Bush launched an international military campaign saying, "Our war on terror begins with Al Qaeda, but it does not end there. It will not end until every terrorist group of global reach has been found, stopped and defeated." The United States immediately engaged in a large-scale military operation, Operation Enduring Freedom. By the end of the operation in December 2014, the "United States and its coalition partners from over forty countries destroyed the leadership and infrastructure of Al Qaeda, thus denying the terrorist organization a safe haven that it used for training members, planning attacks, and conducting operations" (Prunckun and Whitford, 2019, p. 171).

Yet the threat of terrorism continues to characterize international conflict in the post-Cold War period (see Chapter 7), as seen in the rise of the Islamic State of Iraq and Syria (ISIS) that led the U.S. to launch a new military operation, Operation Inherent Resolve, in the Middle East and South Asia. U.S. efforts to confront terrorism have also expanded to include diplomatic, economic, and humanitarian responses. Today, scholars and policymakers agree that the United States and others must develop strategies that address the underlying conditions that give rise to terrorist grievances as well as take a tough stance in combatting extremists (Prunckun and Whitford, 2019).

From Unipolarity to Multipolarity: The Rise of the Rest?

The U.S. National Intelligence Council has projected that "although the unipolar moment is over, the U.S. most likely will remain *primus inter pares* at least until 2030 because of the multifaceted nature of its power and the legacies of its leadership" (Nye, 2013, p. 15). Others see the world from a somewhat different perspective, perceiving a great transformation marked by the ascendance of other great powers in what has been coined a "post-American" world, in which many other state and nonstate actors help to define and direct how we respond to global challenges. "At the politico-military level, we remain in a single-superpower world. But in every other dimension—industrial, financial, educational, social, cultural—the distribution of power is shifting, moving away from American dominance" (Zakaria, 2009, p. 4). As Map 4.3 shows, when we take into account multiple dimensions of what it means to be prosperous, the United States remains in the top tier with many of its Western allies—though it is no longer the single most prosperous country in the world.

Excessive costs to preserve America's empire by military means could prove to burst "the bubble of American supremacy" (Sanger, 2005; see also Rachman, 2012). Overall, defense

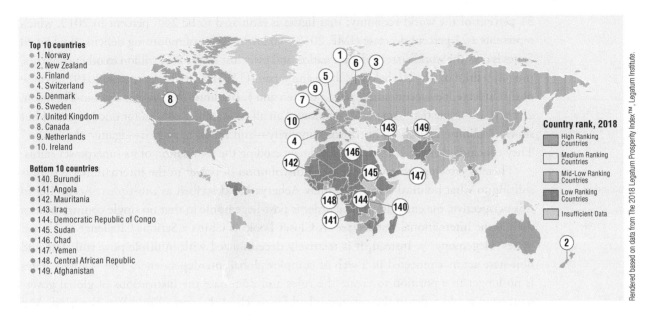

Top 10 countries
- 1. Norway
- 2. New Zealand
- 3. Finland
- 4. Switzerland
- 5. Denmark
- 6. Sweden
- 7. United Kingdom
- 8. Canada
- 9. Netherlands
- 10. Ireland

Bottom 10 countries
- 140. Burundi
- 141. Angola
- 142. Mauritania
- 143. Iraq
- 144. Democratic Republic of Congo
- 145. Sudan
- 146. Chad
- 147. Yemen
- 148. Central African Republic
- 149. Afghanistan

Country rank, 2018
- High Ranking Countries
- Medium Ranking Countries
- Mid-Low Ranking Countries
- Low Ranking Countries
- Insufficient Data

Rendered based on data from The 2018 Legatum Prosperity Index™. Legatum Institute.

MAP 4.3 Global Prosperity Based on eighty-nine measures of wealth and well-being, the 2018 Prosperity Index assesses performance in various areas: the economy, entrepreneurship and opportunity, education, health, governance, safety and security, social capital, and personal freedom. Today, global prosperity is at its highest point since the onset in 2008 of the worst financial crisis in modern times. At the same time, the distribution of prosperity is uneven as the gap between the most and least prosperous countries is the largest that it has ever been. The United States ranks 17ᵗʰ in overall prosperity out of 149 countries; Norway, New Zealand, and Finland enjoy the highest levels of prosperity.

Think It Through What does the ranking of any specific country on the Global Prosperity Index indicate about that country's sphere of influence?

spending by the United States has more than doubled since the terrorist attacks on September 11, 2001, and, when adjusted for inflation, remains at the highest level since World War II. With military expenditures of $649 billion in 2018, the United States spent almost as much on its military as the next eight largest-spending countries combined (SIPRI, 2019). Former U.S. Defense Secretary Robert Gates expressed concerns that the U.S. force structure is likely out of scale to existing threats. "Does the number of warships we have and are building really put America at risk when the U.S. battle fleet is larger than the next thirteen navies combined, eleven of which belong to allies and partners? Is it a dire threat that by 2020 the United States will have only twenty times more advanced stealth fighters than China?"

Trade-offs posed by allocating enormous national resources to military preparedness are reflected in former U.S. President Dwight Eisenhower's warning that "the problem in defense spending is to figure out how far you should go without destroying from within what you are trying to defend from without." Yet it is not only the financial cost of expansive military commitments itself that has some worried about America's ability to sustain its predominant position in the international system; the United States' predominance in the world has been further eroded by the financial crisis of 2008, which originated in the United States and spread throughout the global financial system.

Although the United States continues to rank at the top in terms of the size of its military, other indicators signal a relative decline. For example, in 2000 the United States made up

31 percent of the world economy; that figure is estimated to be 24.5 percent in 2019, which represents a 21 percent decrease (IMF, 2018). Following years of mounting deficits, the United States is now the world's largest debtor nation and owes just under $6.4 trillion to other countries, roughly a third of which is held by China and Japan (U.S. Treasury Department, 2019). Because of this indebtedness, economists Steven Cohen and J. Bradford DeLong (as cited in Thomson, 2011, p. 14) argue that "America has followed an all-too-familiar pattern for once powerful but slowly declining nations by borrowing unwisely—and much too often—against the future." They conclude that the United States is slowly eroding the foundation of its superpower status.

There is growing recognition that the distribution of power in the international system is shifting to what political scientist Amitav Acharya has described as **multiplex**. According to this perspective, the emerging global order is post-hegemonic in that no single country or idea defines the international system (see "A Closer Look: Is China a Serious Challenge to United States' Hegemony?"). Instead, it is relatively decentralized with multiple powerful state and non-state actors connected in a web of complex global interdependence. The "United States is no longer in a position to create the rules and dominate the institutions of global governance and world order in the manner it had for much of the post–World War II period. And while elements of the old liberal order will survive, they will have to accommodate new actors and approaches that do not bend to America's commands and preferences" (Acharya, 2017). Although U.S. involvement remains critical in addressing key international issues, some combination of U.S. imperial overstretch alongside rising economic and political influence by its chief challengers may be transforming the current distribution of global power and giving way to a more complex global system.

multiplex
A global system in which there are multiple consequential actors connected through complex interdependence, but no single power or idea has hegemonic domination.

Looking Ahead: What Does the Future Look Like for the Great Powers?

LO 4-6   Assess potential futures of great-power relations.

There is thus a deepening sense that shifts in the global distribution of power are under way. However, it is difficult to predict what cleavages and partnerships will develop among the great powers in the future because it is hard to foresee what will become the next major axis of conflict.

After years of decline following the Cold War, Russia seeks to restore what it sees as its rightful place as a global leader among the great powers (see "Controversy; A Resurgent Russia?"). Concomitantly, its relations with the United States have oscillated from warm to cool. Collaboration has been evident in the global war on terror, further reductions in nuclear weapons, and Russia's entry into the World Trade Organization. However, tensions also erupted over the Arab Spring, the overthrow of Libya's dictator Muammar al-Qaddafi, and Russia's actions in Georgia and Ukraine. More recently, Russia interfered in the U.S. presidential election in 2016. The "Russian government perceived it would benefit from a Trump presidency and worked to secure that outcome" through cyber-espionage and cyber-driven covert influence operations (Mueller, 2019, p. 1). Michael McFaul, a former U.S. ambassador to Russia, notes, "not only were the Russians able to successfully exploit divisions that already existed in the U.S., they also were able to undermine the legitimacy of the electoral process" (quoted in Brook and

A Closer Look

IS CHINA A SERIOUS CHALLENGE TO UNITED STATES' HEGEMONY?

Today, many see growing economic constraints on American power and question whether the United States has the resources and political will to continue to be the primary provider of international security and other global public goods (Acharya, 2018). At the same time, with China's meteoric rise on the international stage, many wonder about the future of China's role in the international system. "The United States is still the sole reigning superpower, but it is being challenged by the rising power of China, just as ancient Rome was challenged by Carthage, and Britain was challenged by Germany in the years before World War I" (Feldman, 2013, p. xi).

Is China a serious contender to replace the United States as the preeminent world power? Some suggest that we are seeing a true revival of China as a major power with expansion of its global leadership. "Its influence has boomed - along with its economy - in recent years, as the U.S. and Europe nursed the wounds from devastating financial crises" (da Costa, 2018). China's increased economic diplomacy, as evidenced by the Chinese-initiated multilateral Asian Infrastructure Investment Bank (AIIB) and its Belt and Road Initiative to increase trade with Africa, Europe, Latin America and Asia, is a strategic effort to expand its soft power and access to important resources overseas. China's military growth and its increased activity in the strategically vital South China Sea also signal global aspirations. "Not since the hordes of Genghis Khan galloped west in the 13th century have such sweeping transnational ambitions emanated from China" (Campbell, 2017).

So what does this mean for U.S.–China relations? Will the two countries face off in a hostile geopolitical confrontation reminiscent of the Cold War? Alternatively, will they continue to engage each other while seeking to manage peacefully the strategic threat posed by the other? "The Chinese think the U.S. wants to contain them and . . . people in the U.S. think the Chinese want to take over the world," said Director C. Fred Bergsten of the Peterson Institute for International Economics in Washington (da Costa, 2018). Others, however, argue that though China's power in the international system is increasing, the United States will remain a formidable global player and peaceful co-existence is probable. The "United States will almost certainly enjoy military superiority for decades to come, and therefore can afford to accommodate this rise, rather than confront China and thus risk turning it into a challenger by way of a self-fulfilling prophecy" (Maull, 2015, p. 147).

Watch the Carnegie Council Video:

"The U.S.: Shedding Hegemony with Grace"

You Decide:

1. How important is it that the United States continues to play a central role in international politics? If not, should the United States more narrowly define its interests and what should those interests include?

2. Do you think China poses a serious challenge to the United States' hegemony? If so, does this pose a problem for the United States?

3. Is movement to a multiplex system a reflection of declining American power or a result of the rise of the rest? Alternatively, do you think we are seeing a shift toward a bipolar system dominated by the United States and China?

Collins, 2019). By sowing discord, they sought to weaken the United States and hamper its ability to make domestic and foreign policy decisions.

The chill in U.S.-Russian relations has security experts and diplomats concerned about the lack of strategic dialogue to prevent armed conflict. "A bold policy shift is needed to support a strategic re-engagement with Russia and walk back from this perilous precipice. Otherwise, our nations may soon be entrenched in a nuclear standoff more precarious, disorienting and economically costly than the Cold War" (Schultz, Perry, and Nunn, 2019). Nonetheless, the United States and Russia continue to interact around key global issues. In 2019, the presidents of the two countries sought common ground in efforts to peacefully disarm North Korea and establish stronger bilateral trade ties.

China's status as an economic powerhouse has led some to predict that global power is shifting from the United States to China (see "A Closer Look: Is China a Serious Challenge to United States' Hegemony?"). In 2014, China overtook the United States to become the leading economy in terms of gross domestic product (GDP) when measured in terms of **purchasing power parity (PPP)**, which removes differences in countries' price levels. Although it will not surpass the United States in per capita wealth, China's share of global gross domestic product has eclipsed that of the United States and the European Union, leading to speculation that we are entering the "Asian Century." By some estimates, the Chinese economy will reach $61 trillion by 2050, which will far exceed the United States ($41 trillion) and India ($42 trillion), respectively, as the next two largest economies (PWC, 2015). As Kissinger (2012a, p. 546) reminds us, "China does not see itself as a rising but as a returning power. . . . It does not view the prospect of a strong China exercising influence in economic, cultural, political, and military affairs as an unnatural challenge to world order—but rather as a return to a normal state of affairs."

Figure 4.2, which estimates the relative size of the largest economies in 2050, provides some broader context for these debates. The projections show that the rank order of the largest

purchasing power parity (PPP)
An index that calculates the true rate of exchange among currencies when parity—when what can be purchased is the same—is achieved; the index determines what can be bought with a unit of each currency.

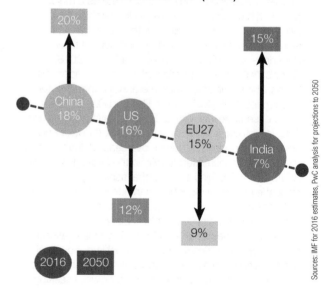

World's Top 10 Economies (GDP at PPPs)

	2016	2050	
China	1	1	China
US	2	2	India
India	3	3	US
Japan	4	4	Indonesia
Germany	5	5	Brazil
Russia	6	6	Russia
Brazil	7	7	Mexico
Indonesia	8	8	Japan
UK	9	9	Germany
France	10	10	UK

◼ E7 economies ◻ G7 economies

Based on "The Long View: How Will the Global Economic Order Change by 2050?" PwC, 2017.

Share of World GDP (PPPs)

20%   15%
China 18%   US 16%   EU27 15%   India 7%
12%   9%

2016   2050

Sources: IMF for 2016 estimates, PwC analysis for projections to 2050

FIGURES 4.2A AND 4.2B Transitions in Wealth and Economic Power, 2016–2050 Current and projected growth indicates that there are significant shifts taking place in the global balance of geopolitical and economic power. Though still one of the strongest economies in the world, the United States was surpassed by China in 2014 for the top ranking in terms of GDP at PPP. The figure on the left shows that by 2050, the top five ranked countries may include the United States plus the emerging market economies of China, India, Indonesia, and Brazil. As shown in the figure on the right, European and U.S. shares of world GDP are projected to decline over the coming decades.

Controversy

A RESURGENT RUSSIA?

Following a period of post-Cold War decline, in recent years Russia has gone to great lengths to project its image "not only as the most important regional power in the Commonwealth of Independent States (CIS) region and a very important one in Europe and Asia, but also a global power enmeshed in a contest with the United States over global

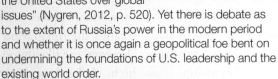

issues" (Nygren, 2012, p. 520). Yet there is debate as to the extent of Russia's power in the modern period and whether it is once again a geopolitical foe bent on undermining the foundations of U.S. leadership and the existing world order.

World politics has long been characterized by rivalry between great powers, and long-cycle theory envisions a transition in world leadership that is prompted, in part, by changes in the relative power of the major global actors (Chase-Dunn and Anderson, 2005). Some see Russia as "pushing back against the political settlement of the Cold War" (Mead, 2014, p. 4) and seeking to upset the United States as the global hegemon by chipping away at the relationships and norms that undergird the status quo. Russia is strongly asserting itself across Eurasia, as seen in the invasion of Ukraine, challenges to U.S. goals in Syria, and regarding Iran's nuclear program, and these efforts are seen as an attempt to dominate the region and threaten the reigning world order.

Others counter that although Russia may challenge U.S. global leadership, it "is not on the rise; to the contrary, it is experiencing one of the greatest geopolitical contractions of any major power in the modern era" (Ikenberry, 2014, p. 2). Its confrontational actions in Crimea, Armenia, and Georgia have been driven to a great extent by geopolitical vulnerability as the West has moved into its backyard. Starting in 2009 with the entry of Poland, Hungary, and the

Czech Republic into NATO—followed by admission between 2004 and 2009 of nine more former members of the Soviet Bloc plus six former Soviet republics participating in NATO's Partnership for Peace program—Russia has seen its sphere of influence and security diminish. U.S. power far surpasses that of Russia, and the liberal international framework that was shaped following World War II continues to underlie the global economy and mechanisms for addressing global problems. Moreover, Russia's own overriding interests "are deeply integrated into the world economy and its governing institutions" (Ikenberry, 2014, p. 2).

Debate about Russian foreign policy and its implications for the rest of the world is ongoing, and it is important that we not reflexively cling to a Cold War prism but intentionally seek an objective and pragmatic lens through which to evaluate Russia's actions (Roberts, 2014). "If its interests and ambitions are legitimate, the West is better off trying to engage Russia as an equal contributor to shaping the global system. If, however, Moscow harbors revisionist plans, it may represent a threat to Western interests and must be either contained or fundamentally transformed" (Tsygankov, 2014, p. 21).

What Do You Think?

1. What insights does realism provide for explaining Russia's foreign policy? What interpretations might liberalism or constructivism provide?

2. If you were Russia's president, what approach would you take to world politics?

3. Are we witnessing the beginning of a second Cold War?

economies by 2050 will be substantially different from today, with emerging markets rising to the top. As shown in Figure 4.3, China's share of global GDP in PPP will increase from 18 percent in 2016 to 20 percent in 2050, and it will remain the world's largest economy throughout. India is also likely to experience significant economic growth over this period, with its share of world GDP in PPP rising from 7 percent in 2016 to about 15 percent in 2050. At the same time, the share of global GDP in PPP for the United States and the EU is expected to decline from a combined 31 percent in 2016 to 21 percent in 2050.

The speed of the transition in global economic power may vary, but the general direction of the trend is clear. Many countries in the Global South, particularly in Asia, are rising in prominence in the global economy. Increasing populations that expand domestic demand and the size of the workforce fuels this economic growth. Over the next three decades, the E7 economies of China, India, Indonesia, Brazil, Russia, Mexico, and Turkey are projected to grow at an annual average rate of almost 3.5 percent compared to 1.6 percent for the advanced G7 nations of the United States, Japan, Germany, United Kingdom, Canada, France, and Italy (PwC, 2017).

In the future, pervasive hostilities could emerge between any pair of powers. For example, competition could escalate between the globe's two major contenders for supremacy, the United States and China, if the United States practices containment to try to prevent China's rise or China threatens U.S. security interests. However, armed rivalry need not develop; cooperation could increase instead (Kissinger, 2012b). Quite different political types of great power relations could emerge in the economic and military spheres. There is the probability of economic rivalry growing as global trade expands the integration of states' economies in an ever-tightening web of interdependence. However, the likelihood of security cooperation for many of these same relationships is also high. Under these circumstances, the danger of *polarization* could be managed if the great powers develop international rules and institutions to manage their fluid, mixed-motive relationships. Such potential for collaboration is reflected in former Chinese Minister of Defense Liang Guanglie's assertion that:

> China's participation in world security cooperation is by no means enlargement of a sphere of influence or territorial expansion. . . . The Chinese military's outreach for international security cooperation is not intended to impair the international system, but to become a player and builder of the system, providing additional public goods to the international community so that the benefit of security can be truly shared by all.

Today the paradox prevails that many pairs of great powers that are the most active trade partners are also the greatest military rivals, but the key question is whether economic cooperation will help to reduce the potential for military competition in the future. The opportunities and challenges we face in the world today call for a multilateral approach, with all of the great powers working cooperatively to achieve global solutions.

concert
A cooperative agreement among great powers to jointly manage the global system.

multilateralism
Cooperative approaches to managing shared problems through collective and coordinated action.

One possibility along these lines is the development of a **concert**, or a cooperative agreement, among the great powers to manage the global system jointly and to prevent international disputes from escalating to war. The Concert of Europe, at its apex between 1815 and 1822, is the epitome of previous great power efforts to pursue this path to peace. The effort to build a great power coalition to wage a war against global terrorism following 9/11 is a more recent example of **multilateralism** to construct a concert through collective action. Some policy makers also recommend that today's great powers unite with the lesser powers in constructing a true system of *collective security*. The formation of the League of Nations in 1919 is the best example of this multilateral approach to peace under conditions of multipolarity, and some believe NATO is representative of a collective security quest to maintain peace through an alliance of powerful countries.

Of course, we have no way of knowing what the future holds. Patterns and practices can change, and it is possible for policy makers to learn from previous mistakes and avoid repeating them. How the great powers react to the eventual emergence of a new global system where power and responsibility are more widely distributed is crucial. It is clear that the choices the great powers make about war and peace will determine the fate of the world. In Chapter 5, we turn your attention from the rich, powerful, and commercially active great powers at the center of the world system to the poorer, weaker, and economically dependent states in the Global South and the emerging powers in the Global East.

IMAGE 4.5 **A New Global Hegemon?** To the West, the notion of a world in which the center of global economic gravity lies in Asia may seem unimaginable. However, according to Chris Patten, a former British governor of Hong Kong, China was the world's leading economic power for eighteen of the past twenty centuries. Shown here, U.S. President Donald Trump meets with Chinese President Xi Jinping in December 2018 to discuss trade relations between the two countries.

> *As much as anything else, the rise and fall of major powers determines the viability of the prevailing order, since changes in economic strength, political cohesion, and military power shape what states can and are willing to do beyond their borders.*
>
> **—RICHARD HAASS, U.S. DIPLOMAT**

Study. Apply. Analyze.

Chapter Summary

4-1 Discuss the cyclical nature of history as portrayed by long-cycle theory. Long-cycle theory contends that the rise and fall of hegemons, or "great powers" which dominate international politics, is recurrent throughout history. Great power rivalries and transitions in global leadership unfold through a series of distinct phases alongside changes in major states' relative power and their relations with one another.

4-2 Explain the causes and consequences of World War I. The causes of this war can be assessed in terms of three levels of analysis. Structuralism takes a realist approach to the systemic level of analysis and connects the seemingly inevitability of war with the anarchical nature of international relations. The state level of analysis includes the rise of nationalism prior to World War I, while the individual level looks at the decisions made by state leaders. World War I changed the face of Europe, and resulted in a profound distaste for war and realist approaches to international relations. Instead, the war set the stage for a rise in liberalism, leading to new international policies and organizations aimed at preventing another "Great War."

4-3 Explain the causes and consequences of World War II.
The various approaches of individual state leaders to shifting power divisions, changes in national identities, and economic turmoil all contributed to the onset of World War II, in which the "grand alliance" fought to stop the fascist coalition of Germany, Italy, and Japan from global expansion. At its close, with the defeat of the Axis Powers, global influence shifted to the United States and the Soviet Union. The other major powers had exhausted themselves and slipped from the heights of the world-power hierarchy.

4-4 Identify the causes and key phases of the Cold War.
Competition between the United States and the Soviet Union for hegemonic leadership gave rise to the Cold War. There is debate as to what factors were most responsible. Systemically, the transition in power that resulted in the United States and the Soviet Union becoming superpowers made their rivalry inescapable. At the state level, their differing ideologies about politics and economics led to mutual disdain. Misperception and distrust affected individual decision making. Over time, the enduring rivalry between the United States and the Soviet Union evolved in distinct phases, from confrontation to peaceful coexistence and détente to renewed confrontation to rapprochement.

4-5 Evaluate shifts in polarity that have occurred since the end of the Cold War.
In the early years of the post-Cold War era, the United States stood alone as the sole hegemon due to its unparalleled military, economic, and cultural influence. However, as time passed, other great powers began to vie for increased influence and visibility in world politics. At the same time, the United States' defense spending exponentially increased and the economies of other countries grew. This led to a change from a unipolar to a multipolar, or multiplex, international system.

4-6 Assess potential futures of great power relations.
There is a deepening sense that shifts in the global distribution of power are under way. One evident change is the shift in global wealth and economic power. China's status as an economic powerhouse has led some to predict that China will be a premier global leader in the twenty-first century. Others point toward Russia's efforts to regain its superpower status. Though the United States will remain a major player, a number of other powerful state and nonstate actors will likely play key roles in shaping our global future.

Key Terms

appeasement	Global War on Terror	long-cycle theory	soft power
bipolarity	(GWOT)	multilateralism	structuralism
Cold War	hegemon	multipolarity	Truman Doctrine
colonialism	ideology	nationalism	unilateralism
concert	imperial	peaceful coexistence	multiplex
containment	overstretch	political economy	unipolarity
détente	irredentism	purchasing power parity (PPP)	Yalta Conference
domino theory	isolationism	rapprochement	
fascism	linkage strategy	selective engagement	

Suggested Readings and Resources

Acharya, Amitav. (2018). *Constructing Global Order: Agency and Change in World Politics*. Cambridge: Cambridge University Press.

Boon, Hoo Tiang. (2018). *China's Global Identity: Considering the Responsibilities of Great Power*. Washington, D.C.: Georgetown University Press.

Graeber, Daniel. (2018). "The Populist Appeal of American Decline." Carnegie Council for Ethics in International Affairs, carnegiecouncil.org/publications/ethics_online/the-populist-appeal-of-american-decline.

Ikenberry, John G. (2014). "The Illusion of Geopolitics: The Enduring Power of the Liberal Order," *Foreign Affairs* (May/June): 2.

Kegley, Charles W. and Gregory A. Raymond. (2020). *The Great Powers and World Order: Patterns and Prospects*. Thousand Oaks, CA: Sage Publishing/CQ Press.

Mankoff, Jeffrey. (2009). *Russian Foreign Policy: The Return of Great Power Politics*. New York: Rowman and Littlefield.

Mead, Walter Russell. (2014). "The Return of Geopolitics: The Revenge of Revisionist Powers," *Foreign Affairs* (May/June): 4.

Nye, Joseph S., Jr. (2015). *Is the American Century Over?* Cambridge, UK: Polity.

Still Out in the Cold: stilloutinthecold.net. A Cold War history blog.

The Atlantic Council: atlanticcouncil.org/ Analysis of political, economic, and security issues pertaining to Asia, the Americas, Europe, and other regions.

The World in 2050: pwc.com/gx/en/world-2050/assets/pwc-the-world-in-2050-full-report-feb-2017.pdf. In-depth view of future global economic shifts.

Carnegie Council Videos

Key Term Videos

- Hegemon
- Structuralism
- Nationalism
- Multipolarity
- Bipolarity
- Cold War
- Truman Doctrine
- Containment
- Soft Power
- Multilateralism
- Multiplex

Additional Videos

- Gelb, Leslie. "Power Rules: How Common Sense Can Rescue American Foreign Policy."
- Matlock, Jack F. "Superpower Illusions: How Myths and False Ideologies Led America Astray—and How to Return to Reality."
- Vocke, William. "The U.S.: Shedding Hegemony with Grace."
- Zelizer, Julian E. "Arsenal of Democracy: The Politics of National Security—from World War II to the War on Terrorism."

Chapter 5

World Politics and the Global South

Yamil Lage/Getty Images

IMAGE 5.1 **Winds of Change** In a world of great powers, the opportunities and challenges faced by countries in the Global South are shaped in part by their position in the global hierarchy. After more than a half-century of hostility, relations between the United States and Cuba have begun to soften, though uncertainty remains as to whether U.S. policy will continue to thaw or revert to one of confrontation. Pictured here in Havana, Cuba, a Cuban wears a shirt with a U.S. flag design.

Learning Objectives

LO 5-1   Describe the historical phases of colonialism, as well as the era of decolonization.
LO 5-2   Discuss the key differences between the Global North and Global South.
LO 5-3   Identify the internal and international causes for underdevelopment in the Global South.
LO 5-4   Assess different approaches taken to facilitate development in the Global South.
LO 5-5   Appraise the prospects for future development in the Global South.

A global human society based on poverty for many and prosperity for a few, characterized by islands of wealth surrounded by a sea of poverty, is unsustainable."
—THABO MBEKI, FORMER PRESIDENT OF SOUTH AFRICA

Earth is divided into two hemispheres, north and south, at the equator. This artificial line of demarcation is, of course, meaningless except for use by cartographers to chart distance and location on maps. Yet this divide also represents a popular way of describing the inequalities that separate rich and poor states as these two groups are generally located on either side of the equator (see Map 5.1).

Common today are the terms **Global North**, which refers to the relatively wealthy industrialized countries that share a commitment to varying forms of democratic political institutions and developed market economies, and **Global South**, which refers to the less developed countries that are mostly located in the Southern Hemisphere. Additionally, these contemporary terms largely correspond to the distinction between *great powers* and **small powers** (Kassimeris, 2009). Among the countries of the Global South, a distinction is also made that recognizes the **emerging powers**, or **middle powers**, as those that seek a more assertive role in international

Global North
A term used to refer to the world's wealthy, industrialized countries located primarily in the Northern Hemisphere.

Global South
A term now often used instead of "Third World" to designate the less developed countries located primarily in the Southern Hemisphere.

small powers
Countries with limited political, military, or economic capabilities and influence.

emerging powers (middle powers)
Countries with rising political and economic capabilities and influence that seek a more assertive role in international affairs.

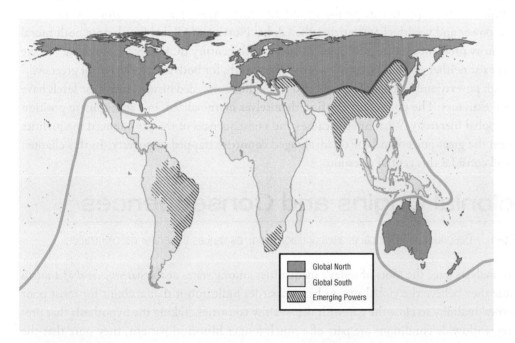

MAP 5.1 The Global North and Global South Global North countries are wealthy and democratic. In contrast, the Global South countries are home to 83.4 percent of the world's population, but the impoverished people living there possess only 35.1 percent of the world's gross domestic product (WDI, 2017). Yet there is considerable variation within the Global South, with some countries enjoying higher levels of prosperity and global influence than others. These "emerging powers" have arisen from the former Global South and now challenge the Global North by seeking a greater role in global governance and institutions.

Think It Through How could colonialism have influenced which countries now fall under the category of Global South?

affairs, possess enough resources to potentially realize their goals, and are experiencing increasing influence in world politics, particularly with regard to the global economy.

The placement of particular states within these categories is not easy. Although journalists, policy makers, and scholars frequently generalize about the Global South, considerable diversity exists within this grouping of states. For example, it includes low-income countries such as Ghana and Haiti, where a majority of the population tries to survive through subsistence agriculture; middle-income countries such as Brazil and Malaysia, which produce manufactured goods; and some countries such as Kuwait and Qatar, whose petroleum exports have generated incomes rivaling those of Global North.

Global South countries are different in other ways as well. Their ranks include both Indonesia—an archipelago nation of more than 17,500 islands scattered across an oceanic expanse larger than the United States—and Timor-Leste, an island state roughly the same size as Connecticut. This category also includes Nigeria, with 191 million inhabitants, and Guinea-Bissau, with just 1.9 million people. In addition to these geographic and demographic differences, Global South countries also vary politically and culturally, ranging from democratic Costa Rica to autocratic Myanmar.

Life for most people in the Northern Hemisphere is very different from that in the Southern Hemisphere. The disparities are profound and, in many places, appear to be growing. The division in power and wealth characterizing the Global North and Global South pose both moral and security problems. As the philosopher Plato in fifth-century BCE Greece counseled, "There should exist neither extreme poverty nor excessive wealth, for both are productive of great evil." Although poverty and inequality have existed throughout recorded history, today the levels have reached extremes. The poor countries find themselves marginalized, in a subordinate position in the global hierarchy. What are the causes and consequences of the pronounced inequalities between the great powers and the disadvantaged countries trapped in poverty? In this chapter, you will consider this central question.

Colonial Origins and Consequences

LO 5-1   Describe the historical phases of colonialism, as well as the era of decolonization.

Many analysts trace the roots of today's inequalities among states at the *systemic level of analysis* because they believe the global system has properties built into it that account for most poor countries' inability to close the gap with the wealthy countries. Taking the hypothesis that prevailing worldwide conditions are part of a much longer historical pattern, they note that the rules governing international politics today were constructed in the 1648 Peace of Westphalia following Europe's Thirty Years' War. These rules were crafted by the most powerful actors on the world stage—the great powers at the time—to serve their parochial self-interests by preserving their predominant positions in the international system and preventing less-powerful states from joining them (Kegley and Raymond, 2002).

As suggested by constructivism, the origins and persistence of the inequalities of states stem in part from the fact that today's modern global system was initially, and remains, a socially constructed reality by, of, and for the most powerful states. The powerful did not design a global system for equals; the great powers followed the prescription of realist thought to seek self-advantage always. Accordingly, they did not build the global system with an eye to preventing the victimization of the weak and the disadvantaged.

Such is not unique to the modern age, of course. Imperialism has repeatedly shaped global relations, with a state seeking through conquest or subversion to exert political, military, cultural, or economic control over others for their own gain. Consider the powerful ancient empires of the Incans, Aztecs, Chinese, and Romans and the empires in the 20th century of Portugal, Spain, Belgium, England, Austria, France, Russia, Turkey, China, and the United States. They were characterized by coercion and exploitation, sometimes supplemented with attempts to establish peace and justice. "In the Incan empire, for example, hunger and poverty were unknown, the people enjoyed a high standard of living, but there was no individual freedom. Western empires, on the other hand, have been characterized by global inequalities between the imperial nations and their colonies" (Eckhard, 1984, p. 299).

So, a good starting place is to begin your inquiry by taking into consideration the legacy of this system today. Many analysts see the history of *colonialism* in the modern world—primarily through the European conquest of **indigenous peoples** and the seizure of their territory for exclusively European gain—as the root source of the problem. They note that almost all of the independent sovereign states in the Global South were at one time colonies and argue that today's inequalities are a product of that past colonization.

The emergence of the Global South as an identifiable group of states is a distinctly contemporary phenomenon. Although most Latin American countries were independent before World War II, not until afterward did other countries of the Global South gain that status. In 1947, Great Britain granted independence to India and Pakistan, after which **decolonization**—the freeing of colonial peoples from their dependent status—gathered speed. Since then, a diverse array of new sovereign states has joined the global community, nearly all carved from the British, Spanish, Portuguese, Dutch, and French empires built under colonialism four hundred years ago.

Today, few colonies exist and the decolonization process is almost complete. However, the effects persist. Most of the ethnic national conflicts that are now so prevalent have colonial roots, as the imperial powers drew borders within and between their domains with little regard for the national identities of the indigenous peoples (see Map 5.2). Similarly, the disparity in wealth between the rich Global North and the poor Global South is attributed in part to unequal and exploitative relations during the colonial period, as is a legacy of mistrust and insecurity that persists not only across this global divide but also within the former colonial countries themselves.

The Congo is but one example of how the colonial experience eroded the strength of a former medieval great power (Gebrekidan, 2010). Four centuries of the slave trade by the Portuguese claimed more than 13 million lives. This was followed in 1885 by decades of further exploitation under the rule of King Leopold II of Belgium, who was, at least indirectly, responsible for 10 million deaths as he turned the country into a virtual labor camp and amassed a personal fortune through the harvest of wild rubber (Haskin, 2005). Although independence was achieved in 1960, peace and prosperity did not follow. Instead, colonial rule was replaced with violent internal divisions. Rising to power in 1965, Mobutu Sese Seko established an

indigenous peoples
The native ethnic and cultural inhabitant populations within countries.

decolonization
The process by which sovereign independence was achieved by countries that were once colonies of the great powers.

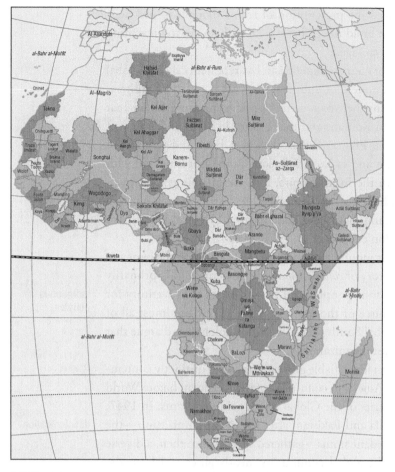

MAP 5.2 A Legacy of Colonialism Before the Europeans arrived, Africa was rich with powerful empires such as the Songhai Empire, which in the 14th century was a global center of learning and culture (Fisher, 2014). However, the stalled economic development of much of Africa today is attributed to the trauma of the European colonial legacy (Nunn, 2007). Shown here, as inspired by Swedish artist Nikolaj Cyon, is how Africa might look if colonialism had never occurred based upon the political and tribal units that existed in the mid-1800s.

 Think It Through How has imperialism shaped the borders of African countries today?

authoritarian state and controlled the people through fear and repression until his overthrow in 1997. Over the course of his reign, Mobutu perpetuated the colonial legacy of exploitation. According to Transparency International, he embezzled more than $5 billion from his country, ranking him as the most corrupt African leader over the past two decades.

The First Wave of European Imperialism

The first wave of European empire building began in the late fifteenth century, as the Dutch, English, French, Portuguese, and Spanish used their naval power to conquer territories for commercial gain. Scientific innovations made the European explorers' adventures possible, and merchants followed in their wake, "quickly seizing upon opportunities to increase their business and profits. In turn, Europe's governments perceived the possibilities for increasing their own power and wealth. Commercial companies were chartered and financed, with military and naval expeditions frequently sent out after them to ensure political control of overseas territories" (Cohen, 1973, p. 20).

The economic strategy underlying the relationship between colonies and colonizers during this era of "classical imperialism" is known as **mercantilism**—an economic philosophy advocating government regulation of economic life to increase state power. European rulers believed that power flowed from the possession of national wealth measured in gold and silver, and that cultivating mining and industry to attain a favorable balance of trade (exporting more than they imported) was the best way to become rich.

mercantilism
A government trade strategy for accumulating state wealth and power by encouraging exports and discouraging imports.

Colonies were desirable in this respect because they afforded an opportunity to shut out commercial competition; they guaranteed exclusive access to untapped markets and sources of cheap materials (as well as, in some instances, direct sources of the precious metals themselves). Each state was determined to monopolize as many of these overseas mercantile opportunities as possible (Cohen, 1973, p. 21).

States adhering to realist justifications of the competitive drive for global power saw the imperial conquest of foreign territory by war as a natural by-product of active government management of the economy.

By the end of the eighteenth century, the European powers had spread themselves, albeit thinly, throughout virtually the entire world. But the colonial empires they had built began to crumble. Britain's thirteen North American colonies declared their independence in 1776, and most of Spain's possessions in South America won their freedom in the early nineteenth century. Nearly one hundred colonial relationships worldwide ceased in the half-century ending in 1825 (Bergesen and Schoenberg, 1980).

As Europe's colonial empires dissolved, belief in the mercantilist philosophy also waned. As liberal political economist Adam Smith argued (1776), national wealth grew not through the accumulation of precious metals but rather from the capital and goods they could buy. Smith's ideas about the benefits of the "invisible hand" of the unregulated marketplace laid much of the intellectual foundation for **classical liberal economic theory**. Following Smith and other liberal free-trade theorists, faith in the precepts of **laissez-faire economics** (minimal government interference in the market) gained widespread acceptance (see also Chapter 10). Henceforth, European powers continued to seek colonies, but the rationale for their imperial policies began to change.

classical liberal economic theory
A body of thought based on Adam Smith's ideas about the forces of supply and demand in the marketplace, emphasizing the social and economic benefits when individuals pursue their own self-interest.

laissez-faire economics
The philosophical principle of free markets and free trade to give people free choices with little government regulation.

> *I hate imperialism. I detest colonialism. And I fear the consequences of their last bitter struggle for life. We are determined, that our nation, and the world as a whole, shall not be the plaything of one small corner of the world.*
>
> **—SUKARNO, FORMER PRESIDENT OF INDONESIA**

The Second Wave of European Imperialism

A second wave of imperialism washed over the world, as Europe—joined later by the United States and Japan—aggressively colonized new territories from the 1870s until the outbreak of World War I. Europeans controlled one-third of the globe in 1800, two-thirds by 1878, and four-fifths by 1914 (Fieldhouse, 1973). As illustrated in Map 5.3, in the last twenty years of the nineteenth century, Africa fell under the control of seven European powers (Belgium, Britain, France, Germany, Italy, Portugal, and Spain), and in all of the Far East and the Pacific, only China, Japan, and Siam (Thailand) were not completely conquered. However, the foreign great powers carved China into separate zones of commerce, which they each individually controlled and exploited for profit. Japan itself also invaded and occupied Korea and Formosa (now Taiwan).

Elsewhere, the United States expanded across its continent, acquired Puerto Rico and the Philippines in the 1898 Spanish-American War, extended its colonial reach west to Hawaii, leased the Panama Canal Zone "in perpetuity" from the new state of Panama (an American

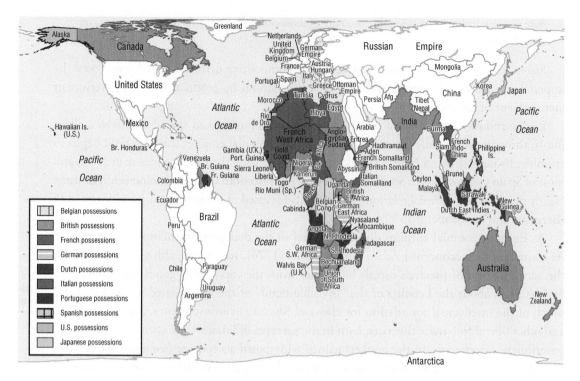

MAP 5.3 Global Imperialism 1914 The ten major imperial powers competed for colonies throughout the globe in the present-day Global South, and on the eve of World War I, their combined territories covered most of the world.

Think It Through   How could the "sun never set" on the British Empire?

communism
The Marxist ideology maintaining that if society is organized so that every person produces according to his or her ability and consumes according to his or her needs, a community without class distinctions will emerge, sovereign states will no longer be needed, and imperial wars of colonial conquest will vanish from history.

creation), and exercised considerable control over several Caribbean islands, notably Cuba. The preeminent imperial power, Great Britain, created an empire that covered one-fifth of the Earth's land area and comprised around one-fourth of its population (Cohen, 1973). As British imperialists proudly proclaimed: The sun never set on the British Empire.

So why did most of the great powers—and those that aspired to great power status—engage in this expensive and often vicious competition to control other peoples and territories? What explains this new imperialism?

One answer lies in the nature of the global economy. With the Industrial Revolution, capitalism grew—emphasizing the free market, private ownership of the means of production, and the accumulation of wealth. Radical theorists following Karl Marx and Vladimir Lenin, who called themselves adherents of **communism**, saw imperialism's aggressive competition as caused by a capitalist need for profitable overseas outlets for surplus production. Sharing a critical perspective of the capitalist world economy, *world-system theory* saw a world division of labor where the (industrial) "core" areas exploit the (nonindustrial) "periphery," and colonization provided a means for imperial control over foreign lands. Liberal economists, by contrast, regarded the new imperialism not as a product of capitalism but, rather, as a response to certain maladjustments that could be corrected. Despite these differences, the three perspectives shared the belief that economics explained the new imperialism: Imperialism was rooted in the material needs of advanced capitalist societies for cheap raw materials and additional markets to consume growing production (see Chapter 2).

Another explanation emphasizes purely political factors as the source of the second wave of imperialism. As liberal British economist J. A. Hobson (1902) argued, jockeying for power and prestige between competitive empires had always characterized the great powers' behavior in the European balance-of-power system. Hobson believed that imperialism through overseas expansion was simply a global extension of this inter-European competition for dominance inspired by the **realpolitik** premise that all states have an unquenchable thirst for more and more power.

By the 1800s, Britain emerged from Europe's perpetual conflict as the world's leading power. By 1870, however, British hegemony began to decline. Germany emerged as a powerful industrial state, as did the United States. Understandably, Britain tried to protect its privileged global position in the face of growing competition from the newly emerging core states. Its efforts to maintain the status quo help to explain the second wave of imperial expansion, especially in Africa, where partition served the imperial powers' purposes to the detriment of the local populations.

realpolitik
The theoretical outlook prescribing that countries should increase their power and wealth in order to compete with and dominate other countries.

Self-Determination and Decolonization in the Twentieth Century

The climate of opinion turned decidedly against imperialism when the 1919 Versailles peace settlement that ended World War I embraced *liberalism*—the body of theoretical thought that stresses the importance of ideas, ideals, and institutions to generate progress, prosperity, and peace. Part of that reform program was the principle of national **self-determination** that U.S. President Woodrow Wilson championed. Self-determination advocated giving indigenous nationalities the moral right to decide which authority would rule them.

self-determination
The liberal doctrine that people should be able to determine the government that will rule them.

Wilson and other *liberal theorists* (see Chapter 2) reasoned that freedom would lead to the creation of states and governments that were content with their territorial boundaries and, therefore, less inclined to make war. In practice, however, the attempt to redraw states' borders to separate nationality groups was applied only to war-torn Europe, where six new states were created from the territory of the former Austrian-Hungarian Empire (Austria, Czechoslovakia, Hungary, Poland, Romania, and the ethnically divided Yugoslavia). Other territorial adjustments were also made in Europe, but the proposition that self-determination should be extended to Europe's overseas empires did not receive serious support.

Still, the colonial territories of the powers defeated in World War I were not simply parceled out among the victorious allies, as had typically happened in the past. Instead, the territories controlled by Germany and the Ottoman Empire were transferred, under League of Nations auspices, to countries that would govern them as "mandates" until their eventual self-rule. Many of these territorial decisions gave rise to subsequent conflicts across the globe. For example, the League of Nations called for the eventual creation of a Jewish national homeland in Palestine and arranged for the transfer of control over Southwest Africa (called Namibia) to what would become the white minority regime of South Africa.

Charles Lomodong/AFP/Getty Images

IMAGE 5.2 Freedom and Self-Determination When World War I broke out, only 62 independent countries existed. With secession from Sudan in July 2011, the emergence of South Sudan as the world's newest nation brought the count to 195, according to the U.S. Department of State. Pictured here, South Sudanese women celebrate their country's independence, though it has been plagued with civil war since 2013.

The principle implicit in the League of Nations mandate system gave birth to the idea that "colonies were a trust rather than simply a property to be exploited and treated as if its peoples had no rights of their own" (Easton, 1964, p. 124). This set an important precedent so that after World War II the defeated powers' territories placed under the United Nations (UN) trusteeship system were not absorbed by others but were promised eventual self-rule. Thus, support for self-determination gained momentum.

The decolonization process accelerated in 1947, when the British consented to the independence of India and Pakistan. War eventually erupted between these newly independent states as each sought to gain control over disputed territory in Kashmir in 1965, in 1971, and again as the nuclear-armed states clashed in 2002. Violence also broke out in Vietnam and Algeria in the 1950s and early 1960s when the French sought to regain control over their pre–World War II colonial territories. Similarly, bloodshed followed closely on the heels of independence in the Congo when the Belgians granted their African colony independence in 1960, and it dogged the unsuccessful efforts of Portugal to battle the winds of decolonization that swept over Africa as the 1960s wore on.

Despite these political convulsions, decolonization was for the most part not only extraordinarily rapid but also remarkably peaceful. This may be explained by the fact that World War II sapped the economic and military vitality of many of the colonial powers. World-system analysts contend that a growing appreciation of the costs of imperialism also eroded support for colonial empires (Strang, 1991). Whatever the underlying cause, colonialism became less acceptable. In a world increasingly dominated by rivalry between East and West, Cold War competition for political allies gave both superpower rivals incentive to lobby for the liberation of overseas empires. Decolonization "triumphed," as Inis Claude (1967, p. 55) explains, in part "because the West [gave] priority to the containment of communism over the perpetuation of colonialism."

As the old order crumbled—and as the leaders in the newly emancipated territories discovered that freedom did not translate automatically into autonomy, economic independence, or domestic prosperity—the conflict between the rich Global North and the emerging states of the Global South began.

North and South Today: Worlds Apart

LO 5-2   Discuss the key differences between the Global North and Global South.

The Global South is sometimes described as a "zone of turmoil" or an "axis of upheaval," in large measure because, in contrast with the peaceful and democratic Global North, most of the people in the Global South face chronic poverty amidst war, tyranny, and anarchy. In the poorest countries of the Global South where dictatorships and dismal financial prospects persist, the odds increase that these countries will experience civil wars and armed conflicts with each other (Ferguson, 2009; Collier, 2005). Indeed, more than 90 percent of inter- and intrastate conflicts and 90 percent of the casualties in the past sixty years occurred within the Global South (see Chapter 7).

Democracy has spread rapidly and widely since the 1980s, becoming the preferred mode of governance throughout much of the Global South as a means of promoting both economic development and peace. Because the Global North's history suggests that "economic and technological development bring a coherent set of social, cultural, and political changes . . . and they also bring growing mass demands for democratic institutions and for more responsive behavior on the part of elites" (Inglehart and Welzel, 2009, p. 39), the continuing expansion of Global South market economies under capitalism appears likely to hasten democratization.

Even so, the continued spread of the liberal democratic community is not guaranteed, with some seeing democracy as failing even while elections become more commonplace. In many places, democratization is only "skin deep." As Oxford economist Paul Collier points out:

> In the average election held among the bottom billion poorest of the world's population, despite the fact that voters usually have many grounds for complaint, the incumbent "wins" a healthy 74 percent of the vote. In elections with particularly weak restraints, it is an even healthier 88 percent. Somehow or other, incumbents in these societies are very good at winning elections (Collier, 2009, p. 149).

Furthermore, many Global South countries lack well-developed domestic market economies based on entrepreneurship and private enterprise. Indeed, the global financial crisis has exacerbated the disappointment of some in the Global South with "the failure of free-market policies to bring significant economic growth and reduce the region's yawning inequality" (Schmidt and Malkin, 2009, p. 5). Consequently, there is renewed interest in the radical ideas of Karl Marx, who would likely have seen the crisis as the natural by-product of "the 'contradictions' inherent in a world comprised of competitive markets, commodity production and financial speculation" (Panitch, 2009, p. 140).

The fact that 83.4 percent of the world's population is poor is both a reflection and cause of these unequally distributed resources. To measure the disparities, we consider **developing countries** as those the World Bank differentiates as "low," "lower-middle" and "upper-middle" income economies, whose average per capita **gross national income (GNI)** in 2017 ranged from $776 to $8,198 annually. **Developed countries** are "high" income countries that averaged $40,404 per capita GNI (WDI, 2019).

developing countries A category used to identify countries according to income, based on World Bank classification of low-income Global South countries with an annual GNI per capita at or below $995, lower-middle income countries with an annual GNI per capita of more than $995 but less than $3,895, and upper-middle income countries with an annual GNI per capita of more than $3,895 but less than $12,055 (WDI, 2019).

gross national income (GNI) A measure of the production of goods and services within a given time period, which is used to delimit the geographic scope of production. GNI measures production by a state's citizens or companies, regardless of where the production occurs.

developed countries A category used by the World Bank to identify Global North countries with an annual GNI per capita of $12,055 or more (WDI, 2019).

Numbers paint pictures and construct images, and the data on the division between the Global North and Global South point to brutal disparities and inequalities. When we compare the differences on some key indicators differentiating developing countries from high-income ones, we discover huge gaps. As Table 5.1 shows, where people live on Earth influences how they live. The situation is much more favorable—and the quality of life is relatively advantageous—in the developed countries of the Global North than it is in the Southern Hemisphere, where nearly all the Global South countries are located.

This picture darkens even more when the focus shifts to the plight of the poorest in the low-income developing countries. More than 732.4 million people (10.28 percent of humanity) live in one of the thirty-four countries at the bottom of the global hierarchy, the **least developed countries (LDCs)** (WDI, 2017). These countries are the very poorest, with little economic growth and rapid population growth that is increasingly straining their overburdened society and environment. These countries are not emerging or reemerging to break the chains of their destitution; they are falling behind the other Global South countries.

The daunting scale of misery and marginalization is thus evident across the Global South, from which only a fraction of its countries have begun to escape. For most Global South countries, the future is bleak, and the opportunities and choices most basic to freedom from fear

least developed countries (LDCs)
The most impoverished countries of the Global South.

TABLE 5.1   Two Worlds of Development: An International Class Divide

Characteristic	Developing Global South	Developed Global North
Number of countries/economies	137	81
Population (millions)	6281.2	1248.4
Average annual population growth rate, 2000–2017	1.5	0.7
Population density (people for each sq km)	83.3	33
Women in parliaments (% of total seats), 2018	22.4	28
Land area (thousands of km²)	92027.8	37882.1
Gross national income per capita (PPP)	4269.2	48254
Average annual % growth of GDP, 2000–2017	5.6	1.6
Net foreign direct investment inflows (% of GDP)	2.2	2.6
Exports—Goods and Services ($ billions)	6873.4	16083.2
Imports—Goods and Services ($ billions)	6826.2	15436.1
Refugees by country of origin (thousands)	19513.5	38.3
Child Measles Immunization Rate (% ages 12–23 months)	85.2	94
Prevalence of undernourishment (% of population)	14.6	3
Health expenditure (% of GDP)	5.1	12.5
Internet users (% of population)	36.2	82.2
Life expectancy at birth (years)	69.6	81
Population living in cities (% of total population)	47.9	81
Mobile cellular subscriptions for each 100 people	93.4	125.5
Electric power consumption per capita (kWh)	1764.0	8834.4
Military expenditure (% of GDP)	2.0	2.7

Source: Based on data from WDI, 2017.

and poverty are unavailable. When we consider that nearly all the population growth in the twenty-first century will occur in the Global South, the poorest countries cut off from circulation in the globalized marketplace, it is hard to imagine how the gap can close and how the soil of poverty can be prevented from producing terrorism and civil war.

This tragic portrayal of unspeakable despair for so many Global South states raises the basic theoretical question: Why does the Global South, at this historical juncture, suffer from such dismal destitution?

Why Do Such Differences Persist?

LO 5-3   Identify the internal and international causes for underdevelopment in the Global South.

Why has the Global South lagged far behind the Global North in its comparative level of well-being and **development**? Furthermore, why have the developmental experiences even within the Global South differed so widely?

The diversity evident in the Global South invites the conclusion that underdevelopment is explained by a combination of factors. Some theorists explain the underdevelopment of most developing economies by looking primarily at *internal* causes within states. Other theorists focus on *international* causes such as the position of developing countries within the global political economy. We take a brief look at each of these schools of thought.

Internal Sources of Underdevelopment

Liberal economic development theories of **modernization** first emerged in the years immediately following World War II. They argued that the Global South countries' own internal characteristics posed major barriers to development. To overcome these barriers, most classical theorists recommended that the wealthy countries supply various "missing components" of development, such as investment capital through foreign aid or private foreign direct investment.

Once sufficient capital accumulated to promote economic growth, these liberal theorists predicted that its benefits would eventually "trickle down" to broad segments of society. Everyone, not just a privileged few, would begin to enjoy rising affluence. Walt W. Rostow (1960), an economic historian and U.S. policy maker, envisioned countries moving through stages of economic growth. He predicted that traditional societies beginning the path to development would inevitably pass through various stages by means of the free market and would eventually "take off" and eventually become similar to the mass-consumption societies of the capitalist Global North. Even though the rich are likely to get richer, it was argued that as incomes in the world as a whole grow, the odds increase that a preindustrialized economy will grow faster and eventually reduce the gap between it and richer countries.

The countries of the Global South rejected that prognosis and the premises on which it was based. Leaders there did not accept the classical liberal argument that the countries of the Global North became prosperous because they concentrated on hard work, innovative inventions of new products, and investments in schooling. Furthermore, by the mid-1970s, it was apparent that assistance from the rich countries of the Global North had not brought about the expected

development
The processes, economic and political, through which a country develops to increase its capacity to meet its citizens' basic human needs and raise their standard of living.

modernization
A view of development popular in the Global North's liberal democracies that wealth is created through efficient production, free enterprise, and free trade, and that countries' relative wealth depends on technological innovation and education more than on natural endowments such as climate and resources.

prosperity or democracy in the Global South. The Global South countries instead found more persuasive a rival theory that attributed their lack of development to international linkages between developing countries and the Global North's leadership in the global political economy.

International Sources of Underdevelopment

Whereas classical theory attributes the causes of most developing countries' underdevelopment to internal conditions within states, *dependency theory* emphasizes international factors, specifically the Global South's dependence on the dominant great powers. As noted in Chapter 2, dependency theory builds on Vladimir Lenin's Marxist critique of imperialism, but it goes beyond it to account for changes that have occurred in recent decades. Its central proposition is that the structure of the capitalist world economy is based on a division of labor between a dominant core and a subordinate periphery. As a result of colonialism, the Global South countries that make up the periphery have been forced into an economic role whereby they export raw materials and import finished goods. Whereas classical liberal theorists submit that specialization in production according to comparative advantage will increase income in an unfettered market and thereby help close the gap between the world's haves and have-nots, dependency theorists maintain that global inequalities cannot be reduced so long as developing countries continue to specialize in producing primary products for which there are often numerous competing suppliers and limited demand.

Breaking out of their dependent status and pursuing their own industrial development remains the greatest foreign policy priority for countries in the Global South. To this end, some countries—particularly those in Latin America—have pursued development through an **import-substitution industrialization** strategy designed to encourage domestic entrepreneurs to manufacture products traditionally imported from abroad. Governments (often dictatorships) became heavily involved in managing their economies, and in some cases became the owners and operators of industry.

Import-substitution industrialization eventually fell from favor, in part because manufacturers often found that they still had to rely on Global North technology to produce goods for their domestic markets. The preference now is for **export-led industrialization**, based on the realization that "what had enriched the rich was not their insulation from imports (rich countries do, in fact, import all sorts of goods) but their success in manufactured exports, where higher prices could be commanded than for [Global South] raw materials" (Sklair, 1991).

Dependency theorists also argue that countries in the Global South are vulnerable to cultural penetration by **multinational corporations (MNCs)** and other outside forces, which saturate them with values alien to their societies. Once such penetration has occurred, the inherently unequal exchanges that bind the exploiters and the exploited are sustained by elites within the penetrated societies who sacrifice their country's welfare for personal gain. The argument that a privileged few benefit from dependency at the expense of their societies underscores the dual nature of many developing countries.

Dualism refers to the existence of two separate economic and social sectors operating side by side. Dual societies typically have a rural, impoverished, and neglected sector operating alongside an urban, developing, or advanced sector—but with little interaction between the two.

import-substitution industrialization
A strategy for economic development that centers on providing investors at home incentives to produce goods so that previously imported products from abroad will decline.

export-led industrialization
A growth strategy that concentrates on developing domestic export industries capable of competing in overseas markets.

multinational corporations (MNCs)
Business enterprises headquartered in one state that invest and operate extensively in many other states.

dualism
The separation of a country into two sectors, the first modern and prosperous and centered in major cities, and the second at the margin, neglected and poor.

Controversy

THEORIES OF DEVELOPMENT—A RETURN TO MODERNIZATION?

Over time, the perceived effectiveness and credibility of development theories have waxed and waned depending, at least in part, on their ability to explain and predict current world events. During its heyday in the 1960s, classical theory prescribed that countries should emulate the path of industrial democracies in order to develop. However, it was apparent by the 1970s that such efforts had not resulted in widespread prosperity or democracy. For example, many countries in Latin America suffered from authoritarian rule and abject poverty. Dependency theory grew in popularity at this time, with its focus on the global capitalist system—rather than the internal problems of the Global South countries—as the reason for persistent underdevelopment. Yet the relevance of this theoretical explanation came to be questioned as well, particularly in light of the success of countries that experienced meaningful growth by participating in the global market and pursuing export-oriented strategies.

As both perspectives fell out of vogue, critics suggested that modernization theory was dead. However, since the end of the Cold War, a nuanced version of modernization theory has emerged and is gaining credibility. Responding to changes in the world such as the demise of communism and the economic success of East Asian countries, its core premise is that producing for the world market enables economic growth; investing the returns in human capital and upgrading the workforce to produce high-tech goods brings higher returns and enlarges the educated middle class; once the middle class becomes large and articulate enough, it presses for liberal democracy—the most effective political system for advanced industrial societies (Inglehart and Welzel, 2009, p. 36).

Like earlier incarnations of modernization theory, this more recent version similarly sees economic development as eliciting important and predictable changes in politics, culture, and society. Yet it provides a more complex understanding in a number of ways (Inglehart and Welzel, 2009):

- **History Matters**. A society's beliefs, values, and traditions shape its larger worldview and its engagement with the forces of modernization.
- **Modernization Is Not Westernization**. The success of industrialization in the Global East challenges earlier ethnocentric assumptions.
- **Modernization Is Not Democratization**. Increases in per capita GDP do not automatically result in democracy.
- **Modernization Is Not Linear**. There are multiple inflection points, as individual phases of modernization tend to be associated with particular changes in society.

What Do You Think?

1. How are liberalism, constructivism, and Marxist perspectives reflected in the various versions of modernization theory?

2. What are the implications of the new modernization theory for the rise of gender equality? For political reform and democratization? For international organizations as instruments of development?

3. New modernization theory suggests that the rise of the middle class is critical for a country's development into a democracy. How might this be an important policy perspective for decision makers, both domestically and internationally?

Multinational corporations contribute to dualism by favoring a minority of well-compensated employees over the rest, which increases gaps in pay, and widens differences between rural and urban economic opportunities.

Although dependency theory has great appeal within the Global South, it cannot easily explain the rapid economic development of what many people refer to as the **newly industrialized countries (NICs)**. Today, the NICs are among the largest exporters of manufactured goods and are leaders in the information processing industry. Neither does it do a good job of explaining the lack of sustained development of countries such as Cuba, Myanmar, and North Korea that focused their economic growth efforts inwardly and have had little involvement in global trade. Recently, however, there has been a reincarnation of modernization theory that once again looks at how internal characteristics, such as social and cultural conditions, may shape political and economic development (see "Controversy: Theories of Development—A Return to Modernization?").

newly industrialized countries (NICs) The most prosperous members of the Global South, which have become important exporters of manufactured goods as well as important markets for the major industrialized countries that export capital goods.

Closing the Gap? The Global South's Prospects in a World of Great Powers

LO 5-4 Assess different approaches taken to facilitate development in the Global South.

The vast political, economic, and social differences separating the Global North and the Global South suggest that the remaining countries in the Global South are increasingly vulnerable, insecure, and defenseless, and that these conditions are products of both internal and international factors. Given the multiple problems standing in the way of the Global South's security and prosperity, ask yourself, were you to become a head of state of a Global South country, how would you approach these immense challenges? Your choices would undoubtedly benefit by considering the different approaches Global South countries have taken to pursue their objectives, particularly in their relationships with the Global North.

Technology and Global Communications

"There is an important relationship between economic growth and research and development, between industry creation and political stability, and between the nurturing of research and sowing the seeds of a middle class in developing nations" (Battelle and *R&D Magazine*, 2013, p. 3). When it comes to technological capabilities, the Global North and the Global South have long differed. "Twenty years ago North America, Europe and Japan produced almost all of the world's science. They were the aristocrats of technical knowledge, presiding over a centuries-old regime" (*The Economist*, 2010b, p. 95). The Global South countries, in contrast, have been slower to develop indigenous technology appropriate to their own resources and have been dependent on powerful Global North multinational corporations (see Chapter 6) to transfer technical expertise.

This means that research and development expenditures are devoted to solving the Global North's problems, with technological advances seldom meeting the needs of the Global South. However, although the Global North remains committed to global research and development, regional shifts are occurring (see Figure 5.1A). The U.S. share of global research and development declined from 34 percent in 2009 to 25 percent in 2019. Similarly, Europe experienced a decline from 26 percent to 20 percent between 2009 and 2019. During the same period, Asia advanced with the regional share expanding from 33 percent to 44 percent. China alone increased from 10 percent to 22 percent (Battelle and R&D Magazine, 2008, 2019).

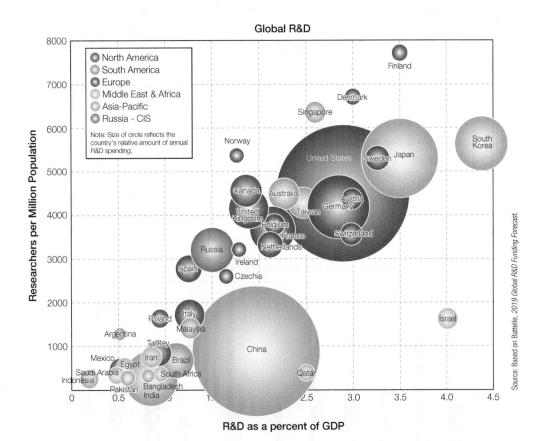

Source: Based on Battelle, *2019 Global R&D Funding Forecast*,

FIGURES 5.1A AND 5.1B Global Research and Development The amount of money a country spends on scientific research and development is one indicator of its global scientific standing. Comparing the gross domestic expenditure on research and development (GERD) as a percentage of a country's total GDP (shown top), this figure indicates that South Korea spent the largest portion on scientific discovery in 2019, with Finland claiming the greatest number of scientists and engineers as a proportion of its total population. Although the United States and the European Union continued to invest in scientific development, R&D investment grew in many Asian countries (shown bottom), further signaling what some see as the "rise of the rest."

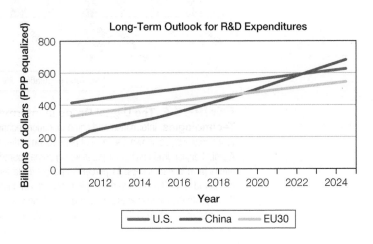

digital divide
The division between the internet-technology rich Global North and the Global South in the proportion of internet users and hosts.

information and communications technology (ICT)
The technological means through which information and communications are transferred.

information technology (IT)
The techniques for storing, retrieving, and disseminating through computerization and the internet recorded data and research knowledge.

Countries in the Global South are making strides in their own technological innovation (see Figure 5.1A). Emerging multinationals in developing countries have made advances and are "spooking the rich world's established multinationals with innovative products and bold acquisitions" (*The Economist*, 2009i, p. 20). Nonetheless, technology is not distributed equally geographically. With the expanding importance of the internet to global commerce and communication, critics fear that the **digital divide** in access to **information and communications technology (ICT)** means that countries in the Global South will be at a disadvantage. At present, the Global North (and particularly the United States, where the internet was developed) remains predominant and the primary beneficiary of the **information technology (IT)** revolution (see Figure 5.1B).

However, the digital divide may shrink as most of the growth in the media and telecommunications industries begins to occur in the Global South. The world's youth, including those in developing countries, are at the forefront of the global digital economy; 71 percent of young people around the world aged 15 to 24 use the internet compared to 48 percent of the total population. In the Global South, this pattern persists with internet use among young people 38.7 percent higher than overall, and this offers hope for a brighter future as ICT is a key enabler of social and economic development. Yet regional differences stand out (see Figure 5.2). Of the 830 million youth online, 320 million are in China and India. Nearly

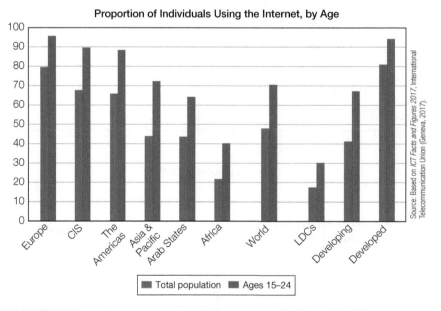

FIGURE 5.2 The Digital Divide in Information and Communication Technologies Information and communication technology (ICT) has spread rapidly in recent years. However, as shown, the level of penetration varies both among and within countries. A global digital divide has emerged in which some countries have high levels of access and others have limited access: 81 percent of people in developed countries use the internet compared to 41.3 percent in developing countries and just 17.5 in the least developed countries. While youth the world over are greater users of the internet, disparities are also evident with 93.3 percent of youth in the Global North and 67.3 percent in the Global South using the internet.

90 percent of the young people who do not use the internet live in Africa, Asia, and the Pacific (ITU, 2017).

Insecurity and Weapons of War

Global South countries must face the fateful question of whether they dare to call for help from the great powers and dominating international organizations when violence, terrorism, and anarchy prevail. The cry for assistance poses risks, because where there is outside involvement, there tends to be outside influence, some of which may be unwelcome. There is a fine line between external involvement and interference. On top of this concern is another: the threat of great power indifference or inability to agree about when, where, why, and how they should collectively become involved within Global South borders where violence, ethnic cleansing, and terrorism occur.

Faced with seemingly endless conflict at home or abroad, and a desire to address military insecurity on their own terms, it is not surprising that the Global South countries have joined the rest of the world's quest to acquire modern weapons of war—including nuclear weapons, as in the cases of China, India, North Korea, and Pakistan (see Chapter 8). As a result, the burden of military spending (measured by the ratio of military expenditures to GDP) is highest among those least able to bear it (SIPRI, 2019). In the Global South, military spending typically exceeds expenditures on health and education; impoverished states facing ethnic, religious, or tribal strife at home are quite prepared to sacrifice economic development to acquire weapons.

Few Global South states produce their own weapons. Instead, most Global South countries have increased their military spending to purchase arms produced in the Global North (SIPRI, 2019). Thus, in responding to a world of powers, the Global South appears to be increasing its dependence for arms purchases on the very same rich states whose military and economic domination they historically have most feared and resented.

Reform of the Economic Order

Although some Global South countries benefit from global economic integration and prosper, others seem unable to take advantage of the alleged benefits of globalization and are especially vulnerable to recessions in the global economy. How to cope with dominance and dependence thus remains a key concern in the Global South.

The emerging Global South countries were born into a political-economic order with rules they had no voice in creating. To gain control over their economic futures, they began coordinating their efforts within the United Nations, where their growing numbers and voting power gave them greater influence than they could otherwise command. In the 1960s, they formed a coalition, the **Group of 77 (G-77)**, and used their voting power to convene the UN Conference on Trade and Development (UNCTAD). UNCTAD later became a permanent UN organization through which the Global South would express its interests concerning development issues. A decade later, the G-77 (then numbering more than 120 countries) again used its numerical majority in the UN to push for a **New International Economic Order (NIEO)** to replace the international economic regime championed by the United States and the other

Group of 77 (G-77)
The coalition of Third World countries that sponsored the 1963 Joint Declaration of Developing Countries calling for reform to allow greater equality in North–South trade.

New International Economic Order (NIEO)
The 1974 UN policy resolution that called for a North–South dialogue to open the way for the less developed countries of the Global South to participate more fully in the making of international economic policy.

capitalist powers since World War II. Motivated by the oil-exporting countries' rising bargaining power, the Global South sought to compel the Global North to abandon practices perceived as perpetuating the Global South's dependence.

Not surprisingly, the Global North rebuffed many of the South's proposals, although some of the issues raised (such as debt relief) remain on the global agenda. Today, disputes about the appropriate intersection between global governance and national sovereignty persist, with the Global North wanting the International Monetary Fund to assume a more overt surveillance responsibility over its member states' macroeconomic policies, whereas the Global South opposes a larger role (Patrick, 2010). In 2009, seven Latin American countries agreed to establish the "Banco del Sur" (Bank of the South) in part to compete directly with the World Bank and circumvent Global North interference by funding big infrastructure projects within the region. Similarly dissatisfied with these Bretton Woods institutions (see Chapter 6), in 2014 the BRICS countries (Brazil, Russia, India, China, and South Africa) established a New Development Bank to mobilize resources for infrastructure and sustainable development projects in emerging economies and developing countries. The "rising economic strength of the BRICS countries has outpaced increases in their voice at the World Bank and the International Monetary Fund (IMF)" (Desai and Vreeland, 2014, p. 1) at the same time that economic cooperation within the Global South has greatly expanded.

Foreign Aid and Remittances

One approach for closing the gap between the Global South and the Global North is the distribution of foreign assistance. Urging the wealthy countries to help the poorest, former Chinese president Hu Jintao declared that "developed countries should assume their responsibilities and obligations, continue to deliver their aid, [keep their] debt relief commitments, maintain

IMAGES 5.3A AND 5.3B **From Rags to Riches** A number of formerly poor Global South countries have catapulted to affluence, either through free markets and aggressive trade or by capitalizing on abundant natural resources. Dubai (shown left) and Kuwait (shown right) are prime examples. In Dubai, the construction of one of the world's largest shopping malls, with the world's largest aquarium and a five-story underwater hotel, demonstrate its wealth. Kuwait enjoys similar good fortunes, with upgrades to the country's infrastructure, including the expansion of Kuwait's international airport and a high-speed international railway set to link up with the proposed Gulf Cooperation Council (GCC) rail network (Oxford Business Group, 2019).

and increase assistance to developing countries and effectively help them maintain financial stability and economic growth."

Some **foreign aid** consists of outright grants of money, some of loans at concessional rates, and some of shared technical expertise. Although most foreign aid is **bilateral** and is termed **official development assistance (ODA)**—meaning the money flows directly from one country to another—an increasing portion is now channeled through global intergovernmental institutions such as the World Bank, and hence is known as "multilateral aid" (see Chapter 6).

The purposes of aid are as varied as its forms. Commonly stated foreign aid goals include not only the reduction of poverty through economic development but also human development, environmental protection, reduced military spending, enhanced economic management, the development of private enterprise, increased women's rights, the promotion of democratic governance and human rights, and humanitarian disaster relief and assistance to refugees (Dimiral-Pegg and Moskowitz, 2009; Woods, 2008; Barrett, 2007). Security objectives have also figured prominently in motives of both economic and military assistance. For example, the United States continues to target Israel and Egypt as major recipients to symbolize friendship, maintain a balance of power, and tilt the scales toward peace in the Middle East. In addition, security was the primary motive behind the doubling of the U.S. foreign assistance budget following 9/11 to provide funds for allies' use in the global war on terrorism.

The assumption that development will support other goals, such as fostering solidarity among allies and promoting commercial advantage, free markets, or democratization, still underpins most donors' assistance programs. The Millennium Challenge Corporation (MCC), which the United States established in 2004, has awarded more than $13 billion in aid to developing countries that govern justly, invest in their people, and encourage economic freedom. This represented the largest increase in U.S. development assistance since the Marshall Plan in 1948. "South-South" foreign aid has also seen unprecedented growth, with Brazil, India, and China all becoming larger donors to low-income countries (Desai and Vreeland, 2014).

The general global trend in the overall amount of foreign aid allocations since 1970 has been toward gradual increases. However, foreign aid as a percentage of a donor country's total gross national income has declined. Most donor countries have not met their targeted ODA levels (see Figure 5.3A). According to OECD Secretary-General Angel Gurría, "This picture of stagnating public aid is particularly worrying as it follows data showing that private development flows are also declining… and this bodes badly for us being able to achieve the 2030 Sustainable Development Goals" adopted by all United Nations members in 2015 as a shared blueprint for global peace and prosperity (OECD, 2019).

Many aid donors have become frustrated with the slow growth rates of numerous Global South recipients and have grown doubtful of the effectiveness of their aid programs, despite strong evidence that foreign aid has had a positive influence (Easterbrook, 2002). Critics particularly resent what they perceive to be an entrenched state of mind in many Global South cultures that stands in the way of development, which—while bemoaning poverty—condemns the profit motive, competition, and consumerism that lie at the heart of capitalism. Donors are especially resentful that the countries seeking aid do not value the core Western values of hard work, economic competition, and entrepreneurial creativity believed to be crucial for progress and prosperity.

foreign aid
Economic assistance in the form of loans and grants provided by a donor country to a recipient country for a variety of purposes.

bilateral
Interactions between two transnational actors.

official development assistance (ODA)
Grants or loans to countries from donor countries, now usually channeled through multilateral aid institutions such as the World Bank for the primary purpose of promoting economic development and welfare.

In response to this viewpoint, donors have grown increasingly insistent on "conditionality," or demands that aid recipients must meet to receive continued assistance. Donors also persist in "tying" development assistance to the donors for their benefit, such as requiring purchases from the donors, even though the World Bank estimates this practice reduces the value of aid by 15 to 30 percent, decreases its efficiency, and violates the same free-market principles that the Global North claims to promote.

On top of this, Global South countries complain that the Global North donors have been promising for the past forty years to allocate 0.7 percent of their gross national product (GNP) to foreign aid, but only a few have kept the promise or even come close (see Figures 5.3A and 5.3B). This is true despite the evidence that more assistance does indeed contribute to development when it is designed properly and delivered in a sustained way to countries with records of improving democratic governance (Sachs, 2005). Recently, however, many Global South leaders have joined Global North critics of foreign aid, interpreting it as an instrument of neocolonialism and neoimperialism and resenting the conditionality criteria for receiving aid imposed by the International Monetary Fund (IMF) and other multilateral institutions. As Rwandan President Paul Kagame explained in May 2009, "We appreciate support from the outside, but it should be support for what we intend to achieve ourselves."

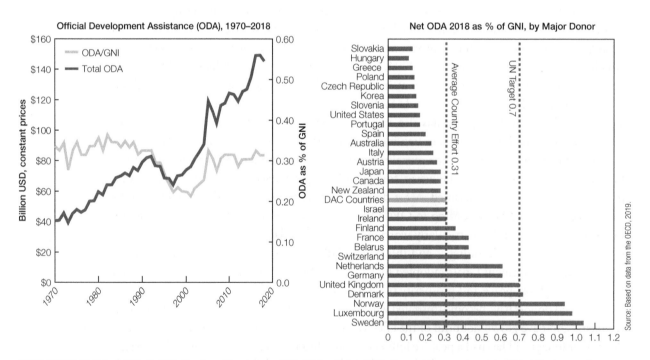

FIGURES 5.3A AND 5.3B Broken Promises With UN Resolution 2626, the wealthy countries of the Global North agreed in 1970 to allocate 0.7 percent of their GNP as aid for the long-term development of the poorer countries of the Global South. While official development assistance in real terms has increased between 1970 and 2018, the same is not true of giving as a percentage of gross national income (shown left). In fact, the global average for ODA as a percentage of GNI in 2018 was less than a third of 1 percent (0.31). In absolute dollars, the United States, Germany, and Britain were the biggest donors; however, in terms of giving relative to the size of the national economy, Denmark, Norway, Luxembourg, and Sweden were the most generous (shown right).

Much more money—more than triple that of foreign aid—is primarily funneled into Global South economies through the **remittances** that migrant laborers working in the Global North faithfully send home to their families. Not as sensitive to economic downturns as private-capital flows, global remittances have risen steadily each year since the 1970s. The World Bank (2019b) estimates that a record $529 billion of total global remittances in 2018 went to developing countries, representing a growth of 9.6 percent for that year alone; the United States is the largest source of remittances, recording around $68 billion in 2017. It is likely that the true amount of remittances is much larger than the official figures as people often send money and goods through informal networks (see Figures 5.4A and 5.4B).

The money received is an important source of family (and national) income in many developing economies, representing in some cases a very relevant percentage of the GDP of the receiving countries. In Tonga and the Kyrgyz Republic, for example, remittances in some years constitute more than a third of their GDP. The World Bank's Chief Economist for South Asia Hans Timmer explains, "The role of remittances in helping lift people out of poverty has always been known, but there is also abundant evidence that migration and remittances are helping countries achieve progress towards … access to education, safe water, sanitation and healthcare."

remittances
The money earned by immigrants working in rich countries (which almost always exceeds the income they could earn working in their home country) that they send to their families in their home country.

Trade and Foreign Direct Investment

Developing countries have long pleaded for "trade, not aid" to improve their global position, turning to the NIC's and the Global East experience to support the view that access to the Global North's markets is critical to Global South economic growth. Requests for greater trade through reduced barriers have generally been successful, and there are almost 300 free-trade agreements in force between and among the Global South and Global North countries (WTO, 2019). Indeed, many countries of the Global South have benefited from a "virtuous cycle" (Blanton and Blanton, 2008) wherein increased trade leads to improved domestic conditions that in turn facilitate trade. Consider some recent developments to promote growth through regional economic agreements:

- **The Americas.** The Central America-Dominican Republic Free Trade Agreement (CAFTA-DR) aims to emulate NAFTA and create a free-trade zone that includes the United States, the Dominican Republic, Guatemala, El Salvador, Nicaragua, Honduras, and Costa Rica. Intent on liberalizing U.S. and Central American markets, the agreement is the first major "subregional" agreement between very unequal trading partners—excluding the United States, the combined GDP of CAFTA-DR members is just above 1 percent of U.S. GDP (WDI, 2019). Mercosur, commonly referred to as the "Common Market of the South," is the largest trading bloc in South America and aims for full economic integration of the region. Full members include Argentina, Brazil, Paraguay, Uruguay, and Venezuela, with Bolivia, Colombia, Ecuador, Peru, and Chile holding associate membership status.

- **Asia.** The association of Asia-Pacific Economic Cooperation (APEC), an informal forum created in 1989, is committed to free trade and regional economic integration. Additionally, the members of the Association of Southeast Asian Nations (ASEAN),

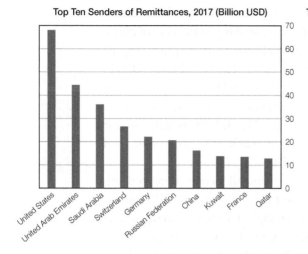

Top Ten Senders of Remittances, 2017 (Billion USD)

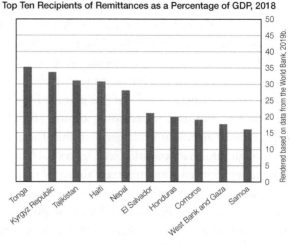

Top Ten Recipients of Remittances as a Percentage of GDP, 2018

FIGURES 5.4A AND 5.4B **Sending Money Back Home** The billions of dollars that migrant workers send home each year are vital to developing countries. With the exception of China, remittances are now the largest source of foreign exchange earnings in the Global South, at more than three times the size of ODA and close to FDI (World Bank, 2019b). The greatest amount of remittances are sent from the United States (shown bottom-left); Low-income countries such as Tonka and the Kyrgyz Republic are among the top recipients of remittances as a share of GDP (shown bottom-right).

 Think It Through What does the fact that Africa and Asia are the largest regional recipients of remittances suggest about their economies?

first established in 1967 by Brunei, Indonesia, Malaysia, the Philippines, Singapore, and Thailand, and now including Vietnam, Cambodia, Laos, and Myanmar, agreed to set up a free-trade area. On a broader scale, the Comprehensive and Progressive Agreement for Trans-Pacific Partnership (CPTPP) was formed when the United States withdrew from the proposed Trans-Pacific Partnership. The CPTPP reduces trade barriers and increases opportunities for investment among a far-flung group of 11 signatories: Brunei, Chile, Singapore, New Zealand, Australia, Canada, Japan, Malaysia, Mexico, Peru, and Vietnam. The agreement "was explicitly written with an eye toward future expansion," (McBride and Chatzky, 2019) with likely future members including South Korea, Thailand, and Colombia.

- **Middle East.** The U.S.-Middle East Free Trade Area (MEFTA) includes agreements between the United States and Bahrain, Israel, Jordan, Morocco, and Oman. The United States proposed the initiative in 2003, and many countries could still become member states very soon, such as Algeria, Kuwait, and Yemen. The Gulf Cooperation Council for the Arab States of the Gulf (GCC) was established in 1981 as a regional common market that also included a defense council. It includes countries with similar political systems rooted in Islamic beliefs, and the founding members included Bahrain, Kuwait, Oman, Qatar, Saudi Arabia, and the United Arab Emirates.

- **Sub-Saharan Africa.** In addition to several long-standing trade associations, most notably the Economic Community of West African States (ECOWAS) and the Southern African Development Community (SADC), 52 African countries currently belong to the African Continental Free Trade Area (AfCFTA). Formed in 2018, this ambitious organization calls for the removal of trade barriers as well as the free movement of investment capital and business travelers throughout the member states.

Will the lofty expectations of these regional politico-economic groups be realized? In the past, political will and shared visions have proven to be indispensable elements in successful regional trade regimes that set rules for members' collaboration. Economic complementarity is another essential component, as the goal is to stimulate greater trade among the members of the free-trade area, not simply between it and other regions.

In an effort to shore up the global economy, global leaders pledged to finance trade, resist protectionist measures, and assist the Global South. There is evidence that these trade initiatives are working, as trade within the Global South continues to expand. In 2016, trade between developing countries made up over one-fifth of the world's merchandise exports, which represents a more than 90 percent increase from 2000 (WTO, 2018). However, the "North-South gap has not narrowed so far during the most recent globalization era" (Reuveny and Thompson, 2008, p. 8). Many Global South countries have not improved their lot: market access remains difficult because domestic pressure groups in these low-growth Global South countries have lobbied their governments to reduce the imports of other countries' products that compete with their own industries. More broadly, many have difficulty diversifying their trade portfolios. They are still heavily dependent on trade in agricultural and mineral commodities, which are prone to economic instability and can even contribute to political instability. Even in manufacturing sectors, global supply chains (see Chapter 11) may put firms in the Global South—who often supply parts or assembly—at a relative disadvantage to their counterparts in the Global North, which reduces the benefits that these countries ultimately derive from trade (UNCTAD, 2018).

In the Global South, another important tactic for escaping destitution and stagnant economic growth has been to attract a greater share of **foreign direct investment (FDI)**. Indeed, "FDI into the Global South has increased more rapidly than trade and surpassed foreign aid as the leading source of capital in developing countries" (Blanton and Blanton, 2012a, p. 1). It is attractive to potential host countries in the Global South as it contributes to capital formation, enhances access to international marketing networks, and provides for the transfer of production technology, skills, and organizational practices between countries (Blanton and Blanton, 2009).

Yet this strategy for economic growth has always been the target of critics who question whether the investment of capital by MNCs (and, to a lesser extent, private investors) into local or domestic business ventures is really a financial remedy. The strategy has always been controversial because there are many hidden costs, or *externalities*, associated with permitting corporations controlled from abroad to set up business within the host state for the purpose

foreign direct investment (FDI) A cross-border investment through which a person or corporation based in one country purchases or constructs an asset such as a factory or bank in another country so that a long-term relationship and control of an enterprise by nonresidents results.

of making a profit. Who is to be the ultimate beneficiary, the foreign investor or the states in which the investments are made? Do ordinary people within the Global South benefit, or are they exploited by corporations and the elite? Such policies entail considerable risks and trade-offs, and they can create conflict between those with competing values and goals.

The primary danger lies in the potential for foreign investments to lead to foreign control and the erosion of the sovereign governments' capacities to regulate the economy within their borders. An additional danger is that the multinational foreign investors might not invest their profits locally but channel them abroad for new investments or disburse them as dividends for their wealthy Global North shareholders. Furthermore, there have long been fears that a "race to the bottom" may occur whereby governments restrict labor rights and human rights in order to enhance a country's attractiveness to foreign investors (Blanton and Blanton, 2012a, 2012b).

However, despite the risks, many developing countries have relaxed restrictions in order to attract foreign investors, with less emphasis placed on liberalizing investment restrictions and encouraging open domestic economic competition than on offering Official Development Assistance taxes and cash enticements and opportunities for joint ventures. This has stimulated a recent surge in the flow of capital investments to the Global South (see Figure 5.5).

The impact of this new infusion of foreign investments in developing countries has been substantial given the Global South's relatively small economies. It has paved the way for emerging markets to expand their rates of economic development—despite the resistance of local

IMAGE 5.4 Making New Friends The fortunes of small powers are increasingly integrated with those of major powers. Despite "political and security risks, China has boosted African oil and mining sectors in exchange for advantageous trade deals. Chinese companies are also diversifying their business pursuits in Africa, in infrastructure, manufacturing, telecommunications, and agricultural sectors" (Albert, 2017). Shown here, patients leave a Chinese-operated hospital in Dar es Salaam in Tanzania.

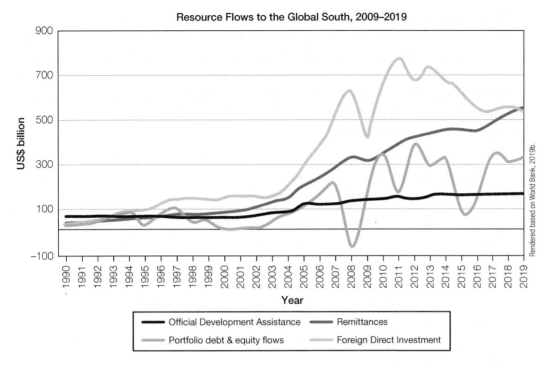

Resource Flows to the Global South, 2009–2019

Rendered based on World Bank, 2019b.

Legend:
— Official Development Assistance — Remittances
— Portfolio debt & equity flows — Foreign Direct Investment

FIGURE 5.5 The Rise and Fall of the Global Economy Over the past decade, foreign capital has been a primary source for growth in the Global South. Private equity, portfolio investment, and FDI experienced great volatility between 2007 and 2017, although remittances and ODA were more stable. As shown, on average, capital flows to the Global South have increased.

industries that are threatened by the new competition and the critics who complain about the increasing income inequalities that the investments are causing. Such fears and consequences notwithstanding, developing countries are intensifying their competition for foreign investment capital to liberate themselves from dependence and destitution. And foreign direct investment is the leading cause of the shift from farm work to service jobs in Global South urban areas (now 47 percent of the developing countries' population) that is lifting millions of people out of poverty while at the same time outsourcing skilled jobs from the Global North (WDI, 2015; 2011).

Debt Management and Governmental Corruption

The prospects for foreign aid, trade, or foreign direct investments to contribute to the future development of, and relief of poverty in, the Global South will depend on a number of other factors. One is the extent to which the level of debt facing many Global South countries can be managed. External debt in developing countries has more than doubled since 2008; on average, the payments to service this debt take up 12.2 percent of the total government revenues in these countries (Jubilee Debt Campaign, 2019). Such debt affects economic health and future growth.

However, national debt is not the only drain on a country's economic and political resources; corruption also undermines essential institutional structures and foments a culture of fear and distrust. "Corruption is much more likely to flourish where democratic foundations are weak and, as we have seen in many countries, where undemocratic and populist politicians can use it to their advantage," observes Delia Ferreira Rubio, chair of Transparency International. The abuse of entrusted power for private gain poses enormous costs on four dimensions (Transparency International, 2019):

- **Political.** Corruption is a barrier to democratic governance and the rule of law. When public officials use their offices for personal gain, they undermine the government's legitimacy and the expectation of accountability.

- **Economic.** Corrupt practices deplete national wealth, with public resources funneled away from the development of infrastructure in areas such as education and health care. Widespread corruption also compromises market structures and discourages investment.

- **Social.** The violation of public trust that results from widespread corruption weakens civil society. Pervasive apathy and disengagement of ordinary citizens enhances the opportunity for public officials to use their position and national assets for personal gain, with bribery becoming a norm.

- **Environmental.** Environmental regulations are often ignored, and environmental projects are often easy to exploit for private gain. As a result, corruption frequently leads to pronounced environmental degradation within a country.

The Global North is not immune to public corruption, but it is a pervasive problem in many countries throughout the Global South (see Map 5.4). "Poorly equipped schools, counterfeit medicine and elections decided by money are just some of the consequences of public sector corruption. Bribes and backroom deals don't just steal resources from the most vulnerable—they undermine justice and economic development, and destroy public trust in government and leaders" (Transparency International, 2014). For example, in the aftermath of the Jasmine Revolution in Tunisia in 2011, the breadth and scope of the corrupt practices by the ruling Ben Ali family came to light. According to a report by the watchdog group Global Financial Integrity, the "amount of illegal money lost from Tunisia due to corruption, bribery, kickbacks, trade mis-pricing and criminal activity between 2000 and 2008 was, on average, over one billion dollars a year" (*The Economist*, 2011h, p. 32). For a country with a GNP that only reaches $80 billion in a single year, this amount was staggering and had enormous implications for the welfare of its citizens.

The Global South's Future

LO 5-5   Appraise the prospects for future development in the Global South.

It is useful to remember the historical trends underlying the emergence of the Global South as an actor on the global stage. Many of the countries share similar characteristics: Most were colonized by people of another race, experience poverty and hunger, and feel powerless in a

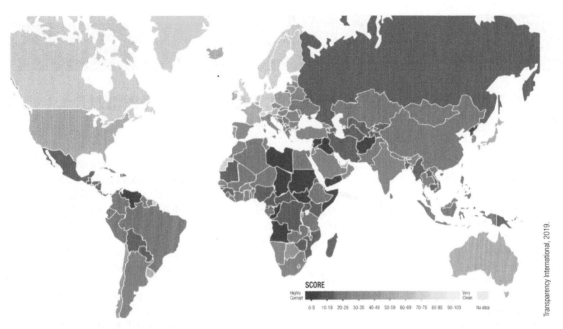

MAP 5.4 The Challenge of Corruption Based on questions regarding kickbacks in public procurement, bribery of public officials, embezzlement of public funds, and the effectiveness of public-sector anticorruption efforts, the 2018 Corruption Perceptions Index assesses the perception of corruption in the public sector. A score of 0 indicates a perception of high corruption and 100 indicates that it is perceived to be very clean. As the map reveals, corruption is a serious problem that is contributing to a crisis in democracy across the globe. More than two-thirds of the 180 countries in the index score below 50, with an average score of 43.

Think It Through In what ways does this map support the idea that the Global South is vulnerable to political instability?

world system dominated by the affluent countries that once controlled them and perhaps still do. Considerable change occurred among the newly emergent states as post–World War II decolonization took place, but much also remained the same.

The relationships between the world's great, middle, and small powers will no doubt continue to change—exactly how remains uncertain. However, the future of Global South development is certain to depend in part on the activities of the Global North (see "A Closer Look: Coming in from the Cold? Diplomacy and Development in Cuba"). A turn inward toward isolationist foreign policies in the Global North could lead to a posture of "benign neglect" of the Global South.

Conversely, a new era of North–South–East cooperation could begin, dedicated to finding solutions to common problems ranging from commercial to environmental and security concerns. As South Korea's former Vice Minister of Foreign Affairs and Trade Sung-han Kim (2013) noted, "Although great powers are useful in mobilizing cooperation, their efforts are insufficient to coordinate all involved actors. Solving today's complex challenges will require 'middle powers' to play a greater, more active role."

Although elements of both approaches are evident, relations between the Global South and the Global North remain dominated by the great powers. That domination is funneled in part through powerful international organizations, such as the United Nations and the World Bank,

A Closer Look

COMING IN FROM THE COLD? DIPLOMACY AND DEVELOPMENT IN CUBA

In 1959, Fidel Castro led a revolution that resulted in the overthrow of the authoritarian dictator Fulgencio Batista and the establishment of communist government in Cuba. With his ascent to power, the government "seized private land, nationalized hundreds of private companies—including several local subsidiaries of U.S. corporations—and taxed American products so heavily that U.S. exports were halved in just two years" (Suddath, 2009). Eliciting further U.S. ire, Cuba aligned with the Soviet Union in the 1960s and allowed the Soviets to place missiles on its territory (resulting in the subsequent Cuban Missile Crisis; see Chapter 9). Vast numbers of Cubans sought refuge in the United States, and organizations such as Human Rights Watch continue to accuse the Cuban government of violating human rights and crushing political dissent (HRW, 2019).

The United States responded to Castro's nationalization of private property by imposing trade restrictions on all goods except medical supplies and food, and in 1962, President John Kennedy made these economic sanctions permanent. When Cuba aligned with the Soviet Union, the United States severed diplomatic ties and made concerted efforts to overthrow and assassinate Castro (Frasquieri, 2011). In 1982, the United States placed Cuba on its list of state sponsors of terrorism because of Cuba's support for armed revolution and leftist guerrilla groups in countries such as Angola, Ethiopia, Colombia, and Spain.

Cuba's relations with the superpower remained strained for over fifty years. Yet in 2014, the two countries moved toward normalization of relations. This transition included the restoration of diplomatic relations, easing of restrictions on remittances, travel, and banking relations, and the removal of Cuba from the U.S. terrorism list. To signal this new era, President

Obama visited Cuba and met with President Raul Castro in 2016, marking the first time a sitting U.S. President had visited Cuba for almost 90 years. Progress came to a halt in 2017, as President Trump enacted several measures to isolate Cuba, such as tightening travel restrictions and more rigorously enforcing existing sanctions. While Trump left many of his predecessors' reforms in place, a Cuban Foreign Ministry official described U.S.-Cuban relations as "seriously deteriorated" (Vela, 2019). Conflicting interests are at play in determining the future of this relationship – while "geographic proximity suggests Cuba and the United States are natural trading partners," (Ermer, 2019) historic grievances and patterns of animosity, rooted in both North/South distrust as well as Cold-War era security interests, are still influential.

Watch the Carnegie Council Video:

"The Cuban Embargo Turns 50: Time to Rethink U.S. Policy?"

You Decide:

1. The United States has had long-standing diplomatic and economic ties with China, Russia, and Vietnam. Why did it treat Cuba differently?

2. How might realism, liberalism, and constructivism each account for changing relations between Cuba and the United States?

3. The prospects of countries in the Global South, such as Cuba, are shaped by both internal and international factors. How might changing relations with the United States affect Cuba's security and prosperity?

which the great powers have created. At the same time, intergovernmental organizations (IGOs) provide an opportunity for the small and middle powers of the Global South to exert influence on world politics. To understand world politics and the roots of changes in international affairs, it is important to understand the impact of these influential IGOs as actors in the global arena. To complete the picture, you also need to inspect the thousands of nongovernmental organizations (NGOs), whose presence and pressure as nonstate actors are also transforming international politics, for both the Global North and the Global South. We turn to both of these transnational actors in Chapter 6.

> *A multipolar world cannot exist without recognizing the status and participation of developing countries.*
>
> **—LI PENG, FORMER CHINESE PREMIER**

Study. Apply. Analyze.

Chapter Summary

5-1 Describe the historical phases of colonialism, as well as the era of decolonization. The roots of today's inequalities among states lie in the structure of the international system, shaped by the great powers' efforts to broaden their power and sphere of influence. Colonialism characterized these power-grabs during the first wave of European empire building that began in the late fifteenth century and during the second wave as Europe, the United States, and Japan aggressively colonized new territories from the 1870s until the outbreak of World War I. However, following World War I, the climate of opinion turned against imperialism with greater support for the principle of national self-determination. Decolonization began, and accelerated following World War II in part because of the diminished economic and military vitality of many colonial powers.

5-2 Discuss the key differences between the Global North and Global South. The Global South and the Global North experience drastically different conditions and circumstances. The Global North generally enjoys democracy and prosperity, while the Global South countries suffer from instability and poverty.

5-3 Identify the internal and international causes for underdevelopment in the Global South. Internally, according to theories of modernization, a lack of characteristics conducive to modernization are barriers to development. Internationally, dependency theory emphasizes the influence that dominant world powers have on the development of Global South countries due to the structure of the global economy.

5-4 Assess different approaches taken to facilitate development in the Global South. The Global South faces a multitude of challenges to improving its social, political, and economic development. One area of emphasis is improving access to information and communications technology. Another is increasing military spending to address insecurity. Foreign aid, remittances, trade, and FDI are all intended to relieve poverty and contribute to development, but at the same time countries in the Global South struggle with corruption, which puts democratization at risk.

5-5 Appraise the prospects for future development in the Global South. The roots of today's inequalities between the Global South and the Global North can be linked to colonialism and slavery, poverty and dependency. These factors and others discussed in this chapter have no doubt shaped the world order and affected the future trajectory of countries in the Global South. Yet while the Global North will continue to influence the development of the Global South, many factors are constantly at play and the landscape of international relations will inevitably host more change in the future.

Key Terms

bilateral

classical liberal economic
  theory

communism

decolonization

developed countries

developing countries

development

digital divide

dualism

emerging powers/middle
  powers

export-led industrialization

foreign aid

foreign direct investment
  (FDI)

Global North

Global South

gross national income (GNI)

Group of 77 (G-77)

import-substitution
  industrialization

indigenous peoples

information technology (IT)

information and
  communications
  technology (ICT)

laissez-faire economics

least developed countries
  (LDCs)

mercantilism

modernization

multinational corporations
  (MNCs)

New International Economic
  Order (NIEO)

newly industrialized countries
  (NICs)

official development assistance
  (ODA)

realpolitik

remittances

self-determination

small powers

Suggested Readings and Resources

Gilley, Bruce, and Andrew O'Neil, eds. (2014). *Middle Powers and the Rise of China*. Washington, D.C.: Georgetown University Press.

Growth Economics Blog: growthecon.wordpress.com. A blog discussing economic development in developing countries.

Halperin, Sandra. (2013). *Re-Envisioning Global Development: A Horizontal Perspective*. New York: Taylor and Francis.

"If You Shouldn't Call It the Third World, What Should You Call It?" npr.org/sections/goatsandsoda/2015/01/04/372684438/if-you-shouldnt-call-it-the-third-world-

what-should-you-call-it. A blog post about labeling countries in the Global North and South.

Millennium Challenge Corporation. mcc.gov. An independent U.S. foreign assistance agency that provides grants to help fight against global poverty.

Prashad, Vijay. (2013). *The Poorer Nations: A Possible History of the Global South*. London, UK: Verso.

Seligson, Mitchell A., and John T. Passe'-Smith, eds. (2014). *Development and Underdevelopment: The Political Economy of Global Inequality*, 5th ed. Boulder, CO: Lynne Ripener.

The Borgen Project: borgenproject.org. A blog about issues in the Global South with a focus on poverty.

Transparency International: transparency.org. A global movement to combat corruption.

World Bank. (2018). *Atlas of Sustainable Development Goals 2018*. Washington, D.C.: World Bank. documents.worldbank.org/curated/en/590681527864542864/Atlas-of-Sustainable-Development-Goals-2018-World-Development-Indicators.

World Education Blog: efareport.wordpress.com/category/developing-countries/. A blog discussing world education progress.

Carnegie Council Videos

Key Term Videos

- Decolonization
- Mercantilism
- Classic Liberal Economy Theory
- Self-Determination

- Development
- Modernization
- Information and Communications Technology

- Information Technology
- Foreign Aid
- Remittances
- Foreign Direct Investment

Additional Videos

- Collier, Paul. "The Bottom Billion: Why the Poorest Countries Are Failing and What Can Be Done About It."
- Friedman, George. "The End of the International Order and the Future of Asia."
- Gao, Qin. "Poverty Reduction & Social Welfare in China, with Qin Gao."
- Myers, Jeanne J. "The New Asian Hemisphere: The Irresistible Shift of Global Power to the East."
- Moyo, Dambisa, "Dead Aid: Why Aid Is Not Working and How There Is a Better Way for Africa."
- Vocke, William. "Development Aid."
- Vocke, William. "International Aid: Does Help Hurt?"

Chapter 6

Nonstate Actors and the Quest for Global Community

Apple White/Alamy Stock Photo

IMAGE 6.1 People Power Shown here is a member of the World Food Programme, an international humanitarian organization, working to deliver food to citizens in Mozambique in response to the destruction wrought in March 2019 by Cyclone Idai. The catastrophic cyclone killed more than 600 people in Mozambique, washed away vital infrastructure, damaged crops, livestock, and fisheries, and left 1.7 million people in need of emergency food assistance. UN Secretary-General Antonio Guterres called on the peoples of the world "to translate into concrete gestures our solidarity with a country affected by one of the worst weather-related catastrophes in African history."

Learning Objectives

LO 6-1   Distinguish between intergovernmental and nongovernmental international organizations.

LO 6-2   Describe the structure and key functions of the UN and the Bretton Woods institutions.

LO 6-3   Describe the structure and key functions of the European Union (EU), and identify other major regional intergovernmental organizations.

LO 6-4   Identify and evaluate prominent types of nongovernmental organizations.

LO 6-5   Identify and evaluate the threat posed by terrorist and transnational crime groups.

LO 6-6   Debate the implications of nonstate actors for state sovereignty and world politics.

> A novel redistribution of power among states, markets, and civil society is underway, ending the steady accumulation of power in the hands of states that began with the Peace of Westphalia in 1648."
>
> **—JESSICA T. MATHEWS, INTERNATIONAL RELATIONS SCHOLAR**

You are a member of the human race, and your future will be determined to a large degree by the capacity of humanity to work together to manage the many common problems confronting the entire world. But how does the world respond to this challenge?

The answer for centuries has primarily relied on sovereign territorial states. As realism posits, countries remain the most influential actors on the world stage. States' foreign policy decisions and interactions, more than any other factor, give rise to trends and transformations in world politics. Today, however, as liberal theory posits, the extraordinary power of states over global destiny is eroding as our world becomes increasingly complex and interdependent, and as nonstate actors continue to multiply and seek greater influence in the global community. Moreover, **responsible sovereignty**, a principle that requires states to protect not only their own people but also to cooperate across borders to protect global resources and address transnational threats, is gaining traction among global leaders. It "entails obligations and duties to one's own citizens and other states" and provides for a greater role by IGOs and NGOs as it "differs from the traditional interpretation of sovereignty (sometimes called Westphalian sovereignty) as noninterference in the internal affairs of states" (Jones, Pascual, and Stedman 2009, p. 9).

A critical question to consider, then, is whether the increased influence of nonstate actors, and the increasingly complex nature of governance, will ultimately prove to be ameliorative for global problems. Conversely, will reducing an individual state's ability to rely on *self-help* measures to address problems unilaterally prove to be a curse?

This chapter provides information and insight to help you evaluate this question. More specifically, it will enable you to confront and assess the theoretical hypothesis advanced by world leader Jean-François Rischard, former World Bank vice president for Europe, who argues, "One thing is sure: global complexity [is creating a] global governance crisis that will have to be solved through new ways of working together globally, and bold departures from old, trusted concepts" (Rischard, 1998).

Global problems often require global solutions. Impressive numbers of nonstate actors on the world stage are increasingly flexing their political muscle in an effort to engineer global changes. This chapter explores two broad types of nonstate actors—international organizations that carry out independent foreign policies as transnational actors and NGOs made up of individual people who band together in coalitions of private citizens to exercise international influence. To introduce this discussion, we begin with a look at the general characteristics of both types of nonstate actors.

responsible sovereignty
A principle that requires states to protect not only their own people but to cooperate across borders to protect global resources and address transnational threats.

> *The quest for international security involves the unconditional surrender by every nation, in a certain measure, of its liberty of action, its sovereignty that is to say, and it is clear beyond all doubt that no other road can lead to such security.*
>
> **—ALBERT EINSTEIN, NOBEL PRIZE–WINNING PHYSICIST**

Nonstate Actors in World Politics

There are two main types of international nonstate actors, *intergovernmental organizations (IGOs)* and *nongovernmental organizations (NGOs)*. What distinguishes the two is that intergovernmental organizations are international organizations whose members are states, whereas nongovernmental organizations are associations composed of private individuals. Both types experienced a sharp increase in their numbers during the twentieth century: In 1909 there were 37 IGOs and 176 NGOs; by 1960 the numbers had risen to 154 IGOs and 1255 NGOs; and at the start of 2017, the numbers had escalated to 285 conventional IGOs and 9404 conventional NGOs (see Figure 6.1). This does not include the 725 unconventional IGOs and 5145 unconventional NGOs (organizations such as international funds and foundations) that are recorded by the *Yearbook of International Organizations* (Union of International Associations, 2019).

Intergovernmental Organizations (IGOs)

IGOs are purposely created by states to solve problems. They are generally regarded as more powerful than NGOs, in part because IGO members are state governments and tend to be more permanent. IGOs meet at regular intervals, and they have established rules for making decisions and a permanent secretariat or headquarters staff.

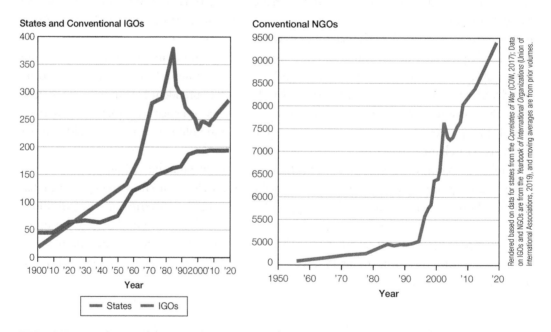

FIGURE 6.1 Trends in the Number of IGOs, NGOs, and States since 1900 Since 1900, the number of independent states has increased dramatically, with growth accelerating after World War II when the decolonization movement began. But note that the number of IGOs has grown even more rapidly in this period, declining only since the late 1980s when a number of formerly independent IGOs began to merge with one another. The number of NGOs has grown even more rapidly, with more than 9400 conventional NGOs worldwide.

IGOs vary widely in size and purpose. Only thirty-seven IGOs qualify as "intercontinental organizations," and only thirty-seven are, like the United Nations (UN), "universal membership" IGOs. The rest, accounting for more than 73 percent of the total, are limited in their scope and confined to particular regions. The variation among the organizations in each subcategory is great, particularly with single-purpose, limited-membership IGOs. The North Atlantic Treaty Organization (NATO), for example, is primarily a military alliance, whereas others, such as the Organization of American States (OAS), promote both economic development and democratic reforms. Still, most IGOs concentrate their activities on specific economic or social issues of special concern to them, such as the management of trade or transportation.

The expansion of IGOs has created a complex network of overlapping international organizations that cooperate with one another to deal with a wide range of global issues. They support one another on issues as varied as trade, defense, disarmament, economic development, agriculture, health, culture, human rights, the arts, illegal drugs, tourism, labor, gender inequality, education, debt, the environment, crime, humanitarian aid, civilian crisis relief, telecommunications, science, globalization, immigration, and refugees.

Nongovernmental Organizations (NGOs)

The term NGO applies to *all* nonstate and nonprofit organizations that operate as intermediaries to build transnational bridges between those with resources and a targeted group. Thus, it is also customary to think of NGOs as intersocietal organizations that contribute to negotiations between and among states in the hope of reaching agreements for global governance on nearly every issue of international public policy.

NGOs link the global society by forming **transnational advocacy networks (TANs)** that bring a collection of actors together around a given issue and work for policy changes (Keck and Sikkink, 2008). According to a constructivist perspective, they are inspired to action by shared interests and values. Broadly put, the goal of TANs is to "mobilize information strategically to help create new issues…and to persuade, pressurize, and gain leverage over much more powerful organizations and governments" (Keck and Sikkink, 1998, p. 89). In terms of international relations theories, TANs are thus at odds with realist theory in that they suggest that weaker nonstate actors may influence state actions and world politics.

transnational advocacy networks (TANs) Group of actors with shared values who work internationally on a common issue.

Like IGOs, NGOs differ widely in their characteristics. For example, some are small with membership in the hundreds; others are huge, with one of the largest being Amnesty International, which in 2019 included more than 2 million members spread across more than 150 countries and regions. In 2019, the Union of International Associations categorized the major "conventional" NGOs as split, with almost 13 percent as "universal," more than 12 percent as "intercontinental," and the vast majority, almost 74 percent, as "regionally oriented." Functionally, NGOs span virtually every facet of political, social, and economic activity in an increasingly borderless globalized world, ranging from earth sciences to ethnic unity, health care, language, history, culture, education, theology, law, ethics, security, and defense.

In general, NGOs are viewed in a positive light as most pursue objectives that are held by large segments of society and, therefore, do not provoke much opposition, at least in principle. This perspective is reflected in the World Bank's definition of NGOs as "private organizations that pursue activities to relieve suffering, promote the interests of the poor, protect the environment, provide basic social services, or undertake community development" (Malena, 1995). For example, NGOs such as Amnesty International, the International Chamber of Commerce, the International Red Cross, Save the Children, and the World Wildlife Federation enjoy widespread popular support. Others, however, are more controversial because they unite people for collective action in ways that can harm others, as in the case of terrorist groups, international drug rings, or transnational pirates.

Many NGOs interact formally with IGOs. For instance, more than 3000 NGOs actively consult with various agencies of the extensive UN system, maintain offices in hundreds of cities, and hold parallel conferences with IGO meetings to which states send representatives. Such partnerships between NGOs and IGOs enable both types to work (and lobby) together in pursuit of common policies and programs. As IGOs and NGOs rise in numbers and influence, a key question to contemplate is whether a "global society" will weaken the traditional state-centric global system and democratize or disrupt global governance.

Prominent Intergovernmental Organizations

LO 6-2   Describe the structure and key functions of the UN and the Bretton Woods institutions.

Let us continue our analysis of nonstate actors in world affairs by examining a few of the most prominent IGOs: the United Nations, the European Union, and various other regional organizations. As we do so, ask yourself whether IGOs' activities are adequate for dealing with the pressing threats to human welfare, whether these IGOs are undermining states' continuing autonomy, and if so, whether an erosion of state power will prove helpful or harmful.

The United Nations

The United Nations (UN) is the best-known global organization. It is distinguishable from most other IGOs as it has nearly universal membership, today including 193 independent member states from across the Global North and Global South. The UN's nearly fourfold growth from the 51 states that joined it at the UN's birth in 1945 has been spectacular but, from the start, political conflicts have shaped the admission process. These conflicts show the extent to which the organization reflects the relationships of the five great powers that created and govern it through veto authority in the Security Council. In principle, any sovereign state that accepts the UN's goals and regulations can join, but the great powers have often let the realist belief that countries should put their own national interest above concern for the global community guide their admissions decision making. This was especially true during the Cold War, when both the United States and the Soviet Union prevented countries aligned with their adversaries from joining.

The UN's Agenda   Peace and security figured prominently in the thinking of the great powers responsible for creating the UN and its predecessor, the League of Nations. These institutional forms were inspired by the liberal conviction that both war and the management of other global problems are best controlled by managing global *anarchy*—the absence of supranational authority to regulate relations between states—on the international scene. The League of Nations sought to prevent a recurrence of the catastrophic World War I by replacing the balance-of-power system with one based on the construction of a *collective security* regime made up of rules for keeping peace (see Chapter 2), guided by the principle that an act of aggression by any state would be met by a collective retaliatory response from the rest. When the league failed to restrain expansionistic aggression by Germany, Japan, and Italy during the 1930s, it collapsed.

During World War II, the U.S., British, and Russian allies began planning for a new international organization, the United Nations, to preserve the postwar peace because it was believed that peace could not be maintained unilaterally by any one great power acting alone. Article 1 of the UN Charter defines the UN's objectives as centered on:

- Maintaining international peace and security.

- Developing friendly relations among states based on respect for the principle of equal rights and the self-determination of peoples.

- Achieving international cooperation in solving international problems of an economic, social, cultural, or humanitarian character and in promoting respect for human rights and fundamental freedoms for all.

- Functioning as a center for harmonizing the actions of countries to attain these common ends.

The more than seventy-year history of the UN reflects the fact that countries from both the Global North and the Global South have successfully used the organization to promote their own foreign policy goals. This record has led to the ratification of more than three hundred treaties and conventions consistent with the UN's "six fundamental values": international freedom, equality, solidarity, tolerance, respect for nature, and a sense of shared responsibility. Although faith in the UN's ability eroded when it became paralyzed by the unforeseen Cold War between the United States and the Soviet Union, in the post–Cold War era it was freed from paralysis and returned to its original mission.

The UN now manages an expanding agenda of urgent military and nonmilitary problems and, in response to these global demands, has evolved over time into a vast administrative machinery (see Map 6.1). To assess the capacity of the United Nations to fulfill its growing responsibilities, let us consider how it is organized.

Organizational Structure   The UN's limitations are perhaps rooted in the ways it is organized for its wide-ranging purposes. The UN structure contains the following six major organs:

- **General Assembly.** Established as the main deliberative body of the United Nations, all members are equally represented according to a one-state/one-vote formula. Decisions are reached by a simple majority vote, except on so-called important questions, which require a two-thirds majority. The resolutions it passes, however, are only recommendations.

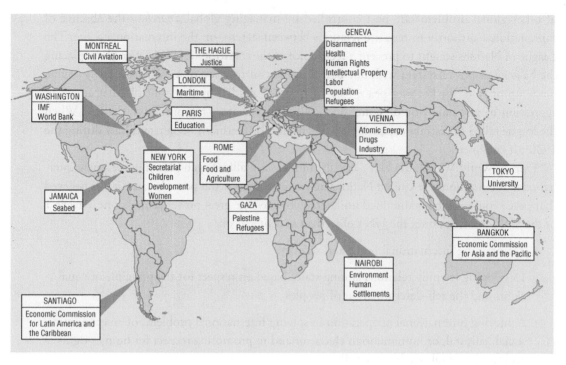

MAP 6.1 The UN's Headquarters and Global Network "The work of the UN is global, touching the lives of billions of people. The work of the organization is, however, mostly done locally, within regions and countries" (United Nations, 2019). As shown here, to reduce the gap between aspiration and accomplishment, the UN has spread its administrative arm to every corner of the globe to fulfill its primary purpose of spearheading international cooperation.

 Think It Through   In what ways is the Global North systematically more highly considered than the Global South within the UN? Given the anarchic nature of the international system, what are some of the UN's limitations in maintaining order and solving global problems?

- **Security Council.** Given primary responsibility by the charter for dealing with threats to international peace and security, the Security Council consists of five permanent members with the power to veto substantive decisions (the United States, the United Kingdom, France, Russia, and China), and ten nonpermanent members elected by the General Assembly for staggered two-year terms.

- **Economic and Social Council.** Responsible for coordinating the UN's social and economic programs, functional commissions, and specialized agencies, its fifty-four members are elected by the General Assembly for staggered three-year terms. This body has been particularly active in addressing economic development and human rights issues.

- **Trusteeship Council.** Charged with supervising the administration of territories that had not achieved self-rule, the Trusteeship Council suspended operation in 1994 when the last remaining trust territory gained independence.

- **International Court of Justice.** The principal judicial organ of the United Nations, the International Court of Justice is composed of fifteen independent judges who are elected for nine-year terms by the General Assembly and Security Council (see Chapter 9). The competence of the court is restricted to disputes between states, and its jurisdiction is based on the consent of the disputants. The court may also give nonbinding advisory opinions on legal questions raised by the General Assembly, Security Council, or other UN agencies.

- **Secretariat.** Led by the secretary-general, the Secretariat contains the international civil servants who perform the administrative and secretarial functions of the UN.

The founders of the UN expected the Security Council to become the organization's primary body, because it was designed to maintain peace and its permanent members were the victorious allied great powers during World War II. It is exclusively permitted by the UN Charter to initiate actions, especially the use of force. The General Assembly, however, can only make recommendations.

Despite the intentions of the founders of the UN, the General Assembly assumed wider responsibilities as countries in the Global South—seizing advantage of their growing numbers under the one-state/one-vote rules of the General Assembly— became increasingly assertive. Since then they have used their dominance in the General Assembly to guide UN involvement in directions of particular concern to them, generally pertaining to issues of economic development and social needs of the Global South. Power within the General Assembly is not in itself sufficient to ensure the Global South's control of the agenda however, as the original five great powers in the Security Council assert their will on issues that they find important. For example, the United States resisted the 2005 proposal to expand the Security Council to twenty-four members because it would dilute American power, and it announced that it would not support extension of the veto power held by the big five permanent members to other members. Similarly, China surprised many with its refusal to support an Indian bid for a permanent seat in 2008.

Budget Controversy   Differences between the Global North and the Global South over perceived priorities are most clearly exhibited in the heated debate over the UN's budget. This controversy centers on how members should interpret the organization's Charter, which states that "expenses of the Organization shall be borne by the members as apportioned by the General Assembly" (UN, 1945).

The UN budget consists of three distinct elements: the core budget, the peacekeeping budget, and the budget for voluntary programs. States contribute to the voluntary programs and some of the peacekeeping activities as they see fit. The core budget and other peacekeeping activities are subject to assessments (see Figures 6.2A and 6.2B).

The precise mechanism by which assessments have been determined is complicated, but largely they are allocated according to states' capacity to pay. Thus the United States, which has the greatest resources, is assessed 22 percent of the UN's regular budget, for a net contribution in 2019 of over $674 million. Yet the poorest 15 percent of the UN's members, or a total of twenty-nine member states, pay the minimum (0.001 percent), each contributing only $30,646 annually and altogether less than 1 percent of the UN's 2019 budget. In comparison, the richest 10 percent of states were assessed to pay almost 83 percent of the UN's 2019 budget. Although this formula is under attack in many wealthy states, it still governs.

Resistance to this budgetary formula for funding UN activities has always existed. It has grown progressively worse in large part because the General Assembly apportions expenses according to majority rule. This raises issues of fairness as those with the most votes (the less developed countries) do not have the money, and the most prosperous countries do not have the votes.

IMAGE 6.2A **Antonio Guterres, 2017–present** With a focus on human dignity, he seeks to broker peace and promote reform.

IMAGE 6.2D **Boutros Boutros-Ghali, 1992–1996** The United States dumped the acerbic and undiplomatic Egyptian after one turbulent term.

IMAGE 6.2G **U Thant, 1961–1971** The placid Thant had a low profile but got flak for pulling UN peacekeepers from Sinai.

IMAGE 6.2B **Ban Ki-Moon, 2007–2016** With a global reputation as someone who will do the right thing, he was one of the most popular leaders of the world.

IMAGE 6.2E **Javier Perez De Cuellar, 1982–1991** He quietly guided the organization out of Cold War paralysis and back into business.

IMAGE 6.2H **Dag Hammarskjold, 1953–1961** The UN's most effective leader. Hammarskjold died on a peacekeeping mission to Congo.

IMAGE 6.2C **Kofi Annan, 1996–2006** He had a quiet charisma, but the Iraq war and the oil-for-food scandal marred his second term.

IMAGE 6.2F **Kurt Waldheim, 1972–1981** An effective bureaucrat, Waldheim is now remembered mainly for his Nazi past.

IMAGE 6.2I **Trygve Lie, 1946–1952** The gruff politician helped create the organization but accomplished little in office.

These disparities have grown: the largest contributors command only 10 votes but pay 69 percent of the cost; the other members pay only 31 percent of the UN budget but command 183 votes. The wealthy members charge that the existing budget procedures institutionalize a system of taxation without fair representation. The critics counter with the argument that, for fairness and justice, the great power members should bear financial responsibilities commensurate with their wealth and influence.

UN Program Budget, 2002–2019

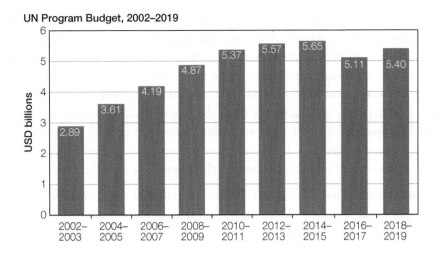

Budget Categories, 2008–2019

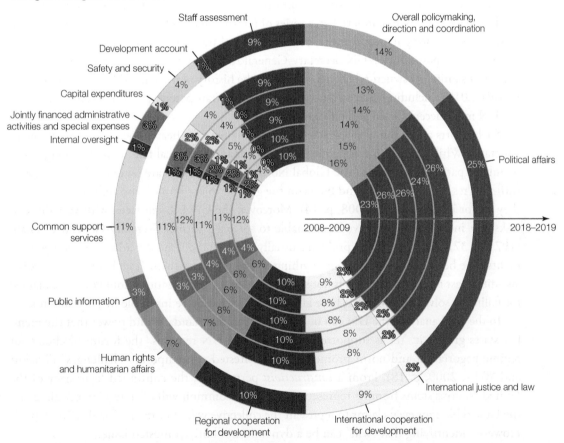

FIGURES 6.2A AND 6.2B   UN Budget Priorities The UN General Assembly approved a program budget of $5.40 billion for the 2018-2019 fiscal year, which was a five percent increase from the previous budget, though below the 2014-2015 amount. Allocation amounts across the various budget categories have been fairly stable for the last five budget cycles. Among the various budget categories (shown bottom), political affairs has consistently been the largest with allocations between 23 and 26 percent of the program budget. (Based on data from the "United Nations Regular Budget 2018–2019.")

Ultimately the money itself is not the issue, as the sums under contention are relatively paltry. In all, the UN and its related funds require about $30 billion annually, which works out to about $4 per person. By way of comparison, at the start of 2018, world military spending was $1.8 trillion—which amounts to an average global per capita spending of $239 (SIPRI, 2019a). The real issues concern which priorities and initiatives are important and which states should have political influence. Poor states argue that need should determine expenditure levels rather than rich countries' interests, and major contributors do not want to pay for programs they oppose. At the beginning of 2019, the United States still owed the UN over $1 billion, arguing that it was bearing an unfair amount of the financial burden (Nichols, 2019).

Future Challenges   The UN's future remains uncertain, and its persistent financial troubles leave it without the resources to combat global problems and carry out the responsibilities assigned to it. However, given the UN's successful history of organizational adaptation to challenges, supporters have reasons to be optimistic about the organization's long-term prospects to live up to its creators' bold mandate to attack world problems (see "A Closer Look: The United Nations and the Syrian Civil War"). Despite some resistance by members of the Global South, who feared that big-donor pressures might prevail and compromise the interests of small powers, the UN has undertaken a series of reforms since 2006 to change its management procedures and bring its recruitment, contracting, and training responsibilities into line with its vast new responsibilities. UN Secretary-General Antonio Guterres put forth what he called "the most significant structural change process in the history of the United Nations" (quoted in Lebada, 2019), including increased accountability and transparency, as well as efforts to make the UN more decentralized and efficient.

Such efforts aside, the UN will likely remain an arena for heated jockeying among member states. While the UN is frequently blamed for failures, the real failure often belongs to its members, particularly those of the Global North. "Those powers are seldom willing to give it sufficient resources, attention and boots on the ground to accomplish the ambitious mandates they set for it" (Fukuyama, 2008, p. 14). Moreover, the UN is often faced with very difficult tasks that individual states have been unable to solve. As former Secretary-General U Thant (1971, p. 37) observed, "Great problems usually come to the United Nations because governments have been unable to think of anything else to do about them. The United Nations is a last-ditch, last resort affair, and it is not surprising that the organization should often be blamed for failing to solve problems that have already been found to be insoluble by governments."

In the final analysis, the UN can be no more than the mandates and power that the member states give to it. Yet as supporters point out, the UN remains "the forum of choice for regime negotiation and norm promotion for contested contemporary challenges" (Thakur and Weiss, 2009, p. 18). From a *constructivist* perspective, the continued legitimacy of the United Nations stems from its representation of the common will of states; "in certain cases, the United Nations even claims to represent the collective will of humanity" (Ellis, 2009, p. 4). However, identifying that "will" can be a dynamic and hotly contested issue.

The UN is well positioned to formulate policies with global relevance and application, as seen in its success in shaming human rights violators through resolutions in the United Nations Commission on Human Rights (Lebovic and Voeten, 2009), its efforts to combat

A Closer Look

THE UNITED NATIONS AND THE SYRIAN CIVIL WAR

Inspired in part by the Arab Spring, hostilities between Syrian rebels and forces loyal to Syrian President Bashar al-Assad began in March 2011 as demonstrators took to the streets in peaceful protest of the imprisonment and torture of a number of young students for antigovernment graffiti. After troops fired on the rioting crowds, the protests turned into armed conflict over the legitimacy of al-Assad's rule. This metastasized into a long, brutal and often one-sided civil war between Syria, with assistance from Russia, and multiple groups of opposition forces. As some of the territory was held by terrorist groups such as the Islamic State (see Chapter 6), several other countries (the United States, Turkey, Iran, Qatar and Saudi Arabia) have been involved, albeit to a more limited extent. It has been both a bloody war and a humanitarian disaster. As of June 2019, the UN estimates that 400,000 people have been killed, and 11.6 million – over 55 percent of the total population – have been displaced by the violence: 6 million have been internally displaced and 5.6 million have fled Syria (Council of Foreign Relations, 2019).

Despite considerable international concern over the conflict in Syria, there was considerable division within the United Nations Security Council over the extent to which it should intervene. The United States and many other Western governments condemned the actions of the Syrian government–which committed rampant violence against civilians and used chemical weapons–and called for al-Assad to step down. Many supporters see UN intervention as supported by the UN Charter, particularly the *Responsibility to Protect* doctrine (see Chapter 2), which calls for armed intervention by the international community if a state fails to protect its citizens from such abuses as war crimes, ethnic cleansing, genocide, or crimes against humanity.

However, critics of intervention–essentially Russia and China–countered that such action is in contradiction to the UN Charter, which rests on the principle of sovereignty and prohibits forceful intervention that violates the political independence and territorial integrity of any state. They see UN actions as constituting intervention into the internal concerns of a sovereign state, although they joined the United States and others in calling for a peace process that would bring an end to the civil war.

This gridlock, and the United Nation's inability to stop the violence in Syria, raises questions about the efficacy of the organization, particularly the difficulties in getting states with different perspectives and political agendas to come together on a given issue. It also highlights the tension between a state's sovereign authority over its territory, its responsibility to protect and provide for the compelling needs of its own people, and the grounds for intervention by the international community.

Watch the Carnegie Council Video:
"Ethics and Humanitarian Intervention"

You Decide:

1. In humanitarian crises, when should the principle of sovereignty be superseded by a responsibility to protect? If so, who should intervene?

2. Do you think that the structure of the Security Council reflects the current power distribution in the world? Should it be changed and, if so, how? Does the UN Security Council have the authority and legitimacy to make these decisions, especially in light of the potential for gridlock?

3. Should the United Nations have intervened in Syria?

global pandemics such as HIV/AIDS (Thakur and Weiss, 2009), and its role in promoting confidence-building measures to prevent future conflicts (Shannon, 2009). Moreover, in the aftermath of several scandals and failures, the UN was able to reform its peacekeeping operations (Goldstein, 2012). Although much maligned, the UN is very much needed. "Only a global organization is capable of meeting global challenges," observed former UN Secretary-General Kofi Annan. "When we act together, we are stronger and less vulnerable to individual calamity" (UN, 1997).

Other Prominent Global IGOs

Beyond the UN, hundreds of other IGOs are active internationally. We look briefly at three of the most prominent of these other IGOs, all of which are specialized in their focus on the international political economy: the World Trade Organization (WTO), the World Bank, and the International Monetary Fund (IMF). Collectively these are also referred to as the "Bretton Woods Institutions," named after the location of the 1944 meeting where these organizations were first discussed and proposed (see Chapters 10 and 11).

Each of these IGOs was created by the great powers in response to their need for a stable international economic order even though it required the voluntary sacrifice of some degree of sovereignty. An underlying issue is why states would give up some of their autonomy when that surrender reduces some of their control over their destiny, in this case their economies. The primary reason is that multilateral cooperation enables those cooperating states to receive benefits that they would not otherwise receive. In the case of international trade, cooperation enables states to achieve higher standards of living than otherwise would be possible. The creation of such **regimes**, as well as authoritative IGO institutions for global governance, can pay dividends. Shared problems often cannot be managed without multilateral cooperation. Unilateral measures on many issues by even the most powerful great power acting independently simply will not work.

regimes
Norms, rules, and procedures for interaction within a given issue or issue area agreed to by a set of states.

The World Trade Organization   Remembering the hardships caused by the Great Depression of 1929, as well as the collapse of the global economy during the 1930s, the Western powers sought to create international economic institutions that would prevent another depression by promoting world trade. The initial proposal was for the International Trade Organization (ITO), conceived as a specialized agency within the overall framework of the UN. While negotiations for the anticipated ITO were dragging on, many people urged immediate action. These calls led to a meeting in 1947 in Geneva where twenty-three states agreed to a number of bilateral tariff concessions between two states. These treaties were written into a final act called the General Agreement on Tariffs and Trade (GATT), which was originally thought of as a temporary arrangement until the ITO came into operation.

When a final agreement on the ITO proved elusive, GATT provided a mechanism for continued multilateral negotiations on reducing tariffs and other barriers to trade. Over the next several decades, eight rounds of negotiations were held to liberalize trade. On January 1, 1995, GATT was superseded by the World Trade Organization (WTO). Although it was not exactly what the ITO envisaged immediately following World War II, it nevertheless represents the most ambitious tariff-reduction institution yet. Unlike GATT, the WTO is a full-fledged IGO with formal dispute-resolution procedures. This mandate gives the WTO authority to enforce trading rules and to adjudicate trade disputes.

Broadly put, the WTO administers an integrated and comprehensive worldwide system of liberal or free trade. This agenda poses a threat to some states and generates controversy. At the heart of their complaint is that the WTO undermines the ability of individual states to manage their own economies, as they are subject to supranational rules. However, it should be kept in mind that these are ultimately voluntary agreements that are beneficial to the members. Nonetheless, adherence to WTO regulations can be politically difficult and it is often argued that "the WTO and democracy are incompatible. To move toward the WTO means to therefore move away from democracy" (Dingwerth, 2014, p. 1129).

The World Bank   In July 1944 at the United Nations Monetary and Financial Conference held in Bretton Woods, New Hampshire, forty-four countries created the World Bank (or International Bank for Reconstruction and Development), which was established to support reconstruction efforts in Europe after World War II. Over the next decade, the United States took a more unilateral approach to reconstruction with the Marshall Plan, and the bank shifted its attention to developmental assistance. Because Global South countries often have difficulty borrowing money to finance projects aimed at promoting economic growth, the bank offers them loans with lower interest rates and longer repayment plans than they could typically obtain from commercial banks.

World Bank projects generally have a medium to long-term focus, and address the two main goals it set to achieve by 2030: reducing extreme poverty (defined as living off of less than $1.90 a day) and fostering income growth for people in the lowest 40 percent in every country (World Bank, 2019). Thus far, these ambitious goals have met with praise from the donor countries.

Administratively, the World Bank has over 10,000 employees who operate in more than 120 offices throughout the world. Decision-making authority is vested in a board of governors, consisting of a governor and an alternate appointed by each of the Bank's 189 member countries. A governor customarily is a member country's minister of finance or an equivalent official. The board meets annually in the bank's Washington, D.C., headquarters to set policy directions and delegate responsibility for the routine operations of the bank to the twenty-four directors of its executive board. The five countries with the largest number of shares in the World Bank's capital stock (the United States, Germany, Japan, France, and the United Kingdom) appoint their own executive directors, and the remaining executive directors are either appointed (Saudi Arabia), elected by their states (China, Russia, and Switzerland), or elected by groups of countries. Voting is weighted by the holdings of the members, which prioritizes the interests of the wealthier countries. The quota of contributions adjusts to changes in a country's economic size and situation.

Over the years, both the self-image and operations of the World Bank have evolved from strictly providing loans to assisting states' development planning and training. David Malpass, upon becoming World Bank president in April 2019, declared "Too many people continue to live in poverty; too many live without access to clean water, health care, or education; too many are not fully included in their local economy. My priority is helping countries get good

IMAGE 6.3 Rage Against Institutional Symbols of Globalization Since the 1990s, protesters have frequently targeted the high-profile meetings of the Bretton Woods institutions. The above picture was taken during one of the protests that took place in Argentina during June 2018, in response to President Mauricio Macri agreeing to a $50 billion loan package from the IMF. As is the norm with the IMF, the agreement is conditional upon the country making unpopular macroeconomic changes to reduce its budget deficit. Argentina has had several financial crises, and many citizens still blame the previous one (which took place in 2001–2002) on IMF programs (The Guardian, 2018).

development outcomes" (Malpass, 2019). This is reflected in the urban safety net program that provides grants to impoverished countries and enables people to work and train for new occupations. The World Bank also has participated increasingly in consortium arrangements for financing private lending institutions while insisting that democratic and anticorruption reforms are made a condition for economic assistance.

The International Monetary Fund   While also a financial institution, the purpose of the International Monetary Fund (IMF) is somewhat distinct from the World Bank, with its purpose being more short-term in nature. Specifically, the primary focus of the IMF is on managing the exchange of money across borders and ensuring that currencies remain convertible through short-term assistance and cooperation on monetary matters. The IMF often functions as a lender of last resort for countries experiencing financial crises. It is also responsible for monitoring and evaluating the fiscal and monetary environments of all their member states as well as the world economy as a whole.

The IMF is now one of the sixteen specialized agencies within the UN system. Each IMF member is represented on its governing board, which meets annually to fix general policy. Day-to-day business is conducted by a twenty-four-member executive board chaired by a managing director, who is also the administrative head of a staff of approximately 2000 employees. The IMF derives its operating funds from its 188 member states. As is the case with the World

Bank, contributions and voting weights are based on a quota system set according to a state's national income, monetary reserves, and other factors affecting each member's ability to contribute. To a large extent the IMF operates like a credit union, as each participant contributes to a common pool of funds from which it can borrow when the need arises.

As the IMF has increasingly functioned as a lender of last resort in times of crises, it has played a growing role in mandating state policies that it reasons are necessary to recover from economic crisis and avoid future ones. These loan conditions–generally a mixture of reduced spending, increased taxes, and increased openness to foreign trade and investment–are controversial, as IMF loan programs have been linked to slower economic growth (Vreeland, 2003), increased human rights violations (Abouharb and Cingranelli, 2007), and deteriorating labor rights practices (Blanton et al., 2015a).

Joseph Stiglitz, a Nobel laureate in economics and former chief economist of the World Bank, complains that the policies can produce damaging results because they are anchored in a free-market dogma that ignores the unique sociocultural contexts of the countries in which they are applied. Given the diversity of the Global South, development strategies for the future should avoid grandiose claims of universality and one-size-fits-all policies. What works in one country may be impractical or undesirable in another. For its part, the IMF is not unaware of these criticisms and has made efforts to be more responsive to the specific needs of the states and less doctrinaire in its approach. However, a recent study of the IMF's actual programs found that its policies have not fundamentally changed, and the "scale and pace of reforms to the IMF's practices do not match the organization's rhetoric" (Kentikelenis et al., 2016).

Regional Intergovernmental Organizations

LO 6-3   Describe the structure and key functions of the European Union (EU), and identify other major regional intergovernmental organizations.

The tug of war between individual states and groups of states within the UN, the WTO, the World Bank, and the IMF are reminders of an underlying principle that IGOs derive their power from the states that join them. This can be at odds with the ability of IGOs to rise above interstate competition and independently pursue their organizational purposes. For this reason, universal IGOs are often viewed from a *realist* perspective as instruments of their members' foreign policies and arenas for debate rather than as independent nonstate actors. As states dominate international organizations like the UN, the prospects for international cooperation are limited because, as realism emphasizes, states are fearful of multilateral organizations that compromise their vital national interests. This limits a given IGO's ability to foster multilateral decision making to engineer global change.

A rival hypothesis—that cooperation among powerful states is possible and international organizations help produce it—emerges from *liberal* theory. From this perspective, the "reality of a world of interconnected and transnational threats is a simple one: You have to cooperate with others to get them to cooperate with you" (Jones et al., 2009, p. 5). This viewpoint is

European Union (EU)
A regional organization created by the merger of the European Coal and Steel Community, the European Atomic Energy Community, and the European Economic Community (called the European Community until 1993) that has since expanded geographically and in its authority.

security community
A group of states whose high level of institutionalized or customary collaboration results in the settlement of disputes by means other than military force.

political integration
The processes and activities by which the populations of many or all states transfer their loyalties to a merged political and economic unit.

widely applicable to regional intergovernmental organizations, most notably the **European Union (EU)**. The EU serves as a model for other regional IGOs to emulate as the globe's most successful example of peaceful cross-border cooperation that has produced an integrated **security community** with a single economy.

The European Union

The EU is not, strictly speaking, a freestanding supranational organization for the collective management of European domestic and foreign affairs. It coexists with a large number of other European IGOs with which it jointly makes decisions. Of these, the Organization for Security and Cooperation in Europe (OSCE) and the Council of Europe stand as regional institutions of equal European partners, free of dividing lines, designed to manage regional security and promote human rights. Even within this overlapping network of European IGOs, the EU stands out as the example of how a powerful organization has transformed itself from a single- to a multiple-purpose IGO.

EU Expansion and Political Integration   As *constructivism* argues, ideas have consequences. Big ideas often come from painful experiences and crises, such as devastating wars. That is what happened after World War II—European leaders conceived of a bold plan to eradicate the curse of war by removing the incentives for war. As former EU official Janvier Solana (2006, p. 4) put it, "Where did we start? As a peace project among adversaries." Their reform program sought the **political integration** of Europe via a new supranational institution that transcended individual European states—to bring about nothing less than the *transformation* of international relations. Arguments in favor of integration included the likelihood of increased economic growth and competitiveness spurred by economies of scale, and reduced conflict due to consistent rules, mutual dependence, and increased trust (Kugler et al., 2015).

European integration began with the European Coal and Steel Community (ECSC) in 1951, the European Atomic Energy Community (Euratom) in 1957, and the European Economic Community (EEC) in 1957. These initiatives centered on trade development. Since the late 1960s, the three have shared a common organization and, through successive steps, have enlarged the EU's mission, becoming "the European Community." The EU's membership grew, and its geographical scope broadened as it expanded in a series of waves to encompass fifteen countries by 1997: Belgium, France, Germany, Italy, Luxembourg, and the Netherlands (the original "six"); Denmark, Ireland, and the United Kingdom (which joined in 1973); Greece (1981); Portugal and Spain (1986); and Austria, Finland, and Sweden (1995). In 2004, the EU reached a new milestone in its path toward enlargement when it formally admitted ten new members (the Czech Republic, Slovakia, Estonia, Hungary, Latvia, Lithuania, Malta, Poland, Slovenia, and the Greek-controlled part of Cyprus). This bold enlargement added 75 million people to create the globe's biggest free-trade bloc and transformed the face of Europe by ending the continent's division. That enlargement process continued when Bulgaria and Romania joined in 2007 and Croatia in 2013, to bring the EU to twenty-eight members (see Map 6.2).

Further expansion is also conceivable because the admission procedures for possible new membership are currently under way for eight additional countries. Turkey began accession

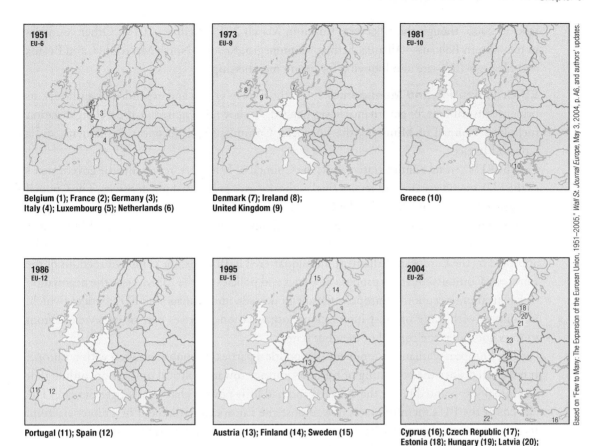

1951 EU-6
Belgium (1); France (2); Germany (3); Italy (4); Luxembourg (5); Netherlands (6)

1973 EU-9
Denmark (7); Ireland (8); United Kingdom (9)

1981 EU-10
Greece (10)

1986 EU-12
Portugal (11); Spain (12)

1995 EU-15
Austria (13); Finland (14); Sweden (15)

2004 EU-25
Cyprus (16); Czech Republic (17); Estonia (18); Hungary (19); Latvia (20); Lithuania (21); Malta (22); Poland (23); Slovakia (24); Slovenia (25)

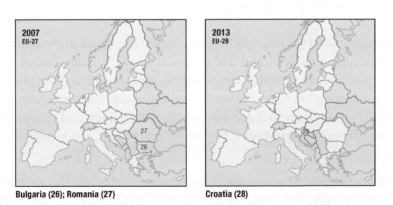

2007 EU-27
Bulgaria (26); Romania (27)

2013 EU-28
Croatia (28)

Based on "Few to Many: The Expansion of the European Union, 1951–2005," *Wall St. Journal Europe*, May 3, 2004, p. A6, and authors' updates.

MAP 6.2 From Few to Many: The Expansion of the European Union, 1951–2019 The European Union is the premier example of the formation and integrative growth of a supranational regional IGO. Expansion has enabled the EU to position itself to become a true superpower. It has grown in eight expansions from six members in 1951 to 28 in 2013, as shown here, and eight other countries, such as Albania and Turkey, waiting in the wings. However, under Brexit, the United Kingdom withdraws from the EU after more than forty-five years of membership.

 Think It Through In what ways will Britain's withdrawal from the EU impact the stability and effectiveness of this IGO?

talks in 2005, though the talks were frozen in March 2019 (Reilhac, 2019). Other countries in the western Balkans—Albania, Serbia, Montenegro, Kosovo, North Macedonia, and Bosnia and Herzegovina—are also lobbying for future membership.

EU Organization and Management   As the EU has grown and expanded its authority, its principal institutions for governance have changed. As shown in Figure 6.3, the EU organization includes a Council of Ministers, the European Commission, a European Parliament, and a Court of Justice.

The EU's central administrative unit, the Council of Ministers, represents the governments of the EU's member states and retains final authority over policy-making decisions. The Council sets general policy guidelines for the **European Commission**, which consists of twenty-eight commissioners (one from each member state). Commissioners are nominated by EU member governments, in consultation with the president of the European Commission, and must be approved by the European Parliament. Headquartered in Brussels, the primary functions of the European Commission are to propose new laws and policies for the EU, oversee the negotiation of EU treaties, execute the European Council's decrees, and manage the EU's budget (which, in contrast with those of most international organizations, derives part of its revenues from sources not under the control of member states).

The European Parliament represents the political parties and public opinion within Europe. It has existed since the beginning of Europe's journey toward political unification, although it was initially appointed rather than elected and had little power. That is no longer the case. The citizens of the EU's member states now choose the European Parliament in a direct election. Its more than 600 deputies debate issues at the monumental glass headquarters in Brussels and at its lavish Strasbourg palace in the same way that democratic national legislative bodies do. The European Parliament shares authority with the Council of Ministers, but the Parliament's influence has increased over time. The elected deputies pass laws with the council, approve the EU's budget, and oversee the European Commission, whose decisions the Parliament can overturn.

The European Court of Justice in Luxembourg has also grown to prominence and power as European integration has developed. The court was founded to adjudicate claims and conflicts among EU governments as well as between those governments and the new institutions the EU created. The court interprets EU law for national courts, rules on legal questions that arise within the EU's institutions, and decides cases concerning individual citizens. The fact that its decisions are binding distinguishes the European Court of Justice from most other international tribunals.

EU Decision-Making Challenges   Disagreement persists over the extent to which the EU should become a single, truly united superstate, a "United States of Europe." Debate continues also over how far and how fast such a process toward **pooled sovereignty** should proceed, and several efforts to further integrate the countries of Europe have met with resistance—the Danes rejected the Maastricht Treaty in 1992, the Irish rejected the Nice Treaty in 2001, and the French and Dutch rejected the EU Constitution in 2005. In 2009, the Lisbon Treaty entered into force. Ostensibly the treaty serves to make the EU more democratic in nature, in that it increases the budgetary power of the European Parliament.

European Commission
The executive organ administratively responsible for the European Union.

pooled sovereignty
Legal authority granted to an IGO by its members to make collective decisions regarding specified aspects of public policy heretofore made exclusively by each sovereign government.

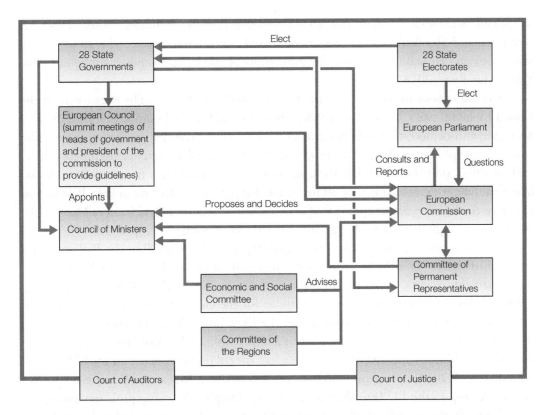

FIGURE 6.3 **The Evolutionary Development of the European Union's Governmental Structure** The EU is a complex organization, with different responsibilities performed by various units. The figure illustrates the principal institutions and the relationships among them that collectively lead to EU decisions and policies.

Given the implications for national sovereignty, it is hardly surprising that EU governance does not escape controversy. As membership increases and the areas of policy coordination continue to expand, so too do the possible areas for contention. Though the EU "has sometimes given the impression of being in perpetual crisis," one journalist noted that now it "is in deeper trouble than ever" (Peet, 2017).

This is due to several related factors. Structurally, as membership has expanded so too have the gaps between these countries in terms of incomes and overall levels of development. Given the redistributive nature of much of the EU budget, this has created a degree of resentment in the wealthier members. Moreover, migration into Europe has skyrocketed since 2010. As of the end of 2016, almost 5.2 million refugees and migrants reached Europe, fleeing conflicts in Syria, Libya, Afghanistan, and Iraq, as well as poor economic conditions in Sub-Saharan Africa (UNHCR, 2019). In addition to placing great stress on countries that were the initial points for the influx of refugees, such as Greece and Italy, these refugee flows created political difficulties, as the Schengen system of open borders among EU members proved unpopular to countries seeking to control their own borders (see Chapter 12).

The backlash to immigration increased the popularity of populist parties that take nationalist stances against both immigration and the EU in general in several European states. More worryingly, the election of right-wing populist governments in several countries has led to democratic backsliding – indeed one study found that four EU members (Poland, Hungary, Lithuania, and Slovakia) were no longer considered "liberal democracies" due to increasing restrictions on personal liberties and the dismantling of checks on the power of the executive branch (Lindberg, 2018).

There are reasons to worry about the future viability of the EU. The Brexit vote in the United Kingdom (see Chapter 2) was a clear indication of British dissatisfaction with the EU. Moreover, anti-democratic trends in some member-states run counter to what some see as the greatest accomplishment of the EU, "the spread of stability and democracy across the continent" (Solana, 2006, p.4). The 2019 EU Parliamentary elections revealed a fragmented and polarized electorate, with increasing support for nationalist parties, particularly in Italy, Poland, and Hungary. At the same time, support for Green parties, which are pro-EU and call for it to be more active in fighting climate change, increased as well (Erlanger and Specia, 2019).

Yet there is also reason for optimism regarding the EU. Regarding the Parliamentary elections, the gains to anti-EU parties were ultimately quite small; they won 25 percent of the Parliamentary seats, which was a gain from their previous level of 20 percent but hardly a wave of domination. Moreover, voter turnout for the election was at its highest level in 20 years, "a sign that political apathy about the EU's future hasn't become the prevailing force amongst the bloc's citizens yet" (Timsit and Bischof, 2019). More broadly, despite the increasing visibility of anti-EU parties and leaders, overall public support for the EU remains quite strong. A 2019 study showed that 61 percent of the European public were supportive of membership in the EU (Eurobarometer, 2019). Despite the many problems facing the EU, ultimately the idea of a single, integrated Europe may be compelling for those who are haunted by the specter of European nationalities and states that have been fighting each other since the Pax Romana collapsed 1800 years ago.

Other Regional IGOs

Since Europe's initial steps toward integration in the 1950s, hundreds of regional IGOs have been created in other parts of the world, notably among states in the Global South (see Chapter 5). Most seek to stimulate regional trade and economic growth (see Chapter 11), but many have expanded from that original single purpose to pursue multiple political and military purposes as well. As indicated in Table 6.1, which shows some of the major regional organizations, regional IGOs have proliferated throughout the world and vary greatly in terms of size and scope. The governments that create them usually concentrate on one or two major goals—such as liberalizing trade or promoting peace within the region—instead of attempting to address the complete range of issues that the members face.

The substantial difficulty most regions have experienced in pursuing the EU's level of institutional integration suggests the enormity of the obstacles to creating new political communities out of previously divided ones. The particular reasons why many regional IGOs sometimes fail and are often ineffective vary. It is not enough that two or more countries choose to interact cooperatively. Chances of political integration wane in the absence of geographical proximity, steady economic growth, similar political systems, supportive public opinion led by enthusiastic

TABLE 6.1   Major Regional Intergovernmental Organizations

Name	Inception	Membership	Purpose(s)
APEC (Asia Pacific Economic Cooperation)	1989	United States plus 21 members from the Asia-Pacific Area	Trade and economic ties
ASEAN (Association of Southeast Asian Nations)	1967	10 members from Southeast Asia	Economic and cultural development; regional security
CAEU (Council of Arab Economic Unity)	1964	18 members from the Middle East and North Africa	Trade, free movement of people and capital among members
CARICOM (Caribbean Community)	1973	15 members, 5 associate members, and 8 observers from the Caribbean region	Trade, coordinate foreign policy
ECOWAS (Economic Community of West African States)	1975	15 members from West Africa	Trade and economic ties; later expanded into security and governance
NATO (North Atlantic Treaty Organization)	1949	28 countries, primarily from Western Europe; also includes the United States and Japan	Military alliance
SADC (Southern African Development Community)	1992	15 members from southern Africa	Trade and economic ties; poverty alleviation; human security

leaders, cultural homogeneity, internal political stability, similar experiences in historical and internal social development, compatible economic systems with supportive business interests, a shared perception of a common external threat, bureaucratic compatibilities, and previous collaborative efforts (Deutsch et al., 1957).

At the root of the barriers is one bottom line: all IGOs are limited by national leaders' reluctance to make politically costly choices that would undermine their political support and their governments' sovereignty. Nonetheless, regional ventures in cooperation demonstrate that many states recognize the benefits of transnational cooperation and accept the fact that they cannot individually manage some of the problems that confront them collectively.

IGOs are not, however, the only nonstate actors leading the potential transformation of world politics. Another set of agents is nongovernmental organizations (NGOs). They include transnational humanitarian organizations, multinational corporations, transnational religious and ethnic groups, and global terrorist and criminal networks. Such NGOs are growing in number and becoming increasingly influential in world politics. Next we evaluate their behavior and global impact.

> *The world's 190-plus states now co-exist with a larger number of powerful non-sovereign and at least partly (and often largely) independent actors, ranging from corporations to non-government organizations (NGOs), from terrorist groups to drug cartels.... The near monopoly of power once enjoyed by sovereign entities is being eroded.*
>
> **—RICHARD N. HAASS, PRESIDENT, COUNCIL ON FOREIGN RELATIONS**

Prominent Types of Nongovernmental Organizations

LO 6-4   Identify and evaluate prominent types of nongovernmental organizations.

Increasing numbers of people have chosen to become international decision makers by electing to join one or more nongovernmental organizations (NGOs). These tens of thousands of activists are influencing the policies of state governments and intergovernmental organizations through a variety of strategies, including direct lobbying, protests, or coordinated strategies as part of transnational advocacy networks (Keck and Sikkink, 1999). As a result, NGO activism is transcending the traditional distinctions between what is local and what is global (Tarrow, 2006). To evaluate how NGOs are contributing to global changes, we examine four of the most visibly active categories of NGOs: **nonstate nations** (ethnic nationalities and indigenous peoples), transnational religious movements, multinational corporations, and issue-advocacy groups.

nonstate nations
National or ethnic groups struggling to obtain power and/or statehood

Nonstate Nations: Ethnic Groups and Indigenous Peoples

Realists often ask us to picture the all-powerful state as an autonomous leader of a unified nation—that is, as a *unitary actor*. But, in truth, that construction can be misleading. Few states, if any, are tightly unified and capable of acting as a single body with a common purpose, as most are divided internally and are highly penetrated from abroad.

Although the state unquestionably remains the most visible global actor, this overlooks the complexity of culture that often exists within a state (Reus-Smit, 2019) as **ethnic nationalism**—people's loyalty to and identification with a particular ethnic nationality group—reduces the relevance of theories that assume a unitary state. Many states are multiethnic and multicultural societies made up of a variety of politically active groups that seek representation, including the protection of group rights and a greater voice in state policies. In some cases, ethnic groups seek a greater level of local control if not outright independence. Although indigenous peoples are located within many of the world's pluralistic states, they also have a transnational dimension because they may be geographically spread across existing state boundaries (see Map 6.3). Individuals who think nationalistically are very likely to pledge their primary allegiance not to the state and the government that rules them but to a politically active ethnic group whose members identify with one another because they perceive themselves as bound together by kinship, language, and a common culture (Fukuyama, 2018a).

ethnic nationalism
Devotion to a cultural, ethnic, or linguistic community.

Ethnicity is socially constructed as members of an ethnic or racial group see themselves as members of that group and thereby perceive their identity as determined by their inherited membership at birth. That perception is reinforced when recognized by other ethnic groups. The presence of distinct ethnic groupings within states is quite common, as three-fourths of the world's larger countries are estimated to contain politically significant minorities.

ethnicity
Perceptions of likeness among members of a particular racial grouping leading them to prejudicially view other nationality groups as outsiders.

As they are often readily identifiable, ethnic groups are often subject to discrimination. Since 1998, 284 minority groups have been classified as "at risk" of persecution by the state in which

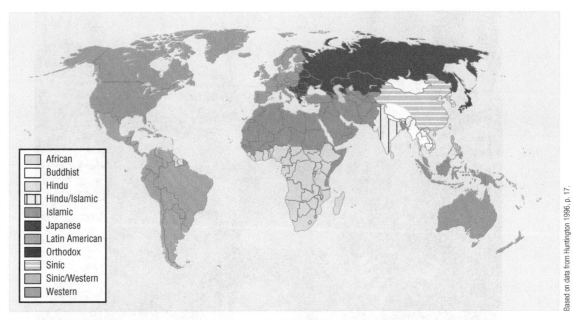

Based on data from Huntington 1996, p. 17.

MAP 6.3 The World's Major Civilizations: Will Their Clash Create Global Disorder? Beyond ethnicity, civilizations are "the broadest level of cultural identity people have" (Huntington, 1993, p. 24). This map shows the location of the world's major civilizations according to the much-debated "clash of civilizations" thesis of Samuel P. Huntington, who predicted that future patterns of conflict would fall along civilizational lines. That prediction proved rather prophetic on September 11, 2001, when the Al Qaeda terrorist network attacked the United States to vent the anger of its extremist Islamic members against the West.

Think It Through How has globalization affected our perception of differences in ethnic identities?

they reside (Minorities At Risk, 2009). For example, China has long been under intense international criticism for its crackdown on ethnic Tibetan groups following its annexing of their territory in 1962. Since then it has closely controlled the area and focused on "re-educating" Tibetans to purge them of their ethnic identity, a move that their spiritual leader the Dalai Lama commonly refers to as "cultural genocide." More recently, China has undertaken similar actions against the Uighur ethnic group in the Western part of the country, including increased monitoring, forced detentions, and "re-education" camps. Violent repression of ethnic groups, considered by some to be state terrorism (see Chapter 7), also occurs in other countries, as evidenced by the ongoing repression of the Kurds in Iraq and Turkey as well as the Rohingya in Myanmar.

Indigenous peoples are ethnic and cultural groups that were the original inhabitants to a particular area. In addition to their common ethnic identity, indigenous peoples often have a very profound bond with their native land. Today an estimated 370 million indigenous people, or about 5.2 percent of the world's population, are scattered in more than seventy countries (International Work Group for Indigenous Affairs, 2019). In most cases, indigenous people were at one time politically sovereign and economically self-sufficient but are now controlled by a state government.

IMAGE 6.4 Protecting Indigenous Peoples Indigenous groups have frequently seen their rights and welfare fall victim to a larger national interest in progress and development as determined by the state government. Pictured here, representatives of local indigenous communities demonstrate in Sao Paulo, Brazil, against the construction of the Belo Monte dam at the Xingu River in the Brazilian Amazon. President Jair Bolsonaro, "who has compared indigenous communities living in protected lands to animals in zoos, took a major step toward undermining the rights of indigenous people just hours after taking office" in January 2019 (Londoño, 2019).

The number of distinct nonstate nations is usually measured by the number of known spoken languages as language provides an ethnic and cultural identity (see Map 6.4). As Edward Sapir and Benjamin Lee Whorf hypothesized in the 1920s (i.e. Wharf, 1929), different languages reflect different views of the world that predispose their speakers toward divergent ways of thought. By this index, indigenous cultures are disappearing. "Some experts maintain that 90 percent of the world's languages will vanish or be replaced by dominant languages by the end of this century" (*Vital Signs*, 2006–2007, p. 112). What this means is that indigenous peoples are at risk, with high percentages of cultures nearing extinction.

Transnational Religious Movements

In addition to language, another basis for common identity is religious affiliation. Politically, societies throughout history have been ordered along religious lines; indeed, a large part of the significance of the Treaty of Westphalia is that it supplanted the church as the primary institution of societal order. While several states are still ruled by religious precepts, it is more common for religious groups to operate as NGOs.

Ideally, religion seems a natural force for global unity and harmony. Religious groups have historically been at the forefront of humanitarian aid and assistance, and continue to play a leading role in this area (Ferris, 2005). Moreover, religious NGOs are often involved in human

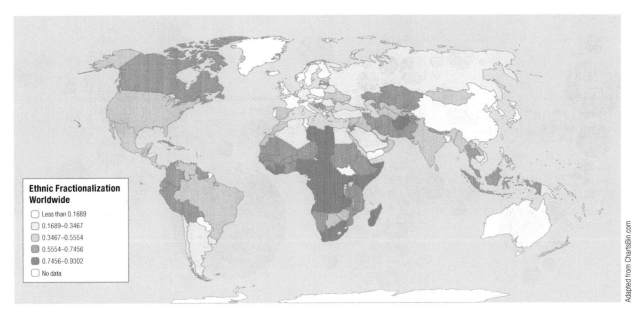

Ethnic Fractionalization Worldwide

- ☐ Less than 0.1689
- ☐ 0.1689–0.3467
- ☐ 0.3467–0.5554
- ☐ 0.5554–0.7456
- ☐ 0.7456–0.9302
- ☐ No data

MAP 6.4 Ethnolinguistic Divisions Differences in language often reflect differences in interests and attitudes. Where there is great diversity, state governments face a formidable challenge to reconcile these differences and generate common identity and goals—and "empirical cross-country studies suggest that linguistic fractionalization hurts economic performance" and quality of government (WDR, 2009, p. 104). As shown here, the diversity of ethnic language groups in Africa and South Asia is very high.

Think It Through In what ways do higher rates of diversity impact a country's politics–both negatively and positively? How are smaller ethnic groups within a given country viewed at the international level?

rights-related causes and "have long shaped discourses on human rights in the United Nations" (Butcher and Hallward, 2018). At the same time, history is replete with examples of religion and violence. The Crusades, which took place between the eleventh and fourteenth centuries, were justified by Pope Urban II in 1095 to combat Muslim aggression. The fighting left millions of Christians and Muslims dead and, "in terms of atrocities, the two sides were about even [as both religions embraced] an ideology in which fighting was an act of self-sanctification" (Riley-Smith, 1995). More recently, the Islamic State has become infamous for the atrocities it has committed within Iraq, Syria, and Libya in its quest to establish an Islamic nation-state (Houry, 2019).

Most of the world's almost 8 billion people are affiliated at some level with **transnational religious movements**. At the most abstract level, a religion is a system of thought shared by a group that provides its members with an object of devotion and a code of behavior by which they can ethically judge their actions. This definition points to commonalities across the great diversity of organized religions in the world, but the world's principal religions also vary greatly in the theological doctrines and beliefs they embrace.

They also differ widely in the geographical locations where they are most prevalent (see Figure 6.4), the extent to which they engage in political efforts to direct international affairs, and the number of adherents. Between 2010 and 2050, the percentage of the world population

transnational religious movements
A set of beliefs, practices, and ideas administered politically by religious organizations to promote the worship of their conception of a transcendent deity and its principles for conduct.

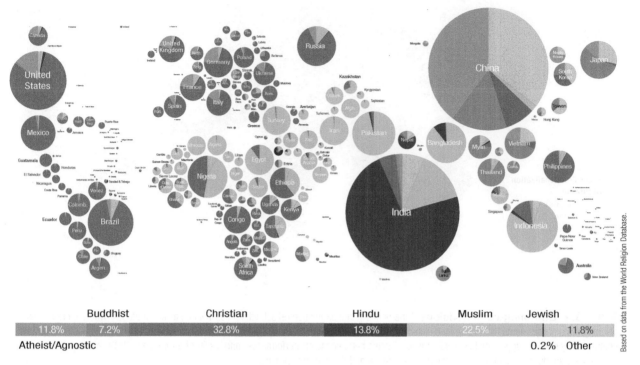

Based on data from the World Religion Database.

Buddhist	Christian	Hindu	Muslim	Jewish
11.8% 7.2%	32.8%	13.8%	22.5%	11.8%

Atheist/Agnostic   0.2% Other

FIGURE 6.4 Major Religions of the World This figure shows the world's religions and how they are distributed between and within countries (the size of the pie chart for each country is a function of population). Several patterns are apparent: Christianity and Islam are the two largest major religions, both in terms of percentage as well as geographic dispersion. The Western Hemisphere, Europe, and the Southern part of Africa are heavily Christian, while Islam is dominant within Northern Africa, the Middle East, and much of South Asia.

that is Buddhist is expected to decline from 7.1 percent to 5.2 percent. The percentage that is Hindu holds steady (15 percent), as do Jewish (0.2 percent), and Christian (31.4 percent) groups. Of all the major religious groups, only Islam is expected to have an increase in the percentage of the world population that are adherents, growing from 23.2 percent to 29.7 percent (PEW, 2019).

These differences make it risky to generalize about the impact of religious movements on world affairs (Haynes, 2004). To a large extent, religious groups function in a manner not unlike other NGOs, as they are subject to broader political pressures and employ the same strategies employed by secular NGOs (Dreier, 2018). Yet unlike secular groups, religious beliefs often provide followers with their main source of identity. This identification with and devotion to their religion springs from the natural human need to find a set of values with which to determine the meaning of life and the consequences of choices. This human need sometimes leads believers to perceive the values of their own religion as superior to those of others, which, sadly, often results in intolerance.

The proponents of most organized religious movements believe their religion should be universal—that is, accepted by everyone throughout the world. To confirm their faith in their religious movement's natural superiority, many organized religions actively proselytize to convert nonbelievers to their faith, engaging in evangelical campaigns to win over nonbelievers and followers of other religions. Conversion is usually achieved through missionary activities. The norm is that such missionary activities are accompanied by some type of assistance or aid, particularly within impoverished areas. Yet conversion has, at times, been achieved though the sword, which has tarnished the reputations of some international religious movements (see "Controversy: Are Religious Movements Causes of War or Sources of Transnational Harmony?").

In evaluating the impact of religious movements on international affairs, it is important to carefully distinguish between the high ideals of doctrines from the activities of the people who head these religious bodies. The two realms are not the same, and each can be judged fairly only against the standards they set for themselves. To condemn what large-scale religious movements sometimes do administratively when they abuse their own religion's principles does not mean that the principles themselves deserve condemnation. Consider the Hindu ideology of tolerance of different religions, which teaches that there are many paths to truth and accepts pluralism among diverse populations. Similarly, Buddhism preaches pacifism, as did early Christianity, which prohibited Christians from serving in the armies of the Roman Empire (later, by the fourth century, when church and state became allies, only Christians were allowed to join Roman military units).

The relationship between transnational religions and states' governments is a major issue in the global community. In most countries, the two realms are politically separate, with legal protection for freedom of religion and little or no state support for a particular established religion. In other countries, however, religion and state are tightly linked and almost indistinguishable. In such a country, termed a **theocracy**, the government is viewed as divinely guided, and religious doctrines permeate the legal system. Currently there are only seven countries that are formal theocracies: Vatican City (which has a population of less than 800), Yemen, Saudi Arabia, Sudan, Iran, Mauritania, and Afghanistan (World Population Review, 2019). As theocratic leaders often claim power in the name of their God, they are much more likely to view themselves as having unlimited power. In practice, this results in severe curtailing of individual liberties and human rights, particularly the rights of women. For example, in Saudi Arabia adult women are essentially treated as permanent legal minors, and must have the approval of their male "guardian" to get married or obtain passports. In some cases they need such approval to obtain work or medical care (Human Rights Watch, 2019).

The most troublesome aspect of religious groups as NGOs, however, are radical religious movements that are enraged, militant, and fanatically dedicated to promote their cause globally through violence and terror (Kifner, 2005). The leaders of extreme **militant religious movements** are convinced that those who do not share their convictions must be punished and that compromise is unacceptable. Underlying this perspective, radical religious movements hold some common beliefs and perceptions:

- They view existing government authority as corrupt and illegitimate because it is secular and not sufficiently rigorous in upholding religious authority or values.

- They attack the inability of government to address the domestic ills of society. In many cases, the religious movement substitutes itself for the government at the local level, involving itself in education, health, and other social welfare programs.

- They subscribe to a particular set of behaviors and opinions that they believe political authority must reflect, promote, and protect in all governmental and social activities.

theocracy
A country whose government is organized around a religious dogma.

militant religious movements
Politically active organizations based on strong religious convictions, whose members are fanatically devoted to the global promotion of their religious beliefs.

- They are universalists that, unlike ethnic movements, tend to see their views as part of the inheritance of every believer worldwide. This is commonly seen as a call to action and in some cases international boundaries are not recognized as barriers to the propagation of the faith, even if this means they must resort to violence.

Controversy

ARE RELIGIOUS MOVEMENTS CAUSES OF WAR OR SOURCES OF TRANSNATIONAL HARMONY?

After 9/11, the debate about the impact of religion on international conflict intensified because of the role the Islamic Al Qaeda global terrorist network played in organizing the attack. As a result, the religious roots of terrorism (Saiya and Scime, 2014) and opposition to democracy in the Global South (Shah, 2004) received much attention, as have religious bodies acting as NGO global actors.

Religious justifications for violence may seem counterintuitive because most religions place a high priority on peace, compassion, and forgiveness rather than hatred or intolerance. Calling on religious leaders to condemn extremists who use religion to justify violence, in 2014 Pope Francis said "To kill in the name of God is a grave sacrilege. To discriminate in the name of God is inhuman." The world's major religious movements voice respect and reverence for the sanctity of life and accept people as equal creations of a deity, regardless of race or color. These are noble ideals.

However, in practice the role of religious NGOs in international affairs is controversial. Some hold the view that religious hostility results from the fact that universalistic religions are managed by organizations that often adopt a particularistic and dogmatic outlook. The virtues that religions uphold can contribute to an ingroup/outgroup dynamic against those who do not hold such views. This constructed reality can inspire an ethic that justifies violence, plunder, and conquest, as followers may feel justified in treating "outsiders" differently. This was demonstrated by the Islamic State's appalling treatment of the Yazidi ethnoreligious group within their occupied territory in Iraq and Syria, in which

women and children were subject to brutal violence and enslavement (Sly, 2019).

Yet it is dangerous to accept stereotypes of religious groups as responsible for relentless barrages of terrorism. Paganistic and atheistic societies recognizing no higher deity have equally long histories of waging violent wars against external enemies and their own people. Moreover, political extremists can readily use religion as a convenient justification for violence and abuse, as reflected by Buddhist nationalists' use of religion to justify the repression of the Rohingya in Myanmar (Albert and Chatzky, 2018). Meanwhile, many religions ably perform the mission of peacemaking and humanitarian assistance (Gaetan, 2013), and in fact most religious bodies have historically coexisted peacefully for centuries. Thus it is important for you to objectively weigh the evidence about the impact of religious NGOs on world affairs.

What Do You Think?

1. If all the world's great religious movements espouse universalistic ideals, why are those same religions increasingly criticized as sources of international conflict—of exclusivism, hatred, terror, and war?

2. Given that many wars have been fought in the name of religion, how might realism view the impact of religious movements on world politics?

3. Which global actors are better suited to address the challenges posed to the global community by violent NGOs? Can states respond more effectively, or IGOs? Why?

- At the same time they are exclusionists in that they often exclude all conflicting opinions on appropriate political and social order. This translates as second-class citizenship–or even repression–for any nonbeliever (Shultz and Olson, 1994, pp. 9–10).

In sum, transnational religious movements not only bring people together but also divide them. Through globalization, religions are transforming social forces that create transnational communities of believers; immigration by adherents to religion brings more faiths into direct contact with one another and forges global networks that transcend borders (Beyer, 2013). Yet while religious groups often play a key role in encouraging peace or even providing humanitarian assistance, their beliefs can be used to divide countries and to justify violence.

Multinational Corporations

Multinational corporations (MNCs) are another major type of NGO. While they have existed for centuries, MNCs have grown dramatically in scope and influence with the globalization of the world political economy since World War II. As a result of their immense resources and power, MNCs have provoked both acceptance and animosity. As advocates of liberal free trade and active contributors to the globalization of world politics, MNCs receive both credit for the positive aspects of free trade and globalization and blame for their costs.

ANDREW MEDICHINI/AFP/Getty Images

IMAGE 6.5 **Papal Diplomacy** Religious leaders can often be important actors on the global stage. Pictured here, Pope Francis visits with Sheikh Mohamed bin Zayed, Crown Prince of Abu Dhabi, in 2019. It marked the first time that a pontiff had ever visited the Arabian Peninsula, a region dominated by Islam where religious freedom for other faiths is highly constrained. In addition to helping build relations with other faiths, the visit was seen as "a rare note of hope for Christians in the Middle East" (Walsh and Horowitz, 2019).

MNCs are influential NGOs because they are the primary agents of the globalization of production and labor (see Chapter 11). MNCs often provide economic opportunities that are not otherwise generated by domestic firms, thus countries within the Global South (as well as the Global North) actively compete for FDI. It is commonplace for countries, or even different regions within countries, to offer rich incentive packages to encourage an MNC to locate in their area (see Chapter 5).

At the same time, there has long been skepticism about the potential political power of MNCs. Part of this derives from their massive size. Table 6.2, which ranks firms by annual sales and states by GNI, provides some perspectives on this. The profile shows that of the world's top

TABLE 6.2   Countries and Corporations: A Ranking by Size of Economy and Revenues

Rank	Country/Corporation	GNI/Revenues (billions of dollars)
1	United States	19,235.4
2	China	12,042.9
3	Japan	4,883.2
4	Germany	3,613.1
5	United Kingdom	2,680.8
6	France	2,560.9
7	India	2,396.3
8	Italy	1,887.6
9	Brazil	1,803.0
10	Canada	1,570.6
11	Republic of Korea	1,460.5
12	Russia	1,354.4
13	Spain	1,265.1
14	Australia	1,263.5
15	Mexico	1,112.4
16	Indonesia	933.4
17	Turkey	883.1
18	Netherlands	803.6
19	Switzerland	685.6
20	Saudi Arabia	661.8
21	Argentina	576.6
22	Sweden	525.7
23	Wal-Mart	514.4
24	Poland	483.6
25	Belgium	478.6
26	Poland	483.6
27	Iran	441.0
28	Sinopec-China Petroleum	399.7
29	Thailand	410.5
30	Norway	401.9

TABLE 6.2   Countries and Corporations: A Ranking by Size of Economy
and Revenues (*continued*)

Rank	Country/Corporation	GNI/Revenues (billions of dollars)
31	Nigeria	400.7
32	Austria	399.0
33	Royal Dutch Shell	382.6
34	Philippines	383.5
35	United Arab Emirates	367.8
36	Hong Kong	342.3
37	Israel	326.3
38	PetroChina	322.8
39	Denmark	319.0
40	Pakistan	311.0
41	South Africa	308.0
42	Singapore	306.0
43	Malaysia	305.2
44	BP	299.1
45	Egypt	293.5
46	Colombia	289.1
47	Exxon Mobil	279.2
48	Volkswagen Group	278.2
49	Toyota Motor	272.1
50	Apple	261.7
51	Ireland	256.8
52	Berkshire Hathaway	247.8
53	Finland	246.5
54	Chile	245.8
55	Bangladesh	242.8
56	Samsung Electronics	221.5
57	Glencore International	219.8
58	Vietnam	206.7
59	Portugal	205.3
60	Greece	197.3
61	Romania	195.8
62	Peru	191.6
63	Czech Republic	190.3
64	New Zealand	185.9
65	Total	184.2
66	Iraq	177.3
67	Algeria	162.8
68	Qatar	159.7
69	Chevron	158.7
70	General Motors	147.0

Source: Gross National Income (GNI), World Bank, 2017 World Development Indicators; MNC revenues, *Forbes*.

thirty-five economic entities, multinationals account for only four. However, MNCs comprise twelve of the next thirty-five. Altogether, MNCs comprise almost 23 percent of the top seventy economic entities. Interestingly enough, the globalization of finance (see Chapter 10)—as indicated by the largest banks in the world—shows that the power of global firms goes beyond that of the MNCs alone. Indeed if banks were listed by the total size of their assets (which includes cash on hand, loans owed to the bank, as well as stocks, bonds, and derivatives owned by the bank), they would occupy the *top twelve* places on the table (Sanders, 2018). This further attests to the major role that firms can play as NGOs within the global system.

In part due to their global reach and economic power, MNC involvement in the domestic political affairs of local or host countries is controversial. In the Global South, this has sometimes taken nefarious forms, with firms being complicit in political violence or human rights abuses. For example, during the Cold War, two MNCs from the United States, the United Fruit Company and International Telephone and Telegraph, reportedly pressured their government to help overthrow regimes in Guatemala and Chile, respectively, that they viewed as harmful to their business interests (Kinzer, 2007; Chapman, 2014; Friedman, 2014). More recent cases of MNCs being either directly or indirectly involved in human rights abuses include Unocal's use of state-provided forced labor in Myanmar or Shell's alleged complicity in the abuses and killings of protesters in Nigeria (Lifsher, 2005; Amnesty International, 2017). Corporations have also come under fire for environmental disasters that occurred in their global subsidiaries, including the infamous Bhopal disaster at a Union Carbide plant in India that resulted in thousands of deaths in 1984 (Taylor, 2014) (see Chapter 14).

Due in no small part to the negative attention and corporate "shaming" generated by these abuses (Spar, 1999), MNCs are increasingly recognizing the importance of corporate social responsibility (CSR). The basic premise is that, contrary to the traditional view that "the social responsibility of business is to increase its profits" (Friedman, 1970), firms are more broadly accountable to the societies in which they operate. More specifically, they are responsible for the so-called triple bottom line—planet, people, and profit (Basham, 2016).

Thus, in addition to the traditional focus on profit, corporations need to be attentive to their environmental impact by either reducing their own pollution or taking steps to improve the environment. For example, Starbucks is providing a million coffee trees to farmers as a part of the Sustainable Coffee Challenge put forth by the environmental NGO Conservation International (Payseno, 2018). The "people" part of the triple bottom line refers to increased attention to human rights and human development. Examples of this include Nike's 2012 launch of girleffect.org, a widely-targeted effort to "get girls onto the global development agenda and to drive massive resources to them" (Nike, 2012), as well as the 5by20 initiative by Coca Cola that aims to empower five million female entrepreneurs in the company's supply chain by 2020 (Manuel, 2018).

On a broader scale, the UN Global Compact was created in 2000. As the world's largest corporate sustainability initiative, it asks signatories to adhere to ten principles, including respect for human rights, workplace-related rights, and enhanced environmental responsibility (United Nations, 2019). While firms enter into the UN Global Compact voluntarily, they are required to submit yearly statements regarding their efforts toward meeting these ten principles. As of 2019, almost 10,000 companies from 159 countries had joined, and over 62,000 reports had been filed. As UN Secretary-General Kofi Annan noted at the founding of the UN Global Compact, "You do not need to wait for governments to pass new laws....You can and should act now, in your own self-interest. The sustainability of globalization is at stake" (quoted in Ruggie, 2017, p. 32).

It is easy to be cynical about such actions. Corporate interests may not always align with human rights or environmental responsibilities (Hafner-Burton and McNamara, 2019), and there are critics who view the compact as a "PR scheme" (Rohwer-Kahlmann, 2017) that corporations use to convince states that they do not need formal regulation. Indeed there are numerous instances of corporate "blue-washing" where firms engage in symbolic but empty efforts to meet the UN Global Compact requirements (Berliner and Prakash, 2015) and "greenwashing" where they similarly make disingenuous efforts to avoid criticism from environmental groups.

Arguably the most egregious example of greenwashing was the "clean diesel" campaign that Volkswagen ran to convince potential buyers that their diesel cars were low emissions vehicles. It turned out the "clean" claims were demonstrably false, as their cars were equipped with software that basically allowed it to mislead emissions tests. In reality, the "clean" diesels were emitting pollutants at up to 40 times more than the legal U.S. limit (Hotten, 2015). Deservedly, this was a disaster for the company, and as of 2019 they had paid over $30 billion in fines (MacDuffie and Zaring, 2019) and multiple executives, including a former CEO, were convicted and imprisoned (Porter, 2019).

Ultimately, as is the case with other NGOs, MNCs can have both positive and negative impact on the global system. While skepticism about MNCs remains, a case can certainly be made that MNCs are increasingly aware of their broader societal responsibilities and take actions to be good global citizens. As political scientist John Ruggie, who served as the UN Special Representative for Business and Human Rights, noted, within a few years "the global business and human rights agenda shifted from a highly polarized and stalemated debate to significant convergence" (Ruggie, 2013: xxi). Whatever the ultimate impact of MNCs, given their size and power they are major actors within the global economy. We now turn to a fourth type of NGOs, issue-advocacy groups.

Issue-Advocacy Groups

As citizens increasingly participate in NGOs to gain a voice in and influence over the institutions that shape the conditions in which they live, issue-advocacy group activity on the global stage has risen to unprecedented levels. "In its simplest form, issue advocacy is about three things: defining a problem (e.g., social, environmental, economic, etc.), identifying and advocating a specific solution, and motivating action" (Hannah, 2009). Greenpeace, Amnesty International, and Doctors Without Borders are just a few examples of nongovernmental issue-advocacy groups that actively seek to influence and change global conditions.

Issue-advocacy groups have had a transformative effect; indeed collectively, they "deliver billions of dollars' worth of social services around the world, pressure other 'global governors' to live up to their commitments, and attempt to reframe the basic values around which global politics might be organized" (Stroup and Wong, 2016, p. 142). They raise fundamental questions about power as they influence state and IGO policies despite their lack of any of the traditional characteristics of power. Issue-advocacy groups suggest that more complex dynamics underlie governance, as they interact with other NGOs (including participation in TANs), IGOs, and states to accomplish their policy agendas. Simply put, it is clear that issue-advocacy groups and the TANs in which they participate have an impact on global politics and have demonstratively contributed to the emergence of a global **civil society**.

As expected by liberalism, issue-advocacy groups derive their authority from various forms of soft power. States may delegate some measure of authority to such NGOs in areas such as delivering humanitarian assistance (Green, 2013). Given their specialized knowledge in particular issue areas, their expertise can be readily seen as a resource for policy insights and ideas. Issue-advocacy groups may also derive authority from being viewed as having the moral "high ground" on an issue, thus their claims and demands may be broadly perceived as legitimate and just (Murdie, 2014). Along constructivist lines, issue-advocacy NGOs and TANs are seen as a common way through which norms are created and transmitted across international actors.

Issue-advocacy groups are very diverse, and have different characteristics, strategies, coalition-building behavior, and networks. There are cases where NGO advocacy efforts have failed to yield progress on a given issue—for instance, various efforts at ending female genital mutilation have met with both successes and failures (Cloward, 2016; Keck and Sikkink, 2014). Sometimes the causes of individual groups, while laudable, simply fail to attract a certain critical mass of attention necessary to enact change, such as caring for children born of wartime rapes or banning thermobaric weapons (Carpenter, 2011; 2009).

civil society
A community that embraces shared norms and ethical standards to collectively manage problems without coercion and through peaceful and democratic procedures for decision making aimed at improving human welfare.

IMAGE 6.6 The Power of Fame In addition to working through NGOs, celebrities can also "function like freelance diplomats" (Avlon, 2011, p. 17). George Clooney has been involved in Sudan for more than a decade in efforts to combat genocide and torture, and worked to help the people of South Sudan achieve independence. Says Clooney, "Celebrity can help focus news media where they have abdicated their responsibility. We can't make policy, but we can 'encourage' politicians more than ever before" (as quoted in Avlon, 2011, p. 17). Pictured here, he speaks with people in a remote village in southern Sudan.

Yet there are numerous areas in which the involvement of issue-advocacy groups has influenced state and IGO policies, whether by influencing new policy initiatives or simply putting new concerns on the global agenda. Some more notable successes include the Mine Ban Treaty, the formation of the International Criminal Court, the protocol banning child soldiers, enhanced tobacco controls, reducing deforestation, and the convention banning cluster munitions (Kim, 2013; Haddad, 2013; Moyes and Nash, 2011; Rodrigues, 2005; Breen, 2003). Moreover, awareness campaigns—particularly "shaming" efforts—have been associated with significant consequences in world politics, such as sanctions and reduction of trade and FDI to offender states (Peterson et al., 2018; Murdie and Peksen, 2013; Barry et al., 2013).

NGOs can be effective agents of change that positively affect many facets of the human condition. Yet the strategies that NGOs take can also be effective for groups that seek to cause harm. As we next discuss, this is particularly the case with terrorist groups that use global networks and coalitions to achieve detrimental goals.

> *Even the weak become strong when they are united.*
>
> —FRIEDRICH SCHILLER, GERMAN PHILOSOPHER

Malevolent Nonstate Actors

LO 6-5   Identify and evaluate the threat posed by terrorist and transnational crime groups.

Are transnational terrorist organizations and global crime organizations correctly seen as a particular category of nonstate actors—as NGOs—on the global stage? Taking a broad conceptualization of NGOs as transnational nongovernmental associations of people, these groups can be seen as a virulent type of NGO. However, others argue that these organizations do not meet expectations for NGOs given their illegal activities and use of violence. No matter how we categorize these groups, they are clearly nonstate actors whose behaviors transcend national boundaries and pose a threat to global well-being (See Chapter 7). Terrorists "operate in the same manner as other non-state actors attempting to affect change in the international system. By exploiting the same technologies and power dynamics, terrorists show clearly that they cannot be discounted as unique and perverse political actors, but rather must be viewed contextually as part of a spectrum of international political action" (Asal et al., 2007, p. 34).

Transnational Terrorist Groups

Terrorism has plagued world politics for centuries and, according to historian Max Boot (2013), such irregular warfare is far older than conventional warfare. Some place the beginnings of terrorism in the first century BCE with the Sicarii Zealots, who violently targeted Jewish high priests whom they saw as collaborating with the Romans in violation of Jewish religious law. Yet terrorism today is arguably much different than in the past. Terrorism now is seen as (Institute for Economics and Peace, I 2014; Sageman, 2004):

terrorism
Premeditated violence perpetrated against noncombatant targets by subnational, transnational groups, or clandestine agents, usually intended to influence an audience.

- Orchestrated by subnational or transnational nonstate actors without state sanction, in ways and by means that erase the classic boundaries between terrorism and a declared war between states.

- Intentionally aimed at securing a religious, political, social, or economic goal, with the incident resulting from a conscious calculation by the perpetrator and falling outside the precepts of international law.

- Characterized by violence or the threat of violence, with an intention to coerce, intimidate, or convey a message to an audience beyond the immediate victims. Terrorists have shifted their tactics from theatrical violent acts to gain media attention to purposeful destruction of a target's property and civilian noncombatants—to destroy and kill for the purpose of instilling fear in as many people as possible.

- Global, in the sense that as new technology redefines limitations of distance, borders no longer serve as barriers to terrorism. Today many terrorist organizations plan their acts through unprecedented levels of communication and coordination across vast networks of terrorist cells.

The events of September 11, 2001, challenged the conventional view of terrorism as a rare and relatively remote threat. The horrors visited on the World Trade Center, the Pentagon, and the crash victims in Pennsylvania forced the world to confront a grim new reality: terrorists were capable of executing catastrophic attacks almost anywhere, even without an arsenal of sophisticated weapons. Not only did groups like Al Qaeda have global reach, but stealth, ingenuity, and meticulous planning could compensate for their lack of firepower. "America is full of fear," proclaimed a jubilant Osama bin Laden. "Nobody in the United States will feel safe."

What arguably made 9/11 a symbolic watershed was that it epitomized a deadly new strain of terrorism. Previously, terrorism was regarded as political theater, a frightening drama where the perpetrators wanted a lot of people watching, not a lot of people dead. Now there seems to be a desire to kill as many people as possible. Driven by searing hatred, annihilating enemies appears more important to global terrorists than winning sympathy for their cause.

IMAGE 6.7 A Terrorist Mastermind Osama Bin Laden, the head of Al Qaeda who was behind the September 11, 2001, terrorist attacks on the United States, was killed by U.S. forces on May 1, 2011. A decade after those atrocious attacks, Americans celebrated as President Obama declared "justice is done."

Universal Images Group/Getty Images

Table 6.3 identifies some of the known terrorist NGOs. As you can see, the primary goals of the various groups are diverse. Some, such as ETA, focus on secular nonreligious objectives such as ethnic self-determination or overthrow of a government. Others, most notably Al Qaeda, Boko Haram, and the self-proclaimed Islamic State, are driven by religious convictions and have more sweeping goals. There is also variation in the manner in which their organizations are structured, with some having a hierarchical structure and newer groups tending to favor networked insulated cells dispersed across the globe. Instead of having a hierarchical command structure, for example, Al Qaeda possesses a decentralized horizontal structure. Although the leadership offers ideological inspiration to small, disparate cells scattered around the world, leaders do not directly plan and execute most of the attacks undertaken in Al Qaeda's name.

What makes the newer breed of terrorists who belong to organizations such as Al Qaeda and the Islamic State more lethal than previous terrorists is their religious fanaticism, which allows them to envision acts of terror on two levels. At one level, terrorism is a means to

TABLE 6.3   Some Terrorist NGOs: Primary Location and Goals

Name	Primary Location	Goal
Al Qaeda	A global network with cells in a number of countries and tied to Sunni extremist networks; heavy concentration in Afghanistan, the border region in Pakistan, Somalia, and Yemen	To establish pan-Islamic rule throughout the world by working with allied Islamic extremist groups to overthrow regimes it deems "non-Islamic" and expel Westerners and non-Muslims from Muslim countries
Boko Haram	Primarily Nigeria, but also active in Chad, Cameroon, and Niger	To establish an Islamic state in Nigeria and oppose westernization
Islamic State (IS)/ Islamic State in Iraq and Syria (ISIS)/ Islamic State in Iraq and the Levant (ISIL)	Formerly in Iraq and Syria; with the loss of its territory, now mostly in sleeper cells	To expand its influence beyond Iraq and Syria and establish an Islamic state across Middle Eastern and African countries
Revolutionary Armed Forces of Colombia (FARC)	Colombia, with some activities in Venezuela, Panama, and Ecuador	To replace the current government with a Marxist regime. In 2016, a peace accord went into effect, with the subsequent UN-monitored demobilization of 11,000 FARC though some dissidents remain
Hezbollah	In the Bekaa Valley, the southern suburbs of Beirut, and southern Lebanon; established cells in Europe, Africa, South America, North America, and Asia	To increase its political power in Lebanon, and opposing Israel and the Middle East peace negotiations
Hamas	Primarily the occupied territories, Israel	To establish an Islamic Palestinian state in place of Israel and gain international acceptance of its rule in Gaza
Basque Fatherland and Liberty (ETA)	Primarily in the Basque autonomous regions of northern Spain and south-western France	To establish an independent homeland based on Marxist principles in the Basque autonomous regions
Real Irish Republican Army (RIRA)	Northern Ireland, Ireland, and the United Kingdom	To create a united Irish state that includes Northern Ireland and Ireland
Liberation Tigers of Tamil Eelam	Sri Lanka	To establish an independent Tamil state. On May 19, 2009, the Sri Lankan government declared an end to the twenty-five-year civil war and a defeat of what had been characterized as the fiercest terrorist force in the world
Sendero Luminoso (Shining Path)	Peru	To destroy existing Peruvian institutions and replace them with a communist peasant revolutionary regime

change the political status quo by punishing those culpable for perceived wrongs. At another level, terrorism is an end in itself, a sacrament performed for its own sake in an eschatological confrontation between good and evil. Functioning only on the first level, most secular terrorist groups employ suicide missions less frequently. Operating on both levels, religious terrorist groups see worldly gain as well as transcendent importance in a martyr's death (Bloom, 2005; Pape, 2003).

Terrorist organizations are largely dominated by men. However, "the number of women implicated in terrorism-related crimes is growing: In 2017, the Global Extremism Monitor registered 100 distinct suicide attacks conducted by 181 female militants, constituting 11 percent of all incidents that year" (Vogelstein and Bigio, 2019). Women are often subjugated and abused by terrorist groups, yet they also advance extremist ideology online, indoctrinate their families, and serve as martyrs. Security personnel tend to target male operatives, and if they "avoid invasively searching women for fear of outraging the local population (based on social norms of women's modesty and the honor code), women are the ideal stealth operatives. If security personnel are too aggressive in searching women, they aid terrorist recruitment by outraging the men in that society and providing the terrorists with propaganda that 'our women' are being violated" (Bloom, 2017).

Though terrorists are popularly portrayed as "madmen" bent on death and destruction, terrorism expert Robert Pape (2003, p. 344) has noted that even "suicide terrorism follows a strategic logic. Even if many suicide attackers are irrational or fanatical, the leadership groups that recruit and direct them are not." Take care to consider how your value judgments can affect your interpretation of the identity and purpose of any group you may believe belongs in this menacing category of nonstate actors. The cliché "one person's terrorist is another person's freedom fighter" springs from the hold of prior and subjective perceptions on many people's definitions of objective realities.

Transnational Crime Organizations

Like terrorist groups, transnational crime groups pose a serious challenge to global security in the twenty-first century and are expected to continue to proliferate because, as Director of the Terrorism, Transnational Crime and Corruption Center Louise Shelly explains, "these crime groups are major beneficiaries of globalization. They take advantage of increased travel, trade, rapid money movements, telecommunications and computer links, and are well positioned for growth."

In general, these groups generate revenue by participating in illicit markets, such as those involving illicit drugs, weapons, human trafficking, and money laundering (see Figure 6.5). Other illegal markets include identity theft, piracy, organ trafficking, nuclear material, and endangered species. However, there are also large illicit markets for goods that are typically considered as legal but may be smuggled to avoid taxation, regulation, tariffs, or sanctions. Illegal markets thus exist for a broad array of legal goods, including caviar, cigarettes, garlic, and even maple syrup (Glenny, 2008; Gomis and Botero, 2016; BBC, 2013; Hamilton, 2013).

Transnational criminal organizations vary in terms of their size, organizational structure, and methods. For example, drug trafficking organizations tend to be male-dominated. They run vertically-integrated businesses in which they are responsible for their products at various stages of distribution and frequently commit violence, both against rival organizations as well as the state (Saviano, 2016; Glenny, 2008). By way of comparison, human trafficking often is accomplished

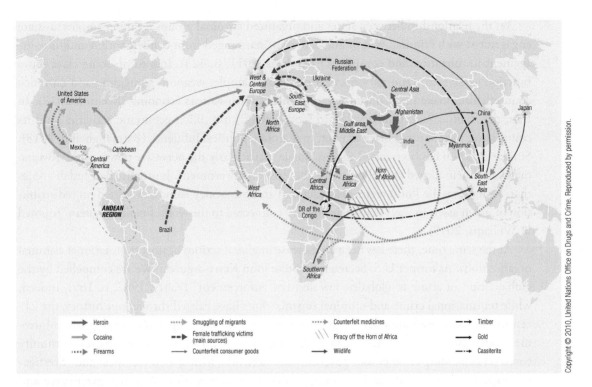

MAP 6.5 Major Global Crime Flows To a certain extent the determinants of illegal markets are not unlike those of their legal counterparts, as products—drugs, weapons, or people—tend to follow demand. According to the UN Office on Drugs and Crime (2010a, p. 3), "Future trends are likely to be affected by global shifts in demographics, migration, urbanization, conflict and economics." It is therefore critical that the international community better understand the way that transnational crime relates to broader social changes.

 What appear to be primary destinations of global crime flows? What do these destinations tend to have in common?

by small groups that operate in a network. In this case the industry structure is decentralized, as a large number of small operators are responsible for specific aspects of the "supply chain" of recruiting, transporting, and employing trafficking victims (see Chapter 13). Moreover, females are well-represented as traffickers—in 2016 over a third of convicted traffickers were women (UN, 2018). While the business is extremely violent toward trafficking victims, violence between trafficking groups is quite rare (Shelley, 2009).

International criminal activity poses a threat to states, including their economies and political authority. Growth in illicit economies may undermine growth in legitimate business activities, particularly in emerging states that are vulnerable to internationally organized crime. Internationally organized crime groups also take a toll on domestic state institutions (Zartner, 2010). According to the U.S. government's National Institute of Justice (2012):

> Transnational crime ring activities weaken economies and financial systems and undermine democracy. These networks often prey on governments that are not powerful enough to oppose them, prospering on illegal activities, such as drug trafficking, that bring them immense profits. In carrying out illegal activities, they upset the peace and stability of nations worldwide, often using bribery, violence, or terror to achieve their goals.

Yet the relationship between states and organized criminal groups is often complex, as state engagement with criminal groups and activities "has ranged from condemnation and discouragement to toleration and complicity" (Andreas, 2011, p. 423). Indeed, in some cases states function as de facto criminal organizations. For example, weapons smuggling and currency counterfeiting make up a substantial portion of North Korea's economy (Bechtol, 2018). In Iran, the Islamic Revolutionary Guard Core (IRGC) uses illicit economic activities, and its control over the country's black market, to maintain political influence (Batmanghelidj, 2018). Similar criticism has been raised against Russia, particularly the pervasive power of the Russian mafia and their alleged complicity with the Russian government. Journalist Ben Judah argues that "At its core, the Putin regime is structured around money laundering based on redistribution of stolen assets in ways that are intimately connected to the world financial system" (quoted in Williams, 2019).

At the same time, there has been an increase in global actions against transnational criminal organizations. As former U.S. Secretary of State John Kerry argued, "We are compelled by the globalization of crime to globalize law and law enforcement" (Kerry, 1997, p. 169). Indeed, while transnational crime and criminal organizations have existed throughout history, the 21st century has witnessed unprecedented efforts at transnational cooperation among law enforcement officials. As a whole, the emergent "transnational criminal law enforcement community based on expanding cross-border governmental networks with shared technical and investigative expertise has become an increasingly important…dimension of global governance and transgovernmental relations" (Andreas and Nadelmann, 2008, p. 9).

At the global level, the United Nations' Office on Drugs and Crime (UNODC) provides standards for harmonizing laws and procedures in such areas as transnational kidnappings, border management, and control of shipping containers. It also provides guidance for the sharing of intelligence related to criminal activities (UN, 2019). The International Criminal Police Organization, commonly referred to as Interpol, has virtually universal membership (194 states). Its primary functions are to offer a common communications network between law enforcement agencies as well as intelligence and investigatory support, particularly in the areas of counter-terrorism, organized crime, and cybercrime. There are also more specialized IGOs that deal with specific areas of criminal activity, such as the Financial Action Task Force (FATF) that deals with money laundering and the World Customs Organization (WCO) that works in areas related to commerce, such as counterfeiting and the illegal weapons trade. There are several regional bodies, including Europol (European Union Agency for Law Enforcement Cooperation), ASEANPOL, AFRIPOL, and the Arab Interior Minister's Council (AIMC).

The United States has been a driving force behind this global response, and it has pushed for both the homogenization of laws—particularly those related to drug trafficking and terrorism—as well as the establishment of cooperative initiatives and organizations. Arguably, "international crime control is one of the most important—and one of the most overlooked—dimensions of U.S. hegemony in world politics" (Andreas and Nadelmann, 2008, p. 10).

As the world grows more interdependent and transactions across state borders increase through the movement of people, information, and traded products, it is likely that world politics will be increasingly affected by the activities of both IGO and NGO nonstate actors. Many work to improve the human condition, but nonstate actors such as terrorists and transnational crime organizations prey on the vulnerabilities and misfortunes of others. Global cooperation is necessary if we are to successfully counter this "dark side" of globalization. Otherwise, the efforts by states and other organizations to fight terrorism and international crime will result in merely displacing the problem from one country to another.

Nonstate Actors and the Future of World Politics

LO 6-6   Debate the implications of nonstate actors for state sovereignty and world politics.

The growth and rising importance of nonstate actors suggests that global governance will become more complex and multifaceted, and continue to undermine the dominance sovereign states have exercised in determining the global system's architecture and rules since the 1648 Peace of Westphalia:

> The idea of sovereign equality reflected a conscious decision governments made 60 years ago that they would be better off if they repudiated the right to meddle in the internal affairs of others. That choice no longer makes sense. In an era of rapid globalization, internal developments in distant states affect our own well-being, even our security. That is what Sept. 11 taught us. Today respect for state sovereignty should be conditional on how states behave at home, not just abroad. Sovereignty carries with it a responsibility to protect citizens against mass violence and a duty to prevent internal developments that threaten others. We need to build an international order that reflects how states organize themselves internally (Daalder and Lindsay, 2004).

Are transnational nonstate actors truly capable of flexing their muscles in ways that can directly challenge states' sovereign control over both their foreign and domestic policies? Does this ultimately translate into more democratic and egalitarian governance, or are NGOs just bothersome interest groups whose impact only matters at the margins? Do they connote a significant weakening of the Westphalian state system (Kegley and Raymond, 2002)?

As you contemplate these questions, keep in mind one clear lesson: It is misleading to think that politics is only about territorial states in interaction with each other, exercising supreme authority within their own borders. The outlines of a future type of multilayer global system may be coming into view, driven simultaneously by the continuing importance of relations between states and by the growing impact of multiple cross-border transactions and channels of communication among nonstate actors.

Are the *liberal* and *constructivist* perspectives on the processes by which trends in world politics are set in motion correct? As nonstate actors "multiply the channels of access to the international system," are they "blurring the boundaries between a state's relations with its own nationals and the recourse both citizens and states have to the international system" (Keck and Sikkink, 2008, p. 222), and thus paving the path for a possible *transformation* of world politics? This change would lead to a hybrid world in which the clout and authority of the governments that rule countries become more diffuse as the relative power of nonstate actors rises.

That said, skeptics counter that nonstate actors have failed to become "a serious rival to the power and processes of the state"—their goals of transforming the dominant processes of policy making and corporate capitalism have not met with success (Price, 2003, p. 591). Indeed, it has been argued that IGOs and NGOs "have helped states retain—and in some instances even increase—their internal and external control, autonomy and legitimacy" (Weir, 2007, p. 618). Seen through *realist theory*, the critical choices that direct global destiny are ultimately made by the most powerful states.

These speculations by no means resolve the question of whether the era of state dominance is coming to an end as nonstate actors increase their clout. Relations between global actors, as well as broader developments in world politics, are the consequence of innumerable decisions made by states, transnational organizations, and individuals. In Part 3, we look more closely at issues that arise in confronting armed aggression. In Chapter 7, you have an opportunity to examine the global character and consequences of violent threats to security. In Chapters 8 and 9, we weigh the rival ideas presented by the realist road to security and the liberal path to peace. In addition, you are invited to consider the insights that alternative constructivist, Marxist, and feminist theories provide in grappling with the challenge of finding solutions to the grave threat of armed conflict.

Study. Apply. Analyze.

Chapter Summary

6-1 Distinguish between intergovernmental and nongovernmental international organizations. Intergovernmental international organizations, or IGOs, are organizations made up of states, while nongovernmental international organizations, or NGOs, are nonstate actors. Both types of organizations serve to aid their members and solve international problems.

6-2 Describe the structure and key functions of the UN and the Bretton Woods institutions. The UN is arguably the most influential IGO in existence today, as it has universal membership and a broad mandate. It has six main governing branches and its functions include protecting global peace and security and addressing transnational problems. The Bretton Woods institutions—the WTO, World Bank, and IMF—maintain economic stability through the promotion of free trade, currency convertibility, and funding for development.

6-3 Describe the structure and key functions of the European Union (EU), and identify other major regional intergovernmental organizations. The European Union is an economic union—an entity with no barriers to trade, investment, or travel among members as well as a common currency—containing 28 European states. The executive functions are fulfilled by the Council of Ministers and European Commission. The European Parliament is its legislative branch, and there is also a Court of Justice. Other regional IGOs include APEC and ASEAN, among many others.

6-4 Identify and evaluate prominent types of nongovernmental organizations. Prominent types of NGOs include ethnic groups, indigenous peoples, religious groups, multinational corporations, and issue-advocacy groups. Ethnic groups and indigenous peoples have a common linguistic or cultural identity. Religious groups have a common object of devotion and code of behavior. MNCs own productive capital in multiple states, while issue-advocacy groups are mobilized around a given concern.

6-5 Identify and evaluate the threat posed by terrorist and transnational crime groups. Terrorists use violence to promote their ideals and spread fear, while transnational crime organizations aim to continue their illegal activities or businesses. Both groups undermine states' security.

6-6 Debate the implications of nonstate actors for state sovereignty and world politics. The increasing prevalence and power of nonstate actors further call into question the state-centric view of world politics, as they suggest that multiple actors at multiple levels influence global governance.

Key Terms

civil society
diasporas
ethnicity
ethnic nationalism
European Commission

European Union (EU)
globally integrated enterprises
militant religious movements
nonstate nations
political integration

pooled sovereignty
regimes
responsible sovereignty
security community
terrorism

theocracy
transnational religious
   movements

Suggested Readings and Resources

Blogs of the European Commissioners: blogs.ec.europa.eu. A website with access to the blogs of sixteen European Commissioners.

Business and Human Rights Resource Centre: business-humanrights.org. Comprehensive resource of news regarding human rights activities of firms, both positive and negative, as well as firm responses to any human-rights related accusations.

Drozdiak, William. (2017). *Fractured Continent: Europe's Crises and the Fate of the West.* WW Norton & Company.

Keck, Margaret, & Sikkink, Kathryn. (2014). *Activists beyond borders: Advocacy networks in international politics.* Cornell University Press.

Mingst, Karen, Margaret Karns, & Alynna Lyon (2018). *The United Nations in the 21st century.* Routledge.

NGO Performance: ngoperformance.org/blog/. A blog on NGOs and various aspects of their performance in global issues.

Patheos: World Religions: patheos.com/blogs/worldreligions/. A blog discussing all world religions and their cultures.

United Nations Blog: blogs.un.org/#sthash.DDAnRFFA.dpbs. Updates on international affairs provided by the United Nations.

Carnegie Council Videos

Key Term Videos

- Responsible Sovereignty
- European Union
- Political Integration
- Nonstate Nations
- Ethnic Group
- Theocracy
- Terrorism

Additional Videos

- Bosco, David L. *"Five to Rule Them All: The UN Security Council and the Making of the Modern World."*
- Brown, Mark Malloch. *"The Unfinished Global Revolution: The Pursuit of a New International Politics."*
- Shanbaum, Elena. *"International Humanitarian Law and Non-State Actors."*
- Sorensen, Gillian, van Puyenbroeck, Robin. *"Facing the Crises of Our Time: The United Nations and the United States in the 21st Century."*
- Vocke, William. *"The EU and Serbia."*

Part 3
Confronting Armed Conflict

When you think about world politics, what is the first image that races to your mind? For many people, world politics is about arms, alliances, and the exercise of military force over rivals and other actors on the global stage. Indeed, this perspective is understandable: An attack by an enemy is the most dangerous direct threat to survival, and preventing such death and destruction is a precondition for attaining all other important values. Yet changes are required in the practices of state and nonstate actors if we are to control armed conflict and reduce its frequency and destructiveness.

In Part 3 of *World Politics*, you have the opportunity to explore many contending ideas and theoretical perspectives about how to best ameliorate armed conflict. Chapter 7 looks at the military threats to international security posed by wars between states, wars within states, and international terrorism. In Chapter 8, the pursuit of national interest defined in terms of military power is examined through the lens of realist approaches to national and international security. In Chapter 9, you will consider liberal ideas for managing international disputes that provide alternatives to fighting on the battlefield.

Stefano Mazzola/Awakening/Alamy Stock Photo

War and Its Alternatives

Placing high importance on power, realists emphasize the need to prepare for war and recommend that it be placed at the very top of a state's concerns. Liberals, and many constructivists, stress a path to peace that embodies progressive ideas and cooperative behavior. They have mobilized to exert pressure to contain arms races, warfare, and world poverty, among other causes. Shown here, demonstrators gather in Venice, Italy in 2018 to call for the nations of the world to seek nonviolent solutions to conflict.

Chapter 7

The Threat of Armed Conflict to the World

IMAGE 7.1 The Global Reach of Armed Conflict Though war between states is now rare, armed conflict within states and involving nonstate actors persists and poses tremendous human cost. Shown here, the Islamic State claimed responsibility for the attacks by jihadist terrorists in Sri Lanka in April 2019 that killed more than 250 people in a series of suicide bombings of hotels and churches. Despite having lost almost all the territory in Iraq and Syria where it had planned to build its caliphate, the Islamic State's goal of establishing a pure Islamic environment continues to attract followers, with radical family terror cells and women increasingly active as perpetrators.

Learning Objectives

LO 7-1 Use a levels-of-analysis approach to examine the causes of armed conflict.

LO 7-2 Describe and assess patterns in the occurrence of armed conflict.

LO 7-3 Discuss and evaluate the leading causes of intrastate conflict.

LO 7-4 Assess the implications of terrorism for the study and prevention of armed conflict.

LO 7-5 Evaluate the broader implications of armed conflict for the future of world politics.

Wars occur because people prepare for conflict, rather than for peace."
—TRYVE LIE, FORMER UN SECRETARY GENERAL

In the calm summer of 2001, complacency had taken hold in the generally peaceful Global North, where many thoughtful observers, noting the disappearance of interstate war among the economic giants, began to ask if war had become obsolete. That mood was shattered shortly thereafter on September 11, 2001, when international terrorists destroyed New York's World Trade Center. The 9/11 attack and the U.S. war in Afghanistan; terrorist attacks elsewhere around the world, such as in Madrid in 2004, London in 2005, Paris in 2015, and Sri Lanka in 2019; the U.S.-led military struggle in Iraq; the 2006 Israeli-Hezbollah War in Lebanon; and a wave of civil wars dashed all prior hopes for sustained peace. Although the 2011 popular protests and demonstrations across much of the Arab world raised hopes that democratization might take place, the violent clashes with state authorities and counterdemonstrators put such reforms in jeopardy and raised concerns about the ubiquity of violence.

Based on even these few events, it becomes understandable why so many people think that armed conflict is the essence of world politics. In *On War*, Prussian strategist Karl von Clausewitz advanced his famous dictum that war is merely an extension of diplomacy by other means, albeit an extreme form. This insight underscores the realist belief that **war** is a policy instrument that transnational actors use to resolve their conflicts. War, however, is the deadliest instrument of conflict resolution, and its onset usually means that persuasion and negotiations have failed.

In international relations, **conflict** regularly occurs when actors interact and disputes over incompatible interests arise. In and of itself, conflict is not necessarily threatening because war and conflict are different. Conflict may be seen as inevitable and occurs whenever two parties perceive differences between themselves and seek to resolve those differences to their own satisfaction. Some conflict results whenever people interact and may be generated by religious, ideological, ethnic, economic, political, or territorial issues; therefore, it should not be regarded as abnormal. Nor should we regard conflict as necessarily destructive. Conflict can promote social solidarity, creative thinking, learning, and communication—all factors critical to the resolution of disputes and the durability of cooperation. However, the costs of conflict do become threatening when the parties take up arms to settle perceived irreconcilable differences or to settle old scores. When that happens, violence occurs, and we enter the sphere of warfare.

This chapter presents information and ideas so you can explore the nature of **armed conflict** in your world—its causes, changing characteristics, and frequency. You will be forced to confront the ethical dilemmas that these military threats create—about when it is moral or immoral to take up arms. *World Politics* spotlights the three most frequent forms of armed conflict today: wars between states, wars within states, and terrorism. You will have the opportunity to review the leading theories that seek to explain the causes of these three types of armed conflict in world politics.

war
A condition arising within states (civil war) or between states (interstate war) when actors use violent means to destroy their opponents or coerce them into submission.

conflict
Discord often arising in international relations over perceived incompatibilities of interest.

armed conflict
Combat between the military forces of two or more states or groups.

> *To build may have to be the slow and laborious task of years. To destroy can be the thoughtless act of a single day.*
>
> **—SIR WINSTON CHURCHILL, BRITISH PRIME MINISTER**

What Causes Armed Conflict?

LO 7-1   Use a levels-of-analysis approach to examine the causes of armed conflict.

Throughout history, efforts have been made to explain why people engage in organized violence. Inventories of war's origins (see Cashman, 2014; Verwimp, Justino, and Bruck, 2009) generally agree that hostilities are rooted in multiple sources found at various *levels of analysis* (recall Chapters 1 and 3). Some causes directly influence the odds of war; others are remote and indirect, creating the context in which any one of a number of more proximate factors may trigger violence. The most commonly cited causes of armed conflict are customarily classified by three broad categories: aggressive traits tied to human nature and individual human behavior, detrimental national attributes that make some states likely to engage in armed conflict, and volatile conditions within the global system that encourage disputes to become militarized.

The Individual Level of Analysis: Human Nature

"At a fundamental level, conflict originates from individuals' behavior and their repeated interactions with their surroundings" (Verwimp, Justino, and Bruck, 2009, p. 307). In a sense, all wars originate from the decisions of the leaders of states or transnational nonstate actors such as terrorist organizations. Leaders' choices, and even their emotions, ultimately determine whether armed conflict will occur (Dolan, 2016; see also Chapter 3). "One would be hard-pressed to find examples of war that occurred without a command decision from the highest level of government authority" (Cashman, 2013, p. 50). So a good starting point for explaining why warfare occurs is to consider the relationship of armed conflict to the choices of individual leaders. For this level of analysis, questions about human nature are central.

The repeated outbreak of war has led some, such as psychiatrist Sigmund Freud, to conclude that aggression is an instinctive part of human nature that stems from humanity's genetic psychological programming. Identifying *Homo sapiens* as the deadliest species, ethologists (those who study animal behavior) such as Konrad Lorenz (1963) similarly argue that humans are one of the few species that practice **intraspecific aggression** (routine killing of their own kind), in comparison with most other species that practice **interspecific aggression** (killing only other species, except in the most unusual circumstances. Realist theorists likewise believe that all humans are born with an innate drive for power that they cannot avoid and that this instinct leads to competition and war. They, therefore, accept the sociological premise suggested by Charles Darwin's theories of evolution and natural selection. Life entails a struggle for survival of the fittest, and natural selection eliminates the traits that interfere with successful competition. To realists, **pacifism** is counterproductive because it is contrary to basic human nature, which they see as aggressive, greedy, and power-seeking. Additionally, by ruling out military action, pacifism rejects the primary realist policy instrument for ensuring state security.

Many question these theories on both empirical and logical grounds. If aggression is truly an inevitable impulse deriving from human nature, then why do not all humans exhibit this genetically determined behavior? Most people, at least outwardly, reject killing as evil based on certain ethical principles. In fact, at some fundamental genetic level, human beings are wired

intraspecific aggression
Killing members of one's own species.

interspecific aggression
Killing others that are not members of one's own species.

pacifism
The liberal idealist school of ethical thought that recognizes no conditions that justify the taking of another human's life, even when authorized by a head of state.

survival of the fittest
A realist concept derived from Charles Darwin's theory of evolution that advises that ruthless competition is ethically acceptable to survive, even if the actions violate moral commands not to kill.

to seek consensus, not conflict. As international theorist Francis Fukuyama argues: "people feel intensely uncomfortable if they live in a society that doesn't have moral rules" (Quoted in Rehak, 1999).

Liberal theory and behavioral social science research suggest that genetics fails to explain why individuals may be belligerent only at certain times. Social Darwinism's interpretation of the biological influences on human behavior can be countered by examining why people cooperate and act morally. As James Q. Wilson (1993, p. 23) argues, Darwinian **survival of the fittest** realist theory overlooks the fact that "the moral sense must have adaptive value; if it did not, natural selection would have worked against people who had such useless traits as sympathy, self-control, or a desire for fairness in favor of those with the opposite tendencies."

Although the **nature versus nurture** debate regarding the biological bases of aggression has not been resolved (McDermott, 2013; Kluger, 2007; Ridley, 2003), most social scientists now strongly disagree with the realist premise that because humans are essentially selfish, they are also aggressive—which then leads them to murder and kill. Instead, they interpret war as a learned cultural habit. Aggression is a propensity acquired early in life as a result of **socialization**. Therefore, aggression is a learned rather than a biologically determined behavior, and "violent human nature is a myth" (Murithi, 2004, pp. 28–32).

Individuals' willingness to sacrifice their lives in war out of a sense of duty to their leaders and country is one of history's puzzles. It appears as though this self-sacrifice stems from learned beliefs that some convictions are worth dying for, such as loyalty to one's own country. "It has been widely observed that soldiers fight—and noncombatants assent to war—not out of aggressiveness but obedience" (Caspary, 1993, p. 423). But this does not make human nature a cause of war, even if learned habits of obedience taught in military training are grounds for participation in aggression authorized by others, and even if at times the mass public's chauvinistic enthusiasm for aggression against foreign adversaries encourages leaders to start wars.

This suggests that factors other than **national character** (the inborn collective traits of particular peoples) may be better suited to explain why certain countries tend to engage in organized violence. Rather, armed conflict occurs most often as a result of the choices leaders make, and not because of the popular preferences of their entire societies. As English statesman Saint Thomas More (1478–1535) remarked, "The common people do not go to war of their own accord, but are driven to it by the madness of kings." Similarly, U.S. diplomat Ralph Bunche argued before the United Nations: "there are no warlike peoples—just warlike leaders."

This idea introduces an important analytic problem. Can the general characteristics of cultures and populations within countries predict the behaviors of the individuals within those groups? No. To generalize from the whole to the part is to commit a logical **ecological fallacy**. Why? Because, unless all members of the group are exactly alike, the characteristics of the collectivity (the entire state or culture, for example) cannot reliably predict the beliefs and behaviors of the individuals in that group.

Do all Americans think alike? All Muslims? All Chinese? Hardly. Such racial and cultural stereotyping is misleading. Rarely can we safely generalize from groups to individuals. However, the opposite, what logicians call the **individualistic fallacy**, is also a mental error. We cannot generalize safely about the beliefs or behavior of individual leaders (Angela Merkel of Germany,

nature versus nurture
The controversy over whether human behavior is determined more by the biological basis of "human nature" than it is nurtured by the environmental conditions that humans experience.

socialization
The processes by which people learn to accept the beliefs, values, and behaviors that prevail in a given society's culture.

national character
The collective characteristics ascribed to the people within a state.

ecological fallacy
The error of assuming that the attributes of an entire population—a culture, a country, or a civilization—are the same attributes and attitudes of each person within it.

individualistic fallacy
The logical error of assuming that an individual leader, who has legal authority to govern, represents the people and opinions of the population governed, so that all citizens are necessarily accountable for the vices and virtues (to be given blame or credit) of the leaders authorized to speak for them.

Xi Jinping of China, or Vladimir Putin of Russia) and ascribe them to the prevailing preferences of the collective cultures and states that each of them heads.

What should be obvious is that leaders do make some immoral foreign policy decisions. Moreover, many of those decisions by countries' leaders are the outcome of flawed decision-making processes; they fail to conform to the *rational choice* model of foreign policy decision making, which assumes that decision makers make choices through cool-headed cost–benefit calculations in order to select the option with the best chance of accomplishing preferred goals. In addition, even intelligent and moral leaders are sometimes prone to make unnecessarily high-risk decisions to wage war because they are pressured through *groupthink* by influential advisers rather than acting on what they personally believe to be the most rational choice.

This observation about the determinants of leaders' choices about war and peace directs attention to the domestic factors that encourage some states to engage in foreign aggression. These internal factors create the context that constrains or enables the policy decisions leaders can make.

The State Level of Analysis: Internal Characteristics

We next examine some theories about the internal characteristics of states that influence leaders' choices regarding the use of force. Implicit in this approach to explaining armed conflict at the *state level of analysis* is the assumption that differences in the types or characteristics of states determine whether they will engage in war. Arguing that the prospects for war are influenced most heavily by national attributes challenges the *structural realism* premise that war is inevitable and that global circumstances, not internal factors, are the most important determinants of warfare.

Geopolitical Factors and Length of Independence   Of all the issues that spark conflict, territorial disputes are the most likely to escalate to war (Wiegand, 2018; Vasquez, 2009). Indeed, when it comes to conflict between states, "two-thirds of dyadic disputes that escalate to war are over territory, less than one-fourth are dyadic disputes over policy, and a very small fraction involve regime disputes" (Cashman, 2014, p. 245). The setting and location of states—including key geographic circumstances, such as low supplies of cropland, fresh water, and treasured natural resources such as oil and gas reserves—and their distances from one another influence the likelihood of disputes and war (Caselli et al., 2015; Gibler, 2007; Starr, 2006). The amount of resources and the market price of those particular resources even influence the intensity of the conflict (van der Ploeg and Rohner, 2012). "When valuable natural resources are discovered in a particular region of a country, the people living in such localities suddenly have an economic incentive to succeed violently if necessary . . . [C]onflict is also more likely in countries that depend heavily on natural resources for their export earnings, in part because rebel groups can extort the gains from this trade to finance their operations" (Collier, 2003, p. 41).

Duration of independence also influences the likelihood of armed conflict and disputes over territory. Newly independent countries usually go through a period of political unrest following their acquisition of independence as sovereign members in the international community of states. They then are likely to seek to resolve long-standing internal grievances and take up arms over contested territories with their neighbors (Rasler and Thompson, 2006). Such foreign disputes frequently expand into larger wars because throughout history they have frequently provoked great power *intervention*, or external interference by other states or nonstate IGOs into the opposed countries' internal affairs. The high levels of **civil wars** and wars between neighboring states throughout the Global South may be explained by the fact that nearly all of these less developed countries have recently gained independence, many through violent revolutions.

civil wars
Wars between opposing groups within the same country or by rebels against the government.

Culture, Nationalism, and Identity Politics   A country's behavior is strongly influenced by the cultural and ethical traditions of its peoples. In the state system, governed by the rules championed by realism, moral constraints on the use of force do not command wide acceptance (Hensel, 2007). Instead, most governments encourage their populations to glorify the state and accept whatever decisions their leaders proclaim as necessary for national security, including warfare against adversaries. To feminists and other constructivist theorists who embrace a cultural interpretation, the penchant for warfare does not evolve in a vacuum but is an outcome of the ways in which societies shape their populations' beliefs and norms. Where cultural norms condone gender discrimination, inequality, and violence toward women, the probability of internal conflict and civil war is high (Hudson, 2012; Pankhurst, 2008).

Advocates of the cultural origins of war argue that when people "acquire an intense commitment to the power and prosperity of the state [and] this commitment is strengthened by national myths emphasizing the moral, physical, and political strength of the state and by individuals' feelings of powerlessness and their consequent tendency to seek their identity and fulfillment through the state, . . . nationalism contributes to war" (Levy, 1989, p. 271). This leads many to criticize *nationalism*, although others defend it as a virtue that creates unity and solidarity within a country.

Nationalism began as a serious force in Europe 350 years ago when monarchical rulers such as Ferdinand and Isabella of Spain engaged in "state building" by fomenting nationalism to mobilize and manage the population, which bred religious and political intolerance, the repression of minorities, and, ultimately, war (Marx, 2003). English essayist Aldous Huxley saw nationalism as "the religion of the twentieth century"—when history's most destructive interstate wars were fought. The linkage between nationalism and war has since grown over time, and "the likelihood of war more than doubles after nationalism has gained a foothold in a political arena" (Wimmer, 2013, p. 5; see also Woodwell, 2008). In East Asia, nationalism plays a role in fomenting hostilities between China and Japan over the disputed South China Sea (Dittmer, 2013).

Today, politics increasingly revolves "around assertions of identity. There has been a widespread populist revolt against globalization, based partly on its unequal economic consequences, but also on the threats to traditional national identities arising from high levels of migration" (Fukuyama, 2018b). **Identity politics** is on the rise in many regions around the world, with people embracing political positions based on their race, ethnicity, religion, or sexuality instead of broader policies. This is a departure from most of the 20th century, when division was largely over political and economic issues regarding the appropriate balance between the state intervening to promote equality versus allowing freedom for individuals and the private sector. Such developments, coupled with a weakening sense of shared national identity, can provide an environment ripe for internal discord and conflict. It also undergirds the trend in world politics

identity politics
The politics of focusing on specific interests and issues based on one's particular ethnic, racial, religious, cultural, sexual, or social identity rather than the concerns and interests of a broader political group.

Central Press/Getty Images

AP Images/U.S. Army

IMAGES 7.2A AND 7.2B Nationalism's Dark and Deadly Past Under the fascist dictatorship of Adolf Hitler (left), the Nazi government glorified the state and claimed that the German people were a superior race. What followed from this extreme form of nationalism was a ruthless German world war and campaign of genocide that exterminated 6 million Jews and other ethnic minorities. U.S. troops under the command of General George Patton (right) liberated the concentration camp at Buchenwald in May 1945, but not in time to save the lives of the prisoners whom the Nazi guards had put to death in the gas chambers.

toward populist nationalism, in which charismatic leaders claim a personal connection to the people, though often defining the group of interest in limited ethnic terms that exclude much of the population (Fukuyama, 2018a). Whatever its consequences, nationalism is a powerful political force in today's world, an idea and *ideology* that animates the constructed images of many around the world.

Poverty, Relative Deprivation, and Demographic Stress A country's level of economic development affects the probability of its involvement in war and armed revolution. Indeed, "underdevelopment is a statistically significant predictor of war" (Lemke, 2003, p. 58), and discontent with globalization and foreign economic liberalization can result in violent protest and civil war (Bussmann and Schneider, 2007).

relative deprivation
Inequality between the wealth and status of individuals and groups, and the outrage of those at the bottom about their perceived exploitation by those at the top.

Armed conflict, often an angry response to frustration, is a product of **relative deprivation**— people's perception that they are unfairly deprived of the wealth and status that they believe they deserve in comparison with more advantaged others. Underlying a great deal of internal armed conflict are people acting out "on their grievances over economic conditions—particularly when they perceive a discord between what they are receiving and what they know is attainable" (Weinberg and Bakker, 2014, p. 3). Violence erupts so frequently because hundreds of millions of people face discrimination or are disadvantaged in comparison to others in their country, with a form of cultural exclusion existing between groups. The same is true for national images of relative deprivation between countries. This is partially why the probability of armed conflict is the highest in the Global South, where people's expectations of what they deserve are rising more rapidly than their material rewards, and the existing gap in the distribution of wealth and opportunities is widening.

Popular support is critical to the success of armed rebellions, and poverty is a great motivator for allegiance to armed groups that promise security and an improved standard of living. Families "in conflict areas draw on local armed groups to protect their economic status when anticipating violence and . . . the poorer the household is at the start of the conflict, the higher is the probability of the household participating and supporting an armed group" (Justino, 2009, p. 315). Indeed, as poverty reduces the "mobilization costs" associated with any social movement, there are fewer disincentives to fight (Kuhn and Weidmann, 2013).

This relationship between poverty and armed conflict is all the more pronounced in countries where there is a **youth bulge**, where a large portion of the population is young and cannot secure jobs, provide for families, and achieve economic security. "Young men—out of school, out of work, and charged with hatred—are the lifeblood of deadly conflict. Countries with a high proportion of adults under thirty have two and a half times the probability of experiencing a new outbreak of civil conflict as do those more mature age structures relative to population size" (Cincotta and Engleman, 2004, p. 18). Furthermore, in countries where there is a pronounced youth bulge, governments are more likely to engage preemptively in coercive action to repress dissent and discontent (Nordås and Davenport, 2013).

So the near future faces an increasing threat—"a clash of generations"—as youth bulges increase the risk of internal armed conflict and political violence (Flückiger and Ludwig, 2018; Urdal, 2011). This will contribute to unrest in the Middle East as the youth unemployment rate continues to hover around 30 percent. Among the highest in the world for the past quarter-century (see Figure 7.1), this level of joblessness is a primary source of the anger that sparked

youth bulge
A burgeoning youth population, thought to make countries more prone to civil conflicts.

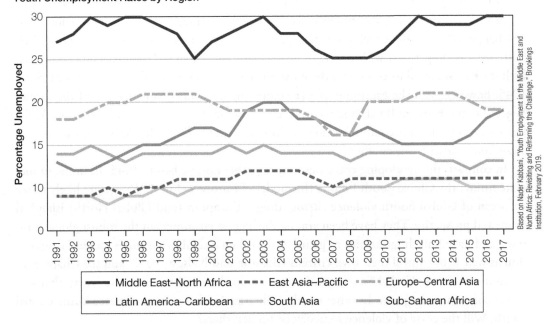

FIGURE 7.1 Unemployment and Unrest Youth in many Global South countries sometimes search for years before securing employment, and their future is grim. "This delayed transition to work affects other pathways to adulthood, including marriage, homeownership, and civic participation. This delay in transition to adulthood has been termed 'waithood,' a term reflecting the waste of youthful energy and potential" (Kabbani, 2019, p.1). As shown above, youth unemployment is particularly high in the Middle East and Africa, where countries are well above the world average of 13 percent.

the Arab Spring (Kabbani, 2019). Yet government policy and changing demographic trends have the potential to alter the outlook in the longer term. Providing education and concomitant employment opportunities might reduce the risk of political violence. Furthermore, the "importance of youth bulges in causing violence is expected to fade in most parts of the world over the next decades because of declining fertility" (Urdal, 2011, p. 9).

Before concluding that poverty always breeds armed conflict, note that the *most* impoverished countries have been the least prone to start wars. The poorest countries cannot vent their frustrations aggressively because they lack the military or economic resources to do so. This does not mean that the poorest countries are always peaceful. If the past is a guide to the future, the impoverished countries that develop economically will be the most likely to acquire arms and engage in future external wars. In particular, states are likely to initiate foreign wars *after* sustained periods of economic growth—that is, during periods of rising prosperity, when they can afford them (Cashman and Robinson, 2007). This signals looming dangers if the most rapidly growing Global South economies direct their growing resources toward armaments rather than investing in sustainable development.

Militarization "If you want peace, prepare for war," realism counsels. It is questionable whether the acquisition of military power leads to peace or to war, but most countries agree with the realists' thesis that weapons contribute to their security. Consider the relationship between changes in military capabilities and war that occurred over centuries in Europe. During the period leading to the peak of the region's development, the world's most frequent and deadly wars occurred in Europe. The major European states armed themselves heavily and were engaged in warfare about 65 percent of the time during the sixteenth and seventeenth centuries (Wright, 1942). Between 1816 and 1945, three-fifths of all interstate wars took place in Europe, with one erupting roughly every other year (Singer, 1991). Not coincidentally, this happened when the developing states of Europe were most energetically building their militaries in competition with one another. Perhaps consequently, the great powers—those with the largest armed forces—were the most involved in, and most often initiated, war. Since 1945, however, with the exception of war among the now-independent states of the former Yugoslavia and between Russia and Georgia, interstate war has not occurred in Europe. As the European countries moved up the ladder of economic and political development, they moved away from war with one another.

In contrast, the developing countries now resemble Europe before 1945. If, in the immediate future, the Global South follows the model of Europe before 1945, we are likely to see an ocean of Global South violence surrounding a European (and Global North) island of peace and prosperity. They have been among the biggest customers in the robust global arms trade and have built huge armies to guard against their neighboring states' potential aggression as well as to control their own citizens (Blanton and Nelson, 2012; and see Chapter 8). As countries in the Global South continue to equip their militaries, many worry that war will become more frequent. In other words, militarization has *not* led to peace in the Global South. Will the curse of violence someday be broken there?

Economic System Does the character of states' economic systems influence the frequency of warfare? The question has provoked controversy for centuries. Particularly since *Marxism* took root in Russia following the Bolshevik Revolution in 1917, communist theoreticians claimed that *capitalism* was the primary cause of imperialistic wars and colonialism. They were fond of quoting Vladimir Lenin's 1916 explanation of World War I as a war caused by imperialistic capitalists' efforts "to divert the attention of the laboring masses from the domestic political crisis" of collapsing incomes under capitalism.

According to the Marxist-Leninist analysis of *imperialism* (see Chapter 2), capitalism suffers from excess production. The need to export this excess provokes wars to capture and protect foreign markets. Thus, *laissez-faire economics*—based on the philosophical principle of free markets with little governmental regulation of the marketplace—rationalized militarism and imperialism for economic gain. Citing the demonstrable frequency with which wealthy capitalist societies militarily intervened on foreign soil for capital gain, Marxists believed, and generally still believe, that the best way to end international war was to end capitalism.

Contrary to Marxist theory, **commercial liberalism** contends that free-market systems promote peace, not war. Defenders of capitalism have long believed that free-market countries that practice free trade abroad are more pacific. They cite many reasons, but they center on the premise that commercial enterprises are natural lobbyists for an **economic peace** because

commercial liberalism
An economic theory advocating free markets and the removal of barriers to the flow of trade and capital as a locomotive for prosperity.

economic peace
The premise that economic institutions associated with a contract-intensive economy are the source of peace between countries.

IMAGE 7.3 Escalating Political Violence   What began as a pro-democracy movement in Yemen, fueled in large part by a perception of corruption as well as a lack of jobs and resources, has deteriorated into an intractable civil war. Rebels comprised largely of the Iran-allied Houthi movement forced the Western-backed Hadi government to flee the country. The neighboring Saudi government formed a coalition of Arab nations to halt the uprising. After three years of war, nearly 10,000 people have died and, according to the United Nations, there are "at least 8.4 million people at risk of starvation and 22.2 million people—75 percent of the population—in need of humanitarian assistance" (BBC News, 2018). Pictured here is a Saudi-led airstrike on Yemen's capital, Sanaa.

their profits depend on it (Mousseau, 2013). War interferes with trade, blocks profit, destroys property, causes inflation, consumes scarce resources, and necessitates big government, counterproductive regulation of business activity, and high taxes. Conflict within a country similarly reduces its international trade (Magee and Massoud, 2011). By extension, this reasoning continues, as government regulation of internal markets declines, prosperity increases and fewer wars will occur.

The evidence for these rival theories, not surprisingly, is mixed. Conclusions depend in part on perceptions regarding economic influences on international behavior because alternative perspectives focus on different dimensions of the linkage. This controversy was at the heart of the ideological debate between the East and the West during the Cold War, when the relative virtues and vices of two radically different economic systems—communism and capitalism—were uppermost in people's minds. The end of the Cold War did not end the historic debate about the link between economics and war. This basic theoretical question commands increasing interest, especially given the "shift in the relevance and usefulness of different power resources, with military power declining and economic power increasing in importance" (Huntington, 1991b, p. 5).

Regime Type   Realist theories discount the importance of government type as an influence on war and peace. Not so with liberalism. As noted in Chapter 2, *liberal theory* assigns great weight to the kinds of political institutions that states create to make policy decisions, and it predicts that the spread of "free" democratically ruled governments would promote peaceful interstate relations.

As Immanuel Kant (1795) argued, when citizens are given basic human rights such as choosing their leaders through ballots as well as civil liberties such as free speech and a free press, these democracies would be far less likely to initiate wars than would countries ruled by dictators and kings. This is because a government accountable to the people would be constrained from waging war by public opinion. Other liberal reformers have since agreed with Kant, such as Thomas Jefferson, James Madison, and Woodrow Wilson. They all believed that an "empire of liberty" (as Madison pictured a growing community of liberal democracies) would be one freed of the curse of war, and that if democratic institutions spread throughout the world, the entire past pattern of belligerent international relations would be replaced by a new pacific pattern.

Much research demonstrates that democracies resolve their differences with one another at the bargaining table rather than the battlefield, and that they are more likely to win wars than are nondemocracies. This pattern provides the cornerstone for the **democratic peace** proposition:

> Democracies are unlikely to engage in any kind of militarized disputes with each other or to let any such disputes escalate into war. They rarely even skirmish. Pairs of democratic states have been only one-eighth as likely as other kinds of states to threaten to use force against each other, and only one-tenth as likely actually to do so. . . . Democracies are more likely to employ "democratic" means of peaceful conflict resolution. They are readier to reciprocate each other's behavior, to accept third-party **mediation** or **good offices** in settling disputes, and to accept binding third-party **arbitration** and *adjudication* (Russett, 2001, p. 235; see also Russett, 2005).

democratic peace
The theory that although democratic states sometimes wage wars against nondemocratic states, they do not fight one another.

mediation
A conflict-resolution procedure in which a third party proposes a nonbinding solution to the disputants.

good offices
Third-party provision of a place for negotiation among disputants; but the third party does not serve as a mediator in the actual negotiations.

arbitration
A conflict-resolution procedure in which a third party makes a binding decision between disputants through a temporary ruling board created for that ruling.

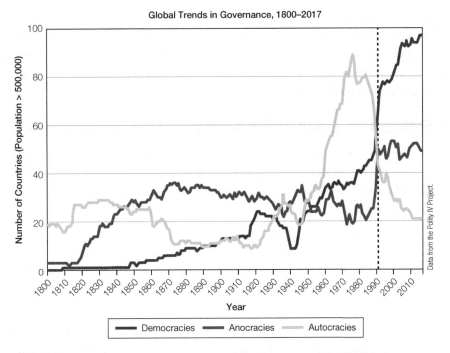

FIGURE 7.2 The Advance of Electoral Democracy, 1800–2017 In the 1800s, most choices about war were made by monarchs, despots, dictators, and autocrats. As this figure shows, that has changed with the growth of "electoral democracy" worldwide, with countries conducting competitive and regular multiparty elections openly and placing constraints on governing authority. The end of the Cold War saw a surge in democratization around the world. Since the early 2000s, however, the number of democracies has plateaued and even shown some signs of decline.

A considerable body of empirical evidence supports the proposition that democracies do not wage war against each other (Dafoe, Oneal, and Russett, 2013; Rasler and Thompson, 2005). Although there is debate about the specific causal mechanisms, it appears that the type of government, specifically multiparty elections, strongly influences foreign policy goals (Ungerer, 2012). Others point to an "us versus them" mentality that leads democracies to band together in the face of a common threat from autocracies (Gartzke and Weisiger, 2013). The democratic peace has also been attributed to a democratic state's "greater ability to more credibly reveal information" than other regime types (Lektzian and Souva, 2009, p. 35).

The impact of government type on propensity for armed conflict has taken on great significance following the conversion of many dictatorships to democratic rule (see Figure 7.2). Yet there is no certainty that liberal democracy will become universal or that democratic reforms will automatically produce a peaceful world order. There is some concern that the global trend toward democracy that began in the mid-1970s and accelerated following the end of the Cold War is experiencing a "global recession" with a decline in the total number of democratic countries (Fukuyama, 2018b; Diamond, 2015). Moreover, emerging democracies are prone to fight wars (Cederman et al., 2012; Mansfield and Snyder, 2005a), and the fact that leaders in elective democracies are accountable to public approval and electoral rejection does not guarantee that they will not use force to settle disputes with other democracies.

This discussion of the characteristics of states that influence their proclivity for war does not exhaust the subject. Many other potential causes internal to the state exist. Yet, however important domestic influences might be as a source of war, many believe that the nature of the *global system* is even more critical. In the next section, we discuss the global context within which actors decide whether to wage armed conflict.

The Systemic Level of Analysis: The Global System

Realism emphasizes that the roots of armed conflict rest in human nature. In contrast, *structural realism*, or *neorealism*, sees war springing from changes at the systemic level of analysis, that is, as a product of the decentralized character of the global system that requires sovereign states to rely on *self-help* for their security:

> Although different realist theories often generate conflicting predictions, they share a core of common assumptions: The key actors in world politics are sovereign states that act rationally to advance their security, power, and wealth in a conflictual international system that lacks a legitimate governmental authority to regulate conflicts or enforce agreements.
>
> For realists, wars can occur not only because some states prefer war to peace, but also because of unintended consequences of actions by those who prefer peace to war and are more interested in preserving their position than in enhancing it. Even defensively motivated efforts by states to provide for their own security through armaments, alliances, and deterrent threats are often perceived as threatening and lead to counteractions and conflict spirals that are difficult to reverse. This is the *security dilemma*—the possibility that a state's actions to provide for its security may result in a decrease in the security of all states, including itself (Levy, 1998, p. 145).

International *anarchy*, or the absence of institutions for global governance, may promote an outbreak of war. However, anarchy fails to provide a complete explanation of changes in the levels of war and peace over time or why particular wars are fought. To capture the many global determinants of armed conflict, also consider how and why global systems change. This requires exploring the impact of such global factors as the distribution of military capabilities, balances (and imbalances) of power, the number of alliances and international organizations, and the rules of international law. At issue is how the system's characteristics and institutions combine to influence changes in war's frequency. You can examine many of these factors in Chapters 8 and 9. Here we focus on cycles of war and peace at the global level.

Does Violence Breed Violence?   Many interpreters of world history have noted that the seeds of future wars are often found in past wars (see Walter, 2004). Renaissance moral philosopher Erasmus of Rotterdam once asked, "What can war beget except war? But good will begets goodwill, equity, equity." Similarly, in his acceptance speech of the 2002 Nobel Peace Prize, former U.S. President Jimmy Carter sadly observed that "violence only begets conditions that beget future violence." For example, World War II was an outgrowth of World War I, the U.S. attack of Iraq in 2003 was an extension of the 1990 Persian Gulf War, and the successive waves of violent protest and brutal state retaliation in the Middle East that began in 2011 were seen by many as a domino effect, with each armed conflict stimulated by its predecessor.

Because the frequency of past wars is correlated with the incidence of wars in later periods, war appears to be contagious and its future outbreaks inevitable. If so, then something within the dynamics of global politics—its anarchical nature, its weak legal system, its uneven

IMAGE 7.4 The Painful Legacy of Armed Conflict Armed struggles within countries occur more frequently than between states, though many intrastate conflicts still have repercussions for world politics more broadly. Pictured here, residents of the Pakistani district of Dir flee the fighting between Taliban militants and the government.

distribution of power, the inevitable destabilizing changes in the principal actors' relative power, or some combination of structural attributes—makes the global system that is centered on states a "war system."

However, it is not accurate to conclude that past wars *cause* later wars. Many scholars reject the deterministic view that history is destiny, with outcomes caused by previous events. Instead, they embrace the **bargaining model of war**, which sees war as a product of a rational choice that weighs anticipated costs against benefits. The decision to engage in warfare—as well as the decision to conclude it—is part of a cost–benefit analysis and bargaining process that occurs between adversaries to settle disputes and disagreements "over scarce goods, such as the placement of a border, the composition of a national government, or control over national resources" (Reiter, 2003, p. 27; see also Reiter, 2009).

War's recurrence throughout history does not necessarily mean we will always have it. War is not a universal institution; some societies have never known war and others have been immune to it for prolonged periods. Moreover, since 1945 the outbreak of armed aggression *between* states has greatly declined, despite the large increase in the number of independent countries. This indicates that armed conflict is not necessarily inevitable and that historical forces do not control people's freedom of choice or experiences.

Power Transitions These trends notwithstanding, when changes have occurred in the major states' military capabilities, war has often resulted. Although not inevitable, war has been likely whenever competitive states' power ratios (the differentials between their capabilities)

bargaining model of war An interpretation of war's onset as a choice by the initiator to bargain through aggression with an enemy in order to win on an issue or to obtain things of value, such as territory or oil.

have narrowed. As Monica Toft (2007, pp. 244–246) concludes, "Peace is clearly a value most states share, but not always, and not always above all other values. . . . Shifts in the distribution of power go a long way toward explaining the likelihood of violence."

power transition theory
The theory that war is likely when a dominant great power is threatened by the rapid growth of a rival's capabilities, which reduces the difference in their relative power.

This hypothesis is known as the **power transition theory**. This theoretical explanation of armed conflict is a central tenet of structural realism, which emphasizes that power distribution is a key determinant of the behavior of states. "According to variants of power transition theory, conflict is most likely when a rising power, dissatisfied with the status quo, approaches parity with the dominant state in a region or the system and is willing to use force to reshape the system's rules and institutions" (Fravel, 2010, p. 505). As Michelle Benson (2007, p. 211) explains, "this theory has proven itself to be the most successful structural theory of war [suggesting] that three simple conditions—power transition, relative power parity, and a dissimilarity of preferences for the status quo—are necessary for great power war."

During the transition from developing to developed status, emergent challengers can use force to achieve the recognition that their newly formed military muscles allow them. Conversely, established powers ruled by risk-acceptant leaders are often willing to employ force to put the brakes on their relative decline. Thus, when advancing and retreating states seek to cope with the changes in their relative power, war between the rising challenger(s) and the declining power(s) becomes especially likely (see Figure 7.3). For example, the rapid changes in the power and status that produced the division of Europe among seven great powers nearly equal in military strength are often (along with the alliances they nurtured) interpreted as the tinderbox from which World War I ignited.

Today, there is much speculation that a power transition is under way that will witness the decline of the United States and the ascendance of emerging non-Western powers, most notably China. "China has quickly strengthened its economic, technological and military power and as a consequence has started to threaten U.S. global hegemony. Accordingly, many scholars now often talk about a declining U.S. hegemony and a forthcoming Chinese hegemony" (Kim, 2019, p. 32; see also Mearsheimer, 2014). The Belt and Road Initiative (BRI) to promote global development through infrastructure projects and investment, the Asian Infrastructure Investment Bank (AIIB), and its "Made in China 2025" industrial development plan are examples of China's efforts that challenge U.S. dominance in the world.

Along with this, there is concern that there may also be a transition in the ideas and principles that underlie the existing global order—with commitment to democracy, free markets, and the acceptability of U.S. military power replaced by alternative illiberal constructions that present an authoritarian capitalist alternative. However, while a global diffusion of wealth and power is occurring, emerging powers are benefiting from the rules and institutions that

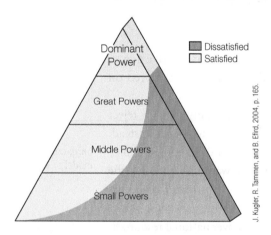

FIGURE 7.3 A Power Transition in the Global Hierarchy Where countries sit in the world pyramid of power predicts their posture toward global change. As this figure suggests, the more favorable a country's position is in the world hierarchy, the more satisfied it is with the international status quo; conversely, states lower in the hierarchy are more dissatisfied and therefore promote change. The power transition theory provides leverage for "anticipating when and where great power and regional wars most likely will occur. With a warning well ahead of time comes the opportunity to construct current policies that can manage the events that lead to future disputes" (Kugler, Tammen, and Efird, 2004, p. 165).

have been largely shaped by the United States and, to date, no viable alternatives have emerged to challenge the current construction of the existing international order.

Cyclical Theories   If war is recurrent but not inevitable, are there global factors other than power transitions that might explain changes over time in the outbreak of armed conflict? The absence of a clear trend in war's frequency since the late fifteenth century, and its periodic outbreak after intermittent stretches of peace, suggests that world history seesaws between long cycles of war and peace. This provides a third systemic explanation of war's onset.

Long-cycle theory seeks to explain the peaks and valleys in the frequency with which major wars have erupted periodically throughout modern history (see Chapter 4). Its advocates argue that cycles of world leadership and global war have existed over the past five centuries, with a "general war" erupting approximately once every century, although at irregular intervals (Ferguson, 2010; Wallerstein, 2005). As indicated by the possession of disproportionate sea power, a single hegemon has regularly arisen after hegemonic wars (see Figure 7.4). Portugal and the Netherlands rose at the beginning of the sixteenth and seventeenth centuries, respectively; Britain climbed to dominance at the beginning of both the eighteenth and nineteenth centuries; and the United States became a world leader at the end of World War II and regained its position of global supremacy after the Cold War ended in 1991. In 2019, a trade war between the United States and China began to escalate, with some speculating that it, along with China's military activity in the South China Sea, could signal a major turning point in the two countries' competition for hegemonic power and foreshadow a transition to a cycle characterized by Chinese hegemony. Now the question remains as to whether or not China's rise is sustainable and, if so, whether or not it signals a transition in yet another cycle of hegemonic dominance (Ogden, 2013; Doran, 2012).

FIGURE 7.4 The Long Cycle of Global Leadership and Global War, 1494–2020 Over the past 500 years, five great powers have risen to control the global system, but in time each former hegemonic leader's top status eventually slipped and a new rival surfaced and waged a global war in an effort to become the next global leader. The troubling question is whether this long cycle of war can be broken in the future when a rising military rival such as China eventually challenges U.S. leadership.

hegemonic stability theory
A body of theory that maintains that the establishment of hegemony for global dominance by a single great power is a necessary condition for global order in commercial transactions and international military security.

During their reigns, these hegemonic powers monopolized military power and trade and determined the system's rules. **Hegemonic stability theory** expects that a stable world order requires sustained global leadership by a single great power. By exercising its preponderance of power, the hegemon establishes the conditions necessary for order in the international system, and discourages aggressors who would challenge the global status quo.

Yet no previous hegemonic power has retained its top-dog position perpetually (see Table 4.1 in Chapter 4). "The best instituted governments," observed British political philosopher Henry St. John in 1738, "carry in them the seeds of their destruction: and, though they grow and improve for a time, they will soon tend visibly to their dissolution. Every hour they live is an hour the less that they have to live." In each cycle, overcommitments, the costs of empire, and ultimately the appearance of rivals have led to the delegitimation of the hegemon's authority and to the deconcentration of power globally. As challengers to the hegemon's rule grew in strength, a "global war" has erupted after a long period of peace in each century since 1400. At the conclusion of each previous general war, a new world leader emerged, and the cyclical process began anew.

> *Peace brings riches; riches bring pride; pride brings anger; anger brings war; war brings poverty; poverty brings humanity; humanity brings peace; peace, as I have said, brings riches, and so the world's affairs go round.*
>
> **—LUIGI DA PORTO, ITALIAN HISTORIAN**

Frequency and Types of Armed Conflict

LO 7-2 Describe and assess patterns in the occurrence of armed conflict.

You have now considered some of the major contending hypotheses and theories about the sources of armed conflict. In a world of seemingly constant change, a grim continuity stands out: violence—or, in the words of former UN Secretary-General Boutros Boutros-Ghali, a "culture of death." Indeed, the belief that "only the dead will see the end of war" is based on the fact that warfare has been an ugly, almost constant factor in a changing world. During the past 600 years, armed conflict has been continual, killing millions, creating hordes of refugees, and costing trillions of dollars, as well as untold human misery. In the relative short term (since 1950), the pattern has shifted to fewer, but more deadly, armed conflicts. These inventories reflect in different ways what the mass media tell us—that violence and global insecurity are inherent in world politics. Armed conflict in 2019 in Syria, Sudan, South Sudan, Yemen, and elsewhere—as well as the tension surrounding the South China Sea dispute—cast a dark shadow.

Figure 7.5 records the changes in both the number of conflicts over the past half-century as well as the type of conflict. In the past, when people thought about armed conflicts, they thought primarily about wars *between* states and secondarily about civil wars *within* existing sovereign states. Both types of wars were frequently under way at similar rates each year between 1816 and World War II. However, since then, internal wars have increasingly defined the global landscape.

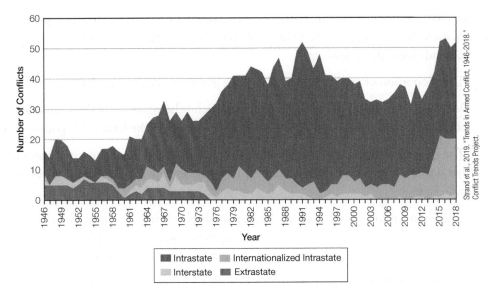

FIGURE 7.5 Changing Frequency and Type of Acts of Armed Conflict Measuring the frequency of armed conflicts each year since 1946, the figure depicts a gradual increase in the frequency of conflicts. The number of armed conflicts peaks in the early 1990s after the end of the Cold War and again in the mid-2010s due to an increase in state-based conflict tied to the growth of the Islamic State. Throughout this period, the type of conflict has changed, with extra-systemic armed aggression becoming, we hope, extinct and interstate conflict becoming very rare. At the same time, however, the occurrence of armed conflict within states has grown, as has the number of internal conflicts where there is intervention from third-party states on one side or the other.

This new pattern of civil wars and armed conflicts that do not involve government forces on at least one side has become especially prevalent since 1990. Indeed, between 1989 and 2014, only 9 of all 144 active armed conflicts worldwide, or 6 percent, were interstate wars between countries (Themnér and Wallensteen, 2014). Of the 52 armed conflicts in 36 different countries in 2018, only two were between states, with India and Pakistan fighting over border issues and active armed conflict arising between Iran and Israel. The number of the major intrastate armed conflicts that are internationalized has increased markedly over the past 15 years. In 2018, 36 percent of the 50 intrastate conflicts involved troops from states that were not primary parties to the conflict aiding one or both sides. These included conflicts involving Afghanistan, Iraq, Syria, Libya, Mali, Nigeria, Rwanda, Somalia, and Uganda (Pettersson et al., 2019; Strand et al., 2019).

Until 9/11, most security analysts expected civil wars to remain the most common type of global violence. However, they have had to revise their strategies and thinking to accommodate changing realities. Today, military planners face two unprecedented security challenges. As described by Henry Kissinger, these challenges are "terror caused by acts until recently considered a matter for internal police forces rather than international policy, and scientific advances and proliferation that allow the survival of countries to be threatened by developments entirely within another state's territory." This suggests an increased risk of further armed aggression, fought by irregular militia and private or semiprivate forces (such as terrorist networks) against the armies of states, or by "shadow warriors" commissioned by states as "outsourced" mercenaries or paid militia.

The characteristics of contemporary warfare appear to be undergoing a major transformation, even though many of the traditional characteristics of armed conflict continue. The general trends show the following:

- The proportion of countries throughout the globe engaged in wars has declined.

- Most wars now occur in the Global South, which is home to the highest number of states, with the largest populations, the least income, and the least stable governments.

- The goal of waging war to conquer foreign territory is no longer a motive; instead, nationalism and Islamic political motivations have emerged as major incentives over the past 30 years.

- Wars between the great powers are becoming obsolete; since 1945 the globe has experienced a **long peace**—the most prolonged period in modern history (since 1500) in which no wars have occurred between the most powerful countries.

- The number of countries where internal conflict has become internationalized is increasing, which is troubling as such interventions tend to translate into greater difficulty in concluding a conflict.

long peace
Extended periods of peace between any of the militarily strongest great powers.

NOORULLAH SHIRZADA/AFP/Getty Images

IMAGE 7.5 The Changing Nature of War The asymmetric struggle in Afghanistan between the world's most powerful military and insurgents raised questions about the conventional understanding of war—in particular, how it is conducted and what constitutes "victory." Almost two decades after the U.S.-led forces toppled its regime, the Taliban insurgency remains active and "the U.S.-backed Afghan government controls only 55 percent of the nation's territory and 65 percent of its population" (Hannah, 2019). Pictured here are U.S. soldiers who, now mostly serving in an advisory role, operate alongside Afghan commando forces during a patrol in Nangarhar province in 2018.

Although in the long term, armed conflict *between* states may disappear, the frequency of armed conflict *inside* established states is growing. Next we examine the characteristics of armed conflict *within* states.

Armed Conflict Within States

LO 7-3   Discuss and evaluate the leading causes of intrastate conflict.

Large-scale civil strife is bred by the failure of state governments to effectively govern within their territorial borders. Mismanagement by governments lacking authority and unable to meet the basic human needs of their citizens is a global trend. This incompetence has led to an epidemic of **fragile states** throughout the globe. Today as many as thirty-one state governments are at high risk of violent internal conflict due to political, social, and economic pressures that have not been well managed by legitimate state institutions (see Map 7.1). Sometimes the armed conflict is confined to local regions that seek secession and independence, and other times fragile states are victims of widespread but episodic fighting by insurgents and warlords. The citizens of fragile states pay the heaviest price for the internal conflict, political violence, and humanitarian catastrophe that commonly befall states that cannot discharge basic functions. The proliferation

fragile states
Countries whose governments have so mismanaged policy that their citizens, in rebellion, threaten revolution to divide the country into separate independent states.

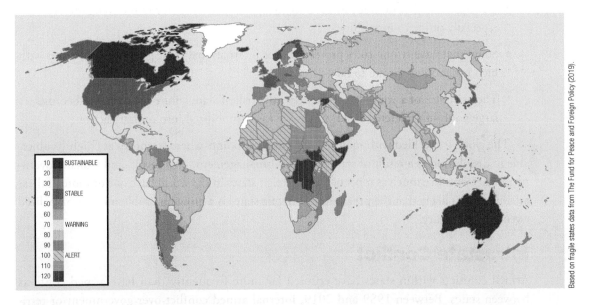

MAP 7.1 The Threat of Fragile States Based upon twelve social, economic, and political indicators, this map assesses countries based on their levels of stability. In 2019, Finland had the strongest score and is one of seven countries falling within the "Very Sustainable" category. State fragility and civil war are particularly evident in the high-risk, weak, and impoverished states in Africa. The most vulnerable countries whose governments are most critically in danger of failing and most likely to collapse in civil war and anarchy are South Sudan, Somalia, Syria, Yemen, and the Democratic Republic of the Congo.

 Think It Through   Does a country's level of internal fragility coincide with its influence at the international level? If so, how?

of fragile states is also a growing global danger because "violent conflict, refugee flow, arms trafficking, and disease are rarely contained within national borders" (Patrick, 2011, p. 55).

There are many causes of state failure and civil disintegration, but fragile states share some key characteristics that make them vulnerable to disintegration, civil war, and terrorism. In general, studies of this global trend suggest the following (Acemoglu and Robinson, 2012; Piazza, 2008):

- A strong predictor of state failure is poverty, but extreme income and gender inequality within countries are even better warning signs.

- The fragile states most vulnerable to internal rebellion are ruled by corrupt governments widely regarded as illegitimate and ineffective.

- Democracy, particularly with a strong parliament, generally lowers the risk of state failure; autocracy increases it.

- Poor or young democracies, however, are more unstable than either wealthy or established democracies or poor nondemocracies; and poor democracies that do not improve living standards are exceptionally vulnerable.

- Population pressures, exacerbated by internally displaced people, refugees, and food scarcity, contribute to state fragility and civil unrest.

- Governments that do not protect human rights, including freedom of religion, are especially prone to instability.

- States that have strong rules protecting free international trade gain stability; states with high inflation are prone to fail.

- The existence of a youth bulge increases the risk of state failure through war because large pools of underemployed youths are easily mobilized into military action.

The globe is speckled with many dangerous flash points where countries are highly vulnerable to dissolution as a result of state failure, mismanagement, civil revolt, and violent government takeovers. Inasmuch as most of the sovereign states in the world have one or more of these attributes, it is likely that the prevalence of fragile states is a growing problem in the globalized twenty-first century.

Intrastate Conflict

Armed conflicts within states have erupted far more frequently than have armed conflicts between states. Between 1989 and 2019, internal armed conflict over government or territory has by far been the most common. For example, of the fifty-two armed conflicts active in thirty-six countries around the world in 2018, all but two were intrastate conflicts involving a government fighting with, in some cases, more than one opposition group at a time (Strand et al., 2019). The outbreak of *civil war*, where the intensity of internal armed conflict reached at least 1000 battle-related deaths per year, has been somewhat irregular, with over 60 percent erupting after 1946 and with the frequency steadily climbing throughout the Cold War before beginning a decline in the post–Cold War years.

Civil wars dominate the global terrain because they start and reignite at a higher rate than they end, and they last longer (Hironaka, 2005). There is a tendency for countries that have undergone a civil war to experience a recurrence, due largely to the continued political exclusion of key groups from the governing process (Call, 2012). This pattern is even more pronounced for conflicts characterized by an **enduring internal rivalry (EIR)**. Empirical evidence shows that "76% of all civil war years from 1946 to 2004 took place in the context of EIRs," and that such civil wars were more likely to recur and be followed by shorter periods of relative peace (DeRouen and Bercovitch, 2008, p. 55). Moreover, the average duration of civil wars once they erupt has increased; one study estimates that 130 civil wars fought worldwide since World War II lasted an average of eleven years (Stark, 2007). Consider examples of long-lasting and resumed civil wars in Afghanistan, Colombia, Congo, Rwanda, Somalia, Sri Lanka, Sudan, and Syria.

enduring internal rivalry (EIR) Protracted violent conflicts between governments and insurgent groups within a state.

Civil wars also have a propensity to diffuse beyond the original state's borders and increase the likelihood of violent internal conflict within its neighbors. Often civil wars are connected, as evident in the wars of decolonization in Africa in the mid-1900s and the civil wars in the Caucasus more recently. The "infection" of other states is most likely when the civil war is a separatist conflict as opposed to one fought over government power, the states are ethnically polarized, and countries are in near proximity to the one fighting a civil war. "This is because such conflicts typically involve regional ethnic groups that have ties to kin across borders, who are more likely to act on demonstration effects" (Forsberg, 2014, p. 190).

Countries with higher levels of state capacity are able to address civil discontent through legal action, prevent unrest from escalating to civil war, and reduce susceptibility to diffusion (Braithwaite, 2010). Although consolidated democracy is likely to reduce the likelihood of civil war, such is not the case for transitioning democracies or authoritarian governments that hold elections. In fact, these countries are often vulnerable to the escalation of internal conflict and more receptive to diffusion across borders. Elections in "dangerous places" are often followed by political violence (Collier, 2009), in part because such societies are often characterized by latent opposition groups (Maves and Braithwaite, 2013). In a competitive political environment (as opposed to a closed political system), ethnicity and group identity tend to be more salient when there are actors that seek to ensure that the government serves the interest of select groups. Moreover, elites may try to mobilize supporters to win elections by emphasizing group differences, inciting hostility, and engaging in discrimination and intimidation. Whereas elections facilitate peaceful competition for political power when the rule of law is credibly guaranteed, they may otherwise be followed by violence if there are perceived irregularities or the official outcome is rejected (Cederman et al., 2012; Collier, 2009).

Another noteworthy characteristic of intrastate armed conflicts is their severity. There are spillover externalities generated by severe civil conflict that spread beyond the original state borders and affect a region broadly, particularly those countries in near proximity. "Practically all 'internal' conflicts have consequences that transcend international borders, by, for example, producing refugee flows or hampering economic growth regionally" (Forsberg, 2014, p. 188). Yet perhaps the most devastating indicator of the severity of internal armed conflict is the number of lives lost (see Figure 7.6).

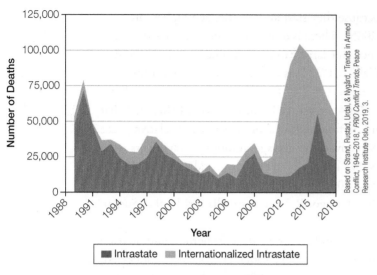

Based on Strand, Rustad, Urdal, & Nygård, "Trends in Armed Conflict, 1946–2018." *PRIO Conflict Trends;* Peace Research Institute Oslo, 2019, 3.

FIGURE 7.6 Lives Lost from Internal Conflict The figure shows the number of battle-related fatalities in countries experiencing intrastate conflict as well as those where intrastate conflict has been internationalized. In 2018, Yemen, Syria, Somalia, and Afghanistan accounted for 82 percent of battle-related casualties, with 49 percent of those occurring in Afghanistan alone. Sometimes conflicts become more brutal when third party countries become involved, such as the Vietnam War. In others, as was the rationale in Libya, international intervention hopes to prevent an escalation of fatalities (Strand et al., 2019).

genocide
The attempt to eliminate, in whole or in part, an ethnic, racial, religious, or national minority group.

Death from civil violence has always been very high, and casualties since World War II have increased at alarming rates, especially among children who have been both innocent victims and major participants. The year 1991 marked a peak in fatalities, with almost 80,000 battle-related deaths, due in large part to the intense war waged in Ethiopia over control of the government. With the turn of the century, deadly conflicts became more common in Africa, Asia, and the Middle East. In 2014, due in large part to the violence in Syria, the number of casualties from organized violence exceed 100,000 people. Since then, the number of deaths has declined, with 53,000 fatalities in 2018 reflecting a 43 percent decrease (Strand et al., 2019). Given that the most lethal intrastate wars in history have erupted recently, the cliché that "the most savage conflicts occur in the home" captures the ugly reality, as **genocide** and mass slaughter aimed at depopulating entire regions have become commonplace in recent civil wars (see "A Closer Look: Sudan and the Human Cost of War").

Another salient characteristic of internal armed conflicts is the resistance to negotiated settlement. Making peace between rival factions that are struggling for power, driven by hatred, and poisoned by the inertia of prolonged killing is difficult. Few domestic enemies fighting in a civil war have succeeded in ending the combat through negotiated compromise.

The reoccurrence of civil war is often due to commitment problems and uncertainties about the military capabilities of the opponent. Typically, a civil war settlement requires insurgents to lay down their arms. This shifts the balance of power in favor of the government, which may be tempted to press its advantage and exploit the cease-fire. "Because the rebels know about the government's incentive to renege on the deal, they are less likely to be willing to sign and maintain a peace agreement" (Mattes and Savun, 2010, p. 512). Therefore, commitment problems arise when the government is not able to credibly obligate itself to a peaceful resolution of the conflict (Hartzell and Hoddie, 2007).

For this reason, states may choose to bind themselves to an international agreement, or make a "credible commitment," by joining institutions such as the International Criminal Court (Simmons and Danner, 2010). Further evidence shows that the concerns of insurgents can be addressed through third-party guarantees, the adoption of institutional safeguards that promote the sharing of power between domestic groups, and transparent information-sharing regarding military capabilities and resolve. "Carefully designed peace agreements can guard

A Closer Look

SÚDAN AND THE HUMAN COST OF WAR

Sudan provides a horrifying example of the mass slaughter of civilians that occurs when government seeks to keep power by destroying minority opposition groups. Since the outbreak of civil war in 1955, Sudan has been in an almost continuous state of violent internal conflict. The first phase of civil war erupted when the Arab-led Khartoum government broke its promises to southerners to create a federal system to ensure their representation and regional autonomy in the newly independent state. Compounded by deep cultural and religious differences, violent aggression raged, eventually claiming the lives of more than a half million people—of which only 20 percent were armed combatants—and displacing hundreds of thousands more. With mediation from religious NGOs, in 1972 the Addis Ababa Agreement was reached, which established a single southern administrative region and brought an end to armed hostilities.

However, the cease-fire proved to be only a fleeting peace. Due to perceived transgression by the north, unrest in the south grew. In 1983, civil war broke out again, fueled by racial and religious tensions, competition over oil resources, and struggles for political power. The Arab-controlled Sudanese government and government-backed Janjaweed militia suspended democracy in 1989 and undertook a divide-and-destroy campaign of **state-sponsored terrorism** against those living in the south.

The historical north-south conflict began to move toward resolution, and eventually a peace agreement was signed in 2005 that called for sharing wealth and power, and included mutual security arrangements.

Yet attacks on non-Arab civilians in the extremely marginalized district of Darfur escalated. In July 2005, U.S. President George W. Bush characterized the situation in Darfur as "clearly genocide." By February 2010, when the Sudanese government signed a cease-fire agreement with the JEM, the largest rebel group in Darfur, UN estimates put the death toll at roughly 300,000 people, with another 2.5 million having fled their homes.

A mostly peaceful process for secession of South Sudan took place in 2011. Yet violence and unrest continues to rage, and the bloodbath throughout Sudan and South Sudan has made this tragic place of death the worst since World War II and raises questions about the prospects for lasting peace.

Watch the Carnegie Council Video:

"Southern Sudan: Would You Declare War?"

You Decide:

1. At what point is war no longer rational? How well does the rational actor model explain the persistence of armed conflict? What insights do other theoretical traditions provide?

2. Given the history of endemic violence in Sudan, under what conditions can a lasting peace be reached?

3. Why have so many noncombatants been targeted, and what responsibility does the international community have to protect them?

against renewed civil war by calling for international monitoring, making the belligerents submit military information to third parties, and providing for verification of this information" (Mattes and Savun, 2010, p. 511). There is evidence that peacekeeping efforts by third parties also can reduce the likelihood of a civil war diffusing to neighboring states as peacekeeping operations can secure borders, prevent large-scale refugee flows, and assist citizens in returning

state-sponsored terrorism
Formal assistance, training, and arming of foreign terrorists by a state in order to achieve foreign policy goals.

IMAGE 7.6 **Warfare and Children** Children have often been the major victims of civil strife and even active participants as child soldiers. They join for many reasons—some are kidnapped and forced to join; others are lured by promises of money; others have lost loved ones and seek vengeance. After putting down arms, says Philippe Houdard, the founder of Developing Minds Foundation, the "biggest challenge is making them emotionally whole again . . . to get them from being killing machines to normal human beings" (Drost, 2009, p. 8). Here we see young children in Angola armed for combat.

to their country (Beardsley, 2011). Third-party arbitration, however, can lead to prolonged violence if, for example, multiple countries with conflicting interests are involved in the negotiations (Aydin and Regan, 2012). This can be seen in the international negotiations—and the opposing perspectives of the United States and Russia—regarding the Syrian civil war. It is to the international dynamics of internal conflict that we now turn.

The International Dimensions of Internal Conflict

The rise of fragile states and their frequent fall into intrastate conflict may make it tempting to think of armed conflict within states as stemming exclusively from conditions within those countries. However, "states do not exist in a vacuum but are influenced by external actors" (Thyne, 2006, p. 937). As George Modelski (1964, p. 41) explained, "war has two faces. . . . Internal wars affect the international system [and] the international system affects internal wars."

An "internal conflict is regarded as internationalized if one or more third party governments are involved with combat personnel in support of the objective of either side" (Strand et al., 2019). Because the major powers have global interests, they have played roles "behind the scenes" in intrastate conflict to support friendly governments and overthrow unfriendly ones. At times, external actors (states and IGOs) have sent armed forces into fragile states to contain and control the civil conflict causing violence and attempt to reestablish governing authority. Neighboring states have also intervened within another country in an effort to thwart the

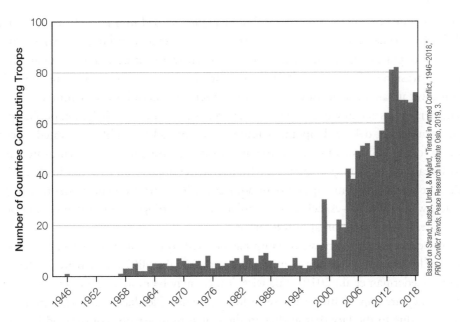

Based on Strand, Rustad, Urdal, & Nygård, "Trends in Armed Conflict, 1946–2018." *PRIO Conflict Trends*, Peace Research Institute Oslo, 2019, 3.

FIGURE 7.7 The Internationalization of Intrastate Conflict One indicator of a country's support for another is its commitment of troops during times of organized violence. As shown, the number of external parties involved in intrastate conflicts has increased notably in the early years of the twenty-first century, with 59 countries involved in the Mali stabilization forces in 2018. Indeed, between 2013 and 2018, more than 30 percent of intrastate conflicts were internationalized – a level previously not reached in the years following World War II (Pettersson, 2019).

diffusion of war across shared boundaries (Kathman, 2010). Outside intervention in intra-state conflict has been fairly common (see Figure 7.7), and has occurred in over a fourth of all intrastate armed conflicts since 1989 (Themnér and Wallensteen, 2012). Of the fifty intrastate conflicts in 2018, troops from external actors were involved in eighteen in support of one or both sides of the conflict (Pettersson et al., 2019).

There is another dimension to the internationalization of intrastate conflict. Many analysts believe that domestic insurrections become internationalized when leaders faced with internal opposition intentionally provoke an international *crisis*, hoping their citizens will become less rebellious if their attention is diverted to the threat of foreign aggression. This proposition has become known as the *diversionary theory of war*. This theory draws a direct connection between civil strife and foreign aggression. It maintains that when leaders sense their country is suffering from conflict at home, they are prone to attempt to contain that domestic strife by waging a war against foreigners—hoping that the international danger will take citizens' attention away from their dissatisfaction with their home leadership. To put it cynically, "when domestic unrest threatens a loss of political support from groups that are politically important to the leadership . . . we expect leaders to try and rally their support through heightened international conflict" (Nicholls, Huth, and Appel, 2010, p. 915).

Indeed, many political advisers have counseled this strategy, as realist theorist Niccolò Machiavelli did in 1513 when he advised leaders to undertake foreign wars whenever turmoil within their state became too great. John Foster Dulles echoed him in 1939 when he recommended before he became U.S. secretary of state that "the easiest and quickest cure of internal dissension is to portray danger from abroad." This strategy was suspected in Ugandan President Idi Amin's invasion of Tanzania in 1978 as an effort, in part, to counter growing domestic dissent and cover up an army mutiny in the southwestern region of his own country.

Whether leaders actually start wars to offset domestic conflict and heighten public approval remains a subject of debate. Unpopular leaders may instead be highly motivated to exercise caution in foreign affairs and to avoid the use of force overseas in order to cultivate a reputation as a peacemaker. It may be better for leaders facing opposition to avoid further criticism that they are intentionally manipulative by addressing domestic problems rather than engaging in reckless wars overseas—especially unpopular wars that trigger protest demonstrations and reduce leaders' public opinion approval ratings.

On the other hand, recent scholarship has pointed to the increased probability to incite hostilities if leaders seek to mobilize supporters by emphasizing differences in group identity and allegiance (Cederman et al., 2012). Likewise, leaders may be more likely to engage in violent conflict if they are approaching their term limit (Zeigler, Pierskalla, and Mazumder, 2013). This may be due to the fact that leaders in their final term are not constrained by the drive for reelection (Williams, 2013). Another potential explanation involves a leader's "conceptual

ABDULAZIZ KETAZ/AFP/Getty Images

IMAGE 7.7 The Globalization of Armed Conflict Over the past two decades, external actors have directly intervened with military force in more than a fourth of all internal armed conflicts. Consider the Syrian war, in which Russia, the United States, Iran, Israel, and Turkey all have played a role. "The Syrian war has now been outsourced," notes Christopher Phillips, a Syria scholar at Queen Mary University of London, with foreign involvement starting as "diplomatic support, then it was economic support, then it was material support for fighters, then it was fighting themselves directly" (quoted in Friedman, 2018). Pictured here, a man rescues a child following air strikes by the regime forces and their allies in Syria on May 30, 2019.

complexity," or the degree to which leaders display awareness of nuanced international relations concepts. A recent study (Foster and Keller, 2014) found that those leaders with low "conceptual complexity" had a greater tendency to use diversionary tactics than those with high "conceptual complexity." This is particularly true if the leader is inclined to view the use of force as a legitimate and effective foreign policy tool.

In sum, intrastate conflicts can become internationalized through both the tendency for them to invite external intervention as well as the propensity for leaders of failing governments to wage wars abroad as a means of preventing rebellion at home. These two trends are making for the globalization of armed conflict. That globalization of conflict is evident in yet another type of armed aggression that characterizes violence in world politics: the threat of global terrorism that knows no borders and that is spreading worldwide.

Terrorism

> **LO 7-4**   Assess the implications of terrorism for the study and prevention of armed conflict.

Since the birth of the modern state system some three and a half centuries ago, national leaders have prepared for wars against other countries. Throughout this period, war has been conceived as large-scale organized violence between the regular armies of sovereign states. Although leaders today still ready their countries for such clashes, they increasingly face the prospect of **asymmetric warfare**—armed conflict between their conventional military forces and guerilla groups or terrorist networks. "Whereas guerilla operations are conducted in unconventional conditions of engagement and directed at military targets, terrorism branched off, striking at noncombatants through murder and kidnapping" (Prunckun and Whitford, 2019, p. 37).

As you learned in Chapter 6, terrorist groups are a type of transnational nonstate actor distinguished by the fact that they use violence as their primary method of exercising influence. Terrorism was well known even in ancient times, as evident in the assassination campaigns conducted by the Sicarii (named after a short dagger, or sica) in Judea during the first century BCE. Indeed, as historian Max Boot (2013, p. 100) explains:

> Pundits and the press too often treat terrorism and guerrilla tactics as something new, a departure from old-fashioned ways of war. But nothing could be further from the truth. Throughout most of our species' long and bloody slog, warfare has primarily been carried out by bands of loosely organized, ill-disciplined, and lightly armed volunteers who disdained open battle in favor of stealthy raids and ambushes: the strategies of both tribal warriors and modern guerrillas and terrorists.

Today, a diverse group of movements (see Chapter 6, Table 6.2) practices terrorism, which can be classified as transnational, international, state, or domestic to contextualize the various acts of political violence (see Table 7.1) (Prunckun and Whitford, 2019). Irrespective of this classification, political terrorism is, as Todd Sandler (2010, p. 205) explains, "the premeditated use or threat to use violence by individuals or subnational groups to obtain a political or social objective through the intimidation of a large audience beyond that of the immediate victims." Because perpetrators of terrorism often strike symbolic targets in a horrific manner,

asymmetric warfare
Armed conflict between belligerents of vastly unequal military strength, in which the weaker side is often a nonstate actor that relies on unconventional tactics.

TABLE 7.1   Types of Terrorism

Classification	Definition	Example
Transnational	Direct political violence carried out in multiple countries by a largely autonomous non-state group, typically with global strategic objectives.	The Islamic State, whose members come from many countries, aims to create a supranational world order and targets multiple countries.
International	Direct political violence carried out in a country by individuals or groups who are not citizens or residents, often under the influence or direction of another sovereign state.	The bombing of New York-bound Pan Am Flight 103 over Lockerbie, Scotland, which is believed to have been carried out by Libyan intelligence officers in retaliation for U.S. actions against then-Libyan dictator Muammar Gaddafi.
State	Direct political violence committed by a government against its citizens.	Argentina's Dirty War in which the Argentine government was responsible for the routine disappearance and torture of real and perceived adversaries.
Domestic	Direct political violence carried out in a country by perpetrators who are citizens or residents of that country.	Influenced by the anti-government sentiment of the right-wing Patriot movement, Timothy McVeigh and Terry Nichols bombed a federal building in Oklahoma City in April 1995, committing the deadliest terrorist assault on U.S. soil prior to 9/11.

the psychological impact of an attack can exceed the physical damage. A mixture of drama and dread, terrorism is not senseless violence; it is a calculated political strategy that threatens people with an impending danger that seems ubiquitous, unavoidable, and unpredictable.

Consider estimates of the growing frequency and intensity of terrorism's threat (see Map 7.2). According to the U.S. Department of State's Office of the Coordinator for Counterterrorism, the yearly number of acts of international terrorism increased steadily from 174 in 1968 to a peak of 666 in 1987, but then began to decline just as steadily to 200 acts in 2002. Many experts believe that the presence of U.S. soldiers on Islamic soil in Iraq counterproductively ignited a new wave of deadly terrorist activity throughout the world. Even after the killing of Al Qaeda leader Osama bin Laden by U.S. Special Forces in May 2011, the threat of terrorist attacks remains. The most recent peak occurred in 2014, with almost 17,000 attacks and over 45,000 total deaths worldwide (START, 2018). Warns terrorism expert Richard Bloom, "the security threat remains consistent. We are still very much at risk" (as quoted in Halsey, 2011).

Terrorism can be used to support or change the political status quo. Governments have used repressive terror, or state terrorism (see Table 7.1), to sustain an existing political order. From the Gestapo (secret state police) in Nazi Germany to the "death squads" in various countries, violence perpetrated by the establishment attempts to defend the prevailing political order by eliminating opposition leaders and by intimidating virtually everyone else. Regimes have even engaged in genocide to maintain power and control (see Chapter 12), such as the mass killing of more than 1.7 million in Cambodia in the mid-1970s under Pol Pot's Khmer Rouge and the slaughter of around 800,000 Tutsi and moderate Hutus in 1994 by the Hutu-led government in Rwanda.

The perpetrators of terrorism are not mindless; they have shown that they have long-term aims and rationally calculate how different operations can accomplish their purposes. Indeed, it is their ability to plan, execute, and learn from these operations that make today's terrorists so

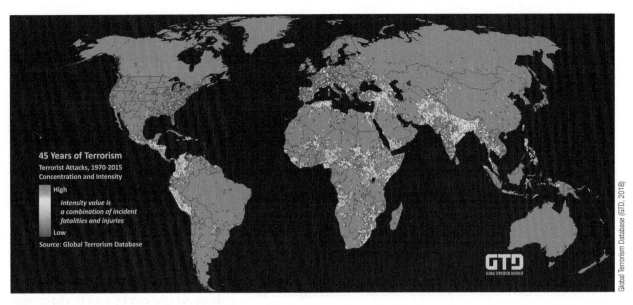

Global Terrorism Database (GTD, 2018)

MAP 7.2 The Persistent Threat of Global Terrorism Shown here are the locations and intensity of terrorist attacks that occurred over a 45-year period from 1970–2015. Counterterrorism measures have reduced fatalities in recent years, with deaths from terrorist violence decreasing by 44 percent in 2017 from the peak in 2014. Yet the occurrence of terrorist incidents remains extremely high in comparison to historical trends. "In the decade prior to the September 11th attacks, the frequency and lethality of terrorist violence each year was less than one-third of what took place in 2017" (START, 2018). Reflecting upon initiatives to combat terrorism, former UN Secretary-General Ban Ki-moon noted that the "complexity and interdependence of these issues mean that no single country or organization can provide solutions alone. Dialogue and cooperation are critical" (see UN, 2010).

Think It Through Explain the relationship between fragile states and rates of active terrorist groups.

dangerous. Moreover, exposure to terrorism can encourage political exclusionism and threaten the principles of democratic governance (Sandler, 2011).

> Alongside the heavy losses and fear, terror creates an enormous challenge to the fabric of demo-cratic societies. In many cases, there is a difficult inner tension between the fundamental need to feel secure and the aspiration to sustain democratic values and preserve democratic culture. More specifically, in times of terrorist threat and severe losses, when direct confrontation with the per-petrators of terrorism is either impossible or does not guarantee public safety, rage is frequently aimed at minority groups and their members. This rage can be easily translated into support for nondemocratic practices in dealing with minorities. Hence, one of the key psychosocial-political consequences of terrorism is the development of hostile feelings, attitudes, and behaviors toward minority groups (Canetti-Nisim et al., 2009, p. 364).

Dissidents who use terrorism to change the political status quo vary considerably. Some groups, like the MPLA (Popular Movement for the Liberation of Angola), used terrorism to expel colonial rulers; others, such as ETA (Basque Homeland and Liberty), adopt terrorism as part of an ethnonational separatist struggle; still others, including Boko Haram, ISIS/ISIL, the Christian Identity Movement, the Sikh group Babbar Khalsa, and Jewish militants belonging to Kach, use terror in the service of what they see as religious imperatives. Finally, groups such as the Japanese Red Army and Italian Black Order turn to terrorism for left- or right-wing

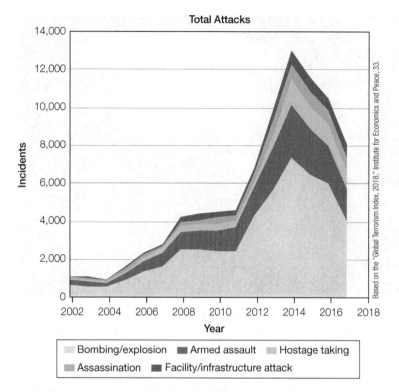

Based on the "Global Terrorism Index, 2018." Institute for Economics and Peace, 33.

FIGURE 7.8 Tools of Terrorist Warfare The figure indicates the major methods used by terrorists worldwide from 2000 through 2017. The pattern of weapons used in terrorist attacks across the globe is relatively constant, with bombings and explosions the most popular terrorist tactic in the fifteen years between 2002 and 2017. Hostage-taking, assassination, and attacks on infrastructure increased more than tenfold during that same period.

ideological reasons. This dissident terror may be grounded in anticolonialism, separatism, religion, or secular ideology.

To accomplish their objectives, terrorists use a variety of tactics, including bombing, assault, hijacking, and taking hostages (see Figure 7.8). About half of recorded terrorist incidents involve the use of explosives. Hijacking and hostage-taking generally involve more complex operations than planting a bomb in a crowded department store or gunning down travelers in a train station. However, such activities do occur and can be seen in the careful planning required by the September 1970 coordinated hijacking of five airliners by Palestinians, which eventually led to one airliner being blown up in Cairo and three others in Jordan. Though suicide attacks are the least frequently used tool of terrorist warfare, Ramadan Shalah of the Palestinian Jihad explained the military logic of suicide tactics through asymmetric warfare by asserting: "Our enemy possesses the most sophisticated weapon in the world. . . . We have nothing . . . except the weapon of martyrdom. It is easy and costs us only our lives."

Beyond the conventional tactics of bombings, assaults, hijacking, and hostage taking, two other threats—what former U.S. Navy Secretary Richard Danzig called "nonexplosive warfare"—could become part of the terrorist repertoire. First, dissidents may acquire weapons of mass destruction to deliver a mortal blow against their enemies. There is widespread fear, for instance, that Pakistan's deteriorating internal political conditions may allow nuclear material to fall into the hands of extremist groups (Clarke, 2013). According to former Director of the U.S. Central Intelligence Agency John Brennan, "The threat of nuclear terrorism is real, it is serious, it is growing, and it constitutes one of the greatest threats to our national security and, indeed, to global security."

Nuclear armaments may be the ultimate terror weapons, but radiological, chemical, and biological weapons also pose extraordinary dangers. Crude radiological weapons can be fabricated by combining ordinary explosives with nuclear waste or radioactive isotopes stolen from hospitals, industrial facilities, or research laboratories. In 2015, Australian intelligence reports indicated that ISIS/ISIL had "seized enough radioactive material from government facilities to suggest it has the capacity to build a large and devastating 'dirty' bomb" (Withnall, 2015) that combines conventional explosives with radioactive material. Rudimentary chemical weapons can be made from herbicides, pesticides, and other toxic substances that are available commercially. Biological weapons based on viral agents are typically more difficult to produce. However, the dispersal of anthrax spores through the mail in 2001 and the inadvertent distribution of live anthrax samples in 2015 from a U.S. military base in Utah to laboratories in nineteen U.S. states, Washington D.C., Australia, Canada, Britain, and South Korea illustrated that low-technology attacks with bacterial agents in powder form are a frightening possibility.

The second tactical innovation on the horizon is cyberterrorism. Not only can the extremists use the internet as a recruiting tool and a means of coordinating their activities with like-minded groups, they can also hack into a foe's computer system to case potential targets. Viruses and other weapons of **information warfare** could also cause havoc if they disable financial institutions. Cyberattacks have risen as a heated issue between the United States and China, with the U.S. charging China with responsibility for high-tech spying in 2013 that compromised more than two dozen major U.S. weapons systems. In 2019, U.S. President Donald Trump signed an executive order that banned U.S. companies and government agencies from using telecommunications equipment that poses a risk to national security. The telecom equipment firm Huawei was affected directly, and the United States pressured other countries to remove Huawei from their cellular networks out of concern that its equipment could be used by Chinese national spy agencies. China contends that it, too, has been subject to extensive hacking from the United States, and that "if the U.S. government wants to keep weapons programs secure, it should not allow them to be accessed online" (Jones, 2013).

Both bioweapons and cyberattacks challenge our thinking about the future of terrorism and war as they pose a strategic quandary: because they are extraordinarily difficult to trace back to the perpetrator, they defy **deterrence** and elude defenses. "The concept of deterrence depends on the threat of certain retaliation that would cause a rational attacker to think twice. So if the attacker can't be found, then the certainty of retaliation dissolves, and deterrence might not be possible" (Hoffman, 2011, p. 78). Moreover, although we tend to expect warning of an impending attack and a chance for defense, as Nobel Prize laureate Joshua Lederberg warned, it is not likely that a perpetrator "is going to give you that opportunity."

Renowned historian and terrorism expert Walter Laqueur sees a future of **postmodern terrorism** that poses a great threat to technologically advanced societies, where terrorists tend to be less ideological, more likely to hold ethnic grievances, and increasingly difficult to distinguish from other criminals. So-called postmodern terrorism is likely to expand because the globalized international environment, without meaningful barriers separating countries, allows terrorists to practice their ancient trade by new rules and methods. The **information age** facilitates transnational networking among terrorists and has made available a variety of new methods of warfare.

Moreover, globalization has encouraged the rapid spread of new weapons and technology across borders, which provides unprecedented opportunities for terrorists to commit atrocities

information warfare
Attacks on an adversary's telecommunications and computer networks to degrade the technological systems vital to its defense and economic well-being.

deterrence
Preventive strategies designed to dissuade an adversary from doing what it would otherwise do.

postmodern terrorism
Terrorism practiced by an expanding set of diverse actors with new weapons "to sow panic in a society, to weaken or even overthrow the incumbents, and to bring about political change" (Laqueur, 1996).

information age
The era in which the rapid creation and global transfer of information through mass communication contribute to the globalization of knowledge.

and to change their tactics in response to successful counterterror operations. The growing difficulty of detecting and deterring the attacks of disciplined globalized terrorist networks is further exacerbated by their ties to international organized crime (IOC) syndicates and internationally linked networks of thousands of gangs, which facilitate their profit in the narcotics trade and provide resources to support terrorist activities.

The activities of nonstate terrorist organizations are likely to remain a troubling feature of world politics also because every spectacular terrorist act generates a powerful shock effect and gains worldwide publicity through the global news media. In an effort to diminish the capacity of terrorists to garner such worldwide attention, U.S. Senator Joe Lieberman (2008) called on Google and others to remove internet video content that was produced by terrorist organizations: "Islamist terrorist organizations use YouTube to disseminate their propaganda, enlist followers, and provide weapons training . . . (and) YouTube also, unwittingly, permits Islamist terrorist groups to maintain an active, pervasive, and amplified voice, despite military setbacks."

Terrorism poses a huge threat to global security. Compounding these challenges is the fact that through state-sponsored terrorism, states have often financed, trained, equipped, and provided sanctuary for terrorists whose activities serve their foreign policy goals. In the throes of the terrorist attack on the United States on September 11, 2001, U.S. President George W. Bush described the threat as a network of terrorist groups as well as the rogue states that harbored them. However, disagreement about the character and causes of global terrorism remains pronounced, and without agreement on these basic characteristics, a consensus on the best response is unlikely. Much like a disease that cannot be treated until it is accurately diagnosed, the plague of new global terrorism cannot be eradicated until its sources are understood. Those persuaded by one image of terrorism are drawn to certain **counterterrorism** policies, whereas those holding a different image recommend contrary policies. As constructivist theorists remind us, what we see depends on what we expect, what we look at, and what we wish to see.

counterterrorism
Strategies and methods used to combat or prevent terrorism.

Consider the diametrically opposed views of whether repression or conciliation is the most effective counterterrorism policy. Those advocating repression see terrorism springing from the cold calculations of extremists who should be neutralized by preemptive surgical strikes. In contrast to this coercive counterterrorism approach, those who see terrorism rooted in frustrations with a lack of civil liberties and human rights (Krueger, 2007) or widespread poverty and poor education (Kavanagh, 2011) urge negotiation and cooperative nonmilitary approaches (Cortright and Lopez, 2008). Rather than condoning military strikes aimed at exterminating the practitioners of terrorism, they endorse conciliatory policies designed to reduce terrorism's appeal.

The debate about how to deal with the new global terrorism has provoked serious concerns about strategies for combating this global threat (see "Controversy: Can the War against Global Terrorism Be Won?"). The debate revolves around a series of interconnected issues: Are repressive counterterrorism policies ethical? Are they compatible with democratic procedures? Do they require multilateral (international) backing to be legal, or can they be conducted unilaterally? Is conciliation more effective than military coercion? What are the relative costs,

Controversy

CAN THE WAR AGAINST GLOBAL TERRORISM BE WON?

In the wake of 9/11, a new conventional wisdom arose—as then-U.S. Secretary of Defense Donald Rumsfeld put it, "if the [United States] learned a single lesson from 9/11, it should be that the only way to defeat terrorists is to attack them. There is no choice. You simply cannot defend in every place at every time against every technique. All the advantage is with the terrorist in that regard, and therefore you have no choice but to go after them where they are."

Others argue that to truly undermine terrorism, we must address the underlying conditions that give it appeal. Efforts to defeat terrorism must include developing governments that can meet the needs of the people and jobs that provide an alternative to fighting. Assessing the prospects of winning the war on terror in Afghanistan, Lieutenant Colonel Brett Jenkinson, commander of the U.S. battalion in the Korengal Valley, explained that "What we need is a better recruiting pitch for disaffected youth. You can't build hope with military might. You build it through development and good governance" (Baker and Kolay, 2009, p. 27).

Exactly what approach to take to control the new global terrorism remains controversial. To conduct a worldwide war requires an enduring commitment at high costs. Moreover, strategists often fail to distinguish different types of terrorist movements and their diverse origins. Therefore, they construct counterterrorism strategies in the abstract—with a single formula—rather than tailoring approaches for dealing with terrorism's alternate modes. As the conflict continues, "means become ends, tactics become strategy, boundaries are

blurred, and the search for a perfect peace replaces reality" (Cronin, 2013, p. 174).

In evaluating proposed methods to fight the latest wave of global terrorism, you need to confront a series of incompatible conclusions: "concessions only encourage terrorists' appetite for further terrorism," as opposed to "concessions can redress the grievances that lead to terrorism." Your search for solutions will necessarily spring from assumptions you make about terrorism's nature and sources, and these assumptions will strongly affect your conclusions about the wisdom or futility of contemplated remedies.

Keep in mind that what may appear to be a policy around which an effective counterterrorism program might be constructed could potentially make the problem worse. Counterterrorism is controversial because one person's solution is another person's problem, the answers are often unclear, and the ethical criteria for applying just-war theory to counterterrorism needs clarification (Patterson, 2005).

What Do You Think?

1. How does armed aggression, such as terrorism, by nonstate actors change the circumstances of war for policy makers? How does it change the circumstances of intervention for policy makers?

2. What would you advise governments about the best methods of fighting terrorism? Keep in mind the promises and perils of each possible solution.

3. How might intergovernmental organizations such as the United Nations complement, or hinder, states' abilities to fight terrorism?

risks, and benefits of these contending approaches to combat terrorism? Although most experts would agree that it is not possible to wipe terrorism from the face of the globe, "it should be possible to reduce the incidence and effectiveness of terrorism" (Mentan, 2004, p. 364; Bapat, 2011).

IMAGE 7.8 **Terrorists Behind Masks** Shown here is the faceless militia that targets armies in uniforms: looking like self-funded criminal gangs with no ranks and uncertain allegiances, many terrorist groups hide their identity and report to no superiors.

Armed Conflict and Its Future

LO 7-5   Evaluate the broader implications of armed conflict for the future of world politics.

You have now inspected three trends in the major types of armed conflict in the world: wars between states, wars within states, and global terrorism. Some of these trends, you have noticed, are promising. War between states is disappearing, and this inspires optimists who hope that it will vanish from human interaction altogether. As some security studies experts predict, "Unlike breathing, eating or sex, war is not something that is somehow required by the human condition or by the forces of history. Accordingly, war can shrivel up and disappear, and it seems to be in the process of doing so" (Mueller, 2004, p. 4).

However, that threat remains, and because armed conflict between and within states threatens everyone in the borderless globalized world, all of humanity is at risk. Between 2008 and 2018, the level of peace in the world declined by 2.38 percent (see Map 7.3), deteriorating in eighty-five countries around the world and improving in only seventy-five. "Terrorism and internal conflict have been the biggest contributors to the global deterioration in peacefulness over the decade. One hundred countries experienced increased terrorist activity, with only thirty-eight improving, and total conflict deaths increased by 264 percent" (Institute for Economics and Peace, 2018, pp. 2–3). There is no sure guide to what the future will hold. But the sad news is that your life and livelihood are certain to be threatened by the continuing onset of armed conflict. That threat imperils the future and affects *all* other aspects of world politics—which is why much of world history is written about the causes and consequences of

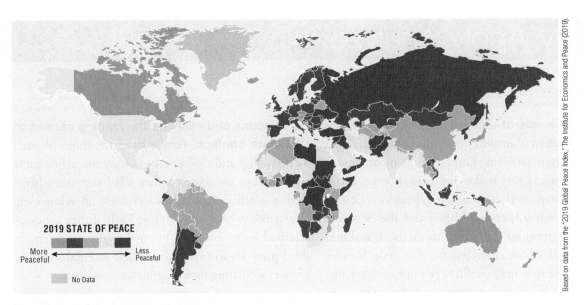

Based on data from the "2019 Global Peace Index," The Institute for Economics and Peace (2019).

2019 STATE OF PEACE

More
Peaceful ←——→ Less
Peaceful

No Data

MAP 7.3 The Quest for Global Peace Based on twenty-three indicators across 163 countries that are home to 99.7 percent of the globe's population, the 2019 Global Peace Index gauges peacefulness in terms of the extent to which countries are involved in international and intrastate conflicts, their degree of militarization, and the level of safety and security within a state. Scores show that the world is considerably less peaceful now than in the past decade, declining by 3.78 percent since 2008. Iceland continues to be the most peaceful country, and Europe is the most peaceful region. The least peaceful countries include Afghanistan, Syria, South Sudan, Yemen, and Iraq.

Think It Through According to this map, are any countries potentially at risk by their proximity to a fragile state?

armed conflict from the vantage point of all peoples' and professions' perspectives. As British poet Percy B. Shelley framed it:

> War is the statesman's game, the priest's delight,
> The lawyer's jest, the hired assassin's trade,
> And, to those royal murderers, whose mean thrones
> Are brought by crimes of treachery and gore,
> The bread they eat, the staff on which they lean.

Lucius Annaeus Seneca, a Roman statesman and philosopher in the first century CE, wryly noted that "Of war men ask the outcome, not the cause." Yet in order for us to reduce and possibly eliminate the plague of armed conflict in the world, it is necessary for us to first understand what drives violent conflict. The correlates of war speak to the correlates of peace. Thus, in this chapter you also have been given the opportunity to examine the many leading causes of armed conflict that theorists have constructed to explain why political violence in its various forms erupts.

We next consider the alternative potential paths to peace, security, and world order. In Chapter 8, we examine the vision realism advances about dealing with the threat of war, specifically as it deals with arms, military strategy, alliances, and the balance of power.

> *Peace cannot be kept by force; it can only be achieved by understanding.*
>
> **—ALBERT EINSTEIN, NOBEL PRIZE–WINNING PHYSICIST**

Study. Apply. Analyze.

Chapter Summary

7-1 Use a levels-of-analysis approach to examine the causes of armed conflict. At the individual level of analysis, analyzing human nature is paramount in understanding why leaders instigate violence. There are many explanations regarding leaders' choices, including their inherent fallibility and the existence of external pressures that influence decision making. At the state level are characteristics that make it more or less prone to armed conflict. For instance, territorial disputes have often instigated conflict. There are numerous other factors, including cultural influences, economic system, and regime type. At the systemic level, the decentralized structure requires actors to rely on self-help for their security. Realism provides insights and informs power transition theory, long cycle theory, and hegemonic stability theory. Considering each level provides a multidimensional view of the causes of armed conflict, as naming one universal cause of war would be inaccurate.

7-2 Describe and assess patterns in the occurrence of armed conflict. Violent conflict within states rather than war between them comprises the largest portion of armed conflict in the world. Increasingly, conflicts are internationalized as external countries support or directly participate in armed hostilities. There has also been an increase in political violence by nonstate actors, such as insurgency forces and terrorist groups.

7-3 Discuss and evaluate the leading causes of intrastate conflict. Fragile states are those plagued by instability and civil unrest, and are frequently most vulnerable to intrastate conflict. Civil wars often beget further conflict, leading to a seemingly unending cycle of violence, which is even more likely if they are characterized by an enduring internal rivalry. Increasingly, third-party actors intervene in these internal conflicts, often exacerbating their length and intensity.

7-4 Assess the implications of terrorism for the study and prevention of armed conflict. Though governments sometimes engage in state terrorism, most terrorist groups are nonstate actors that strategically use violence as their primary method of exercising influence. Over time, the frequency and severity of terrorist attacks have increased, and globalization has facilitated terrorism by reducing meaningful barriers and enhancing opportunities for transnational networking. It is important to identify the character and causes of terrorism in order to enact effective counterterrorism efforts.

7-5 Evaluate the broader implications of armed conflict for the future of world politics. As wars between states diminish, there is hope for enduring global peace. However, intrastate conflict and terrorism are on the rise, and fragile states are not the only ones impacted by this shift. In our borderless globalized world, all of humanity is at risk.

Key Terms

arbitration	deterrence	individualistic fallacy	pacifism
armed conflict	ecological fallacy	information age	postmodern terrorism
asymmetric warfare	economic peace	information warfare	power transition theory
bargaining model of war	enduring internal rivalry (EIR)	interspecific aggression	relative deprivation
civil war	fragile states	intraspecific aggression	socialization
commercial liberalism	genocide	long peace	state-sponsored terrorism
conflict	good offices	mediation	survival of the fittest
counterterrorism	hegemonic stability theory	national character	war
democratic peace	identity politics	nature versus nurture	youth bulge

Suggested Readings and Resources

Cashman, Greg. (2014). *What Causes War? An Introduction to Theories of International Conflict.* Lanham, MD: Rowman and Littlefield.

National Consortium for the Study of Terrorism and Responses to Terrorism (START). (2018). *Global Terrorism Database.* An open-source database of information on terrorist events around the world between 1970 and 2017: start.umd.edu/gtd.

Kegley, Charles W., ed. (2003). *The New Global Terrorism: Characteristics, Causes, Controls.* Upper Saddle River, NJ: Prentice Hall.

Levy, Jack, and William R. Thompson. (2010). *Causes of War.* Malden, MA: Wiley-Blackwell.

Monitoring South Sudan. An up-to-date timeline of activity involving South Sudan: blogs.prio.org/MonitoringSouthSudan/.

Prunckun, Henry and Troy Whitford. (2019). *Terrorism and Counterterrorism: A Comprehensive Introduction to Actors and Actions.* Boulder: Lynne Rienner Publishers.

Sandler, Todd. (2011). "New Frontiers of Terrorism Research: An Introduction," *Journal of Peace Research* 48: 279–286.

Transatlantic Dialogue on International Law and Armed Conflict: A Blog Series. A website listing blog posts highlighting armed conflict and the laws surrounding it: ejiltalk.org/transatlantic-dialogue-on-international-law-and-armed-conflict-a-blog-series/.

Wallensteen, Peter. (2011). *Understanding Conflict Resolution: War, Peace, and the Global System.* London: Sage.

Carnegie Council Videos

Key Term Videos

- War
- Conflict
- Armed Conflict
- Socialization
- National Character
- Commercial Liberalism
- Power Transition Theory
- Failed States
- Asymmetric Warfare
- Information Warfare
- Deterrence

Additional Videos

- Bacevich, Andrew J. "Washington Rules: America's Path to Permanent War."
- Betts, Richard K. "The World Ahead: Conflict or Cooperation?"
- Reiss, Mitchell B. "Negotiating with Evil: When to Talk to Terrorists."

Chapter 8

The Pursuit of Power Through Arms and Alliances

IMAGE 8.1 Missiles, Bombs, and Bullets, Oh My! Throughout history, countries have used weapons to back their enemies into surrender. Realists regard the prudent use of armed force as a powerful instrument for maintaining security and stability in world politics. Shown here is one controversial example: unmanned predator drones such as this were used by the United States between 2004 and 2019 for an estimated 6786 confirmed strikes in Pakistan, Yemen, Somalia, and Afghanistan with a death toll of at least 8459 people (BIJ, 2019).

Learning Objectives

LO 8-1 Describe the distribution of military power among states, and evaluate the dilemmas raised by the pursuit of military power.

LO 8-2 Identify and evaluate the implications of the global arms trade and nuclear weapons for world politics, and assess recent developments in weapons technology.

LO 8-3 Examine patterns in military intervention and factors that contribute to its effectiveness.

LO 8-4 Discuss the implications of alliances for global security.

LO 8-5 Summarize the strategies and difficulties associated with balancing.

LO 8-6 Extrapolate the future prospects for alliances and balancing in world politics.

" *The adversaries of the world are not in conflict because they are armed. They are armed because they are in conflict and have not yet learned peaceful ways to resolve their conflicting interests.* "

—RICHARD M. NIXON, FORMER U.S. PRESIDENT

I magine yourself someday becoming the next secretary-general of the United Nations. You would face the awesome responsibility for fulfilling the UN's charter to preserve world peace. But looking at the globe, you would likely see that many countries are engaged in armed conflict and that those wars are destroying life and property. Moreover, you would undoubtedly also be distressed by the countries and possibly some transnational terrorist groups with the new capacity to annihilate their enemies with weapons of mass destruction. And you shudder at the realization that many states are living in constant fear of threats to their security, while at the same time these armed actors are increasing the military power in their arsenals.

As a result of the escalating destructive power of modern weapons, you cannot help but notice that the UN members most feverishly working to increase their capacity to resist threats to their physical survival are the same countries whose **national security**, or psychological freedom from fear of foreign aggression, seems to be declining the most rapidly. Taking a picture of the pregnant fears circulating the globe, you conclude that as a consequence, a true *security dilemma* has been created: the armaments amassed by states for what they claim to be defensive purposes are seen by others as threatening, and this has driven the alarmed competitors to undertake, as countermeasures, additional military buildups—with the result that the arming states' insecurities are increasing even as their military strength increases.

As you watch the jockeying for power and position among the UN members, you also notice that countries tend to forge partnerships, based on converging and clashing interests and values. As realist policy maker Steven Rosen (1970) remarked, "It is the existence of an enemy that gives rise to the need for allies, and [it] is for the advantageous conduct of fighting that alliances are formed." And when relationships and conditions change, new alliances form and established alliances dissolve as transnational actors—all obsessed with the power of their rivals—realign.

What course should you counsel the UN's members to pursue in order to escape the dilemma of rising insecurity in which they have imprisoned themselves? Alas, your options are limited and your advice ignored. Why? Because when the topic of war and peace is debated, and in periods when international tensions are high, policy makers (and theorists) turn to realist theory for guidance.

national security
A country's psychological freedom from fears that the state will be unable to resist threats to its survival and national values emanating from abroad or at home.

> *We have not eternal allies and we have not perpetual enemies. Our interests are eternal and perpetual and those interests it is our duty to follow.*
>
> **—LORD PALMERSTON, BRITISH PRIME MINISTER**

Power in World Politics

LO 8-1 Describe the distribution of military power among states, and evaluate the dilemmas raised by the pursuit of military power.

Nearly all states continue to believe that the anarchical global system requires them to rely on *self-help* and depend only on themselves for security. They have been schooled in the lessons constructed from *realism*—the school of thought that teaches that the drive for power and the domination of others for self-advantage is a universal and permanent motive throughout world history. For this reason, most states follow the realist roads to national and international security. This worldview, or *paradigm*, for organizing perceptions pictures the available and practical choices for states primarily among three time-honored options: (1) arming themselves, (2) forming or severing alliances with other countries, or (3) constructing strategies for controlling their destinies through military approaches and **coercive diplomacy**, such as acts of military intervention that target their enemies.

coercive diplomacy
The use of threats or limited armed force to persuade an adversary to alter its foreign or domestic policies.

In this chapter, you will explore states' efforts to follow the realist recipes for reducing threats to their national security by creating a favorable balance of power. In the spirit of seventeenth-century English philosopher Thomas Hobbes, who viewed the natural human condition as one of "war of all against all" and advised that successful states are those that hold the "posture of Gladiators; having their weapons pointing, and their eyes fixed on one another," this chapter introduces the acquisition and use of arms, major trends in weaponry, and the role of alliances in ensuring that national security and national interests are served and a balance of power persists among rivals that prevents any one transnational actor from using force against the others.

The Elements of State Power

This discussion begins by underscoring the high importance that realists place on *power*, which they believe has, throughout history, been key in driving world politics. National security is truly a paramount priority for the policy makers responsible for constructing their country's foreign policy agendas. Because the threat of armed conflict persists, realism recommends that war be placed at the very top of a state's concerns and that, to contain dangers, the pursuit of power must be the top priority. As Table 8.1 demonstrates, this emphasis is part and parcel

TABLE 8.1   Realist Roads to Security: Premises and Policy Recommendations

Realist Perspective of the Global Environment
Primary global condition: anarchy; or the absence of authoritative governing institutions
Probability of system change/reform: low, except in response to extraordinary events, such as 9/11
Primary transnational actors: states and especially great powers
Principal actor goals: power over others, self-preservation, and physical security
Predominant pattern of actor interaction: competition and conflict
Pervasive concern: national security
Prevalent state priorities: acquiring military capabilities
Popular state practice: use of armed force for coercive diplomacy
Policy Premises
If you want peace, prepare for war.
No state is to be trusted further than its national interest.
Standards of right and wrong apply to individuals but not to states; in world affairs amoral actions are sometimes necessary for security.
Isolationism is not an alternative to active global involvement.
Strive to increase military capabilities and fight rather than submit to subordination.
Do not let any other state or coalition of states become predominant.
Negotiate alliances to maintain a favorable military balance.

of a much broader range of foreign policy recommendations realists embrace to chart the safest routes to national and international security (see also Chapter 2).

Realist theorists since antiquity have based their thinking and policy recommendations on the belief that all people and states seek power. Even texts such as the Bible reflect this assumption, as it observes and warns that people seem born to sin, and the drive for power to dominate others is one of their inalterable compulsions. That said, the abstraction called power, which realists assume to be humanity's primary objective, defies precise definition. Constructivists recognize that in the broadest sense power is usually interpreted as the political capacity of one actor to exercise influence over another actor to the first's benefit.

Most leaders follow *realpolitik* and operate from the traditional construction that conceives of power as a combination of factors that gives states the capability to promote national interests, to win in international bargaining, and to shape the rules governing interaction in the global system. As former Secretary of State Condoleezza Rice observed, "Power is nothing unless you can turn it into influence." However, beyond the semantic definition of power as *politics*—the exercise of influence to control others—power is an ambiguous concept, and difficult to measure. A dictionary definition begs the question: What factors most enable an actor to control or coerce another?

Of all the components of state power, realists see military capability as by far the most important. Thus, realists reject the view of liberal strategic thinkers who maintain that under conditions of globalization, which links countries economically, politically, and culturally in webs of interdependence, economic resources are becoming increasingly more critical to national strength and security than are military capabilities (Nye, 2008).

Following tradition, one way to estimate the **power potential** of states is to compare their military expenditures. On this dimension, the United States is the undisputed military powerhouse of the world, with defense spending that leaves all other countries far behind. Figure 8.1 shows the trend in U.S. defense budgets over seven decades that has made America unsurpassed in military spending: at $671 billion in 2018, the United States was responsible for 36 percent of all of the world's military expenditures for that year. Between 2010 and 2017, the United States has decreased its expenditures in real terms by 22.8 percent. However, its military expenditures continue to be at historically high levels, in line in real terms with its previous spending peak in the late 1980s. Furthermore, in 2020, U.S. military spending increased to $718.3 billion to include funds for U.S. border security and emergency reconstruction efforts. The U.S. Department of Defense expects that between fiscal years 2021 and 2024, the United States will spend more than $2.93 trillion in defense (SIPRI, 2019a; DOD, 2019).

Power potential also derives from factors other than military expenditures. Among the so-called elements of power, analysts also consider such capabilities as the relative size of a state's economy, its population and territorial size, geographic position, raw materials, technological capacity, political culture and values, efficiency of governmental decision making, volume of trade, educational level, national morale, and internal solidarity. For example, if power potential were measured by territorial size, Russia, which is twice as large as its closest rivals (Canada, China, the United States, Brazil, and Australia, in that order), would be the globe's most powerful country. Likewise, if power were measured by the UN's projections for countries' populations by the year 2025, India, China, the United States, Indonesia,

power potential
The capabilities or resources held by a state that are considered necessary to its asserting influence over others.

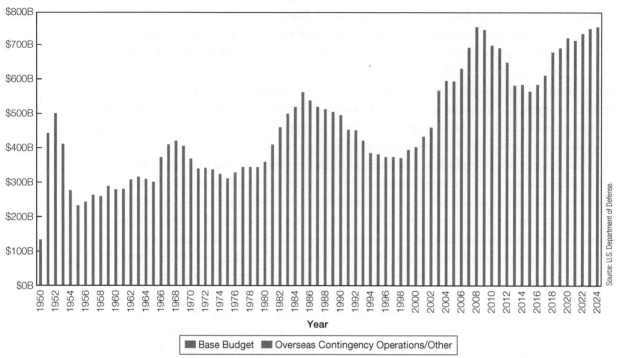

FIGURE 8.1 Over Seven Decades of U.S. Military Spending America's military expenditures spiked during the Korean and Vietnam Wars, expanded in the 1980s under President Ronald Reagan, dipped after the end of the Cold War, and have risen rapidly since 9/11 and the start of its global "war on terror." Due in part to its extensive military capabilities, the United States continues to be regarded as a hegemonic power, without rival. In 2020, U.S. military spending is expected to include $545 billion in base budget, plus an additional $173 billion for Overseas Contingency Operations and border security. To keep up with Chinese and Russian military and technological advances, the 2020 budget includes the "largest research and development request in seventy years" (DOD, 2019). This includes an investment of $927 million in artificial intelligence and machine learning, as well as $2.6 billion in hypersonics research.

Nigeria, Pakistan, and Brazil, in that order, would be the most powerful (UN, 2019a). In a similar comparison, the rankings of countries' expenditures on research and development (as a percentage of GDP) to fund future economic growth and military strength would rank Austria, Israel, Japan, South Korea, Sweden, and Switzerland as the countries with the brightest future (WDI, 2017). Clearly, strength is relative. The leading countries in some dimensions of power potential are not leaders in others because power comes in many forms (see Maps 8.1A and 8.1B).

Thus, there is little consensus on how best to weigh the various factors that contribute to military capability and national power. History is replete with examples of weaker transnational actors prevailing in armed conflicts against much more militarily powerful enemies. Consider the seventeenth century, for example, with Switzerland against the Hapsburg Empire, the Netherlands against Spain, and Greece against the Ottomans. In the more recent past, Vietnam succeeded against a vastly stronger France and, later, the United States. Similarly, the United States' superior military power did not prevent Iran from taking American diplomats as hostages or the Al Qaeda terrorist network's 9/11 attack. Intangible factors, such as the will of the target population to resist a more powerful army and their willingness to die for their cause, were key elements in the capacity of each of these weaker actors to combat a much stronger military force.

Chapter 8   **239**

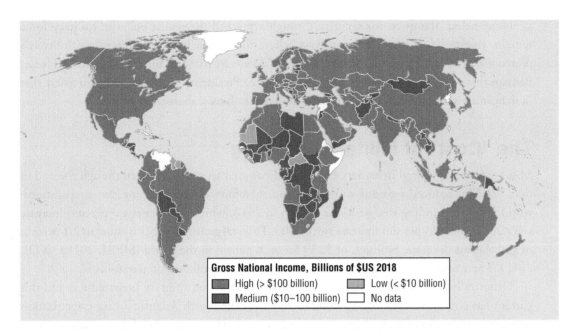

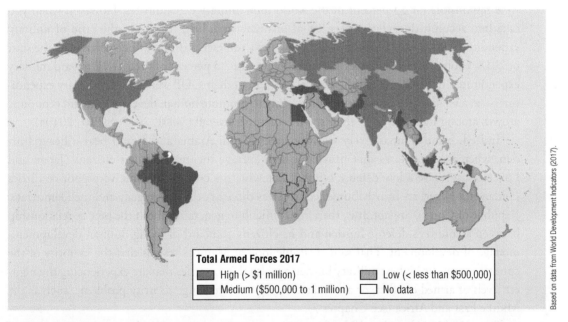

Based on data from World Development Indicators (2017).

MAPS 8.1A AND 8.1B Two Measures of Power Potential: State Wealth and Size of National

Armies The map on top measures gross national income (GNI) across countries to estimate the differences in national wealth that contribute to state power, and the distribution categorizes differences in the size of states' economies that separate the rich from the poor (and the strong from the weak). Another measure of power projection is the number of uniform personnel in states' armies, navies, and air forces. The map on the bottom classifies the varying size of each country's armed forces available for military operations.

Think It Through Is there a correlation between Gross National Income and Total Armed Forces? Why or why not?

Nonetheless, the quest for security through arms and the realist belief in military force remain widespread. Most security analysts believe that this is because military capability is a prerequisite for the successful exercise of *coercive diplomacy* through the threat of limited force. Perhaps this conviction is what inspired former U.S. President George W. Bush to assert that "a dangerous and uncertain world requires America to have a sharpened sword."

The "Cost" of Military Spending

Military power is central in leaders' concepts of national security, and even though the end of the Cold War reduced tensions worldwide and therefore the need for military preparations, world military spending rose to $1.82 trillion in 2018, which represents a 3 percent increase since 2011, and a 65 percent increase since 2000. This staggering number is equal to 2.1 percent of global gross domestic product, or $239 for each person in the world (SIPRI, 2019a; WDI, 2017). The world is spending $6,930,708 each *minute* for military preparations.

Historically, rich countries have spent the most money on military preparedness and this pattern has continued. The twenty-nine members of the North Atlantic Treaty Organization spent $963 billion in military expenditures in 2018—that is, 15 percent of the world's countries were responsible for 53 percent of the world total military expenditures. However, when you take into account the **relative burden of military spending** and assess the ratio of military expenditures to GDP within the country, we get a somewhat different perspective. At the start of 2018, Global North countries allocated on average 2.3 percent of their GDP toward military expenditure. In the Global South, almost 2 percent of their GDP went toward military expenditures—at a relatively greater sacrifice of funding to promote human development and economic growth among the poor given their small economies overall (WDI, 2017; SIPRI, 2019a).

relative burden of military spending
Measure of the economic burden of military activities calculated by the share of each state's gross domestic product allocated to military expenditures.

Indeed, some comparatively wealthy states (Saudi Arabia and Israel) bear a heavy burden, whereas other states that provide a high average income for their citizens (Japan and Luxembourg) have a low defense burden. Likewise, the citizens of some very poor countries (Sudan and Niger) are heavily burdened, whereas those of others (Paraguay and the Democratic Republic of Congo) are not. It is, therefore, difficult to generalize about the precise relationship between a country's defense burden and its citizens' standard of living, human development, or stage of development. That said, a simple look at Map 8.2 reveals that the majority of the countries with the highest military burden are also the countries that are experiencing the highest levels of armed conflict, or are located in regions with huge security problems, such as the Middle East and Africa (see Chapter 7).

Since 1945, only a handful of states have borne enormous military costs in terms of total dollars. Figure 8.2A shows that U.S. military spending accounted for 36 percent of the world total in 2018, followed by China with 14 percent, Saudi Arabia and India each with 3.7 percent, France with 3.5 percent, and Russia with 3.4 percent. It was the first time since 2010 that the United States increased its military spending, because of the implementation of a new arms procurement program under U.S. President Donald Trump. China increased its military spending for the twenty-fourth year in a row, with spending in 2018 almost ten times as high as that in 1994 (SIPRI, 2019c). Figure 8.2B shows that the Americas comprise the largest regional component of world military expenditures, driven largely by U.S.

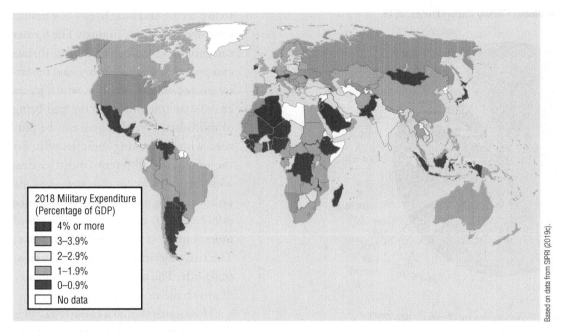

Based on data from SIPRI (2019c).

MAP 8.2 Military Expenditures as a Percentage of GDP As the map shows, wide variations exist in the percentage of a country's gross domestic product that is allocated toward military spending. Many countries allocate a high proportion of their total GDP to defense, and others spend their wealth to enhance human security. In 2018, Saudi Arabia had the highest relative burden of military spending with 8.8 percent of its GDP going to defense, followed by Oman (8.1 percent), Algeria (5.3 percent), Kuwait (5.1 percent), and Lebanon (5 percent) (SIPRI, 2019a).

Think It Through In what ways does the relative burden of military spending cyclically harm fragile states?

expenditures. Military spending in Asia and Oceania has risen every year since 1988, having increased over the course of thirty years from 9 percent of the world total to 28 percent in 2018. This has been spurred by tensions between countries within the region as well as between the United States and China (SIPRI, 2019a).

Many countries, however, have gained a relative competitive edge by investing in research on the development of goods to export abroad, while conserving resources by relying on allies and global institutions to provide defense against potential threats. The United States is somewhat of an exception: In addition to its high military spending, the United States has also been the dominant investor in research and development funding. Its emphasis, however, has been on military preparation, which comprises most of U.S. federal R&D spending (Battelle and R&D Magazine, 2019).

Military expenditures incur **opportunity costs**—when what is gained for one purpose is lost for other purposes—so that any particular choice means the cost of some lost opportunity must be paid. Military spending, for example, retards economic growth and creates fiscal deficits. The substantial costs of defense can also erode national welfare—the very thing that policy makers hope to defend with military might. "Guns versus butter"—how to allocate scarce finances for military preparedness as opposed to meeting the human needs of citizens and enabling them

opportunity costs
The sacrifices that result when the decision to select one option means that the opportunity to realize gains from another option is lost.

human security
A measure popular in liberal theory of the degree to which the welfare of individuals is protected and promoted, in contrast to realist theory's emphasis on putting the state's interests in military and national security ahead of all other goals.

Shares of Global Military Expenditures, 2018

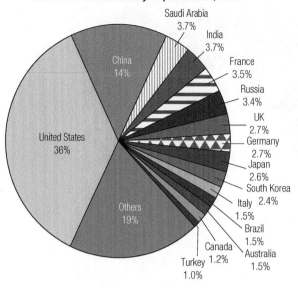

World Military Expenditures by Region, 1988–2018*

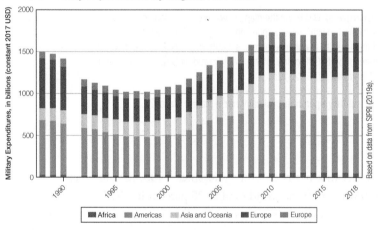

*No total can be calculated for 1991 as no data for the Soviet Union is available for that year

FIGURES 8.2A AND 8.2B   Rising Global Military Expenditures Global military budgets have fluctuated since 1960, with total expenditures worldwide peaking in 1987, after which they fell about a third until the 9/11 terrorist attacks in 2001. As shown on top, U.S. military expenditures continue to far exceed those of any other country and are almost three times more than the expenditures of the next closest country—China. However, as shown on bottom, the military budget of the Global South's developing countries, particularly in Asia and Oceania, has grown to command a significant portion of world military expenditures, amounting to more than a fourth of the world total at the start of 2019.

to live secure and long lives—is a serious controversy in every country. The former category looks to arms to combat threats and preserve *national security*, and the latter stresses **human security**, which places an emphasis on protecting the well-being of individuals. Neither goal can be pursued without making some sacrifice for the other, and different countries deal with this dilemma in different ways. As political scientist Richard Rosecrance (1997, p. 210) notes, "States can afford more 'butter' if they need fewer 'guns'. The two objectives sometimes represent trade-offs: The achievement of one may diminish the realization of the other."

How much should a country sacrifice for national security? For many realists, the price is never too high. Others caution, however, that leaders should take heed of U.S. civil rights activist Martin Luther King Jr.'s warning: "A nation that continues year after year to spend more money on military defense than on programs of social uplift is approaching spiritual doom." These skeptics of high military spending believe the high costs can easily reduce the human security found within a particular country. "It is important to remember that every defense dollar spent to over-insure against a remote or diminishing risk," cautioned former U.S. Secretary of Defense Robert Gates, "is a dollar not available to take care of our people, reset the force, win the wars we are in, and improve capabilities in areas where we are underinvested and potentially vulnerable." Consider how, given the U.S. choice to prioritize military spending, the United States ranks on various nonmilitary measures of human security (see Table 8.2).

These rankings raise serious questions about the true costs of national security. The choices in balancing the need for defense against the need to provide for the common welfare are difficult because they entail a necessary trade-off between competing values. Examination of

TABLE 8.2   Human Security: How the U.S. Ranks in the World

Indicator	Rank
GNI for each person	11
Unemployment rate (% of labor force)	55
Human development (HDI)	13
Gender inequality (GII)	41
Life expectancy	38
Carbon dioxide emissions (per capita)	9
Under age 5 mortality rate	45
Total health expenditure (% of GDP)	23

Based on data from World Development Indicators (2017); Human Development Report (UN, 2018h).

national budgets discloses an unmistakable pattern: although the sources of global political power may be changing, many states continue to seek security by spending substantial portions of their national treasures on arms.

> *Every gun that is made, every warship launched, every rocket fired, signifies in the final sense a theft from those who hunger and are not fed, those who are cold and are not clothed.*
>
> **—DWIGHT D. EISENHOWER, FORMER U.S. PRESIDENT**

Changes in Military Capabilities

LO 8-2   Identify and evaluate the implications of the global arms trade and nuclear weapons for world politics, and assess recent developments in weapons technology.

The growing militarization of the United States, the other great powers, and now mobilized nonstate terrorist groups has altered the global distribution of military capabilities. Part of the reason is that weapons production capabilities are more widespread than ever, with even Global South countries and terrorist organizations participating in the business of manufacturing modern aircraft, tanks, and small arms. Furthermore, a growing trend since the beginning of the Iraq War has been the increased use of **private military services**, which enhances a state's military capabilities by allowing the government to conduct operations with fewer troops than would otherwise be needed.

private military services
Outsourcing activities of a military-specific nature to private companies, such as armed security, equipment maintenance, IT services, logistics, and intelligence services.

Trends in the Weapons Trade

During the Cold War, many states sought to increase their security by purchasing arms produced by suppliers eagerly seeking allies as well as profits from exports. In 1961, the world arms trade was valued at $4 billion. Thereafter, the traffic in arms imports climbed rapidly and peaked in 1987 at $82 billion (U.S. ACDA, 1997, pp. 10, 100). The end of the Cold War did not end the arms trade, however. Since 1991 when the Cold War ended, and continuing

Global Share of Major Arms Imports, 2014–2018

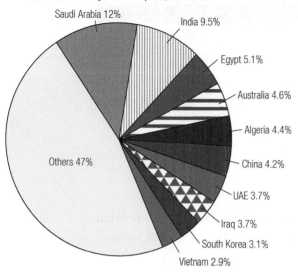

Global Share of Major Arms Exports, 2014–2018

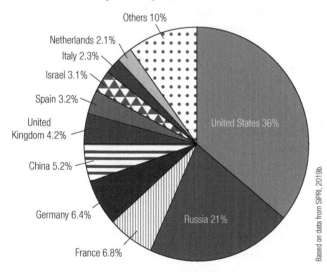

Based on data from SIPRI, 2019b.

FIGURES 8.3A AND 8.3B   Major Players in the Global Weapons Bazaar The ongoing global arms trade has led to the globalization of military capabilities throughout the Global North and Global South. Of the ten largest arms recipients (shown top), half are in Asia and Oceania. As shown on bottom, the United States is the top supplier in the business of war, responsible for more than a third of major arms exports globally.

throughout the era of global terrorism that began on 9/11, the magnitude of the weapons trade continues to increase. The volume of international transfers of major arms, estimated in 2018 to be at least $95 billion, is 23 percent higher than ten years earlier (SIPRI, 2019a; SIPRI 2019b).

There have been troubling trends in the global arms trade in recent years. Between 2014 and 2018, major weapons were imported by 155 countries. Overall, the major recipients of global arms shipments remain heavily concentrated in a subset of Global South arms purchasers. The top five arms recipients, which accounted for 35 percent of arms imports, included Saudi Arabia, India, Egypt, Australia, and Algeria (see Figure 8.3A). The stream of weapons to these insecure and eager buyers with money to spend is not likely to end soon, and the short- and long-term consequences of arms transfers to countries experiencing internal conflict is a concern. In 2018, Pakistan purchased thirty combat helicopters and four frigates from Turkey. In its ongoing efforts to combat Islamic State forces, Iraq received a wide variety of major arms—such as combat aircraft—mainly from the United States and Russia (SIPRI, 2019b).

Along with the changing demands of arms importers, changes in the activities of arms suppliers are also important. During the Cold War, the superpowers dominated the arms export market. Between 1975 and 1989, the U.S.-Soviet share of global arms exports varied between one-half and three-fourths, and the United States alone had cornered 40 percent of the world arms export market when the Cold War ended (U.S. ACDA, 1997). In that period, the two superpowers together "supplied an estimated $325 billion worth of arms and ammunition to the Third World" (Klare, 1994, p. 139). In the post-9/11 global war on terrorism, the United States increased its worldwide supply of weapons to countries that agreed to be partners in the "coalition of the willing" in wars in Afghanistan and Iraq. Interestingly, it is still the United States and Russia that dominate the arms export market, supplying 36 and 21 percent of all conventional weapons exports, respectively, between 2014 and 2018 (see Figure 8.3B). Together with China, Germany, and France, these top five arms suppliers account for 75 percent of global arms exports (SIPRI, 2019b).

TABLE 8.3   Sellers of Security or Merchants of Death? Top 20 Arms-Producing Companies

Rank	Company (Country)	2017
1	Lockheed Martin (USA)	44.9
2	Boeing (USA)	26.9
3	Raytheon (USA)	23.9
4	BAE Systems (UK)	22.9
5	Northrop Grumman (USA)	22.4
6	General Dynamics (USA)	19.5
7	Airbus Group (Trans-European)	11.3
8	Thales (France)	9.0
9	Leonardo (Italy)	8.9
10	Almaz-Antey (Russia)	8.6
11	United Technologies Corp. (USA)	7.8
12	L-3 Communications (USA)	7.8
13	Huntington Ingalls Industries (USA)	6.5
14	United Aircraft Corp. (Russia)	6.4
15	United Shipbuilding Corp. (Russia)	5.0
16	Honeywell International (USA)	4.5
17	Rolls-Royce (UK)	4.4
18	Leidos (USA)	4.4
19	Naval Group (France)	4.1
20	Textron (USA)	4.1

Based on data from SIPRI (2018).

Although countries themselves are typically identified as global suppliers of arms, in some countries private companies are major producers of weapons and compete in the profitable arms marketplace (see Table 8.3). Sales of arms and military services by the world's 100 largest arms-producing and military services companies exceeded $398 billion in 2017 (SIPRI, 2018). That year, the $44.9 billion in arms sales of Lockheed Martin, an American-based company, were greater than the GDPs of 123 countries. The sales of weapons by U.S.-based Boeing (at $26.9 billion) exceed the baseline budget of the Marine Corps in 2017 by roughly $3.3 billion.

Another development in the post–Cold War era, which has been likened to modern-day mercenaries, is the growth in companies that provide private military services for hire on the global market. The outsourcing of military-like activities enables governments to maintain their force structure for a lower cost than otherwise would be possible. However, relying on private contractors in war zones may compromise democratic accountability and the state's monopoly on the use of force, as well as raise issues about legal status (see "A Closer Look: Private Soldiers and the Conduct of War").

The Strategic Consequences of Arms Sales

The transfer of arms across borders has produced some unintended and counterproductive consequences. For example, during the Cold War, the United States and the Soviet Union thought they could maintain peace by spreading arms to strategically important countries. Yet many of

A Closer Look

PRIVATE SOLDIERS AND THE CONDUCT OF WAR

On September 16, 2007, Blackwater private security contractors guarding U.S. diplomats in Iraq opened fire in Nisoor Square, a crowded Baghdad intersection. An angry Iraqi government blamed them for the shooting deaths of seventeen civilians and the injuries of twenty others—some of whom were women and children. Although Blackwater said the guards were responding to an ambush by insurgents and were innocent of any crime, others said the shooting was unprovoked and the Blackwater guards fired indiscriminately. The incident inflamed anti-American sentiment in the country (Blackwater renamed itself Xe Services in an effort to distance its brand from the incident) and raised questions about the role and accountability of private military companies in war zones.

Iraq is not the only place where private soldiers have been prevalent; in 2011 Muammar al-Qaddafi's government recruited mercenaries from Guinea and Nigeria, offering up to $2,000, to quash the ongoing protests in Libya against his regime. Supporters of private military services point out that private contractors like Blackwater (Xe Services), Triple Canopy, and DynCorp are not of the same ilk as al-Qaddafi's mercenary forces that come from informal networks of former civil war combatants. Military contractors from reputable companies tend to be professional, efficient, and effective. Hiring private soldiers for a single mission is less expensive than maintaining a standing army, and it has been argued that they may be less likely to maltreat civilians "than public soldiers precisely because their motivation is pecuniary and not ideological or rooted in loyalties to a nation, group, clan or tribe" (Leander, 2005, p. 609). Moreover, "they are bound to follow the laws of the countries where they are based

zffoto/Shutterstock.com

and operate and, in theory, are only hired for noncombat operations like guard duty (though that line is often a thin one in war zones)" (Keating, 2011).

Critics, however, point out that private military companies operate in a legal gray area and that they do not receive adequate monitoring and evaluation. In the Blackwater case, it was unclear whether the employees were subject to Iraqi, U.S., civilian, or military law. And even if employees are found culpable, it is difficult to establish corporate liability unless it can be proven that the company itself intended to break the law. Others worry that private military services have a financial incentive for armed conflicts to persist and that the outsourcing process for lucrative government contracts is not sufficiently competitive, with private military companies effectively establishing a monopoly once they are awarded a long-term contract (Markusen, 2003).

Watch the Carnegie Council Video:
"Paying Others to Fight Our Battles"

You Decide:

1. Does hiring private military services encourage the use of force to resolve conflicts, and make it easier for us to look the other way when it comes to death and destruction in war?

2. Do private military services compromise the states' monopoly on the use of force? Do you think reliance on such services should continue?

3. Are there areas where private contractors could prove particularly useful?

these recipients went to war with their neighbors or experienced internal rebellion. Of the top twenty arms importers in 1988, more than half "had governments noted for the frequent use of violence" (Sivard, 1991, p. 17).

Undoubtedly, the import of such huge arsenals of weapons aided this level of destruction. As the arms exporters "peddle death to the poor," they seldom acknowledge how this scouting

JOEL SAGET/Getty Images

IMAGE 8.2 A World Awash with Guns The sale of arms is a big transborder business. Part of its growth has occurred because the line between legal and illegal trades is blurred—there is a vibrant black market for the sale of arms to illicit groups, though "almost every firearm on the black market was originally traded legally" (De Soysa, Jackson, and Ormhaug, 2009, p. 88). Shown here is an example of the thriving international trade in weapons: one of the many "arms bazaars" in the global weapons marketplace. There are over 857 million civilian-held firearms in circulation (Karp, 2018), and as Nobel Laureate Oscar Arias Sanchez (1996, p.i) sadly noted, "The greatest percentage of violent deaths occurs from the use of light weapons and small arms."

for customers contradicts other proclaimed foreign policy goals. For instance, while seeking to promote democratization, less democratic countries receive the greatest amounts of U.S. arms (Blanton, 2005). Between 2010 and 2018, the United States was responsible for 33 percent of all global arms exports, with major weapons delivered to ninety-eight countries, including many with human rights problems such as the UAE, Qatar, and Saudi Arabia (SIPRI, 2019b). Speaking to a similar pattern of exporting arms to countries with poor human rights records, former British Defense Minister Sir John Stanley cautioned that the "scale of the extant strategic licenses to . . . countries of human rights concern puts into stark relief the inherent conflict between the government's arms exports and human rights policies." He further admonished that the "government should apply significantly more cautious judgments when considering arms export license applications for goods to authoritarian regimes, which might be used to facilitate internal repression, in contravention of the government's stated policy" (as quoted in Norton-Taylor, 2013).

The inability of arms suppliers to control the uses of their military hardware is troubling. Friends can become foes, and supplying weapons can backfire—generating what the CIA calls **blowback** to describe what can happen when foreign activities such as covert shipments of arms are later used in retaliations against the supplier (Daase and Friesendorf, 2010). The United States learned this painful lesson the hard way. The weapons it shipped to Iraq when Saddam Hussein was fighting Iran in the 1980s were later used against U.S. forces in the Persian Gulf War. This also happened when the Stinger missiles the United States supplied to Taliban forces resisting the Soviet Union's 1979 invasion in Afghanistan fell into the hands of terrorists who

blowback
The propensity for actions undertaken for national security to have the unintended consequence of provoking retaliatory attacks when relations later sour.

later used them against the United States. Likewise, in 1982 Great Britain found itself shipping military equipment to Argentina just eight days before Argentina's attack on the British-controlled Falkland Islands; and in 1998 U.S. military technology sold to China was exported to Pakistan, making its nuclear weapons test possible.

Such developments have long-term consequences and are particularly alarming, as in the case of Pakistan, where there is grave concern about the ability of the state to ensure the security of nuclear material. According to Graham Allison, a leading nuclear expert, "[t]he nuclear security of the arsenal is now a lot better than it was. But the unknown variable here is the future of Pakistan itself, because it's not hard to envision a situation in which the state's authority falls apart, and you're not sure who's in control of the weapons, the nuclear labs, the materials" (as quoted in Sanger, 2009).

Nuclear Weapons

Technological research and development has radically expanded the destructive power of national arsenals. Albert Einstein, the Nobel Prize–winning physicist whose ideas were the basis for the development of nuclear weapons, was alarmed by the threat they posed. He professed uncertainty about the weapons that would be used in a third world war but was confident that in a fourth world war they would be "sticks and stones." He warned in May 1946 that inasmuch as "the unleashed power of the atom has changed everything save our modes of thinking we thus drift toward unparalleled catastrophe."

IMAGE 8.3 **Unleashing the Atom** On August 6, 1945, the United States dropped the world's first deployed atomic bomb over the Japanese city of Hiroshima, wiping out 90 percent of the city, immediately killing 80,000 people, and causing radiation that would result in the deaths of 140,000 more by the year's end. The next day, the *New York Times* sagely reflected that "Man unleashed the atom to destroy man, and another chapter in human history opened." Pictured here is the destruction of the Museum of Science and Industry shortly after the blast.

The use of nuclear weapons could not only destroy entire cities and countries but also, conceivably, the world's entire population. The largest "blockbuster" bombs of World War II delivered the power of 10 tons of TNT. The atomic bomb that leveled Hiroshima had the power of over 15,000 tons of TNT. Less than twenty years later, the Soviet Union built a nuclear bomb with the explosive force of 57,000,000 tons of TNT.

Since 1945, more than 130,000 nuclear warheads have been built, all but 2 percent by the United States (which has built 55 percent) and the Soviet Union (43 percent). Most have been dismantled since the 1986 peak but, as shown in Table 8.4, as many as 3750 remained deployed at the start of 2019. The United States, Russia, France, and Britain all continue to possess deployed warheads. Other countries have warheads, but do not have them deployed such as China, India, Pakistan, and Israel. The size of North Korea's nuclear weapons inventory remains uncertain.

In addition, as many as twenty-one other states (such as Iran and Brazil) or NGO terrorist organizations are widely believed to be seeking to join the nuclear club. The **proliferation** of arms is a serious global concern, because the so-called **Nth country problem** (the addition of new nuclear states) is expected to become increasingly probable. Both **horizontal nuclear proliferation** (increase in the number of nuclear states) and **vertical nuclear proliferation** (increases in the capabilities of existing nuclear powers) are likely.

Consider North Korea's nuclear tests, as well as Iran's and Syria's self-proclaimed aims to acquire nuclear weapons. Nuclear proliferation is likely to continue as states face strong incentives to join the nuclear club and acquire missiles and bombers for their delivery. As long as they do, the threat remains that Argentina, Brazil, Libya, and Taiwan, which once had active nuclear programs, could revive these capabilities to manufacture nuclear weapons.

Likewise, there is widespread international concern regarding the expansion of existing nuclear programs. Though making limited reductions to their nuclear forces as called for by the **Strategic Arms Reduction Treaty (START)** (see Chapter 9), both the United States and Russia have long-term plans to replace and modernize their nuclear warheads, nuclear weapon production facilities, and missile and aircraft delivery systems. China, India, and Pakistan are

proliferation
The spread of weapon capabilities from a few to many states in a chain reaction, so that increasing numbers of states gain the ability to launch an attack on other states with devastating (e.g., nuclear) weapons.

Nth country problem
The expansion of additional new nuclear weapon states.

horizontal nuclear proliferation
An increase in the number of states that possess nuclear weapons.

vertical nuclear proliferation
The expansion of the capabilities of existing nuclear powers to inflict increasing destruction with their nuclear weapons.

Strategic Arms Reduction Treaty (START)
The U.S.–Russian series of negotiations that began in 1993 and with the 1997 START-III by Russia in 2000, which pledged to cut the nuclear arsenals of both sides by 80 percent of the Cold War peak to lower the risk of nuclear war.

TABLE 8.4   Nuclear Forces Worldwide, 2019

Country	Deployed Warheads*	Other Warheads**	Total
United States	1750	4435	6185
Russia	1600	4900	6500
United Kingdom	120	95	215
France	280	20	300
China		290	290
India		130–140	130–140
Pakistan		140–150	140–150
Israel		80	80
North Korea	..	..	(20–30)
Total	**3750**	**10,110**	**13,890**

*Placed on missiles or bases with operational forces.
**Stored and retired warheads awaiting dismantlement.
Based on data from FAS (2019).

IMAGE 8.4 **A Rogue Nuclear Power** Shown here, in April 2012, North Korea launched a ballistic missile in defiance of UN Security Council resolutions and an agreement with the United States. According to former U.S. Ambassador to South Korea Donald Gregg, "This is [Kim Jong-un's] way of demonstrating to the people of North Korea he is in charge and his country is capable of high tech things. It is a manifestation of his power." Although the launch ended in failure, it generated international condemnation—as did North Korea's test in 2017 of a thermonuclear bomb thought to be as much as eight times stronger than the one dropped on Hiroshima in 1945.

Nuclear Nonproliferation Treaty (NPT)

An international agreement that seeks to prevent horizontal proliferation by prohibiting further nuclear weapons sales, acquisitions, or production.

also all modernizing their nuclear weapon delivery systems and expanding their nuclear weapon stockpiles. Ongoing tensions between India and Pakistan, which in 2019 involved air strikes in each other's territories for the first time by the two nuclear-armed nations, sparked concerns about nuclear confrontation. "The renewed focus on the strategic importance of nuclear deterrence and capacity is a very worrying trend," observed former Swedish ambassador Jan Eliasson.

"Grounded in the tradition of realist and security-based approaches to nuclear proliferation and nuclear deterrence," the rationale behind the decision to acquire nuclear weapons is clear, since "nuclear weapons on average and across a broad variety of indicators enhance the security and diplomatic influence of their possessors" (Gartzke and Kroenig, 2009, p. 152). The complaint of former French President Charles de Gaulle, who argued that without an independent nuclear capability France could not "command its own destiny," reflects the strong incentive of nonnuclear states to develop weapons similar to those of the existing nuclear club. Similarly, in 1960 Britain's Aneurin Bevan asserted that without the bomb, Britain would go "naked into the council chambers of the world."

This sentiment continues to be reflected today by aspiring nuclear powers, as seen in North Korea's declaration that "[i]t has become an absolutely impossible option for (North Korea) to even think about giving up its nuclear weapons" (Fackler, 2009, p. A12). In 2017, North Korea conducted a test of what it said was a thermonuclear weapon and two new types of long-range ballistic missile delivery systems. Assessing the impact of North Korea's advancements in missile technology, the commander of U.S. Army forces in the Pacific General Vincent Brooks warned in 2015 that North Korea "now represents a 'physical threat' to the United States" (Crawford, 2015).

Because of the widespread conviction, rooted in realism, that military power confers political stature, many countries, such as Iran and North Korea, regard the **Nuclear Nonproliferation Treaty (NPT)** as hypocritical because it provides a seal of approval to the United States, Russia, China, Britain, and France for possessing nuclear weapons while denying it to all others. The underlying belief that it is acceptable to develop a nuclear capacity for deterrence, political influence, and prestige was expressed in 1999 at the Munich Security Conference by Brajesh

Mishra, India's national security adviser. He justified India's nuclear program by asserting that "in the 21st century a new security order is likely to arise in the Asia-Pacific region" and that India should be granted as much respect and deference as is China.

Although the underlying demand for nuclear weapons is rather straightforward, the supply of nuclear weapons does not appear to make as much sense. Aside from economic motivations, it is less clear why nuclear-capable states themselves have contributed to the global spread of nuclear weapons by providing sensitive nuclear know-how to non-nuclear states. Consider, for example, that Israel built its first nuclear weapon just two years after receiving nuclear assistance from France in the early 1960s. Similarly, after receiving assistance from China in the early 1980s with its nuclear program, Pakistan constructed its first nuclear weapon. Pakistani scientist A. Q. Khan operated a black market nuclear proliferation ring in the late 1990s, and this is thought to have aided Libya, Iran, and North Korea in their efforts to develop nuclear weapons.

Focusing on the supply side of nuclear proliferation, political scientist Matthew Kroenig (2009, p. 114) identifies three basic conditions under which states are likely to share sensitive nuclear assistance:

> First, the more powerful a state is relative to a potential nuclear recipient, the less likely it is to provide sensitive nuclear assistance. Second, states are more likely to provide sensitive nuclear assistance to states with which they share a common enemy. Third, states that are less vulnerable to superpower pressure are more likely to provide sensitive nuclear assistance.

These strategic characteristics of the supplier provide some insight into the nuclear proliferation problem, which is also exacerbated by the widespread availability of materials needed to make a nuclear weapon. This is partly because of the widespread use of nuclear technology for generating electricity. Today, almost 451 nuclear-power reactors are in operation in thirty-four countries throughout the world. The number of new operational nuclear reactors is certain to increase because about 55 new nuclear reactors are now planned or under construction (IAEA, 2019). Conversion of peacetime nuclear energy programs to military purposes can occur either overtly or, as in the case of India and Pakistan, covertly. The safeguards built into the **nonproliferation regime** are simply inadequate to detect and prevent secret nuclear weapons development programs.

It is very unlikely that the nuclear threat will disappear (see Figure 8.4). As Matthew Bunn, editor of *Arms Control Today*, explains, "There's not a snowball's chance in hell we'll eliminate all nuclear weapons from the face of the Earth. That genie is long since out of the bottle and there's no chance of ever getting him back in."

nonproliferation regime
Rules to contain arms races so that weapons or technology do not spread to states that do not have them.

The Revolution in Military Technology

Another trend that is increasing the lethality of the weapons of war is the rapidity of technological refinements that increase the capacity of states to send their weapons great distances with ever-greater accuracy. Missiles can now send weapons from as far away as 11,000 miles to within one hundred feet of their targets in less than thirty minutes. One example is the development by the United States and Russia of the ability to equip their ballistic missiles with

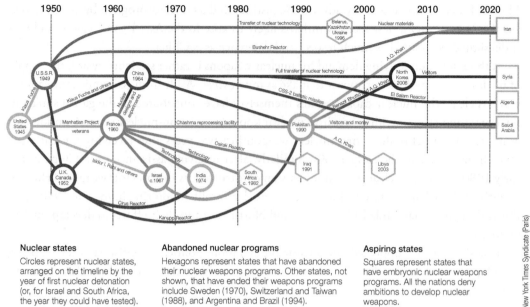

Nuclear states

Circles represent nuclear states, arranged on the timeline by the year of first nuclear detonation (or, for Israel and South Africa, the year they could have tested).

Abandoned nuclear programs

Hexagons represent states that have abandoned their nuclear weapons programs. Other states, not shown, that have ended their weapons programs include Sweden (1970), Switzerland and Taiwan (1988), and Argentina and Brazil (1994).

Aspiring states

Squares represent states that have embryonic nuclear weapons programs. All the nations deny ambitions to develop nuclear weapons.

New York Times Syndicate (Paris)

FIGURE 8.4 A Chain Reaction of Proliferation Since the dawn of the nuclear age, the secrets for making nuclear weapons have spread, either through intentional transfer, leak, or espionage. The connections depicted above indicate the flow of information and technology, through either one-way or two-way transfers. Today there are five official nuclear states (the United States, Russia, the United Kingdom, China, and France) and four additional de facto nuclear states (India, Pakistan, North Korea, and Israel). Many others are poised to join the club of nuclear weapon powers, as this figure shows. Halting nuclear proliferation continues to be seen as one of the most urgent challenges facing the world.

multiple independently targetable reentry vehicles (MIRVs)
A technological innovation permitting many weapons to be delivered from a single missile.

nonlethal weapons (NLWs)
The wide array of "soft kill," low-intensity methods of incapacitating an enemy's people, vehicles, communications systems, or entire cities without killing either combatants or noncombatants.

revolution in military technology (RMT)
The sophisticated new weapons technologies that make fighting war without mass armies possible.

multiple independently targetable reentry vehicles (MIRVs). This allows these countries to launch many warheads on a single missile toward different targets simultaneously and accurately. One MIRV U.S. MX Peacekeeper missile could carry ten nuclear warheads—enough to wipe out a city and everything else within a fifty-mile radius.

Other technological improvements have led to steady increases in the speed, accuracy, range, and effectiveness of weapons. Laser weapons, nuclear-armed tactical air-to-surface missiles (TASMs), stealth air-launched cruise missiles (ACMs), and antisatellite (ASAT) weapons that can project force and wage war from outer space have become a part of the military landscape.

The global terrain is being transformed by another sea change in the kinds of arms being developed to wage war: the new high-tech **nonlethal weapons (NLWs)** made possible by the **revolution in military technology (RMT)**. The new generation includes sounds, shocks, and smells to disperse or incapacitate crowds. For example, the Long Range Acoustic Device (LRAD) blasts sounds at a deafening 150 decibels to incapacitate everyone within 300 meters by giving them an instant and intense headache. Another example is the U.S. Air Force's "active denial technology" that uses electromagnetic radiation to penetrate clothing and cause water molecules to vibrate and burn skin tissue. And it's humorous, but true, that the Pentagon has considered various nonlethal chemical weapons to disrupt enemy discipline and morale, including an aphrodisiac chemical weapon "that would make enemy soldiers sexually irresistible to one another" (Hecht, 2007).

More seriously, NLWs are already deployed in information-warfare squadrons to protect military computer networks from electronic sneak attacks. Other forms of these weapons include energy pulses to knock out or take down enemies without necessarily killing them, biofeedback, beamed electromagnetic and sonic wavelengths that can modify the human behavior of targets (for example, putting people to sleep through electromagnetic heat and magnetic radiation), and ground-penetrating **smart bombs**, which can penetrate a buried bunker at 1000 feet per second and, at the proper millisecond, detonate 500 pounds of explosive to destroy an adversary's inventory of buried chemical and biological weapons.

The precision and power of today's conventional weapons have expanded exponentially, at precisely the moment when the revolution in military technology is leading to "the end of infantry" in the computer age. Countries (and now, terrorist groups) increasingly rely on a variety of new cyberstrategies using innovation in information technology to deter and demobilize enemies (Dombrowski and Gholz, 2007). Examples include such futuristic weapons as the electromagnetic pulse (EMP) bomb, which can be hand-delivered in a suitcase and can immobilize an entire city's computer and communications systems; computer viruses that can eliminate a country's telephone system; and logic bombs that can confuse and redirect traffic on the target country's air and rail systems.

> **smart bombs**
> Precision-guided military technology that enables a bomb to search for its target and detonate at the precise time it can do the most damage.

Artificial Intelligence and Autonomous Weapons Systems

A revolution in the role of **artificial intelligence** (AI) in warfare is also already under way and development of autonomous weapons systems (AWS) is fast becoming a focus of global competition. "AI weaponization is evident across the board: navigating and utilizing unmanned naval, aerial, and terrain vehicles, producing collateral-damage estimations, deploying 'fire-and-forget' missile systems and using stationary systems to automate everything from personnel systems and equipment maintenance to the deployment of surveillance drones, robots, and more" (Pandya, 2019).

> **artificial intelligence**
> The ability of computer systems to perform tasks commonly requiring intelligence, such as audio recognition, visual perception, and decision making.

Unmanned systems such as the forty-two-pound PackBot have been used in Iraq and Afghanistan to detect improvised explosive devices. Altogether, at least twenty-two different robot systems are now in use on the ground, with prototypes for a variety of others, from automated machine guns to robotic stretcher bearers to lethal robots the size of insects. Robot soldiers that can think, see, and react like human beings are based on nanotechnology (the science of very small structures) and, predicts Robert Finkelstein, a veteran engineer who leads Robotic Technologies Inc., by "2035 we will have robots as fully capable as human soldiers on the battlefield" (Singer, 2013).

On the rapidly evolving landscape of robotic weaponry, the acquisition and use of unmanned aerial vehicles—more commonly known as drones—is also on the rise (see "Controversy: Should Drones Be Used in the Conduct of Warfare?"). By the start of 2019, nine countries had used armed drones, with many other countries developing and enlarging their drone capabilities. India has indicated that it is equipping its drones with precision-guided munitions "to conduct cross-border attacks on suspected terrorists. Pakistan, not to be outdone by its rival, has declared that it will develop armed drones on its own or with China's help in order to target the Taliban and Al Qaeda in its lawless tribal areas" (Kreps and Zenko, 2014, p. 72). Of growing concern is that countries might use drones in ways that they would not use manned aircraft, and that this might lead to an escalation of disputes. China flies drones over the Senkaku/Diaoyu Islands, eight

Controversy

SHOULD DRONES BE USED IN THE CONDUCT OF WARFARE?

A major development in the conduct of warfare has been the widespread use of unmanned aerial vehicles (UAV), commonly referred to as drones.* Drones have extensive surveillance capabilities, as they are able to fly at 17,500 feet and still observe 15 square miles in a single image with enough clarity to identify the kind of cell phone an individual is carrying (Gayle, 2013). While the bulk of drones deployed around the world function as tools for unarmed surveillance, the United States has provoked controversy over its growing use of drones as lethal robots of war both on and off the battlefield. Between 2004 and mid-2019, the United States had conducted 6786 strikes in Yemen, Afghanistan, Somalia, and Iraq (BIJ, 2019). Yet the "U.S. is ahead, but not alone, in using drones. Nine countries have already used armed drones in combat, and at least 20 more are developing lethal drone programs – including Russia and China" (Parker, 2018).

Such capabilities raise important questions about the limitations that should, or should not, be placed on the use of drones. Addressing the privacy concerns of ordinary civilians, proponents of drones point out that they are operated by trained personnel as part of a security strategy; they are not controlled by voyeuristic amateurs. Furthermore, given their strategic utility for targeted strikes, drones save human lives because they remove the risk that a pilot could be shot down and, due to their accuracy, arguably minimize collateral damage (Shwayder and Mahapatra, 2013). Drones are also cost-effective because they eliminate the need for a fighter pilot to be trained and deployed.

Detractors paint a very different picture. While drone pilots are not at risk of physical harm, there is increasing evidence that the operation of drones may be psychologically damaging to the pilots (Press, 2018). There are also questions about the moral and

Arthimedes/Shutterstock.com

legal basis for the use of drones—with critics pointing out that the legal parameters concerning their use are vague, government usage is generally shrouded in secrecy, and signature strikes of anonymous military-aged males in targeted-killings fail to meet the legal principal of distinction to engage only valid military targets (Davis et al., 2013; Zenko, 2013). Using drones to strike targets abroad may also be counterproductive as such attacks anger the populace, which might create more enemies as these people decide to take up arms (Shwayder and Mahapatra, 2013). Moreover, there is growing concern about the extent to which drones are used to observe domestic noncombatants for nonmilitary security purposes. Naomi Gilens, of the American Civil Liberties Union, cautions that as "drone use becomes more and more common, it is crucial that the government's use of these spying machines be transparent and accountable to the American people. . . . We should not have to guess whether our government is using these eyes in the sky to spy on us" (Gilens, 2013). This sentiment may be directed toward a host of entities. In the United States, the Federal Aviation Administration estimated that by 2020 there will be 7 million drones in that country alone (Doctor, 2016).

What Do You Think?

1. Weighing the pros and cons of drones, are they an effective weapon of war?

2. Do secret drone programs place too much power in the hands of leaders?

3. With drone production under way around the world, are they the weapon of the future? To what extent is there a risk that the rights of ordinary people will be violated?

*Prepared with the advice and assistance of William Wagstaff, Ph.D.

uninhabited islands in a strategically important location that lie at the heart of a continuing territorial row with Japan and have contributed to tensions between the two countries. In response, Japan has developed drone-specific rules of engagement and indicated that it would be less hesitant to shoot a Chinese drone out of the sky than a piloted aircraft (Kreps and Zenko, 2014).

This revolution in military technology is reshaping the conduct of war, in part because weapons that are symbols of military might like stealth bombers and nuclear submarines are of little use in today's *asymmetric warfare*, in which individual soldiers equipped with the latest technologies are needed for search-and-destroy missions against guerrilla militias. Moreover, robotic forces are not vulnerable to human frailties. Gordon Johnson, of the Pentagon's Joint Forces Command, notes the appeal of robotic forces. "They're not afraid. They don't forget their orders. They don't care if the guy next to them has just been shot. Will they do a better job than humans? Yes." Technological advances thus may make obsolete current ways of classifying weapons systems and measuring power ratios.

Even though these new weapons have been heralded as a way to accomplish the mission without exposing soldiers to the risks of combat, there are concerns about long-term implications. General Robert E. Lee famously observed, "It is good that we find war so horrible, or else we would become fond of it." Some worry that times are changing, and that war waged by remote control will become too easy and irresistibly tempting as a means to resolve conflicts. It is all the more alarming as we contemplate the prospect of the evolving ability to delegate the decision to kill to machines. "The prospect of machines with the discretion and power to take human life is morally repugnant," says UN Secretary-General Antonio Guterres. Mirroring this concern, twenty-six countries have called for an explicit ban on AI weapons "that requires some form of human control in the use of force. But the prospects for an AI weapons ban are low. Several influential countries including the United States are unwilling to place limits while the technology is still in development (Satariano, 2018). Significant advances in AI weaponization are sure to occur over the next couple of decades, and as former director of the U.S. Central Intelligence Agency John Brennan points out, "If we want other nations to use these technologies responsibly, we must use them responsibly."

Biological and Chemical Weapons

Biological and chemical weapons pose a special and growing threat, particularly in the hands of terrorists aiming for mass destruction rather than influencing public opinion. These unconventional weapons of mass destruction (WMD) are sometimes regarded as a "poor man's atomic bomb" because they can be built at comparatively little cost and cause widespread injury and death. Chemical weapons are toxic chemicals contained in a delivery mechanism such as a shell or bomb that have immediate consequence at the point of skin contact or inhalation. They kill or injure through toxic effects on the lungs, skin, blood, nerves, eyes, or other organs and are typically categorized as choking, blister, blood, or nerve agents; examples of each, respectively, include chlorine, mustard gas, hydrogen cyanide, and sarin. Biological weapons are infectious agents that cause disease or death, the release and effects of which may not be apparent until days after the weapon has been dispersed. These weapons are categorized as bacterial, viral, or toxic agents and include anthrax, smallpox, yellow fever, pneumonic plague, and botulism.

IMAGE 8.5 **Remote-Control Warfare?** The United States is building a new generation of technologically sophisticated weapons. Shown here, U.S. soldiers with land mine detectors wait as another soldier maneuvers a robot into a cave to check for mines, traps, and other weapons that may have been hidden by Taliban or Al Qaeda fugitives in the eastern border town of Qiqay, Afghanistan. The war in Afghanistan is the first time that robots have been used by the U.S. military for combat purposes. They are intended to help prevent U.S. casualties.

Chemical and biological weapons proliferation is of worldwide concern. In addition to the United States, which led the way in building these weapons, twelve other states have declared past production of chemical weapons, still others are suspected of secret production, and many terrorists claim they intend to acquire and use them. Following the 9/11 terrorist attacks on the United States, for example, there were fears that the spread of anthrax through the U.S. mail system was the first step in an endless series of future biological warfare attacks by terrorist networks. Advances in biotechnology have made it easier and cheaper to develop dangerous bacteria, viruses, and toxins, and this has increased the likelihood that such weapons will proliferate not only to an increasing number of countries but that nonstate actors also will develop or acquire these weapons of mass destruction and use them to attack civilian populations.

International law prohibits the use of chemical and biological weapons. The 1925 Geneva Protocol banned the use of chemical and biological weapons in warfare, though some signatories indicated that they would not abide by the prohibitions if their enemies used such weapons. Ratified by 189 (96 percent) of the world's countries, the Chemical Weapons Convention has addressed chemical weapons further by requiring the destruction of existing stocks. Israel signed the treaty in 1993, but as of August 3, 2019, had yet to ratify it. Only North Korea, Angola, Egypt, and South Sudan have declined to sign or accede to the Chemical Weapons Convention. The 1972 Biological and Toxin Weapons Convention extends the 1925 Geneva

IMAGE 8.6 Insidious Weapons of War Pervasive insecurity haunts much of the world because real supranational controls over the proliferation of biological and chemical weapons do not exist. Shown here are unexploded artillery shells from World War I that are believed to contain chemical warfare agents and are still being cleared from the border area between France and Germany. In light of the more recent use of chemical weapons in Syria—with some incidents committed by the Syrian government and others attributed to the Islamic State—Australia's former foreign minister Julie Bishop said, "The fact that atrocities such as this continue to occur shows that we must remain vigilant to the threat of chemical and biological weapons."

Protocol's restriction on the use of biological weapons to also prohibit the acquisition, development, production, and stockpiling of biological weapons.

Although there is concerted global attention to the threats of chemical and biological weapons, the ability to verify and thwart their development and use is limited. Iran's and Iraq's use of gas in their eight-year 1980s war against each other, Iraq's 1989 use of chemical weapons against its own Kurdish population, and Syria's use of sarin and chloride against unarmed civilians demonstrate the weaknesses of this, and similar, legal barriers. In addition, many radical extremists, often beyond the control of weak state governments, see chemical and biological weapons as a cheap and efficient terrorist method.

In response to military dangers, many leaders today still adhere to the realist axiom that "if you want peace prepare for war." Security, realists insist, requires military capabilities. However, because the possession of overpowering military capabilities does not automatically result in their prudent use, realists counsel that what matters greatly in the pursuit of national security are the *methods* on which states rely to use the capabilities they have acquired. How can weapons be most effectively used to promote national interests and exercise international influence? This question underscores the vital importance of choices about the types of military strategies employed.

Military Strategies

The most important event distinguishing pre– from post–World War II politics occurred on August 6, 1945, when the United States dropped the first atomic bomb on Hiroshima, Japan. In the blinding flash of a single weapon and the shadow of its mushroom cloud, the world was transformed from a "balance-of-power" to a "balance-of-terror" system. Since then, policy makers have had to grapple with two central policy questions: (1) whether they should use weapons of mass destruction and (2) how to prevent others from using them.

The search for answers is critical because both the immediate and delayed effects of weapons of mass destruction are terrifying to contemplate. Consider that even a short war using a tiny fraction of any great power's nuclear arsenal would destroy all life as we know it. A **nuclear winter** would result, with devastating consequences that could make the planet uninhabitable. Even a more limited nuclear conflict would greatly affect the atmosphere, with the sun at least partially blocked by large patches of dense smoke that would move around the world (Westing, 2013). It has been estimated that "the missiles on board a single [U.S.] SLBM submarine may be enough to initiate nuclear winter" (Quester, 1992, p. 43)—enough to end human existence.

Since World War II, not only have nuclear arsenals and the number of states that possess nuclear capabilities grown, but many have also come to think of biological, chemical, and radiological weapons as weapons of mass destruction because of their capacity for large-scale devastation and casualties. Rogue states and nonstate actors, such as terrorist organizations, also pose a threat to global security with their potential use of WMDs. Military strategies that respond to changes in technologies, defense needs, capabilities, and global actors and conditions are critical. For analytical convenience, we consider three broad postures: compellence, deterrence, and preemption.

Compellence   Countries that possess military preeminence often think of weapons as instruments in diplomatic bargaining. Military capabilities do not have to be used for them to be instrumental; a country can exercise influence over enemies simply by demonstrating the power of its weapons and signaling its willingness to use them. Through a show of force, or a convincing threat of force, countries can use **compellence** as a strategy to convince others to do what they might not otherwise do.

The United States, the world's first and for many years unchallenged nuclear power, adopted the strategy of compellence when it enjoyed a clear-cut nuclear superiority over the Soviet Union. The United States sought to gain bargaining leverage by giving the impression that it would actually use its nuclear weapons. This posture was especially evident during the Eisenhower administration, when Secretary of State John Foster Dulles practiced **brinkmanship**, deliberately threatening U.S. adversaries with nuclear destruction so that, on the brink of war, they would concede to U.S. demands. Brinkmanship was part of the overall U.S. strategic doctrine known as **massive retaliation**. To contain communism and Soviet expansionism, this doctrine called for aiming U.S. nuclear weapons at what the Soviets valued most—their population and industrial centers.

Massive retaliation heightened fears in the Kremlin that a nuclear exchange would destroy the Soviet Union but permit the survival of the United States. In addition to responding by increasing their nuclear capabilities, Soviet leaders accelerated their space program and

nuclear winter
The expected freeze that would occur in the Earth's climate from the fallout of smoke and dust in the event nuclear weapons were used, blocking out sunlight and destroying the plant and animal life that survived the original blast.

compellence
A method of coercive diplomacy usually involving an act of war or threat to force an adversary to make concessions against its will.

brinkmanship
The intentional, reckless taking of huge risks in bargaining with an enemy, such as threatening a nuclear attack, to compel its submission.

massive retaliation
The Eisenhower administration's policy doctrine for containing Soviet communism by pledging to respond to any act of aggression with the most destructive capabilities available, including nuclear weapons.

successfully launched the world's first space satellite (Sputnik). This demonstrated Moscow's ability to deliver nuclear weapons beyond the Eurasian landmass. Thus, the superpowers' strategic competition took a new turn as the United States for the first time faced a nuclear threat to its homeland.

Deterrence   Whereas a strategy of compellence relies on an offensive threat aimed at persuading an adversary to relinquish something without resistance, *deterrence* seeks to dissuade an adversary from undertaking some future action. The chief assumption of deterrence theory is that the defender has the ability to punish an adversary with unacceptably high costs if it launches an attack. The key elements of deterrence are:

- **Capabilities.** The possession of military resources that signal to the adversary that threats of military retaliation are possible.
- **Credibility.** The belief that the actor is willing to act on its declared threats.
- **Communication.** The ability to send a potential aggressor the clear message that the threat will be carried out.

A deterrence strategy depends on obtaining the unquestionable ability to inflict intolerable damage on an opponent. This means that a state seeking to deter an enemy must build its weapons to acquire a **second-strike capability**, which necessitates having sufficient destructive weapons to ensure that the country can withstand an adversary's first strike and still retaliate with a devastating counterattack. To guarantee that an adversary is aware that a second-strike capability exists, deterrence rationalizes an unrestrained search for sophisticated retaliatory capabilities. As President Kennedy explained in his Inaugural Address in 1961, "only when arms are sufficient beyond doubt can we be certain without doubt that they will never be employed."

The phrase **mutual assured destruction (MAD)** was coined to describe the strategic balance that emerged between the United States and the Soviet Union after the near nuclear exchange during the 1962 Cuban Missile Crisis. Regardless of who struck first, the other side could destroy the attacker. Under these circumstances, initiating a nuclear war was not a *rational choice*; the frightening costs outweighed any conceivable benefits. As Soviet leader Nikita Khrushchev put it, "If you reach for the push button, you reach for suicide." Safety, in former British Prime Minister Winston Churchill's words, was "the sturdy child of terror and survival the twin brother of annihilation."

Today, a strategy of deterrence is reflected in U.S.-led efforts to construct a defensive shield against ballistic missiles (see Map 8.3). Using an integrated system of ground, sea, and space-based radars and weapons, this defense technology detects, intercepts, and destroys weapons launched in fear, anger, or by accident. The goal of **ballistic missile defense (BMD)**, in U.S. President Reagan's words, is to make nuclear weapons "impotent and obsolete" and to shift nuclear strategy away from mutual assured destruction. In support of the United States' pursuit of antiballistic missile defense, Congress appropriated more than $200 billion for missile defense between 1985 and 2019 (ACA, 2019).

Critics question the allocation of resources to BMD. There is debate about the scope of the ballistic missile threat, the cost-effectiveness of the BMD system, and its technical capability to defend the United States against enemy attack under realistic conditions. Others worry that

second-strike capability
A state's capacity to retaliate after absorbing an adversary's first-strike attack with weapons of mass destruction.

mutual assured destruction (MAD)
A condition of mutual deterrence in which both sides possess the ability to survive a first strike with weapons of mass destruction and launch a devastating retaliatory attack.

ballistic missile defense (BMD)
A planned antiballistic missile system using space-based lasers that would destroy enemy nuclear missiles before they could enter Earth's atmosphere.

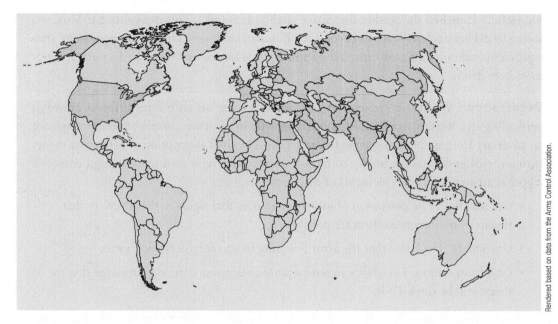

Rendered based on data from the Arms Control Association.

MAP 8.3 Global Ballistic Missile Capabilities The map above shows countries with ballistic missiles. At the start of 2018, thirty-one countries possessed ballistic missiles. Short- and medium-range ballistic missiles are called theater ballistic missiles; intercontinental and long-range missiles are referred to as strategic ballistic missiles because of the significant distance they can travel. Although the direct threat is limited, such military capacity is widely feared.

Think It Through What does the increasing number of states that have access to nuclear weapons indicate about the future of warfare?

BMD undermines the deterrence strategy, rather than complements it, and may lead to more nuclear missiles worldwide instead of fewer.

preemptive warfare
A quick first-strike attack that seeks to defeat an adversary before it can organize an initial attack or a retaliatory response.

preventive warfare
Strictly outlawed by international law, a war undertaken by choice against an enemy to prevent it from suspected intentions to attack sometime in the distant future—if and when the enemy might acquire the necessary military capabilities.

Preemption   Strategic planning continues to find new ways of dealing with the constant danger of emergent military threats. The United States has led the way in forging new strategies to deal with global terrorism and belligerent enemies in the post-9/11 world. From that threat has emerged the **preemptive warfare** strategy, which calls for striking a potential enemy before it undertakes armed aggression.

As posited in the 2002 *U.S. National Security Strategy*, "traditional concepts of deterrence will not work against a terrorist enemy whose avowed tactics are wanton destruction and the targeting of innocents; whose so-called soldiers seek martyrdom in death; and whose most potent protection is statelessness." A preemptive strategy calls for attacking a potential enemy before it engages in armed aggression, either with or without the support of allies and international institutions. "We must take the battle to the enemy," President George W. Bush exhorted, "and confront the worst threats before they emerge."

Although international law affords states the legal right to defend themselves against aggression as well as imminent attacks, critics charge that beneath the language of military preemption lies a more radical policy of preventive war (see Chapter 9). A preemptive military attack entails the use of force to quell or mitigate an impending strike by an adversary. **Preventive warfare** entails the use of force to eliminate any possible future strike, even if there is no reason to believe that the capacity to launch an attack currently exists. Whereas the grounds for preemption lie in evidence of a credible, imminent threat, the basis for prevention rests on the suspicion of an incipient, contingent threat (Kegley and Raymond, 2004).

According to critics, the preventive use of military force sets a dangerous precedent. Predicting an adversary's future behavior is difficult because its leadership's intentions are hard to discern, information about long-term goals may be shrouded in secrecy, and signals of its policy direction may be missed in an oversupply of unimportant intelligence information. If suspicions about an adversary become a justifiable cause for military action, then every truculent leader would have a rough-and-ready pretext for ordering a first strike.

The ever-present threat of armed aggression raises timeless questions about the conditions under which, and the purposes for which, using military force is justified. What does prudent caution require when ruthless countries and nameless, faceless enemies pursue indiscriminate, suicidal attacks against innocent noncombatants? How can force be used to influence an adversary's decision-making calculus? What conditions affect the success of coercive diplomacy?

Coercive Diplomacy through Military Intervention

LO 8-3   Examine patterns in military intervention and factors that contribute to its effectiveness.

Coercive diplomacy in international bargaining is the threat or use of limited force to persuade an opponent to stop pursuing an activity it is already undertaking. Drawing on aspects of a strategy of compellence, threats to use arms are made to force an adversary to reach a compromise or, even better, to reverse its policies. The goal is to alter the target state's costs and benefits calculation, so that the enemy is convinced that acceding to demands will be better than defying them. This result may be accomplished by delivering an ultimatum that promises immediate and significant escalation, or by issuing a warning and gradually increasing pressure on the target.

Coercive diplomacy's reliance on the threat of force is designed to avoid the bloodshed and expense associated with traditional military campaigns. Orchestrating the mix of threats and armed aggression can be done in various ways. The methods range from traditional **gun-boat diplomacy** to threaten an enemy by positioning navies and/or armies near its borders to "tomahawk diplomacy" by striking an adversary with precision-guided cruise missiles. These are among the instruments of coercive diplomacy in the arsenal of military options envisioned by realist policy makers to pursue power.

Intervention can be practiced in various ways—physically through direct entry of military forces into another country, indirectly by broadcasting propaganda to the target's population, or through **covert operations**. Global actors also can take a *unilateral* or *multilateral* approach to intervention. Overt military intervention is the most visible method of interference inside the borders of another country. For that reason, it is also the most controversial and costly.

Interventions have been frequently, if episodically, occurring since World War II. States send their troops into the sovereign territory of other states in order to influence the target,

gun-boat diplomacy
A show of military force, historically naval force, to intimidate an adversary.

covert operations
Secret activities undertaken by a state outside its borders through clandestine means to achieve specific political or military goals with respect to another state.

even though military intervention is under most circumstances prohibited by international law. The frequency of this forceful coercive diplomacy fluctuates from year to year, and suggests that military interventions rise and fall in response to both changing global circumstances and shifting perceptions about the advantages and disadvantages of intervention as an effective method of coercive diplomacy.

Each act of military intervention had a different rationale and produced different results. Past cases raise tough questions about the use of military intervention for coercive diplomacy. Does the record show that the actions met the goals of the intervening states, such as successfully punishing countries so that they no longer violated their citizens' human rights? Have they for the most part restored order to war-torn societies? Or, on the whole, have they made circumstances worse?

These questions are hotly debated now because of the prevalence of fragile states. The great powers have not reached a consensus about whether to intervene in sovereign states when tyrants victimize innocent civilians. Why? Primarily because these interventions undermine state sovereignty and the deeply entrenched **nonintervention norm**. The United Nations' call for a "new commitment to intervention" stirred up the percolating debate about military intervention, even in the name of morality, justice, and human rights.

nonintervention norm
A fundamental international legal principle, now being challenged, that traditionally has defined interference by one state in the domestic affairs of another as illegal.

Today, policy makers disagree about the appropriate use of military coercion. Research on coercive diplomacy suggests that its success depends upon each specific context. The following conditions are thought to favor the effective use of coercive diplomacy (Art, 2005; George, 1992):

- **Clarity of user objectives.** The coercing power's demands must be clearly understood by the target state.

- **Asymmetry of motivation favoring the user.** The coercing power must be more highly motivated than the target by what is at stake. Military coercion tends to be effective when it occurs prior to the target making a firm commitment on the issue at hand, and when factions exist within the target state's government.

- **Opponent's fear of escalation and belief in the urgency for compliance.** The coercing power must convince the adversary mind that compliance with its demand is an urgent matter. Two factors are important in affecting an adversary's perceptions: (1) the coercing power's reputation for successfully using armed force in the past, and (2) its capability to increase pressure to a level that the target would find intolerable.

- **Adequate domestic and international support for the user.** In addition to having political support at home, the coercing power is helped when it can also count on support from key states and international organizations.

- **Clarity on the precise terms of settlement.** The coercing power must be able to articulate the specific conditions for ending the crisis, as well as assure that it will not formulate new demands for greater concessions once the target capitulates.

Although these conditions improve the odds of successful coercive diplomacy, they do not guarantee success. History shows that leaders who rely on military intervention for coercive diplomacy often start a process that they later find they cannot control, and many states that have ventured down this path have come to regret it. Although often undertaken to address severe human rights conditions, there is evidence that military intervention instead "contributes to the rise of state repression by enhancing the state's coercive power and encouraging more repressive behavior" (Peksen, 2012, p. 558). In the aftermath of failed interventions, confidence in this military method of coercive diplomacy frequently vanishes, and the search for other means to exercise power in world politics has intensified.

Most realists, and many others, continue to put lasting faith in the realist premise that it is safer to rely on the force of arms than on the force of arguments to successfully resolve disputes. Yet security may depend as much on the control of force as on its pursuit. At issue is whether the traditional realist emphasis on arms and military strategies that require either the threat or actual use of weapons for coercive diplomacy is the best and safest route to national and international security. To be sure, the traditional realist reliance on military capabilities to increase national security continues to resonate in world capitals. However, other realists recommend an alternative path—one that sees national interests served most, not by the acquisition and use of arms but by the acquisition of allies in order to maintain a balance of power among rivals that will prevent any transnational actor from using force against the others. This, these other realists believe, provides the safest path to security. Are they right?

> *Warfare is not a question of brute strength, but rather of winning and losing friends.*
>
> **—COUNT DIEGO SARMIENTO GONDOMAR, SPANISH AMBASSADOR TO LONDON IN 1618**

Realist Interpretations of Alliances in World Politics

LO 8-4   Discuss the implications of alliances for global security.

Alliances in world politics require agreements between parties in order for them to cooperate. For that reason, it may seem that *liberal theory*, with its emphasis on the possibility of self-sacrifice for mutual gain, might provide a key to understanding why and how states join together in alliances. According to liberal theory, states may form an alliance even if their immediate interest is not realized in order to maximize their long-term collective interest.

Realism, however, provides the dominant lens through which the dynamics of alliance formation and decay, and the impact of these dynamics on global security, are most often interpreted. As you have learned, realism portrays world politics as a struggle for power under conditions of anarchy by competitive rivals pursuing only their own self-interests (and *not* for moral principles and global ideals such as improving the security and welfare of *all* throughout the globe). Realists picture **alliances** as temporary, opportunistic agreements to cooperate that predictably come into being when two or more parties face a common security threat (see Map 8.4). "An alliance (or alignment) is a formal (or informal) commitment for security cooperation between two or more states, intended to augment each member's power, security, and/or influence" (Walt, 2009, p. 86).

Realism provides the most compelling explanation of the coldly calculating motives underlying decisions about alliances, which realists see first and foremost as a method for states to protect themselves from threats posed by predatory common enemies and as a mechanism by which a "balance of power" can be maintained. "Regarding the origins and purposes of alliances,

alliances
Coalitions of two or more states that combine their military capabilities and promise to coordinate their policies to increase mutual security.

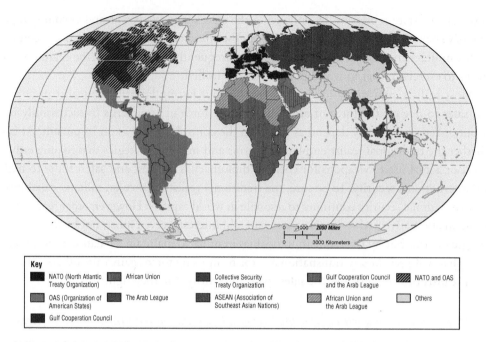

MAP 8.4 Partnerships for Security The map above shows a number of alliances that were created, in part, to integrate joint regional military or economic security interests and promote cooperation. Highlighting the importance of alliances in the 2010 U.S. National Security Strategy, U.S. President Obama once said "We will be steadfast in strengthening those old alliances that have served us so well. . . . As influence extends to more countries and capitals, we must also build new partnerships, and shape stronger international standards and institutions."

Think It Through How might a realist account for the formation and continuation of these alliances?

realists are doggedly parsimonious, taking states as rational, security-maximizing actors whose self-interested behavior is largely determined by the structure of the international system" (Byrne, 2013). Realism posits that military alliances are forged when the parties perceive that the advantages of an alliance outweigh the disadvantages. When facing a common threat, alliances provide their members with the means of reducing their probability of being attacked (deterrence), obtaining greater strength in case of attack (defense), and precluding their allies from aligning with the enemy (Snyder, 1991).

These advantages notwithstanding, realists often see a downside and counsel against forming alliances, as Britain's Lord Palmerston did in 1848 when he advised that states "should have no eternal allies and no perpetual enemies." Under anarchy a state must rely on *self-help* for its own security, and cannot really count on allies to come to its defense if attacked. Moreover, alliances bind a state to a commitment that may later become disadvantageous.

As realist theoretician Thucydides counseled, "One has to behave as friend or foe according to the circumstances," and these choices are made on a complex geostrategic playing field in which today's enemy may be tomorrow's ally and where fears of entrapment, abandonment, or betrayal are ever present. This is why "wise and experienced statesmen usually shy away from commitments likely to constitute limitations on a government's behavior at unknown dates in the future in the face of unpredictable situations" (Kennan, 1984, p. 238). Because conditions are certain to change sooner or later and the usefulness of all alliances is certain to change once the common threat that brought the allies together declines, the realist tradition advises states not to take a fixed position on temporary convergences of national interests and, instead, to forge alliances only to deal with immediate threats.

When considering whether joining a new alliance is a rational choice in which the benefits outweigh the costs, heads of state usually recognize that allies can easily do more harm than good. Arguing that whereas a state "may safely trust to temporary alliances for extraordinary emergencies" it is an illusion "to expect or calculate real favors from nation to nation," the first president of the United States, George Washington, advised that the United States should "steer clear of permanent alliances." Many realists similarly advise states against forming alliances for defense, basing their fears on five fundamental flaws:

- Alliances enable aggressive states to combine military capabilities for war.

- Alliances threaten enemies and provoke the creation of counteralliances, which reduces the security of both coalitions.

- Alliance formation may draw otherwise neutral parties into opposed coalitions.

- Once states join forces, they must control the behavior of their own allies to discourage each member from reckless aggression against its enemies, which would undermine the security of the alliance's other members.

- The possibility always exists that today's ally might become tomorrow's enemy.

Despite their uncertain usefulness, many states throughout history have chosen to ally because, the risks notwithstanding, the perceived benefits to security in a time of threat justified the decision. The United States has formal military partnerships with more than sixty countries, and these alliances not only "provide a global platform for the projection of U.S. power, but they also distribute the burden of providing security" (Ikenberry, 2014).

To best picture how alliances affect global security, it is instructive to move from the state level of analysis, which views alliance decisions from the perspective of an individual state's security, to the global level of analysis by looking at the impact of alliances on the frequency of interstate war. This view focuses attention on the possible contribution of alliance formation to maintaining the balance of power.

Realism and the Balancing of Power

LO 8-5 Summarize the strategies and difficulties associated with balancing.

The concept of a balance of power has a long and controversial history. Supporters envision it as an equilibrating process that maintains peace by counterbalancing any state that seeks military superiority, distributing global power evenly through **alignments** or shifts by nonaligned states to one or the other opposed coalitions. Critics deny the effectiveness of the balance of power, arguing that it breeds jealousy, intrigue, and antagonism.

alignments
The acceptance by a neutral state threatened by foreign enemies of a special relationship short of formal alliance with a stronger power able to protect it from attack.

At the core of "balance of power" is the idea that national security is enhanced when military capabilities are distributed so that no single state is strong enough to dominate all others. If one state gains inordinate power, balance-of-power theory predicts that it will take advantage of its strength and attack weaker neighbors, thereby giving compelling incentive for those threatened to unite in a defensive coalition. According to the theory, the threatened states' combined military strength would then deter (or, if need be, defeat) the state seeking to expand. Thus, for realists, laissez-faire competition among states striving to maximize their national power yields an international equilibrium, ensuring the survival of all by checking the hegemonic ambitions of any.

The use of alliances to balance power is intrinsically tied to shifts in the global structure of the international system. Military power can be distributed around one or more power centers in different ways—an idea scholars call *polarity* (see Chapter 4). Historically, these have ranged from *unipolarity*, where there is a high concentration of power in the hands of a single hegemon, to *multipolarity*, where the power distribution is highly dispersed among multiple actors. Examples of unipolarity include regional empires such as the Roman Empire, as well as the United States in the years immediately following World War II when it was without rival and no state could counterbalance it. An example of multipolarity is the approximate equality of power held by the European powers at the conclusion of the Napoleonic Wars in 1815.

In between these two ends of the continuum is *bipolarity*—the division of the balance of power into two coalitions headed by rival powers, each seeking to contain the other's expansion. In 1949, when the Soviets broke the U.S. monopoly on atomic weapons, a redistribution of power began to emerge. Military capabilities became concentrated in the hands of two competitive "superpowers" whose capacities to destroy anyone else made comparisons with the other great powers meaningless. Both attached great importance to balancing power by recruiting new allies. The formation of the **North Atlantic Treaty Organization (NATO)**, linking the United States to the defense of Western Europe, and the Warsaw Pact, linking the former Soviet Union in a formal alliance with its Eastern European client states, occurred due to this *polarization*. Two opposing blocs formed in part because the superpowers competed for allies and in part because the less powerful states looked to one superpower or the other for protection.

To balance power, realists recognize that national actors need to see the value of rapidly shifting alliances (see Map 8.5). Although balancing is occasionally described as an automatic, self-adjusting process, most realists see it as the result of deliberate choices undertaken by national leaders to maintain equilibrium among contending states. All leaders must constantly monitor changes in states' relative capabilities so that policies about arms and allies can be adjusted to rectify power imbalances. Such choices must be made by rational, self-interested actors who recognize the costs and benefits of various strategic options.

The resistance of Germany, France, and many other countries to the 2003 U.S. decision to launch a preemptive war to prevent Iraq from acquiring and using weapons of mass destruction illustrates the balancing process—especially as evidence of Iraq's possession of such weapons, ties to the 9/11 terrorist attacks, or intention to wage war were all highly questionable. The alarm of countries in the Baltic, such as Estonia, Latvia, and Lithuania, to France's decision to sell Mistral-class assault ships to Russia that would enter service in 2015 provides another example.

North Atlantic Treaty Organization (NATO)
A military alliance created in 1949 to deter a Soviet attack on Western Europe that since has expanded and redefined its mission to emphasize not only the maintenance of peace but also the promotion of democracy.

| 1812 NAPOLEON'S EMPIRE | 1879–1914 EUROPE'S FIRST PEACETIME ALLIANCES | 1949–1991 THE COLD WAR |

Empire and allied states
States allied against Napoleon

The Triple Alliance
The Triple Entente

Original NATO members
Joined NATO after 1952
Warsaw Pact countries (Albania withdrew in 1968)

Past European alliances from *U.S. News and World Report,* July 14, 1997. Copyright © 1997, *U.S. News and World Report,* L.P. Reprinted with permission.

MAP 8.5 Changing European Alliances When relationships and conditions change, new alliances form and established alliances dissolve as transnational actors—all obsessed with the power of their rivals—realign. Pictured here are three distributions of power in past European alliances.

Think It Through How have alliances changed—or remained the same—since the end of the Cold War?

As realism prescribes, when faced with unbalanced power, leaders of states should mobilize their domestic resources or ally with others to bring the international distribution of power back into equilibrium (Elman and Jensen, 2014; Waltz, 1979). As Joseph Nye (2007, p. 65) phrased it, "Balance of power is a policy of helping the underdog because if you help the top dog, it may eventually turn around and eat you."

Can balancing power help to preserve world order, as most realists believe? Critics of balance-of-power theory raise several objections to the proposition that balancing promotes peace:

- Scholars argue that the theory's rules for behavior are contradictory. On one hand, states are urged to increase their power. On the other hand, they are told to oppose anyone seeking preponderance. Yet sometimes **bandwagoning** with (rather than balancing against) the dominant state can increase a weaker country's capabilities by allowing it to share in the spoils of a future victory. History suggests that states that are most content with the status quo tend to balance against rising powers more than do dissatisfied states.

- Balance-of-power theory assumes policy makers possess accurate, timely information about other states. Recall that the concept of "power" has multiple meanings. Tangible factors are hard to compare, such as the performance capabilities of the different types of weapons found in an adversary's arsenal. Intangible factors, such as leadership skills, troop morale, or public support for adventuresome or aggressive foreign policies, are even more difficult to gauge. The uncertainty of power balances due to difficulties in

bandwagoning
The tendency for weak states to seek alliance with the strongest power, irrespective of that power's ideology or type of government, in order to increase their security.

determining the strength of adversaries and the trustworthiness of allies frequently causes military planners to engage in worst-case analysis. This, in turn, prompts each side to expand the quantity and enhance the quality of its weaponry. Critics of realism warn that if a serious dispute occurs between states locked in relentless arms competition under conditions of mutually assured suspicions, the probability of war increases.

• Balance-of-power theory assumes that decision makers are risk-averse—when confronted with countervailing power, they refrain from fighting because the dangers of taking on an equal are too great. Yet, as *prospect theory* (see Chapter 3) illuminates, national leaders evaluate risks differently. Some are risk-acceptant. Rather than being deterred by equivalent power, they prefer gambling on the chance of winning a victory, even if the odds are long. Marshaling comparable power against adversaries with a high tolerance for risk will not have the same effect as it would on those who avoid risks.

• The past performance of balance-of-power theory is checkered. If the theory's assumptions are correct, historical periods during which its rules were followed should also have been periods in which war was less frequent. Yet a striking feature of those periods is their record of warfare. After the 1648 Peace of Westphalia created the global system of independent territorial states, the great powers participated in a series of increasingly destructive general wars that threatened to engulf and destroy

Kremlin Pool/Alamy Stock Photo

IMAGE 8.7 Fast Friends or Temporary Playmates? In July 2018, the BRICS (Brazil, Russia, India, China, and South Africa) held their tenth annual summit in Johannesburg, South Africa. Seen as a balancing maneuver, this cooperative venture between the five countries is a product of the desire to have greater influence in shaping the global economy and the political order. This picture shows, from left to right, Chinese President Xi Jinping, Indian Prime Minister Narendra Modi, South African President Cyril Ramaphosa, Brazilian President Michel Temer, and Russian President Vladimir Putin.

the entire multistate global system. As Inis L. Claude (1989, p. 78) soberly concludes, it is difficult to consider these wars "as anything other than catastrophic failures, total collapses, of the balance-of-power system. They are hardly to be classified as stabilizing maneuvers or equilibrating processes, and one cannot take seriously any claim of maintaining international stability that does not entail the prevention of such disasters." Indeed, the historical record has led some theorists to construct the *hegemonic stability theory* as an alternative to the balance-of-power theory, postulating that a single, dominant hegemon can guarantee peace better than a rough equality of military capabilities among competing great powers (see Chapter 7).

A significant problem with the balance-of-power system is its haphazard character. The potential for great power harmony to be replaced by great power rivalry is what alarms many realist observers. A dangerous power vacuum could result if the world witnesses "the end of alliances," when formal military ties fade away and are replaced by informal shifting alignments among the competitors (Menon, 2007). These difficulties associated with balancing power lead most realists to conclude that international conflict and competition is a permanent feature of world politics.

What Lies Ahead?

LO 8-6 Extrapolate the future prospects for alliances and balancing in world politics.

Sooner or later, America's predominance will inevitably fade, and some new distribution of power will develop. Much counterbalancing and shifting in flexible and fluid alliances is occurring, and the probable consequences of such a transformation in world politics are not clear.

An enlarged global chessboard of multiple geostrategic relationships is developing, and may lead to uncertainty about others' allegiances. The major players align together against others on particular issues, as their interests dictate. But behind the diplomatic smiles and handshakes, one-time friends and allies begin to grow apart, formally "specialized" relations begin to dissolve, and former enemies forge friendly ties and begin making a common cause against other common threats. "In this complex international reality, fixed alliances and formal organizations may count for less than shifting coalitions of interest" (Patrick, 2010, p. 51).

For example, friction grew between the United States and its closest allies over how to pursue the war on terrorism, particularly with regard to the war in Iraq. As a measure of how sensitive particular issues can be among great powers, both the European Union's foreign affairs commissioner, Christopher Pattern, and the German foreign minister, Joschka Fischer, at the time castigated President Bush for treating America's coalition partners as subordinate "satellites." In an effort to renew partnerships that had been strained because of the Iraq War, at a NATO summit marking the sixtieth anniversary of the alliance, President Obama called for all countries to play a part in fighting Al Qaeda, reminding the leaders of the alliance that "we have a mutual interest in ensuring that organizations like Al Qaeda cannot operate."

It is difficult to confidently predict what the twenty-first century will look like and whether it will be chaotic or stable. Realists insist that the tragic struggle for security among great powers

IMAGE 8.8 Make New Friends but Keep the Old Global summits provide foreign leaders with an opportunity to meet and listen to each other and strengthen alliances. Pictured here are military representatives from the member states at the opening ceremony for the NATO summit in Brussels, Belgium on July 11, 2018. Leaders gathered to discuss the alliance's three core tasks: collective defense, cooperative security, and crisis management.

will continue (Mearsheimer, 2001). Their expectations have been strengthened by China's rapid rise toward becoming the globe's biggest economy and the growing fears that this coming financial clout will translate into Chinese *hard power* and a military threat. If the future belongs to China, counterbalancing by the other great powers in an anti-Chinese coalition is likely (Kugler, 2006). Likewise, realists think that great power competition will continue because the American military giant is unlikely to quietly accept a diminished stature.

Whatever ensues, this crucial question is certain to command attention at the center of debate: whether international security is best served by states' military search for their own national security or whether, instead, the military pursuit of security through arms, alliances, and the balance of power will sow the seeds of the world's destruction. In the next chapter of *World Politics*, turn your attention away from the balance-of-power politics of realism to examine what liberal theorists say about institutional reforms that they contend lead to a more orderly world.

> *Those who scoff at "balance-of-power diplomacy" should recognize that the alternative to a balance of power is an imbalance of power—and history shows us that nothing so drastically escalates the danger of war as such an imbalance.*
>
> —RICHARD M. NIXON, FORMER U.S. PRESIDENT

Study. Apply. Analyze.

Chapter Summary

8-1 Describe the distribution of military power among states, and evaluate the dilemmas raised by the pursuit of military power. As necessitated by an anarchical global system in which actors must rely on self-help to ensure security, realism instructs states to focus on military power. Yet the extent to which countries invest in military spending varies greatly depending on a number of factors such as relative size of their economy, population, territorial size, and governmental decision making, among others. Yet regardless of whether a state is rich or poor, government spending entails opportunity costs, or trade-offs. When the government spends money on the military, they are giving up the opportunity to invest in social spending.

8-2 Identify and evaluate the implications of the global arms trade and nuclear weapons for world politics, and assess recent developments in weapons technology. Militarization across the globe, including within the great powers, is steadily increasing and this translates into the expansion of the global arms trade. Major powers often export weapons to the Global South for profit and influence. However, the transfer of weapons facilitates armed conflict, can exacerbate the level of destruction and violence, and results in blowback. Nonetheless, research and development of military technology has expanded the destructive power of arsenals, producing nuclear weapons, autonomous weapons systems, and chemical and biological weapons.

8-3 Examine patterns in military intervention and factors that contribute to its effectiveness. Coercive diplomacy is the threat or use of limited force to persuade an opponent to stop pursuing an activity it is already undertaking. While this tactic relies on the actor having a strong and capable military, it aims to prevent outright conflict and fighting through approaches such as gunboat diplomacy, covert operations, and intervention.

Certain conditions increase the likelihood of successful coercive diplomacy, including clarity of user objectives, level of motivation, opponent's fear of escalation, level of domestic and international support, and clarity of terms of settlement.

8-4 Discuss the implications of alliances for global security. According to realism, world politics is a struggle for power under conditions of anarchy by competitive rivals pursuing only their own self-interests. Through this lens, alliances are self-serving, temporary, and opportunistic agreements that are made in response to a common threat. Alliances are forged when the advantages are calculated as higher than the disadvantages, and may contribute to a balance of power in the international system.

8-5 Summarize the strategies and difficulties associated with balancing. At the core of the realist concept of balance of power is the idea that security is enhanced when military capabilities are distributed so that no single state is strong enough to dominate all others. Accordingly, threatened states combine their power to deter a state seeking to expand. Yet there are difficulties associated with balancing, such as the potential value of bandwagoning with the dominant power, uncertainty in determining power balances, different levels of risk acceptance among actors, and the prospect that balancing may not be an equilibrating process.

8-6 Extrapolate the future prospects for alliances and balancing in world politics. Considerable counterbalancing and shifting in alliances is occurring. Realists insist that the struggle for power and security will continue, and anticipate competition among the major powers for status and influence. Military preparation and alliances will play a role in determining dominance in world politics.

Key Terms

alignments

alliance

artificial intelligence

ballistic missile defense
   (BMD)

bandwagoning

blowback

brinkmanship

coercive diplomacy

compellence

covert operations

gunboat diplomacy

horizontal nuclear
   proliferation

human security

massive retaliation

multiple independently
   targetable reentry vehicles
   (MIRVs)

mutual assured destruction
   (MAD)

national security

nonintervention norm

nonlethal weapons (NLWs)

nonproliferation regime

North Atlantic Treaty
   Organization (NATO)

Nth country problem

Nuclear Nonproliferation
   Treaty (NPT)

nuclear winter

opportunity costs

power potential

preemptive warfare

preventive warfare

private military services

proliferation

relative burden of military
   spending

revolution in military
   technology (RMT)

second-strike capability

smart bombs

Strategic Arms Reduction
   Treaty (START)

vertical nuclear proliferation

Suggested Readings and Resources

Coker, Christopher. (2012). *Warrior Geeks: How 21st Century Technology Is Changing the Way We Fight and Think About War*. New York: Columbia University Press.

Drone Analyst: droneanalyst.com/blog/. A blog about commercial drones as well as unmanned robots.

How Military Spending Has Changed Since 9/11: nationalpriorities.org/campaigns/how-military-spending-has-changed/. A website post documenting the increase in military spending since 9/11.

Larsen, Jeffrey A., and Kerry M. Kartchner, eds. (2014). *On Limited Nuclear War in the 21st Century*. Stanford, CA: Stanford University Press.

Mearsheimer, John. (2018). *The Great Delusion: Liberal Dreams and International Realities*. New Haven: Yale University Press.

Small Arms Survey: smallarmssurvey.org. A project of the Graduate Institute of International and Development Studies in Geneva, Switzerland that addresses small arms and armed violence.

Singer, P. W. (2009). *Wired for War: The Robotics Revolution and Conflict in the 21st Century*. New York: Penguin Press.

Shearman, Peter. (2013). *Power Transition and International Order in Asia: Issues and Challenges*. New York: Routledge.

Walt, Stephen M. (2009). "Alliances in a Unipolar World," *World Politics* 611(1): 86–120.

Carnegie Council Videos

Key Term Videos

- Coercive Diplomacy
- Power Potential
- Military-Industrial Complex
- Private Military Services
- Proliferation

- Nuclear Nonproliferation Treaty
- Nonproliferation Treaty
- Nonproliferation Regime
- Revolution in Military Technology
- Preemptive Warfare

- Preventive Warfare
- Nonintervention Norm
- Alliances
- Alignments
- North Atlantic Treaty Organization

Additional Videos

- Bacevich, Andrew J., "Washington Rules: America's Path to Permanent War."
- Cha, Victor D., "North Korea: What Next?"
- Doyle, Michael W., and Harold H. Koh, "Striking First: Preemption and Prevention in International Conflict."
- Jentleson, Bruce W., "The End of Arrogance: America in the Global Competition of Ideas."
- Rose, Gideon, "How Wars End: Why We Always Fight the Last Battle."

Chapter 9

The Quest for Peace Through International Law and Collective Security

Marco Rubino/Shutterstock.com

IMAGE 9.1 **Seeking Alternatives to War** Liberals, and many constructivists, are dissatisfied with the world and would like to change it. Progressive ideas and global cooperation create the possibility of a world without violence. Shown here is the sculpture by Swedish artist Carl Fredrik Reuterswärd, known as "The Knotted Gun" or "Non-Violence," which was given to the United Nations in 1988 by the government of Luxembourg and symbolizes hope for peace.

Learning Objectives

LO 9-1 Link liberal and constructivist ideas to the development of peaceful norms, laws, and institutions.

LO 9-2 Evaluate the effectiveness of arms control and disarmament in the prevention of armed conflict.

LO 9-3 Apply the principles of collective security to international organizations, and assess their effectiveness along these lines.

LO 9-4 Describe the core principles of international law, and evaluate its effectiveness in the global system.

LO 9-5 Survey laws relating to the conduct of war and military intervention, and describe methods for the negotiated settlement of international disputes.

> " *Today the real test of power is not capacity to make war but capacity to prevent it.* "
>
> **—ANNE O'HARE McCORMICK,**
> **AMERICAN JOURNALIST AND PULITZER PRIZE WINNER**

You overlook the incredibly low chances, purchase a lottery ticket, and hit an enormous jackpot. You are now very, very rich! What next? Remembering your pledge to try to make the world a better place before you die, you decide to put your ethical principles above power. To make a difference, you decide to invest your newfound wealth in projects that will "give peace a chance." Congratulations! You are joining Andrew Carnegie, Bill Gates, Warren Buffett, and other exceptionally wealthy philanthropists who generously chose to give large portions of their fortunes to causes that attempt to change the world for the better.

On what ventures should you invest your fortune? There are numerous choices. You could seek, for example, to provide humanitarian relief for refugees, fight worldwide poverty and disease, join others in seeking to stem the threat of global warming, or subsidize a global campaign to educate all youth throughout the world. The needs are endless. Sorting through your moral values, however, you conclude that the greatest threat to the world is the danger of armed conflict. Acting on this conviction, you make it your mission to help others find better ways than violence to settle conflict. Reliance on weapons of war and balances of power has been tried since the beginning of time, but never with lasting success. So now you have found your cause—finding peaceful methods for settling potentially violent disputes.

In the quest to better understand nonviolent approaches to world security, you draw insights from policy makers and philosophers who have spent their lifetimes probing the same question you are now asking yourself—how to do good in a wicked world. This chapter presents some of the major ways in which liberal international thought directly challenges the assumptions underlying realist thinking about world politics. Also, from constructivist and identity perspectives, it looks at the importance of progressive ideas and norms in shaping international behavior and collective conceptions of world politics. What are the consequences if liberal and constructivist roads to world order—specifically disarmament, collective security through international organizations, and the management of conflict through negotiation and international law—are pursued? These questions guide our discussion.

> *There are only two forces in the world, the sword and the spirit. In the long run the sword will always be conquered by the spirit.*
>
> **—NAPOLEON BONAPARTE, FORMER FRENCH EMPEROR**

Liberal and Constructivist Routes to International Peace

LO 9-1 Link liberal and constructivist ideas to the development of peaceful norms, laws, and institutions.

The various paths to peace that *liberalism* and *constructivism* envision differ in meaningful ways from those of *realism* and offer alternative perspectives on how to address armed conflict (see Chapter 2).

"Unlike the realists . . . who tend to view international relations as the amoral, rational pursuit of narrow self-interest by rational unitary sovereign states, liberals emphasize interdependence and the possibility of cooperation, while constructivists stress the centrality of ideas as important for explaining and understanding international relations." (Hudson, 2009, p. 1).

The realist road to national security counsels, "If you want peace, prepare for war." On the surface this makes intuitive sense. If a country is militarily stronger than its rivals, it is not very likely to be attacked. However, what would be the likely consequences if all countries adhered to this advice? It is possible that a country would become less secure, not more, as it builds its military might.

That is the deduction of liberal thought. In this construction, the *security dilemma* figures prominently—when a country builds armaments, alarmed neighbors mistrust its claims that the weapons are only for defensive purposes and out of fear begin to vigorously arm themselves. This results in an **arms race** that leaves no state more secure. All of the arming parties are now more vulnerable—wanting peace, war preparations increase the likelihood of war. Jesus Christ expressed this liberal conviction when he warned, "For all those who take up the sword perish by the sword" (Matthew 26:52). Centuries earlier, the Hebrew prophet Isaiah similarly voiced a recommendation that is now inscribed on the United Nations (UN) headquarters in New York City: "The nations shall beat their swords into plowshares" (Isaiah 2:4).

This liberal axiom and advice have been echoed many times. For example, Sir John Frederick Maurice wrote in his memoirs, "I went into the British Army believing that if you want peace you must prepare for war. I now believe that if you prepare thoroughly for war you will get it." The French political philosopher Charles de Montesquieu expressed the same liberal conviction when he observed that the quest for a preponderance of power in relation to rivals "inevitably becomes a contagious disease; for, as soon as one state increases what it calls its forces, the others immediately increase theirs, so that nothing is gained except mutual ruination."

The destructiveness of today's weapons has inspired many people to embrace the conclusion that reducing the weapons of war can increase the prospects for global peace. Although there is no single constructivist position on armaments or armed conflict, there is a widespread interest in moving beyond a limited traditional conception of security to one that takes into account the consequence of progressive ideas and human creativity. Constructivists "argue that violent political behavior and thereby its resolution and future prevention could be explained and even understood by focusing on the role of norms and ideas as determinants of such behavior" (Conteh-Morgan, 2005, p. 72; see also Adler, 2013).

Along these lines, many feminist scholars are critical of the role of weapons of mass destruction

arms race
The buildup of weapons and armed forces by two or more states that threaten each other, with the competition driven by the conviction that gaining a lead is necessary for security.

IMAGE 9.2 **A Fervent Call for Peace** Liberal and constructivist views on war and peace are influenced by the importance of shared ethics and morality around the globe. Shown here, mourners gather to remember the eleven victims of a bomb blast at a café in Pune, India. Many Indians blame Pakistan, and a previously unheard of Pakistani militant group, Lashkar-e-Taiba Al Alami, claimed responsibility.

in ensuring global security. In particular, the "antiwar feminist" tradition rejects and tries to change the social processes that associate norms of masculinity with militarized violence and war making (see Chapter 2). "It calls for ways of thinking that reveal the complicated effects on possessor societies of developing and deploying these weapons, that portray the terror and potential suffering of target societies, and that grapple with the moral implications of the willingness to risk such massive destruction" (Cohn and Ruddick, 2008, p. 459).

There is optimism that by reducing the supply of arms, armed conflict will be less likely and will result in a more secure world. These reforms are advanced even while liberal policy makers accept the notion that it is morally defensible to use constrained and proportional armed force to repel an imminent military attack by an adversary (Mapel, 2007). But in thinking about the control of the spread of weapons around the world, keep in mind that it is not strictly a tenet of liberal or constructivist theory. Although realists are reluctant to view arms control as a path to peace, most policy makers who have negotiated arms limitations have been realists who perceived such treaties as prudent tools to promote security by balancing military power to minimize the threat of war.

Keep these perspectives in mind as you contemplate the benefits and liabilities of alternative roads to peace. Here, rivet your focus on the hope that reduction in armaments will lead to less armed conflict and a safer and more secure world.

Beating Swords into Plowshares

LO 9-2   Evaluate the effectiveness of arms control and disarmament in the prevention of armed conflict.

disarmament
Agreements to reduce or destroy weapons or other means of attack.

arms control
Multilateral or bilateral agreements to contain arms races by setting limits on the number and types of weapons states are permitted.

Both liberalism and realism see limitations on weapons as useful. Where they part ways is in their respective postures toward the advantages of disarmament versus arms control. **Disarmament** is ambitious. It aims to reduce or eliminate armaments or classes of armaments completely, usually by negotiated reciprocal agreements between two or more rivals, in an effort to prevent their use in warfare. **Arms control** is less ambitious. Arms control is designed to regulate arms levels either by limiting their growth or by restricting how they might be used. It results from agreements between potential enemies to cooperate in order to reduce the probability that conflicting interests will erupt in warfare, and to reduce the scope of violence in any armed conflict that may nonetheless occur. Liberals are more willing to take a leap of faith and consider disarmament as a workable possibility for peace. Because arms control is based on the recognition that a true conflict of interest between rivals exists, it is favored by realists who see a positive contribution potentially made when enemies negotiate an agreement to balance their weapons and through that balancing build mutual confidence.

Controlling war by reducing weapons inventories is hardly a novel idea. Yet, until recently, few states have negotiated disarmament agreements. True, some countries in the past have reduced their armaments. For example, in 600 BCE the Chinese states formed a disarmament league that produced a peaceful century for the league's members. Canada and the United States disarmed the Great Lakes region through the 1817 Rush–Bagot Agreement. Nonetheless, these kinds of achievements have been relatively rare in history. Most disarmaments have been involuntary, the product of reductions imposed by the victors in the immediate aftermath of a war, as when the Allied powers attempted to disarm a defeated Germany after World War I.

In addition to differentiating between arms control and disarmament, it is important to distinguish between **bilateral agreements** and **multilateral agreements**. Because the former involves only two countries, such agreements are often easier to negotiate and to enforce than are the latter, which are agreements between three or more countries. By far the most revealing examples are the superpower agreements to control nuclear weapons. This chapter looks briefly at the record of Soviet–American negotiations before examining the checkered history of multilateral arms control and disarmament.

Bilateral Arms Control and Disarmament

The Cold War between the Soviet Union and the United States never degenerated into a direct trial of military strength. One of the reasons was the series of more than twenty-five arms control agreements that Moscow and Washington negotiated in the wake of the Cuban Missile Crisis. Beginning with the 1963 Hot Line Agreement, which established a direct radio and telegraph communications system between the two governments, Soviet and American leaders reached a series of modest agreements aimed at stabilizing the military balance and reducing the risk of war. Each of these bilateral treaties lowered tensions and helped build a climate of trust that encouraged efforts to negotiate further agreements.

The most important agreements between the superpowers were the **Strategic Arms Limitation Talks (SALT)** of 1972 and 1979; the **Intermediate-Range Nuclear Forces (INF) Treaty** of 1987; the *Strategic Arms Reduction Treaty (START)* of 1991, 1993, 1997, and 2010 (see also Chapter 8); and the **Strategic Offensive Reductions Treaty (SORT)** of 2002. The first two agreements stabilized the nuclear arms race, and the remaining agreements reduced each side's stockpile of nuclear weapons. Even with these initial steps, at the end of the Cold War in 1991, the United States still had more than 9500 nuclear warheads and Russia had about 8000. It was then that disarmament began in earnest (see Figure 9.1).

Since their 1986 peak of approximately 70,300 nuclear weapons, the sizes of the two superpowers' nuclear arsenals have declined by over 80 percent to an estimated 13,890 in early-2019 (Kristensen and Korda, 2019). This achievement inspired other nuclear powers to discontinue building and expanding their nuclear arsenals. Most nuclear powers have not increased their stockpile of nuclear weapons, and forty countries that have the technical ability to construct nuclear arsenals have renounced nuclear weapons. That said, there is always a temptation to rearm in response to new threats, and as a result many fear that continued disarmament is a tenuous prospect (Gramer and Seligson, 2019).

Indeed, compared to the 1990s, the pace of reduction has slowed significantly. In fact, the progress achieved by both Russia and the United States in limiting their nuclear arsenals is threatened as, rather than striving for nuclear disarmament, they "appear to plan to retain large arsenals for the indefinite future, are adding new nuclear weapons, and are increasing the role that such weapons play in their national strategies" (Kristensen and Korda, 2019). The United States decision in 2019 to withdraw from the INF Treaty, which U.S. President Donald Trump characterized as a "bad deal" and attributed his country's withdrawal to Russia's noncompliance with the terms of the treaty, raised concerns that "the exit could trigger a

bilateral agreements Exchanges between two states, such as arms control agreements negotiated cooperatively to set ceilings on military force levels.

multilateral agreements Cooperative compacts among three or more states to ensure that a concerted policy is implemented toward alleviating a common problem, such as levels of future weapons capabilities.

Strategic Arms Limitation Talks (SALT) Two sets of agreements reached during the 1970s between the United States and the Soviet Union that established limits on strategic nuclear delivery systems.

Intermediate-Range Nuclear Forces (INF) Treaty The U.S.–Russian agreement to eliminate an entire class of nuclear weapons by removing all intermediate and short-range ground-based missiles and launchers with ranges between 300 and 3500 miles from Europe.

Strategic Offensive Reductions Treaty (SORT) The U.S.–Russian agreement to reduce the number of strategic warheads to between 1700 and 2200 for each country by 2012.

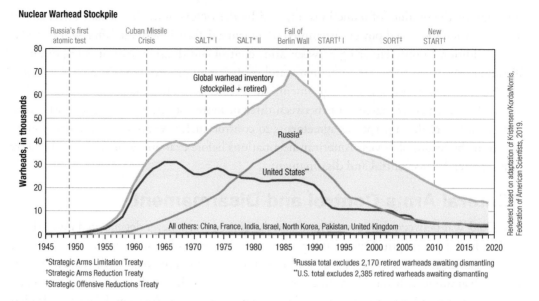

FIGURE 9.1 Shrinking the Stockpile, 1945–2019 The overall record of successful bilateral arms control and even disarmament between the United States and Russia attests to the possibilities for rival military powers to contain by agreement a dangerous arms race. As shown here, the nuclear warhead stockpiles of both countries have been reduced significantly in the post–Cold War period. However, the fragility of these agreements underscores the difficulties associated with maintaining and implementing such commitments, and both countries have slowed their disarmament in recent years.

new nuclear arms race with Washington's former Cold Rival" (Gramer and Seligman, 2019). There are also worries that it could jeopardize the New Start Treaty that was adopted in 2010 and cast a shadow over the prospect of both governments agreeing to extend that treaty past 2021. Nonetheless, the progress made by the United States and Russia in reducing their nuclear weapons stockpiles illustrates the possibility for rival military powers to take steps to de-escalate a risky arms race.

Multilateral Arms Control and Disarmament

History provides many examples of multilateral arms control and disarmament efforts. As early as the eleventh century, the Second Lateran Council prohibited the use of crossbows in fighting. The 1868 St. Petersburg Declaration prohibited the use of explosive bullets. In 1899 and 1907, International Peace Conferences at The Hague restricted the use of some weapons and prohibited others. The leaders of the United States, Britain, Japan, France, and Italy signed treaties at the Washington Naval Conferences (1921–1922) agreeing to adjust the relative tonnage of their fleets. The 1925 Geneva Protocol banned the use of biological and chemical weapons in warfare.

Nearly thirty major multilateral agreements have been signed since World War II (see Table 9.1). They have addressed critical aspects of arms control and disarmament, such as the Biological Weapons Convention (BWC) adopted in 1972 as the first multilateral disarmament treaty to ban the production and storage of an entire category of weapons of mass destruction. The Chemical Weapons Convention (CWC) opened for signature in 1993 following twelve years of negotiation and similarly prohibited the development and production of chemical weapons and called for the destruction of existing stockpiles.

TABLE 9.1   Major Multilateral Arms Control Treaties Since 1945

Date	Agreement	Number of Parties (signed or acceded, 2019)	Principal Objectives
1959	Antarctic Treaty	49	Prevents the military use of the Antarctic, including the testing of nuclear weapons
1963	Partial Test Ban Treaty	137	Prohibits nuclear weapons in the atmosphere, outer space, and underwater
1967	Outer Space Treaty	127	Outlaws the use of outer space for testing or stationing any weapons, as well as for military maneuvers
1967	Treaty of Tlatelolco	33	Creates the Latin American Nuclear Free Zone by prohibiting the testing and possession of nuclear facilities for military purposes
1968	Nuclear Nonproliferation Treaty (NPT)	190	Prevents the spread of nuclear weapons and nuclear-weapons-production technologies to nonnuclear weapons states
1971	Seabed Treaty	117	Prohibits the development of weapons of mass destruction and nuclear weapons on the seabed beyond a 12-mile coastal limit
1972	Biological Weapons Convention (BWC)	177	Prohibits the production and storage of biological toxins; calls for the destruction of biological weapon stockpiles
1977	Environmental Modifications Convention (ENMOD Convention)	85	Bans the use of technologies that could alter Earth's weather patterns, ocean currents, ozone layer, or ecology
1980	Protection of Nuclear Material Convention	146	Obligates protection of peaceful nuclear material during transport on ships or aircraft
1981	Inhumane Weapons Convention	115	Prohibits the use of such weapons as fragmentation bombs, incendiary weapons, booby traps, and mines to which civilians could be exposed
1985	South Pacific Nuclear Free Zone (Roratonga) Treaty	13	Prohibits the testing, acquisition, or deployment of nuclear weapons in the South Pacific
1987	Missile Technology Control Regime (MTCR)	34	Restricts export of ballistic missiles and production facilities
1990	Conventional Forces in Europe (CFE)	30	Places limits on five categories of weapons in Europe and lowers force levels
1990	Confidence- and Security-Building Measures Agreement	53	Improves measures for exchanging detailed information on weapons, forces, and military exercises
1991	UN Register of Conventional Arms	101	Calls on all states to submit information on seven categories of major weapons exported or imported during the previous year
1992	Open Skies Treaty	35	Permits flights by unarmed surveillance aircraft over the territory of the signatory states
1993	Chemical Weapons Convention (CWC)	190	Requires all stockpiles of chemical weapons to be destroyed
1995	Treaty of Bangkok	10	Creates a nuclear-weapon-free zone in Southeast Asia
1995	Wassenaar Export-Control Treaty	40	Regulates transfers of sensitive dual-use technologies to nonparticipating countries
1996	Southeast Asian Nuclear Free Zone Treaty	10	Prevents signatories in Southeast Asia from making, possessing, storing, or testing nuclear weapons
1996	Comprehensive Test Ban Treaty (CTBT)	183	Bans all testing of nuclear weapons
1996	Treaty of Pelindaba	52	Creates an African nuclear-weapon-free zone
1997	Antipersonnel Landmines Treaty (APLT)	161	Bans the production and export of landmines and pledges plans to remove them

(Continued)

TABLE 9.1   Major Multilateral Arms Control Treaties Since 1945 (*continued*)

Date	Agreement	Number of Parties (signed or acceded, 2019)	Principal Objectives
1998	Protocol IV of the Inhumane Weapons Convention	100	Bans some types of laser weapons that cause permanent loss of eyesight
1999	Inter-American Convention on Transparency in Conventional Weapons Acquisitions	21	Requires all thirty-four members of the Organization of American States (OAS) to annually report all weapons acquisitions, exports, and imports
2007	Treaty on Nuclear Free Zone in Central Asia (Treaty of Semipolinsk)	5	Obligates parties not to acquire nuclear weapons
2008	Convention on Cluster Munitions	110	Prohibits the use, production, stockpiling, and transfer of cluster munitions
2014	Arms Trade Treaty	130	Regulates the international trade in conventional arms
2017	Treaty on the Prohibition of Nuclear Weapons	70	Prohibits the use, threat of use, production, possession, and transfer of nuclear weapons

Based on data from U.S. Department of State, 2019; Arms Control Association, 2019.

The Comprehensive Test Ban Treaty (CTBT), adopted in 1996, expanded prohibitions on weapons development to ban testing of all nuclear weapons. It must still be ratified by China, Pakistan, India, Israel, Egypt, Iran, North Korea, and the United States before it can formally enter into force. The United States sought middle ground in its 2018 Nuclear Posture Review, declaring that "Although the United States will not seek ratification of the Comprehensive Nuclear Test Ban Treaty . . . The United States will not resume nuclear explosive testing unless necessary to ensure the safety and effectiveness of the U.S. nuclear arsenal, and calls on all states possessing nuclear weapons to declare or maintain a moratorium on nuclear testing."

Of the multilateral arms agreements, the 1968 Nuclear Nonproliferation Treaty (NPT), which prohibited the transfer of nuclear weapons and production technologies to nonnuclear weapons states, stands out as particularly important. This 2400-word contract that some say saved the world is historically the most symbolic multilateral arms control agreement. With 190 signatory countries, the NPT has had considerable success promoting nuclear nonproliferation, and efforts to bolster and extend this nonproliferation persist. It has also promoted cooperation on the peaceful use of nuclear energy.

However, though the United States and Russia have reduced their nuclear arsenals significantly, the non-nuclear states have expressed frustration with the current status quo and the lack of further progress toward disarmament as called for by the NPT. There have been no new agreements between these major nuclear powers since New START was signed in 2010, the United States withdrew from the INF treaty with Russia in 2019, and the nuclear weapons states are actively seeking to modernize and diversify their nuclear arsenals rather than eliminate them.

At the same time, public anxiety about the salience of nuclear threats has increased amidst several notable setbacks to the NPT (Erästö and Cronberg, 2018). Though not signatories, in 1998 India and Pakistan broke the NPT's barriers to become nuclear powers and are presently locked in a spiraling arms race (see "A Closer Look: The Future of Nuclear Weapons"). Likewise, despite initially signing the treaty, North Korea violated the NPT with its secret development of nuclear weapons. It has further increased tensions with its intercontinental ballistic missile

A Closer Look

THE FUTURE OF NUCLEAR WEAPONS

According to realism, the dynamics of arms competition are rooted in the security dilemma. Recall that in an anarchic international system, each country must ensure its own survival—and this demands that countries strive to become more powerful than their potential opponents. Yet, as described by the imagery of the **spiral model**, this enhancement of military capabilities for defensive purposes tends to result in escalating arms races that diminish the security of all. Sir Edward Grey, British foreign secretary before World War I, described this process well:

> The increase in armaments, that is intended in each nation to produce consciousness of strength and a sense of security, does not produce these efforts. On the contrary, it produces a consciousness of the strength of other nations and a sense of fear. Fear begets suspicion and distrust and evil imaginings of all sorts, 'til each government feels it would be criminal and a betrayal of its own country not to take every precaution, while every government regards every precaution of every other government as evidence of hostile intent (Wight, 2002, p. 254).

Consider the ongoing arms competition between Pakistan and India. In 2012, both states test-launched nuclear-capable missiles (Abbot, 2012). Their rivalry was exacerbated further in 2018 when India revealed its first domestic-built nuclear-powered submarine and announced plans to build three more. The submarines enhance its second-strike capability by enabling India to deliver nuclear missiles from air, land, and sea. "India's decision to produce nuclear-powered submarines

is a major escalation in the nuclear field . . . Pakistan will certainly try to match in kind," said Talat Masood, a retired lieutenant general in Islamabad. It also raises the prospect of a response from China as the country has a geopolitical interest to counter India's military moves and is an ally of Pakistan (Bokhari, 2018).

Liberal theory posits that security may depend as much on the control of force as its pursuit. So how do countries avoid or pull out of an arms race? Expanding confidence-building measures that reduce fear and suspicion—including increased transparency and a global culture of disclosure—is critical to countering the uncertainties of the security dilemma and establishing a foundation of trust for future disarmament. In a world where nuclear proliferation and arms competition continue to pose a threat to global security, in the words of U.S. President Dwight D. Eisenhower, "disarmament, with mutual honor and confidence, is a continuing imperative."

Watch the Carnegie Council Video:

"The Irony of Nuclear Weapons?"

You Decide:

1. Are nuclear weapons the scourge of international relations? Or, do they provide a valuable deterrent effect?

2. Are arms races doomed to end in violent conflict? What measures can be taken to ameliorate such competition?

3. Will disarmament bring about a more peaceful world?

(ICBM) tests in 2017 and its short-range ballistic missile tests in 2019. Russia's annexation of Crimea, coupled with its nuclear rhetoric, has likewise increased the perception of threat by European countries and led to concern that Russia might be willing to use tactical nuclear weapons in the event of a conflict with NATO.

spiral model
A metaphor used to describe the tendency of efforts to enhance defense to result in escalating arms races.

Fears of nuclear proliferation were also inflamed by Iran's pursuit of nuclear capabilities. In September 2009, Iran test-fired missiles capable of striking Israel, Europe, and American bases in the Persian Gulf. The United Nations subsequently adopted new sanctions against Iran, including a prohibition on Iranian investment in uranium mining and activity involving ballistic missiles capable of delivering nuclear weapons. In 2015, Iran engaged in negotiations with the United States and five other major powers regarding reductions in its existing stockpile of nuclear fuel and limiting its capacity to produce new fuel in exchange for relief from international sanctions. The nuclear accord signaled an interest and willingness of Iran to collaborate and pursue a path to peace with members of the global community. However, there is worry that the 2015 Iran nuclear deal may completely unravel and instability in the region will increase following the United States withdrawal from the agreement in 2018 (Erästö, 2019).

Thus, more than a half-century after adoption of the NPT, nuclear weapons still exist and there is frustration that the commitment of the nuclear-armed states to disarmament is tenuous. To challenge the status quo, in 2017 the Treaty on the Prohibition of Nuclear Weapons (TPNW) was adopted with, as of mid-2019, at least 70 signatories. It calls for the total elimination of nuclear weapons and is opposed by all the nuclear-armed members of the NPT—the United States, Russia, China, France, and the United Kingdom—in the current security environment. Proponents of disarmament recognize that the TPNW will not eliminate nuclear weapons in the short term, but the "expectation is that this stigmatization will weaken the association between nuclear weapons and prestige, and thus create a new kind of pressure for disarmament" (Erästö and Cronbert, 2018, p. 5).

The Problematic Future of Arms Control and Disarmament

The control and disarmament of nuclear arms faces three intimidating obstacles—the insecurity of states, the idea that nuclear weapons are the great equalizer, and the proliferation risk that occurs when a nuclear power builds civilian reactors for a nonnuclear state (Ferguson, 2010). Though expressing commitment to the idea of disarmament, the nuclear-armed states see the security environment as prohibiting further progress. The United States points to the expansion of Russian and Chinese arsenals, Russia perceives challenges to strategic stability caused by the U.S. missile defense and deployment of weapons in space, and China argues that those two countries with the largest nuclear arsenals must accomplish further substantive reductions before conditions exist for other nuclear weapon states to disarm (Erästö, 2019).

Amongst non-nuclear powers, some states that signed the original agreement wonder whether the deal they were handed by the "nuclear club" in 1968 was fair. They observe the failure of the original nuclear powers to honor their pledge to disarm and perceive the NPT as "an instrument for the haves to deny the have-nots" (Allison, 2010, p. 80). Countries in the Global South such as Saudi Arabia, the United Arab Emirates, and Egypt have indicated intent to explore nuclear options, albeit peaceful ones (Coll, 2009). Given this trend, it is all the more alarming that "new nuclear states, with a nascent arsenal and lack of experience in nuclearized disputes, play the 'nuclear card' significantly more often than their more experienced nuclear counterparts, making them more likely to reciprocate militarized disputes" (Horowitz, 2009, p. 235).

Another problem with arms control and disarmament is that these agreements frequently regulate only obsolete armaments or ones that the parties to the agreement have little incentive to continue developing in the first place. Even when agreements are reached on modern, sophisticated weapons, the parties often set ceilings higher than the number of weapons currently deployed, so they do not have to slash their inventories. A second pitfall is the propensity of limits on one type of weapon system to prompt developments in another system. Like a balloon that is squeezed at one end but simply expands at the other, constraints on certain parts of a country's arsenal can lead to enhancements elsewhere. An example can be seen in the 1972 SALT I agreement, which limited the number of intercontinental ballistic missiles possessed by the United States and the Soviet Union. Although the number of missiles was restricted, no limits were placed on the number of nuclear warheads that could be placed on each missile. Consequently, both sides developed *multiple independently targeted reentry vehicles* (MIRVs). In short, the quantitative freeze on launchers led to qualitative improvements in their warhead delivery systems.

Furthermore, the slow and ineffective ability of the global community to ban some of the most dangerous and counterproductive weapons reduces optimism in the future of meaningful arms control. Consider the case of **antipersonnel landmines (APLs)** that cannot discriminate between soldiers and civilians. It is thought that more than 100 to 300 million landmines are scattered in more than seventy countries (with another 100 million in stockpiles). It is estimated that about one mine exists for every fifty people in the world and that each year they kill or maim more than 26,000 people—almost all of them civilians. That is a rate of one victim occurring every twenty minutes.

In 1994, not a single state would endorse a prohibition on these deadly weapons. It took peace activist Jody Williams to organize the International Campaign to Ban Landmines, which led to the *Convention on the Prohibition of the Use, Stockpiling, Production and Transfer of Antipersonnel Mines*, which opened for signature in December 1997. For her efforts, Williams received the Nobel Peace Prize. But the United States, Russia, and other great powers stubbornly resisted the APL convention until a coalition of NGO peace groups mounted sufficient pressure for them to produce this important treaty. Now signed by 161 states, the challenge of enforcing the ban and removing APLs remains staggering, in part because of continued support of landmines as a deterrent against ground invasion. Though the United States still has not accepted the treaty, it has indicated that it will "no

antipersonnel landmines (APLs) Weapons buried below the surface of the soil that explode on contact when any person—soldier or citizen—steps on them.

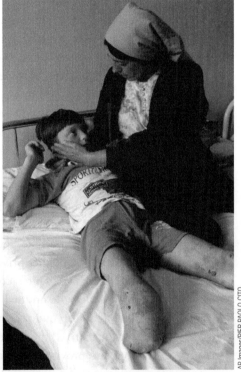

IMAGE 9.3 **A Legacy of War** Antipersonnel mines are triggered by the contact or presence of a person. Indiscriminate weapons of war that do not recognize a cease-fire or termination of hostilities, they kill or cause injuries such as destroyed limbs, burns, and blindness. Pictured here is a twelve-year-old victim, Burin, in a hospital with his mother where he is being treated for the loss of his right leg and other serious wounds that he received while picking strawberries in a field in southern Kosovo.

longer produce or acquire antipersonnel land mines or replace old ones that expire, which will have the practical effect of reducing the estimated 10 million mines in the American stockpile" (Gladstone, 2014).

A final problem facing those advocating arms control and disarmament is continuous innovation in the defense industry. By the time that limits are negotiated on one type of weapon, a new generation of weapons has emerged. Modern technology is creating an ever-widening range of novel weapons—increasingly smaller, deadlier, and easier to conceal.

Why do states often make decisions to arm that apparently imprison them in the grip of perpetual insecurity? On the surface, the incentives for meaningful arms control seem numerous. Significant controls would save money, reduce tension, decrease environmental hazards, and diminish the potential destructiveness of war. However, most countries are reluctant to limit their armaments because the self-help international system requires each state to protect itself. Thus, states find themselves caught in a vicious cycle summarized by two basic principles: (1) "Don't negotiate when you are behind. Why accept a permanent position of number two?" and (2) "Don't negotiate when you are ahead. Why accept a freeze in an area of military competition when the other side has not kept up with you?" (Barnet, 1977).

The logic underlying the well-known "Prisoner's Dilemma" illuminates the circumstantial barriers to international cooperation that exist among distrustful transnational actors (see Figure 9.2). To illustrate, imagine that two suspects following an armed robbery are taken into police custody and placed in separate cells by the district attorney, who is certain that they are guilty but only has sufficient evidence to convict them on an illegal weapons charge. The district attorney tells both prisoners that there are two choices: confess to the robbery or remain silent. If one prisoner confesses and the other doesn't, he will be given immunity from prosecution for providing evidence, whereas his accomplice will get a sentence of ten years in prison. If both confess, they will be given a reduced sentence of five years. If neither confesses, they each will be convicted on the weapons charge but serve only six months in prison.

Faced with this situation, what should each prisoner do? They both want as little time behind bars as possible, and they are being interrogated separately so they cannot communicate. Furthermore, neither prisoner is sure that he can trust the other. This situation, which can be roughly applied to interactions between transnational actors, has some interesting consequences.

Although the optimal strategy for both prisoners would be to tacitly cooperate with each other and keep quiet so each receives only a six-month sentence (the win-win outcome of 2, 2 in the matrix), the suspects face incentives in this situation that incline each to turn on the other and provide incriminating evidence to the district attorney. First, there is an offensive incentive to defect by confessing and thereby securing an outcome for oneself (immunity) that is even better than the one available if the partners stick together (a six-month prison sentence for both). Second, there is a defensive incentive to defect grounded in the fear of being double-crossed by an accomplice who squeals and thereby winding up with the worst outcome (ten years in prison) while the partner goes free.

Not wanting to be a "sucker" who spends a decade incarcerated while his partner goes free, according to the logic of the Prisoner's Dilemma, both prisoners conclude that it is in their self-interest to defect and testify against one another in an effort to "win more." Consequently, they both receive a less optimal result (the lose-lose outcome 3, 3 in the matrix—five years in prison) than if they had tacitly cooperated and remained silent. The dilemma is that seemingly rational calculations by each individual actor can yield collectively worse results for both than had they chosen other strategies.

Many realist theorists liken arms races to the Prisoner's Dilemma. Instead of prisoners, consider two countries that have roughly equal military capabilities, are uncertain of whether they can trust one another, and are currently facing two choices: cooperate in lowering arms spending or defect by increasing arms spending. Suppose that each country prefers to have a military advantage over the other and fears being at a serious disadvantage, which would happen if one increased arms spending while the other reduced expenditures (the win more-lose more outcomes 4, 1 and 1, 4 depicted in Figure 9.2). By cooperating to lower arms spending they could devote more resources to other national needs such as education and health care (the outcome 2, 2), but given offensive and

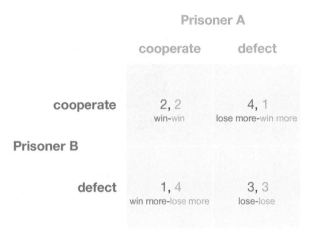

FIGURE 9.2 The Prisoner's Dilemma The matrix depicts the results that will occur depending on whether each prisoner chooses to cooperate with his accomplice by remaining silent or defect by confessing to the district attorney. Because both prisoners want to spend as little time incarcerated as possible, their preferences are rank ordered from the most preferred outcome to the least preferred as follows: (1) immunity from prosecution; (2) six months in prison; (3) five years in prison; and (4) ten years in prison. The first number shown in each cell is Actor A's outcome; the second number is B's outcome.

defensive incentives that are similar to those tempting the two prisoners in our earlier example, they both conclude that it is in their individual self-interest to play it safe and arm. As a result of their joint defection (outcome 3, 3), they end up worse off by locking themselves into an expensive arms race that may destabilize the prevailing balance of power.

Although this version of the Prisoner's Dilemma game is a simplification that does not take into account what might happen in repeated plays over time (see Axelrod, 1984), it highlights for you some of the difficulties in reaching mutually beneficial arms control agreements among self-interested actors who distrust their peers. This mind-set was very evident in U.S. decisions at the turn of the century to reject an array of international treaties designed to control the threat of nuclear weapons. During 2001 alone, the United States decided to abrogate the 1972 Anti-Ballistic Missile (ABM) Treaty, withdraw from a UN conference to impose limits on illegal small arms trafficking, and reject proposed enforcement measures for the 1972 Biological Weapons Convention. This disregard for arms control set a standard for other states to follow.

Especially troubling was the U.S. repudiation of the 1972 ABM treaty, which was regarded by many as the cornerstone of nuclear arms control, as that announcement was the first time in modern history that the United States had renounced a major international accord. It ignited fears that a global chain reaction of massive repudiations of arms control agreements by other states would follow. For example, in 2007 Russia threatened to quit the INF missile treaty and to place a moratorium on the CFE treaty. Yet it was instead the United States that, in 2019, withdrew from the INF missile treaty, again stoking fears that abandonment of a key bilateral treaty could erode support for other arms control agreements and foreshadow a renewed arms race with Russia.

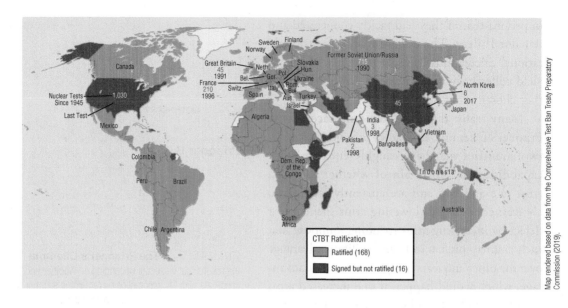

Map rendered based on data from the Comprehensive Test Ban Treaty Preparatory Commission (2019).

Nuclear Weapons Tests

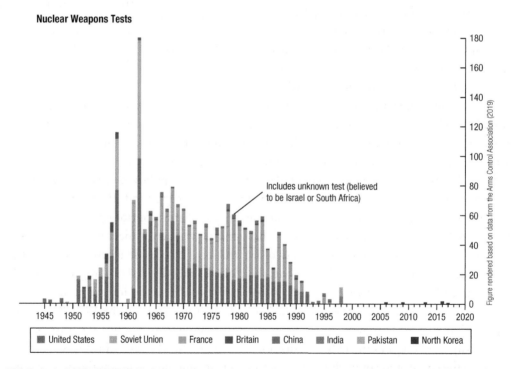

Figure rendered based on data from the Arms Control Association (2019)

MAP 9.1 AND FIGURE 9.3 Trick or Treaty? Can Arms Control Stop the Proliferation of Weapons?   As indicated in the timeline, nuclear testing has declined dramatically since the 1960s. This commitment to arms control is reflected in support for the Comprehensive Test Ban Treaty. Shown in the map, as of June 2019, 184 states had signed the Comprehensive Test Ban Treaty (CTBT); 168 had ratified it. However, 12 states still have not signed, including Pakistan, India, and North Korea. Twenty of the countries that have signed have yet to ratify the treaty, including the United States, China, Iran, and Israel. Fears of intensified nuclear arms rivalry and a potential wave of new testing remain.

Think It Through Based on current circumstances, does a country's ratification and/or signing of the CTBT appear to influence their proliferation of nuclear weapons? Why or why not?

The tendency of states to prioritize improving their weapons over controlling them is illustrated by the prevalence of nuclear tests (see Map 9.1 and Figure 9.3). At the start of 2019, eight known nuclear states had conducted a total of 2056 nuclear explosions since 1945—an average of one test every thirteen days, though there is suspicion that many tests are not reported (ACA, 2019). Both China and the United States regularly conduct zero-yield nuclear experiments and are suspected of conducting explosive tests so small that they cannot be detected. North Korea conducted its first nuclear test in 2006 and its latest in 2017, showing no sign of abandoning its nuclear ambitions despite its pledge to denuclearize (Ali, 2019).

The past record of arms control and disarmament has dispirited liberal and constructivist reformers who hope that negotiated compromises will curtail the global arms race. It appears that realism, and its abiding emphasis on peace through military preparations, is trumping liberalism's premise that weapons acquisitions are not a safe road toward world order. As long as the threat of armed conflict haunts the world, leaders are unlikely to think it prudent to disarm. Someday, however, Woodrow Wilson's cause of world disarmament may yet triumph. The non-nuclear states' support for the TPNW reflects a countervailing trend "to delegitimize and stigmatize nuclear weapons and thereby contribute to achieving the ultimate goal of nuclear disarmament" (Kile and Erästö, 2018). However, many liberals and constructivists perceive other paths to peace as more promising. The construction of international organizations for collective security benefits from a more encouraging history, in part because so many military crises require multilateral cooperation to be peacefully managed.

Maintaining Collective Security Through International Organizations

LO 9-3   Apply the principles of collective security to international organizations, and assess their effectiveness along these lines.

One of the prime rationales for the formation of *international organizations* is the preservation of peace. An institutional pathway to international peace is sculpted in liberal and constructivist thinking, with liberals focusing on interdependence and cooperation and constructivists emphasizing the centrality of ideas and norms. These approaches are voiced as alternatives to the balancing of power advocated by realist thinkers. The global community has usually trodden down paths to peace through international organizations when each previous balance of power has collapsed in large-scale warfare (as all past balances of power have done sooner or later).

Note that classical realism vigorously opposes relying on international organizations. Realism, it should be recalled, prizes the sovereign independence of states as a core value and berates any international organization as a barrier to states' foreign policy autonomy, freedom, and flexibility of unilateral action. Indeed, realism rejects prescriptions for the global community to "get organized" by creating institutions *above* states as a route to global stability. The only exception to this realist posture is when great powers have elected to create supranational multilateral institutions to manage military power in international relations, and this *only* when the great powers forming them were certain that the organizations would be managed authoritatively *by* them for their own self-interests.

For liberal and constructivist reformers, *collective security* is conceived as an alternative to the balance-of-power politics favored by realists. By definition, collective security requires collective decisions for collective goals, such as containing armed conflict, which is guided by the principle that an act of aggression by any state will be met with a unified response from the rest. As former U.S. Secretary of State Henry Kissinger (1991) explained, the twin assumptions of collective security are "that nations perceive each threat in the same way and are prepared to run identical risks" to preserve it. International organizations are seen as key to peaceful conflict management as "organizations with interventionist capabilities encourage disputing members to attempt peaceful conflict resolution" (Shannon, 2009, p. 145).

Collective security is based on a creed similar to that voiced by Alexandre Dumas's d'Artagnan and his fellow Musketeers: "One for all and all for one!" In order for collective security to function in the rough-and-tumble international arena, its advocates usually translate the Musketeer creed into the following rules of statecraft:

- **All threats to peace must be a common concern to everyone.** Peace, collective security theory assumes, is indivisible. If aggression anywhere is ignored, it eventually will spread to other countries and become more difficult to stop; hence, an attack on any one state must be regarded as an attack on all states.

- **Every member of the global system should join the collective security organization.** Instead of maneuvering against one another in rival alliances, states should link up in a single "uniting" alliance. Such a universal collectivity, it is assumed, would possess the international legitimacy and strength to keep the peace.

- **Members of the organization should pledge to settle their disputes through peaceful means.** Collective security is not wedded to the status quo. It assumes that peaceful change is possible when institutions are available to resolve conflicts of interest. In addition to providing a mechanism for the mediation of disagreements, the collective security organization would also contain a judicial organ authorized to issue binding verdicts on contentious disputes.

- **If a breach of the peace occurs, the organization should apply timely and robust sanctions to punish the aggressor.** A final assumption underpinning this theory holds that members of the collective security organization would be willing and able to give mutual assistance to any state suffering an attack. Sanctions could range from public condemnation to economic boycott to military retaliation.

Putting the pieces of these premises together, this approach to international peace through collective security organizations aims to control anarchical self-help warfare by guaranteeing every state's defenses through collective regulation. Perhaps ironically, therefore, liberal reformers accept the use of military might—not to expand state power, but rather to deter potential aggressors by confronting them with armed force organized by the united opposition of the entire global community. Might *can* be used to fight for right.

The League of Nations, United Nations, and Collective Security

Perhaps more than any other event, World War I discredited the realist argument that peace was a by-product of a stable balance of power. Citing arms races, secret treaties, and competing alliances as sources of divisive tension, many liberals viewed power balancing as a *cause* of war instead of as an instrument for its prevention. U.S. President Woodrow Wilson voiced the strongest opposition to balance-of-power politics; Point XIV of his Fourteen Points proposal for post-war peace called for "a general association of nations for the purpose of preserving the political independence and territorial integrity of great and small states alike." This plea led to the formation of the League of Nations, a precursor to the

IMAGE 9.4 **With a Little Help from Friends** Embodying the liberal vision of collective security, UN peacekeepers continue a 70-year history of service. Today they are "called upon not only to maintain peace and security, but also to facilitate the political process, protect civilians, assist in the disarmament, demobilization and reintegration of former combatants; support the organization of elections, protect and promote human rights and assist in restoring the rule of law" (UN, 2019c). Pictured here, members of the United Nations Stabilization Mission in Haiti (MINUSTAH) help a child collect water that is safe to consume.

United Nations, to replace the balance of power with a global governance system for world order in which aggression by any state would be met by a united response.

Yet long before Wilson and other reformers called for the establishment of a League of Nations, the idea of collective security had been expressed in various peace plans. Between the eleventh and thirteenth centuries, for example, French ecclesiastic councils held in Poitiers (1000), Limoges (1031), and Toulouse (1210) discussed rudimentary versions of collective security. Similar proposals surfaced in the writings of Pierre Dubois (1306), King George Podebrad of Bohemia (1462), the Duc de Sully (1560–1641), and the Abbé de Saint-Pierre (1713). The belief that an organized "community" of power would be more effective in preserving peace than shifting alliances aimed at balancing power served as a foundation for these proposals.

To the disappointment of its advocates, the League of Nations never became an effective collective security system. It was not endorsed by the United States, the very power that had most championed it in the waning months of World War I. Moreover, its members disagreed over how to define "aggression," as well as how to share the costs and risks of mounting an organized response to potential aggressors. Although the league failed to realize its lofty goal, the principles of collective security embedded in the League of Nations guided the subsequent formation of the United Nations.

Like the League, the United Nations was established to promote international peace and security after a gruesome world war. The goal was to construct, in the words of U.S. President Harry Truman, "a permanent partnership . . . among the peoples of the world for their common

peacekeeping
The efforts by third parties such as the United Nations to intervene in civil wars and/or interstate wars or to prevent hostilities between potential belligerents from escalating, so that by acting as a buffer, a negotiated settlement of the dispute can be reached.

preventive diplomacy
Diplomatic actions taken in advance of a predictable crisis to prevent or limit violence.

peacemaking
The process of diplomacy, mediation, negotiation, or other forms of peaceful settlement that arranges an end to a dispute and resolves the issues that led to conflict.

peace building
Post-conflict actions, predominantly diplomatic and economic, that strengthen and rebuild governmental infrastructure and institutions in order to avoid renewed recourse to armed conflict.

peace operations
A general category encompassing both peacekeeping and peace enforcement operations, undertaken to establish and maintain peace between disputants.

peace and common well-being." The architects of the United Nations were painfully aware of the league's disappointing experience with collective security. They hoped a new structure would make the United Nations more effective than the defunct League.

Recall from Chapter 6 that the UN Charter established a Security Council of fifteen members, a General Assembly composed of representatives from all member states, and an administrative apparatus (or Secretariat) under the leadership of a secretary-general. Although the UN's founders voiced support for collective security, they were heavily influenced by the idea of a *concert* of great powers that together would manage global issues. The UN Charter permitted any of the Security Council's five permanent members (the United States, the Soviet Union [now Russia], United Kingdom, France, and China) to veto and thereby block proposed military actions.

Because the Security Council could approve military actions only when the permanent members fully agreed, the United Nations was hamstrung by great power rivalries, especially between the United States and the Soviet Union. During the Cold War, "it became a formula for political paralysis" (Urquhart, 2010, p. 26), with more than 230 Security Council vetoes stopping action of any type on about one-third of the UN's resolutions. Because the UN's structure limited its ability to function as a true collective security organization, during the Cold War the United Nations fell short of many of its ambitious ideals.

Nevertheless, like any adaptive institution, the United Nations found other ways to overcome its compromising legal restrictions and lack of great power cooperation that inhibited its capacity to preserve world order. For example, in contrast to peace enforcement as in the Korean War, the United Nations undertook a new approach, termed **peacekeeping**, that aimed "to prevent undue violence from occurring in countries plagued by civil war" (Powers et al., 2015, p. 46). The UN Emergency Force (UNEF), authorized in 1956 by the *Uniting for Peace Resolution* in the General Assembly in response to the Suez crisis, was the first of many peacekeeping operations (see Map 9.2). The United Nations' peacekeeping activities have been credited with successfully containing conflict by "decreasing the tactical advantage of mobility for the rebels, by obstructing the movement of armed actors, and by altering the ability for governments to seek and confront rebel actors" (Beardsley and Gleditsch, 2015, p. 67).

Furthermore, in 1960 Secretary-General Dag Hammarskjöld sought to manage security through what he termed **preventive diplomacy** by attempting to resolve conflicts before they became a crisis, in contrast to ending wars once they erupted. Frustrated with the superpowers' prevention of the United Nations from playing "as effective and decisive a role as the charter certainly envisaged for it," in 1989 Secretary-General Javier Pérez de Cuéllar pursued **peacemaking** initiatives. These programs were designed to end fighting so that the UN Security Council could then establish operations to keep the peace. Later, UN Secretary-General Kofi Annan concentrated the UN's efforts on **peace building** by creating conditions that would make renewed war unlikely, while at the same time working on peacemaking (ending fighting already under way) and managing the UN's **peace operations** to police those conflicts in which the threat of renewed fighting between enemies is high. These endeavors have emphasized **peace enforcement** operations, relying on UN forces that are trained and equipped to use military force if necessary, without the prior consent of the disputants.

For over four decades, the United Nations was a victim of superpower rivalry. However, the end of the Cold War removed many of the impediments to the UN's ability to act to preserve peace. For example, in 1999, the Security Council swung into action to authorize military coercion to force Iraq to withdraw from Kuwait, which it had invaded. This successful collective security initiative jump-started optimism for the usefulness of the UN's peacekeeping leadership. After 1990, the United Nations launched over three times as many peacekeeping missions as it had in the previous forty years of its existence (see Map 9.2).

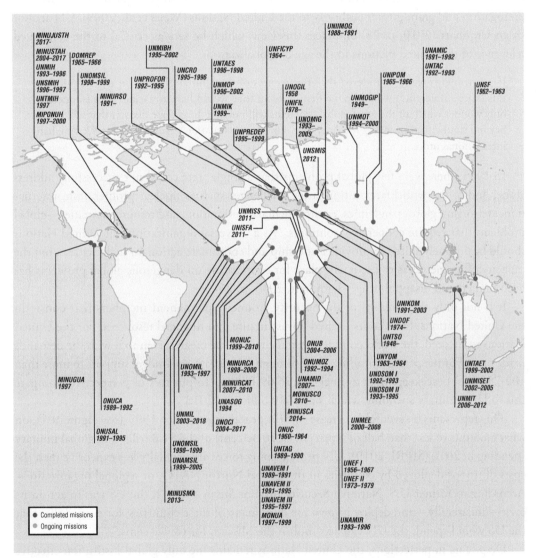

MAP 9.2 UN Peace Missions, 1948–2019 In its first forty years, the United Nations undertook a mere eighteen peacekeeping operations. But since 1990, the United Nations has been much more active, sending peacekeepers to fifty-eight flash points. As the map shows, most of the seventy-one missions between 1948 and 2019 lasted at least a decade. As of June 2019, fourteen peacekeeping missions were deployed.

 Think It Through What does the increasing number of peacekeeping operations over time indicate about the evolving role of collective security?

Although liberals have great hope for the United Nations as a means of promoting human rights and a global rule of law (Mertus, 2009b), the constraints that it faces as an organization may be due in part to its continued emphasis on sovereignty and dependence on power politics. From a realist perspective, the "UN was founded to perpetuate the global dominance of Britain and America while accommodating the unwelcome emergence of the Soviet Union . . . as an institution whereby power politics could be pursued by other means" (Gray, 2010, p. 79; Mazower, 2009). In order to fundamentally enhance the ability of the United Nations to function as a truly global authority, its members may need to relinquish their individual prerogatives and grant greater authority to the United Nations (Weiss et al., 2009). UN analyst Brian Urquhart (2010, p. 28) embraces this view, which he sees as critical to the continued relevance of the United Nations in the age of globalization:

> If governments really considered the effectiveness of the United Nations an urgent priority, this (state sovereignty) would be the first problem they would have to tackle. As it is, one can only wonder which of the great global problems will provide the cosmic disaster that will prove beyond doubt, and probably too late, that our present situation demands a post-Westphalian international order.

In 1945, there were few global problems that a single state could not successfully address alone. Today, the world faces intimidating challenges such as nuclear proliferation, international terrorism, global pandemics, environmental deterioration, and resource scarcities—global problems that require cooperative solutions. "As a universal organization, the United Nations should be uniquely suited to provide leadership and coordinate action on such matters, but the capacity of its members to use it as a place for cooperating on dangerous global problems has been limited and disappointing" (Urquhart, 2010, p. 26).

It is not only the interests of the Security Council's permanent members that constrain the United Nations, but also its limited infrastructure and financial resources. For the United Nations to succeed, the world community must match the means given to it with the demands made on it. For the period from July 2018 through June 2019, the budget support to more than 102,736 UN peacekeeping personnel was $6.69 billion. To put this in perspective, compare this to U.S. military spending which was $649 billion in 2018.

This represents a sevenfold increase in UN peacekeepers since 1999 (see Figure 9.4), on what amounts to less than half of 1 percent (0.26 percent) of the $1.8 trillion in global military spending in 2018 (SIPRI, 2019). UN peacekeeping forces are generally less expensive than the costs of troops deployed by countries in the Global North, NATO, or regional organizations. According to former U.S. National Security Advisor Susan Rice, "If the US was to act on its own—unilaterally—and deploy its own forces in many of these countries; for every dollar that the US would spend, the UN can accomplish the Mission for twelve cents."

Despite its imperfections, the United Nations remains the only global institution effective at organizing international collaboration to meet security crises in situations where states are unwilling or unprepared to act alone. However, the use of regional security organizations is rising as regional IGOs are stepping into the breach in those situations where UN Blue Helmets have not been given the necessary support to do the job.

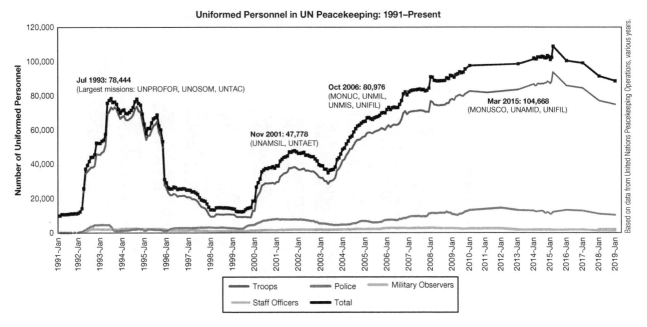

Uniformed Personnel in UN Peacekeeping: 1991–Present

Jul 1993: 78,444
(Largest missions: UNPROFOR, UNOSOM, UNTAC)

Oct 2006: 80,976
(MONUC, UNMIL, UNMIS, UNIFIL)

Nov 2001: 47,778
(UNAMSIL, UNTAET)

Mar 2015: 104,668
(MONUSCO, UNAMID, UNIFIL)

Based on data from United Nations Peacekeeping Operations, various years.

Troops   Police   Military Observers
Staff Officers   Total

FIGURE 9.4 **The Increasing Demand for "Peace"** The chart shows a clear trend in the demand for peacekeepers over time, as the total number of personnel involved in peacekeeping missions—often referred to as "Blue Helmets" because of their blue helmets or berets—has increased sevenfold since 1999. The other trend lines show two of the other key functions increasingly performed by these personnel: military observers (who monitor conditions on the ground and have no mandate to engage militarily) and police. In March 2019, uniformed personnel included 74,874 troops, 10,316 police, and 1271 military observers who were contributed by 122 countries (UN, 2019c).

Regional Security Organizations and Collective Defense

If the United Nations reflects the lack of shared values and common purpose characteristic of a divided global community, perhaps regional organizations, whose members already share some interests and cultural traditions, offer better prospects. The kinds of wars raging today do not lend themselves to being controlled by a worldwide body because these conflicts are now almost entirely civil wars. The United Nations was designed to manage international wars *between* states; it was not organized or legally authorized to intervene in internal battles *within* sovereign borders.

Regional IGOs are different. Regional IGOs see their security interests vitally affected by armed conflicts within countries in their area, and historically they have shown the determination and discipline to police these bitter intrastate conflicts. The "regionalization" of peace operations is a global trend. As 2019 began, no less than fifty peace missions served by 66,278 military and civilian personnel were carried out by regional organizations and ad hoc UN-sanctioned coalitions of states (SIPRI, 2019). Hence, regional security organizations can be expected to play an increasingly larger role in the future security affairs of their regions (see Figure 9.5).

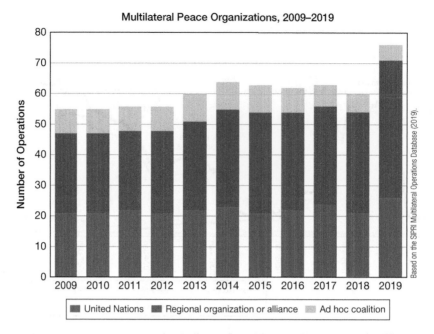

Multilateral Peace Organizations, 2009–2019

Based on the SIPRI Multilateral Operations Database (2019).

FIGURE 9.5 Pitching In to Protect the Peace Collective security depends on members of the international community coming together to resolve conflicts and support peaceful change. As shown above, fifty multilateral missions and operations took place during May 2019, with twenty-six conducted by the UN, forty-five by regional organizations and alliances, and five by ad hoc coalitions of states. Of these, 58 percent were deployed in Africa, 42 percent in Europe, and 24 percent in the Middle East.

The North Atlantic Treaty Organization (NATO) is the best-known regional security organization. Others include the Organization for Security and Cooperation in Europe (OSCE), the ANZUS pact (Australia, New Zealand, and the United States), and the Southeast Asia Treaty Organization (SEATO). Regional organizations with somewhat broader political mandates beyond defense include the Organization of American States (OAS), the League of Arab States, the Organization of African Unity (OAU), the Nordic Council, the Association of Southeast Asian Nations (ASEAN), and the Gulf Cooperation Council.

Many of today's regional security organizations face the challenge of preserving consensus and solidarity without a clear sense of its mission. Consider NATO. In the years since the end of the Cold War, the ambiguous European security setting has been marked by ethnic and religious conflicts that NATO was not originally designed to handle. Its original charter envisioned only one purpose—mutual self-protection from the Soviet Union. It never defined policing intrastate conflict as a goal.

Consequently, until 1995, when NATO took charge of all military operations in Bosnia-Herzegovina from the United Nations, it was uncertain whether the alliance could adapt to the new security environment. Since that intervention, NATO *has* redefined itself. It intervened to police the civil violence in Kosovo in 1999. For the first time invoking its Article 5, which requires collective defense of a member under attack, NATO joined the war in Afghanistan in 2001 in a strong show of support for the United States following the terrorist attacks on 9/11. In March 2011, NATO took over responsibility for military operations in Libya that were initially conducted by the United States, France, and Britain. In 2014, NATO condemned Russia's annexation of Crimea and the destabilization of eastern Ukraine by Russia and Russian-backed separatists as a violation of international law. The alliance declared its support for the sovereignty and territorial integrity of Ukraine, and agreed to help Ukraine provide for its security. NATO also carried out a peace operation in Iraq in 2018.

Today, NATO has grown considerably, with its membership expanding from the twelve founding members in 1949 to the current twenty-nine members through six rounds of enlargement in 1952, 1955, 1982, 1999, 2004, 2009, and 2017 (see Map 9.3). A number of countries in Eastern Europe are candidates for future membership, with North Macedonia signing an accession accord in February 2019. NATO Secretary General Jens Stoltenberg emphasized

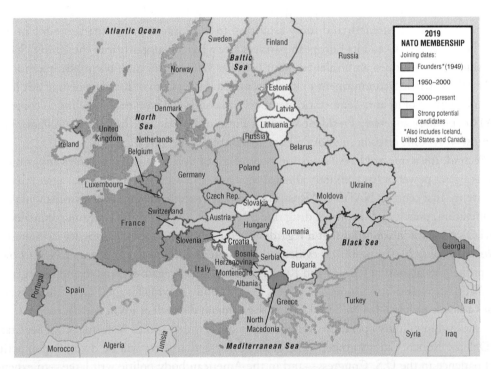

MAP 9.3 The Enlarged NATO in the New Geostrategic Balance of Power The twenty-first-century geostrategic landscape has been transformed by NATO's expansion to twenty-nine full members, with Montenegro formally joining as the newest member on April 28, 2017. Ratification of North Macedonia's membership is expected in 2020, which will bring membership to thirty full members. As shown in this map, NATO now casts its security umbrella across and beyond Europe in its endeavor to create a collective security regime, including states that were once its enemies.

 Think It Through What does NATO's spread to East European countries suggest about the organization's future?

the continued importance of security through multinational cooperation, proclaiming that "NATO's door remains open for countries that meet NATO standards and that adhere to the NATO values of democracy, the rule of law and individual liberty."

Additionally, NATO has transformed itself to become a *military* alliance for security both between states and within them and for containing the spread of global terrorism, as well as a *political* alliance that encourages the spread of democracy. Although NATO is widely seen as a proxy for the Global North, collective security operations under its authority convey a legitimacy that *unilateral* interventions tend to lack. "This is particularly the case for Britain and France, whose colonial histories bring enormous baggage in the Middle East and North Africa—not to mention the United States, with its own more recent complicated history in the region" (Joyner, 2011).

Nonetheless, as is the case with the United Nations and other regional organizations, NATO faces barriers to its success as a collective security organization. NATO is most capable of conducting successful operations only when its most powerful members are in agreement with one another. For most of the last seventy years, the United States has viewed Europe as a vital partner and seen its strength and unity as critical to U.S. interests. For the first time in history, however, NATO and its European partners face a lack of support from the United States. "President Trump's open ambivalence about NATO's value to the U.S., his public questioning of America's Article 5 commitment to its allies, persistent criticism of Europe's democratic leaders and embrace of its anti-democratic members and continued weakness in failing to confront NATO's primary adversary President Vladimir Putin of Russia, have hurtled the Alliance into its most worrisome crisis in memory" (Lute and Burns, 2019, p. 2).

Second, the scope of NATO's mission is constrained as it is unlikely to target any country that is a great power or has a military alliance with one. Its traditional foe, Russia, agrees that in the twenty-first century, NATO and Russia should work together to confront terrorism, nuclear proliferation, piracy, and the illegal drug trade. However, "Russia is still far from reconciled to NATO's presence in countries that it regards as being within its 'sphere of privileged interests'" (*The Economist*, 2010a, p. 67), as evidenced by the tension between Russia and NATO over the military escalation in Crimea and Russia's military action against Ukraine and Georgia.

The reluctance of its European members to sufficiently provide for their own militaries also poses a major problem for NATO. Instead, they remain dependent upon the United States to take the lead in military operations and provide most of the weapons. As former U.S. Secretary of Defense Robert Gates warned, "The blunt reality is that there will be dwindling appetite and patience in the U.S. Congress—and in the American body politic writ large—to expend increasingly precious funds on behalf of nations that are apparently unwilling to devote the necessary resources or make the necessary changes to be serious and capable partners in their own defense." Thus, President Trump echoed previous U.S. leaders when he complained about the imbalance as the United States accounts for almost three-fourths of all military spending by NATO countries. As U.S. Ambassadors Douglas Lute and Nicholas Burns explain, "It is simply unfair that only five of the twenty-nine allies are currently spending at least 2 percent of their gross domestic product (GDP) on their military budgets, while the U.S. is spending 3.5 percent and shouldering much of the defense burden" (Lute and Burns, 2019, p. 3). Further, the limited investment by other NATO members is frequently matched by limited political will. In Afghanistan, many European states were reluctant participants in NATO's International Security Assistance Force (ISAF). American fighting forces ruefully quipped that the alliance mission's initials equated to "I Saw America Fight." NATO is an important institution that has shown an ability to adapt to changing global circumstances, but this will be tested if the United States shifts its interests away from Europe and toward Asia in the years to come (*The Economist*, 2012b).

Collective security organizations represent a major liberal path to international peace. Liberals have also long advocated that international law be strengthened in order to more capably provide for world order. Let us now consider the place of international law in world politics and the rules that have been fashioned to control by legal methods armed conflict within and between states.

Law at the International Level

LO 9-4   Describe the core principles of international law, and evaluate its effectiveness in the global system.

While one might expect the international community to have an obligation to protect states from attack and innocent citizens from abuse, the idea that it should do so has only gained ground in recent history. International law has been conceived and written mostly by realists, who have placed the privileges of the powerful as their primary concern and have historically advocated that the use of force should be an acceptable practice to protect a dominant state's position in the global hierarchy. As Henry Wheaton (1846) wrote, "every state has a right to force."

No principle of international law is more important than *state sovereignty*. Recall that sovereignty means that no authority is legally above the state, except that which the state voluntarily confers. Ever since the 1648 Treaty of Westphalia, states have tried to preserve the right to perform within their territories in any way the government chooses. That norm is the basis for all other legal rules; the key concepts in international law all speak to the rules by which sovereign states say they wish to abide. In fact, as conceived by theoreticians schooled in the realist tradition since the seventeenth century, the rules of international law express codes of conduct designed to protect a state's freedom to preserve its sovereign independence and act in terms of their perceived national interests.

Although the 1948 *Universal Declaration of Human Rights* addressed concerns about the state's treatment of individual people, states remain supreme. Accordingly, most rules address the rights and duties of states, not people. For instance, the principle of **sovereign equality** entitles each state to full respect by other states as well as equal protection by the system's legal rules. The right of independence also guarantees states' autonomy in their domestic affairs and external relations, under the logic that the independence of each presumes the independence of all. Similarly, the doctrine of **neutrality** permits states to avoid involvement in others' conflicts and coalitions.

Furthermore, the noninterference principle forms the basis for the *nonintervention norm*, which requires states to refrain from uninvited activities within another country's territory. This sometimes-abused classic rule gives governments the right to exercise jurisdiction over

sovereign equality
The principle that states are legally equal in protection under international law.

neutrality
The legal doctrine that provides rights for states to remain nonaligned with adversaries waging war against each other.

practically all things on, under, or above their bounded territory. In fact, international law was so permissive toward the state's control of its own domestic affairs that, before 1952, "there was no precedent in international law for a nation-state to assume responsibility for the crimes it committed against a minority within its jurisdiction" (Wise, 1993). A citizen was not protected against the state's abuse of human rights or **crimes against humanity**.

crimes against humanity
A category of activities, made illegal at the Nuremberg war crime trials, condemning states that abuse human rights.

Although international law has deficiencies, this does not mean that it is irrelevant or useless. States themselves find international law useful and expend a lot of effort to shape its evolution. This behavior demonstrates that countries interpret international law as real law and obey it most of the time (Joyner, 2005). Consider this analogy: Children playing "tag" in the backyard create rules of the game. These rules might designate that the tree is out of bounds, the swing set is a safe base, once touched a player is "frozen" and cannot move, and so forth. There is no enforcement mechanism or real punishment for violating the rules, but the rules help organize the game, create certain expectations, and make it a pleasurable interaction.

Along these same lines, a primary reason why states value international law and affirm their commitment to it is that, as constructivist theory elucidates, they need a common understanding of the "rules of the game." Law helps shape expectations, and rules reduce uncertainty, which enhances predictability in international affairs (Morrow, 2014). These communication functions serve every member of the global system by allowing for states to trust one another.

Even the most powerful states usually abide by international laws because they recognize that adherence pays benefits that often outweigh the costs of expedient rule violation. Those international actors that obey the rules receive rewards, whereas those that ignore international law or opportunistically break customary norms engender penalties for doing as they please. International reputations are important, and contribute to a state's *soft power*. States that routinely violate international legal rules are likely to find that other countries will be reluctant to cooperate with them. Violators also must fear the retaliation of those they victimize, as well as the loss of prestige. For this reason, only the most ambitious or reckless state is apt to flagrantly disregard accepted standards of conduct.

Nigel Treblin/Getty Images

IMAGE 9.5 Following the Rules of the Game In world politics, as in ordinary life, there are norms and expectations of state and nonstate behavior. As liberalism and constructivism contend, such principles help to create order and predictability which contribute to global peace. Following Syria's formal accession to the Chemical Weapons Convention, the OPCW that oversees implementation of the treaty determined that "almost 98 percent of Syria's declared stockpile of 1,308 metric tons of sulfur mustard agent and precursor chemicals had been destroyed" by October 2014 (Walker, 2014). Shown here, workers carefully carry neutralized chemical agents.

Limitations of the International Legal System

Legal theoretician William Coplin (1965, pp. 618–619) observed that "international law is an institutional device for communicating to the policymakers of various states a consensus on the nature of the international system." Nonetheless, to liberal theoreticians, putting the state ahead of the global community was a serious flaw that undermined international law's potential effectiveness. Many theorists consider the international legal system institutionally defective due to its dependence on state participation. Because formal legal institutions are weak at the global level, critics point to several major limitations.

First, in world politics, no legislative body is capable of making truly binding laws. Rules apply only when states willingly observe or embrace them in the treaties to which they voluntarily subscribe. Generally accepted as the authoritative definition of the "sources of international law," Article 38 of the Statute of the International Court of Justice declares that international law derives from (1) custom, (2) international treaties and agreements, (3) national and international court decisions, (4) the writings of legal authorities and specialists, and (5) the "general principles" of law recognized since the Roman Empire as part of "natural law" and "right reason."

Second, in world politics, no judicial body exists to authoritatively identify and record the rules accepted by states, interpret when and how the rules apply, and then identify violations. Instead, states are responsible for performing these tasks themselves. The World Court does not have the power to perform these functions without the state's consent, and the United Nations cannot speak on judicial matters for the global community as a whole (even though it has defined a new scope for Chapter VII of the UN Charter that claims the right to make quasi-judicial authoritative interpretations of global laws).

Finally, in world politics there is no executive body capable of enforcing the rules. Enforcement usually occurs through the unilateral self-help actions of the victims of a transgression or with the assistance of their allies or other interested parties. No centralized enforcement procedures exist, and compliance is voluntary. The whole system rests, therefore, on states' willingness to abide by the rules to which they consent and on the ability of each to use retaliatory measures to punish violations of the norms and behaviors they value.

Beyond the barriers to legal institutions that sovereignty poses, further weaknesses reduce confidence in international law:

- **International law lacks universality.** An effective legal system must represent the norms shared by those it governs. According to the precept of Roman law, *ubi societas, ibi jus* (where there is society, there is law), shared community values are a minimal precondition for forming a legal system. Yet the contemporary international order is incredibly diverse culturally and ideologically and, as a consequence, lacks consensus on common values. The simultaneous functioning of often-incompatible legal traditions throughout the world undermines the creation of a universal, cosmopolitan culture and legal system.

- **Under international law, legality and legitimacy do not always go hand in hand.** As in any legal system, in world politics what is legal is not necessarily legitimate. Although legality is important in determining an action's legitimacy, other values play a role—such as popular normative acceptance of international law as having authority. Moreover, the legality of an action does not always imply wisdom or usefulness. "The UN Security Council's decision to deny weapons to victims of ethnic and religious abuse in Yugoslavia in the early 1990s, for example, was legal but arguably illegitimate, whereas NATO's unauthorized use of force to prevent abuses in Kosovo was illegal but arguably legitimate" (Sofaer, 2010, p. 117).

- **International law is an instrument of the powerful to oppress the weak.** In a voluntary consent system, the rules to which the powerful willingly agree are those that serve their interests. These rules therefore preserve the existing global hierarchy (Goldsmith and Posner, 2005). As Marxist theory posits, "the form of international law consists of the struggle between states' views of legal right, and the view that prevails will depend on which state happens to be stronger" (Carty, 2008, p. 122).

- **International law is little more than a justification of existing practices.** When a particular behavior pattern becomes widespread, it becomes legally obligatory; rules of behavior become rules *for* behavior (Leopard, 2010). Eminent legal scholar Hans Kelsen's (2009, p. 369) contention that "states ought to behave as they have customarily behaved" reflects the **positivist legal theory** that when a type of behavior occurs frequently, it becomes legal. In fact, positive legal theory stresses that law is socially constructed. States' customary practices are the most important source from which laws derive in the absence of formal machinery for creating international rules.

- **International law's ambiguity reduces law to a policy tool for propaganda purposes.** The vague, elastic wording of international law makes it easy for states to define and interpret almost any action as legitimate. "The problem here," observes Samuel S. Kim (1991, p. 111), "is the lack of clarity and coherence [that enables] international law [to be] easily stretched, . . . to be a flexible fig leaf or a propaganda instrument." This ambivalence makes it possible for states to exploit international law to get what they can and to justify what they have obtained.

positivist legal theory
A theory that stresses states' customs and habitual ways of behaving as the most important source of law.

Consequently, states themselves—not a higher authority—determine what the rules are, when they apply, and how they should be enforced. This raises the question that most concerns liberal advocates of world law: When all are above the law, are any truly ruled by it? It is precisely this problem that prompts reformers to restrict the sovereign freedom of states and expand their common pursuit of shared legal norms in order to advance collective global interests over the interests of individual states.

The Judicial Framework of International Law

To be sure, liberal and constructivist reformers have a long way to go in order to fulfill their dream of seeing international law strengthen so that it can more effectively police international conflict. However, reformers take heart from recent trends that have enabled international law to increase its capacity to manage the threat of war within states, between states, and through global terrorism—and they question those cynics who still contend that international law is and should remain irrelevant to states' use of armed force. Reformers make the following arguments:

- International law is not intended to prevent *all* warfare. Aggressive war is illegal, but defensive war is not. It is a mistake, therefore, to claim that international law is broken whenever war breaks out—though whether a war is seen as defensive or aggressive is often a matter of which side the participant is on in the conflict.

- Instead of doing away with war, international law preserves it as a sanction against breaking rules. Thus, war is a method of last resort to punish aggressors and thereby maintain the global system's legal framework.

- International law is an institutional substitute for war. Legal procedures exist to resolve conflicts before they erupt into open hostilities. Although law cannot prevent war, legal procedures often make recourse to violence unnecessary by resolving disputes that might otherwise escalate to war.

For the rule of law to gain strength in world politics, it is also necessary to strengthen the international adjudicative machinery to enhance its effectiveness and legitimacy. The **International Court of Justice (ICJ)**, known as the World Court, was created in 1945 as the highest judicial body on Earth—the only international court with universal scope and general jurisdiction. Composed of fifteen judges who are elected by the UN General Assembly and the Security Council, the court settles legal disputes submitted by states and offers advisory opinions on legal questions submitted by the United Nations.

The court is highly regarded in principle: 193 states are party to the statute of the court, and more than 300 bilateral or multilateral treaties have given the World Court jurisdiction in resolving disputes arising from the interpretation and application of international law. However, a weakness is that it can make rulings only on disputes freely submitted by the states themselves; the court cannot rule on cases that states do not bring forward. State sovereignty is protected, and many states have traditionally been hesitant to use the court because ICJ decisions are considered final—there is no opportunity to appeal. This is why between 1947 and January 2019, states granted the court permission to hear only 176 cases, about one-fourth of which were withdrawn by disputants before the court could make a ruling.

The trends in the World Court's activity are not encouraging to advocates of world law. Whereas the number of sovereign states since 1950 has tripled, the court's caseload has not seen a similar increase. To illustrate, over half of today's states have never appeared before the ICJ. Moreover, once the court has ruled on cases, the disputants have complied with ICJ judgments only a little more than half of the time. This record suggests that although approval for using the court of law to resolve international conflicts is increasingly voiced, most states remain reluctant to voluntarily use judicial procedures to settle their most important international disputes.

International Court of Justice (ICJ) The primary court established by the United Nations for resolving legal disputes between states and providing advisory opinions to international agencies and the UN General Assembly.

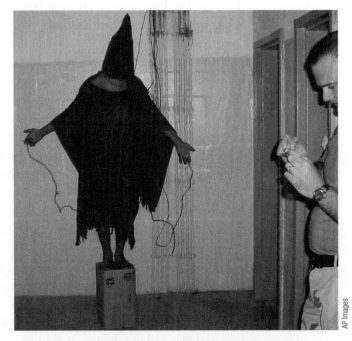

IMAGE 9.6 War Crimes and the Loss of Global Legitimacy In 2004, scandal erupted when more than 1000 graphic photos taken at the Abu Ghraib prison in Baghdad were televised worldwide, ostensibly showing U.S. personnel torturing Iraqi prisoners. Similar methods—including electric shocks, prolonged exposure to frigid temperatures, and simulated drowning—were purportedly used to interrogate terror suspects detained at the U.S. Guantanamo Naval Base. Both became a negative symbol of U.S. power in the Muslim world, and cast doubt upon the United States' commitment to moral and ethical principles.

war crimes
Acts performed during war that the international community defines as crimes against humanity, including atrocities committed against an enemy's prisoners of war, civilians, or the state's own minority population.

However, it bodes well that the global community has radically revised international law to prevent the horror of civilian casualties and contain the mass slaughter that has increasingly taken place, and it now holds leaders of countries accountable for **war crimes** as war criminals. International law prohibits leaders from allowing their militaries to undertake actions in violation of certain principles accepted by the international community, such as the protection of innocent noncombatants.

Before these recent developments in international law, when violations occurred, little could be done except to verbally condemn those acts because international law exempted leaders from legal jurisdiction under the doctrine of "sovereign immunity." This was true even when their commands ignored the laws of the appropriate conduct of war. Although they might behave as criminals, leaders traditionally have been treated with respect (perhaps because they were the only people with whom negotiations could be held to settle disputes). This tradition has now been rejected on legal grounds, as reflected in the premise of the Nuremberg International Military Tribunal (which tried World War II German Nazi war criminals) that "crimes against international law are committed by men, not by abstract entities, and only by punishing individuals who commit such crimes can the provisions of international law be enforced" (Kirsch, 2006, p. 3).

international criminal tribunals
Special tribunals established by the United Nations to prosecute those responsible for wartime atrocities and genocide, bring justice to victims, and deter such crimes in the future.

Attempts to bring armed conflict under more potent legal controls are now spread across the jurisdiction of several international judicial bodies. The **international criminal tribunals** formed in 1993 signaled to would-be perpetrators that the global community would not tolerate these atrocities. The International Criminal Tribunal for the former Yugoslavia (ICTY) was established in 1993, followed by the International Criminal Tribunal for Rwanda (ICTR) in 1994. One of the most famous tribunal detainees was Slobodan Milosevic. Milosevic was the former Yugoslav president who perpetrated four wars in the 1990s that killed more than 250,000 and tore the Balkans apart—he died of a heart attack in March 2006 in his Hague prison cell while facing trial. Both the ICTY and the ICTR were set up by the United Nations on an ad hoc basis for a limited time period and a specific jurisdiction, and underscored the need for a permanent global criminal court.

International Criminal Court (ICC)
A court established by international treaty for indicting and administering justice to people committing war crimes.

In 2002, the Rome Statute launched the **International Criminal Court (ICC)** as an independent court of last resort that investigates and prosecutes terrible mass crimes such as genocide, crimes against humanity, and war crimes that have been committed since the court's inception. The ICC only pursues a case when a state's courts are unwilling or unable to do so, and brings charges only against individuals as opposed to states. As of June 2019, 122 states had ratified the treaty (139 are signatories) and joined the ICC, although the United States, Russia, and China had not (see Map 9.4).

Though the United States has long been a leader in developing standards for international law and supports the prosecution of atrocities—and directly endorsed the ICC's investigation of such crimes in Sudan—in 2002 it suspended its signature of the Rome Statute and declared that it did not intend to become a member of the ICC due to concerns over the court's statute, accountability, and jurisdiction. Reflecting concerns for preserving the sovereignty of the United States, the Heritage Foundation (an American conservative think tank) argued that U.S. participation in the ICC would be "unconstitutional because it would allow the trial of American citizens for crimes committed on American soil, which are otherwise entirely within the judicial power of the United States." The United States' opposition to the ICC is also due to the conviction that its citizens would be treated unfairly by the court and would be vulnerable targets of political retribution against the United States government for its influence and intervention

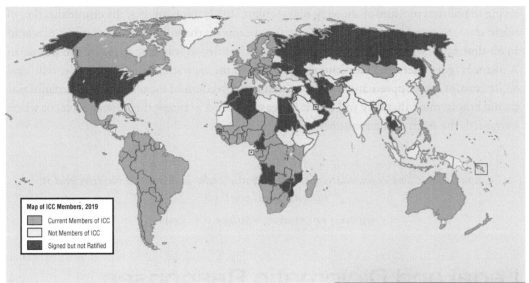

IMAGE 9.7 AND MAP 9.4 Which World

Court? The International Court of Justice (ICJ), which is known as the World Court, is the primary judicial body of the United Nations with global jurisdiction to settle legal disputes between states and provide advisory opinions to international agencies. Shown (right) is its home, the Peace Palace, in The Hague, Netherlands. The International Criminal Court (ICC), also commonly referred to as a "world court," is a court of last resort that is legally independent of the UN and tries those accused of committing the most horrendous of mass crimes. As shown in the map, with Palestine's ratification on January 2, 2015, 122 countries have formally joined the ICC.

Think It Through Could the ICC hold more influence at the global level over time, or has it reached its limit of authority? Explain.

in other countries around the world. Though criticized as violating the Nuremburg principle of individual accountability, the United States sought to guarantee that Americans would be immune to the court's jurisdiction and pressed other states for bilateral immunity agreements that take into account its concerns. More recently, however, the United States has become less hostile to the ICC and has agreed to cooperate with the court on a case-by-case basis.

The ICC is gaining legitimacy as the appropriate court of last resort for cases involving crimes against humanity, genocide, and war crimes. To date, the ICC has opened investigations into atrocities in Uganda, the Democratic Republic of Congo, the Central African Republic, Kenya, Mali, Libya, Cote d'Ivoire, Darfur, Georgia, Burundi, and Afghanistan. In a case that stood as a milestone in international justice and a deterrent of war crimes, in March 2012 Thomas Lubanga Dyilo became the first person convicted by the ICC. The Congolese militia leader was found guilty of conscripting and using child soldiers.

However, the ICC is criticized for the length of time it takes for cases to be brought to trial, and it lacks the independent ability to enforce its decisions or physically detain the accused. Given the politically complex nature of its mission, it is critical that the ICC avoid accusations of caving to political pressure or showing bias (Struett, 2012). Nonetheless, the criminalization of rulers' *state-sponsored terrorism* raises the legal restraints on the initiation and conduct of war to an all-time high, widening the scope of acts now classified as war crimes. As British politician William Hague observed, "Governments that block the aspirations of their people, that steal or are corrupt, that oppress and torture or that deny freedom of expression and human rights should bear in mind that they will find it increasingly hard to escape their own people, or where warranted, the reach of international law."

> *Law is the essential foundation of stability and order both within societies and in international relations.*
>
> **—J. WILLIAM FULBRIGHT, FORMER U.S. SENATOR**

Legal and Diplomatic Responses to Armed Conflict

LO 9-5   Survey laws relating to the conduct of war and military intervention, and describe methods for the negotiated settlement of international disputes.

Many people are confused by international law because it both prohibits and justifies the use of force. The confusion derives, in part, from the just war tradition in "Christian realism," in which the rules of war are philosophically based on **morals** (principles of behavior) and **ethics** (explanations of why these principles are proper). Therefore, it is important to understand the origins of just war theory and the way it is evolving today, and to also consider how the rules of law shape military interventions and negotiated solutions to international disputes.

In the fourth century, St. Augustine questioned the strict view that those who take another's life to defend the state necessarily violate the commandment "Thou shalt not kill." He (Saint Augustine, 2018, p. 553) counseled that "it is the wrong-doing of the opposing party which compels the wise man to wage just wars." The Christian was obligated, he felt, to fight against evil and wickedness. To St. Augustine, the City of Man was inherently sinful, in contrast to the perfect City of God. Thus, in the secular world, it was sometimes permissible to kill—to punish a sin by an aggressive enemy (while still loving the sinner) to achieve a "just peace." Pope Nicholas I extended this realist logic in 866 when he proclaimed that any defensive war was just.

Though there are references to just war principles in classical Greek political thought, as reflected in Aristotle's reference to "war that is by nature just" and Ciceros' writings on *bellum justum* (O'Driscoll, 2015, p. 1), the modern **just war doctrine** was heavily influenced by early Christian doctrine and further developed by such humanist reformers as Hugo Grotius. He challenged the warring Catholic and Protestant Christian powers in the Thirty Years' War (1618–1648) to abide by humane standards of conduct and sought to replace the two "cities," or ethical realms of St. Augustine, with a single global society under law. For Grotius, a just war was only one fought in self-defense to punish damages caused by an adversary's blatant act of

morals
Principles clarifying the difference between good and evil and the situations in which they are opposed.

ethics
Criteria for evaluating right and wrong behavior and the motives of individuals and groups.

just war doctrine
The moral criteria identifying when a just war may be undertaken and how it should be fought once it begins.

violence: "No other just cause for undertaking war can there be excepting injury received."

For war to be moral it must also be fought by just means without harm to innocent noncombatants. The modern version of just war doctrine evolved from this distinction and consists of two categories, **jus ad bellum** (the justice of a war) and **jus in bello** (justice in a war). The former sets the legal criteria by which a leader may initiate a war. The latter specifies restraints on the range of permissible tactics to be used in fighting a just war. Christian theologian St. Thomas More (1478–1535) contended that the assassination of an evil leader responsible for starting a war was justified if it would prevent the loss of innocent lives. This premise shapes contemporary discussions of public international law (Wills, 2004) and provides the foundation for a number of other key principles:

IMAGE 9.8 War and the Birth of Modern International Law Enraged by the inhumane international conditions that he witnessed during his lifetime, Dutch reformer Hugo Grotius (1583–1645) wrote *De Jure Belli et Pacis (On the Law of War and Peace)* in 1625 in the midst of the Thirty Years' War. His treatise called on the great powers to resolve their conflicts by judicial procedures rather than on the battlefield and specified the legal principles he felt could encourage cooperation, peace, and more humane treatment of people.

- All other means to a morally just solution of conflict must be exhausted before a resort to arms can be justified.

- War can be just only if employed to defend a stable political order or a morally preferable cause against a real threat or to restore justice after a real injury has been sustained.

- A just war must have a reasonable chance of succeeding in these limited goals.

- Only a legitimate government authority can proclaim a just war.

- War must be waged for the purpose of correcting a wrong rather than for revenge.

- Negotiations to end a war must be continued as long as fighting continues.

- Particular people in the population, especially noncombatants, must be immune from intentional attack.

- Only legal and moral means may be employed to conduct a just war.

- The damage likely to be incurred from a war may not be disproportionate to the injury suffered.

- The final goal of the war must be to reestablish peace and justice.

jus ad bellum
A component of just war doctrine that establishes criteria under which a just war may be initiated.

jus in bello
A component of just war doctrine that sets limits on the acceptable use of force.

These ethical criteria continue to color thinking about the rules of warfare and the circumstances under which the use of armed force is legally permissible. U.S. President Theodore Roosevelt counseled that "a just war is in the long run far better for a nation's soul than a most prosperous peace obtained by acquiescence in wrong and injustice." However, the advent of nuclear, chemical, and biological weapons of mass destruction that violate many of these

QuintLox/Leemage/LISZT COLLECTION/Bridgeman Images

principles has created a heated debate about the relevance of the just war doctrine (Hensel, 2007), which has been further exacerbated by the trend toward intrastate conflicts involving both state and nonstate actors (Hudson, 2009).

Advanced technological innovations have blurred many of the lines between acceptable and unacceptable conduct in war. For example, insurgent terrorists and now the armies fighting them are increasingly relying on improvised explosive devices (IEDs) planted on animal carcasses, mobile cell phones, or human cadavers in order to kill with minimal risk to the attacker. With advancements in robotics and artificial intelligence, it becomes even more difficult to assign immediate responsibility for the decision to kill. How can international law control such innovative new ways of perpetrating violence when the aggressors using them cannot be treated as criminals? Because the containment and prevention of violence has become the chief purpose of armies today, leaders and scholars are struggling to revise just war doctrine to deal with the new strategic realities of contemporary weapons and warfare (J. Johnson, 2005).

As Figure 9.5 shows, since World War I the international community has increasingly rejected the traditional right of states to use military force to achieve their foreign policy objectives. Just war theory reflects the continuing quest to place legal constraints on the use of armed force in order to create a moral consensus about the conditions under which ends justify means, even though vehement disagreements continue today about what criteria should be accepted. These differences became especially evident in the heated debate after the U.S. preemptive invasion of Iraq in 2003. Many condemned the U.S. invasion as a breach of international law, calling the United States a "rogue nation" and an outlaw state (Hathaway, 2007; Paust, 2007). Others disagreed (Elshtain, 2003), however, with some suggesting that U.S. intent in waging war was justifiable as Saddam Hussein intentionally let the United States believe Iraq had weapons of mass destruction.

The U.S. invasion of Iraq raised concerns about the legality of preemptive and preventive use of force. The Bush administration's support for preventive action that included the use of force against states that either supported or failed to oppose terrorism was particularly controversial because such use of force is generally viewed as a violation of international law. "The International Court of Justice (ICJ) and most international legal authorities currently construe the United Nations Charter as prohibiting any use of force not sanctioned by the UN Security Council, with the exception of actions taken in self-defense against an actual or imminent state-sponsored 'armed attack'" (Sofaer, 2010, p. 110). However, the doctrine of **military necessity** still accepts the use of military force as legal—though only as a last recourse for defense (Raymond, 1999).

Liberal paths to the control of armed conflict embrace the conviction that war and international instability are primarily caused by deeply rooted global institutional deficiencies that reduce incentives for international cooperation (Barrett, 2007). Thus, liberals advocate institutional methods that pool sovereignty to collectively manage global problems. With the expansion of global norms that support collective solutions to conflicts in world politics, constructivists envision greater possibilities for the peaceful resolution of situations that might otherwise lead to armed aggression. Here, consider the ways in which changing conceptions of sovereignty and global responsibility are shaping state responses to military intervention and the diplomatic resolution of crises.

military necessity
The legal principle that violation of the rules of warfare may be excused for defensive purposes during periods of extreme emergency.

New Rules for Military Intervention

International law has recently begun to revise its traditional prohibition against military intervention and the belief that governments have a right, even an obligation, to intervene in the affairs of other states under certain conditions for humanitarian purposes has won advocates. This global norm of a *responsibility to protect* has been advocated by former Australian foreign minister Gareth Evans, who counsels that our goal should be "to institutionalize the idea that all states have an obligation to shield their own citizens from mass atrocities, and that if a state fails to do so, it falls to other states to take on that obligation" (Malcomson, 2008, p. 9; see also Doyle, 2011). Contemporary international law has defined military intervention as a right and a duty to alleviate human suffering, stop genocide and ethnic cleansing, and prevent states from repressing basic human rights and civil liberties (Feinstein and Slaughter, 2004; Finnemore, 2003).

The result has been the collapse of the Westphalian principle that what a state does within its own borders is its own business. International law has relaxed its restrictive definition that delimits when the global community can legally use military intervention to intervene in other states. The world has made a choice on genocide and has declared organized savagery illegal. Over the last fifty years, near-universal support for humanitarian intervention has emerged as a legal right to protect *human rights*—political rights and civil liberties are now recognized by the global community as inalienable and universally applicable. This shift permits states and international organizations to punish acts of genocide by reinterpreting the traditional rule against external interference in another state's domestic affairs to make outside intervention permissible. This includes even the right to military invasion and occupation.

This sea change suggests that international law develops and changes most rapidly when global problems arise that require collective solutions and legal remedies. The spread of genocide and atrocities in failed states and countries ruled by tyrants has spawned new sets of legal rules that attempt to arrest these dangers and to permit interventions within these countries. Likewise, the rising frequency of global crises has pushed efforts to rewrite international law so as to facilitate diplomatic negotiations that bring about a nonviolent settlement of disputes.

AP Images/Aaron Favila

IMAGE 9.9 A Responsibility to Protect? Although many states and IGOs have been reluctant to intervene militarily in internal conflicts outside their spheres of influence, in 2011 NATO intervened in Libya in response to what many saw as a clear case for when the global community should decisively uphold the *responsibility to protect (R to P)*. The UN Security Council argued that Muammar al-Qaddafi's response to the popular uprising—replete with his promise to "cleanse Libya house by house" of the rebel "cockroaches"—posed an imminent threat of mass atrocities. Yet this intervention was not without controversy, as demonstrated by this picture of protestors calling for the withdrawal of U.S. and NATO troops from Libya.

International Crises and the Negotiated Settlement of Disputes

Crises have been very frequent in modern history. When a crisis erupts, the capacity for reaching coolheaded rational decisions is reduced. The threat of force causes stress and reduces the amount of time available to reach decisions that might successfully end the **crisis** peacefully.

Consider the 1962 Cuban Missile Crisis, which occurred when the Soviet Union installed medium-range nuclear missiles in Cuba and the United States responded with a naval blockade. The danger of nuclear war rose quickly. After the fact, U.S. President John F. Kennedy estimated that the odds were 50–50 that a nuclear exchange could have destroyed the entire world. Often, such crises resulting from *coercive diplomacy* have escalated to the use of force when bargaining failed and the adversaries took up arms.

The problem that liberal reformers identify is that these crises and armed conflicts could potentially have been settled by diplomatic negotiations had that avenue for dispute settlement been tried. To liberals, it is always better to talk about divisive issues at a negotiating table than to let anger and anxieties sizzle and tempt the disputants to take up arms. Only through discussion and bargaining can positions be clarified and, possibly, concessions and compromises be reached that terminate the threat of warfare.

Embedded in international law, **negotiation** is a process of bargaining between two or more actors in an effort to deal with an issue or situation and reach an agreement. At a basic, elementary level, negotiation entails an exchange of communications, with discussion flowing back and forth between the bargaining parties. As an approach to conflict management, the goal is to facilitate communication between the parties regarding their intentions and goals, and to produce options that address the interests of those involved. In the give-and-take required to negotiate a solution, there is a strong tendency for some level of reciprocity to emerge from the action-and-reaction sequence of communications—to return in kind or degree the kind of friendly or hostile communication received from the other party.

Note that, for this reason, reciprocated communications can produce greater cooperation or greater conflict. The Chinese translation of the word "crisis" means both "opportunity" and "danger," and efforts to negotiate compromises provide an opportunity to produce a positive agreement or to produce a dangerous negative outcome that heightens threats and tensions. That is why negotiation is not a sure-fire way to resolve global conflicts and crises.

Still, negotiations make the settlement of disputes possible by providing reciprocated concessions between disputants. Russia's President Vladimir Putin offered wise counsel, saying that "Today to be successful, one must be able to reach agreements. The ability to compromise is not a diplomatic politeness but rather taking into account and respecting your partner's legitimate interests." Reciprocated gestures of goodwill and empathy for the opponent's situation pave the way for a compromise. Indeed, a common bargaining approach to induce the other party to reach agreements is through a **tit-for-tat strategy** that responds to any cooperative offer by immediately reciprocating it with an equal offer; the reward through repetitive concessions can facilitate a mutually satisfactory agreement.

British diplomatic historian Sir Harold Nicolson defined diplomacy as "the management of the relations between independent states by the process of negotiation." Diplomacy aims to

---

crisis
A situation in which the threat of escalation to warfare is high and the time available for making decisions and reaching compromised solutions in negotiations is compressed.

negotiation
Diplomatic dialogue and discussion between two or more parties with the goal of resolving, through give-and-take bargaining, perceived differences of interests and the conflicts they cause.

tit-for-tat strategy
A bargaining approach that consistently reciprocates in kind the offers or threats made by the other party in a negotiation, with equivalent rewards returned and equivalent punishing communications returned in retaliation.

IMAGE 9.10A Winston Churchill, Franklin D. Roosevelt, and Joseph Stalin, 1945

IMAGE 9.10B Richard Nixon and Leonid Brezhnev, 1972

IMAGE 9.10C Ronald Reagan and Mikhail Gorbachev, 1988

IMAGE 9.10D Boris Yeltsin and Bill Clinton, 1994

IMAGE 9.10E Dmitri Medvedev and Barack Obama, 2009

IMAGE 9.10F Donald Trump and Vladimir Putin, 2018

IMAGES 9.10A–9.10F Diplomacy Dialogues To liberal reformers, direct negotiations between adversaries are a crucial step on the path to make peace a possibility. As shown here, despite times of open hostility and opposing interests, diplomatic summits between the United States and Russia help to keep conflicts between the two great military powers "cold." Although tensions persist, diplomacy is "worth a try. For this truth hasn't changed since the Cold War: when Russia and the United States don't get along, the rest of the world has every right to feel uneasy" (Ghosh, 2009, p. 14).

resolve international disputes peacefully, which is why liberals favor it. Conversely, realists, for whom the state's primary interest is the pursuit of power, believe that threats of war preserve peace better than diplomatic efforts. Marxism takes a similarly pessimistic view of diplomatic approaches to peace, declaring, "when equal rights collide, force decides" (Carty, 2008, p. 122). Chinese former foreign minister Zhou Enlai spoke to this view when he echoed Clausewitz, saying "all diplomacy is the continuation of war by other means."

Diplomacy requires great intelligence, information, imagination, flexibility, ingenuity, and honesty to successfully maintain peaceful negotiations. Compounding the challenge is the common liability that while diplomats are sent to negotiate for their countries, no matter what their skill or sincerity, they cannot succeed unless they have the full backing of their government's authority. Furthermore, public scrutiny can cripple negotiations. Sometimes secrecy is necessary to make concessions and reach compromises without losing face; "unless covenants are arrived at secretly," warned U.S. President Richard M. Nixon, "there will be none to agree to openly." As former UN Secretary-General Dag Hammarskjöld similarly cautioned, "The best results of negotiation cannot be achieved in international life any more than in our private world in the full glare of publicity with current debate of all moves, unavoidable misunderstandings,

Photo Courtesy of Charles Kegley, Jr.

IMAGE 9.11 Negotiating with a Negotiator about Negotiation U.S. President George H. W. Bush meets with Charles Kegley, one of the authors of *World Politics*. The major topics they discussed: the uses and limits of methods of dispute settlement without the use of military force. These methods include diplomatic negotiations, international courts, collective security, and other methods of conflict resolution that are advocated by policy makers whose image of world politics is informed by liberal and constructivist theories.

inescapable freezing of positions due to considerations of prestige and the temptation to utilize public opinion as an element integrated into the negotiation itself."

These problems, potholes, and pitfalls notwithstanding, liberals prefer negotiation when trying to facilitate international peace. There is even evidence that greater involvement of women in international negotiations may enhance the prospects for dispute resolution (see "Controversy: Can Women Improve Global Negotiations and the Prospects for World Peace?"). If gender differences produce different processes and outcomes in international negotiation, then many hypothesize that increasing the number of women involved in decision making may bring fresh perspectives to conflict management (Anderlini, 2007). Rooted in the premise that women bring certain values to negotiation and mediation that are derived from their gendered socialization experiences, and that these insights and policy prescriptions have been absent due to the exclusionary nature of international negotiations (Hudson, 2005), the intent of the adoption in 2000 of UN Resolution 1325 was to "increase the participation of women at decision-making levels in conflict resolution and peace processes" in the interest of generating new perspectives and options for lasting conflict resolutions.

Fortunately, those playing the game of international politics have been inventive in creating supplementary methods that enable negotiations to reduce the threat of war. All are now nested in laws accepted by the global community:

- **Good offices.** When two conflicting parties have a history of relatively peaceful negotiations, often a "good office" will be provided by a third party as neutral ground for negotiation. In these circumstances, the good office provider does not participate in the actual negotiations.

- **Conciliation.** When two or more conflicting parties wish to negotiate a dispute resolution but wish to maintain control over the final compromise, often a third party will assist both sides during the negotiations and attempt to offer unbiased opinions and suggestions to help achieve a solution while remaining neutral and refraining from proposing a solution.

Controversy

CAN WOMEN IMPROVE GLOBAL NEGOTIATIONS AND THE PROSPECTS FOR WORLD PEACE?

Feminist theory stresses the importance of gender in studying world politics, and explores the extent to which a "masculine" conceptualization of key ideas—such as power, interest, and security—shapes the way transnational actors conduct foreign affairs. While recognizing the influence of a masculine tradition in world politics, some feminist scholarship posits that in practice there is on average no significant difference in the capabilities of men and women. Others, however, claim that differences exist and are contextual, with each gender being more capable than the other in certain endeavors. Does this apply to international negotiation? Do women bring strengths to the bargaining table and enhance the prospects for conflict resolution? Or are men better suited to conflict management?

Arthimedes/Shutterstock.com

Since the 1990s, feminist scholars have pointed to the different ways in which gender identity shapes international decision making (Sjoberg, 2013; Bolzendahl, 2009; Peterson and Runyan, 2010). With its emphasis on the role of power in an amoral pursuit of narrow self-interest by rational actors, realism portrays a competitive world in which a masculine approach to decision making reigns. The accumulation of power is achieved through greater strength and authority, and at the expense of others. Men often have independent self-schemas that lead them to define themselves as distinct from others, and "tend to focus on end gains, making the achievement of personal preferences and goals the primary negotiation objective" (Boyer et al., 2009, p. 27). Thus, men are often comfortable negotiating in situations in which controlled conflict is expected.

Some argue that, due to their traditional social roles, women have interdependent self-schemas and a nurturing orientation that gives them valuable perspectives that are an asset to conflict negotiation and mediation. Rather than focusing on competition, they tend to be more inclined to a liberal view of mutual gain. How women frame and conduct negotiations is influenced by "a relational view of others, an embedded view of agency, an understanding of control through empowerment, and problem-solving through dialogue" (Kolb, 1996, p. 139). As women are likely to "define themselves more through their relationships than do men, their actions and rhetoric within the negotiation process may be more oriented toward maintaining and protecting these relationships" (Boyer et al., 2009, p. 27). Moreover, "increasing the flow of information between the negotiators is essential to achieving a superior solution in an integrative bargain . . . and women are more likely to use these methods" (Babcock and Laschever, 2003, pp. 169–170).

For social constructivists, "men and women's roles are not inherent or predetermined, but rather a social fact that can change through practice, interaction, and the evolution of ideas and norms" (Boyer et al., 2009, p. 26). Perhaps if greater numbers of women are included in international negotiations where men have traditionally dominated, both will benefit from the perspectives of the other, and the role of diplomacy in preventing and resolving conflict will be enhanced.

What Do You Think?

1. As a lead mediator trying to resolve an intractable conflict between two countries, what value would you place on having women at the bargaining table?

2. Might the role of women in negotiation vary across different regions of the world? How might culture influence the empowerment and legitimacy of women at the negotiating table?

3. Consider two recent U.S. foreign policy figures: former Secretary of State Hillary Clinton and President Donald Trump. How would you categorize their negotiating tendencies? Do they fit the gender mold as described here? Why or why not? What lessons for conflict resolution do they have to offer?

- **Arbitration.** When disputing parties are willing to allow a third party to make a binding decision to resolve their dispute, a temporary ruling board considers both sides' arguments and reaches a decision.

- **Adjudication.** Perhaps the most formal of the dispute resolution options, this approach is roughly the equivalent of arguing a case in court and accepting a binding decision or ruling by a judge.

- **Mediation.** When a third-party outside actor, either another state or a group of states in an intergovernmental organization (IGO), participates directly in negotiations between the disputants to aid them in recognizing their shared interests and proposing solutions based on these common interests.

Mediation has a particularly strong track record of terminating international crises and history shows that it works best when democracies or international institutions conduct the negotiating service, due in part to the influence of democratic social norms of conflict resolution (Shannon, 2009; Mitchell et al., 2008). For success, particularly in cases where the effectiveness and legitimacy of existing governance is viewed as deeply inadequate, it is important

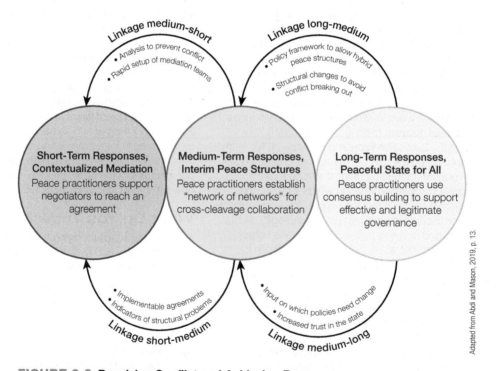

Adapted from Abdi and Mason, 2019, p. 13.

FIGURE 9.6 Resolving Conflict and Achieving Peace

In a polarized conflict, a framework for peace must create linkages, help deal with complexity, and create a path for moving beyond the point of agreement. As shown here, small steps across multiple phases are important, with mediation helping to reach an agreement and governance-building helping to establish rules, norms, institutions, and processes for the future.

to contextualize mediation and emphasize efforts to address the immediate conflict as well as the structural factors that fueled it. As explained by global peacemaker and mediator Dekha Ibrahim Abdi (Abdi and Mason, 2019, p. 12):

> [Working for peace] requires a holistic approach that links all levels and sectors from top to bottom, from political and economic to social, deep spiritual soul searching and development. . . . We were naïve to think that we were at the end of the road when we had a deal, when we had a group who all agreed and who disseminated the information in the agreement. You also have to find a strategy for any new emerging conflict.

In order to achieve lasting peace, mediation needs to set the stage for governance-building and discussion of critical policy questions regarding services and security for everyone (see Figure 9.6). The alternative to peaceful resolution of disputes—the coercive use of military power—is ethically unacceptable to people seeking to avoid war.

Future generations will likely judge whether disarmament agreements, multilateral international organizations, and international law can lead to a collective response to the multitude of global needs. What is clear is that countries are making bold efforts to unite in a common civic culture behind common values to construct global institutions to jointly protect themselves against the many problems they face in common. They appear to increasingly accept the once radical liberal view that, as former UN Secretary General Kofi Annan (1999) argued, "a new, broader definition of national interest is needed" that will unify states to work on common goals that transcend national interests.

> *The quest for international security involves the unconditional surrender by every nation, in a certain measure, of its liberty of action, its sovereignty that is to say, and it is clear beyond all doubt that no other road can lead to such security.*
>
> **—ALBERT EINSTEIN, NOBEL PRIZE-WINNING PHYSICIST**

If the paths you have explored in this chapter are pursued, will the belief that peace is best preserved through ethical policies break the violent historical pattern? The world waits for an answer. But what is clear at this time is that the global agenda facing the world is huge. The biggest problems facing humanity are transnational, and none can be solved effectively with a unilateral national response. A multilateral approach is required to address the staggering number of global problems that require peaceful management through collective solutions.

In Part 4, you will have an opportunity to look at trends in the economic, human, and environmental conditions that prevail as the cascading globalization of world politics accelerates. This survey can aid in understanding the world as it presently exists and allow you to contemplate, as a caring and responsible global citizen, the prospects for transformations that could create a better world.

Study. Apply. Analyze.

Chapter Summary

9-1 Link liberal and constructivist ideas to the development of peaceful norms, laws, and institutions. In the face of armed conflict, liberalism favors cooperation and regulation in order to achieve and maintain peace. The constructivist perspective often compliments the liberal emphasis on normative and institutional paths to peace, and the idea that constraints on weapons of war are essential to global security.

9-2 Evaluate the effectiveness of arms control and disarmament in the prevention of armed conflict. In response to the threat of war, arms control and disarmament are often pursued through bilateral or multilateral agreements. These agreements attempt to enforce accountability, reduce or eliminate weapons, and discourage arms races. While there has been some success, these methods have more often than not proved insufficient against the rapid spread of arms throughout the world. The ability and will of global actors to ensure world disarmament is limited, and it appears that realism's emphasis on peace through military preparations may triumph.

9-3 Apply the principles of collective security to international organizations and assess their effectiveness along these lines. From liberalism and constructivist perspectives, collective security is an alternative to the balance-of-power politics and self-help warfare favored by realists in an anarchical international system. The goal of international organizations is to maintain peace by guaranteeing security through collective action. More than seventy years ago, the United Nations was created to promote international peace and security. Additionally, regional security organizations, such as NATO, address conflict and collective defense for countries with which they tend to share strategic interests and cultural traditions.

9-4 Describe the core principles of international law, and evaluate its effectiveness in the global system. Sovereign equality, neutrality, and noninterference comprise core principles of international law, and provide a foundation for the norm that states should refrain from intervening uninvited into another's internal affairs. Yet international law places constraints on the use of armed force and increasingly reflects the emerging norm that the international community has a responsibility to protect populations from crimes against humanity. Numerous institutions have been created to provide a judicial framework for international law, and global actors largely abide by international law because it shapes expectations and reduces uncertainty in world politics. However, international law falters in its ability to actually enforce its standards and react effectively to any infractions.

9-5 Survey laws relating to the conduct of war and military intervention, and describe methods for the negotiated settlement of international disputes. The just war doctrine contends that for a war to be moral, it must be fought for just purposes and by just means without harm to innocent noncombatants. This doctrine reflects the continuing quest to place legal constraints on the use of armed force in order to create a moral consensus about the conditions under which ends justify means. In the wake of terrorism and crimes against humanity, international law has begun to revise its traditional prohibition against military intervention. It has also evolved to facilitate diplomatic solutions to global crises, through such methods as negotiation, mediation, conciliation, good offices, arbitration, and adjudication.

Key Terms

antipersonnel landmines (APLs)

arms control

arms race

bilateral agreements

crimes against humanity

crisis

disarmament

ethics

Intermediate-Range Nuclear Forces (INF) Treaty

International Criminal Court (ICC)

International Court of Justice (ICJ)

international criminal tribunals

jus ad bellum

jus in bello

just war doctrine

military necessity

morals

multilateral agreements

negotiation

neutrality

peace building

peace enforcement

peacekeeping

peacemaking

peace operations

positivist legal theory

preventive diplomacy

sovereign equality

spiral model

Strategic Arms Limitation Talks (SALT)

Strategic Offensive Reductions Treaty (SORT)

tit-for-tat strategy

war crimes

Suggested Readings and Resources

Abdi, Dekha Ibrahim and Simon J.A. Mason (2019). *Mediation and Governance in Fragile Contexts: Small Steps to Peace.* Boulder: Kumarian Press.

Beyond the Hague: beyondthehague.com. A blog about international justice from the Hague and more.

Chatterjee, Deen K., ed. (2013). *The Ethics of Preventive War.* Cambridge, UK: Cambridge University Press.

GAPW Blog: gapwblog.wordpress.com. A "UN-based" blog discussing the measures of preventing war.

Morrow, James D. (2014). *Order within Anarchy: The Laws of War as an International Institution.* New York: Cambridge University Press.

Nardin, Terry. (2011). "Middle-Ground Ethics: Can One be Politically Realistic without being a Political Realist?" *Ethics & International Affairs*, 25 (1).

Puchala, Donald, Katie Verlin Laatikainen, and Roger A. Coate. (2007). *United Nations Politics.* Upper Saddle River, NJ: Prentice Hall.

Scott, Shirley V. (2017). *International Law in World Politics: An Introduction.* Boulder: Lynne Rienner Publishers.

UN Dispatch: www.undispatch.com. A website with the world's latest news and news analysis.

Carnegie Council Videos

Key Term Videos

- Disarmament
- Arms Control
- Peacekeeping
- Preventive Diplomacy
- Peace Enforcement
- Crimes against Humanity
- War Crimes
- Ethics
- *Jus ad Bellum*
- *Jus in Bello*
- Crisis
- Negotiation

Additional Videos

- Betts, Richard K. "The World Ahead: Conflict or Cooperation?"
- Dhanapala, Jayantha, and David C. Speedie. "After START—What Next? David Speedie Interviews Jayantha Dhanapala."
- Doyle, Michael W., and Harold H. Koh. "Striking First: Preemption and Prevention in International Conflict."
- Kupchan, Charles A. "How Enemies Become Friends: The Sources of Stable Peace."
- Romano, Cesare P. R., Stephen M. Schwebel, and Daniel Terris. "The International Judge: An Introduction to the Men and Women Who Decide the World's Cases."
- Vocke, William. "Can Moral Injury Be a Wound of War?"

Part 4

Human Security, Prosperity, and Responsibility

As money, goods, and people travel across national borders with blinding speed, globalization is transforming world politics. The chapters in Part 4 explore the global condition and the ways in which eroding national borders are transforming international relations and affecting global welfare throughout the world. Each chapter explores some facet of the challenges to prosperity and human security that we face in our globalized world, and the extent to which we have the ability, and responsibility, to respond and seek solutions to them.

Chapter 10 inspects how the globalization of finance is altering the international economic landscape, and Chapter 11 considers how the globalization of international trade is transforming the world. Chapter 12 then examines the demographic dimensions of globalization as well as how increased access to information is shaping culture and perceptions of identity. Chapter 13 looks at the human condition, and how global actors and their activities affect the welfare and basic rights of all humanity. Finally, Chapter 14 considers threats to the global environment that pose a serious challenge to the planet and humanity's continued survival.

Mutual Understanding in a Globalized World
The growing web of globalization enhances the prospect and need for mutual toleration and cooperation. Shown here are the opening ceremonies of the PyeongChang 2018 Winter Olympics. Originally founded to promote peace and bridge cultural divides, the renaissance spirit of the Olympic Games was apparent in 2018, particularly as the delegates from North and South Korea marched together under the Korean Unification Flag. As Lee-Hee Boem, President of the Olympic Organizing Committee, noted, "Just as the Seoul 1988 Olympic Games broke down the Cold War barrier between East and West thirty years ago, we hope that the two Koreas participating together in the PyeongChang 2018 Olympic Winter Games will once again bring peace over our land" (Olympic.com, 2018). Perhaps, as Nelson Mandela stirringly noted years earlier, "sport can change the world."

Chapter 10

The Globalization of International Finance

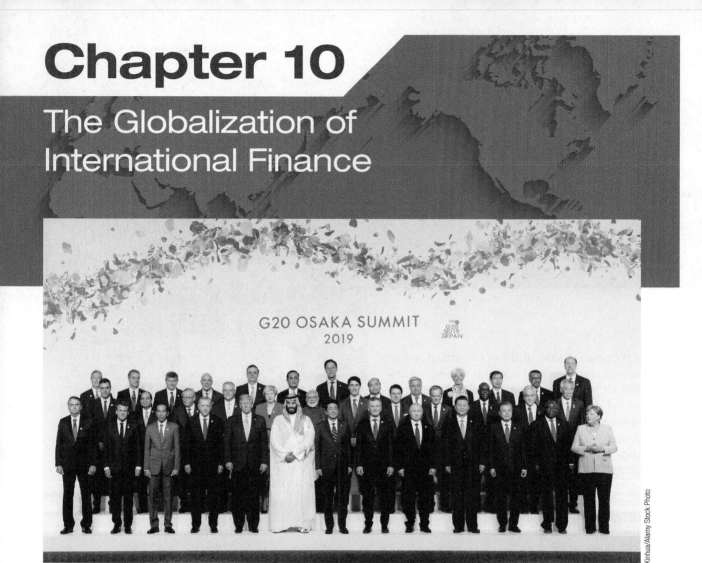

IMAGE 10.1 Seeking Global Financial Stability and Growth In the wake of the 2008 global financial crisis, the leaders of the G-20—an informal group of the twenty largest economies that meets periodically to discuss the coordination of financial policy— expanded their agenda to facilitate discussion of the world's most pressing problems. Shown above, they met in Osaka, Japan, in June 2019 to discuss innovation and sustainable growth, as well as the U.S.-China trade conflict, North Korea's nuclear program, and reform of the World Trade Organization. The larger message of the G-20 meetings is that "international cooperation still matters, as do the platforms that facilitate such cooperation" (Albright and Malcorra, 2019).

Learning Objectives

LO 10-1 Define globalization and explain its implications for the global economy.

LO 10-2 Describe the facets of global finance, and assess the policy tools available to states.

LO 10-3 Explain the Bretton Woods system, and discuss the financial order that followed it.

LO 10-4 Describe the stages of the 2008 financial crisis, and assess its impact on the global economy.

LO 10-5 Critique the global financial arrangements that have emerged since the 2008 crisis, and evaluate the current status of the global financial architecture.

—KOFI ANNAN, FORMER UN SECRETARY-GENERAL

"Money makes the world go 'round." "Money is the root of all evil." "All that glitters is not gold." "Money can't buy you happiness." "There's hell in not making money." You have heard all of these old sayings at one time or another. Even though such aphorisms and clichés are somewhat contradictory, they all contain elements of truth. Your challenge is to separate fact from fiction by determining the place of money in your life and in the world around you. This task will depend heavily on your personal values and preferences. However, the quality of your conclusions will depend on your analytic skills in evaluating how money affects the many dimensions of world politics—and your own personal financial fate.

Today, more than ever, money truly *is* moving around the world, and with increasing speed. The rapidity of global finance directly affects your quality of life. When you make a purchase, the odds are now very high that the goods have been produced overseas. What is more, when you buy a sandwich, a sweater, a car, or the gasoline to make it run, the cost is very likely to be affected by the rate at which your own country's currency is valued and exchanged for the currency of the producer abroad. Should you have the opportunity to travel abroad, you will instantly discover how the global exchange of national currencies will determine whether you can afford to attend a concert or buy that extra bottle of wine.

This chapter introduces you to the global financial system. It looks at the processes governing currency exchanges, particularly on how the transfer of money across borders affects levels of national prosperity and human security. Note that this topic is part of the larger issue of international economics in general, and it serves as an introduction to international trade, which is discussed in Chapter 11. Neither dimension of international economics—money or trade—can be considered without the other. They are inextricably linked, and only by looking at both together can you understand how money and markets drive the rise and fall of individual and national wealth. You will be looking at a phenomenon as old as recorded history and inspecting how it influences life in the twenty-first century.

> *Financial markets are like the mirror of mankind, revealing every hour of each working day the way we value ourselves and the resources of the world around us.*
>
> **—NIALL FERGUSON, BRITISH HISTORIAN**

Interpreting Contemporary Economic Change

LO 10-1 Define globalization and explain its implications for the global economy.

When changes occur in the world, they force people to think about and interpret world politics in fresh ways. Of all the many recent changes, perhaps none has been more continually invasive and far reaching than those occurring in the economic world. In fact, to some analysts, **geo-economics** (the geographic distribution of wealth) will replace *geopolitics* (the distribution

geo-economics
The relationship between geography and the economic conditions and behavior of states that define their levels of production, trade, and consumption of goods and services.

globalization
The integration of states through increasing contact, communication, and trade, as well as increased global awareness of such integration.

of strategic military and political power) as the most important axis around which international competition, and ultimately the globe's destiny, will revolve (see Chapter 4).

The growth of interdependence between each state's economy can be viewed as part of a trend toward **globalization** that began more than a century ago, and as states' economies have become more closely linked, traditional ideas about states, currency exchange mechanisms, trade, and markets have had to be reexamined in a new light (see Map 10.1). Bond purchases by Chinese investors, or even statements about future purchases, influence the relative value of currencies worldwide. Financial crises in the United States can likewise create turbulence in markets around the world. Revolutionary activity in the Middle East causes rapid increases in world oil prices. These are only a few of the consequences of globalization, and the undercurrents of the global economy have assumed increasing importance as they are inextricably linked to world politics.

Although some regard globalization as little more than a euphemism for capitalism (Petras and Veltmeyer, 2004), it is a multifaceted phenomenon that encompasses the development of interconnected material relations, the increasing rapidity with which they take place, and the shift in public perception of these changes. These multiple facets are evident in sociologist Fran

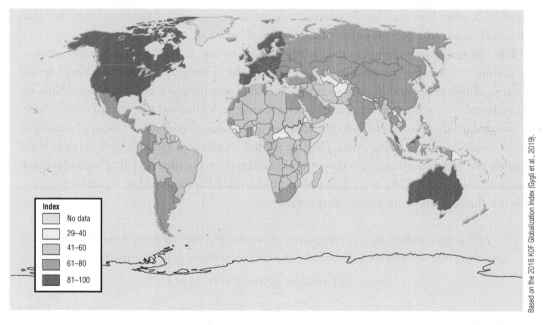

Index
No data
29–40
41–60
61–80
81–100

Based on the 2018 KOF Globalization Index (Gygli et al., 2019).

MAP 10.1 Globalization Around the World This map depicts the extent of globalization across the globe and is rendered from the 2018 Globalization Index released by the KOF Swiss Economic Institute. The index is based on forty-two different measures of economic, social, and political aspects of globalization, such as trade flows, personal contacts across borders, and participation in international organizations. As shown here, globalization varies across countries and regions. European countries are among the most global (eighteen of the twenty most globalized countries are from that region). The United States ranked twenty-third, with a globalization index score of 82.1 out of 100. There are also some trends among the least globalized, as they tend to be underdeveloped and largely autocratic regimes such as Bhutan, Liberia, and Somalia.

Think It Through   What does the map suggest about the relationship between globalization and development?

Tonkiss' (2012) definition of economic globalization as "the increasing integration of circuits of goods, production, image, information, and money across national borders . . . characterized not only by high level of trade, but by increasing levels of foreign direct investment and outsourcing, as well as the complex linkage of financial transactions across space."

Globalization is thus shorthand for a cluster of interconnected phenomena, and you will find the term used to describe a process, a policy, a predicament, or the product of vast international forces producing massive worldwide changes. Moreover, some analysts argue that globalization is a permanent trend furthering a probable *transformation* of world politics—the end of one historic pattern and the beginning of a new one. Political journalist Thomas L. Friedman (2007, pp. 48–49) argues that globalization will have a profound impact on the global system as a whole:

> This new era of globalization will prove to be such a difference of degree that it will be seen, in time, as a difference in kind . . . it will be remembered as one of those fundamental changes—like the rise of the nation-state or the Industrial Revolution—each of which, in its day, produced changes in the role of individuals, the role and form of governments, the way we innovated [and] the way we conducted business.

Given the broad and multifaceted scope of globalization, this chapter, as well as the remaining chapters in *World Politics*, deals with different dimensions of globalization and their implications. Nowhere is this integration more apparent than in the world of international finance and capital. We next focus our attention on the dynamics of the **international monetary system** through which currencies and credits are calculated as capital moves freely across national boundaries by way of investments, trade, foreign aid, and loans.

> *The importance of money flows from it being a link between the present and the future.*
>
> **—JOHN MAYNARD KEYNES, BRITISH ECONOMIST**

international monetary system
The financial procedures used to calculate the value of currencies and credits when capital is transferred across borders through trade, investment, foreign aid, and loans.

Money Matters: The Transnational Exchange of Money

LO 10-2 Describe the facets of global finance, and assess the policy tools available to states.

Part of the equation on which global economic destiny depends is the character of *laissez-faire* capitalism, which posits that free-market mechanisms—with a minimum of state intervention—are foundational to the "dynamism that produces capitalism's vast economic and cultural benefits" (Muller, 2013, p. 31). For its part, the state seeks to provide some operational rules for the system as well as measures to mitigate the more disruptive effects of the marketplace upon its citizenry. In the area of currency exchanges, a number of governments have taken some tentative steps in creating rules for adjusting their currencies with one another and stabilizing wide fluctuations in their exchange rates.

However, the process through which money is exchanged between countries does not have strong supranational regulatory institutions. Moreover, states often have very limited ability to control either those transactions or the relative value of their currencies on the world market. At the same time, these transactions, as noted above, are escalating at a furious rate. But what does this really mean, and what are its implications?

The Globalization of Finance

Global finance encompasses a broad variety of transactions, including international loans, foreign aid, remittances, and currency trading, as well as cross-border investments such as the purchase of stocks, bonds, or derivatives. It also includes financial services that are conducted across borders. Another major facet of global finance is *foreign direct investment* (FDI)—transactions "involving significant control of producing enterprises" (Cohen, 2005) ranging from the purchase of a substantial share of a foreign company's stock to setting up production facilities in another country (see Chapters 5 and 6).

globalization of finance
The increasing transnationalization of national markets through the worldwide integration of capital flows.

This **globalization of finance** refers to the increasing transnationalization and centralization of these markets through integrating worldwide capital flows. The most fundamental characteristic of this emerging system of financial arrangements is that it is not centered on any single state. Thus, globalization implies the growth of a single, unified *global* market. Whereas telecommunications specialists talk about the "death of distance," financial specialists talk about the "end of geography" because geographic location is no longer a barrier to finance.

Evidence of financial globalization abounds. Although trade has grown dramatically, since World War II the volume of cross-border capital flows has increased even more. In 2018 there were $1.2 trillion in global FDI flows. Although this is still below the levels reached before the 2008 global financial crisis, it is triple the level of FDI in 1997 and almost ten times the amount of FDI in 1980 (UNCTAD, 2019b; OECD, 2013).

arbitrage
The selling of one currency (or product) and purchase of another to make a profit on changing exchange rates.

Moreover, growth in the **arbitrage** market, in which currencies are bought and sold for profit based off differences and fluctuations in their relative values, has been truly staggering. Since 1973 this market has grown more than sixty times faster than the value of world trade (McGrew, 2008), and it routinely handles over $5 trillion worth of currency on a daily basis (Bank of International Settlements, 2016). By way of comparison, the total value of all goods and services produced in the United States during 2017—its **gross domestic product (GDP)**—was $19.5 trillion (World Bank, 2019c). Viewed another way, the amount of currency that circulates in four days is greater than the total yearly production of the U.S. economy.

gross domestic product (GDP)
Total value of all goods and services produced in a country within a year.

Today, even more speculative financial instruments have exponentially increased the size and scope of these capital flows. For example, by 2017 the total value of all the stock markets in the world was $78 trillion, which was somewhat less than actual global GDP of $80.9 trillion. During that same time, the bond market (the means through which governments and corporations accumulate debt) was valued at $237 trillion, or almost triple the value of global GDP (Nasdaq, 2018; World Bank, 2019c; Institute for International Finance, 2018). Yet the value of the derivatives market—financial instruments that are essentially "side bets" placed on the prospective future value of assets such as stocks and bonds—was $532 trillion (Bank for International Settlements, 2018). In other words, the market for these purely speculative financial instruments was almost seven times larger than the actual amount of goods and services produced in the world! In short, "Planet Finance is beginning to dwarf Planet Earth" (Ferguson, 2008, p. 4).

Global flows of capital are not entirely new. In an early form of globalization, a network of financial centers flourished along the Baltic and North seas, and city-states such as Lübeck, Hamburg, and Bergen dominated finance and trading. At the turn of the nineteenth century, London replaced Amsterdam as the world's leading financial center, and by the early twentieth century New York began to rival London—antecedents of today's shifting of financial hubs to Beijing, Tokyo, Singapore, and Dubai. Neither are international financial crises new; economist Charles Kindleberger (2000) notes that the "manics, panics, and crashes" of global finance began in the early seventeenth century, with twenty-seven major financial crises occurring before the beginning of the twentieth century.

What is different are the speed and breadth of finance capital flows throughout the entire globe. For example, many stock purchases are handled by high-frequency trading firms (HFTs) that rely on computer programs to execute many trades in a short period of time—some firms measure their trading speed in picoseconds; that is, trillionths of a second (Malmgren and Stys, 2011). The combination of rapid, computer-driven trading and the sheer volume of shares processed can produce rapid swings in global stock markets for very idiosyncratic reasons. Indeed, there are ways (some of which are illegal) in which traders can profit solely from their ability to trade faster than other traders (Lewis, 2014).

For example, a momentary crash occurred around 1:08 p.m. on April 23, 2013, when someone hacked the Associated Press Twitter account and reported that two explosions had just occurred at the U.S. White House and that President Obama had been hurt. Over the course of two minutes the U.S. stock market plummeted $200 billion. By 1:13 p.m., as investors discovered the story was false, the stock market recovered and the Dow Jones Industrial Average (an index widely used to evaluate how the stock market is doing) closed the day at a net gain (Lauricella et al., 2013).

To some extent, the global capital market reflects larger patterns in economic and political power. For example, Table 10.1 lists the twenty largest stock market exchanges in the world, expressed in terms of market capitalization (the total value of all stocks traded on a given exchange). Although this is only part of global finance, it does provide some indication of the centers of global finance. A clear pattern is continued U.S. dominance, as its two largest exchanges, the NYSE and NASDAQ, are larger in size than the next eight exchanges combined. At the same time, Chinese exchanges are growing, as they host three of the ten largest exchanges. There is also some indication of emerging economic powers, including India, South Korea, South Africa, Taiwan, and Brazil. Broader patterns in stock exchanges beyond the twenty reveal almost universal participation in this aspect of global finance, as only nine countries in the world have no stock exchanges. Thus, although power centers remain, an increasing number of countries are participating in the stock exchange system.

Though the structure of financial markets is somewhat indicative of a state's economic power, other aspects of the global capital market reveal limitations in the power of the state. For example, the volume of currencies traded far exceeds the actual amount of reserve currencies held by governments, which limits the ability of governments to influence exchange

TABLE 10.1   The Twenty Largest Stock Exchanges in the World, 2019

Exchange Name	Country	Market Capitalization (Trillions ($US))*
NYSE (New York Stock Exchange)	United States	22.477
NASDAQ OMX	United States	11.770
Japan Exchange Group, Tokyo	Japan	5.608
Shanghai Stock Exchange	China	5.014
Hong Kong Exchanges	China	4.378
Euronext	EU	4.268
London Stock Exchange Group	UK	4.038
Shenzhen Stock Exchange	China	3.355
TMX Group	Canada	2.281
Bombay Stock Exchange	India	2.186
National Stock Exchange India	India	2.156
Deutsche Börse	Germany	1.989
SIX Swiss Exchange	Switzerland	1.621
NASDAQ Nordic Exchanges	Various	1.471
Korea Exchange	South Korea	1.468
Australian Securities Exchange	Australia	1.384
Taiwan Stock Exchange	Taiwan	1.042
JSE Limited	South Africa	0.983
B3	Brazil	0.979
Bolsas y Mercados Españoles	Spain	0.790

*As of April 30, 2019.
Data from the World Federation of Exchanges (2019).

rates. Indeed, the value of a country's currency can fluctuate wildly no matter the wishes of a particular country. For example, the value of the Russian ruble decreased 85 percent during 2014 (Clinch, 2015) and has since stayed around that level, which greatly increased the economic cost associated with its assertiveness in the Ukraine. During the Asian financial crisis, Malaysian prime minister Mahathir bin Mohamad famously called international financier George Soros a "menace" to his country and argued that "currency trading is unnecessary, unproductive and immoral" (Friedman, 1997).

The globalization of finance also has implications for international trade (see Chapter 11) because the currency exchange rate directly affects the price of goods traded internationally. The international monetary system is a critical factor facilitating international trade, as such transactions could not exist without a stable and predictable method for calculating the value of sales and investments. However, monetary issues can precipitate trade conflict, and vice-versa. For example, currency values have long been a key issue of contention between the United States and China, with several instances of U.S. officials contending that China undervalues its currency. As currency values set the relative prices for goods, a lower exchange rate would serve to make Chinese products relatively cheaper, and thus put them at a relative advantage to U.S. goods. China has also used monetary policies to counteract trade conflict. In the summer of 2018, China let the value of its currency decline by about 9 percent in response to U.S. tariffs on

Chinese imports. The shift in currency values essentially made Chinese imports less expensive, which effectively counteracted U.S. tariffs (which would have otherwise made Chinese goods more expensive). As noted by economist Robin Brooks, "It was a signal to Washington that . . . if you keep slapping on tariffs, our currency is going to weaken significantly, and you're going to have a currency war on top of a trade war" (quoted in Johnson, 2018).

It is important to note that such "conflicts" are still within the context of mutually beneficial economic relations. Commercial liberals, the branch of liberalism that focuses on the positive spillovers that result from economic ties, argue that the open exchanges of currencies across borders benefits all countries. Yet the globalization of finance does not affect all countries equally. Though a majority of global capital goes to the Global North, all countries are mutually vulnerable to rapid transfers of capital in this globalized system.

As the financial crisis of 2008 has shown, the Global North is hardly without its problems (Laeven and Valencia, 2012). Yet historically the Global South has been the most dependent and vulnerable to shifts in the financial marketplace. Of the 461 systemic banking, currency, or debt crises that have occurred since 1970, 371 have been in the developing world (Laeven and Valencia, 2018). In accordance with neoliberal institutionalist approaches, this multitude of crises suggests why bankers and economists have called for more reliable multilateral mechanisms for policy coordination to better manage the massive movement of cross-border capital. This was the raison d'être for the G-20, a grouping of the twenty largest economies that was formed in the aftermath of the Asian financial crisis.

Broadly put, crises—like many of the fluctuations in global financial markets—connote limitations in the ability of a state to control its financial markets. There is also a significant portion of global finance that avoids the purview of states and global financial institutions altogether, whether to finance illegal activities or simply to avoid taxation. We next turn to this area of global finance, illicit financial markets.

Dark Money: Globalization and Illicit Financial Flows

The difficulties of controlling global financial flows are particularly apparent in **illicit financial flows (IFFs)**, defined as "money that is illegally earned, used or moved and which crosses an international border" (Global Financial Integrity, 2019). While IIFs are commonly associated with organized crime groups, such as drug traffickers, terrorist groups, or weapons dealers, many individuals and corporations participate in some aspect of illicit financial flows. While these flows are often used to support criminal activities, in many cases IFFs are more ambiguous legally, as actors use differences in legal regimes or tax rates across countries to maximize their personal wealth.

illicit financial flows
Money that is either illegally earned, used or moved across borders.

Controlling IFFs is particularly difficult given the speed in which money can cross borders, the many ways in which money can avoid attention, and the sheer volume of the flows. In 2014, an estimated $2 trillion to $3.5 trillion in illicit funds crossed borders. IFFs are growing rapidly; one admittedly "conservative" estimate reports that illicit flows grew between 8.5 and 10.4 percent annually between 2005 and 2015 (Golubski, 2017). Additionally, IFFs to and from the developing world have exceeded the yearly combined value of FDI and foreign aid into these countries since 2008 (Kar and Spanjers, 2014). These flows can have a corrosive effect on societies. At the least, they represent lost tax revenues that could have been devoted to public investment such as education or health. At the worst, these resources can finance criminal activity, terrorism, or armed conflicts (Shelley, 2018).

money laundering
Financial and legal processing designed to hide the criminal origins of money.

There are three primary categories of IFFs: tax evasion, **money laundering**, and trade mis-invoicing. Tax evasion occurs when individuals or businesses transfer capital abroad to avoid paying taxes. The basic dynamic is that assets or earnings are essentially moved from the higher-tax location where they were earned into locations with lower or nonexistent tax rates. There are many ways in which this can be done. One commonly-used method is to create fictitious "shell corporations" in low-tax locations and then divert assets or earnings into them under the guise of conducting business between the two "firms." This is essentially a "shell game" in that money can be moved into multiple fictitious firms to avoid detection and thus tax payments. For example, the Panama Papers case—in which data on money laundering and tax evasion operations taking place in a leading tax haven were leaked to journalists—revealed that one single Panamanian law firm created 214,000 corporations to help its clients avoid taxation or legal accountability (Transparency International, 2017). While these transactions can be quasi-legal (as they may not violate laws in all of the countries involved), they place a drain on the global economy. One study found that 8 percent of global private wealth was held in tax havens, and that the use of these havens reduced global tax revenues by approximately $200 billion per year (Konrad and Stolper, 2016).

Money laundering is the "processing of criminal proceeds to disguise their illegal origin" (Financial Action Task Force, 2019). It consists of three basic steps—placement, layering, and integration. In the first stage the launderer introduces the assets into the financial system, usually in such a way as to avoid attention, such as setting up numerous smaller accounts or off-shore accounts in shell corporations. In the layering phase the origin of the money is disguised through a variety of transactions or investments. Finally, the assets are integrated back into the legitimate economy, either as "clean" money or through investments in real estate, businesses, or tangible assets such as fine art. While the process is often bafflingly complex, in some cases it can be as straightforward as purchasing a legitimate business, layering "dirty" money in with legitimately-earned business revenues, and reporting profits that include money from both sources. For example, Operation Car Wash, the massive corruption and money laundering scandal in Brazil that brought about the indictments of hundreds of business and political leaders including two former presidents, began at a car wash that was used to launder money (Watts, 2017).

Trade misinvoicing is a commonly used method for facilitating IFFs in which money is illegally moved through falsifying the stated values, volume, or quality of goods that are traded across countries. For example, exporters can avoid paying taxes through under-reporting the value of their goods, while over-reporting the value of goods can be an effective way to launder or even extort money out of a given country. The general pattern is the same, with the actual invoice providing an inaccurate picture of the actual transaction, with the balance of the actual exchange (the under or over-payment) being completed through other channels, including shell corporations or personal exchanges. In practice this can be very difficult to detect, particularly if the perpetrators only make relatively small (in terms of percentages) altera-tions to the records; that is, while inspectors may notice goods that are drastically overpriced, a ten percent gap may not draw much attention. The volume of money laundered through trade misinvoicing is significant – according to some estimates trade misinvoicing accounts for over one-fifth of the total value of all trade between developed and developing countries (Global Financial Integrity, 2019).

There are several major obstacles to responding to IFFs. First, a coordinated global response is limited. The leading global organization in this area, the Financial Action Task Force, has no enforcement power as its primary purposes are to monitor state actions (or lack thereof) and develop international standards for combatting money laundering. While global organizations such as the UN and IMF encourage adherence to these standards, it is ultimately up to the states to enforce relevant laws and establish their own regulations in areas such as financial standards and taxation. Even with coordination, it is virtually impossible to police comprehensively the extensive number of actors who facilitate IFFs, including banks, shipping companies, law firms and sometimes the political leaders themselves. Ultimately, many of the same factors that help the legitimate global economy flourish—capital mobility, the relative anonymity of many transactions, and the numerous options for investment—create opportunities for illicit activity.

Taken as a whole, IFFs flourish by successfully exploiting the inherent complexity of global finance. While many of these interactions—both licit and illicit—may be quite intricate, useful insights can be gained from understanding the fundamentals of global finance. With that in mind, we next examine the core concepts of the global monetary system, some of the key issues and dilemmas surrounding monetary policy, and its recent historical context.

Monetary Policy: Key Concepts and Issues

Monetary and financial policies are woven into a complex set of relationships between states and the global system and involve fairly esoteric terminology. To help you to better understand these issues, Table 10.2 lays out some of the key concepts related to monetary policy and the role of currency. As you consider these explanations, keep in mind that these are not separate phenomena but a related set of factors through which the global financial system operates.

To begin to put together how these factors are related, and the importance of a state's **monetary policy** in determining its well-being, we consider why a country's **exchange rate** fluctuates frequently and the challenges states face in dealing with these fluctuations. As you will see, states face a variety of trade-offs in navigating monetary policies and must seek a difficult balance between competing values, goals, and priorities. Moreover, states are ultimately limited in their ability to control monetary outcomes.

Money works in several ways and serves different purposes:

- Money must be widely accepted, so that people earning it can use it to buy goods and services from others.

- Money must store value, so that people will be willing to keep some of their wealth in the form of that particular currency.

- Money must act as a standard of deferred payment, so that people will be willing to lend money knowing that, when the money is repaid in the future, it will still have purchasing power.

monetary policy
The decisions made by states' central banks to change the country's money supply to manage the national economy and control inflation, such as changing the amount of money in circulation and raising or lowering interest rates.

exchange rate
The rate at which one state's currency is exchanged for another state's currency in the global marketplace.

TABLE 10.2 Understanding Currency: Basic Terms and Concepts

Term	Concept
Balance of Payments	A calculation summarizing a country's financial transactions with the external world, determined by the level of credits (export earnings, profits from foreign investment, receipts of foreign aid) minus the country's total international debits (imports, interest payments on international debts, foreign direct investments, and the like).
Budget Deficit	Yearly amount of debt necessary to fund a balance-of-payments deficit. Money is most commonly raised by selling bonds to foreign and domestic investors.
National Debt	Cumulative amount of debt that a country owes its various bondholders, both foreign and domestic.
Balance of Trade	The difference in the value of the goods a country sells (exports) minus the goods it purchases (imports). If a country imports more than it exports, it is said to have a balance-of-trade deficit. For example, in April 2019 the United States exported $207 billion in goods and services and imported $258 billion, for a balance-of-trade deficit of about $51 billion (BEA, 2019).
Central Bank	The primary monetary authority within a state. It is responsible for issuing currency, setting monetary policy, acting as a bank for the government, and helping to administer the state's banking industry.
Monetary Policy	Central bank policy tools for managing economies. Policies fall into two basic categories: altering the money supply (the amount of money in circulation) and adjusting interest rates (the relative "price" for using money). An expansionary monetary policy would entail such things as selling additional bonds and lowering interest rates. Such policies would make money relatively more plentiful and less expensive to borrow.
Fiscal Policy	Governmental policy tools for managing economies. Basic policy options are taxation and spending. An expansionary fiscal policy would consist of lowering taxes and/or increasing spending, whereas a "tight" or contractionary policy would involve raising taxes and/or decreasing spending.
Devaluation	The lowering of the official exchange rate of one country's currency relative to other currencies. This is generally done to increase exports, as devaluation lowers the relative prices of a country's exports. However, it can also reduce the spending power of citizens within that country.
Exchange Rate	The rate at which one state's currency is exchanged for another state's currency in the global marketplace. For example, on June 8, 2019, for one U.S. dollar you would have received 0.88 euro or 19.62 Mexican pesos. Exchange rates are subject to constant fluctuations. Daily changes are generally quite small, although they can vary greatly over the long run. For example, on June 28, 2001, the U.S. dollar was worth 1.17 euros and 9.08 Mexican pesos.
Fixed Exchange Rate	A system in which a government sets the value of its currency at a fixed rate for exchange in relation to another country's currency or another measure of value (such as a group of different currencies or a precious metal such as gold) so that the exchange value is not free to fluctuate in the global money market.
Floating Exchange Rate	System in which the relative value of a country's currency is set by market forces. In principle, the value of a country's currency is indicative of the underlying strengths and weaknesses of its economy.
Fixed-but-Adjustable Exchange Rate System	A system in which a government fixes its currency in relation to that of another country's currency but may still change the fixed price to reflect changes in the underlying strengths and weaknesses of its economy. The general expectation is that such changes are rare and only occur under specially defined circumstances.

(Continues)

TABLE 10.2   Understanding Currency: Basic Terms and Concepts (*continued*)

Term	Concept
Inflation	A decrease in the value of money, which increases the prices paid for goods and services. It is generally expressed in percentages and calculated on a yearly basis. Inflation reduces the buying power of citizens, as it decreases the value of their currency. Very high levels of inflation (hyperinflation) can cause severe disruptions within a society, as the currency becomes largely worthless. For example, in 2018 the inflation rate for Venezuela was over 1,000,000 percent.
Capital Controls	Government attempts to limit or prevent global capital transactions. Examples range from placing taxes on foreign exchanges to outright bans on the movement of capital out of a country. These policies are generally intended as a means to "insulate" an economy from the global capital market.

Movements in a state's exchange rate occur, in part, when changes develop in the people's assessment of a national currency's underlying economic strength or the ability of its government to maintain the value of its money. A deficit in a country's balance of payments, for example, would likely cause a decline in the value of its currency relative to that of other countries. This happens when the supply of the currency is greater than the demand for it. Similarly, when those engaged in international economic transactions change their expectations about a currency's future value, they might reschedule their lending and borrowing. Fluctuations in the exchange rate could then follow.

Arbitrage speculators who buy and sell money also affect the international stability of a country's currency. Speculators make money by guessing the future value of currencies. If, for instance, they believe that the Japanese yen will be worth more in three months than it is now, they can buy yen today and sell them for a profit three months later. Conversely, if they believe that the yen will be worth less in three months, they can sell yen today for a certain number of dollars and then buy back the same yen in three months for less money. As is the case with global capital flows, the globalization of finance allows investors to rapidly move funds from one currency to another in order to realize gains from differences in states' interest rates and the declining value of other currencies.

In the same way that governments try to protect the value of their currencies at home, they often try to protect them internationally by intervening in currency markets. Their willingness to do so is important to importers and exporters, whose success may depend on predictability in the value of the currencies in which they deal to carry out transnational exchanges. Governments intervene when their central banks buy or sell currencies to change the relative value of their own. Unlike speculators, however, governments should not try to manipulate exchange rates so as to gain unfair advantages because that could damage their credibility as custodians of monetary stability. In any event, the extent to which governments can ultimately affect the value of their currency in the face of large transnational movements of capital is increasingly questionable (see Figures 10.1A and 10.1B).

Within this system, governments are faced with the difficult task of balancing the demands of the global currency market with the need to manage their economies. There are many difficulties in navigating these channels, and states face three main sets of competing values, or trade-offs: inflation versus unemployment, strong versus weak currency valuation strategies, and the competing values of stability versus autonomy (see Table 10.3).

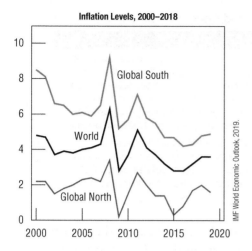

Inflation Levels, 2000–2018

IMF World Economic Outlook, 2019.

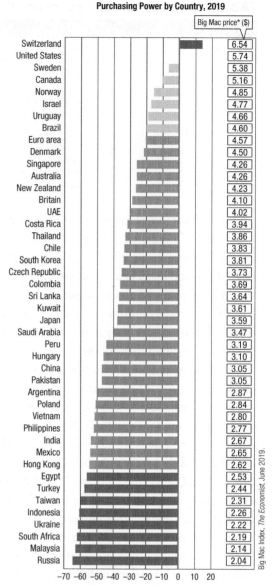

Purchasing Power by Country, 2019

Big Mac Index, *The Economist*, June 2019.

*At market exchange rate

FIGURES 10.1A AND 10.1B
Calculating the Changing Costs of Goods in the Global Economy People who travel abroad use currency exchange rates to convert the price of their purchases abroad to the value of their home currencies, and sometimes they are alarmed at the higher price. Economists usually calculate currency exchange rates in terms of purchasing power parity (PPP) as that index measures the cost of identical goods or services in any two countries. Shown on the right, this index uses a McDonald's Big Mac, which is available for sale in more than 130 countries. As of June 2019, the least expensive burger could be purchased in Russia for $2.04 versus an average price of $5.74 in the United States. In Switzerland, the same burger costs $6.54. Inflation also affects the cost of goods and services, as a general increase in the level of prices means that each unit of currency purchases less. The figure on the left shows how global inflation has fluctuated since 2000. It shows that inflation is consistently higher in the Global South than the Global North.

money supply
The total amount of currency in circulation, calculated to include demand deposits, such as checking accounts in commercial banks, and time deposits, such as savings accounts and bonds.

Governments attempt to manage their currencies to prevent inflation. Inflation occurs when the government creates too much money in relation to the goods and services produced in its economy. As explained in Table 10.3, high degrees of inflation can undercut the ability of a currency to effectively serve as a store of value or medium of exchange. However, the creation of money—whether directly through increasing the **money supply** or indirectly through expansionary fiscal policies that necessitate the creation of more money—stimulates the economy. Alternatively, restrictive monetary policy is very useful in curbing inflation or helping the government reduce debt. Yet such actions slow an economy down, which can result in increased

TABLE 10.3 Conflicting Goals in Financial Policy

Trade-Off	Policy Tools	Dilemma
Inflation vs. unemployment	Monetary policy (interest rates and money supply)	Stimulative (expansionary) policies may create inflation. Restrictive (tight) monetary policies may cause unemployment.
Strong vs. weak currency	Capital controls Choice of exchange rate regime Currency devaluation Monetary policy	Any choice hurts some segments within the country, such as exporting industries or consumers.
Currency stability vs. policy autonomy	Choice of exchange rate regime	Cannot have both stability and autonomy in an open economy.

unemployment and even recessions. This is one of the most commonly noted trade-offs associated with monetary policy—inflation versus unemployment.

A related dilemma regards currency values, specifically whether states should seek to maintain "strong" or relatively "weak" currencies. In a flexible exchange rate regime, the exchange rate for a given currency ideally reflects the health of its economy (or lack thereof). As mentioned, states are generally expected to refrain from manipulating the value of their currencies, or the currencies of other countries, in order to maintain predictability and stability. However, there are benefits to maintaining a weak currency, through such means as capital controls, fixing exchange rates, or even currency devaluations. Although a weaker currency has a negative effect on the spending power of domestic consumers, it makes exporting industries more competitive because their goods become relatively less expensive in the global marketplace as compared to those countries with a stronger currency. This has been a major source of controversy regarding the Chinese currency, as critics contend that China maintains an unduly low exchange rate that creates unfair competition in the global marketplace. Alternatively, currencies that are relatively strong face the opposite dilemma—though their consumers have relatively more spending power, both at home and abroad, their exporting industries suffer, and they are more likely to run a balance-of-trade deficit.

This speaks to the trade-off that is at the core of global monetary policy, namely, the choice between currency stability and policy autonomy. The basic problem is that in a system in which capital flows freely (that is, there are no substantial capital controls), it is impossible to have both stability and autonomy. In principle, each has advantages. Stable exchange rates ensure that a country's currency can perform the primary functions of a currency (cited earlier), and the lack of volatility provides both policy makers and potential investors with expectations for the future. Autonomy gives states the flexibility to pursue monetary policies that best suit their particular economic situation, such as the use of expansionary policies to stimulate growth.

A flexible exchange rate regime gives states autonomy to conduct their own monetary policies. For example, all else being equal, the market would respond to expansionary monetary policy by lowering the exchange rate of a currency (as the currency would be relatively more plentiful and/or offer lower interest rates). In this case, autonomy is gained, although there is no guarantee of stability, as the currency is subject to the vicissitudes of the global currency markets.

A fixed exchange rate regime provides currency stability, yet it gives states practically no freedom to conduct monetary policy. For example, if a country with a fixed exchange rate were to lower interest rates, the exchange rate could not move to take the decreased demand for the currency into account. As a result, the country would have a balance-of-payments deficit. To fill this deficit, the country would need to intervene in the foreign exchange market to reduce the oversupply of currency—a "tight" monetary policy that would essentially undo the initial policy—or get rid of the fixed exchange rate altogether. The United States near the end of the Bretton Woods era, Argentina in the late 1990s, and Greece since 2010 have faced such dilemmas.

States thus have to balance competing interests when creating monetary policy—the desire to help their economy grow with the necessity to maintain their currencies, the relative utility of strong versus weak currency valuation, and the incompatibility of stability and policy autonomy. Moreover, all states face these dilemmas within the context of a global monetary system over which they have very little actual control. It is helpful to keep these trade-offs and limitations on state power in mind as you consider the monetary policies of the Bretton Woods era, as well as some of the current issues in international finance.

Bretton Woods and Beyond

LO 10-3 Explain the Bretton Woods system, and discuss the financial order that followed it.

In July 1944, forty-four of the states allied against the Axis powers met at Bretton Woods, a New Hampshire resort, to devise new rules and institutions that would govern international trade and monetary relations after World War II. As the world's preeminent economic and military power, the United States played the leading role.

The perceived causes of the economic catastrophes of the previous decade, as well as the states' beliefs about the need for active U.S. leadership, shaped the proposals. The United States sought free trade, open markets, and monetary stability—all central tenets of what would become the "Bretton Woods system"—based on the theoretical premises of *commercial liberalism*, which advocates free markets with few barriers to trade and capital flows.

Britain also played an important role at the conference. Led by John Maynard Keynes—whose theories about the state's role in managing inflation, unemployment, and growth still influence economic thinking around the world—the British delegation won support for the principle of strong government action when states face economic problems. This ideology conforms less closely with liberalism than with the principles of *mercantilism*, which assigns states a greater role in managing economic interactions as a strategy for acquiring national wealth (see Chapter 5 and Chapter 11).

Despite these differences, the rules established at Bretton Woods reflected a remarkable level of agreement. They rested on three political bases. First, power was concentrated in the rich Western European and North American countries, which reduced the number of states needed to reach decisions. The onset of the Cold War helped cement Western unity along these lines. Second, a compromise was reached between the contrasting ideologies of the United States and Britain. In particular, the emergent order honored both commercial liberal

Lou-Foto/Alamy Stock Photo

IMAGE 10.2 Growing from Economic Integration New skyscrapers—a symbol of economic growth—dot the skyline of Beijing, China, which is recognized as one of the globe's leading financial centers. Former World Trade Organization Director-General Pascal Lamy remarked that "the wealth of the great Merchant Cities extends far beyond money. As cities open to trade and traders, these communities have served as centers for the exchange of ideas and culture as well as goods and services."

preferences for an open international economy and the more mercantilist desires for active state involvement in their domestic economies. This mix of ideologies that underpinned the Bretton Woods order was eventually termed **embedded liberalism** (Ruggie, 1982). Third, Bretton Woods worked because the United States assumed the burdens of hegemonic leadership, which others willingly accepted.

Commercial liberalism's preference for open markets spread worldwide during this time and remains dominant today. Thus, it is still useful to characterize the contemporary international economic system as a **Liberal International Economic Order (LIEO)**—one based on such free-market principles as openness and free trade. Three institutions were formed to maintain the LIEO. The General Agreement on Tariffs and Trade (GATT), which later became the World Trade Organization (WTO), was formed to encourage trade liberalization. The International Bank for Reconstruction and Development, which later became the World Bank, and the International Monetary Fund (IMF) were created to bolster financial and monetary relations (see Chapter 5).

Financial and Monetary Aspects of the Bretton Woods System

The global economic collapse of the 1930s provided important lessons for monetary relations. In particular, as the major economies contracted in the late 1920s, they found themselves unable to maintain their fixed exchange rate regimes. The resulting flexible currency regime

embedded liberalism
Dominant economic approach during the Bretton Woods system, which combined open international markets with domestic state intervention to attain such goals as full employment and social welfare.

Liberal International Economic Order (LIEO)
The set of regimes created after World War II, designed to promote monetary stability and reduce barriers to the free flow of trade and capital.

speculative attacks

Massive sales of a country's currency, caused by the anticipation of a future decline in its value.

fixed exchange rates

A system in which a government sets the value of its currency in relation to another country's currency at a fixed rate of exchange and does not allow it to fluctuate in the global money market.

was highly unstable, replete with **speculative attacks** on currencies and currency devaluations. Eventually states began to isolate their monetary and trade regimes from the global market, and the global economy collapsed into "closed imperial blocks" (Ravenhill, 2008, p. 12).

To avoid repeating history, the leaders sought to construct a common set of practices regarding monetary and currency policy to help simplify international trade and finance. The negotiating parties agreed that the postwar monetary regime should be based on **fixed exchange rates**, and governments were tasked with maintaining this new currency regime. To provide a stabilization fund to help countries offset short-term balance-of-payments problems, they set up what eventually became the International Monetary Fund (IMF). The IMF was to function somewhat like a global credit union—countries contributed to the fund and were able to draw capital from it to help them maintain a balance-of-payments equilibrium, and hence exchange rate stability. Along somewhat similar lines, they established the International Bank for Reconstruction and Development, later known as the World Bank, to provide capital for longer-term development and recovery projects.

Today the IMF and World Bank continue to be important, if controversial, players in the global monetary and financial systems. Eighty-five percent of their state members belong to both intergovernmental organizations (IGOs), which serve as "lenders of last resort" to members facing financial crises if those seeking assistance agree to meet the often-painful loan conditions. In the period immediately after World War II, these institutions commanded too little authority and too few resources to cope with the enormous devastation of the war.

The United States stepped into the breach. The U.S. dollar became the key to the hegemonic role that the United States eagerly assumed as manager of the international monetary system. Backed by a vigorous and healthy economy, a fixed relationship between gold and the dollar (pegged at $35 per ounce of gold), and the U.S. commitment to exchange gold for dollars at any time (known as "dollar convertibility"), the dollar became a universally accepted parallel currency. It was used in exchange markets as the reserve used by monetary authorities

IMAGES 10.3A AND 10.3B Money Matters Currency now moves effortlessly across borders, and the globalization of international finance is wreaking havoc on the efforts of state governments to control rapid fluctuations in economic conditions. Shown here is an example of how financial policies sometimes unleash hostile feelings: As part of the Occupy Wall Street movement, May Day protestors expressed popular outrage and frustration over the corrupt and fraudulent practices of financial institutions, as well as the failure of governments to hold them accountable. Pictured left, around 32,000 people took to the streets in Tokyo on May 1, 2013, to protest economic conditions for the common man. Pictured right, a police lieutenant confronts protestors in New York City.

in most countries and by private banks, corporations, and individuals for international trade and capital transactions.

To maintain the value of their currencies, central banks in other countries used the dollar to raise or depress their value. Thus, the Bretton Woods monetary regime was based on fixed-but-adjustable exchange rates that were pegged to the dollar and gold, which ultimately required government intervention to maintain.

To get U.S. dollars into the hands of those who needed them most, the Marshall Plan provided Western European states billions of dollars in aid to buy the U.S. goods necessary to rebuild their war-torn economies. The United States also encouraged deficits in its own balance of payments as a way of providing **international liquidity**. Such liquidity was intended to enable these countries to pursue expansionary monetary and fiscal policies, as well as to facilitate their participation in the global economy.

international liquidity
Reserve assets used to settle international accounts.

Controversy

CRYPTOCURRENCIES—FAD OR THE FUTURE OF FINANCE?

Bitcoin and other so-called "cryptocurrencies" (also referred to as digital or virtual currencies) have become increasingly visible in global finance. Though none of these currencies is over ten years old, their use has expanded greatly, as has their value. By far the largest of these currencies, and the best known, is bitcoin. As of June 2019, bitcoin was used in approximately 340,000 transactions per day, and its market capitalization (the number of bitcoins multiplied by the exchange rate) was over $140 billion. As its usage has expanded, its exchange rate has skyrocketed – it reached parity with the dollar (each bitcoin was valued on exchange markets at one dollar) in 2010, and in 2019 a single bitcoin traded at approximately $8,000. Assessments of these currencies vary wildly—while cryptocurrencies have been derided as "the greatest scam in history" (Harris, 2018), others contend that "the future of cryptocurrencies is bright" (Zalewska, 2018). The prevalence of bitcoin and other cryptocurrencies raises important issues about the functions of currencies, the future evolution of money, and the role of the state in these developments.

Arthimedes/Shutterstock.com

Bitcoin functions similarly to other currencies in that consumers can use money from their electronic "wallet" to sell or purchase goods and services. The process is otherwise very different. Rather than being printed by a central bank, currency is created by a complex and labor-intensive process called "mining," in which users solve complex mathematical problems and help to verify other user purchases in exchange for new currency. Transactions are monitored and verified by blockchain, an innovative decentralized ledger system. Most notably, the issuance of the currency, its value, as well as the conditions surrounding its use are totally driven by its users and investors—while states can take broad measures to either encourage or discourage its use, bitcoin is essentially outside of government control.

Given these characteristics, there is debate over whether bitcoin is a "real" currency. Economist David Yermack asserts that it fails to achieve any of the criteria of a currency and has "scant transaction volume" in comparison with other currencies. Also, given its volatile exchange rate—its value fell from $19,499 in

(Continued)

December 2017 to $8,401 in less than two months (blockchain.com, 2019)—bitcoin behaves "more like a speculative investment than a currency" (Yermack, 2015, p. 31) and is thus not a suitable store of value or means for deferred payment. Others counter that it is in fact readily usable, as there is a controlled supply of the currency, and it is perfectly exchangeable, durable, and mobile. They see the problems cited by mainstream economists as short-term difficulties that will be surpassed as the currency continues to evolve. Somewhat hyperbolically, advocates argue that the bitcoin "may be the best form of money we have ever used" (Blasetti, 2017) as it is completely "censorship-free" since no "single government, corporation or nation controls bitcoin" (bitcoin.com, 2019).

Cryptocurrencies also raise many political concerns. As its value is completely user and investor-driven, the value of bitcoin is not determined by state actions, such as imprudent fiscal and monetary policies. Yet this also means that there is ultimately no safety net for the currency. Unlike the dollar, bitcoin is not backed by the "full faith and credit" of any country. As a result, prices may fluctuate for no reason other than flows of speculative investment (Bianchi, 2019). The anonymous nature of bitcoin can be problematic, in that it is useful for terrorist groups, criminal organizations, or rogue states such as North Korea (Panda, 2018). While bitcoin transactions are secure, their unregulated nature and wild fluctuations in exchange rates creates fertile ground for cryptocurrency-related theft and fraud, such as hacking of personal currency codes, fraudulent ICO's (initial currency offerings), pyramid or Ponzi schemes,

and fraud relating to cryptocurrency exchanges or mining arrangements (Bianchi, 2019; Kshetr, 2019).

These issues point to two main problems underlying cryptocurrencies. First, it is problematic for a currency to be both a medium of exchange and a vehicle for speculative investment. Moreover, while the need to have some regulation over these currencies is broadly noted (Rundell, 2019), cryptocurrencies are specifically designed to be free from such control. Despite these issues and persistent doubts about the viability of cryptocurrencies, some mainstream organizations, including Facebook, banks such as JP Morgan, and organizations such as the IMF and World Bank, are considering their own versions of cryptocurrency (Salami, 2019). Similarly, some states are looking into developing their own digital currencies, citing reduced transaction costs as well as better tracking of illicit transactions—which is a particular problem with physical currency (Rundell, 2019). Ultimately, while controversy continues, it appears that digital currencies in one form or another will play a part in the future of global finance.

What Do You Think?

1. Do you think cryptocurrencies are "real" currencies? Why or why not?

2. Are cryptocurrencies a threat to conventional currencies such as the dollar?

3. How would the global financial system change if cryptocurrencies were as prevalent as dollars or Euros? How would this prevalence affect the fiscal and monetary policies of states?

Note: Prepared with the advice and assistance of Robert G. Blanton, PhD.

In addition to providing liquidity, the United States assumed a disproportionate share of the burden in rejuvenating Western Europe and Japan. It supported European and Japanese trade competitiveness, permitted certain forms of protectionism (such as Japanese restrictions on importing U.S. products), and accepted dollar discrimination (as the European Payments Union did by promoting trade within Europe at the expense of trade with the United States). The United States willingly agreed to pay these costs of leadership because subsidizing economic growth in Europe and Japan increased the U.S. export markets and strengthened the West against communism's possible popular appeal.

The End of Bretton Woods

Although this system worked well initially, it grew overly burdensome. By the 1960s, it had become apparent that the system would ultimately be unsustainable. As use of the dollar—as well as the amount of dollars in circulation—continued to expand, the resulting U.S.

balance-of-payments deficit became increasingly problematic. Unlike other countries, the United States was not able to adjust the value of its currency because it was pegged to gold. Although strict adherence to a fixed exchange regime supposedly limits the policy autonomy of a state, the United States nonetheless began to pursue expansionary macroeconomic policies during the 1960s to finance the Vietnam War and to increase social spending. Such spending further exacerbated the balance-of-payments deficit. By 1970, the total amount of foreign claims for dollars, $47 billion, was over four times the value of gold holdings in the United States (Oatley, 2012, p. 217). This gap between the amount of dollars in circulation and the amount of dollars actually supported by gold holdings was known as **dollar overhang**. Simply put, although the dollar was officially "as good as gold," the monetary reality was far different.

This left the Bretton Woods system in a tenuous position, and the United States with few options. Tight monetary policies on behalf of the United States would have reduced the balance-of-payments deficit. However, given the scope of the deficit, such cuts would have dealt a major shock to the U.S. economy. Such policies would have international ramifications as well because reducing the supply of dollars would damage countries that relied on the dollar for liquidity purposes. Another potential option, currency devaluation, could conceivably have reduced the balance-of-payments problem. This option was also problematic, as its effect could be undone if other states likewise devalued their currencies (so as not to give the United States any advantage in selling goods on the world marketplace). Although some of the other major economies were willing to intervene to support the dollar, there were limits to what these countries would do, and it was widely known that the status quo was not sustainable.

dollar overhang
The condition that precipitated the end of the Bretton Woods era, in which total holdings of dollars outside of the U.S. central bank exceeded the amount of dollars actually backed by gold.

> *The architecture of the international finance system must be reformed to reduce the susceptibility to crises. The ultimate key is not economics or finance, but politics—the art of developing support for strong policy.*
>
> **—ROBERT RUBIN, FORMER U.S. SECRETARY OF THE TREASURY**

Floating Exchange Rates and Financial Crises

In 1971, U.S. President Richard Nixon cut this Gordian knot by abruptly announcing—without consulting allies—that the United States would no longer exchange dollars for gold. With the price of gold no longer fixed and dollar convertibility no longer guaranteed, the Bretton Woods system gave way to a system based on **floating exchange rates**. Market forces, rather than government intervention, now determined currency values. A country experiencing adverse economic conditions now sees the value of its currency fall in response to the choices of traders, bankers, and businesspeople. This was expected to make exports cheaper and imports more expensive, which in turn would pull the currency's value back toward equilibrium—all without the need for central bankers to support the value of its currency.

Although flexible exchange rates give governments the autonomy to conduct their own fiscal and monetary policies, these same market forces hold governments accountable for their policies and actions. Exposure to the market thus exerts a "disciplinary effect on the conduct of policies, because international capital flows adversely respond to imprudent macroeconomic

floating exchange rates
An unmanaged process in which governments neither establish an official rate for their currencies nor intervene to affect the value of their currencies and instead allow market forces and private investors to influence the relative rate of exchange for currencies between countries.

policies" (IMF, 2005). As a result, states should be forced to closely monitor their fiscal and monetary policies to avoid balance-of-payments deficits and inflation.

Those expectations were not met. Beginning in the late 1970s, escalating through the 1980s, and persisting to the present, a wave of financial crises—both in currency and banking—occurred (see Map 10.2). In the Global South, the situation was particularly grim during the 1980s and 1990s. A massive debt crisis in Latin America, as well as unsustainable debt levels throughout the developing and transitioning economies, raised alarms throughout the global financial system.

Yet the debt picture within the developing world has improved markedly during the twenty-first century. Debt reduction programs such as the Heavily Indebted Poor Countries (HIPC) Initiative, which began in 1996 and targeted debt levels in forty developing countries whose debt load was at least 280 percent of their GDP, as well as the Multilateral Debt Relief Initiative (MDRI), which provided debt forgiveness for developing countries, contributed to this improvement. Increased export performance, as well as higher prices for many of the commodities sold by these countries, similarly enhanced economic conditions. Overall, the external debt of the Global South decreased from 37.9 percent of GNI (Gross National Income) in 2000 to 25 percent in 2017 (WDI, 2019).

Yet high debt levels have been endemic in many developed countries since the turn of the century, due in no small part to the 2008 global financial crisis. In the G-7 countries in the Global North, government debt is 117 percent of GNP, almost seven times the level

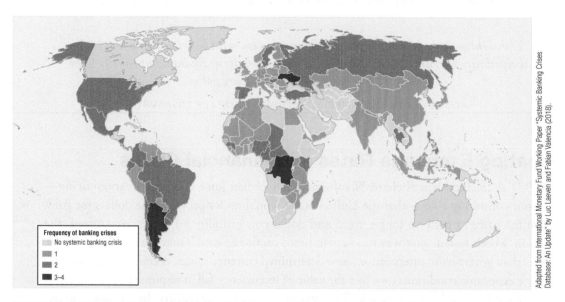

Frequency of banking crises
- No systemic banking crisis
- 1
- 2
- 3–4

Adapted from International Monetary Fund Working Paper "Systemic Banking Crises Database: An Update" by Luc Laeven and Fabian Valencia (2018).

MAP 10.2 Financial Crises since Bretton Woods This map shows the global distribution and frequency of systemic banking crises, a type of financial crisis, marked by significant financial distress in the banking system such as bank runs and liquidations. In all, 151 banking crises occurred between 1970 and 2017. Most tend to have a regional focus and, until the 2008 global financial crisis, generally took place in the Global South.

Think It Through What patterns are there for states that have been able to completely avoid financial crisis?

for countries in the Global South (IMF, 2019d). Greece, for example, has perennially dealt with debt issues, and controversy still surrounds the tight fiscal policies that the country was forced to enact to reduce its debt. Indeed, Greece cut its total government spending by more than 32 percent between 2009 and 2011 (Trading Economics, 2013). These cuts have translated into massive layoffs of government employees, decreased spending on social services—including a 40 percent reduction in public health expenditures (Stuckler and Basu, 2013)—increased taxes, and higher ages for retirement. Unfortunately, Greece still has a debt ratio of 174 percent (IMF, 2019e; see also "A Closer Look: The Greek Financial Crisis"). In addition to generating controversy, such measures have shrunk the Greek economy and increased unemployment, which remains over 20 percent. Moreover, unemployment among youth is around 40 percent (Jordan, 2015).

Even the most powerful countries are vulnerable. The United States may be the reigning hegemon with the globe's largest economy, but its total debt at the beginning of 2019 was just over $22 trillion, which is 107 percent of the total U.S. GDP (NPR, 2019; IMF, 2019).

Given the large volumes of debt, as well as the rapidity with which currencies flow across borders, conditions have been ripe for financial crises, whether due to poor government practices (such as taking on too much debt or cutting debt too rapidly) or the massive "boom and bust" patterns of global investment and currency markets. Since the demise of the Bretton Woods monetary system, there have been 471 financial crises that have directly affected as many as 120 countries around the world. The total losses in these crises have been great. Since 1970, output losses of each crisis—that is, the deviation of post-crisis GDP growth from growth patterns before the crises—averaged 23 percent of GDP (Laeven and Valencia, 2012). To put such loss in perspective, in the absence of a financial crisis, these countries would have produced almost a quarter more goods and services.

To better understand the dynamics and far-reaching effects of financial crises, the next section focuses on the causes and effects of one of the largest financial collapses in history—the 2008 global financial crisis. This crisis, which began in the United States and quickly spread worldwide, has produced subsequent crises in more than twenty other countries (Laeven and Valancia, 2012), and has set the tone for many of the issues and challenges still facing the global financial system today.

The 2008 Global Financial Crisis

LO 10-4 Describe the stages of the 2008 financial crisis, and assess its impact on the global economy.

Myriad economic and political factors caused the global financial crisis, and the particulars of the crash, especially the investment instruments themselves, are incredibly complex. Indeed, former chair of the U.S. Federal Reserve Alan Greenspan noted that a key cause of the crisis was the inability of the world's "most sophisticated investors" and regulators—the people who actually created and worked with these instruments—to understand them (Comisky and Madhogarhia, 2009).

A Closer Look

THE GREEK FINANCIAL CRISIS

Since 2010, Athens has been rocked with protests and riots. Demonstrators have thrown furniture, rocks, and even yogurt at police, who have responded with the widespread use of tear gas and clubs to disperse the crowds. Such protests are a response to the passage of austerity measures, including massive cutbacks in health and education spending, layoffs of public employees, the privatization of state-run industries, and tax increases on such items as heating oil (Donadio, 2011). The worst of the crisis is arguably over, as Greece completed its last bailout program in 2018, and Prime Minister Alexis Tsipras—who campaigned heavily against austerity programs and had even discussed leaving the Euro—declared that Greece was "once again becoming a normal country" (The Economist, 2018). However, though it has balanced its budget, the Greek economy is still quite weak. As of June 2019, its official unemployment rate is 18 percent overall (almost three times the EU average) and almost 40.3 percent for workers under age 25. While this constitutes a decrease from the 2013 highs of 28 and 60 percent, it is still indicative of a struggling economy (Trading Economics, 2019).

zffoto/Shutterstock.com

Throughout the crisis the Greek government passed painful measures to avoid defaulting on Greece's foreign debt, which had risen to about $418 billion (173 percent of total GDP) by the beginning of 2015 (Trading Economics, 2015). While the 2019 debt level is somewhat lower ($403 billion), it is noteworthy that Greece has only repaid about ten percent of the debt it assumed as a result of the crisis (The Balance, 2019). The crisis was initially set off in December 2009 when President Papandreou "revised" his estimate of the Greek budget deficit from 6.7 percent of GDP to 12.7 percent, which severely undercut confidence in his government. Yet the accumulation of this debt was driven by several longer-term factors, including heavy government spending, an inefficient and corrupt tax collection system, a largely uncompetitive industrial base, ready access to cheap credit, and lax enforcement of EU financial rules (Nelson, Belkin, and Mix, 2010). To avoid default (failure to repay debts), Greece had to rapidly change its budget deficit to a budget surplus—it ran a 13.2 percent deficit in 2013 and had a small surplus by 2016 (Trading Economics, 2019). These macroeconomic improvements have come at a large cost, as the "long-term effects of the austerity programs over the past eight years are so deep-rooted that poverty as a way of life . . . is the real prospect for a huge percentage of the population" (Pine, 2018).

In assessing the crisis, revelations about the role of private investment banks, such as Goldman Sachs, have generated controversy. During the crisis, reports indicated that over the past decade they had helped Greece hide portions of its debt from public view through a complex array of derivatives and side deals, such as paying Greece to trade away future rights to long-term government revenues such as airport fees and lottery proceeds. Indeed, Greece's "original sin" regarding its entry into the euro zone was to hide debt through these methods in order to meet entrance requirements (Story, Thomas, and Schwartz, 2010). Yet such measures are legal, as there are no regulations that govern how a country handles its sovereign debt. As one IMF analyst noted, "if a government wants to cheat, it can cheat" (Story et al., 2010).

Watch the Carnegie Council Video:

"Greece, Goldman, and Financial Transparency?"

You Decide:

1. What policies should the Greek government enact?

2. What role do international institutions play in preventing, or facilitating recovery from, financial crises?

3. What does this situation reveal about the global financial system?

Yet the broad dynamics of the crisis are hardly unprecedented, as they resemble the basic cycle described in Kindleberger's sweeping history of financial crises (Kindleberger, Aliber, and Solow, 2005). The first phase of a crisis cycle is "displacement," which refers to a change in the system that alters profit opportunities and creates new opportunities for financial gain. There were several developments that brought increased attention to the mortgage and securities markets during the beginning of the century, including massive cash holdings by states such as China and the OPEC members, the real estate boom in the United States, extremely low interest rates in the United States, and new investment instruments that banks and investment firms had created for themselves. These factors were inextricably linked—the initial dilemma that led to this crisis was how to put to use the "giant pool of money" held by China, the OPEC states, and other investors (Glass and Davidson, 2008).

U.S. interest rates were extremely low, which meant that investing in dollars—traditionally considered the safest move for investors with large amounts of money—was not sufficiently profitable (U.S. Treasury bills at the time were only yielding 1 percent). At the same time, the low interest rates also meant that mortgages were less expensive for U.S. homeowners and that businesses had access to very inexpensive loans that could be leveraged for investment purchases. As housing prices were increasing, buying new or larger homes (financed by mortgages) was a good investment. Sensing opportunity, banks and other financial institutions created financial instruments to link the "pool" of money to the housing market, by selling securities based off of the value of these mortgages to large investors. In addition to banks, non-bank institutions—so-called **shadow banks**—were able to insert themselves into these processes by financing and investing in mortgages, thus increasing the amount of capital in circulation. Shadow banks include a wide variety of financial institutions, such as mortgage brokers, hedge funds, insurance companies, and investment firms. While they are not necessarily "shadowy" in nature, they are not subject to the same oversights and regulations as traditional banks.

shadow banks
Financial entities outside of the formal banking structure that engage in lending and credit-issuing activities.

As a result of this new securities market, the investors made a higher rate of return from the mortgages, homeowners reaped the benefits of lower interest rates, and everyone in this chain of economic interactions, from mortgage brokers to investment banks, made billions of dollars as intermediaries. Moreover, as the investments were backed by houses—whose values had been steadily increasing—many of these securities were highly rated by the credit agencies. Thus, the perception was that these investments were almost as safe as a money market account.

The second phase of the crisis—the so-called boom period in which money pours into these new opportunities—thus began. As the investors and bankers continued to reap profits, the "pool of money" became ever larger, and trillions of dollars continued to flow into this market. To further service the "pool," banks began to invent more investment instruments (essentially different ways to bundle these mortgages and securities together), and huge derivative markets based on the performance of these instruments began to emerge.

This led to the "overtrading" stage, which involves "pure speculation for a price rise, an overestimate of prospective returns," and excessive leveraging or "gearing," where additional debt is taken on purely for the purposes of making investments (Kindleberger, 2000). At some point in this process, the market for traditional mortgages became saturated; basically, everyone who was willing and able to purchase and/or refinance a home had already done so. Yet the "pool" continued to grow, and demand for these securities continued to increase.

To keep the market going, banks began to sell mortgages to "subprime" buyers who would have never qualified for mortgages under normal circumstances. Lending regulations were loosened so that prospective borrowers no longer had to provide proof of their ability to actually pay off their mortgages. Now, rather than having to show proof of income, such as paycheck stubs or bank statements, borrowers were only asked to provide estimates of their financial holdings and future earnings (these were disparagingly known as "liar's loans"). The rationalization for doing this was that even if some loans were not repaid, there would still be a sufficient flow of capital to keep the overall securities serviced. Even if the loans defaulted, the banks would get the real estate, which was considered at the time to be an ever-appreciating asset.

For their part, investment banks and related institutions continued to use an array of speculative instruments based off the mortgage securities, including derivatives linked to the performance of mortgage-backed securities, as well as so-called synthetic securities, which were essentially repackaged derivatives based off the derivatives based on the securities themselves. The market for collateralized debt obligations (CDOs), which functioned as de facto insurance for the mortgage-backed securities and the various derivatives, boomed. Given the panoply of instruments and their cross purposes, for many investment banks it was a "no lose" situation—they made fees for processing all of these investment flows, and even if the securities crashed, they could still recoup their losses via the CDOs. Thus their "bets" were effectively covered, and they stood to make a profit regardless of the actual outcome of the investment. Investment banks further maximized their profits, as well as their exposure, through excessive

AP Images/Thanassis Stavrakis

IMAGE 10.4 Responding to Crises—"All Pain No Gain?" Financial crises are "periods of dramatic change" (Chwieroth, 2010, p. 496) during which much of the economic and political status quo—including the competency of the state—may be called into question. Post-crises policies may exacerbate this situation, as they commonly entail debt reduction measures that are recessionary and can produce a politically difficult combination of increased unemployment, higher taxes, and fewer government services. Shown above are protestors outside Parliament in Athens, Greece, who are acting in response to the austerity policies enacted in the wake of their financial crisis. Though Greece finally emerged from austerity programs in 2018, its economy still faces major problems.

use of leveraging to obtain additional investments. By 2007, the five largest investment banks (Bear Stearns, Goldman Sachs, Lehman Brothers, Merrill Lynch, and Morgan Stanley) were leveraged at an average of over thirty to one, meaning that they owned assets, purchased through taking out loans, worth over thirty times the total equity of their firms (Government Accounting Office, 2009).

However, in 2007 and 2008, the "revulsion" or "panic" stage set in due to several directly related factors: increasing loan defaults by homeowners, plummeting real estate values, and severe liquidity problems of banks that were too entangled in this process. As homeowners failed to repay the mortgages, banks quickly found themselves without a stream of income from mortgage holders and holding properties of declining value that they were unable to sell. For their part, the highly-leveraged investment banks found themselves facing debt loads worth many times greater than their own net worth. As the mortgage market began to fall, the speculative markets and instruments built around it—whose total cash value was many times more than the value of the mortgages themselves—also collapsed. As a result, banks and investors literally ran out of money, and the credit market in the United States, and much of the financial world, collapsed.

Recovery and Reform: Challenges Facing Global Finance

LO 10-5 Critique the global financial arrangements that have emerged since the 2008 crisis, and evaluate the current status of the global financial architecture.

Though financial crises are not new to the global financial system, the 2008 crisis had a particularly profound and broad-based impact that is still apparent in global finance. Most immediately, the sheer amount of money involved was staggering—according to some estimates, the U.S. government alone devoted $13 trillion to help bail out its own financial sector, including direct financial assistance to the banks as well as selling bonds to help increase the supply of money (French, 2009). The crisis drove global FDI and trade to unprecedented declines in 2009—FDI outflows fell approximately 42 percent, and world trade slipped over 12 percent. In all, total global output, as measured by GDP, contracted by 2.3 percent in 2009—the worst worldwide decrease since World War II (WTO, 2010; IMF Survey, 2009). The longer-term economic impact is even more troubling. Some aspects of global commerce, such as global FDI and trade openness (trade as a percentage of GDP), remain below pre-crisis levels. In terms of economic growth rates, the world economy as a whole is still underperforming relative to pre-crisis levels. Overall, "the scars are largely healed but growth is still slow" (Blanchard, 2016).

Given these persistent and widespread consequences, the crisis and its aftermath also raise broader concerns about some of the fundamentals of the global financial system, including the leadership of the United States and the dominance of the dollar, the relevance of commercial liberal perspectives and policies, and the challenges in governing the global financial system. We now turn to these issues, which figure prominently in assessing the future of global finance.

U.S. Leadership and the Future of the Dollar

Unlike previous crises, which primarily struck developing or emerging countries, the 2008 crisis hit the developed countries the hardest, thus increasing trends toward a more multipolar financial order (Eichengreen, 2009). Although Germany and Canada remained strong, the United States entered a multiyear recession. Several countries in Europe, including the United Kingdom, Portugal, Ireland, Spain, Italy, and Greece, are still struggling with slow growth and high unemployment (see "A Closer Look: The Greek Financial Crisis"). At the same time, the Global South was much less affected by the immediate crisis and experienced rapid economic growth in its wake. Indeed, annual economic growth rates of less developed countries have been approximately two to four times that of their developed counterparts in the years since the crisis (IMF, 2019b).

The legacy of the 2008 crisis is complex and remains contentious. It originated in the United States, and early analyses noted "much of the world . . . blames U.S. financial excesses for the global recession" (Altman, 2009, p. 2). In the immediate aftermath, the United States was unable to get a policy consensus around expansionary macroeconomic policies among the G-20 states, which raised doubts about its influence (Drezner, 2014). However, more recent assessments counter that U.S. leadership—particularly the role of the Federal Reserve Bank in supporting European Central Banks (Tooze, 2018) and the United States' key role in convincing the G-20 to invest over a trillion dollars into emergency spending through the IMF—"proved crucial in crisis response" (Rediker, 2018).

In addition to raising questions about U.S. leadership, the crisis had broad geopolitical implications. Most significantly, it improved the relative global position of China as well as other emerging economies. China passed the United States as the largest economy (in terms of purchasing power parity) in 2016, and is the world's largest exporter. It is also the largest holder of U.S. foreign debt, with over $1.1 trillion in debt securities (U.S. Department of Treasury, 2019). The differential growth rates between the developed and developing economies have hastened the trend toward a broad multipolar financial order, with countries such as India, Indonesia, and Brazil taking their place among the world's largest economies (Price Waterhouse, 2017).

These developments have also raised questions about the continued role of the dollar as the world's leading currency. The dollar is still the dominant currency in the global financial system, and such dominance gives the United States significant leverage in the global economy. According to the IMF, it is the leading **reserve currency**. At the end of 2018, 62 percent of all foreign exchange reserves (money that states hold to help them maintain their balance of payments) were in dollars (IMF, 2019c). This implies that countries place a great deal of trust in the dollar, in that they use it as a store of value. Seven countries use the dollar as their currency, and another thirty-two anchor, or "peg," the value of their currency to the dollar in some way (IMF, 2018). Moreover, it is by far the most commonly used currency in global transactions, as 90 percent of all foreign exchange trading involves the dollar and 40 percent of the global bond market is issued in dollars (Amadeo, 2019).

Although the value of the dollar on the world market has been stable, some of the leading economies in the world, most notably China, have suggested that the dollar be replaced—or at

reserve currency
Currency held in large amounts by governments for the purpose of settling international debts and supporting the value of their national currency.

least supplanted—as the major currency of the global marketplace. Indeed, there are predictions that the dollar will decline as the dominant currency, and some argue that a more "multipolar" currency system would be viable as transaction costs become increasingly minimal (Eichengreen et al., 2017). More specifically, the Chinese renminbi, the euro, and the SDR (Special Drawing Rights) used by the IMF have been suggested as possibilities (Amadeo, 2019; Ocampo, 2019).

Yet none are presently a practical alternative. The EU has had severe problems with several member states, and some even argue that the fate of the euro is in question (Pisani-Ferry, 2014). SDRs would be impractical for individual countries to use, as they are not a true currency so much as a composite index of currencies used for reserve purposes by the IMF (Bosco, 2011). The currency most often mentioned as a potential replacement is the Chinese renminbi (Cukierman, 2015; Prasad, 2014). China has made concerted efforts to increase the global circulation of its currency and reportedly aspires to raise the global stature of the renminbi (Amadeo, 2019). However, the renminbi is problematic since global access to it remains restricted and doubts continue because of the repressive nature of the Chinese government. As one economist bluntly argued, "I could go there (China) and disappear. This doesn't inspire confidence. Once you start that kind of politics, you cannot be serious as a global currency" (Goodman, 2019).

Ultimately, despite these potential changes in the economic balance of power, the dominance of the dollar is unlikely to wane anytime soon. Paradoxically, the financial crisis served to increase support for the dollar. The foreign exchange reserves of emerging economies, including Brazil, Taiwan, India, and particularly China, were depleted as a result of the crisis and dollars were seen as a relatively risk-free way to replenish them (Prasad, 2014). In the developed world, the Federal Reserve Bank was energetic about circulating dollars into Europe in the aftermath of the crisis. Despite the blame that the United States received for the 2008 crisis, "the collapse reinforced the financial supremacy of Washington and New York" and "gave an entirely new dimension to the global dollar" (Tooze, 2018, p. xx).

Many countries worry about the long-term future of the U.S. economy given its sizeable debt, somewhat unresponsive political system, and increasingly antagonistic and unpredictable trade policy (IMF, 2019; Eichengreen, 2014). Despite these issues, the power of the dollar has deep historical roots as the "endurance of the dollar has been a foundational truism in global affairs since the end of World War II" (Goodman, 2019). Such dominance is not easy to overcome. While countries may signal an interest in lessening dependence on the dollar, ultimately the "U.S. dollar greases the wheels of global commerce, and legitimate businesses cannot risk losing access to it" (Rosenberg and Saravalle, 2018; see also Eichengreen et al., 2018). Thus though the dollar may be "unloved" (McKinnon, 2013), it "will remain the dominant reserve currency for a long time, mainly for want of better alternatives" (Prasad, 2014).

The End of the Liberal Consensus?

The crisis also ushered in a period of increased doubts about the ideological underpinnings of the global financial system: the free-market–oriented "Washington Consensus." Although the open exchanges of currencies and free movement of capital are viewed as foundational to liberal economics, the financial crisis undercut basic beliefs regarding the efficacy of the marketplace. Though globalization is generally related to positive outcomes such as economic growth and development (Wolf, 2004), in this instance the countries that fared better were the ones that were less integrated into the financial system. Among the larger economies of the world, India and China fared best. Interestingly, Moldova, a very small country with a rather primitive "cash-only system" of finance—banks and credit cards are largely nonexistent and savings are generally stored under mattresses or in drawers—was ranked by a leading financial journal as the fifth most stable economy in the world the year after the crisis (Tayler, 2009).

In the wake of the crisis, Roger Altman, a former U.S. Treasury Department official, remarked, "the long movement towards market liberalization has stopped," and "globalization itself is reversing. The long-standing wisdom that everyone wins in a single world market has been undermined." Micah White, co-founder of the Occupy Wall Street advocacy group, argued that "what broke in 2008 wasn't primarily the economy: it was the people's faith in the reigning world order" (White, 2018). Similarly, journalist Robert Kuttner (2018) posited that "the crash demonstrated the emptiness of the claim that markets could regulate themselves."

Such contentions are striking rebuttals of the commercial liberal perspective and the set of policy recommendations that emerged from this outlook, often referred to as "neoliberalism" or the "Washington Consensus." Foundational to this perspective is the efficacy of free markets, with minimal intervention—either regulatory or economic—from the state. Simply put, the economy should be governed more by voluntary market exchanges and "the primary role of government is to protect individuals and their property from aggression by others" (Gwartney, Lawson, and Hall, 2014, p. 1). The crisis served to undermine both the inherent trust in the market as well as the purported benefits of minimal state intervention, particularly as a key cause of the crisis was the failure of the state to properly regulate its financial markets.

Somewhat ironically, while the crisis represented "a shocking overturning of the prevailing laissez-faire ideology," in the response to the crisis "the ideology prevailed" (Tooze, 2018). This was readily apparent in the prevalence of austerity measures. Simply put, austerity is "the cutting of the state's budget to promote growth" (Blyth, 2014, p. 8). The general idea is that reducing state spending will allow for increased private investment for two reasons—businesses will be heartened by the smaller budget deficits that accompany reductions in government spending, and the smaller amount of state spending will no longer "crowd out" private investment. The end product is an improved business environment as well as balanced budgets. To a large extent, this approach effectively denies that the "inflation vs. unemployment" tradeoff (see Table 10.3) exists, as restrictive policies are viewed as a way to spur economic growth.

In the wake of the crisis, several European countries, including Portugal, Ireland, Italy, Greece, Spain, and to a lesser extent the United Kingdom, implemented these policies, instituting massive budget cuts in hopes of reducing their budget deficits and thus spurring economic growth. However, most analysts argue that these policies were counterproductive. Not only were the sometimes draconian cuts politically unpopular—former Greek Finance Minister Giannis Varoufakis referred to it as "fiscal waterboarding"—but they failed to reduce budget deficits. On the contrary, the cuts resulted in decreased tax revenues, which increased debt levels (Krugman, 2015; Blyth, 2013; Schui, 2014). Indeed, as economist Martin Wolf (2013) concluded "Austerity has failed. It turned a nascent recovery into stagnation."

Economists have long argued over the proper mixture of fiscal and monetary tools that a state should use to recover from an economic shock, and the controversy over austerity is no exception (Skidelsky, 2019; Alesina et al., 2019). Problems with austerity demonstrate the dangers of applying a common policy solution to financial situations that may be different, the dilemmas inherent in balancing fiscal and monetary policy tools, as well as the difficult nature of determining how active a state should be in its economy.

At the least, the widespread support of neoliberal policies has become more qualified, and many are arguing that we are currently witnessing the emergence of a "new heterogeneity" (Kirshner, 2014) as policy makers look to multiple ways to manage their economies. Some argue that the response to the crisis—particularly the juxtaposition of austerity measures with little real recourse against the financial institutions that helped to precipitate the crisis—is a root cause of much of the political upheavals in the developed world, particularly the rise of populist and nationalist movements (Tooze, 2018; White, 2018). Snyder (2019) argues that many states "broke" the promises of embedded liberalism and recommends "a revival of the basic practices of postwar liberalism: national-level democratic accountability, economic coordination through international institutions, and compromise on competing priorities" of providing social benefits while supporting open economies. Outside of the developed countries, a "Beijing Consensus" is seen by some as a possible alternative to the Washington Consensus (Kurlantzick, 2015). Though precise definitions of this consensus vary (Ferchen, 2013), it is generally portrayed as a more developmental and pragmatic approach in which the state plays a much heavier role in the marketplace and is particularly mindful of the distributional effects of its policies. As one Chinese economist noted, "When reforms drastically change the distribution of wealth or power in society, the government must take a stand and address challenges from the less favored" (Yao, 2011).

Regarding alternate theories of world politics, the crisis and its aftermath revealed strengths in perspectives critical of commercial liberalism. Marxists have long noted the inherent instability of capitalism, its susceptibility to speculative panics, and the need for strong state intervention in the financial system. Along these lines, the crisis revealed deep structural flaws in the capitalist order, particularly the tendency to overinvest, which creates an inherently unstable system (Kotz, 2013). As one analyst concluded, global capitalism is "in an ideological tailspin," and the crisis "has spawned a resurgence of interest in Karl Marx" (Panitch, 2009, p. 140).

For their part, feminist scholars note the gendered nature of the crisis and that the predominantly male culture in finance remains an impediment to meaningful reform. The banking sector of the economy has traditionally been driven by males (Griffin, 2013), and "male" traits—risk taking, aggression, and hypercompetitiveness—were driving factors behind the speculative surges that helped to create the

IMAGES 10.5A AND 10.5B **Women and Global Finance** Only 5.2 percent of Fortune 500 companies have a woman as CEO, and all of the large banks—from Citigroup to Goldman Sachs—employ just a few women in senior positions. Within the U.S. finance and insurance industries, women comprise only 14 percent of executive officers and board directors (Goudreau, 2013). Pictured left is Marillyn Hewson, President and CEO of defense contractor Lockheed-Martin, who has been ranked as the most powerful woman CEO of a Fortune 500 company. Pictured right is Christine Lagarde, a former French minister of finance and current president of the European Central Bank, who was the first woman to serve as managing director of the IMF.

financial crisis. Many critically pointed to "a testosterone-filled trading culture" (Scherer, 2010) and wondered if "the presence of more women on Wall Street might have averted the downturn" (Kay and Shipman, 2009).

Despite the widespread impact of the failures of the banking sector, there is little indication of meaningful change. A study of the British financial sector by their Commons Treasury committee found the industry to be quite resistant to change, as "an alpha-male culture is still prevalent in finance" (Morgan, 2018). In the United States, there were decidedly gendered elements in the responses of the bank leaders—who were exclusively male—to female investigators. Tellingly, Jamie Dimon, CEO of JPMorgan Chase, told a group of business leaders "he didn't know if" U.S. Senator Elizabeth Warren—a former professor of bankruptcy law at Harvard Law School who supervised the government rescue of troubled banks in 2008—"fully understands the global banking system" (Chipman, 2015). For her part, Warren noted that it "was not an accident" that none of the major banks were led by women. Regarding her expertise in the area, she noted that "The finance guys argue that if you're never in the club, you can't understand it, but I think they have it backward. Not being in the club means not drinking the Kool-Aid."

> *For the great difference between an ordinary casino where you can go into or stay away from, and the global casino of high finance, is that in the latter all of us are involuntarily engaged in the days' play.*
>
> **—SUSAN STRANGE, ECONOMIST AND INTERNATIONAL RELATIONS SCHOLAR**

Whither the International Financial Architecture?

The crisis revealed many underlying weaknesses in the global financial system, particularly the speed at which the crisis could spread, the true extent to which the world's financial markets are interconnected, and difficulties in controlling the global markets. Indeed, it is argued that the 2008 crisis was a "watershed" moment in history, as it was the first truly "systemic" crisis of the twenty-first century (Goldin and Mariathasan, 2015). Yet, ultimately, the major economies were able to avoid another Great Depression. Drezner (2014) argues that the system worked, as global trade did not implode and capital markets were able to provide liquidity to counteract the immediate effects of the crisis.

The general consensus is that the most effective institution in responding to the crisis was the U.S. Federal Reserve, which provided liquidity to the U.S. and European markets (Tooze, 2018; Kirshner, 2014). However, it was not a collective response so much as the "ad-hoc improvisation by the agency of a great power" (Kirshner, as quoted in Farrell, 2015). Despite the remarkable nature of the crisis itself, the policy response and recovery from the "crisis was a strangely conservative event" (Helleiner, 2014, p. 8) that threatened, though ultimately did not change, the status quo. Indeed, while some minor reforms were made, and "many holes in our (the United States') financial regulatory system are now plugged" (Merle, 2018), the underlying systemic factors that allowed the crisis to occur still exist.

Given these potential problems, various suggestions have been made for reforming the international financial architecture. Some argue that the banking system itself—specifically the use of leveraging—is fundamentally flawed and that much higher capital requirements should be imposed for banks; that is, they should be required to keep more money on hand and thus have less to devote to risky investment tools (LaGarde, 2015). As explained by Federal Reserve official Neel Kashkari, this would "make the banks fund themselves with their own money instead of borrowed money" and reduce the need for government-funded bailouts (quoted in Goldstein, 2016). Some suggest that automatic mechanisms should exist to account for current account imbalances, because currency prices should have some type of relationship to the external debt (or surplus) of a country (White, 2015).

As for financial institutions, there has been considerable criticism of the IMF, including its policies and internal practices such as underrepresenting emerging economies. There have also been calls to empower the IMF and World Bank to have stronger abilities to address imbalances and currency valuation issues (Kahn, 2015), as well as create an emergency fund that would enable them to quickly distribute financial support in times of crisis (Gregorio et al., 2018).

For its part, the IMF is aware of the widespread criticism of its policies and practices, and has made substantial efforts at reform. In particular, it has sought to give individual countries more flexibility by loosening the conditionality requirements to better take into account the specific needs of each recipient (IMF, 2009). It has also been very forthright in admitting its failure to foresee the 2008 global financial crisis and is trying to develop a more effective "early warning system" (Beattie, 2011; IMF, 2011). In 2010, the IMF approved reforms to its voting system, increasing the influence of China and India in line with their increasing financial contributions to the IGO (IMF, 2019f). The IMF also increased country representation of emerging markets on its board, and moved that all board members should be elected. Finally, the IMF voted to double its quotas (the amount of money that the IMF holds) to over $750 billion. Ostensibly these reforms increase the ability of the IMF to respond to crises, and counter the criticism that the United States and Europe largely run the organization (Mallaby, 2011).

In 2014, two important regional development banks emerged as alternatives to the IMF and World Bank (Engen and Prizzon, 2018). The BRICS countries launched the New Development Bank (see Chapter 5), with a capital base of $100 billion (Maasdorp, 2015). It is on track to disperse $40 billion in startup capital for "sustainable development" projects by 2021 (Silk Road Briefing, 2019). While the BRICS countries emphasize that it is intended as a complement rather than a rival to the IMF and World Bank, the NDB nonetheless represents a new assertiveness on the part of these countries.

That same year the Asia Infrastructure Investment Bank (AIIB), led by China, was also formed. Despite active lobbying by the United States to discourage membership, it has eighty-six members, including the United Kingdom, France, Germany, and Italy, giving it the second-largest global membership of any development bank—the World Bank is first with over 180 members (Gutner, 2018). Its purpose is to provide infrastructure loans for Asian countries and, as is the case with the NDB, to provide another alternative to the IMF.

The founding of the NDB and AIIB was driven in no small part by frustration with the existing system, particularly at the perceived underrepresentation of the emerging economies. Chinese leadership in both these ventures is also significant, as it evidences its

AP Images/MUCHTAR ZAKARIA

IMAGE 10.6 **Surrendering to the IMF?** A controversy surrounding multilateral institutions, such as the IMF, is that their policies are seen as another way in which powerful states of the Global North seek domination over those in the Global South. In this picture, taken January 15, 1998, Indonesian President Suharto signs an agreement for a $43 billion assistance and reform package, while IMF Managing Director Michel Camdessus looks on. This picture proved damaging for both Suharto and the IMF. Indonesians, who place a great value on symbolism and body language, viewed the picture as a humiliating loss of face for the president, who was forced out of office four months later. It was also an economic and public relations disaster for the IMF, helping to solidify negative opinions of the IMF within the developing world (Camdessus later apologized for his arm-crossing and his stance).

increased power and assertiveness in the global financial order. Political motivations aside, there are potential advantages to regional banks. First, they could function as a "lender of last resort" that could be "better placed to coordinate economic actions" (Desai and Vreeland, 2011, p. 114) given their proximity to the country in need of relief. Ideally, they could work alongside the IMF or the World Bank to resolve problems. Along those lines, it may be the case that a regional body could be better suited to help troubled countries maintain their credit ratings, as they are better situated to use informal pressure, rather than strict conditionality measures, to encourage countries to service their debts. Within the developing world, such organizations could also help foster a regional identity; unlike the IMF and World Bank, they would not be perceived as being driven by a few developed countries. Efforts also have been made to develop regional funds in Latin America, Africa, and the Middle East. Although regional banks represent a "challenge to the existing global economic order" (Kahn, 2015), they could potentially supplement the efforts of the IMF and the World Bank in seeking financial stability and economic growth. Promisingly, the IMF has delineated policies for how to best coordinate with these banks on related or common projects (Gregorio et al., 2018).

Though such organizations may prove useful in helping countries to respond to financial difficulties, many of the factors underlying the instability of the global financial system persist.

Thus, "the opportunity of securing a more prosperous and integrated global economy surely remains . . . [and] the challenge of achieving it now seems more intractable" (Wolf, 2014, p. 12). As UN Secretary-General Antonio Gutterres (UN, 2019g, p. xv) observed in 2019:

> Global levels of public and private debt continue to rise. Economic growth is often failing to reach the people who need it most. The essential transition towards environmentally sustainable production and consumption is not happening fast enough, and the impacts of climate change are growing more widespread and severe . . . Decisive policy action relies on multilateral, cooperative approaches in key areas such as pursuing climate action, mobilizing sustainable finance and redressing inequality.

At the same time, a growing portion of the global financial system is taking place completely outside of state control, as illicit global finance and tax havens continue to proliferate. Indeed, as shown in Figure 10.2, it is telling that world uncertainty—as indicated by a measure that systematically assesses the use of the word "uncertainty" in economic reports and assessments since 1996—reached a record high in 2019 (Hagan, 2019).

The debate over currency and monetary policies will remain as intense as ever, while global finance becomes increasingly complex and interconnected. Further adding to this turbulence is the related, and contentious, arena of international trade. It is that twin dimension of economic globalization that we consider next in Chapter 11.

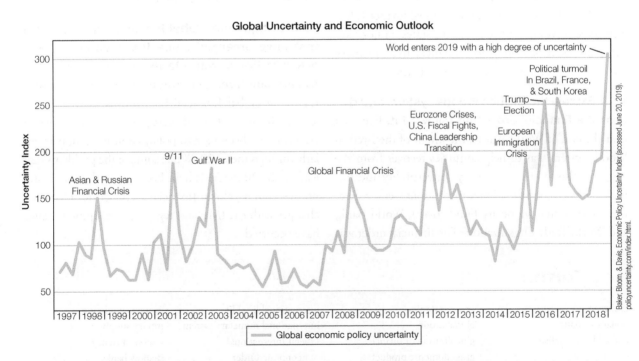

FIGURE 10.2 A Global Economy On Edge There are growing "concerns over the sustainability of global economic growth in the face of rising financial, social and environmental challenges" (UN, 2019d). Based on analysis of uncertainty as indicated in newspapers in twenty countries across the world, the World Uncertainty Index shown here indicates a rising level of consumer concern over unpredictability regarding economic policy and the global economy. In 2019, this uncertainty was fanned by trade tensions between the United States and China and the slowing of economic growth in the European Union.

Study. Apply. Analyze.

Chapter Summary

10-1 Define globalization and explain its implications for the global economy. Globalization refers to the integration or bringing together of states through increasing contact, communication, and trade, as well as increased global awareness of such integration. It implies that economies throughout the world are more intertwined and that states may be further limited in the extent that they can control their own economies.

10-2 Describe the facets of global finance, and assess the policy tools available to states. Global finance encompasses a broad variety of cross-border transactions, including international loans, foreign aid, remittances, and currency trading. It also includes investments such as the purchase of stocks, bonds, or derivatives. Another major facet of global finance is foreign direct investment (FDI). While states do not have complete control over global finance, their primary policy tools are monetary and fiscal policies.

10-3 Explain the Bretton Woods system, and discuss the financial order that followed it. Founded near the end of World War II, the intent of the Bretton Woods system was to help countries recover from the war, and also to ensure currency convertibility and free trade between countries. Three institutions were created: the International Monetary Fund (IMF), World Bank, and World Trade Organization. The financial order was

premised on liberal trade and the financial leadership of the United States.

10-4 Describe the stages of the 2008 financial crisis, and assess its impact on the global economy. There were four basic stages of the financial crisis: displacement, boom, overtrading, and revulsion. The first stage was marked by the advent of mortgage-backed securities as an investment tool. In the second stage, money poured into these tools, eventually reaching the overtrading phase as the investments became increasingly risky. In the revulsion stage the market, which was largely premised on mortgage-backed securities and the related investment tools, collapsed. The crisis caused trillions of dollars of damage to the world economy.

10-5 Critique the global financial arrangements that have emerged since the 2008 crisis, and evaluate the current status of the global financial architecture. The crisis raised multiple questions regarding global financial institutions as well as the leadership of the United States. Since then, increased attention has been paid to policy coordination, particularly through the G-20. While some of the problems that lead to the 2008 Crisis have been resolved, there is still no overarching global financial architecture. However, changes with the IMF and regional development banks have occurred.

Key Terms

arbitrage
dollar overhang
embedded liberalism
exchange rate
fixed exchange rates
floating exchange rates

geo-economics
globalization
globalization of finance
gross domestic product
    (GDP)
illicit financial flows

international liquidity
international monetary system
Liberal International
    Economic Order
    (LIEO)
monetary policy

money laundering
money supply
reserve currency
shadow banks
speculative attacks

Suggested Readings and Resources

Collier, Paul. (2018). *The Future of Capitalism: Facing the New Anxieties.* London, England: Penguin UK.

Diamond, Jared. (2019). *Upheaval: Turning Points for Nations in Crisis.* New York: Little, Brown and Company.

Eichengreen, Barry, Mehl, Arnaud, & Chitu, Livia. (2019). *How global currencies work: past, present, and future.* Princeton, NJ: Princeton University Press.

IMFdirect: blog-imfdirect.imf.org. A blog/forum sponsored by the International Monetary Fund.

Mattli, Walter. (2019). *Darkness by Design: The Hidden Power in Global Capital Markets.* Princeton, NJ: Princeton University Press.

Project Syndicate: project-syndicate.org/section/economics. Selection of short opinion pieces and longer articles from wide range of academics and policymakers.

Shelley, Louise. (2018). *Dark Commerce: How a New Illicit Economy is Threatening Our Future.* Princeton, NJ: Princeton University Press.

Tooze, Adam. (2018). *Crashed: How a decade of financial crises changed the world.* London, England: Penguin.

Carnegie Council Videos

Key Term Videos

- Geo-economics
- Globalization
- International Monetary System

Additional Videos

- Devin Stewart Interviews Ian Bremmer. "The End of the Free Market."
- Donaldson, Thomas, Neal Flieger, Stephen Jordan, Seamus McMahon, and Christian Menegatti. "Restoring Trust in the Global Financial System."
- Eisenman, Joshua. "China, Surveillance and 'Belt & Road'"
- Farmer, Roger E. A. "How the Economy Works: Confidence, Crashes and Self-Fulfilling Prophecies."
- Rollert, John Paul. "Greed, Movies and Capitalism."
- Sormon, Guy. "Economics Does Not Lie: A Defense of the Free Market in a Time of Crisis."
- Stiglitz, Joseph E., Bert Koenders, and Jose Antonio Ocampo. "Reform of the International Monetary and Financial System."
- Vocke, William. "The Power of Economic Models."

Chapter 11

International Trade in the Global Marketplace

IMAGE 11.1 Globalization and Carbonation Multinational corporations are major players in the globalization of the world economy. Coca-Cola—one of the most recognizable brands in the world—illustrates this, with over 1.9 billion servings consumed daily. Shown here are some of its products in China, which is one of its most important growth markets. Coca-Cola was the first foreign company allowed into China after the Communist Revolution in 1949 and recently celebrated its 40th year of doing business there (Fahs, 2019). Coca-Cola employs over 51,000 local Chinese workers in forty-five plants located in China (Jing, 2018).

Learning Objectives

LO 11-1 Evaluate the deepening of trade ties between countries, and articulate how these ties relate to multinational production processes and global labor.

LO 11-2 Explain the major facets of economic liberalism, and contrast with mercantilism.

LO 11-3 Specify the political implications of trade, and apply the insights of hegemonic stability theory to the global trade order.

LO 11-4 Identify and assess the tools of state policy in the area of international trade as well as their economic effects.

LO 11-5 Assess the role of the World Trade Organization (WTO) in facilitating global trade, and appraise future prospects for the global trade order.

" *Globalization has changed us into a company that searches the world, not just to sell or to source, but to find intellectual capital—the world's best talents and greatest ideas.*"

—JACK WELCH, FORMER CEO OF GENERAL ELECTRIC

As you struggle to make payments on your college tuition, your father calls with some bad news: his employer has decided to move its production to India in order to save money by hiring lower-paid foreign workers where there are no trade unions. Now your father faces unemployment. The downside of globalized international trade has been brought home, and you fear a decline in your quality of life. Or so it would appear as you contemplate your future clad in Levi jeans no longer produced in the United States and Calvin Klein shirts made in China. Trying to find meaning in the whirlwind of international trade going on around you, you race off to your international economics course, where you hope you can derive some insight. And you are in luck. Your professor's lesson today: "The Impact of International Trade on Global and National Circumstances." She introduces her topic by telling you that trade across national borders is the biggest part of the globalization of world politics. She begins by quoting former World Bank president Paul Wolfowitz: "I like globalization; I want to say it works, but it's hard to say that when 600,000,000 people are slipping backwards."

You learn that scholars also hold competing views about the consequences of the globalization of international trade. To construct an objective evaluation of these rival interpretations, consider leading ideas about various trade policies rooted in past thinking. In this chapter, you will focus on the contest between liberalism and mercantilism, two dominant sets of values that underlie the different trade strategies states pursue in their quest for power and wealth. However, the best place to start is by identifying emerging trends in the globalization of international trade.

> *We must ensure that the global market is embedded in broadly shared values and practices that reflect global social needs, and that all the world's people share the benefits of globalization.*
>
> **—KOFI ANNAN, FORMER SECRETARY-GENERAL OF THE UNITED NATIONS**

Globalization and Trade

LO 11-1 Evaluate the deepening of trade ties between countries, and articulate how these ties relate to multinational production processes and global labor.

Evidence of global trade is as close to you as the clothes you wear and the coffee you drink. Yet how can we gauge the true extent to which commerce has become more global? Is the increase in international trade really significant, or is it just an artifact of the increased amount of total goods—both foreign and domestic—now available to us? One relatively straightforward proxy is the degree of **trade integration** in the world economy, which is simply the extent to which the growth rate in world trade increases faster than the growth rate of world *gross domestic product* (GDP). As trade integration grows, so does globalization, because states' interdependence increases as their exports

trade integration
The difference between growth rates in trade and gross domestic product (GDP).

account for an increasing percentage of their GDP (the value of the goods and services produced within a given country).

The index of trade integration reveals that international trade has continually expanded over the past decades. For example, since World War II, the world economy (as measured by GDP) has expanded by a factor of six while global trade has increased twenty times. Moreover, trade makes up an increasingly large portion of states' economies. Since 1960, world exports, as a percentage of GDP, have increased from just under 12 percent to almost 30 percent. In 2017, world exports amounted to $22.9 trillion (World Bank, 2018a). As shown in Figure 11.1, these trends persist. Despite recent declines, growth in world trade still exceeds the growth of global GDP. Although the general trend is toward greater integration, countries differ in the degree to which their economies participate in global commerce.

Growth in World Trade and GDP, 1981–2017

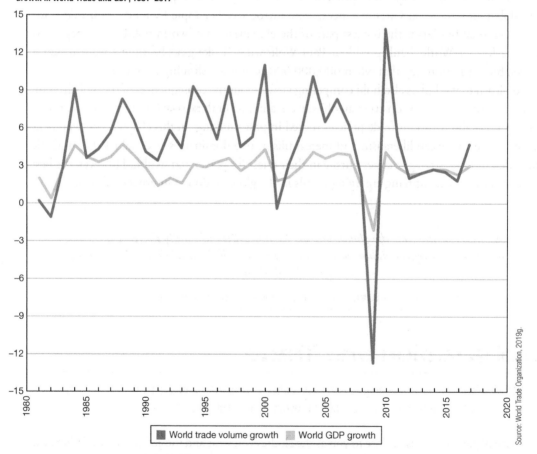

Source: World Trade Organization, 2019g.

FIGURE 11.1 The Growth of Global Trade Integration 1981–2017 When the annual percentage change in the volume of world trade grows faster than the annual growth rate of the combined world economy, trade integration increases. As shown in this figure, world trade generally grows faster than GDP (as noted by values of over one on the yellow points for each year). However, in 2009 world trade declined dramatically, by 12.2 percent, a casualty of the 2008 financial crisis. The 2010 rebound was just as dramatic, with a 13.8 percent surge in trade volume. Yet overall trade integration has lagged since then, finally returning to the historical average level of 1.5 in 2017.

Global trade integration has become most rapid as a result of the increasing participation of the Global South in world trade; their share of global exports grew from 10 percent in 1980 to almost 43 percent in 2017 (WTO, 2019b), fueled predominantly by Asia's growth in the share of new export products.

Trade is one of the most prevalent and visible aspects of the globalized world economy. However, globalization is a multifaceted phenomenon, encompassing a variety of often inter-related actions. There is a close relationship between trade and the global financial markets, as exchange rates set the values for traded goods, and capital flows are often necessary to finance these commercial activities. Trade is also inextricably linked to two other important aspects of globalization: the globalization of production and the globalization of labor. Understanding these components of globalization, as well as their relationship with trade, is important to understanding the complex world economy.

> *Global interdependence today means that economic disasters in developing countries could create a backlash on developed countries.*
>
> **—ATAL BIHARI VAJPAYEE, FORMER PRIME MINISTER OF INDIA**

Trade, Multinational Corporations, and the Globalization of Production

Selling products to consumers in another country often requires companies to establish a presence abroad, where they can produce goods and offer services. Traditionally, the overseas operations of *multinational corporations* (MNCs) (see Chapters 5 and 6) were "appendages" of a centralized hub. Today the pattern is more diffuse. Made feasible by the revolution in communication and transportation, production facilities are located around the world.

Consider the global nature of the production of Dell computers, whose supply chain involves eight countries outside of the United States (see Map 11.1). Every Dell computer that is sold, in effect, generates trade between nine different countries. The automobile industry is even more complex—on average automobiles contain over 20,000 parts, which can be obtained from thousands of suppliers from locations around the world (Kapadia, 2018). As economist Richard Baldwin notes, "the formation of global production networks and supply chains has changed the center of gravity of the world economy" (Baldwin et al., 2013, p. 3). Trade is no longer viewed as a bilateral interaction but as part of a broader, multi-country chain of production and commerce.

This **globalization of production** has transformed the global economy. It once made sense to count trade in terms of flows between countries, and that practice continues because national account statistics are still gathered using states as the unit of analysis. But that picture increasingly fails to portray current realities. Countries do not really trade with each other; corporations do. Altogether MNCs are now responsible for about one-fourth of the world's production and two-thirds of global exports. Indeed, a substantial portion of current global trade is **intra-firm trade**, that is, commerce that takes place *between* an MNC's cross-border

globalization of production
Transnationalization of the production process, in which finished goods rely on inputs from multiple countries outside of their final market.

intra-firm trade
Cross-national trade of intermediate goods and services within the same firm.

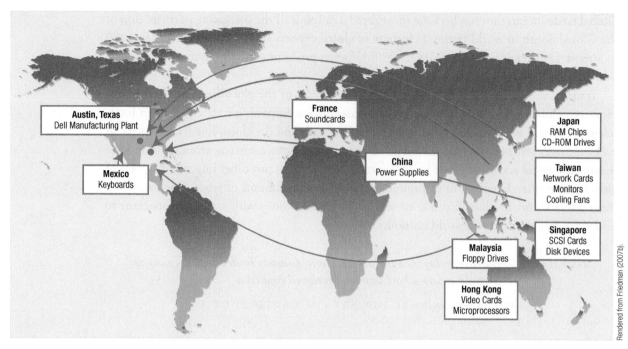

MAP 11.1 The Global Supply Chain The globalization of production means that it is often hard to discern exactly where a good is "from." This map shows the supply chain for the production of Dell computers. Supply chains such as this have a significant influence on the world economy, reflecting increasing levels of cross-border integration and the "networked" nature of interdependence. Thomas Friedman even goes so far as to offer a "Dell Theory" of conflict prevention, which posits that states that are part of common major supply chains are less likely to go to war.

Think It Through   Based on the map, where is a Dell computer "from"?

affiliates. For example, almost 50 percent of U.S. imports are of this nature (World Bank, 2017; Lanz and Miroudot, 2011).

MNCs are the primary agents in the globalization of production. Due to their size and scope, they are often massive nongovernmental organizations (NGOs) that rival states in financial resources (see Table 6.1). As they facilitate large commercial flows across national borders, these global conglomerates are also integrating national economies into the worldwide market. In the process, the movement of investments across borders is facilitating a level of social homogeneity by causing "countries to adopt similar institutions and practices to organize economic life. . . . FDI is a conveyor of norms, technologies, and corporate practices" (Prakash and Potoski, 2007, p. 738). In short, foreign direct investment (FDI) affects global identities as well as global trade.

Although the effects of FDI are controversial (see Chapter 5), many agree that the *globalization of production* will only increase. FDI flows—the amount of new investment entering a country in a given year—increased one-hundred-fold from 1970 to 2000, peaking at over $1.9 trillion in 2007. FDI levels plummeted to $1.1 trillion in 2009 as a result of the global financial crisis of 2008. They recovered to $1.65 trillion in 2011 (WDI, 2013), and declined again to $1.3 trillion by 2018 (UNCTAD, 2019c).

Within these broad trends, the rise of the Global South as a fully engaged participant in FDI stands out. Developing countries are increasingly the recipients of investments from abroad. Between 1995 and 2014, net inflows of FDI to developing countries increased over sevenfold, from $98 billion to over $706 billion. The Global South countries are also investing outside of their own borders. In 2018, net outflows of FDI from developing countries reached record levels of 54 percent of total FDI outflows (UNCTAD, 2019c).

The recent financial crisis has heightened this pattern. Although the developed countries experienced a 25 percent drop in FDI inflows, investment into the Global South continued to grow, and its post-crisis growth has outstripped that of the developed world (UNCTAD, 2015). However, large differences exist among the companies investing overseas to expand their global financial presence and trade, as well as among the targets of FDI inflows (see Figures 11.2A and 11.2B).

FDI Inflows, 1995-2018 ($US billion)

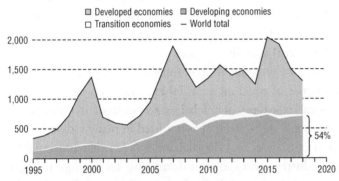

Top 20 Host Economies, 2017 and 2018 ($US billion)

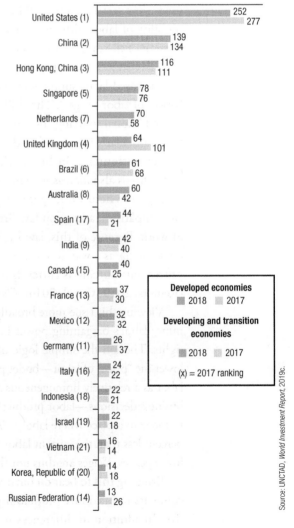

FIGURES 11.2A AND FIGURE 11.2B **The Shifting Distribution of Foreign Direct Investments** As the figure (left) demonstrates, despite the longer-term growth of FDI, the market is still recovering from the 2008 financial crisis (see Chapter 10). Historically, while FDI growth averaged 21 percent per year in the 1990s and eight percent from 2000 to 2007, since then it has averaged one percent. The slow-down is due to a variety of political and economic factors, including increased restrictions on FDI in the transition economies as well as reduced profits. Moreover, FDI in the developing countries surpassed investment in the Global North in 2014 and 2018. Shown on the right are the most popular FDI destinations in 2017 and 2018, based on the volume of FDI inflows. Developing and transition economies make up five of the top ten host countries for FDI and reflect a growing interest for investing in developing and transition economies.

Source: UNCTAD, *World Investment Report*, 2019c.

The Globalization of Labor

globalization of labor
Integration of labor markets, predicated by the global nature of production as well as the increased size and mobility of the global labor force.

Goods cannot be produced without labor. The globalization of production is thus inextricably linked to the **globalization of labor**. Labor is a particularly contentious aspect of globalization because it directly links individuals with the global economy, as illustrated by issues such as undocumented immigration (see Chapter 12), the use of child labor, and *outsourcing*.

The globalization of labor has emerged as a result of related changes in the world economy and global demographics. As evident from the growing volume of global FDI, an increasing amount of productive capital is mobile and can readily change locations according to the firm's desires as well as the perceived advantages of prospective host countries. Businesses are increasingly able to use labor from multiple countries and to switch locations when conditions change.

At the same time, there is mobility in the workforce as individuals move from one country to another. Although completely accurate estimates of migrant flows are virtually impossible to obtain, the UN (2018a) estimates that around 244 million people work outside of their home countries. Moreover, the overall size of the global workforce has increased greatly over the past few decades. By 2017, the total global labor force was 3.46 billion people, having increased more than fourfold since 1980 (WDI, 2019). Comparing these two figures reveals that the mobility of labor, although substantial, is far less than the mobility of capital, as only a small portion of the overall labor pool (.07 percent) actually relocates to another country.

Taken at face value, this does not bode well for global labor. In terms of supply and demand, the increased labor supply—in the absence of equal increases in demand—acts to depress the "price" of labor (wages). The ability of capital to seek out global sources of labor at a lower cost, termed "global sourcing" or more commonly outsourcing, has occurred in many industrial sectors, particularly in lower-skilled manufacturing sectors where labor is more readily substitutable.

Yet outsourcing in higher-skill industry areas—from information technology to legal research—is also increasingly prominent. In Gurgaon, India, for example, lawyer Ritu Solanki earns $50 an hour working for a legal-outsourcing company to draft contracts and legal memos. By comparison, a London law firm would likely charge up to $400 an hour for the same type of work. Because of this, law firms and corporate legal departments are beginning to look to outsourcing as a way to cut costs. According to recent estimates, the global market for legal-process outsourcing is currently $4.6 billion, and is predicted to reach $24.1 billion by 2024 (Reuters, 2019; Gogel, 2014; *The Economist*, 2010e, p. 69).

Viewing this issue more broadly, the key question is the extent to which globalization undermines labor's bargaining power in seeking to obtain two main goals: living wages and worker rights. Though the simple logic of supply and demand—that increased labor supply serves to lower the "price" of labor—bodes poorly for wage levels, it oversimplifies the situation by treating labor as a relatively homogeneous and interchangeable good. Such a view ignores a key factor in business decisions—labor productivity. For example, it would not make sense for a corporation to move to a place where labor is 50 percent less expensive if the productivity of that labor is 75 percent less than the current labor force, as such a move would result in a net increase in operating expenses. Wages are thus not the only factor that determines where global capital will locate.

Bringing this to bear on outsourcing—which involves corporate use of gaps in wages across countries to maximize profitability—there is evidence that the practice is becoming less effective. In addition to differences in productivity across countries, some firms are beginning to

Kham/Reuters

IMAGE 11.2 Struggles with Globalization After decades of communist rule, Vietnam has opened up to the global economy, enjoying rapid growth since 1990. This is due in part to the influx of foreign capital, as Vietnam is known as a "cheaper-than-China" location for foreign direct investment (Bloomberg, 2011). Yet difficulties remain, and repression of labor rights is endemic. This is particularly the case among the female labor force, which provides a majority of the labor in light-manufacturing industries. Shown above, employees work on an assembly line in a shoe factory in a village outside of Hanoi.

rediscover the advantages of producing goods close to where they are ultimately sold, as higher labor costs may be offset by other factors such as lower inventory requirements, quicker customer service, lower transport costs, and lower risk of supply chain interruptions.

Similar trends are apparent in the service industries, particularly the high-tech sector. Technology firms such as IBM and HP led the **outsourcing** charge during the 1980s and 1990s, moving such services as data management, call centers, and software assistance abroad. Yet in addition to some of the issues faced in manufacturing, service industries have "become keener to the social and political ramifications of outsourcing" (Saginor, 2012), particularly consumer backlash from the practice. As a result, outsourcing is on the decline across many industrial sectors, and the practice of **near-sourcing** is on the rise. Although this does not represent a complete reversal in the global nature of the supply chain, it does appear that many businesses have rediscovered the importance of location as they seek to "find the perfect mix of jobs that can be moved to foreign countries or be performed locally" (Hutchins, 2015).

Further supporting these trends, there is evidence that the gap between labor costs across countries may be lessening. As skill and education levels, and thus productivity, have increased in the Global South, countries that have traditionally been abundant sources of cheap labor have seen sharp increases in labor costs over the past few years. For example, accounting for productivity levels, manufacturing labor costs in China in 2018 were 24 percent higher than in Mexico and 51 percent higher than in Vietnam (Duffin, 2019). Such trends accelerated due to the 2008 global financial crisis, as post-crisis wage levels in the Global North have stagnated, while wages in the

outsourcing
Transfer of jobs by a corporation usually headquartered in a Global North country to a Global South country able to supply trained workers at lower wages.

near-sourcing
Locating production or services closer to where the goods or services are sold, in order to increase efficiency.

Global South, particularly the emerging economies, have risen significantly (ILO, 2015). To the extent that rising wages connote the expansion of a middle class in the Global South, such trends offer support for the liberal economic perspective that global commerce—despite its disruptive effects in the short term—may lead to development and economic prosperity in the long run.

That said, empirical studies of this issue indicate that globalization is problematic for low-skilled labor, which is more readily interchangeable across countries. Yet even though some workers may face lower wages, globalization acts to increase the purchasing power of these workers. In concordance with liberal economic theory, global commerce enables consumers to purchase a greater selection of goods at lower prices than would be the case without globalization. Indeed, an IMF study found that though globalization had lowered the wage levels in some states, the losses were offset by increases in their purchasing power. In short, though globalization "reduced labor's share of the pie, it has made the whole pie bigger" (*The Economist*, 2007, p. 84).

A similar dynamic occurs between the globalization of labor and labor rights. In this case the concern is that competition for capital and the increased supply of labor could have an adverse effect on labor rights, including the right to form unions (collective bargaining) and to legal protections from morally questionable labor practices such as the use of child labor and slave labor. Anecdotal evidence about "sweatshops" and the repression of union rights in the name of profit abound; companies as varied as Unocal, Walt Disney, Nike, and Apple have suffered embarrassment and financial costs for their associations with poor labor practices.

Yet comprehensive studies reveal a more complex reality. Although some liberal reforms, such as those associated with IMF and World Bank programs (see Chapter 6), are damaging to labor rights (Blanton, Blanton, and Peksen, 2015a), other aspects of globalization are more amenable to labor. MNCs, for example, often bring in better technology and labor policies than domestic corporations (Greenhill, Mosley, and Prakash, 2009; Graham, 2000). To the extent that they are drawn to skilled labor pools, they can also encourage countries to increase the skill and productivity of their labor force via education and health care reforms (Blanton and Blanton, 2012a; Mosley, 2011). Increased foreign investment has also been found to be related to decreased incidents of child labor (Neumayer and de Soysa, 2005).

Though most studies have found the *globalization of production* and the *globalization of labor* to be—on balance—positive developments for societies, the gains have not been spread equally across or within societies. As noted by economist Dani Rodrik (2008), "[g]lobalization has exposed a deep fault line between groups who have the

IMAGE 11.3 Child Labor in a Global System
Globalization is sped not only by the rapid expansion of technology but by the availability of cheap labor in some countries that take advantage of their people's low wages to make products highly competitive in the globalized marketplace. Here, a child labors under hazardous conditions and at extremely low wages in Bangladesh, producing goods that cost less than those made where labor unions protect workers.

AP Images/PAVEL RAHMAN

skills and mobility to flourish in global markets and those who either do not have these advantages or perceive the expansion of unregulated markets as inimical to social stability." This inequity has proven persistent, as there is rampant backlash against globalization, and "even globalization's biggest boosters now concede that it has produced lopsided benefits and that something will have to change" (Rodrik, 2019).

Whatever the overall influence of globalization on social well-being, fears about globalization persist. Though it creates winners and losers, the negative consequences of globalization—companies outsourcing their work or using child labor—are quite visible and strike people profoundly. A statement by an American whose software-testing job was outsourced to India is telling: "The fact that they not only outsourced my job, but my entire industry, makes me feel powerless and paralyzed. . . . Frankly, this situation has created problems that are way too big for one person like me to solve" (Cook and Nyhan, 2004). Alternatively, the gains from globalization, such as less expensive products and the gradual diffusion of technologies, are often unnoticed as their benefits are widely dispersed and shared by all. Thus, though globalization may be good for societies as a whole, the losers of globalization attract much more attention than the winners. As we will see, similar dynamics are apparent in many of the controversies surrounding trade policy.

Contending Trade Strategies

LO 11-2 Explain the major facets of economic liberalism, and contrast with mercantilism.

International trade is a far-reaching and hotly debated dimension of globalization, and the differing sides of the trade debates each offer their own set of policy prescriptions. To understand the trade strategies that states may pursue, it is important to understand the aspects of economic liberalism and mercantilism, and the historical context of the global trade order that guides their international economic decisions.

The Shadow of the Great Depression

The institutional basis for the post–World War II economic order began at the 1944 meeting at Bretton Woods, New Hampshire (see Chapters 6 and 10). Over the course of the next three years, the leaders founded the liberal economic order based around convertible currencies and free trade. While the International Monetary Fund and the World Bank emerged as the leading financial institutions, the task of liberalizing world trade later fell to the General Agreement on Tariffs and Trade (GATT).

The basic mission of the GATT was to encourage free trade among countries by reducing trade barriers and serving as a common forum for resolving trade disputes. The GATT had three primary principles: reciprocity, nondiscrimination, and transparency. **Reciprocity** calls for the mutual lowering of trade barriers, so countries that lowered their tariffs could expect their trading partners to do the same. According to the **nondiscrimination** principle, all members have the same level of access to the markets of other member states. In practice, nondiscrimination had two specific forms, the **most-favored nation (MFN) principle** and national treatment. The MFN principle holds that the tariff preferences granted to one state must be granted to all others—in other words, there could be no "favored nation" among members. National

reciprocity
Mutual or reciprocal lowering of trade barriers.

nondiscrimination
Principle that goods produced by all member states should receive equal treatment, as embodied in the ideas of most favored nation (MFN) and national treatment.

most-favored nation (MFN) principle
WTO rule requiring any advantage given by one WTO member also be extended to all other WTO members, thus disallowing "favored nations."

Iain Masterton/Alamy Stock Photo

IMAGE 11.4 Cascading Globalization: Communist China Chooses to Convert to Capitalism and Consumerism Shown here is one example of China's growing consumerism: a view of the huge South China Mall in Dongguan, the world's biggest shopping center. Opened in 2005, the mall has 7.1 million feet of leasable shopping area, and includes windmills and theme parks. In all, China has two of the world's largest malls (Emporis, 2012). China has long embraced America's "shop-'til-you-drop" ethos and is overtaking the United States in many areas of consumer spending (Ranasinghe, 2013).

transparency
With regard to free trade, the principle that barriers to trade must be visible and thus easy to target.

treatment means that foreign goods are treated the same as domestic goods, and that countries are not able to enact policies, such as taxes or other regulations, to give their domestic products any advantage over foreign products. Finally, the GATT called for **transparency** in trade policy, meaning that trade regulations and barriers need to be clearly articulated.

Overall, the GATT was successful in liberalizing trade. When the institution was formed, the primary barrier to trade was tariffs (taxes on imported goods). In a series of successive meetings, or "rounds," held from 1947 to 1994, the average tariff levels were lowered from 40 percent to just below 5 percent. When the Uruguay Round was concluded in 1994, the GATT became the World Trade Organization (WTO), which further strengthened the organization by giving it the power to settle disputes between members. This dispute settlement mechanism gave the WTO the ability to enforce its rules, and the WTO has settled hundreds of disputes among its members since 1994. In addition to gaining additional power as an institution, the organization has grown stronger in terms of members—since 1947 its membership has grown from 23 countries to 164.

Although liberalization has spread as a policy principle around the world (Simmons, Dobbin, and Garrett, 2006), not all states consistently support the liberal tenet that governments should not actively manage trade flows. Indeed, *commercial liberalism* (see Chapter 10) is under attack in many states, including some of liberalism's supposed proponents, which are under domestic pressure to protect industries and employment at home.

Next, we review the basic philosophical beliefs that undergird trade policy and the role of trade within the global political system before turning to the specific policy tools that states use in international trade.

The Clash Between Liberal and Mercantilist Values

How should states cope in the globalized political economy to best manage economic change? Broadly put, governments need state cooperation in liberalizing trade to maximize their wealth. At the same time, states have political incentives to put their own welfare first, thus undermining such cooperation. Thus many controversies in the international political economy are ultimately reducible to differences between liberalism and mercantilism. A comparison of their divergent theoretical positions on five central questions illuminates the issues of debate that divide these schools today (see Table 11.1).

TABLE 11.1 Key Differences between Liberalism and Mercantilism

	Liberalism	Mercantilism
Economic Relations	Harmonious	Conflictual
Major Actors	Households, firms	States
Goal of Economic Activity	Maximize global welfare	Serve the national interest
Priority of Economics vs. Politics	Economics determines politics	Politics determines economics
Explanation for Global Change	A dynamic, ever-adjusting equilibrium	The product of shifts in the distribution of states' relative power

Commercial Liberalism Commercial liberalism proceeds from the idea that humans are naturally inclined to cooperate. Thus, progress through mutually beneficial exchanges is possible, both to increase prosperity and to enlarge individual liberty under the law. In commercial liberalism, economic activity can contribute to global welfare, and the major problems of capitalism (boom-and-bust cycles, trade wars, poverty, and income inequalities) can be managed. One of the globe's "great causes" (Bhagwati, 2004) is to promote free international trade to lift the poor from poverty and to expand political liberties.

Adam Smith laid the foundations for commercial liberalism in 1776 when he wrote the now-classic *The Wealth of Nations*. In it, he argued how the "invisible hand" of an unregulated market, guided by humanity's natural tendency to "truck, barter, and exchange" in pursuit of private interest, could serve the globe's collective, or public, interest by creating efficiency and gains. According to Smith, if individuals rationally pursue their own self-interest, they will maximize societal interests as well.

Regarding trade between states, the key concept Smith fostered was the idea of **absolute advantage**, the belief that countries should produce goods in which their cost of production is lowest in comparison with other countries. As Smith (1902 [1776], p. 162) reasoned, "If a foreign country can supply us with a commodity cheaper than we ourselves can make it, better buy it off them with some part of the produce of our own industry, employed in a way in which we have some advantage." Though the idea was revolutionary, it raises an obvious dilemma—what if a country does not have an absolute advantage in anything?

David Ricardo, an eighteenth-century political economist, addressed this issue with his concept of **comparative advantage**. Ricardo argued that all parties, even those with no absolute advantage in anything, can benefit from trade. How? According to the principle of comparative advantage, countries should specialize in whichever good has a lower *opportunity cost* (the value of whatever the country forgoes producing). In other words, a country should focus on the production of goods that it produces comparatively cheaply, rather than other goods that it could conceivably produce but only at a relatively higher cost.

This was a profound concept with important implications for liberal theory as well as the discipline of economics. In a famous incident, economist and Nobel laureate Paul Samuelson was challenged by a mathematician to name a proposition in the social sciences that was both "true and nontrivial." Sometime after that question was posed, he arrived at his answer: comparative advantage. As he reasoned, "that it is logically true need not be argued before a mathematician; that it is not trivial is attested by the thousands of important and intelligent men who have never been able to grasp the doctrine for themselves or to believe it after it was explained

absolute advantage
The liberal economic concept that a state should specialize in the production of goods in which their costs of production are lowest compared with those of other countries.

comparative advantage
The concept in liberal economics that every state will benefit if it specializes in the production of goods that it can produce at a lower opportunity cost relative to other goods.

TABLE 11.2 Comparative Advantage and the Gains from Trade

Country	Work Productivity per Hour		Before Specialization		Specialization, No Trade		Specialization with Trade	
	Textiles	Autos	Textiles	Autos	Textiles	Autos	Textiles	Autos
China	9	3	900	300	990	270	910	300
United States	4	2	400	200	320	240	400	210

to them" (Samuelson, 1969, p. 683). For our purposes, comparative advantage shows that trade benefits all parties that partake in it. This principle is the basis for commercial liberalism's claim that free trade will enable all countries to achieve economic progress together.

To show how trade can produce benefits for both partners, consider a brief hypothetical situation involving China and the United States, each of which produces textiles and automobiles, but with different worker productivity (output per hour) for each country, as shown in the first column of Table 11.2.

Clearly, China has an absolute advantage in both products, as its workers are more productive at producing both textiles and automobiles than American workers. Does that mean that two countries cannot benefit from trading with each other? No. As long as the two countries have some difference in the relative costs they face in producing the goods, they can still both gain from specialization and trade.

Following the logic of comparative advantage, each country should produce the item for which it has the lower opportunity cost relative to the other country. Viewing the first column in terms of opportunity cost, the "cost" of China producing each additional automobile is three units of textiles. Alternatively, by producing one less automobile, China can produce three more units of textiles. However, it only "costs" the United States two units of textiles for each additional automobile, and the United States only gains two units of textiles by producing one less automobile. The United States thus has a smaller disadvantage in automobile production, as its opportunity cost for automobile production (two units of textiles) is less than the opportunity cost faced by China for the same production (three units of textiles). Put another way, though the United States is at a disadvantage in the production of both goods, its disadvantage is comparatively less in automobiles.

The remaining scenarios show specifically how trade can benefit each country by enabling it to further specialize in producing the good in which it has a comparative advantage. Imagine a hundred workers in each industry without specialization or trade (the second column). Next, specialize production by shifting ten Chinese workers from automobile to textile production and twenty Americans from textile production to automobiles (third column). The fourth column shows how both countries can then benefit from trade. If we permit trade between the two countries, then eighty units of textiles are sold or exported to the United States, and thirty U.S. automobiles are exported to China. By shifting Chinese resources into textiles, U.S. resources into automobiles, and allowing trade, the same total allocations will cause both textile and automobile output to increase by ten units each. Resources are now being used more efficiently and both countries benefit—China ends up with more textiles than before specialization and trade, and with the same number of automobiles. The United States finds itself with more automobiles and the same number of textiles. Achieving greater output with the same number of workers means that both countries enjoy higher living standards (see Figure 11.3).

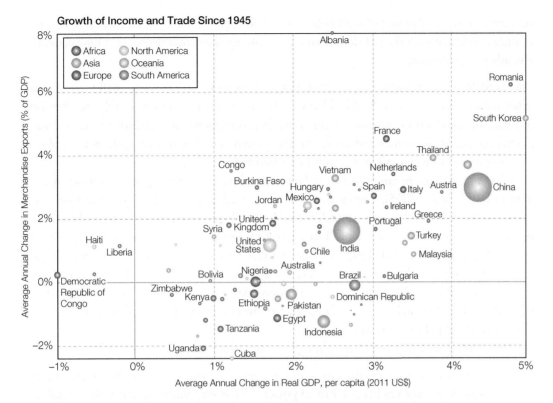

Growth of Income and Trade Since 1945

FIGURE 11.3 Trade Openness and Economic Growth Since World War II Liberalism views trade as a mutually-beneficial interaction for all participating countries. This figure depicts the long-run linkage between average trade openness and annual economic growth between 1945 and 2014. The size of the dots reflects the average population of the countries over that time. The general pattern is quite clear—countries that are more open to trade such as South Korea, China, and the Netherlands tend to have higher average levels of economic growth, as opposed to countries closed to trade such as Uganda and Tanzania.

The assumption implicit in liberalism is that markets succeed according to their own logic. This provides a fairly straightforward set of policy recommendations. For liberals, minimal state regulation of the national economy will maximize growth and prosperity. The best government is one that stays out of business, and politics should be separate from the economic market. A free market is the foundation for broad-based, steady economic growth that allows democratic institutions to flourish (Naím, 2007). As Benjamin Franklin once quipped, "No nation was ever ruined by trade."

There is at least one problem, however. Although liberal theory promises that the "invisible hand" will maximize efficiency so that everyone will gain, it does not promise that everyone will gain equally. Instead, "everyone will gain in accordance with his or her contribution to the whole, but . . . not everyone will gain equally because individual productivities differ. Under free exchange, society as a whole will be more wealthy, but individuals will be rewarded in terms of their marginal productivity and relative contribution to the overall social product" (Gilpin, 2001).

This holds true between states as much as within them. The gains from international trade are distributed quite unequally, even if the states are acting in accordance with comparative advantage. Globalization has not benefited middle-income countries as much as richer and poorer states (Garrett, 2004). Commercial liberal theory ignores these differences, as it is most concerned with *absolute gains* for all rather than *relative gains*. Mercantilist theory, in contrast, is more concerned with the political competition among states that determines how economic rewards are distributed.

Mercantilism   Also known as economic nationalism, *mercantilism* is essentially an economic extension of realist thinking. Unlike liberals, who focus on the rationality of the marketplace, mutual gains, and a minimal role for the state, mercantilists see the need for power politics as a determinant of economics and posit that the government has an important role to play in ensuring the state's economic well-being (see Chapter 5).

Classic mercantilism emerged in the late fifteenth century during the first wave of colonialism (Wallerstein, 2005). Classic mercantilists viewed gold and silver accumulation as the route to state power and wealth, and advocated imperialism as a means to that end. In the early nineteenth century, what we now call mercantilism emerged largely as a response to the rise of liberalism. Indeed, one of the leading mercantilist works, Friedrich List's *National System of Political Economy*, can be seen as a direct critique of Smith's *The Wealth of Nations*. Although economic nationalists draw from some of the core ideas of liberalism, such as the importance of productivity, the benefits of specialization, and the efficiency of the marketplace, they draw a different set of political conclusions.

Mercantilists diverge from liberal thought in three main ways:

- Whereas liberals view wealth and economic growth as ends in themselves, mercantilists view them as instruments of national power. This is very much in line with the realist emphasis on national interest, which posits that "economic activities are and should be subordinate to the goal of state building and the interests of the state" (Gilpin, 2001).

- Although liberal thought expounds the gains of specialization, it implicitly treats all specializations as equal in value. Mercantilists question this assumption, positing that "the power of producing wealth is therefore infinitely more important than wealth itself" (List, 1841, p. 108). For example, during the early years of the United States, Treasury Secretary Alexander Hamilton recommended that the United States specialize in manufacturing instead of agriculture, as it would better serve U.S. national interests. As opposed to agriculture, manufacturing required higher levels of technological advancement. Such industrialization would thus increase the "diversity of talents" in the country and, as a result, industrial capabilities would more readily convert to military might.

- Mercantilists view the state as playing an active and vital role in the economy. Since some specializations are superior to others, states can encourage the development of certain industries by subsidizing them and "protecting" them from foreign competition. As Hamilton (1791) noted, in key instances of national interest, the "public purse must supply the deficiency of private resources."

This perspective yields a different set of economic policies. Whereas commercial liberals emphasize the mutual benefits of cooperative economic agreements, mercantilists focus on *zero-sum* competition and are therefore more concerned that the gains realized by one party in a trade exchange will come at the expense of the other trade partner. For mercantilists, relative gains are more important than both parties' absolute gains. Although mercantilists recognize the superior efficiency of free trade, they have a more guarded view of its political benefits. They view free trade as an acceptable practice for a powerful country, in that it often serves to solidify that country's power. For growing countries, trade ties can sometimes be manipulated to the economic advantage of the more powerful, more developed state (Hirschman, 1945).

In many instances, practicing liberal trade can undermine national security and long-term economic development. Indeed, as mercantilists point out, powerful countries who profess liberal ideals, most notably the United States and the United Kingdom, were quite protectionist when their industries were developing. U.S. President Abraham Lincoln was an ardent protectionist who doubted the benefits of international trade and viewed tariffs as a way to protect the U.S. industrial base. He succinctly noted that his "politics are short and sweet, like the old woman's dance. I am in favor of a national bank . . . and a high protective tariff." In short, "(w)hile American industry was developing, the country had no time for laissez-faire. After it had grown strong, the United States began preaching laissez-faire to the rest of the world" (Fallows, 1993).

Trade and Global Politics

LO 11-3   Specify the political implications of trade, and apply the insights of hegemonic stability theory to the global trade order.

Trade plays a central role in the global system. In addition to being a key facet of economic globalization, it has many implications for the global political system. Indeed, a lot of scholarship on the global political economy deals with some aspect of the relationship between trade and world politics. With that in mind, let us briefly touch upon some of the key concepts and issues at the systemic and state levels of analysis.

At the systemic level, one of the most influential theories of global trade is *hegemonic stability theory*. Hegemonic stability theory, which is also used in theories of global conflict (see Chapter 7), is based on the proposition that free trade and international peace depend upon a single predominant great power, or *hegemon*, that is willing and able to use its economic and military might to enforce rules for international interaction. A hegemon is much more than a powerful state; rather, it refers to an instance in which a single state has a preponderance of economic and military power, a dominant ideology shared by the world, and the willingness to exert its power and influence.

The underlying assumption of hegemonic stability theory is that a stable and prosperous global economy approximates a collective or **public good** in that it provides shared benefits from which no one can be excluded. If all share a public good, why does it require a hegemon to provide it? This is due to the problematic nature of providing public goods, or the **collective action dilemma**. In this dilemma, the provision of public goods is problematic due to two basic problems: accountability and rationality. First, although a public good generates benefits, there are certain costs associated with providing or maintaining it. If the benefit has a large group of potential recipients, it is not possible to hold any single party accountable for paying its portion of the cost to provide this good. The recipients are thus faced with a dilemma: Why should they have to pay for the good when they can enjoy it without paying for it? If we assume

public good
Collective goods, such as clean air or sunlight, whose use is nonexclusive and nonrival in nature; thus, if anyone can use the good, it is available to all.

collective action dilemma
Paradox regarding the provision of collective goods in which, if there is no accountability for paying the costs of maintaining or providing the good, it may cease to exist.

that the actors are rational, then they would seek to enjoy the good as free riders that reap the benefits without paying any of the cost. However, if everyone is "rational," then no one will pay to maintain the good, and it will eventually disappear.

Thinking about the cost of a public park helps to clarify this principle. If there were no central government to provide for park maintenance, individuals themselves would have to cooperate to keep the park in order (the trees trimmed, the lawn mowed, litter removed, and so on). Some, however, may try to come and enjoy the benefits of the park without pitching in. If enough people realize that they can get away with this—that they can enjoy a beautiful park without helping to maintain it—it will not be long before the once beautiful park looks shabby. If even this basic form of cooperation is hard to sustain, imagine the difficulties in perpetuating cooperation in the international system.

The same logic applies to the collective good of the liberal international economy. Because many states enjoy the collective good of an orderly, open, free-market economy, there are often free riders. A hegemon, however, may tolerate free riders, partly because the benefits that the hegemon provides, such as a stable global currency, encourage other states to accept the hegemon's dictates. Moreover, the hegemon may view maintaining the system as worthwhile, even if it bears a disproportionate share of the cost. Thus, both the hegemon and the smaller states gain from the situation. If the costs of leadership begin to multiply, however, a hegemon tends to become less tolerant of free riders. In such a situation, cooperation is increasingly seen as one-sided, or zero-sum, because most of the benefits come at the expense of the hegemon. The open global economy could then crumble amid a competitive race for individual gain at others' expense.

The theory is thus quite parsimonious in that it explains very broad political and economic trends on the basis of one condition—hegemonic leadership. Although theorists may disagree about how many instances of hegemony have existed throughout history, there is widespread agreement about the most recent case—the United States during the post–World War II period. Studies within this area have considered the issue of a U.S. decline from hegemony, and its implication for the world economic order (Shifrinson and Beckley, 2013; Zakaria, 2009; Wallerstein, 2002).

At the state level of analysis, studies have assessed the relationship between trade and military conflict, with the preponderance supporting the commercial liberalism argument that trade ties tend to discourage military conflict (Copeland, 2014; Mousseau, 2013; Hegre, Oneal, and Russett, 2010). The basic argument is that trade interdependence increases the opportunity costs of violence—in addition to the more obvious costs that accompany military conflict, the presence of trade ties implies that a country would also forgo the benefits of trade if it takes military action against a trading partner (see "Controversy: China and Taiwan—Can Economic Ties Overcome Strategic Rivalry?"). On a broader scale, Oneal and Russett (2001) posit that trade, alongside democracy and international organizations, is a key part of the "Kantian triad" that encourages lasting peace between states.

Within states, trade liberalization is beneficial to societies, as it is positively related to economic growth, levels of democratization, life expectancy, education, human rights, and food security, and negatively related to child labor, poverty, and environmental degradation (Bhagwati, 2008b; Wolfe, 2005). "Despite all the misgivings about international trade, the fact

Controversy

CHINA AND TAIWAN—CAN ECONOMIC TIES OVERCOME STRATEGIC RIVALRY?

In 1949 Chiang Kai-shek and his party, the Kuomintang (KMT), were defeated in the Communist Revolution and fled mainland China to Taiwan with one to two million followers and troops. Since then, Taiwan has exercised *de facto*, if not *de jure*, sovereignty in international affairs. Ever since it lost its status as a recognized member of the United Nations (UN) in 1971, Taiwan has long sought broad international recognition as a sovereign state. For its part, China views Taiwan as a "breakaway province" that is rightfully a part of China. The Chinese emphatically adhere to the "One China" principle—that there is only one Chinese nation, of which Taiwan is a part. As such, any formal declaration of Taiwanese independence is viewed as an act of war. In 2005 China passed an Anti-Secession Law, which formalized this long-standing commitment to use "nonpeaceful means" if Taiwan declares formal independence.

Arthimedes/Shutterstock.com

Given these fundamental political differences, relations between China and Taiwan, or "Cross-Strait" relations, have been tarnished with suspicion and hostility. At its worst, the area has been on the brink of outright war. In 1958, China bombarded several offshore islands that are part of Taiwan, which nearly brought the United States, a close military ally of Taiwan, into war with China. Before Taiwan's first democratic elections in 1996, China test-fired missiles near two major Taiwanese ports, again risking military hostilities with both Taiwan and the United States. President Clinton responded by deploying aircraft carrier battle groups in the area.

The current strategic situation remains precarious in many respects. Reports indicate that China has a growing arsenal of almost 2,000 missiles pointed at Taiwan (Tzu-ti, 2018). Despite its much smaller size, Taiwan has a powerful military—one report ranks it as the twenty-second most powerful in the world (globalfirepower.com, 2019), and the fourth-leading

recipient of U.S. arms (Zhang, 2019). In addition to its stockpile of defensive missiles, it is currently producing land-attack cruise missiles, and completing development of a missile with a range of over 1,200 miles (Missile Defense Project, 2018).

Yet at the same time, the economies of China and Taiwan have become ever-more closely integrated. Bilateral trade has increased dramatically since 2000, from $31.3 billion to $150.5 billion in 2018 (Albert, 2019). China is currently Taiwan's largest trading partner, responsible for almost 30 percent of Taiwan's total trade volume, and Taiwan ranks as China's fifth largest trading partner. China is also Taiwan's leading location for FDI, having hosted over $140 billion in investment since 1988 (Jennings, 2019). China and Taiwan have signed multiple trade agreements, the most substantial being the Economic Cooperation Framework Agreement in 2010.

How can these contrasting patterns—traditionally labeled as "hot economics, cold politics"—be reconciled? From the theoretical viewpoint of liberalism, we would expect that economic interdependence may be reducing the probability of military conflict between the two countries. Given the close integration between both sides, any military conflict would be very costly to both countries, as it would damage large portions of both economies. Moreover, economic ties serve to empower business interests that have a vested concern in maintaining peaceful relations between the two countries. This could eventually cause the policy preferences of both countries to converge (Kastner, 2010). Finally, economic interdependence provides each country with a means to engage in "costly signaling," that is, a way to have conflicts through economic rather than political means. Indeed, one study cites such ties as a reason that the 2000 elections in Taiwan did not attract the same military action as the 1996 elections (Gartzke and Li, 2003).

Taken as a whole, political relations between Taiwan and China have waxed and waned over the years, driven in no small part by which political party is in power in Taiwan, the KMT (Kuomintang) or the DPP (Democratic Progressive Party). The KMT, long the dominant party in Taiwan, supports the "one country, two systems" doctrine that it worked out with the mainland in 1992 that precludes formal Taiwanese independence. The DPP does not support this doctrine; as current President Tsai Ing-wen (DPP) argued "China must face the reality of the existence of the Republic of China (Taiwan), and not deny the democratic system that the people of Taiwan have established together" (Office of the President, 2019). For its part, China treats administrations from the two parties quite differently. For example Chinese President Xi Jinping personally met with Ma Ying-jeou (KMT) during his tenure in office — the first time the leaders of these two countries had ever met. Since Tsai took office, China has imposed

a partial tourism ban and had a brief military standoff when two Chinese planes entered Taiwanese airspace (Zhang, 2019). Thus political relationships remain uneasy, and many issues remain unresolved, even in the face of economic integration. Furthermore, rising tensions about territorial claims in the South China Sea may embroil Taiwan and China in conflict. Time will tell whether the optimists or pessimists are correct.

What Do You Think?

1. What does this case suggest about the ability of economic ties to prevent military conflict?

2. What insights would a realist or constructivist perspective have on this case?

3. As the United States is closely integrated with both countries, what policies do you think it should follow regarding cross-strait relations?

Note: Prepared with the advice and assistance of William C. Vocke, PhD.

remains that countries in which the share of economic activity related to exports is rising grow one and a half times faster than those with more stagnant exports" (Naím, 2007, p. 95). This accounts for the continuing popularity of the liberal belief that the exponential growth of trade contributes enormously to economic prosperity, as the last sixty years suggest.

These payoffs notwithstanding, states still have many reasons to try to increase their own domestic standard of living through trade protectionism. Some states feel as though free trade is neither free nor fair because it does not benefit everyone equally. Although the longer-term trend is toward increased liberalization, many states remain unwilling to open their domestic markets to foreign competition because they are also unwilling to reform their home markets. According to the Heritage Foundation's 2019 Index of Economic Freedom, only six countries, or about 3 percent, of the 185 states were "free." Twenty-nine (16 percent) were "mostly free," and the remaining countries (81 percent) were "moderately free," "mostly unfree," or "repressed" (see Map 11.2).

Although governments may face political pressure to close off their economies, such policies frequently have negative consequences. Economically closed countries tend to be the poorest and the most corrupt. Indeed, many countries with low levels of economic freedom, such as South Sudan, Somalia, and North Korea, are also some of the most corrupt countries in the world (Transparency International, 2019). These patterns underscore the influence of a state's internal conditions on its international economic policies, and suggest that the future preservation of a global free-trade regime may be compromised in the absence of increasing numbers of free governments and free economies.

Trade can also function as a foreign policy tool for states, and it is readily used as both a "carrot" and a "stick" in interstate relations. Trade ties and granting of preferential access to markets are commonly established with developing countries as a way to help them compete in

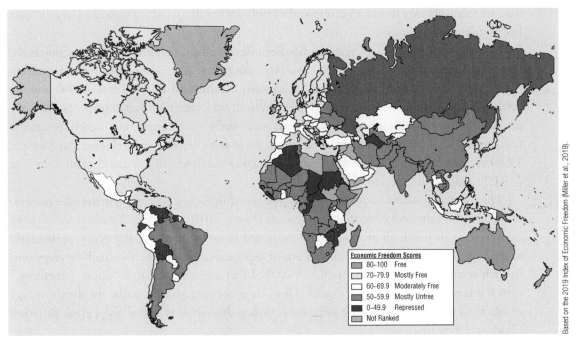

Based on the 2019 Index of Economic Freedom (Miller et al., 2019).

Economic Freedom Scores
- 80–100 Free
- 70–79.9 Mostly Free
- 60–69.9 Moderately Free
- 50–59.9 Mostly Unfree
- 0–49.9 Repressed
- Not Ranked

MAP 11.2 Economic Freedom in the World Economic liberals and mercantilists portray two different visions of international economics, one in which the market has virtually free reign and the other in which the state actively intervenes to regulate and manipulate market forces. Yet the reality is more nuanced, as there are differences in the degree to which free markets operate within each state. This map depicts economic freedom as measured by the 2019 Index of Economic Freedom. By using measures across 13 economic areas, including government policies on trade, labor, investment, and property rights, the Economic Freedom Index assesses the extent to which countries promote competition, individual empowerment, and nondiscrimination. Although there are differences in the degree to which economic freedom is enjoyed across countries, there appears to be a strong relationship between economic freedom and prosperity.

 Think It Through When comparing Global North and Global South average levels of economic freedom, how is the impact of labor and production outsourcing reflected?

the global market and thereby achieve economic growth. Leading examples include the WTO's Generalized System of Preferences, which exempts developing countries from some of the non-discrimination and reciprocity principles of the organization; and the Lomé Convention, which gives seventy-one developing countries preferential access to the EU markets.

Economic sanctions—deliberate actions against a target country to deprive it of the benefits of economic relations—are the most common way that trade can be used as a "stick" for *coercive diplomacy.* Sanctions have a long history; as President Woodrow Wilson argued in 1919, "A nation that is boycotted is a nation that is in sight of surrender. Apply this economic, peaceful, silent, deadly remedy and there will be no need for force. . . . It does not cost a life outside the nation boycotted but it brings a pressure upon the nation which, in my judgment, no modern nation could resist" (Hufbauer et al., 2007; see also Rowe, 2010).

Sanctions are used frequently and have proliferated rapidly since the end of the Cold War. Indeed, the number of sanctions imposed since 1990 is roughly equal to the number imposed between 1900 and 1990 (Drezner, 2011a). Politically, sanctions are an expedient tool because

economic sanctions
Punitive economic actions, such as the cessation of trade or financial ties, by one global actor against another to retaliate for objectionable behavior.

they are relatively easy to enact (as opposed to military conflict) and are viewed as largely "cost free" by the sender country.

A considerable amount of research has been devoted to sanctions, and most scholars are skeptical of their utility as a strategic tool. First, sanctions "are seldom effective in impairing the military potential" of their targets (Hufbauer, Schott, and Elliot, 1990, p. 94) and are rarely successful as a substitute for warfare, or even in achieving their stated policy goals. They can often impose significant unintended costs on citizens. For example, U.S. sanctions against Iraq during the 1990s were argued to be "sanctions of mass destruction" (Mueller and Mueller, 1999) because resultant food and medicine shortages were linked to the deaths of an estimated 250,000 Iraqi children (Garfield, 1999).

The focus on success versus failure may be too simplistic a way to view the effectiveness of sanctions, or any tool of economic statecraft (Rowe, 2010). Policy makers have a variety of tools at their disposal, all of which have costs and benefits. Stated policy goals, particularly strategic goals such as territorial concessions or regime change, may be too costly to carry out. In such cases, sanctions may be used as a symbol that a given country is "doing something," even if it is not likely to achieve its goal. Thus, "it is not enough to describe the disadvantages of sanctions; one must show that some other policy alternative is better" for a given situation (Baldwin 1999/2000, p. 84).

IMAGE 11.5 **Sanctions: Taming the Russian Bear?** Shown here in 2015, leaders of the G-7 states discuss sanctions imposed against Russia for its intervention in Ukraine. The continuing sanctions—imposed by the United States as well as the EU—cover a wide range of strategically important industries, including oil technology, arms sales, and shipments of dual use technology (goods that have both military and consumer uses). They also freeze the assets of dozens of Russian officials. For its part the U.S. has imposed more than 60 different sanctions on Russian firms, wealthy oligarchs, and government agencies (Newlin and Mankoff, 2018). Though the sanctions have driven the value of the ruble down substantially and are a drain on the Russian economy, their impact on Russian policy is hard to ascertain.

The Fate of Free Trade

LO 11-4   Identify and assess the tools of state policy in the area of international trade as well as their economic effects.

While global trade continues to proliferate, "we live in a time of protectionist backlash" (Scheve and Slaughter, 2018). Skepticism against globalization, which became very apparent in the wake of the 2008 financial crisis, has played no small role in the wave of anti-trade and anti-immigrant populism in the United States as well as Europe. Societal feelings of insecurity, bolstered by rising income inequality further contribute to this response.

As is the case with international finance (see Chapter 10), there is an esoteric vocabulary attached to trade policy issues. Before assessing current issues facing the world trading order, it is helpful to develop an understanding of the "trade tricks" countries can use to influence trade flows.

Trade Tricks

Trade liberalization has played a key role in the growth of the global economy since World War II, and there is virtual unanimity among economists regarding the potential benefits of free trade. As Nobel Prize–winning economist Paul Krugman (1987, p. 131) noted, "If there were an Economist's Creed, it would surely contain the affirmations 'I Understand the Principle of Comparative Advantage' and 'I Advocate Free Trade.'"

However, free trade is politically less attractive than mercantilism because of the nature of the costs and benefits that accompany free trade. In the aggregate, the societal benefits of free trade greatly outweigh the costs. Yet these benefits, particularly the consumer gains from imports, are spread throughout an entire society and are often not noticed. For example, although foreign trade may enable you to save $10 on a sweatshirt, you are probably unaware that imports are the reason behind your savings. There is thus little incentive to politically organize in the interests of imports—if you discovered that the price of sweatshirts had risen by $10, you probably would not take the time to organize "pro-import" protest marches.

However, the "costs" of free trade are quite concentrated and visible. It is quite common, for example, to hear about plants closing and people losing jobs due to competition with cheaper imports. There are thus greater political incentives to organize against free trade and for these forces to influence the political process. In short, "bad economics is often the cornerstone of good politics" (Drezner, 2000, p. 70).

Given this dilemma, trade squabbles are a constant fixture, as states have political incentives to enact mercantilist policies. This section explains some of these policy tools, all of which fall under the broad rubric of **protectionism**—policies designed to "protect" domestic industries from foreign competition.

- **Tariffs**—taxes placed on imported goods—are the most well-known protectionist policy tools. For example, in 2018 and 2019, the Trump Administration either threatened or enacted tariffs against Canada, the EU, Mexico, and China.

protectionism
Barriers to foreign trade, such as tariffs and quotas, which protect local industries from foreign competition.

tariffs
Tax assessed on goods imported into a country.

import quotas
Numerical limit on the quantity of particular products that can be imported.

export quotas
Barriers to free trade agreed to by two trading states to protect their domestic producers.

orderly market arrangements (OMAs)
Voluntary export restrictions through government-to-government agreements to follow specific trading rules.

voluntary export restrictions (VERs)
Protectionist measure in which exporting countries agree to restrict shipments of a particular product to a country to deter it from imposing an even more burdensome import quota.

nontariff barriers (NTBs)
Measures other than tariffs that discriminate against imports.

countervailing duties
Government tariffs to offset suspected subsidies provided by foreign governments to their producers.

antidumping duties
Taxes placed on another exporting state's alleged selling of a product at a price below the cost to produce it.

- **Import quotas** limit the quantity of a particular product that can be imported from abroad. In the late 1950s, for example, the United States established import quotas on oil, arguing that they were necessary to protect U.S. national security. Hence the government, rather than the marketplace, determined the amount and source of imports.

- **Export quotas** usually result from negotiated agreements between producers and consumers and restrict the flow of products (for example, shoes or sugar) from the former to the latter. Along those lines, **orderly market arrangements (OMAs)** are formal agreements through which a country accepts limiting the export of products that might impair workers in the importing country, often under specific rules designed to monitor and manage trade flows. Exporting countries are willing to accept such restrictions in exchange for concessions from the would-be importing countries. The Multi-Fiber Arrangement (MFA) was an example of an elaborate OMA that restricted exports of textiles and apparel. It originated in the early 1960s, when the United States formalized **voluntary export restrictions (VERs)** with Japan and Hong Kong to protect domestic producers from cheap cotton imports. The quota system was later extended to other importing and exporting countries and then, in the 1970s, to other fibers, when it became the MFA. The MFA expired in 1995.

- As quotas and tariffs have been reduced, a broader category of trade restrictions known as **nontariff barriers (NTBs)** has been created to impede imports without direct tax levies. These cover a wide range of creative government regulations designed to shelter particular domestic industries from foreign competition, including health and safety regulations, government purchasing procedures, and subsidies. Unlike tariffs and quotas, NTBs are more difficult to detect and dismantle.

- NTBs can also take the form of contingent trade-protective measures which are intended to offset policies of exporting countries. The two most common of these measures are **countervailing duties** and **antidumping duties**. Countervailing duties impose tariffs to offset alleged subsidies, and their use is fairly common to offset agricultural subsidies. Antidumping duties counter competitors' sale of products below their cost of production. For example, in March 2015, Indonesia filed a suit with the WTO over countervailing duties on paper products imposed by the United States, which the United States argued were in response to Indonesian dumping of these products.

- **Subsidies**—government-provided financial assistance to industries—are a very common form of NTB. In this case the government simply provides some type of financial support, including direct payments, preferential access to finance, or tax breaks. They can either be intended to support the business itself or to encourage certain practices (most often exporting), and be used in combination with other measures.

- Among developing countries, whose domestic industrialization goals may be hindered by the absence of protection from the Global North's more efficient firms, the

infant industry argument is often used to justify mercantilist trade policies. According to this argument, subsidies, tariffs, or other forms of protection are necessary to nurture young industries until they eventually mature and lower production costs to successfully compete in the global marketplace. *Import-substitution industrialization* policies, which were once popular in Latin America and elsewhere, often depended on protection of infant industries (see Chapter 5).

- In the Global North, creating comparative advantages now motivates what is known as **strategic trade policy** as a mercantilist method to ensure that a country's industries remain competitive. Strategic trade policies focus government subsidies toward particular industries so they gain comparative advantages over foreign producers. A notable example of this strategy is Airbus, a European company that builds wide-bodied airplanes. The company was founded in large part by France, Germany, and the United Kingdom, and has been heavily subsidized during much of its existence.

Although economic liberalism is based on free trade, realist theory helps to account for the state's impulse to pursue mercantilist policies. Recall that realism argues that states often compete rather than cooperate because international anarchy without global governance feeds states' distrust of each other. Moreover, states seek self-advantage and economic primacy. In this sense, mercantilist strategic trade is a prime example of this realist explanation of states' concern for self-interest and relative gains, as it "focuses on economic development as a matter of strategic significance" (Holstein, 2005).

The Uneasy Coexistence of Liberalism and Mercantilism

Given the political advantages of mercantilism, states often have a hard time resisting the calls of domestic industries and interest groups for protection. They do so even if, according to liberalism, their relations with their trade partners will deteriorate and all will suffer in the long run, as trade partners retaliate with the many clever and innovative counter-protectionist actions.

The result is that states simultaneously pursue liberalism and mercantilism. Such a paradoxical approach to trade policy reflects the state's determination to reap the benefits of interdependence while minimizing costs. It also reveals the tension between states and markets, between the promise that everyone will benefit and the fear that the benefits will not be equally distributed. The absence of a world government encourages each state to be more concerned with how it fares as compared to other states—its relative gains—than collectively with its absolute gains.

America's trade competitors have long noted that the United States, the principal advocate of free trade in the post–World War II era, has often failed to live up to its own rhetoric. For instance, almost a third of U.S. foreign aid is tied to the purchase of U.S. goods and services, the highest level among the major donor states (Lawson and Morgenstern, 2019). The specific ways in which aid may be tied are complex and may vary with the type of aid, and the political power of the industry that dispenses the aid. Agricultural aid is rife with such conditions. According to U.S. law, 75 percent of U.S. food aid has to be shipped on U.S. vessels, of which 75 percent of the crew are U.S. citizens. Also, a sizeable portion of food aid is simply "monetized"; that is, the government buys the food directly from farmers, sells it to other countries, and

subsidies
Government-directed financial support for a firm, usually intended to encourage increased exports and/or decreased imports.

infant industry
Newly established industries ("infants") that are not yet strong enough to compete against mature foreign producers in the global environment.

strategic trade policy
Government support for particular domestic industries to help them gain competitive advantages over foreign producers.

AP Images/Elaine Thompson

IMAGE 11.6 "Invisible Hands" Holding Shovels A key assumption of liberalism is that the state should step aside and let the "invisible hand" of the marketplace operate as freely as possible. Yet the economic reality is much more "hands on" because states take an active role in supporting many industries. Shown here are several Boeing officials as well as two U.S. senators in a "ground-breaking" ceremony at a new Boeing factory in Everett, Washington. The state of Washington gave Boeing $8.7 billion in tax breaks to encourage the company to locate there. The EU successfully filed a complaint with the WTO over these policies, arguing that that they are "market-distorting" and put European competitors at a "massive disadvantage" (Zarocostas, 2014).

then donates the proceeds to international charities. In short, "food aid programs have become a buffet for special interest groups" (Pincin and Brenberg, 2013). Such processes reveal a mercantilist nature, as they turn foreign aid into a *de facto* subsidy for domestic corporations.

Additionally, although overall tariff levels in the United States are lower than those in the developing world, the United States, like the rest of the developed countries, still protects several key sectors, most notably agriculture. Between 1995 and 2017, farmers in the United States received around $205 billion in agriculture subsidies. Moreover, the distribution of the assistance is skewed toward large agribusinesses rather than small farmers. During this time, the top 1 percent of the recipients received 26 percent of the assistance, and 77 percent of the assistance went to the top 10 percent (Amadeo, 2019b). Such mercantilist tactics are damaging to the liberal trade regime, given U.S. liberal rhetoric and its stature as the world's leading economic superpower. This is particularly troubling for developing countries, as they often have very powerful agricultural sectors as well. The gap between the ideals and the actions of the Global North also brings back vestiges of colonialism and past hypocrisy on the part of the rich countries. It also has negative domestic implications, as the skewed distribution of benefits feeds into the impression that the overall system of assistance is rigged and even corrupt.

Triumph or Trouble for the Global Economy

LO 11-5   Assess the role of the World Trade Organization (WTO) in facilitating global trade, and appraise future prospects for the global trade order.

The global trade order is at a troubling juncture. On one hand "rapid globalization has done nothing to undermine the confidence liberals have always placed in trade," and "(n)o serious economist questions the case for international integration through flows of goods and services" (Crook, 2003, p. 3). Yet such "confidence" is not broadly shared by the public. One poll found that while 81 percent of the respondents across 44 countries thought that international trade is good in general, only 45 percent thought that it actually increased wages and only 26 percent believed that trade actually lowered consumer prices (Stokes, 2014). This indicates that while the public supports trade in principle, they are unsure about its tangible benefits. Reflecting this perspective, protectionist policies are on the rise. To better assess this dilemma, we examine the progression of the liberal trade order, as well as the current issues it faces.

The Development of the WTO

Although it is difficult to maintain a liberal trade regime, and there are problems with the global trading system, it has a better developed architecture than the global financial system. As discussed in Chapter 10, the financial arrangement established by the Bretton Woods order broke down in 1971, and the current system is prone to "manics, panics, and crashes" (Kindleberger, 2000); currencies fluctuate according to the dictates of the markets, there are only discussion forums to address issues of financial and monetary cooperation, and the IMF merely monitors financial systems and provides crisis management for countries that are in dire financial straits. It does not set broad-based, enforceable rules and practices for global financial flows.

By contrast, the WTO provides a well-developed institutional structure for the world trading system. The GATT/WTO has had a rather tumultuous and uneven history and has been criticized for its lack of progress throughout its existence. The 1950s were declared a "lost decade," and "postmortems" were written during the Uruguay Round negotiations (Pakpahan, 2013; Stiles, 2005). In the aftermath of the financial crisis, legal scholar Richard Steinberg declared that "[a]s a location for trade negotiation, the WTO is dead" (Steinberg, 2009). His assertion proved prophetic as the Doha Round is currently "dead in all but name" (*The Economist*, 2015c).

Yet to paraphrase Mark Twain, rumors of the institution's death have been "greatly exaggerated" and while it is no longer able to pass comprehensive multilateral liberalization measures, and faces challenges as an IGO, it is still an asset to the global trade order. During the Bretton Woods era, successive meetings of the GATT were very successful in cutting tariffs. The initial Geneva Round of negotiations in 1947 reduced tariffs by 35 percent, and successive rounds of negotiations in the 1950s, 1960s (the Kennedy Round), 1970s (Tokyo Round), and the 1980s and 1990s (Uruguay Round) virtually eliminated tariffs on manufactured goods. Currently, the global average tariff rate stands at a historical low of 2.59 percent (World Bank, 2019e).

The Uruguay Round transformed the GATT into the WTO, a rules-based regime with a powerful dispute resolution mechanism that arbitrates trade-related conflicts among members and holds them accountable for mercantilist measures. The WTO currently has 164 members, and another 23 states have "observer" status and have taken significant measures toward gaining WTO membership. The WTO has handled almost 500 disputes since 1995 (WTO, 2019c) and can hold even its most powerful members accountable for their trade practices. For example, the WTO played a pivotal role in forcing the United States to rescind its 2002 steel tariffs (Becker, 2003). At the same time, it benefits the United States, which has filed 115 complaints through the WTO against other countries (see Map 11.3).

In addition to having policy "sticks" to bring member states in line, the "carrot" of WTO membership, which brings with it access to the markets of the 164 member states, can itself be beneficial to states. The trade reforms necessary for accession are related to higher economic growth (Bernier et al., 2018) and can also serve to improve the quality of state governance. For example, recent additions to the WTO—Russia, Laos, China, and Saudi Arabia—underwent reform of their trading regimes, including increased accountability and transparency of their trade policies, in order to make it through the accession process to join the WTO. According to Peter Sutherland (2008, p. 127), a founding director of the WTO, countries change "dramatically—and mostly for the better—in the context of acceding to the WTO." Political

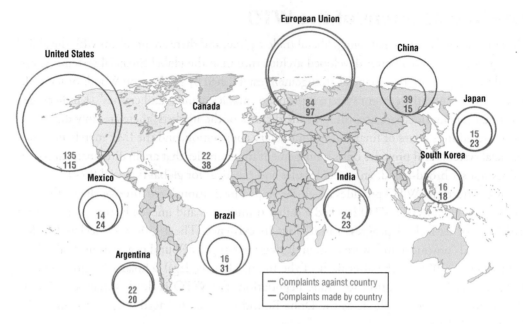

MAP 11.3 Dispute Resolution at the WTO An important aspect of the GATT becoming the WTO was the development of its dispute settlement mechanism (DSM), which offered states a global forum in which to present trade disputes. This map shows the countries that are the most involved in the DSM on either side of a given trade conflict. The more powerful economies are the most likely to use the DSM (particularly the United States and the EU), and frequent defenders are likewise more active in pressing their own complaints.

Think It Through   To what extent does this map indicate that the WTO may be becoming more "multipolar"?

effects continue after accession, and studies have found WTO membership to be positively related to some democratic processes, such as political participation and free and fair elections (Aaronson and Abouharb, 2011; Aaronson and Zimmerman, 2007).

Yet the WTO is to some extent a victim of its success. When the GATT was formed, it contained twenty-three members and was charged with one central goal—reducing tariffs. As tariffs have declined as a policy tool across most industrial sectors, the WTO has turned its attention to industries that previous rounds had left largely untouched and has begun to address a broad variety of nontariff barriers (NTBs) that impede foreign trade. Expansion into each of these areas has proven politically difficult, albeit for somewhat different reasons.

Despite the economic advantages of liberal trade, it is often politically advantageous to protect industries through mercantilist policies. The so-called "cotton wars" between the United States and Brazil illustrate the competing pressures highlighted by liberalism and mercantilism, as well as the role of the WTO in adjudicating disputes. The United States has long subsidized cotton production, and Brazil, seeking access to the U.S. market, has filed—and won—many disputes with the WTO (Schnepf, 2011). However, the United States continually appealed these rulings and refused to remove the subsidies. After eight years of disputes, Brazil finally presented the United States with an ultimatum: either end cotton subsidies or face punitive tariffs on a wide variety of goods it exports to Brazil, ranging from beauty products to automobiles

(Politi and Wheatley, 2010). It is noteworthy that though the WTO has no direct enforcement abilities, Brazil was able to credibly make the tariff threat due to the WTO ruling, which gives the measure legal legitimacy under global trade rules. Faced with two difficult options, the United States found a rather innovative solution. In exchange for Brazil dropping its trade dispute, it agreed to make payments to both the U.S. and Brazilian cotton farmers. That is, in addition to retaining their multibillion dollar subsidies to U.S. farmers, U.S. trade officials agreed to provide Brazilian cotton producers with annual payments of over $150 million (Joffe-Walt, 2013). In 2014, the United States and Brazil officially concluded the dispute, with Brazil dropping its case in exchange for a final payment of $300 million (Hufbauer, 2014).

As the WTO has begun to focus on nontariff barriers to trade, it has found itself addressing issues that go beyond the traditional dichotomy of free trade versus protectionism. For example, concerns related to labor and environmental standards link trade to broader controversies about core human rights and development (see "A Closer Look: Trade and the Environment"). As trade policy specialist I. M. Destler posits, a "new politics" of international trade has emerged. These new issues involve "not the balance to be struck among economic interests and goals, but rather the proper balance between economic concerns and other societal values." (Destler, 2005, p. 253). Often brought together under the umbrella of fair trade, these other goals and values do not neatly fall into arguments for or against free trade; survey research indicates even supporters of liberal trade still view fair trade measures, such as labor and environmental rights protections, as important (Ehrlich, 2011). These matters are far more difficult to reconcile, and pose "a challenge that longstanding trade policy institutions were ill-equipped to meet or even to understand" (Destler, 2005, p. 253).

Additionally, increased WTO membership has created further challenges. Traditionally GATT/WTO negotiations followed a "club model" (Esty, 2002) in which a small group of trade officials—typically the United States, European Union, and Japan—ironed out policy, with other countries largely following their lead. Rounds were largely private affairs, with the public paying little or no attention to them. For example, the conclusion of the Tokyo Round in 1979, which was widely heralded by experts as a sweeping victory for trade liberalization, was reported on page 18 of the Business Section (Section D) of the *Washington Post*—hardly prime placement for news items.

This is no longer the case. As evidenced by the massive protests that have become ubiquitous at every meeting, WTO rounds now attract

IMAGE 11.7 Does the WTO "Kill" Farmers? The liberalization of agriculture has been one of the most intractable items on the WTO agenda and often triggers visceral responses to any potential "threat" to the status quo. South Korea is certainly no exception to this, particularly with regard to its rice market. This photo, taken at the 2003 WTO Ministerial Conference in Cancun, Mexico, shows South Korean rice farmer Lee Kyung Hae (at left, with sign) protesting rice liberalization. Shortly after this picture was taken, Lee, a longtime advocate for rice farmers, publicly stabbed himself in the heart as a dramatic display of his opposition to trade liberalization; he died shortly thereafter.

a great deal of public attention. At the same time, the power structure in the organization has become much more *multipolar*. The Global South has been very active in the international trade system, accounting for more than 43 percent of all goods traded in the world (WTO, 2018). Thus, developing states, particularly the "G-5" emerging economies—China, India, Brazil, Mexico, and South Africa—have become very assertive in trade negotiations (Meltzer, 2011).

A Closer Look

TRADE AND THE ENVIRONMENT

A great deal of controversy surrounds the relationship between trade and the environment. Critics charge that globalization, of which free trade is a part, leads to a "race to the bottom" in environmental standards because countries are encouraged to enhance their competitiveness by lessening environmental regulations. Yet many studies find that trade can lead to improved environmental conditions, as it contributes to the diffusion of advanced technologies and environmentally friendly practices, a process termed the "California effect" (Prakash and Potoski, 2007; Vogel, 1995).

At the root of the trade–environment controversy is a substantial gap in global governance. While the WTO views climate change as "the biggest sustainable development challenge the international community has had to tackle to date" (WTO, 2019d), it has only two vague mandates that relate to the environment. The Marrakesh Agreement, which founded the WTO, calls for the organization to "protect and preserve the environment." Moreover, Article XX of the original GATT mandate allows for countries to enforce trade laws "necessary to protect human, animal or plant life or health" and that relate "to the conservation of exhaustible natural resources." In the absence of explicit environmental rules, the principle of national treatment implies that goods are to be treated equally for trade purposes, no matter how they were made. Thus, to discriminate against a country's product because of the way it is manufactured constitutes protectionism. For example, the WTO ruled that U.S. labeling of "dolphin safe" tuna unfairly discriminated against Mexican tuna, which did not use dolphin-safe nets. The WTO also ruled against other U.S. environmental laws, such as provisions for "turtle-safe" shrimp harvesting methods and gasoline standards—although supporting the laws themselves, the panel nonetheless ruled that they were being enforced in a manner that unfairly targeted certain countries. Given these weaknesses, it is increasingly common for regional trade agreements to include environmental provisions (Martinez-Zarzozo, 2018).

This highlights a key dilemma. States obviously have a right to maintain environmental standards and practices, yet there is wide variance in how states choose to do this. Given these differences, how can the line be drawn between legitimate environmental regulation and attempts to use such regulation as a "convenient additional excuse for raising trade barriers" (Anderson, 1996)?

Watch the Carnegie Council Video:

"Climate Protectionism and Competitiveness"

You Decide:

1. What does this reveal about the difficulties of reconciling free trade and the environment?

2. How can global trade be reconciled with the need to protect the environment?

3. Is the WTO the best forum to decide these issues?

The WTO thus faces an interesting dilemma—having largely succeeded in its goal of lowering tariffs, and having attracted almost every state into the organization, it is now tasked with getting an increasing number of states to agree on a large number of very difficult and contentious issues. The most recent round of WTO negotiations, the Doha Round, was begun only after seven years of pre-negotiations and essentially ended without an agreement in 2015, due in no small part to the complexities raised above. On the positive side, they did reach a very limited accord. Specifically, the Bali Agreement concluded in December 2013, which covered trade facilitation measures such as streamlining customs requirements. Even this agreement was contentious, as some countries raised concerns about their ability to pay for the necessary improvements to their customs procedures (*The Economist*, 2013). These institutional struggles have taken place in a particularly challenging economic environment. We next turn to some of the major challenges facing the world trading order, as well as potential ways in which they may be addressed.

World Trade and the Global Financial Crisis

In assessing world trade, it is important to keep the global context in mind, particularly the sweeping and persistent impact of the 2008 financial crisis. World trade fell 9 percent in 2008—the first time annual world trade had decreased since 1982—and declined an additional 12.2 percent in 2009. This decrease in trade was steeper and more sudden than the drop that accompanied the Great Depression (Eichengreen and O'Rourke, 2009). Global trade came back very strongly in 2010 and 2011, growing 13.8 and 6.6 percent respectively, though subsequent trade growth has averaged only 3.5 percent per year (World Bank, 2019). Examining the effects of the 2008 global financial crisis on world trade can provide an understanding of how facets of economic globalization, particularly trade and finance, interact. It also demonstrates the resilience of liberal trade norms even in times of economic crisis, as well as how threats to these norms arise. Finally, it provides the context to assess future prospects for the global trading order.

The 2008 global financial crisis caused a historic drop in world trade levels due to three primary factors. First, the crisis led to a downturn in the overall world economy, which created a huge fall in consumer demand. There was less of a market for foreign goods, as well as products in general. The globalization of production, in particular the nature of supply chains, further magnified this effect. Recalling Map 11.1, for each unit decrease in the sales of Dell computers in the United States, trade between nine countries is reduced. Global supply chains mean that trade reduction has a "multiplier effect," and that the pain of trade contractions is shared among a large group of companies and states.

Additionally, with the collapse in credit markets, trade finance dried up; international trade often requires short- to medium-term credit that was no longer readily available. Exporters, for example, may need short-term loans during the time period between when their goods are produced and when the revenue from their sales makes it back. In some instances, if neither seller nor buyer can obtain credit to facilitate the transactions, trade will not occur (Chauffour and Malouche, 2011; Auboin, 2009). The end result was a contraction in trade that was "sudden, severe, and synchronized" (Baldwin and Evenett, 2009) across the major trading states.

Economic downturns tend to encourage protectionism. The Great Depression pushed the United States to enact the Smoot-Hawley Act of 1932, which increased U.S. tariffs by 50 percent and contributed to a collapse in world trade. There were some short-term responses that raised concerns. Of particular note was the emergence of **murky protectionism** (Aggarwal and Evenett, 2013; Baldwin and Evenett, 2009). This refers to more subtle NTBs that may not be direct violations of WTO laws but are, rather, "abuses of legitimate discretion" on behalf of policy makers that serve to reduce trade. An example of this was the bailout of U.S. automobile industries in the wake of the 2008 financial crisis; while it was not intended specifically as a trade measure, it was nonetheless an NTB as it represented a $30 billion subsidy from the U.S. government.

murky protectionism
Nontariff barriers to trade that may be "hidden" in government policies not directly related to trade, such as environmental initiatives and government spending.

Yet despite these difficulties, a rush toward broader protectionism during the immediate aftermath did not occur, as world trade rebounded rapidly in 2010. There were several reasons global trade did not fall prey to protectionism and collapse during that time. Although some protectionist policies were enacted, they were narrowly focused measures; at the peak of the crisis, the various protectionist measures only affected 2 percent of world imports. As former WTO director-general Pascal Lamy noted, "governments acted with great restraint" (Lamy, 2011).

Moreover, the changing nature of world trade, particularly the use of global supply chains, weighs in favor of liberal trade. An increasing portion of world trade, particularly in emerging economies such as BRICS countries, is within larger supply chains. More than 70 percent of world merchandise trade is trade in components, that is, parts of finished products that represent portions of a larger production chain (OECD, 2019). Since the production processes are increasingly split across different countries, participation in global trade becomes less a matter of shipping finished products and more one of participating in global supply chain networks. Within this context, liberalization—through regional or even unilateral measures—is now the key to joining these chains as they develop.

The increased importance of supply chains has significance for state policies as well as the WTO. Multinational corporations control many of these chains, hence FDI as well as its relation to global trade becomes increasingly important to potential host countries. For the WTO, this underscores the need to change its emphasis from trade issues such as tariffs and agriculture to those more directly related to the formation of supply chains, including FDI policies as well as trade facilitation—the administrative "nuts and bolts of international trade" (Lamy, 2013), including customs and shipping regulations. Indeed, the only real progress that the WTO has made, the 2013 Bali Agreement, was in this area. However useful, these incremental advances are taking place within the broader context of an increasingly fractured world trade order. It is to these conflicts that we now turn.

The Protectionist Backlash and Current Trade Conflicts

To a certain extent, the longer-term impact of the 2008 financial crisis on global trade is somewhat analogous to its impact on finance (see Chapter 10). In each case while short-term economic disasters were avoided, the underlying structural factors uncovered by the crisis were never resolved and suspicion regarding the broader global system persisted. In global finance, such concerns are apparent in increased market uncertainty as well as persistent doubts that the global financial architecture has sufficiently evolved to avoid subsequent crises. In global trade, these grievances are readily apparent in the resurgence of protectionist measures as well as a current wave of trade conflicts, most notably between the U.S. and China.

Protectionism is on the rise, with discriminatory trade interventions (subsidies, tariffs, and quotas) far outnumbering liberalization measures (see Figures 11.4A and 11.4B). These measures are particularly common among the G-20 economies, with over 73 percent of all protectionist measures implemented by this group of states (Evenett, 2019, p. 18). Discriminatory measures are more narrowly focused and less transparent. For example, rather than declaring across-the-board trade restrictions (as during the Great Depression), states now tend to employ a variety of more limited NTB measures. In short, "there has been no Smoot Hawley 'moment,' but that did not stop the scale of crisis-era protectionism mounting up significantly over time" (Evenett 2019, p. 21). That said, one particular conflict—between the United States and China—has the potential to develop into such a "Smoot-Hawley 'moment.'"

Despite the increased use of protectionist measures, trade wars had been averted in the aftermath of the 2008 financial crisis. However, since 2017, the threat of a trade war between the United States and China and trade conflicts between the United States and many of its major trading partners, including the EU, Canada, Mexico, Japan, and India, have raised uncertainty in global markets. To a large extent, U.S. actions are historically unprecedented. "Trump is the first president going back to the 1930s to launch a multi-pronged trade war against America's A-list trading partners. The U.S. hasn't seen this kind of rough-and-tumble trade action since the Great Depression" (Rapoza, 2019). As of June 2019, the United States had imposed tariffs on $282 billion dollars of imported products, which constituted 12 percent of total U.S. imports. A vast majority of these tariffs have targeted Chinese products. For its part, China has

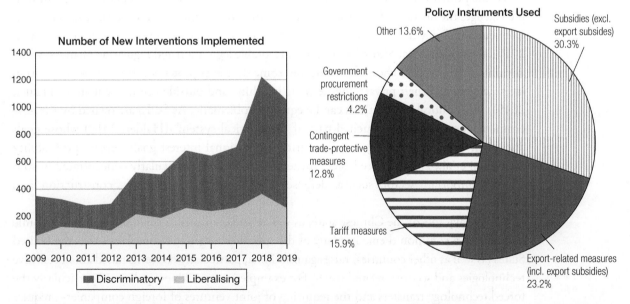

FIGURES 11.4A AND 11.4B **Trends and Policies in Trade Protectionism: Mercantilism versus Liberalism**
State policies reflect a mixture of mercantilism and liberalism, as they enact a variety of measures to either encourage or impede trade. The graph (shown left) shows the relative prominence of each type of policy since the 2008 financial crisis. State interventions in trade have increased rapidly since 2008 with an increasing proportion of them discriminatory (protectionist) in intent. Between 2009 and 2019, states implemented a total of 13,572 discriminatory interventions and only 5,050 liberalizing ones. Shown right, the figure indicates the mix of protectionist policies that are used. Tariffs comprised 16.3 percent, export-related measures were 23.6 percent, and subsidies were 29.1 percent. The overall picture is troubling for advocates of liberalism.

imposed retaliatory tariffs on over $100 billion of U.S. products. In total, the U.S. faces tariffs on 8 percent of its total exports (Williams et al., 2019).

To some extent, these measures and threats are due to the personal idiosyncrasies of the Trump Administration. Yet the conflict with China is more substantial due to its underlying causes, as well as the degree of disruption it can pose to global trade and potentially the WTO system as a whole. While the United States lists a total of 142 trade-related demands on China (Behusdi, 2018), many reflect a common underlying concern—the pervasive mercantilism of the Chinese economic system. Since coming into office, President Xi Jinping has orchestrated a "third revolution" that is undoing many of the pro-market reforms that took place under his predecessors. His policies represent "a reassertion of the state in Chinese political and economic life at home, and a more ambitious and expansive role for China abroad" (Economy, 2018, p. 10). The economics of this "reassertion" raise profound questions for global trade.

state-owned enterprise (SOE)
A business directly owned or partially owned by the government.

A vast majority of the major MNCs in China are **state-owned enterprises** (SOEs) "where the state has significant control through full, majority, or significant minority ownership" (Sturesson et al., 2015, p. 8). The Chinese government owns a total of 51,000 enterprises, which are collectively valued at over $29 trillion and employ over 20 million people. By way of comparison, the country with the second-largest number of SOEs is Hungary, which has 370 (OECD, 2017). Practically all of the major Chinese MNCs are SOEs; of the twenty-one Chinese companies large enough to place in the Fortune 100, eighteen are state-owned (Murphy et al., 2019).

As the presence and prevalence of state-owned enterprises are unambiguously mercantilist, it challenges the liberal trading order. Economically, while China espouses the idea of "competitive neutrality," in which state-owned enterprises and private companies compete equally (Lee, 2019), the reality is that SOEs "benefit from favorable legislation and regulation changes, virtually unlimited access to cheap financing and some degree of protection from anti-competition laws…advantages their private counterparts in China and outside can rarely match" (Halder, 2019). The political implications can be equally problematic. As SOEs are owned by the government, they are "an entrenched part of the political system" (Halder, 2019) whose goals and incentives can ultimately entail security and national interest goals beyond profitability (Amighini et al., 2013). Indeed, state-owned enterprises are particularly concentrated in strategically important sectors such as defense, energy, telecommunications, construction, and aviation.

The heavy role of the Chinese state, as well as the mercantilist orientation of its economic policies, are a common theme in many of the specific charges and complaints that the United States (as well as other countries) raise against China, particularly concerns raised about sensitive technologies and security-related issues. For example, many Chinese policies—particularly the forced technology transfers and the requiring of joint ventures of foreign companies—require foreign companies investing in China to transfer proprietary technology to Chinese stakeholders as a precondition for doing business. That is, the companies have to give away their key technological "edge" to their Chinese counterparts. Industrial espionage is also a problem; the U.S. Department of Justice recently reported that 90 percent of the industrial espionage cases that they investigated from 2011 to 2018 involved China (Maza, 2018). As a whole, while economists note that SOEs are ultimately more inefficient than their private-sector counterparts, a mercantilist government—particularly one with a large and growing economy—can essentially ignore these problems in the interests of broader strategic goals.

Thus, while the entry of China into the world economy has been welcomed for decades, countries are beginning to note the difficulties of incorporating a large economy that is run by fundamentally different principles into a largely liberal trading system. The United States is not alone in recognizing the broader problems China poses to global trade. For example, the Federation of German Industries (2019, p. 4) argued that "China's state-dominated economic system conflicts in many respects with the liberal social economy principles of the EU and many other countries. While in Europe the market is the organizing principle of the economy, China seems to regard market mechanisms and a means to be applied selectively and gradually."

The scope of this problem is particularly troubling, as it implies that these trade disputes are not an isolated conflict over a particular industry, but rather a pervasive problem whose effective resolution would "demand serious structural changes in China" (Savage and Harris, 2019). The short-term impact of the tariffs is already beginning to be felt in the United States, particularly in industries that depend on exports to China, most notably agriculture, or firms that rely on imports of steel. For example, a recent study by the Center for Automotive Research estimated that the tariffs—which increase prices on many of the necessary components for automobiles—could cost the auto industry almost 370,000 jobs (Schultz et al., 2019).

Given the relative sizes of the U.S. and Chinese economies, as well as the nature of global supply chains, these trade conflicts could mark a "history-altering moment" since the "partnership between the U.S. and China anything but assured, businesses are redrawing the map of global production" (Schuman, 2019). While supply chains are mobile, they value stable relations and reduced risk, both of which are threatened by these conflicts. Some firms are already starting to relocate their supply chains. Foxconn, one of Apple's largest suppliers, recently announced that they would no longer produce in China, and Apple is looking into drastically cutting back its production facilities in China (Schuman, 2019). More broadly, the increased uncertainty surrounding this issue has had a negative effect on global trade flows. Between 2017 and 2019, the annual growth in global trade declined by more than 44 percent (from 4.6 to 2.6). As WTO Director-General Roberto Azevêdo (2019) concluded, "With trade tensions running high, no one should be surprised by this outlook. Trade cannot play its full role in driving growth when we see such high levels of uncertainty." Ostensibly, the WTO could function as a forum for dealing with these issues, given its universal membership as well as the DSM. Yet this has not been the case in practice, as the WTO faces struggles on several fronts.

WTO: Future Threats and Prospects

There are reasons to be concerned about the effectiveness and future prospects of the multilateral trade system. The Doha Round yielded no major deals and a subsequent ministerial meeting in 2017 yielded "no major deliverables" (Cimino-Isaacs, 2019, p. 1). To some, the U.S. decision to pursue trade conflict directly with China instead of through the WTO—despite the repeated attempts of both countries to resolve issues through the dispute settlement mechanism—marked "the day the WTO died" (Alden, 2018).

In defending U.S. actions against China, U.S. Trade Representative Robert Lighthizer argued that the dispute settlement mechanism, while useful in narrowly-targeted disputes, "is not effective in addressing a trade regime that broadly conflicts with the fundamental underpinnings of the WTO system" (U.S. Trade Representative, 2018, p. 5). At the same time, the DSM itself has been hamstrung by unilateral U.S. actions, specifically its decision to completely block all judicial reappointments at the appellate level of the DSM and accuse it of judicial overreach and unfairness. With no ability to add judges, the DSM could ostensibly "paralyze the dispute settlement function of the WTO" when the terms of the existing judges expire (Payosova et al., 2018).

Beyond these potentially existential threats, members have expressed concerns about the ability of the organization to reach consensus or make meaningful progress on other pressing issues, including intellectual property rights, human rights, and environmental protections. Critics also note the inability of the WTO to "modernize" to better take into account the emerging economies and reach out into different areas of the world economy (Lamy, 2011). Arguably, these problems are somewhat due to the increasingly difficult nature of these trade-related issues as well as inherent challenges in reaching a consensus with the increased membership.

Nonetheless, there are still many areas in which the WTO is useful and relevant. As WTO Deputy Director General Alan Wolff notes, much of global trade continues to be conducted in accordance with WTO rules, and none of the 164 member countries has opted to leave the organization. Moreover, he notes that the overriding wishes of member-states are to make the organization stronger and to resolve the current problems with the dispute settlement mechanism. Though there is no shortage of challenges, he argues that history has shown that "mercantilism has its limits" as economic policy and "national politics will ultimately align with the underlying reality that it is in the fundamental interest of all countries to have a well-functioning world trading system" (Wolff, 2018, pp. 3–4).

The broad support for the WTO connotes a need for the international governance of global trade. Given the size of the WTO, it may be the case that alternate governance structures—regional, plurilateral, or bilateral—may be more viable vehicles for advancing trade liberalization. We next consider these alternative governance structures, paying particular attention to regional trade agreements (RTAs) as the most prevalent trade institutions.

Regional and Plurilateral Trade Arrangements: Supplement or Substitute for the WTO?

In the absence of progress by the WTO, regional and bilateral trade agreements—efforts by pairs or small groups of states to deepen their trade ties with one another—have become a popular alternative for governing commerce (see Map 11.4). The EU was the earliest and most successful example of regional integration, and similar, albeit less successful, initiatives occurred in the Global South during the 1960s and 1970s (see Chapter 5). However, the rapid proliferation of **regional trade agreements (RTAs)** and bilateral trade agreements did not begin in earnest until the early 1990s. According to the WTO, the number of trade agreements in force increased more than tenfold since 1990. As of January 2019, the WTO had been notified of 473 RTAs, and 294 agreements were in force (WTO, 2019f).

Such agreements are ubiquitous; only South Sudan, Somalia, the Democratic Republic of the Congo, and Mauritania remain unaffiliated with any RTA. There is also some evidence

regional trade agreements (RTAs)
Treaties that integrate the economies of members through the reduction of trade barriers.

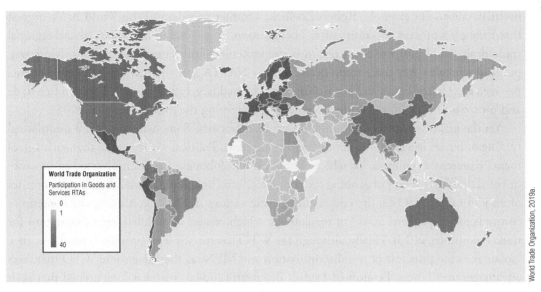

MAP 11.4 Membership in Regional Trade Agreements RTAs have proliferated since the 1990s and have emerged worldwide as a means of expanding trade ties between groups of states. As shown here, many states join multiple RTAs and membership often falls along geographic lines. For example, most of the RTAs to which the United States belongs are within the Western Hemisphere. RTAs may also codify groups of countries that have traditionally had trade relations, as evidenced by the Lomé Convention, which joins EU members and the wide variety of states that were formerly colonial holdings.

Think It Through Why might countries in the Global North belong to more RTAs than their counterparts in the Global South?

that RTAs increase trade among members. For example, trade among the full members of Mercosur—Argentina, Brazil, Paraguay, and Uruguay (there are also six associate members)—increased to $73.6 billion in 2018 from only $8 billion in 1990 (Global Edge, 2015; Felter and Renwick, 2018). Another large trade block, the ten-member Association of Southeast Asian Nations (ASEAN), has seen expansion of trade among its members, with a total of $590 billion in intra-ASEAN trade in 2017 (ASEAN, 2018). It also served as the political impetus for the larger Regional Comprehensive Economic Partnership (RCEP), which also included China, Japan, South Korea, India, Australia, and New Zealand.

As regional intergovernmental organizations (IGOs), RTAs are "a dominant mode of international cooperation in many issue areas" (Schneider, 2017). Politically, regional trade agreements are much easier to implement because they involve fewer actors and are often encouraged by politically powerful export-oriented industrial sectors (Dur, 2010). Given their smaller membership, RTAs offer increased flexibility to negotiate and make subsequent improvements in additional nontrade issues such as human rights, worker rights, democracy promotion, environmental protection measures, or anti-corruption statutes (Schneider, 2017; Milewicz, 2016). Along the lines of liberal theory, the development of RTAs also serves to strengthen foreign policy ties among member states and reduce the probability of conflict (Mousseau, 2013; Aydin, 2010).

Many RTAs are consistent with WTO principles and are viewed as catalysts to trade because they encourage trade liberalization, albeit among smaller groups of states. Indeed, political leaders commonly assume that there is no natural conflict between bilateralism, regionalism, and multilateralism. For example, Robert Zoellick, a former president of the World Bank, argued that through a process of "competitive liberalization," the formation of bilateral and regional trade deals could pressure countries into strengthening multilateral institutions. Moreover, political struggles over these trade deals, such as NAFTA and the bilateral trade agreements between the United States and South Korea, are framed largely as a struggle between free trade and protectionism, with the trade agreements representing the former (Destler, 2005).

Yet the push toward RTAs is not without its detractors. Some who support a multilateral trading order are less sanguine about these agreements. Politically, they argue that such agreements represent a "chimera" in which "attention and lobbying has been diverted to inconsequential deals" at the cost of pushing for multilateralism (Bhagwati, 2008a). Legally, as countries often join multiple RTAs, the end result of these various deals is a confusing and sometimes contradictory "spaghetti bowl" of regulations, which creates a muddled legal foundation for trade (Suominen, 2013). Finally, although the WTO has specific legal provisions for RTAs, they violate the core principle of nondiscrimination and MFN, as they give some WTO members advantages over others. Economist Jagdish Bhagwati (2008a), who has long argued that such agreements are "termites in the trading system," humorously noted:

> I discovered that the European Union, which started the pandemic (of regionalism) . . . applied its MFN tariff to only six countries—Australia, New Zealand, Canada, Japan, Taiwan, and the United States—with all other nations enjoying more favorable tariffs. I asked Pascal Lamy, who was then the E.U. trade commissioner, "Why not call it the LFN (least favored nation) tariff?"

plurilateral agreements
Treaties between a subset of WTO members that apply only to a specific issue.

Plurilateral agreements, issue-specific treaties created between WTO members, represent a more "à la carte" approach to trade liberalization (Hoekman and Mavroidis, 2015). WTO statutes have long allowed for these agreements, which were originally referred to as "codes." These agreements are growing in popularity. Examples include the 2013 Bali Agreement of the WTO, the Information Technology Agreement (ITA) which began in 1996 between twenty-nine countries, and the Government Procurement Agreement (GPA) which was also enacted in 1996 and currently has forty-three members.

Some see these agreements as a promising way forward for the WTO in that they provide a more flexible forum for addressing a single issue of contention (Bacchus, 2012). Plurilateral negotiations are open to all WTO members, though participation is voluntary and only those who specifically sign onto the agreement are subject to enforcement. It thus brings together countries that share at least some agreement over a given issue. Given the smaller membership, these agreements are also more flexible and quicker to implement or change (Hoekman and Mavriodis, 2015; Nakatomi, 2013).

Ideally, a plurilateral approach can be helpful to the WTO, as agreement in a given area could spread and provide the impetus to attain a "critical mass" of support within the organization as a whole (Saner, 2012). Moreover, unlike PTAs, plurilateral agreements are negotiated within the context of the WTO, thus reducing the chance of potential contradictions between these agreements and broader WTO statutes. Some economists note that plurilateralism could be applied to a broad variety of trade-related issues such as services, trade-related investment measures, and electronic commerce (Nakatomi, 2013).

Overall, although the liberal commercial order remains intact, the global trade order faces many challenges. The WTO encounters continued difficulties in maintaining its power and legitimacy within a more multipolar system, and alternate structures of governing world trade are proliferating. Such problems provide some corroboration to the realist viewpoint that there are definite limits to the strength of international organizations, as countries will focus on their domestic interests when threats arise, be they economic or political. At the same time, a liberal case can be made—for the WTO to maintain legitimacy during such tumultuous times attests to its underlying strength and utility within the global economy. Whatever the current balance between the two, the perennial battle between mercantilism and liberalism will continue, and countries and organizations will continue to grapple with how to balance trade interests with noneconomic concerns such as human rights and the environment.

This chapter, as well as the previous one, has shown that globalization is a "double-edged sword"—the same processes and ties that help our economies grow also ensure that crises have a diffuse effect. Moreover, you have seen the interdependent nature of the various facets of economic globalization, such as the linkages between global finance, production, labor, and trade. Yet globalization is more than just economics; it involves individuals and cultures. To understand that part of the broader puzzle of globalization, the next chapter takes you beyond the economics of globalization and addresses the cultural and demographic dimensions of our global society.

Study. Apply. Analyze.

Chapter Summary

11-1 Evaluate the deepening of trade ties between countries, and articulate how these ties relate to multinational production processes and global labor. World trade continues to grow, albeit at a slowing rate. Trade ties have increased in complexity due to global production processes, particularly global supply chains. This can have mixed implications for global labor.

11-2 Explain the major facets of economic liberalism, and contrast with mercantilism. Economic liberalism focuses on the mutual gains that can occur due to free trade, and encourages open markets with a minimum of government intervention. Mercantilism calls for a much more active role for the state, and views trade ties in terms of relative gains.

11-3 Specify the political implications of trade, and apply the insights of hegemonic stability theory to the global trade order. At the aggregate level, trade is mutually beneficial. However, it is politically difficult as the "losers" of trade are much easier to identify

than the "winners." There is thus a political incentive to engage in mercantilist behaviors despite the economic disadvantages. A global hegemon can ensure an open trade order by setting up the necessary markets and institutions to help keep such actions from occurring.

11-4 Identify and assess the tools of state policy in the area of international trade as well as their economic effects. States have a variety of tools they can use to either encourage their own products or discourage the products of others, including tariffs and quotas as well as a wide variety of NTBs (non-tariffs barriers). While these measures all result in an aggregate loss, they can provide targeted gains for individual firms or sectors of an economy.

11-5 Assess the role of the World Trade Organization (WTO) in facilitating global trade, and appraise future prospects for the global trade order. The WTO sets rules for conducting open trade and provides a forum for resolving trade disputes. Though there is a need for international governance over global trade, members have expressed concerns about the ability of the organization to make meaningful progress on complex trade issues as well as other issues such as intellectual property rights, human rights, and environmental protections. The WTO members largely wish to make the organization stronger and to resolve the current problems with the dispute settlement mechanism. However, in light of the shortcomings of the WTO, regional and bilateral trade agreements have become a popular alternative for governing commerce.

Key Terms

absolute advantage

antidumping duties

collective action dilemma

comparative advantage

countervailing duties

economic sanctions

export quotas

globalization of labor

globalization of production

import quotas

infant industry

intra-firm trade

most-favored nation (MFN)
   principle

murky protectionism

near-sourcing

nondiscrimination

nontariff barriers (NTBs)

orderly market arrangements
   (OMAs)

outsourcing

plurilateral agreements

protectionism

public good

reciprocity

regional trade
   agreements (RTAs)

state owned enterprise (SOE)

strategic trade policy

subsidies

tariffs

trade integration

transparency

voluntary export
   restrictions (VERs)

Suggested Readings and Resources

Economy, E. (2018). *The Third Revolution: Xi Jinping and the New Chinese State.* New York: Oxford University Press.

Globalization of the Economy: www.globalpolicy.org/globalization/globalization-of-the-economy-2-1.html. A blog by the Global Policy Forum with links for different aspects of the global economy.

Hopewell, Kristen. (2016). *Breaking the WTO: How Emerging Powers Disrupted the Neoliberal Project.* Stanford: Stanford University Press.

International Political Economy Zone: ipezone.blogspot.com/. Blog on the field of international political economy (IPE) including book reviews.

Irwin, Douglas. (2015). *Free Trade under Fire,* 4th ed. Princeton, NJ: Princeton University Press.

Rivoli, Pietra. (2014). *The Travels of a T-Shirt in the Global Economy: An Economist Examines the Markets, Power, and Politics of World Trade.* New York: Wiley.

Rodrik, Dani. (2017). *Straight Talk on Trade: Ideas for a Sane World Economy.* Princeton, NJ: Princeton University Press.

Ruggie, John. (2013). *Just Business: Multinational Corporations and Human Rights.* New York: W. W. Norton.

Stiglitz, J. (2017). *Globalization and Its Discontents Revisited: Anti-Globalization in the Age of Trump.* New York: W.W. Norton.

World Trade Organization. (2018). *World Trade Report 2018.* Geneva: WTO.

Carnegie Council Videos

Key Term Videos

- Globalization of Labor
- Globalization of Production
- Economic Sanctions
- Protectionism
- Regional Trade Agreements
- Strategic Trade Policy

Additional Videos

- Judis, John. "The Populist Explosion: How the Great Recession Transformed American and European Politics."
- Vocke, William. "Global Ethics Corner: Populism, Protectionism, and China."
- Vocke, William. "Global Ethics Corner: Buy American? Is There a Choice?"

Chapter 12

The Demographic and Cultural Dimensions of Globalization

Jonas Bendiksen/Magnum Photos

IMAGE 12.1 **The Difference between Haves and Have-Nots** Of the almost 8 billion people in the world, one out of every seven lives in slums. Pictured here, children dance in one of the squatter communities that surround Caracas, a city and metro area of more than 2.9 million people in Venezuela. The provision of better housing, social services, and education is a major challenge to improving human security and realizing benefits from urbanization.

Learning Objectives

LO 12-1 Survey current trends in global demographics.

LO 12-2 Examine global migration patterns, and discuss the significance of global urbanization.

LO 12-3 Explain how infectious disease can lead to health crises around the world.

LO 12-4 Describe the expansion of global information flows, and outline the political and social implications.

LO 12-5 Evaluate the multiple facets of globalization, and appraise their implications for the future of world politics.

> *In the globalized world that is ours, maybe we are moving towards a global village, but that global village brings in a lot of different people, a lot of different ideas, lots of different backgrounds, lots of different aspirations."*
>
> **—LAKHDAR BRAHIMI, UN ENVOY AND ADVISER**

Everyone in the world is becoming more alike each and every day. It really is a small world, after all. As you probably have at one time or another imagined, beneath the skin every human being is essentially similar. We all share the same planet. And we all tend to respond to the same experiences that almost everyone feels at one time or another—love, fear, alienation, or a sense of a common community and destiny. Everyone also certainly shares a similar aspiration for a better world, as expressed by world futurist Rafael M. Salas (1985, p. 111): "The final binding thought is to shape a more satisfying future for the coming generations, a global society in which individuals can develop their full potential, free of capricious inequalities and threats of environmental degradation."

There is increasing optimism that this hope will be fulfilled. Why? One explanation is that growing numbers of people throughout the world are pursuing these human goals because globalization is bringing all humanity together as never before in bonds of interdependence. Do you, like them, think that breaking down barriers and boundaries can bring people together in a human family that recognizes no East, West, North, or South, but every individual as part of the same human race? Should you, therefore, practice morality instead of cutthroat politics? And if that goal is your passion, should you, like many others joining together in *nongovernmental organizations* (NGOs) across the globe, promote progress toward more prudent policies rather than blind partisanship?

Is this rising global awareness and activism warranted? Is the vision by which people are increasingly defining themselves as global citizens reasonable? Will a truly global society come into being in your lifetime, propelled by the pressure of cascading globalization that is tearing down visions of separate states, nations, and races that throughout history have so divided humanity? This chapter opens a door to evaluating the prospect for such a jaw-dropping development. You will be asked to consider whether global trends might transform the world, and the world politics that condition this.

> *Once you have glimpsed the world as it might be, as it ought to be, as it's going to be (however that vision appears to you), it is impossible to live compliant and complacent anymore in the world as it is.*
>
> **—VICTORIA SAFFORD, UNITARIAN MINISTER**

Population Change as a Global Challenge

LO 12-1   Survey current trends in global demographics.

demography
The study of population changes, their sources, and their impact.

To formulate your interpretation of this human dimension of globalization and world politics, it is instructive to first look at how changes in world population are a part of the globalization of world politics. "Chances are," notes an expert in **demography**, Jeffrey Kluger (2006), "that you will never meet any of the estimated 247 human beings who were born in the past minute. . . .

In the minute before last, however, there were another 247. In the minutes to come, there will be another, then another, then another. By next year at this time, all those minutes will have produced millions of newcomers in the great human mosh pit. That kind of crowd is very hard to miss."

As the population on this planet increases, globalization is bringing us closer together in a crowded **global village** where transnational challenges characterize our borderless world. Evidence strongly suggests that unrestrained population growth will result in strife and environmental degradation (see Chapters 7 and 14). Population change also forces reconsideration of standards for ethics (the criteria by which right and wrong behavior and motives should be distinguished). Some people regard the freedom to parent as a human right. Others claim that controls on family size are necessary because an unregulated population will "parent" a crowded and unlivable future world without the resources necessary to sustain life for all people. For this reason, politics—the exercise of influence in an attempt to resolve controversial issues in one's favor—surrounds debate about population policies. To understand why the globalization of population has become such a controversial issue, it is helpful to trace the global trends in population growth that have made this topic so problematic.

global village
A popular cosmopolitan perspective describing the growth of awareness that all people share a common fate because the world is becoming an integrated and interdependent whole.

World Population Growth Rates

The rapid growth of world population is described by a simple mathematical principle that Reverend Thomas Malthus noticed in 1798: unchecked, population increases in a geometric or exponential ratio (1 to 2, 2 to 4, 4 to 8), whereas subsistence increases in only an arithmetic ratio (1 to 2, 2 to 3, 3 to 4). When population increases at such a geometric rate, the acceleration can be staggering. Carl Sagan illustrated this principle that governs growth rates with a parable he termed "The Secret of the Persian Chessboard":

> The way I first heard the story, it happened in ancient Persia. But it may have been India, or even China. Anyway, it happened a long time ago. The Grand Vizier, the principal adviser to the King, had invented a new game. It was played with moving pieces on a board of 64 squares. The most important piece was the King. The next most important piece was the Grand Vizier— just what we might expect of a game invented by a Grand Vizier. The object of the game was to capture the enemy King, and so the game was called, in Persian, shahmat—shah for king, mat for dead. Death to the King. In Russia it is still called shakhmaty, which perhaps conveys a lingering revolutionary ardor. Even in English there is an echo of the name—the final move is called "checkmate." The game, of course, is chess.
>
> As time passed, the pieces, their moves and the rules evolved. There is, for example, no longer a piece called the Grand Vizier—it has become transmogrified into a Queen, with much more formidable powers.
>
> Why a king should delight in the creation of a game called "Death to the King" is a mystery. But, the story goes, he was so pleased that he asked the Grand Vizier to name his own reward for such a splendid invention. The Grand Vizier had his answer ready: He was a humble man, he told the King. He wished only for a humble reward. Gesturing to the eight columns and eight rows of squares on the board he devised, he asked that he be given a single grain of wheat on the first square, twice that on the second square, twice that on the third, and so on, until each square had its complement of wheat.
>
> No, the King remonstrated. This is too modest a prize for so important an invention. He offered jewels, dancing girls, palaces. But the Grand Vizier, his eyes becomingly lowered, refused them all. It was little piles of wheat he wanted. So, secretly marveling at the unselfishness of his counselor, the King graciously consented.

When the Master of the Royal Granary began to count out the grains, however, the King was in for a rude surprise. The number of grains starts small enough: 1, 2, 4, 8, 16, 32, 64, 128, 256, 512, 1,024. . . . But by the time the 64th square is approached, the number becomes colossal, staggering. In fact, the number is nearly 18.5 quintillion grains of wheat. Maybe the Grand Vizier was on a high fiber diet.

How much does 18.5 quintillion grains of wheat weigh? If each grain were 2 millimeters in size, then all the grains together would weigh around 75 billion metric tons, which far exceeds what could have been stored in the King's granaries. In fact, this is the equivalent of about 150 years of the world's present wheat production (Sagan, 1989, p. 14).

The story of population growth is told in its statistics. The annual rate of population growth in the twentieth century increased from less than 1 percent in 1900 to a peak of 2.2 percent in 1964. It has since dropped to about 1.1 percent and is expected to drop slightly less than 1 percent between 2020 and 2025, when 78 million new people (nearly equivalent to the population of Iran or Germany) will be added each year. In terms of absolute numbers, the world population has grown dramatically in the twentieth century. Even in the past twenty years the population has grown from 6.1 billion in 2000 to 7 billion in 2011 and is expected to reach 8.5 billion by 2030 (WDI, 2019). Robert S. McNamara, as World Bank president, noted that "If one postulates that the human race began with a single pair of parents, the population has had to double only thirty-one times to reach its huge total." Plainly, the planet is certain to have many people by the mid-twenty-first century, well beyond the roughly 7.7 billion in 2019.

replacement-level fertility
One couple replacing themselves on average with two children so that a country's population will remain stable if this rate prevails.

The size of the global population is shaped by worldwide fertility rates and cannot stabilize until it falls below **replacement-level fertility**. That will happen after the total **fertility rate**, the worldwide average number of children born to a woman, falls to 2.1. Such is the case in many countries already as "nearly half of all people now live in countries where women, on average, give birth to fewer than 2.1 babies" (Teitelbaum and Winter, 2014, p. 1). Indeed, as evidenced by a decline in global total fertility rates from 4.8 in 1965 to 2.4 today, a "global reduction in childbearing and birth rates is now under way" (Eberstadt, 2010, p. 55).

fertility rate
The average number of children born to a woman (or group of women) during her lifetime.

Nonetheless, world population is projected to continue to surge because of "population momentum" resulting from a large number of women now entering their childbearing years. Like the inertia of a descending airliner when it first touches down on the runway, population growth simply cannot be halted even with an immediate, full application of the brakes. "Large families in an earlier generation mean that there will be more mothers in the current one and therefore more children, even if families are smaller and the underlying impetus towards growth has dropped" (Parker, 2010, p. 28). Moreover, even "when the absolute size of a national population declines, the drop often turns out to be short-lived, and in aggregate numbers usually is so slight as to be of little significance" (Teitelbaum and Winter, 2014, p. 3). Not until the size of the generation giving birth to children is no larger than the generation among which deaths are occurring will the population "airplane" come to a halt.

Changes in life expectancy also account for global population growth. "Over the course of the twentieth century, global life expectancy at birth more than doubled, soaring from about 30 years in 1900 to about 65 years in 2000" (Eberstadt, 2010, p. 55). By 2017, less than two decades later, life expectancy at birth had reached 72 years. Improvements in general health conditions have led to declines in mortality, and the global population has grown as people have lived longer lives.

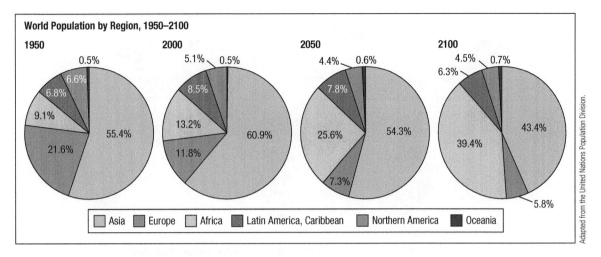

FIGURE 12.1 World Population Growth Projections to the Year 2100 It took until the early 1800s for world population to reach 1 billion people, and today another billion people are added every twelve to fourteen years. World population is expected to reach 9.7 billion in 2050 and continue to rise to 10.9 billion by 2100. The distribution of world population is also anticipated to change significantly. As the figure shows, Africa is expected to experience rapid population growth and account for over a third of global population by 2100; Europe is expected to continue to decline from almost 22 percent in 1950 to less than 6 percent in 2100.

World population will reach 8.5 billion by 2030 and 9.7 billion by 2050, at which point it is expected to stabilize. In the meantime, regional differences will become more prominent, portending the fulfillment of a demographic divide (see Figure 12.1). Population is expected to decline in Europe by almost 1 percent by 2030. In the Global South, Africa is projected to account for more than 40 percent of the increase in population so that almost one in five people will be from the region (UN, 2019a).

Demographic Divisions: Youth Bulges and Aging Populations

Consider the demographic divide between the Global South and Global North as a whole. Fertility rates in the Global South are, on average, almost a full 1 percent higher than the Global North. Because each cohort is typically larger than the one before it, the number of young men and women entering their reproductive years continues to grow. Continued population growth in the Global South also reflects the progress that has been made to combat infectious and childhood disease in developing countries around the world. In the Global North, population is stabilizing or declining, despite increasingly longer life spans.

Sub-Saharan Africa and Western Europe illustrate the force of two different pictures of population momentum (see Map 12.1). Africa's demographic profile is one of rapid population growth, as each new age group (cohort) contains more people than the one before it. Africa's population will continue to grow because there are now more women of childbearing age than ever before. Furthermore, the highest national fertility rates are concentrated in Africa, where thirty-five of the countries with fertility rates of four or more children per woman are located.

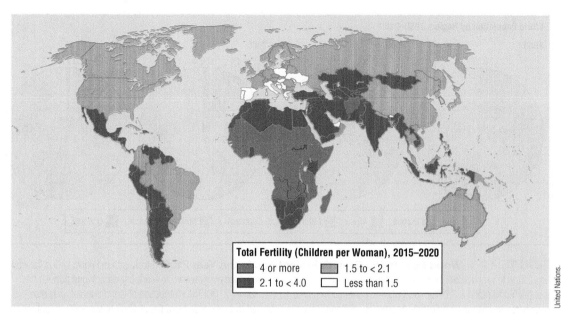

Total Fertility (Children per Woman), 2015–2020

■ 4 or more	■ 1.5 to < 2.1
■ 2.1 to < 4.0	☐ Less than 1.5

United Nations.

MAP 12.1 A Geographic Population Divide Although world population growth is anticipated to decelerate in the latter half of the twenty-first century, it is expected to reach 10.9 billion by 2100. UN predictions of growth rates are based on expectations of replacement-level fertility and declining mortality across most regions of the globe. Depicting trends over time, the graph shows that total fertility remains highest in Africa throughout most of this century.

 Think It Through What does the significant growth in the population of Africa over time suggest about the continent's future in international relations?

The population of sub-Saharan Africa has expanded from 228 million in 1950 to 1.3 billion in 2020, and is expected to double again by 2055 (UNDESA, 2019).

In contrast, Europe's population is growing slowly because recent generations have been smaller than preceding ones. In many European countries, the number of women of reproductive age is expected to decline by at least 10 percent by 2030, with the region already facing below replacement-level fertility rates (UN, 2015). A product of an extended period of low birthrates, low death rates, and increased longevity, Europe is best described as an aging society, where the low birthrates and aging populations have caused alarm that the number of European newborns will not be sufficient to renew populations or bear the financial burden of supporting an aging society.

In addition to population size and rate of growth, a demographic divide is also reflected in age distribution with some countries experiencing a *youth bulge* and others an aging population. The youth population is highest in Asia, though it may be surpassed by Africa around 2080 (see Figure 12.2). In Africa, the number of youth is escalating and expected to increase by 32 percent over the next eleven years, from 252 million in 2019 to over 333 million in 2030 (UNDESA, 2019). In Europe and North America, the proportion of people sixty years of age or older is advancing the fastest due to changes in fertility and mortality rates.

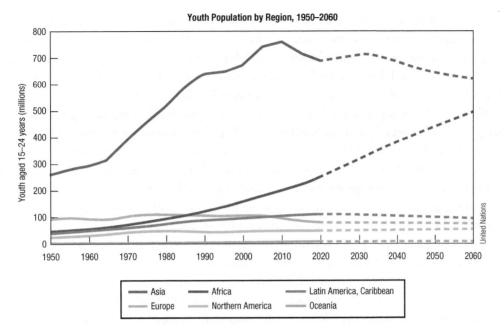

Youth Population by Region, 1950–2060

FIGURE 12.2 Baby Boom or Bust As global population grows, so too does the number of youth. In 2015 there were 1.2 billion young people aged fifteen to twenty-four years; by 2030, the number is expected to increase by 7 percent to reach almost 1.3 billion. Yet the rate of growth varies across regions, as shown in the graph above. Youth populations are expected to stabilize in Europe, North America, Latin America, and Oceania over the coming decades. Asia and Africa will experience the greatest changes, with Africa's youth population projected to more than double between 2015 and 2060 (UNDESA, 2019).

For countries that struggle to educate and employ their young people, a burgeoning youth population poses challenges for economic growth and political stability. It is difficult for public policy to meet citizens' needs and generate national wealth as "soaring unemployment, endemic poverty, and flailing schools are quite simply impossible to combat when every year adds more and more people" (Potts and Campbell, 2009, p. 30). Furthermore, as an enlarged youth population in the Global South faces poor economic conditions and a lack of resources to provide for a family, many are turning to religious fundamentalism to counter their frustration and despair and are propelling an Islamic revival. Particularly in conjunction with economic stagnation, youth bulges have been linked to a greater involvement in terrorism, crime, and civil conflict (Flückiger and Ludwig, 2018; Lombardi et al., 2015). As Michelle Gavin, an international affairs fellow with the Council on Foreign Relations, explains: "If you have no other options and not much else going on, the opportunity cost of joining an armed movement may be low."

At the same time, a revolution in longevity is unfolding, with life expectancy at birth worldwide at a record high of seventy-two years and rising (WDI, 2017a). This is creating an increasingly aged world population, and changing the contours of the global community. By 2025, 8.4 percent of the population in the Global South will be sixty-five or older. In the Global North, this demographic trend is even more pronounced, with about 21.1 percent of the population likely to be sixty-five years or older by 2025 (UNDESA, 2019).

Global aging is occurring at rates never before seen, in part because of improvements in medicine and health care, with some physicians now distinguishing between chronological and biological aging. Even the number of people who reach age eighty is on the rise. In 1950, 14.3 million people had seen their eightieth birthday. By 2009, the number had risen to 104.1 million, and by 2050, the number is expected to be more than 426 million (UNDESA, 2019).

Although the "aging and graying" of the human population is a global population trend that poses its own set of public policy dilemmas, it is more pronounced in the Global North than the Global South (see Map 12.2). There are concerns that, due to its rapidly aging populations, the Global North will be especially burdened by rising old-age dependency and face an array of economic, budgetary, and social challenges. Although the effects are expected to vary among developed countries, these could include a decreasing labor supply; a decline in economic growth and per capita income; increased demand for public expenditures on health care, long-term care, and pensions; and an increased need to invest in the human capital of future generations in order to boost overall productivity.

Resolving this dilemma in the Global North will require, in part, the promotion of demographic renewal by creating better conditions for families. Over the past few years, there has been growing debate within the Global North, particularly Europe, as to whether policy makers

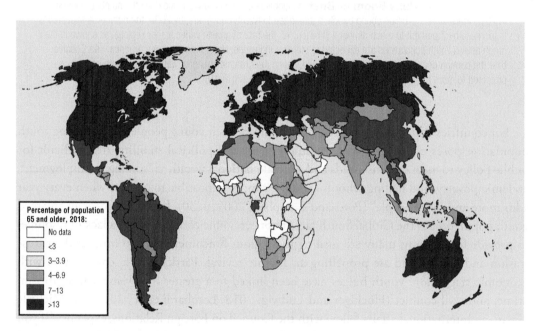

MAP 12.2 Aging and Graying Around the World As falling fertility is met with rising life expectancy, the world moves toward a major demographic transformation—global aging—wherein elderly people constitute an increasing percentage of a state's population. "It will challenge the ability of many countries to provide a decent standard of living for the old without imposing too big a burden on the young" (Jackson, 2013). As the map shows, this transformation is already well under way in the Global North. In Germany, for example, 22 percent of the population is sixty-five or above as compared to only 2 percent in Angola.

 Think It Through In what ways will shifting global demographics change the way states interact politically and economically? For instance, how will the youth bulge in the Global South impact world trade?

should adopt "pro-natal" policies designed to stimulate increased birthrates and combat norms for small families. French families with at least three children benefit from tax breaks and discounts such as reduced train fares. Russia, where the population declined for two decades, has begun a sustained effort to encourage marriage and childbearing by offering financial incentives to women who have multiple children. In Japan, the government estimates that the population will decline from 127 million in 2014 to 86.7 million by 2060, with people over sixty-five comprising 40 percent of the population (Gray, 2015). To boost the country's fertility rate, the government has created a number of policies, including the promotion of speed-dating events.

It will also hinge on reforming age-related public expenditures in the Global North, in particular health care, long-term care, and government-supported retirement pensions. As described by the European Commission:

> An aging population raises challenges for our societies and economies, culturally, organizationally and from an economic point of view. Policy makers worry about how living standards will be affected as each worker has to provide for the consumption needs of a growing number of elderly dependents. Markets worry about fiscal sustainability and the ability of policy makers to address timely and sufficiently these challenges in several Member States. The seriousness of the challenge depends on how our economies and societies respond and adapt to these changing demographic conditions. Looking ahead, policy makers need to ensure long-term fiscal sustainability in the face of large but predictable challenges, as well as significant uncertainty. This is all the more true as Europe has experienced the deepest recession in decades, which is putting an unprecedented stress on workers and enterprises and has had a major negative impact on public finances (European Commission, 2012, p. 21).

The resulting differences in demographic momentums are producing quite different population profiles in the developed and the developing worlds, and "twenty-first century international security will depend less on how many people inhabit the world than on how the global population is composed and distributed: where populations are declining and where they are growing, which countries are relatively older and which are more youthful, and how demographics will influence population movements across regions" (Goldstone, 2010, p. 31). The poor Global South is home to a surplus of youth, with rising birthrates and growing populations; the rich Global North is aging, with falling birthrates and declining populations. In the Global South, the working-age population will shoulder the burden of dependent children for years to come, whereas in the Global North it is the growing proportion of elderly adults who will pose a dependency burden.

IMAGE 12.2 **From Russia with Love** In response to Russia's demographic crisis, policy makers are offering married couples incentives to procreate. From its low of 1.2 in 1999, the Russian fertility rate increased to a little more than 1.8 in 2020. However, due to a declining number of women of childbearing age, the actual number of births continues to drop, from 9.36 million between 2010 and 2015 to 9.29 million between 2015 and 2020 (UNDESA, 2019). President Vladimir Putin announced government plans to spend $8.6 billion, starting in 2018, to encourage Russians to have more children. Anticipated to last at least three years, the government policy provides for mortgage subsidies and payments to new and growing families (TMT, 2018). Shown here is a couple on the Bench of Reconciliation in a Moscow park, which is curved to promote physical contact and help couples to work out their differences.

It is easy to see how this facet of globalization is *not* making people in the world more alike. Variation in the geographical distribution of population is increasing the differences in the quality of life experienced around the planet, and this demographic diversity is the result of different changes in the key determinants of population growth and structure—fertility, mortality, and migration. Let us now consider how the movement of people, both across and within countries, shapes global population structures.

Global Migration Trends

LO 12-2 Examine global migration patterns, and discuss the significance of global urbanization.

The movement of populations across borders has reached unprecedented proportions, with 244 million international migrants in 2015, an increase of 3.3 percent from 2010 (UN, 2018b). The United States, Germany, Russia, Saudi Arabia, and the United Kingdom are the top five migrant destinations, while India, Mexico, Russia, China, and Bangladesh are the largest countries of origin (UN, 2018b). The Mexico-U.S. corridor is the most frequent migrant path, accounting for 13 million migrants in 2013. The second largest migration corridor is Russia-Ukraine, followed by Bangladesh-India (World Bank, 2015a). Contrary to popular belief, migration between countries in the Global South (37 percent of global migration) is larger than migration from the Global South to the Global North (35 percent of global migration) (UN, 2018c).

The migration of people between countries has raised a host of moral issues, such as the ethnic balance inside host countries, the meaning of citizenship and sovereignty, the distribution of income, labor supply, **xenophobia**, the impact of multiculturalism, and protection of basic human rights and prevention of exploitation. Furthermore, large flows of migrants and refugees from *fragile states*—countries whose governments no longer enjoy support from their rebelling citizens and from displaced peoples who either flee the country or organize revolts to divide the state into smaller independent units—can undermine democratic governance and state stability and poses a potential threat (see Chapters 6 and 7). The governments of sovereign states have difficulty regulating the movement of foreigners inside their borders, and no multilateral intergovernmental organizations (IGOs) for meaningful global governance exist to deal with the consequences of the escalating migration of people (and labor) around the globe. Porous borders create ambiguous ethics about mass migration movements, but one consequence is clear: there are both winners and losers through the globalization of migration.

xenophobia
Antipathy for members of a foreign nationality, ethnic, or linguistic group.

A Quest for Sustenance and Freedom

People most commonly migrate in search of better jobs. For host countries, this can contribute to economic growth. For the home countries, many of which are poor Global South countries, the growing flow of *remittances* (see Chapter 5), or money that migrants earn while working abroad and then send to their families in their home countries, provides one of the biggest sources of foreign currency (Lopez et al., 2010; Singer, 2010). Remittances sent home by migrants from the Global South are projected to be at least $529 billion in 2018, with global remittances for both developing and developed countries reaching $689 billion (World Bank, 2019b).

Factors that influence migration may reflect broader demographic trends, as working-age people in "younger" countries within the Global South move to fill employment needs of "graying" countries in the Global North. Yet there are inevitable worries that migration may reduce the job opportunities for citizens and place a strain on public services. Weak or uncertain economic conditions tend to exacerbate such fears. Given the uncertainty of the current global economic order (see Chapters 10 and 11), immigration flows have become increasingly controversial and many countries have adopted measures intended to stem the flow of peoples across borders (Traynor and Hooper, 2011; Koser, 2010). In the EU, while the Schengen Agreement officially dismantled borders within member countries, several members, including Austria, Denmark, France, Germany, Norway, and Sweden, have cited "national security" reasons for instituting border controls (BBC, 2019a). The United States has severely cut programs dealing with multiple types of immigration, including family-based immigration and refugees (Krogstad and Gonzalez-Barrera, 2019).

At the same time, another trend in our "age of migration" is the flight of people not in search of economic opportunity but out of fear of persecution. **Refugees** are individuals whose race, religion, nationality, membership in a particular social group, or political opinions make them

refugees
People who flee for safety to another country because of a well-founded fear of political persecution, environmental degradation, or famine.

IMAGES 12.3A AND 12.3B Growing Up as a Refugee Children make up a large portion of the refugee population; in 2018, about half of the total global refugee population was under the age of eighteen (UN, 2019a). As refugees, children face additional challenges. Given the lack of economic opportunities for their families, many children must beg for money, particularly in urban areas. Pictured right is a Syrian refugee child begging on the streets of Beirut, Lebanon, a city where this in an endemic problem. Securing educational opportunities for children is vital to their growth and future prospects, though resources for doing so are often scarce. Shown above is the Sunflower temporary learning centre in Kutupalong Extension Camp 4 in south-east Bangladesh. The centre, run by the UN, offers a few hours of primary education to three shifts of students daily (Gluck and Yeasmine, 2019).

internally displaced persons (IDPs) People who have been forced to flee their homes, but remain within their country of origin.

targets of persecution in their homelands and who, therefore, migrate from their country of origin, unable to return. According to the UN High Commissioner for Refugees (UNHCR), at the start of 2019, the world's refugee population was an unprecedented 25.9 million, of whom 20.4 million fell under UNHCR's mandate and 5.5 million Palestinian refugees fell under the responsibility of the United Nations Relief and Works Agency for Palestinian Refugees in the Near East (UNRWA). Other "persons of concern" are **internally displaced persons (IDPs)**, which the UNHCR estimated as increasing by 10.8 million over the prior year to total a staggering 41.3 million worldwide (see Figure 12.3). Additionally, though not considered displaced per se, there are about 3.9 million stateless people worldwide and 3.5 million asylum seekers (UNHCR, 2019). According to UN Secretary-General António Guterres, "we are witnessing a paradigm change, an unchecked slide into an era in which the scale of global forced displacement as well as the response required is now clearly dwarfing anything seen before."

ethnic cleansing The extermination of an ethnic minority group by a state.

Refugees and displaced persons alike are often the victims of war, political violence, and human rights repression (see Chapter 13). For example, the *genocide* in Rwanda in 1994 drove more than 1.7 million refugees from their homeland; the persecution, **ethnic cleansing**, and armed conflict that accompanied the breakup of the former Yugoslavia uprooted nearly 3 million victims, moving Europe to the list of continents with large numbers of refugees—over 6 million—for the first time since World War II. More recently, the UNHCR estimates that Syrian, Afghan, and South Sudanese refugees comprise more than half of all refugees. At

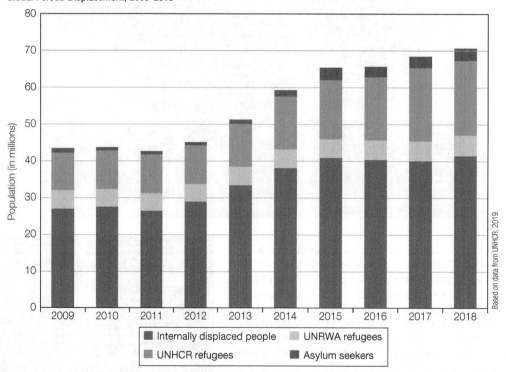

Global Forced Displacement, 2009–2018

Based on data from UNHCR, 2019.

FIGURE 12.3 The Chronic Global Refugee Crisis The UN Refugee Agency (UNHCR) defines "persons of concern" as refugees, internally displaced persons (IDPs), stateless people, and asylum seekers. The problem is huge and has become steadily worse since 2004, climbing to a record high of 70.8 million forcibly displaced people at the end of 2018 (UNHCR, 2019). Turkey continues as the largest refugee-hosting country, followed by Pakistan and Uganda. The Global South hosted 84 percent of refugees worldwide.

the start of 2019, 6.7 million Syrians—over 30 percent of their pre-civil war population—and 2.7 million Afghans sought refuge in other countries (UNHCR, 2019).

A large proportion of the world's refugees and displaced people flee their own homelands when ethnic and religious conflicts erupt in fragile states where governments fail to preserve law and order. In addition, millions of refugees flee their homelands because when disaster strikes, they are denied basic human rights such as police protection, access to fair trials in courts, and public assistance. A combination of push-and-pull forces now propels migration trends. Human rights violations, environmental degradation, unemployment, overpopulation, famine, war, and ethnic conflict and **atrocities** within states all push millions beyond their homelands (see Map 12.3).

atrocities
Brutal and savage acts against targeted citizen groups or prisoners of war, defined as illegal under international law.

Migrants are also pulled abroad by the promise of political freedom elsewhere, particularly in the democratically ruled Global North countries. Yet today's refugees face increased difficulty in finding safe havens; shutting the door is increasingly viewed as the preferred solution, and xenophobia is on the rise (see "A Closer Look: Global Migration and the Quest for Security"). Among both developed and developing countries, there is a growing unwillingness to provide refuge for those seeking a better life. With a weakening global economy, people are ever-more resistant to foreigners competing for domestic jobs and resources. Moreover, as security concerns since 9/11 have escalated worldwide, the perceived linkage between refugees and the probability of terrorism has tightened immigration controls.

Not only have countries in the Global North restricted the flow of people across borders, but the Global South is also increasingly unwilling to bear the burden of hosting refugees. This places the blame for insecurity on the victims—refugees seeking refuge—because "as a general

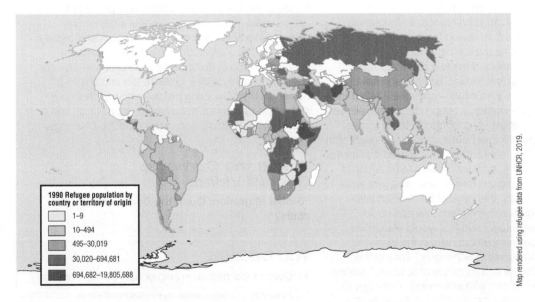

MAP rendered using refugee data from UNHCR, 2019.

MAP 12.3 From Whence Do They Flee? Oppressive and violent conditions cause many people to leave their homes in the interest of security and survival. At the start of 2019, there were 70.8 million forcibly displaced people worldwide, with the vast majority fleeing dangerous conditions in Africa and the Middle East. Although it is commonly assumed that states in the Global North admit the most refugees from conflict, evidence indicates instead that the majority flee to neighboring countries in the Global South. Indeed, the UNHCR estimates that 80 percent remain within their region of origin.

 Think It Through The refugee crisis is a fast-growing global issue. However, what limitations of international intervention exist here?

A Closer Look

GLOBAL MIGRATION AND THE QUEST FOR SECURITY

As unrest flowed across northern Africa in the spring of 2011, more than 25,000 migrants fled to Italy by way of the tiny island of Lampedusa. To Italy's frustration, the other members of the EU were unwilling to share the illegal immigration burden. Italy's request that the EU apply an emergency rule that would relocate the refugees across the various EU member states was blocked. In an effort to address its immigration crisis, Italy repatriated some of the migrants to their home country. For thousands of others, it issued national residence permits. This not only allowed the North Africans to remain in Italy, but it also enabled them to travel within Europe's border-free Schengen area to other countries.

This latter action angered France, as thousands of migrants traveled from Italy in the hopes of joining relatives in France. As tension between Italy and France accelerated, the leaders of the two countries at the time—French President Nicolas Sarkozy and Italian Prime Minister Silvio Berlusconi—collectively called for reform of the open-border Schengen treaty that allowed legal residents of most EU countries to travel across borders with only minimal border checks. Although both wished to see the treaty persist, they argued that it was necessary to allow temporary controls to be enacted when exceptional circumstances arise. In a joint letter to senior EU officials, they argued that the "situation concerning migration in the Mediterranean could rapidly transform into a crisis that would undermine the trust that our compatriots have in the [principle] of freedom of travel within Schengen." They further sought commitment to a "principle of solidarity" among the EU member states, with assurances that other EU countries would assist the southern states along the Mediterranean in dealing with problems posed by mass immigration.

This initial issue was a precursor to subsequent difficulties, as it brought to a head a key governance challenge in the EU: how to coordinate immigration policy among a group of countries that have been

at "a crossroads of human mobility since ancient times" (IOM, 2019). The problem only increased in significance as record numbers of people risked—and sometimes lost—their lives crossing the Mediterranean to seek refuge from conflict, persecution, and poverty in Africa, the Middle East, and Southeast Asia. Today, the "crisis" phase in Europe is essentially over—yearly migration flows peaked at just over a million in 2015 and by 2018 the number of new arrivals had fallen to 150,000 (BBC, 2018; Balmer, 2019). However, the political struggles persist. Surveys indicate that only 14 percent of Europeans think that the EU did an effective job of handling the crisis (Balmer, 2019), and populist and anti-immigrant parties have become increasingly powerful in several countries. As Lampedusa's deputy mayor, Damiano Sferlazzo, stated, "We have an economic union in Europe, not a political one. Europe needs to see this is their problem too and help out" (Tayler, 2014). Navigating precisely how to "help out" in the face of competing humanitarian, political, and economic interests remains an unresolved challenge.

Watch the Carnegie Council Video:

"Global Migration: Open the Doors or Build the Walls?"

You Decide:

1. Does global migration help or hurt the host country?

2. How can democracies reconcile conflicting principles—support for the fundamental right of people to emigrate versus a commitment to the absolute right of sovereign states to control their borders?

3. Is your stance on global migration compatible with the principle of a global "Responsibility to Protect"?

rule, individuals and communities do not abandon their homes unless they are confronted with serious threats to their lives and liberty. Flight from one's country is the ultimate survival strategy. . . . Refugees serve both as an index of internal disorder and the violation of human rights and humanitarian standards" (Loescher, 2005, p. 47).

That said, efforts to stem the tide of migrants have not reversed the trend of people seeking **sanctuary**. During 2018, 1.7 million new applications for **asylum** were submitted to governments and UNHCR offices in 158 countries (UNHCR, 2019), with a total of 3.5 million people still awaiting asylum decisions. With more than 254,300 asylum applications, the United States was the world's largest recipient of individual applications in 2018. Peru was the second largest recipient of asylum applications, followed by Germany, France, and Turkey (UNHCR, 2019).

The ethical issue is whether in the future the wealthy countries will respond to the plight of the needy with indifference or with compassion. How will *human security* be reconciled with *national security*? The welfare and survival of everyday people are endangered, and the need for their protection is increasing.

sanctuary
A place of refuge and protection.

asylum
The provision of sanctuary to safeguard refugees escaping from the threat of persecution in the country where they hold citizenship.

Urbanization

When considering migration patterns and interpreting demographic projections, it is also important to examine the geographic concentration of people within countries. Known as **population density**, this measures how closely together people are living. Some countries and regions are very crowded and others are not. For example, Monaco is the most congested sovereign state in the world, with 19,196 people for each square kilometer, and people in Greenland have the most space to spread out, with less than one person for each square kilometer (WDI, 2019).

Today, more than half the world lives in cities, and the urbanization of the world is accelerating and spreading. Worldwide, 4 billion people (about 54 percent of the total global population) live in urban areas, with a projected urban population growth rate of 2.0 percent (WDI, 2017a). The United Nations predicts that by 2050, 6.7 billion people—more than two-thirds of the population—will live in an urban environment (UNDESA, 2018).

Referring to rapid urbanization, also known as **turbo-urbanization**, economist Edward Glaeser (2011) quips that "the world isn't flat, it's paved." From 1990 to 2016, the percentage of people living in a city with a population of over a million increased almost 28 percent (WDI, 2017a). Moreover, cities are growing fastest in the Global South. "Every month 5 million people move from the countryside to a city somewhere in the developing world" *(The Economist,* 2011d, p. 91). According to UN estimates, 90 percent of future population growth will take place in the sprawling cities and slums of the Global South (Muggah, 2015). This is particularly evident in Asia and the Pacific, where three of the world's ten most global cities are located.

This urbanizing trend is producing a related kind of demographic divide: the increasing concentration of people in giant **megacities** where populations exceed 10 million (see Figure 12.4). As the percentage of world population residing in dense urban agglomerations increases worldwide, the "dualism" between city dwellers and those living in the rural and poor periphery will make the urbanized core cities more similar to each other in outlooks, values, and lifestyles. People in megacities are already communicating with one another more frequently than they do with people living in the countryside within their own states. "The process of urbanization, through

population density
The number of people within each country, region, or city, measuring the geographical concentration of the population as a ratio of the average space available for each resident.

turbo-urbanization
Extremely rapid and unregulated urban growth.

megacities
Metropolitan areas in which the population is more than 10 million people.

Top Twenty-Five Global Cities

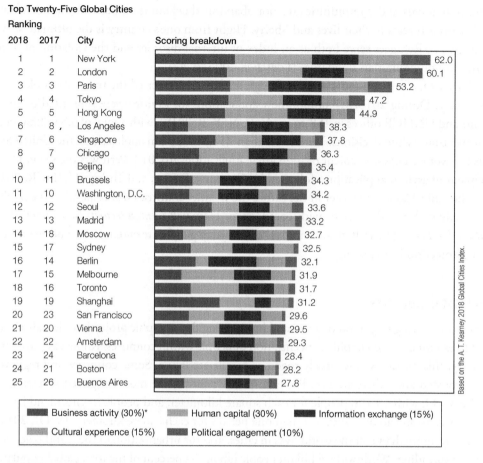

Ranking

2018	2017	City	Scoring breakdown
1	1	New York	62.0
2	2	London	60.1
3	3	Paris	53.2
4	4	Tokyo	47.2
5	5	Hong Kong	44.9
6	8	Los Angeles	38.3
7	6	Singapore	37.8
8	7	Chicago	36.3
9	9	Beijing	35.4
10	11	Brussels	34.3
11	10	Washington, D.C.	34.2
12	12	Seoul	33.6
13	13	Madrid	33.2
14	18	Moscow	32.7
15	17	Sydney	32.5
16	14	Berlin	32.1
17	15	Melbourne	31.9
18	16	Toronto	31.7
19	19	Shanghai	31.2
20	23	San Francisco	29.6
21	20	Vienna	29.5
22	22	Amsterdam	29.3
23	24	Barcelona	28.4
24	21	Boston	28.2
25	26	Buenos Aires	27.8

Based on the A. T. Kearney 2018 Global Cities Index.

- Business activity (30%)*
- Human capital (30%)
- Information exchange (15%)
- Cultural experience (15%)
- Political engagement (10%)

FIGURE 12.4 The Top Twenty-Five Global Cities "Cities are becoming stronger and increasingly exerting a sphere of influence that transcends country borders" (Hales et al., 2015, p. 5). This figure depicts global engagement of major world metropolitan areas across five dimensions: business activity, human capital, information exchange, cultural experience, and political engagement. There is stability at the top of the rankings, with New York, London, Paris, Tokyo, and Hong Kong placing in the top five ranked cities across both time periods. Within the top twenty-five in 2018, nine are in the Asia Pacific region, nine are in Europe, and seven are in the Americas.

which populations are increasingly concentrated in towns and cities, is an apparently inexorable transition and associated with rising living standards. No highly developed society is primarily rural" (Skeldon, 2010, p. 25). Indeed, many positive externalities can result from urbanization: "proximity makes people more inventive, as bright minds feed off one another; more productive, as scale gives rise to finer degrees of specialization; and kinder to the planet, as city-dwellers are more likely to go by foot, bus or train" (*The Economist*, 2011d, p. 91; Glaeser, 2011).

The world is witnessing a surge in urbanization, where capital flows, supply chains, and telecommunications link global cities and denationalize international relations. "The world today is more about cities than countries, and a place like Seoul has more in common with Singapore and Hong Kong than it does with smaller Korean cities" (Hales and Pena, 2012, p. 4). The power and influence of cities, however, are not unique to the contemporary period. Sociologist Saskia Sassen (2008) points out that, in ages past, nations and empires did not restrain cities but instead used cities as filters for their global ambitions. In Europe, it was in the largely autonomous Renaissance cities of Bruges and Antwerp that the innovative legal foundations for a transnational stock exchange were first developed, providing a basis for international credit and global trade networks and reflecting the ability of the cities to conduct their own "sovereign" diplomacy (Khanna, 2010).

However, urbanization and the growth of megacities can pose challenges for national governance. Balance-of-power politics falls short in helping us to understand the implications of how globalization enables major cities to challenge national sovereignty and pull away from their home states:

> Taken together, the advent of global hubs and megacities forces us to rethink whether state sovereignty or economic might is the new prerequisite for participating in global diplomacy. The answer is of course both, but while sovereignty is eroding and shifting, cities are now competing for global influence alongside states (Khanna, 2010, p. 126).

Though cities can serve as engines for growth and development, they can also pose risks to human security. Millions of urban squatters pour into megacities each year, and economic inequality and urban blight is rampant in major metropolitan areas. Migrants live in slums in destitution and squalor next to stunning high rises and private gated communities in cities such

IMAGE 12.4 Feeling the Pulse of Humanity At almost 8 billion people at the start of 2020, the world's population continues to grow. More than half live in cities, and urbanization continues to rise. In 1975, only three cities in the world exceeded 10 million people. The UN predicts that by 2030 there will be forty-three megacities, and the fastest growing urban areas will be in Asia and Africa (United Nations, 2018d). Pictured here, vendors, pedestrians, and vehicles vie for space on the streets of Kolkata, India, a city and metro area of more than 15 million people.

fragile cities
Cities in a state of violent crisis, with the municipal government incapable or unwilling to govern and provide public services.

as Sao Paulo, Shanghai, and Istanbul. In **fragile cities**, the social contract between municipal governments and their people has deteriorated, and urban violence is rampant.

So why do some cities spiral into crisis while others prosper? A key factor connected to insecurity and violence in cities appears to be turbo-urbanization, characterized by extremely rapid urbanization and unregulated growth. Another factor is the presence of a youth bulge that leaves large numbers of young people, particularly males, undereducated and unemployed. The Pakistani city of Karachi stands out as a fragile city, having expanded from a half million people in 1947 to 16 million today. Though it generates almost 15 percent of the country's GDP, it is one of the most violent megacities in the world (World Bank, 2018b).

population implosion
A rapid reduction of population that reverses a previous trend toward progressively larger populations; a severe reduction in the world's population.

The impact of global urbanization is also likely to aggravate health and environmental problems, straining supplies of clean water, shelter, and sanitation. If urbanization throughout the global community continues at its current pace, which is almost certain, this trend will lead to still another kind of *transformation* in the world. Threats, such as the outbreak of a widespread and deadly disease, could produce a **population implosion**. Next, we look at examples of life-threatening diseases that are sweeping a globe without borders.

New Plagues? The Global Impact of Disease

LO 12-3   Explain how infectious disease can lead to health crises around the world.

Although infant and child mortality rates remain discouragingly high in many developing countries, at least they are decreasing. On a global level, life expectancy at birth has increased each year since 1950, climbing by UN estimates to seventy-two years (WDI, 2017a). However, this rising longevity could reverse if globally transmittable diseases cut into the life spans made possible by improvements in health care, nutrition, water quality, and public sanitation.

Throughout history, the spread of bacteria, parasites, viruses, plagues, and diseases to various ecospheres, regardless of state borders, has suspended the development of or brought down once-mighty states and empires (Kolbert, 2005). In our age of globalization, a disease such as drug-resistant strains of tuberculosis (TB), which affects 134 out of every 100,000 people around the world (WDI, 2017a), knows no borders. It can spread with a sneeze or a cough on an international flight. Likewise, there are about 198 million cases of malaria each year, leading to more than 435,000 deaths in 2017 (WHO Malaria Report, 2018b). Because communicable diseases cause 20 percent of deaths worldwide (WDI, 2017a), global health is a concern and a threat to human security (see Figure 12.5).

acquired immune deficiency syndrome (AIDS)
An often fatal condition that can result from infection with the human immunodeficiency virus (HIV).

The grim possibility that virulent disease will decimate the world's population because we all share a common global environment is evident in the spread of the human immunodeficiency virus (HIV), which causes **acquired immune deficiency syndrome (AIDS)**. Since the 1970s onset of the AIDS pandemic, the UN estimates that "every day more than 8,000 people die of AIDS. Every hour almost 600 people become infected. Every minute a child dies of the virus." Today, nearly 8 percent of people worldwide between the ages of fifteen and forty-nine have HIV (WDI, 2017a).

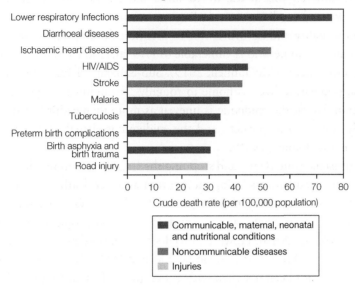

Leading Causes of Death, Low-Income Countries

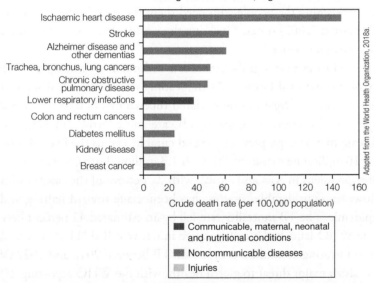

Leading Causes of Death, High-Income Countries

Adapted from the World Health Organization, 2018a.

FIGURE 12.5 The Burden of Disease Globally, almost 20 percent of deaths are due to communicable, maternal, neonatal, and nutrition conditions collectively. Noncommunicable diseases account for 71 percent of deaths globally. Yet a death divide is apparent between the Global North and the Global South. Shown on the top, low-income countries are most affected by risks associated with poverty such as undernutrition, poor sanitation, and unsafe water and are highly vulnerable to communicable disease. Shown on the bottom, in the Global North, people face health risks due to physical inactivity, diet-related factors, and tobacco-related factors and die from noncommunicable conditions such as cardiovascular disease and cancer.

However, some regions of the world suffer more from the disease as "local economic, cultural, and political conditions—including rates of male circumcision, drug use, and attitudes toward homosexuality and sex work, not to mention funding for prevention and treatment programs—can determine who is vulnerable to HIV infection and how people living with the disease access treatment" (McDonnell, 2019). Sub-Saharan Africa, where just over 14 percent of the global population lives, is home to roughly 25 million HIV-positive people. Yet even in sub-Saharan Africa, the epidemic is uneven as more than a third of those infected live in small, highly concentrated pockets, and the epidemic is virtually nonexistent across most of the continent (McDonnell, 2019).

The circumstances are tragic, and stopping the tragedy is "a moral duty." Fortunately, there are signs that this pandemic is losing momentum as fewer deaths are occurring due to HIV/AIDS every year. During 2017, 940,000 people died from AIDS-related illnesses—down from a peak of 1.9 million in 2004—and a record 21.7 million people are receiving treatment for the disease (UNAIDS, 2018). However, this does not mean that the epidemic is vanishing. As UNAIDS Executive Director Michel Sidibé informs, "There is a prevention crisis. The success in saving lives has not been matched with equal success in reducing new HIV infections . . . HIV prevention services are not being provided on an adequate scale and with sufficient intensity and are not reaching the people who need them the most." Thus, as world public health expert Laurie Garrett (2007) notes, "Tackling the world's diseases has become a key feature of many nations' foreign policies."

Sadly, many diseases pose significant threats to human well-being and remind us of the permeability of our national borders. As the leading cause of death from a single infectious agent, the World Health Organization declared tuberculosis (TB) a major health emergency and since 1993 has led efforts to improve TB care and control. Tuberculosis is an airborne infectious disease that, though preventable and curable, claims the lives of millions of people. An estimated 10 million new cases of TB, with 1.3 million deaths, were reported in 2017. The disease is most prevalent in Asia and Africa, with 27 percent of the cases worldwide occurring in India. However, considerable progress has been made toward halting and reversing the global TB epidemic. The TB mortality rate fell by an estimated 42 percent between 2000 and 2017, and the WHO launched a collaborative initiative called "Find. Treat. All." with a goal of detecting and treating 40 million people with TB between 2018 and 2022 (WHO, 2018a).

Malaria is also a major threat to global health, with the WHO reporting 219 million cases and 435,000 related deaths in 2017 (WHO, 2018b). This is tragic because the disease, which mosquitoes transmit to human beings, is largely preventable and treatable. Efforts to combat the spread of the disease include distributing millions of insecticide-treated bed nets. In May 2015, the World Health Assembly adopted a new global strategy for malaria that emphasizes universal access to malaria prevention, treatment, and diagnosis. The member states set an ambitious target of reducing global malaria incidence and mortality rates by 90 percent by 2030.

Over the past decade, deadly outbreaks of influenza have also generated global concern. What makes influenza different from other global diseases is the frightening ease with which it spreads. Some strains, such as avian flu, spread from birds to human beings. Experts believe that this disease spreads through the direct handling of chickens and the processing of meat, and worry that a new strand may spread easily from human to human (Mo, 2013). Another recent deadly strain, known as H1N1, or swine flu, crossed the species barrier between pigs and people. First appearing in Mexico in March 2009 and then spreading quickly to the United States, by its peak in 2010 it had appeared in at least 214 countries and overseas territories. Although the pandemic is now over, it highlighted the challenges faced by public officials as they seek to identify and enact protective measures for the population. A number of countries, particularly China and Russia, took vigorous quarantine measures against people who had traveled to countries suffering from high numbers of infected people.

Several African countries have suffered from outbreaks of the Ebola virus, a disease with a very high fatality rate that is transmitted from wild animals to people and also spreads through human-to-human transmission involving body fluids. Though discovered in 1976, the first major outbreak occurred in 2014. At that time, the World Health Organization declared the Ebola outbreak in West Africa a global public health emergency. Beginning in Guinea, the disease spread rapidly, claiming lives in the Democratic Republic of Congo (DRC), Gabon, South Sudan, Cote d'Ivoire, Uganda, Republic of the Congo (ROC), Guinea, and Liberia.

By the time the outbreak was halted in 2016, there had been almost 27,000 cases and 11,325 deaths (CDC, 2019). The initial response to the outbreak was slow, exacerbated by the political and economic shortcomings of the host states, including the lack of adequate health care infrastructure, political violence, population density in urban areas, and the mobile

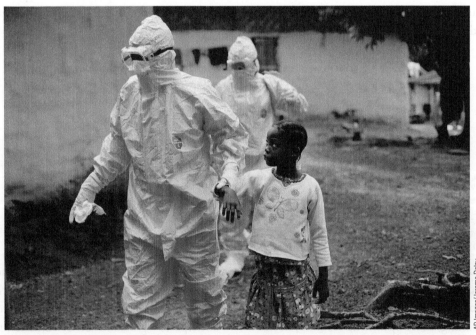

IMAGE 12.5 Does Globalization Make the Whole World Sick? The dangerous threat of a global pandemic "is arguably one of the greatest threats to global stability and security" (Monaco and Gupta, 2018). Shown here, a nine-year-old girl in Liberia is ushered away by health care workers after showing signs of being infected with Ebola. Most of the health care facilities in the region are underfunded and have limited resources. American businessman and philanthropist Bill Gates urges the international community to better guard against and prepare for future health pandemics, much like how we "prepare ourselves for war."

nature of much of the population. Though lauded for its later efforts, the WHO was criticized for being slow to declare the outbreak an official Public Health Emergency of International Concern (PHEIC) and thus tardy in mobilizing international support (WHO, 2015). In all, though "the initial outbreak response was slow and inadequate, once established the response demonstrated unprecedented and impressive levels of international cooperation" among countries, health organizations, and individual caregivers (Coltart et al., 2017).

Yet, of great concern, the underlying biological, economic, and political conditions that enabled the 2014-2016 outbreak are largely unchanged. In 2018, cases of Ebola resurfaced in the Democratic Republic of Congo and spread to Uganda by the following year. This marks the tenth Ebola outbreak in the Democratic Republic of Congo since the disease was discovered. As of July 2019, over 1,200 deaths had been reported in this most recent outbreak (Doctors Without Borders, 2019). There is hope, however, in light of very successful drug trials of two new Ebola treatments that hold the promise of a cure (Christensen and Yeung, 2019).

The spread and control of infectious diseases such as AIDS, tuberculosis, malaria, cholera, Middle East respiratory syndrome (MERS), Ebola, lymphatic filariasis, avian flu, mad cow disease, and swine flu have established themselves on the radar screen of policy makers throughout the world. Additionally, noncommunicable diseases—such as cancer, stroke, and diabetes—are on the rise, and it is estimated that by 2030 they will be the "leading cause of death and disability in every region of the world" (Bollyky, 2012). These diseases will not vanish from sight anytime soon and are a stark reminder of the transnational threats that remain ever-present in our borderless world and necessitate global cooperation and coordination. "In a globalized world, we're only as strong as the weakest health link" (Walsh, 2016, p. 10).

A relationship exists between the health of individuals within a state and that state's national security. A population's health is of utmost importance to the state's ability to survive.

—JEREMY YOUDE, GLOBAL HEALTH EXPERT

The Global Information Age

LO 12-4 Describe the expansion of global information flows, and outline the political and social implications.

cosmopolitan
An outlook that values viewing the cosmos or entire world as the best polity or unit for political governance and personal identity, as opposed to other polities such as one's local metropolis or city of residence.

Pessimists predict that one result of globalization will be competition between states as they seek to preserve their sovereign independence, retain the allegiance of their citizens, resist the homogenizing forces now sweeping the world, and ensure their own national security. In a contrasting, more optimistic scenario, *liberal theory* anticipates a globalization of cultures that transcends contemporary geopolitical boundaries and erodes the meaning of national identity and sovereignty by creating "global citizens" who assign loyalty to the common interests of all peoples. Trends in the cultural dimension of globalization are generating changes in how people construct their identities and encourage a more **cosmopolitan** perspective. The major source of this global transformation is the growing speed and flow of communications, which is a hallmark of the *global village*—a metaphor used by many to portray a future in which borders will vanish and the world will become a single community.

In the age of global communication, the meaning of "home" and "abroad" and of "near" and "far" vanishes, promoting changes in people's images of community and their own identity. Will cellular phones, the internet, blogs, and other means of transnational communication portend consensus and, perhaps, an integrated global village? Or is this vision, in which shared information breeds understanding and peace, unattainable? Worse, will the unconstrained interconnectedness of globalization do away with private life, erasing what remains of identity, individualism, and independence?

The Evolution of Global Communications

The increased ease and volume of international communications is creating "the death of distance" and radically altering people's decisions about where to work and live, as well as their constructed images of "us" and "them." No area of the world and no arena of politics, economics, society, or culture are immune from the pervasive influence of *communication technology*. "Since 1969, when the first bit of data was transmitted over what would come to be known as the Internet, that global network has evolved from linking mainframe computers to connecting personal computers and now mobile devices. By 2010, the number of computers on the Internet had surpassed the number of people on earth" (Gershenfeld and Vasseur, 2014, p. 60). Personal computers and the "wireless world" of mobile phones have facilitated communication

IMAGE 12.6 **The World at One's Fingertips** As a primary information highway, the internet fuels globalization and allows individuals to become part of a "digital public" that transcends national borders and identities (Tiessen, 2010). More than 82.2 percent of citizens in the Global North are internet users, as are 41.9 percent of people in the Global South (WDI, 2017a), and internet usage continues to grow. This photo of a Huli tribal chief from Papua New Guinea presenting his new website illustrates how the spread of information technology facilitates the global flow of ideas and information.

between people in areas as diverse as rural communities in the Global South and the technology-intensive countries in the Global North. "More than 50 percent of the world's population has access to some combination of cell phones (5 billion users) and the Internet (2 billion). These people communicate within and across borders, forming virtual communities that empower citizens" (Schmidt and Cohen, 2010, p. 75).

cyberspace
A metaphor used to describe the global electronic web of people, ideas, and interactions on the internet, which is unencumbered by the borders of the geopolitical world.

The result of this expanding worldwide use of the internet is the creation of **cyberspace**, a global information superhighway allowing people everywhere to communicate freely as they surf the Web, exchange emails, and join social networking sites. The increasing number of internet users is promoting a cultural revolution by giving most of the world access to unfiltered information. This creates a single globe, united in shared information. This face of globalization submerges borders and breaks barriers. It lays the foundation for a smaller, shrinking, and flatter world and propels "an exciting new era of global interconnectedness that will spread ideas and innovations around the world faster than ever before" (Giles, 2010, p. 4).

If one constant stands out, it is continuous change in technological innovation. The rapid pace of *information technology* development drives globalization. It will make today's methods of communicating look ancient in a few years and, in the process it will transform how people communicate as well as which countries lead (and prosper) and which follow. The digital and physical worlds are also beginning to be linked, as the things around us go online as part of the **Internet of Things (IoT)**

Internet of Things (IoT)
The networked connectivity of objects or devices that have unique identifiers and the ability to transfer data without requiring human interaction.

. Technological innovation has made it possible to embed small computers in everyday objects so that they can send and receive information through the internet, in essence becoming independently intelligent:

> Shelves and pill bottles connected to the Internet can alert a forgetful patient when to take a pill, a pharmacist to make a refill, and a doctor when a dose is missed. Floors can call for help if a senior citizen has fallen, helping the elderly live independently. . . . A coffeemaker can turn on when a person gets out of bed and turn off when a cup is loaded into a dishwasher, a stoplight can communicate with roads to route cars around traffic, a building can operate more efficiently by knowing where people are and what they're doing, and even the health of the whole planet can be monitored in real time by aggregating the data from all such devices (Gershenfeld and Vasseur, 2014, pp. 60–61).

Enthusiasts believe that the advantages of the global communications revolution are a blessing for humanity. When people and things around the world are connected through the revolution in digital communications, the shared information propels human development and productivity. Proponents also see the globalized digital revolution as producing many side payoffs: reducing oppressive dictators' authority, allowing small businesses to compete globally, empowering transnational activists to exercise more influence, and providing opportunities for a diversity of voices and cultures. For example, in 2011, using information technology such as Twitter, Facebook, and YouTube, Egyptians were able to organize protest demonstrations, document to the world images of repression, and bring to life a digital people's movement for freedom. These actions ultimately toppled Egyptian President Hosni Mubarak from power. As famous actor and Twitter enthusiast Ashton Kutcher optimistically noted at the time, "the word *revolution* is spelled with 140 characters." Echoing this sentiment, former UN Secretary-General Ban Ki-moon observed that some dictators "are more afraid of tweets than they are of opposing armies."

The Dark Side of the Global Communications Revolution

However, though advances in *information and communications technology* have made information far more accessible to ordinary people and have consequently facilitated greater global debate, there are challenges that cast a shadow over our increasingly extensive information interconnectivity. Historian Niall Ferguson (2011, p. 9) notes, "social networks might promote democracy, but they also empower the enemies of freedom." Critics complain that the growing electronic network has created a new global condition known as **virtuality**. In such a world, one can conceal one's true identity, which threatens to make the activities of international organized crime, terrorist groups, and other malevolent actors easier:

> The world's most repressive regimes and violent transnational groups—from al Qaeda and the Mexican drug cartels to the Mafia and the Taliban—are effectively using technology to bring on new recruits, terrify local populations, and threaten democratic institutions. The Mexican drug cartels, in order to illustrate the consequences of opposition, spread graphic videos showing decapitations of those who cooperate with law enforcement, and al Qaeda and its affiliates have created viral videos showing the killings of foreigners held hostage in Iraq (Schmidt and Cohen, 2010, p. 78).

virtuality
Imagery created by computer technology of objects and phenomena that produces an imaginary picture of actual things, people, and experiences.

Some also worry that "privateness will become passé [through] the spread of surveillance technology and the rise of websites like YouTube, which receives more than 65,000 video uploads daily and is driving a trend toward cyber-exhibitionism" (*Futurist*, 2007, p. 6). New privacy concerns are likely to arise as analysts and corporations figure out how to use all of the information about a user's location and preferences that can be determined through information technology services offered by internet providers and cell phone companies. "You may use your phone to find friends and restaurants, but somebody else may be using your phone to find you and find out about you" (Markoff, 2009, p. 1). Similarly, online social networks, such as Facebook, which has a global membership that would place it as the world's most populous country, encourage users to share information. Then, the networks mine the data on members' personal preferences (Fletcher, 2010). Some fear that big internet companies are abusing their power, and in a landmark ruling in 2014 the European Court of Justice supported "the right to be forgotten" by asking Google to honor requests by individuals to remove old links to posts about them (*The Economist*, 2014a).

In the name of national security, governments are also developing extensive surveillance systems that discreetly and covertly monitor activities, many in public spaces. One example is the high-tech surveillance program in China, known as "Golden Shield," which can identify dissent and allow the government to address it before it turns into a mass movement. Using people-tracking technology supplied by American corporations such as General Electric, IBM, and Honeywell, the goal is to create "a single, nationwide network, an all-seeing system that will be capable of tracking and identifying anyone who comes within its range" (Klein, 2008, p. 60).

The United States' extensive surveillance of internet communications, which became the focus of considerable international criticism in 2013, is another example. The U.S. National Security Agency (NSA), Federal Bureau of Investigation (FBI), and Central Intelligence Agency (CIA) secretly collected millions of records from U.S. telecommunications and technology firms. Some defended the program as a necessary violation of privacy to fight terrorism and major crime, but critics charged that it was an overreach of authority and a threat to democracy. Adding further to global furor, evidence emerged indicating that the emails and phone messages of national delegates at the G-20 economic meetings in 2009 were intercepted by the British signals intelligence agency (GCHQ) in order to give their country an advantage at the meetings (MacAskill et al., 2013).

Reflecting deep concern for the threat that surveillance and interception of communications poses to human rights, in December 2013 the United Nations adopted a resolution that called for states to respect and protect the right to privacy in digital communication. In 2018, the European Union took a more rigorous stand in protection of individual data privacy by passing the General Data Protection Regulation (GDPR). It gave individuals more control over their personal data and compelled organizations to ensure the security of the way they collect, process, and store personal information. The EU defended these new rules as "necessary to protect consumers in an era of huge cyberattacks and data leaks" (Kottasová, 2018).

disinformation
False information that is intentionally disseminated to harm an individual, organization, or state.

Perhaps even more alarming than mass surveillance is the pervasiveness and increasing sophistication of **disinformation** campaigns intended to cause deliberate harm through false and misleading information. Russia has used such techniques to influence societies and undermine democracies. "There is nothing new about state propaganda and other means of political subversion . . . But, digital and social media, in combination with more traditional methods, offer new means to achieve traditional ends" (Polyakova and Freid, 2019, p. 1). For years, the Ukraine, Georgia, and the Baltic states have faced Russian disinformation attacks. More recently, Russia successfully targeted the United States' 2016 presidential election, the Dutch referendum, and possibly the Brexit vote (Mueller, 2019; Thorington, 2019; Holton, 2017).

There are worries that not only are other malicious actors, such as Iran, North Korea, and political extremist groups, emulating Russian tactics but also that disinformation techniques continue to evolve. Advances in *artificial intelligence* are responsible for:

> "deepfakes" and other "synthetic media" products—video and audio manipulation with the capability to manufacture the appearance of reality, such as nonexistent, but real-looking, remarks by a political leader. As these tools become more low cost and accessible, they will become perfect weapons for information warfare . . . it may be increasingly difficult to disentangle foreign-origin disinformation from domestic social media conversations. Rather than trying to break through the noise, the new strategy aims to blend in with the noise—obfuscating manipulative activity and blurring the line between authentic and inauthentic content (Polyakova and Freid, 2019, p. 2).

In light of these developments, there is increased national and international attention to policies and processes to limit the influx of disinformation. "The EU first recognized this threat in 2015 by establishing the East Strategic Communication Task Force which responds to Russian disinformation efforts in Eastern Europe by exposing false Russian narratives and strengthening independent media in the region" (Thorington, 2019). Companies such as Facebook, Twitter, Google, and YouTube have agreed to address the spread of fake news and hate speech. There is also a growing effort to build resilience by improving social awareness of disinformation and improving the ability to recognize fabricated or deceptive content and sources. The "Learn to Discern" project in Ukraine, implemented in 2018, is one example that aims to educate children as part of a national effort to counter Russian disinformation and cyber-warfare. Students who received the training "were twice as likely to detect hate speech, 18 percent better at identifying fake news stories, 16 percent better at sorting out fact from opinion, and 14 percent more knowledgeable about the role of the news media industry" (Cain, 2019). In a digital age when information moves freely and often anonymously, it is increasingly important to be a perceptive consumer.

The Business of Global Communication

Despite the increase in state and non-state actors who create and disseminate information, the more than $1 trillion global telecommunications industry remains a major vehicle for the rapid spread of ideas, information, and images worldwide. That impact accelerated after the World Trade Organization created the World Telecom Pact in 1997. This *regime* ended government and private telecommunications monopolies in many states, and the resulting cuts in phone costs were widely seen as a catalyst of the world economy's expansion.

Advances in information technology and the expansive scope of global media have augmented this development. Yet, contrary to conventional wisdom that the media has the ability to drive a country's foreign policy, the type of power that media wields over international affairs is arguably limited. Scholarship shows that the media influence what people think *about* more than what they think. In this way, the media primarily function to set the agenda of public discussion about public affairs instead of determining public opinion.

It is through **agenda setting** that the media demonstrably shape international public policy (Eshbaugh-Soha and Linebarger, 2014). For example, global broadcasts of the ruthless repression and illegitimate tactics associated with Mugabe's bid for reelection in Zimbabwe in 2008 ignited a worldwide chain reaction to aid that country's refugees and pressure the government to reform. Similarly, reports by professional journalists and individual activists helped to fan Iranian resistance and protest over the declared electoral victory of incumbent president Mahmoud Ahmadinejad in 2009. Likewise, in 2011, social media helped fan popular dissent and organize demonstrations by providing communication and inspiration during the "Arab Spring."

These examples of the power of information technology in international politics aside, some people caution that this kind of "virtual diplomacy" has real limitations. Not only can it constrain the policy options available to global decision makers, it can provide biased or incomplete information that may contribute to an inaccurate or limited understanding of global problems. Moreover, though ours is often described as the information age, a remarkably large portion of the available information is controlled by a **cartel** of huge multinational media corporations. Headquartered mostly in the rich Global North, these industry leaders are merging to combine their resources and, in the process, are expanding their global reach. The world's population is a captive audience, and the information presented by these corporate giants shapes our values and our images of what the world is like.

A counterpoint to the "McWorld" of transnational media consumerism is "jihad"—a world driven by "parochial hatreds," not "universalizing markets" (Ram, 2008; Barber, 1995). Because globalized communications and information may be used as tools for terrorism and revolution as well as for community and peace, the creation of a world without boundaries, where everybody will know everything about anybody's activities, will not necessarily be a better world. You should ask: Would the world be better or worse if it were to become an increasingly impersonal place, with rootless individuals who have declining connections to their own country's culture and history?

agenda setting
The thesis that by their ability to identify and publicize issues, the communications media determine the problems that receive attention from governments and international organizations.

cartel
A convergence of independent commercial enterprises or political groups that combine for collective action, such as limiting competition, setting prices for their services, or forming a coalition to advance their group's interests.

> *People from all over the world will draw knowledge and inspiration from the same technology platform, but different cultures will flourish on it. It is the same soil, but different trees will grow. The next phase of globalization is going to be more glocalization—more and more local content made global.*
>
> —THOMAS L. FRIEDMAN, INTERNATIONAL JOURNALIST

Globalization and the Global Future

LO 12-5 Evaluate the multiple facets of globalization, and appraise their implications for the future of world politics.

Rapid globalization, propelled in large measure by revolutions in technology, is almost certain to continue. Expect the controversies about globalization's alleged virtues and vices to heighten as finance, trade, population, labor, communications, and cultures continue to converge globally.

Although globalization has narrowed the distance between the world's people, some have gained and others have lost ground. The global village is not proving to be an equally hospitable home for everyone. Indeed, levels of satisfaction with cascading globalization vary widely, as do the levels to which countries and people are linked by globalization's multiple forces (see Figure 12.6). Winners in the game downplay the cost of global integration, and critics deny

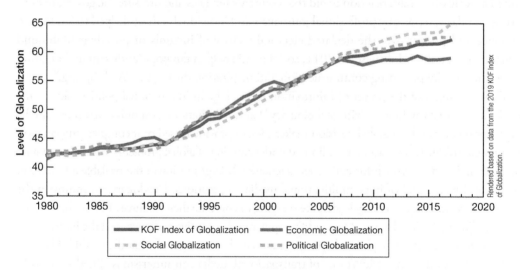

FIGURE 12.6 Levels of Globalization In an effort to take stock of globalization's progress, the *2019 KOF Index of Globalization* examines the political, social, and economic dimensions of globalization by looking at multiple indicators spanning trade, business, politics, and information technology to determine the ranking of 187 countries. Since the 1970s, there has been an upward trend in all three dimensions of globalization, with a strong increase after the end of the Cold War. The latest global economic and financial crisis has slowed the pace of the economic globalization process, although social and political globalization continue to rise.

globalization's benefits. The debate about globalization's problematic impact is intensifying, but without resolution, as contenders are hardening their positions without listening to the counterarguments.

You have now taken into account a number of the dimensions of globalization—in international economics, demography, global communication, and the potential spread of universal values for the entire world. If the trends you have surveyed do culminate for the first time in a global consensus uniting all of humanity, these values and understandings might unify all people on Earth in a common global culture. This could conceivably prepare the way for a global *civil society*, even with the eventual emergence of supranational institutions to govern all of humanity.

Yet this worldview and set of predictions strike fear into the hearts of many people who experience *cognitive dissonance* when they confront a frightening vision that challenges their customary way of thinking about world affairs. These people (and there are multitudes) strenuously reject the idea that the traditional system of independent sovereign states can or should be replaced by a global community with strong supranational regulatory institutions that enhance global governance.

So, conclude your inspection of globalization's influence on world politics by evaluating the available evidence and sorting out the balance sheet of globalization's costs and benefits (see "Controversy: Is Globalization Helpful or Harmful?"). What do prevailing trends tell you? Is Thomas Friedman's (2007b) "flat world" concept that globalization has emasculated the state just as an "electronic herd" tramples down traditional state borders valid? Or is Daniel Drezner (2007) more accurate in arguing that "states make the rules" and that powerful governments are still in control of shaping global destiny because "great powers cajole and coerce those who disagree with them into accepting the same rulebook"?

Globalization is real, for better or for worse. Many people recommend globalization for international public policy, because they believe that its consequences are basically good for humankind. However, critics argue that globalization's costs far outweigh its benefits. As the pace of globalization has become a recognized force in world politics, it also has become a topic of heated debate. Globalization has hit a political speed bump, provoking intense critical

IMAGE 12.7 The Making of a Global Culture? Some people regard globalization as little more than the spread of values and beliefs of the world's reigning hegemon, the United States. Shown here is one image that fuels that point of view—an enormous inflated Santa Claus in front of a hotel in downtown Hanoi, Vietnam—a predominantly Buddhist city still subscribing to communist principles that emphasize the greed of market capitalism and the class divisions it is believed to create. The sale of Christmas trees is rising there too.

Controversy

IS GLOBALIZATION HELPFUL OR HARMFUL?

To many students of international relations, globalization has two faces, one positive and one negative. To those whose perceptions focus on globalization's benefits, globalization helps to break down traditional divisions of humanity—between races, nations, and cultures—that are barriers to peace, prosperity, and justice. To others, globalization is a harmful phenomenon, breeding such things as global disease and threats to local job security, and therefore a force to be resisted.

Imagine yourself writing a report such as the evaluation that the International Labour Organization undertook when it challenged itself to provide "new thinking to break the deadlock and bridge the divide about the globalization debate." To frame your analysis, see if your evaluation would support or question the World Commission's conclusion:

> Globalization can and must change. [We acknowledge] globalization's potential for good—promoting open societies, open economies, and freer exchange of goods, knowledge, and ideas. But the Commission also found deep-seated and persistent imbalances in the current workings of the global economy that are ethically unacceptable and politically unsustainable. The gap between people's income in the richest and poorest countries has never been wider. . . . More than one billion people are either unemployed, underemployed, or working poor. Clearly, globalization's benefits are out of reach for far too many people (Somavia, 2004, p. 6).

An alternative exercise would be to make an ethical assessment about the morality of globalization. This is what the philosopher Peter Singer (2004) did in applying as a criterion the utilitarian principle that it is a moral duty to maximize the happiness and welfare of all human beings and even animal welfare. Singer sees great benefit from the erosion of state sovereignty and the idea that the entire world should be the unit of ethical analysis. His conclusion springs from a UN report that observed (as cited in Pinstrup-Andersen, 2007, p. 23), "In the global village, someone else's poverty very soon becomes one's own problem: illegal immigration, pollution, contagious disease, insecurity, fanaticism, terrorism." Under globalization, altruism and concern for others pay dividends, whereas narrow selfish behavior causes the selfish competitor counterproductive harm.

Alternatively, think like an economist. Would your economic analysis of globalization agree with the conclusions of famous social scientist Jagdish Bhagwati (2004)? Richard N. Cooper (2004, pp. 152–153) summarizes Bhagwati's liberal theoretical position and propositions:

> (Bhagwati) addresses a slate of charges against globalization . . . before turning to fixes for globalization's downsides: improving governance, accelerating social agendas, and managing the speed of transitions. He concedes a few points to globalization's critics but, wielding logic and fact, demolishes most of the allegations made against it. His conclusion: that the world, particularly its poorest regions, needs more globalization, not less. . . . To the claim that globalization increases poverty, Bhagwati's response is, "rubbish."

What Do You Think?

1. On balance, do you think the benefits of globalization outweigh the costs?

2. As globalization creates both winners and losers, what policies do you think should be enacted to better protect the "losers" of globalization?

3. How do you think realists would view the debate over globalization? To what extent would they part company with liberal and constructivist interpretations of globalization?

evaluation of globalization's causes, characteristics, and consequences, and inspiring fresh ethical examination of the elevated interdependence of countries and human beings. The uncertain wisdom and morality of globalization may be the most discussed issue on today's global agenda, receiving even more attention than poverty, disease, urbanization, or the preservation of identity.

The age of globalization has far-reaching implications for humanity. In the next chapter of *World Politics*, we consider the circumstances of the almost 8 billion human beings striving throughout the world to sustain themselves, improve the human condition, and protect their right to life, liberty, and happiness.

Study. Apply. Analyze.

Chapter Summary

12-1 Survey current trends in global demographics. Changes in world population trends have significant implications for the future of international relations. Total global population is increasing, particularly within the Global South, though the rate of population growth will slow. Other trends include graying, mostly in the Global North, due to an increasingly high percentage of the elderly population, as well as youth bulges within some countries in the Global South.

12-2 Examine global migration patterns, and discuss the significance of global urbanization. Global migration continues to increase each year, and this trend is likely to persist. While economic concerns undergird most migration, there are also unprecedented numbers of refugees who flee threatening conditions. Additionally, urbanization is changing where and how people live within their states. Urban cities are on the rise all over the world, leading to a disconnect from rural populations.

12-3 Explain how infectious disease can lead to health crises around the world. One unfortunate aspect of globalization has been the threat of infectious diseases that can spread rapidly throughout the world with no regard for borders. Rapidly responding to these diseases can be particularly challenging in the Global South, and must address both the prevention of disease and treatment for those who are ill.

12-4 Describe the expansion of global information flows, and outline the political and social implications. Global communication has rapidly evolved, and people share ideas and information instantaneously throughout the world and interact like never before. The political and social implications are mixed, as information flows can be used for both productive and destructive purposes.

12-5 Evaluate the multiple facets of globalization, and appraise their implications for the future of world politics. While globalization has resulted in many positive outcomes, it can create public insecurities and challenges for political leaders. The future of international interconnectedness is uncertain, and states have begun to criticize some of the effects that globalization has on the world.

Key Terms

acquired immune deficiency
 syndrome (AIDS)

agenda setting

asylum

atrocities

cartel

cosmopolitan

cyberspace

demography

disinformation

ethnic cleansing

fertility rate

fragile cities

global village

internally-displaced persons
 (IDPs)

Internet of Things (IoT)

megacities

population density

population implosion

refugees

replacement-level fertility

sanctuary

turbo-urbanization

virtuality

xenophobia

Suggested Readings and Resources

Bricker, D., & Ibbitson, J. (2019). *Empty Planet: The Shock of Global Population Decline*. New York: Random House.

CDC Our Global Voices Blog: blogs.cdc.gov/global/. A blog that examines global disease and health security issues.

Choucri, Nazli. (2012). *Cyberpolitics in International Relations*. Cambridge, MA: MIT Press.

General Analysis on Globalization of the Economy: globalpolicy.org. A website examining economic globalization.

Glaeser, Edward. (2011). *Triumph of the City: How Our Greatest Invention Makes Us Richer, Smarter, Greener, Healthier and Happier*. New York: Penguin.

Global Culture Blog: modelpeopleinc.com/globalcultureblog/. A blog discussing world culture topics from around the globe.

Martin, Susan F. (2014). *International Migration: Evolving Trends from the Early Twentieth Century to the Present*. New York: Cambridge.

Morland, P. (2019). *The Human Tide: How Population Shaped the Modern World*. New York: Public Affairs.

People Move Blog: blogs.worldbank.org/peoplemove. A World Bank blog discussing development, migration, and remittances.

en.unesco.org/fightfakenews. UNESCO resource on disinformation in the digital age.

Carnegie Council Videos

Key Term Videos

- Demography
- Fertility Rate
- Xenophobia
- Refugees

- Ethnic Cleansing
- Globalization
- Acquired Immune Deficiency Syndrome (AIDS)

- Virtuality
- Agenda Setting

Additional Videos

- Grewal, David Singh. "Network Power: The Social Dynamics of Globalization."
- Kotkin, Joel. "The Next Hundred Million: America in 2050."
- Vocke, William. "Egypt: Democracy or Demography?"
- Vocke, William. "How Real Is Virtual?"

Chapter 13

The Promotion of Human Development and Human Rights

IMAGE 13.1 **Life Without Liberty** Abuses of women's rights often take place outside of the political sphere as "the crucial economic, social, and cultural power relationship for most women is not one directly with the state but with men" (Gideon, 2006, p. 1272). In 2018, the Indian Supreme Court ruled that women could enter the Sabarimala temple, a popular Hindu pilgrimage destination. However, protesters—arguing that women of menstrual age were "unpure" and should be denied entry—violently blocked the temple entrance. As a counter protest, on January 1, 2019, several *million* women joined hands in a 385-mile long "women's wall" to raise awareness of gender equality. As one participant argued, "it's time for awareness and for change" (Thiagarajan, 2019).

Learning Objectives

LO 13-1 Describe the role of individual rights in the global system.

LO 13-2 Explain the concepts of human security and human development.

LO 13-3 Describe the globally recognized facets of human rights, and examine ways in which these rights are threatened.

LO 13-4 Appraise the methods through which human rights may be promoted, and evaluate the challenges faced in enforcing these rights.

To deny people their human rights is to challenge their very humanity."
—NELSON MANDELA, FORMER PRESIDENT OF SOUTH AFRICA

Surf the Web any night, and you will come across a number of news articles depicting the daily horrors some people face. From living in conditions of squalor and poverty to suffering the raping and pillaging of paramilitary forces, you would be stunned and sickened at the trials and tribulations that many less fortunate people must endure. Like most people, you hope for a better future for all humanity. So, what can be done to promote moral values and reform world politics?

For many people the future is bleak, resembling what the English political philosopher Thomas Hobbes described when he talked of life as "solitary, poor, nasty, brutish, and short." The opportunities and choices that are most basic to freedom from fear and poverty are unavailable for most people in the Global South's poorest countries. They experience slower rates of development and less *human security* than in the Global North, and the prospects of the "have-nots" are not improving.

Given the serious deprivations facing so many people, there are many reasons for concern. The denial of the inalienable rights to which all humans are presumably entitled—the "life, liberty, and the pursuit of happiness" of which the U.S. Declaration of Independence speaks—attests to the extent that fundamental human security is not being met. This problem prompted Mary Robinson (2002), the former United Nations (UN) high commissioner for human rights, to "call on global actors—corporations, governments and the international financial organizations—to join with globalized civil society and share responsibility for humanizing globalization."

> *If you are neutral in a situation of injustice, you have chosen the side of the oppressor.*
>
> **—ARCHBISHOP DESMUND TUTU, NOBEL PRIZE WINNER**

Putting People into the Picture

LO 13-1 Describe the role of individual rights in the global system.

Until relatively recently in the theoretical study of world politics, the needs of the faceless billions of everyday people were neglected. That past theoretical legacy pictured the mass of humanity as marginalized victims or left them invisible by painting their fates as controlled by forces over which hapless people have little influence. French world-systems historian Fernand Braudel (1973, p. 1244) wrote that "when I think of the individual, I am always inclined to see him imprisoned within a destiny in which he himself has little hand, fixed in a landscape in which the infinite perspectives of the long term stretch into the distance both behind and before."

When thinking about world affairs, the average person has long been relegated to a mere "subject" whom rulers were traditionally permitted to manipulate to advance their states' interests. That vision has been rejected throughout the world. A consensus has emerged that now supports the view that people are important, that they have worth, and, therefore, that *ethics* and *morals* belong in the study of international relations. As ethicist Ronald Dworkin (2001, p. 485) defined these terms, "Ethics includes convictions about what kinds of lives are good or bad for a person to lead, and morality includes principles about how a person should treat other people." These principles apply to interstate relations, and they are at the heart of analyses of human security in world politics.

That consensus notwithstanding, many observers embrace the traditional realist assumption that vast global forces render people powerless. Realists recognize that people participate politically but claim they have no real power because an invisible set of powerful forces described before as the "system" gives most human beings only superficial involvement without granting real influence.

Denying the importance and influence of individual human *agency* seems increasingly strange; classic thinking about the world has long been concentrated on people and the essential characteristics of human nature. As anthropologist Robert Redfield (1962) argued, "Human nature is itself a part of the method [of all analysis]. One must use one's own humanity as a means to understanding. The physicist need not sympathize with his atoms, nor the biologist with his fruit flies, but the student of people and institutions must employ [one's] natural sympathies in order to discover what people think or feel." This requires a humanistic interpretation that gives people status and value. Moreover, in the global community, a *civil society* is emerging. A normative consensus has emerged concerning the inherent moral worth and status of humans and the concomitant obligation of states to recognize and protect that status (Calhoun, 2011).

How can we create a world that is free of poverty and persecution? If you, as a student of international affairs, are to understand the forces behind the prevailing trends in world politics, it is important to consider the conditions that humanity faces (see Map 13.1 and Figure 13.1). This chapter introduces information about the human condition to enable you to evaluate the unfolding debate about the role of humans as actors on the global stage, the prospect for human development, and the ethics of **human rights**. Will humanity be valued? Will human welfare and human rights be protected? And more broadly, what is the best way to view human security and reconcile it with national security (see "Controversy: What Is Security?")?

These are critical questions. Where does humanity fit into the prevailing and most popular *paradigms* or theoretical orientations that policy makers and scholars construct about world politics? For the most part, classical realism focuses solely upon the state and its ruler's sovereign freedom and, except for building its image of international reality from a pessimistic conception of human nature, it ignores the role of leaders and the *nongovernmental organizations* (NGOs) that people form. Liberals attach more importance to humans, following the ethical precept of German philosopher Immanuel Kant that people should be treated as ends and not means, and that human rights and human dignity should be safeguarded. *Constructivism* goes further; it makes humanity the primary level of analysis and emphasizes how human ideas define identities that in turn impart meaning to material capabilities and the behavior of actors (see Chapter 2).

human rights
The political rights and civil liberties recognized by the international community as inalienable and valid for individuals in all countries by virtue of their humanity.

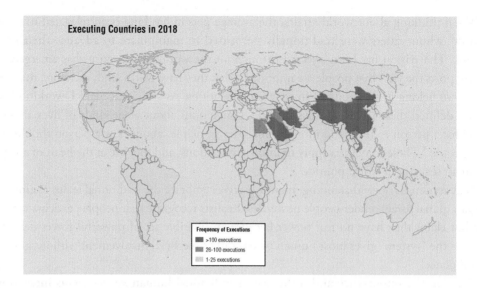

Executing Countries in 2018

Frequency of Executions
- >100 executions
- 26-100 executions
- 1-25 executions

Number of Countries Conducting Executions, 1995–2018

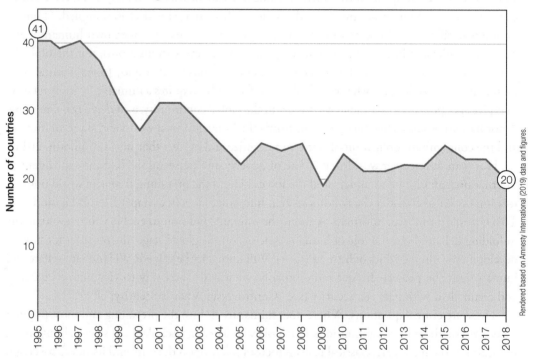

Rendered based on Amnesty International (2019) data and figures.

MAP 13.1 AND FIGURE 13.1 **Human Rights** *versus* **States' Rights** Although more than two-thirds of countries have abolished the death penalty in practice or in law, the thirteen countries shown in the map have repeatedly executed prisoners between 2014 and 2018. As shown in the figure, in 2018 alone, twenty countries committed at least 690 executions—not including those carried out in China. While this represents a 31 percent decrease from 2017, at least 2,531 new death sentences were imposed that same year in fifty-four countries (Amnesty International, 2019). The five countries with the greatest number of executions in 2018 were China (though it refuses to divulge figures, it is known that thousands of executions take place), Iran (at least 253), Saudi Arabia (at least 149), Vietnam (at least 85), and Iraq (at least 52).

 Think it Through At what point does an individual state's issue, such as implementation of the death penalty, become an international one?

How Does Humanity Fare? The Human Condition Today

LO 13-2 Explain the concepts of human security and human development.

"Man is born free, and everywhere he is in chains," bemoaned political philosopher Jean Jacques Rousseau in his famous 1762 book, *Social Contract*. Times have since changed, but in many respects, Rousseau's characterization of the human condition remains accurate. How should we evaluate the depth of human deprivation and despair against this fact? Can the poorest proportion of humanity sever their chains of disadvantage in order to realize their human potential and obtain the high ideals of human security, freedom, and dignity?

The inequalities and disparities evident in people's standards of living cannot help but to evoke sympathy for the difficult conditions many people face, especially in the less developed Global South countries. One American graduate student, when working on his PhD, confronted this reality during his field research in South America. Brian Wallace found a reality far different from his own experience of growing up in the southern United States. In 1978, he was moved to write:

> I spent the first 24 years of my life in South Carolina. When I left for Colombia [South America], I fully expected Bogotá to be like any large U.S. city, only with citizens who spoke Spanish. When I arrived there I found my expectations were wrong. I was not in the U.S., I was on Mars! I was a victim of culture shock. As a personal experience this shock was occasionally funny and sometimes sad. But after all the laughing and the crying were over, it forced me to reevaluate both my life and the society in which I live.
>
> Colombia is a poor country by American standards. It has a per capita GNP of $550 and a very unequal distribution of income. These were the facts that I knew before I left.
>
> But to "know" these things intellectually is much different from experiencing firsthand how they affect people's lives. It is one thing to lecture in air conditioned classrooms about the problems of world poverty. It is quite another to see four-year-old children begging or sleeping in the streets.
>
> It tore me apart emotionally to see the reality of what I had studied for so long: "low per capita GNP and maldistribution of income." What this means in human terms is children with dirty faces who beg for bread money or turn into pickpockets because the principle of private property gets blurred by empty stomachs.
>
> It means other children whose minds and bodies will never develop fully because they were malnourished as infants. It means street vendors who sell candy and cigarettes 14 hours a day in order to feed their families.
>
> It also means well-dressed businessmen and petty bureaucrats who indifferently pass this poverty every day as they seek asylum in their fortified houses to the north of the city.
>
> It means rich people who prefer not to see the poor, except for maids and security guards. It means foreigners like me who come to Colombia and spend more in one month than the average Colombian earns in a year.
>
> It means politicians across the ideological spectrum who are so full of abstract solutions or personal greed that they forget that it is real people they are dealing with.
>
> Somewhere within the polemics of the politicians and the "objectivity" of the social scientists, the human being has been lost.

Controversy

WHAT IS SECURITY?

How should security be defined? Policy makers disagree. Some see it primarily in military terms, others in human welfare terms. Underlying the disagreement is a different conception of what is most important on the global agenda. One tradition gives states first priority and assumes that protecting their territorial integrity must be foremost in the minds of national leaders. Others challenge this conception and place primacy on the security of individual people, arguing that social and environmental protection must be a global priority.

In considering this question, remember the traditional realist view that national security is essentially the freedom from fear of attack by another country or nonstate terrorists. Realists maintain that armed aggression is the paramount security threat and that preparing for war to prevent war overrides all other security concerns. Safeguarding the state by military force matters most. Therefore, realists define "security" primarily in terms of each country's capacity to resist armed threats. This definition puts the protection of entire states' interests above those of individual people.

In contrast, "human security" has risen as a concept that focuses on protecting individuals (as distinct from states) from threat. The Human Security Centre (2006, p. 35) elaborates this perspective that derives from liberal thought, explaining that "secure states do not automatically mean secure peoples." Protecting citizens from foreign attack may be a necessary condition for the security of individuals, but it is not a sufficient one. Indeed, during the last one hundred years far more people have been killed by their own governments than by foreign armies.

All proponents of human security agree that the primary goal is protection of individuals. Although there is a lack of consensus regarding the specific threats against which individuals need protection, some see a synergy between the security of individuals and the security of the state. According to the United Nations (2015b), "human security underscores the universality and interdependence of a set of freedoms that are fundamental to human life: freedom from fear, freedom from want and freedom to live in dignity. As a result, human security acknowledges the interlinkages between security, development and human rights and considers these to be the building blocks of human and, therefore, national security."

What Do You Think?

1. To what extent are the "national security" approaches emphasized by realists and the "human security" approaches favored by liberals contradictory and in competition with one another? Might they instead be complementary and mutually reinforcing?

2. What are some considerations that a feminist theorist would include in this debate?

3. How might this affect your perception of security?

4. As a policy maker, which aspects of security would you emphasize as the most likely guarantor of your country's well-being? Why?

Despite wide differences that enable a proportion of humanity to enjoy unprecedented standards of living, the daunting scale of poverty and misery is evident throughout the world, from which only a small fraction of people have any hope of escaping in the near term. We must view human development in terms of "building human capabilities—not just for a few, not even for most, but for everyone" (UNDP, 2018, p. 1). To do this, let us consider how to best assess human welfare—its level and the prospects for humanity's escape from poverty—so that we can think analytically about human progress not only in terms of economic resources but also in terms of broader human security that firmly places people and human development as the core of development policies and strategies.

Human Development and Human Security

One indicator of human well-being around the world is money. According to the World Bank's definition of extreme poverty as income of $1.90 or less a day, about 731 million people (about 10 percent of the world) live in extreme poverty (WDI, 2017b). This is a dramatic improvement since 1990, when 35.9 percent of the world's people lived on no more than $1.90 a day (see Figures 13.2A and 13.2B).

However, this remarkable achievement notwithstanding, an expanded view of poverty shows that many still live on meager resources. More than 26 percent of the world's population lives on less than $3.20 per day, and almost 46 percent live on less than $5.50 per day (World Bank, 2018c). Income inequality, both between and within countries, also remains a serious global problem from which many other difficulties and disputes result, and that problem is deeply entrenched. Consumption patterns show that the division between the rich and the poor is growing. About one-fifth of the globe's wealthiest people consume anywhere from two-thirds to nine-tenths of its resources.

Economic indicators such as the average income for each person in a country are important proxies for a decent standard of living. However, income is only a means to human development, not an end. It is not the sum total of human life. Thus, it is important to consider other aspects of human development that go beyond material possessions and more comprehensively indicate the extent to which basic **human needs** are met.

human needs
Those basic physical, social, and political needs, such as food and freedom, that are required for survival and security.

The extreme suffering of people in many parts of the world, especially in the low-income countries of the Global South, manifests itself in many areas and affects their ability to live a long and healthy life, become educated, and achieve a decent standard of living. Life expectancy in the Global South averages almost seventy-one years, whereas in the Global North it is eighty-one years. In the Global South, the average infant mortality rate—the number of infant deaths per 1000 live births—is twenty-seven, as compared to an infant mortality rate of five in the Global North. The health and well-being of pregnant women is also precarious in the Global South, where the maternal mortality rate is 177 per 100,000 live births. In comparison, the maternal mortality rate in the Global North is thirteen (WDI, 2017a).

When we look at the ability of countries to contribute to the human development of the people living within their borders, we see a revealing picture of the way they provide for personal welfare (see Figure 13.3). These indicators show that consumption is not the same as human welfare and that economic growth does not automatically produce human development.

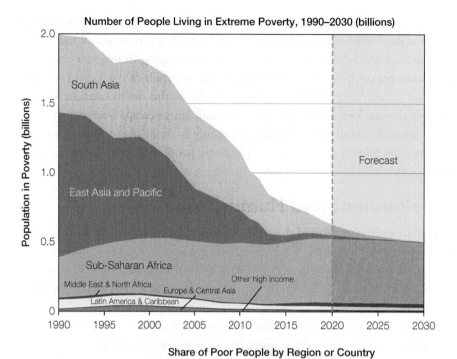

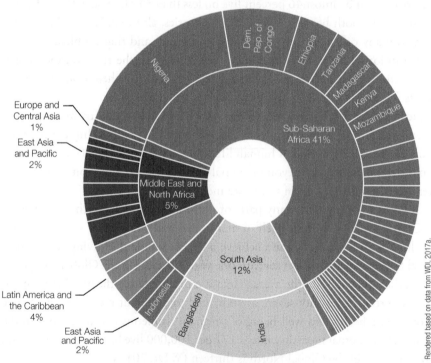

FIGURES 13.2A AND 13.2B **Where Poverty Prevails in the World** Shown here are distributions of where people live in conditions of extreme poverty, defined as subsisting on less than $1.90 per day. As shown above, the overall trends are encouraging, as the total number of people living in extreme poverty, about 731 million people, represents more than a 60 percent decrease from 1990. Future projections indicate that extreme poverty may disappear outside of sub-Saharan Africa. As shown below, almost half of the extremely poor worldwide—368 million—live in just five countries: India, Nigeria, Democratic Republic of Congo, Ethiopia, and Bangladesh. While challenges remain, this is a positive development for human security. Former World Bank President Jim Yong Kim called this reduction in poverty "one of the greatest human achievements of our time," (World Bank, 2018d).

As indicated by the United Nations' **Human Development Index (HDI)**—which provides a more holistic measure of human security and welfare in terms of life expectancy, literacy, education, and income—some countries enjoy very high human development such as Norway, Switzerland, Australia, Ireland, and Germany. Human development is far lower in others, such as the lowest-scored countries of Burundi, Chad, South Sudan, the Central African Republic, and Niger.

To assess human welfare further, we must also take into account the effect of inequality in the distribution of health, education, and income upon human development within a society. "Inequality reduces the pace of human development, and can even bring it to a halt" (UNDP, 2014, p. 37). In Latin America, there is a 33.2 percent regional drop in human development due to inequality in income. Differences in life expectancy across sub-Saharan Africa are linked

Human Development Index (HDI)
An index that uses life expectancy, literacy, average number of years of schooling, and income to assess a country's performance in providing for its people's welfare and security.

Measuring Human Development

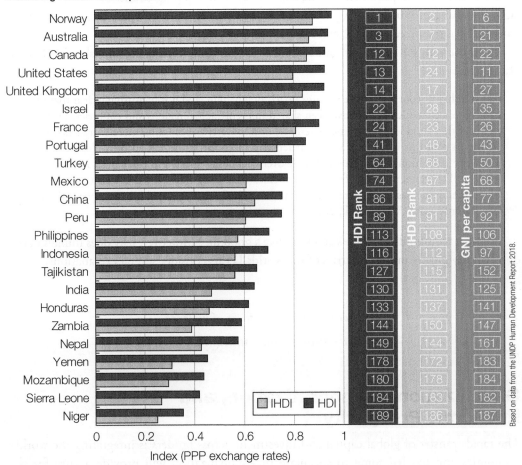

FIGURE 13.3 **Measuring Human Development: What Is Quality of Life?** When using the Human Development Index to measure the human welfare and development of people within various populations, notice how countries can rank somewhat differently than when using an aggregate measure such as the gross national income (GNI) per capita. The Inequality-adjusted Human Development Index further takes into account the effect of variation in the human condition within a country upon human development. Norway ranks very high and Niger ranks very low on all three measures, while other countries, such as Indonesia and Turkey, show more variation across the HDI and GNI measures.

to a 30.8 percent decrease in human development for those with the lowest expected length of life. In South Asia, high levels of inequality in education have a profound negative effect—up to a 37.7 percent decrease—upon the human development of some of its people (UNDP, 2018). Generally, countries that have lower levels of human development suffer from higher levels of multidimensional inequality. Conversely, countries in the Global North experience the least inequality in human development.

Against this grim picture are trends that inspire hope. For some segments of humanity, things have improved: On average, people in developing countries are healthier, better educated, and less impoverished—and they are more likely to live in a multiparty democracy. In the quarter of a century from 1990 to 2015, the global poverty rate declined by more than 25 percent, roughly 1 percent or 76 million people less per year. The world's goal of reducing the 1990 poverty rate by half by 2015 was met six years ahead of schedule, and the world is set to reach the poverty target of 9 percent by 2020 (World Bank, 2018c). In other areas of human welfare, there has also been improvement as life expectancy in developing countries has increased by eight years since 1990, from sixty-three to seventy-one. In the same period, primary school completion rates increased to 92 percent from 78 percent.

These human development gains should not be underestimated, nor should they be exaggerated:

> The number of poor worldwide remains unacceptably high, and it is increasingly clear that the benefits of economic growth have been shared unevenly across regions and countries. Even as much of the world leaves extreme poverty behind, poverty is becoming more entrenched and harder to root out in certain areas, particularly in countries burdened by violent conflict and weak institutions. Poor households are overwhelmingly located in rural areas, have a large number of children, and suffer from a lack of education. They are ill served in essential elements of well-being such as health care and sanitation, and often are exposed to natural hazards and physical insecurity (World Bank, 2018c, p. 1).

So, what factors affect people's ability to live a good life? Moreover, why does human development vary greatly in the countries of the world? Let us consider several explanations.

> *Poverty is the worst form of violence.*
>
> **—MAHATMA GANDHI, INDIAN NATIONALIST LEADER**

Globalization, Democratization, and Economic Prosperity

The rapid transfer of global capital and investment across borders is integrating the world's economies and has led some to speculate that globalization will provide a cure for the chronic poverty faced by the majority of humanity. There exists "a widely shared image of globalization—a worldwide process of converging incomes and lifestyles driven by ever-larger international flows of goods, images, capital, and people as formidable equalizers [because] greater economic openness has made small parts of the changing world full-fledged members of the global village . . . so that globalized islands of prosperity are thriving in many developing nations" (Heredia, 1999).

However, critics of globalization complain that it is the culprit—that globalization actually causes relative deprivation rather than cures it. They see globalization as a part of the problem of human suffering, not the solution. Capital may flow more freely around the world, but it flows most slowly to the places and people where it is most scarce. In their constructed image of the consequences of globalization, a more global economy increases inequality in some countries, particularly in the Global South.

Critics decry the "human harms" wrought by globalization, arguing that "nothing is more certain than the inequality and exploitation generated by a totally free market. The inequalities that global capitalism generates are inequities because they violate the principles of egalitarian individualism ..." and create "risks of injury and incapacitation that strike at the very being of human beings" (Boli, Elliott, and Bieri, 2004, p. 395). Similarly, Pope Francis I has argued that "human rights are not only violated by terrorism, repression or assassination, but also by unfair economic structures that create huge inequalities." Economist John Maynard Keynes noted these tensions, stating that the "political problem of mankind is to combine three things: economic efficiency, social justice and individual liberty." It is argued that not only does globalization fail to benefit the people that most need help, but the poor "are paying the price for everyone else's prosperity" (McGurn, 2002).

Yet, where human development has expanded, one factor stands out—the degree to which countries rule themselves democratically and protect citizens' civil liberties. Where democracy thrives, human development and human rights also tend to thrive. At the start of 2019, 145 countries—well over half of the countries in the world (74 percent)—were either free or partly free, providing their citizens with a broad range of political liberties (Freedom House, 2019).

Now consider the location where people benefit from such freedom with Map 13.2, which shows the various levels of human development in countries across the globe. The two go hand in hand: Where democracy flourishes, human development flourishes. But in autocratic governments not ruled by the will of the people, human development fails to occur and human rights are frequently denied.

Along with democratization, rising economic prosperity within a country clearly increases the pace of human development, as previously shown in Figure 13.3, which displays the wealth of each person for countries based on *purchasing power parity* (PPP) exchange-rate comparisons. This is why levels of human development are generally highest in the Global North, where economic prosperity on average is also highest (as opposed to the low-income Global South). Although it is still a source of debate, evidence also supports the conclusion that those countries that respect human rights encourage trade that reduces poverty (Ibrahim, 2013; Blanton and Blanton, 2007). But the exceptions demonstrate the general rule that a country's regime type, and its protection of the civil and political liberties of its population, make a crucial difference in achieving levels of human development.

Some question the "trickle-down" hypothesis (that if the rich first get richer, eventually the benefits will trickle down to help the poor) while accepting the evidence that meeting basic human needs ultimately promotes long-term economic growth. Others maintain that

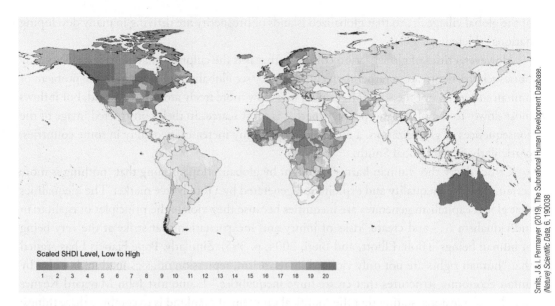

Smits, J & I. Permanyer (2019). The Subnational Human Development Database. *(Nature) Scientific Data.* 6, 190038

Scaled SHDI Level, Low to High

1   2   3   4   5   6   7   8   9   10   11   12   13   14   15   16   17   18   19   20

MAP 13.2   A Subnational Map of Human Development   Measures of human development typically are depicted at the state level, yet there are often significant variations in human development within states. Providing a more nuanced picture, as shown here, the Subnational Human Development Index (SHDI) portrays human development across 1635 regions within 160 countries, representing more than 99 percent of the global population (Smits and Permanyer, 2019; Permanyer and Smits, 2018). At the state level, countries within the Global North tend to have higher levels of human development. At the same time, both within the Global North and Global South, there is substantial variation within countries, particularly between urban and rural areas, with the urban areas generally having higher levels of human development (see Chapter 12).

 Think it Through   What do these patterns tell us about inequality between and within states? What role do you think geography plays in determining differences in human development?

redistributive policies aimed at enhancing human welfare and growth-oriented policies focusing on "trickle-down" benefits function at cross-purposes because the latter can only be attained at the expense of the former.

Many now recommend fostering human development through a strategy that combines the efficiency of a free-enterprise capitalistic market with the compassion of governmental economic planning and regulation in an effort to cooperatively produce the greatest good for the greatest number. Proponents agree that this mixed approach would enable a free market to generate rapid growth while providing a safety net for those most in need of assistance, and that this formula is the best solution for engineering economic growth with a moral human purpose.

Inequality is growing. And people are questioning a world in which a handful of people hold the same wealth as half of humanity.

—ANTONIO GUTERRES, UN SECRETARY-GENERAL

Human Rights and the Protection of People

"Prior to the second half of the seventeenth century, the idea that all human beings, simply because they are human, have rights that they may exercise against the state and society received no substantial political endorsement anywhere in the world" (Donnelly, 2013, p. 75). The 1648 Treaty of Westphalia, which marked the end of the Thirty Years' War, recognized limited religious rights for select Christian minorities. International campaigns in the mid-1800s against slavery were a form of human rights advocacy and, following World War I, labor rights and minority rights were addressed by the International Labor Organization and the League of Nations. However, it was not until after World War II, with the creation of the United Nations in 1945, that human rights decisively entered international discourse and states began to publicly embrace universal human rights (Donnelly, 2013).

"Everyone has human rights, and responsibilities to respect and protect these rights may, in principle, extend across political and social boundaries" (Beitz, 2009, p. 1). This premise was expressed in the ringing words of the 1948 Universal Declaration of Human Rights: "Recognition of the inherent dignity and of the equal and inalienable rights of all members of the human family is the foundation of freedom, justice, and peace in the world." This treaty expressed the idea that people should be empowered and therefore no longer reduced to "simply hapless victims of fate, devoid of any historical agency" (Saurin, 2000).

Internationally Recognized Human Rights

The body of legal rules and norms designed to protect individual human beings is anchored in the ethical requirement that every person should be treated with equal concern and respect. As the most authoritative statement of these norms, the 1948 Universal Declaration of Human Rights "establishes a broad range of civil and political rights, including freedom of assembly, freedom of thought and expression, and the right to participate in government. The declaration also proclaims that social and economic rights are indispensable, including the right to education, the right to work, and the right to participate in the cultural life of the community. In addition, the preamble boldly asserts that 'it is essential, if man is not to be compelled to have recourse, as a last resort, to rebellion against tyranny and oppression, that human rights should be protected by the rule of law'" (Clapham, 2001).

These rights have since been codified and extended in a series of treaties, most notably the *International Covenant on Civil and Political Rights* and the *International Covenant on Economic, Social, and Cultural Rights*. There are many ways to classify the rights listed in these treaties. International ethicist Charles Beitz (2001, p. 271) groups them into five categories:

- **Rights of the person.** "Life, liberty, and security of the person; privacy and freedom of movement; ownership of property; freedom of thought, conscience, and religion, including freedom of religious teaching and practice 'in public and private'; and prohibition of slavery, torture, and cruel or degrading punishment."

- **Rights associated with the rule of law.** "Equal recognition before the law and equal protection of the law, effective legal remedy for violation of legal rights, impartial hearing and trial, presumption of innocence, and prohibition of arbitrary arrest."

- **Political rights.** "Freedom of expression, assembly, and association; the right to take part in government; and periodic and genuine elections by universal and equal suffrage."

- **Economic and social rights.** "An adequate standard of living; free choice of employment; protection against unemployment; 'just and favorable remuneration'; the right to join trade unions; 'reasonable limitation of working hours'; free elementary education; social security; and the 'highest attainable standard of physical and mental health.'"

- **Rights of communities.** "Self-determination and protection of minority cultures."

Although the multilateral treaties enumerating these rights are legally binding on the states ratifying them, many have either not ratified them or have done so only with significant caveats. When states specify caveats, they are expressing agreement with the broad declarations of principle contained in these treaties while indicating that they object to certain specific provisions

IMAGE 13.2 Cruel and Unusual, or Simply Usual? The UN Human Rights Commission holds annual sessions that deal with accusations that some UN members are violating human rights treaties. This photo shows the kind of human rights abuse that some countries practice: a man being punished for gambling by Sharia law authorities in Jantho, Aceh Province, in Indonesia. Stipulated in Islam's holy book, the Quran, caning is practiced in some Muslim countries.

and elect not to be bound by them. The United States, for example, ratified the *International Covenant on Civil and Political Rights* with reservations in 1992, but it has not ratified the *International Covenant on Economic, Social, and Cultural Rights.* Countries that agree with the general principle that all human beings possess certain rights that cannot be withheld may still disagree on the scope of these rights. Thus, some emphasize rights associated with the rule of law and political rights, whereas others stress the importance of economic and social rights.

Unfortunately, not everyone enjoys the human rights recognized by international law. Three groups for whom respect for human rights remains particularly problematic are indigenous peoples, women, and children.

> *Freedom means the supremacy of human rights everywhere. Our support goes to those who struggle to gain those rights or keep them.*
>
> **—FRANKLIN DELANO ROOSEVELT, FORMER U.S. PRESIDENT**

The Precarious Life of Indigenous Peoples

As *nonstate actors* (see Chapter 6), *indigenous peoples* are representative of one type of ethnic and cultural group that were once native to a geographic location. In most cases indigenous peoples were at one time politically sovereign and economically self-sufficient. Today, largely without a homeland or self-rule, an estimated 370 million indigenous peoples are living in more than ninety countries worldwide, each of which has a unique language and culture and strong, often spiritual, ties to an ancestral homeland (UNDESA, 2019a).

Many indigenous peoples feel persecuted because their livelihoods, lands, and cultures are threatened. The Turkish mass killing of Armenians, Hitler's slaughter of Jews (and other groups), the Khmer Rouge slaughter of Cambodians, and the Hutu slaughter of the Tutsi of Rwanda all exemplify the atrocities committed during the twentieth century.

In describing the tragedy of the Nazi holocaust, Polish jurist Raphael Lemkin coined the word *genocide* from the Greek word *genos* (race, people) and the Latin *caedere* (to kill), and called for it to be singled out as the most grievous violation of human rights, a heinous crime that the international community would be morally responsible for punishing. "When any state or movement claims the right to decide what groups have the right to exist, it poses a threat to all groups" (Smith, 2010, p. 434). Genocide focuses on the destruction of groups, not individuals per se, and has several dimensions, including physical (the annihilation of members of a group), biological (measures taken to reduce the reproductive capacity of a group), and cultural (efforts to eliminate a group's language, literature, art, and other institutions). **Ethnocentrism** often underlies genocidal policies. "Brute force realpolitik," concludes Manus Midlarsky (2006), "often provides a rationale rooted in ethnocentrism for the physical extermination of victim minorities by leaders claiming genocide is a necessary 'altruistic punishment' for the good of the dominant nationality."

Various native peoples are now fighting back across the globe against the injustice they believe states have perpetrated against them. The members of these nonstate nations, however, are often outnumbered and divided about their objectives. Most indigenous movements only

ethnocentrism
A propensity to see one's nationality or state as the center of the world and therefore special, with the result that the values and perspectives of other groups are misunderstood and ridiculed.

IMAGE 13.3 **Ethnic Cleansing, Rape, and War** Ethnic conflict is often accompanied by widespread sexual violence. For example, during the 1998–1999 war in Kosovo, an estimated 20,000 Albanian women (and some men) were raped by Serbian police and military personnel, often in front of their own families (Rames, 2013). Shown above are over 5000 skirts, which were hung in a football stadium in Pristina, the capital of Kosovo, in June 2015 to honor the victims of sexual violence. Kosovo-born artist Alketa Xhafa-Mripa, who organized the display to increase awareness of these war crimes, noted the symbolism of the skirts: "The laundry is washed clean, like the women who are clean and pure—they carry no stain" (Cole, 2015).

seek a greater voice in redirecting the policies and allocation of resources within existing states and are eliciting the support of NGOs and *intergovernmental organizations* (IGOs) to pressure states to recognize their claims and protect their rights.

Substantial numbers of indigenous movements in the last decade have successfully negotiated settlements resulting in **devolution**—the granting of regional political power that increases local self-governance. Examples include the Miskitos in Nicaragua, the Gagauz in Moldova, and most regional separatists in Ethiopia as well as in India's Assam region. Yet, as suggested by the hostilities between the Chechens and the Russian Federation, resolving clashes between aspiring peoples and established states can be extremely difficult.

The goal expressed in the UN Charter of promoting "universal respect for, and observance of, human rights and fundamental freedoms" is very challenging for many nationally diverse countries. The division of these states along ethnic and cultural lines makes them inherently fragile. Consider the degree to which minority groups compose many states: for example, the share of indigenous populations in Bolivia is as high as 48 percent and in the Philippines 20 percent (IWGIA, 2019). Or consider that there are 5000 different indigenous cultures across ninety countries, with 7000 different languages spoken worldwide (UNDESA, 2019b). Conspicuous examples include Papua New Guinea's 830 languages, Indonesia's 719, Nigeria's 514, India's 438, China's 292, and Mexico's 291 (*The Economist*, 2012c).

devolution
States' granting of political power to minority ethnic groups and indigenous people in particular national regions under the expectation that greater autonomy will curtail the groups' quest for independence as a new state.

Racism and intolerance are hothouses for fanaticism and violence. The belief that one's nationality is superior to all others undermines human rights. Although interethnic competition is a phenomenon that dates back to biblical times, it remains a contemporary plague. According to the Minorities at Risk Project (2009), since 1998, more than 284 politically motivated minority groups throughout the globe suffered in their home countries from organized discriminatory treatment and mobilized in collective action to defend and promote their self-defined interests. Some analysts predict that conflict within and between ethnically divided states will become a major axis on which twenty-first-century world politics will revolve.

Efforts to toughen domestic refugee legislation and criteria for granting asylum raise important ethical issues. Where will the homeless, the desperate, the weak, and the poor find *sanctuary*—a safe place to live where human rights are safeguarded? Will the rich countries act with compassion or respond with indifference? The policy proposals crafted to address these questions may involve controversial trade-offs, and point to the difficulties in appropriately responding to the global refugee crisis in particular (see Chapter 12), and human rights abuse in general.

Gender Inequality and Its Consequences

A global consensus has emerged that the status of women needs to improve if human rights and development are to progress. For more than three decades, global conferences have highlighted the critical role of women's human rights concerns (see Table 13.1). These conferences are signposts that increasingly depict gender equality and empowerment across political, social, and economic arenas as a fundamental right. They have introduced the world to the incontrovertible evidence that women's status in society, and especially their education, profoundly influences human development and that the treatment of women is a global rights issue that affects everyone.

As measured by the UNDP's **Gender Inequality Index (GII)**, women throughout the world continue to be disadvantaged relative to men across a broad spectrum (UNDP, 2019b). The composite measure, which ranges from zero (no inequality) to one (extreme inequality), indicates that disparities between men and women persist across three dimensions: reproductive health, empowerment, and the labor market. **Gender inequality**—difference in living standards between men and women—erodes human development and human rights, and is reflected in differences found in female mortality and fertility rates, political power and educational attainment, and participation in the workforce. Women generally enjoy less access to advanced study and training in professional fields, are frequently relegated to less prestigious jobs, face formidable barriers to political involvement, and typically receive less pay than men.

Gender inequality varies enormously around the world, and is especially prevalent in three Global South regions: South Asia, the Middle East, and sub-Saharan Africa. At the start of 2018, gender inequality in the Netherlands was nominal, as indicated by a GII score of .044, whereas inequality was very high in Yemen and Niger, as shown by GII scores of .834 and .649, respectively (UNDP, 2018).

The need to extend equal human rights to women is clear-cut. "When women are educated and can earn and control income, a number of good results follow: infant mortality declines, child health and nutrition improve, agricultural productivity rises, population growth slows,

Gender Inequality Index (GII)
An index that uses female reproductive health, political and educational empowerment, and participation in the labor market to assess the extent to which gender inequality erodes a country's human development achievements.

gender inequality
Differences between men and women in opportunity and reward that are determined by the values that guide states' foreign and domestic policies.

TABLE 13.1 Important Steps on the Path toward Human Rights and Women's Rights

Year	Conference	Key Passage
1975	World Conference on International Women's Year (Mexico City)	Launched a global dialogue on gender equality and led to the establishment of the United Nations Development Fund for Women (UNIFEM)
1979	Convention on the Elimination of All Forms of Discrimination against Women (Women's Convention, New York)	Article 12 calls on countries to "take all appropriate measures to eliminate discrimination against women in the field of health care in order to ensure, on a basis of equality of men and women, access to health care services, including those related to family planning"
1980	Second World Conference on Women (Copenhagen)	Calls for governments to enact stronger measures that will ensure women's ownership and control of property, and will improve women's rights to inheritance, child custody, and recognition of nationality
1985	Third World Conference on Women (Nairobi)	Recognized the need for governments to bring gender concerns into the mainstream and develop institutional mechanisms to promote broad-based gender equality and empowerment of women
1993	United Nations World Conference on Human Rights (Vienna)	The Vienna Declaration includes nine paragraphs on "The Equal Status and Human Rights of Women," and for the first time recognizes that "violence against women is a human-rights abuse"
1995	United Nations Fourth World Conference on Women (Beijing)	Sets a wide-ranging, ambitious agenda for promoting human development by addressing gender inequality and women's rights
2004	NATO Conference on Trafficking in Humans (Brussels)	Seeks a convention to contain the growing problem of human trafficking and export of people across borders—particularly women and children
2004	United Nations Conference on Sexual and Reproductive Rights (New York)	Launches action plan to uphold women's "fundamental human rights including sexual and reproductive rights"
2005	United Nations World Conference on Women (Beijing)	110 Platform for Action charts strategies for empowerment of women and girls
2010	Commission on the Status of Women (New York)	Conducts a fifteen-year review of the implementation of the Beijing Declaration, and assesses the Platform for Action
2015	Commission on the Status of Women, Beijing+20 (New York)	Conducts a twenty-year review and appraisal of the implementation of the Beijing Declaration and Platform for Action
2015	Planet 50-50 by 2030: Step It Up for Gender Equality	A major campaign launched by the United Nations that calls upon governments to make concrete commitments to gender equality and women's empowerment
2020	Commission on the Status of Women, Beijing+25 (New York)	Conducts a twenty-five-year review and appraisal of the implementation of the Beijing Declaration and Platform for Action

economies expand, and cycles of poverty are broken" (Coleman, 2010b, p. 13). When women and girls earn income, they reinvest 90 percent of it in the welfare of their families, buying books, bed nets, and medicines—as compared to men, who allocate only 30 to 40 percent of their income to fulfill similar functions (Gibbs, 2011).

Yet despite the fact that "since the eighteenth century feminists, scholars, and activists have taken up the task of revealing just how much political life has been built on presumptions about femininity and masculinity there is abundant evidence now that regimes and the states beneath them in fact have taken deliberate steps to sustain a sort of hierarchical gendered division of labor that provides them with cheap-end, often completely unpaid, women's productive labor"

(Enloe, 2001, p. 311). Women continue to be responsible for the bulk of family labor and care work and are underrepresented in positions of power in business, academia, media, and law. "The disadvantages facing women and girls are a major source of inequality" (UNDP, 2019b). Social constructs that shape the options women have and the choices they make largely perpetuate a gendered division of labor, and public policies that facilitate participatory parity are needed to interrupt this gender inequality (Markovits and Bickford, 2014).

Much the same holds true in politics: since 1900, only 15 percent of the world's countries have had one or more female heads of state (*Harper's*, 2008). Today, women continue to be vastly underrepresented in decision-making positions in government, even in democracies and developed countries. Gender differences in parliaments around the world are highly skewed in favor of men. At the start of 2018, women accounted for only 24 percent of all seats in parliament around the world, up from a mere 13 percent in 1990 (WDI, 2018; see also Map 13.3).

In most societies, politics is seen "as a largely male sport—unarmed combat—and women are very often ignored or pushed aside in an effort to gain or consolidate power," explained former U.S. Secretary of State Hillary Clinton. Moreover, she continued, "where women are disempowered and dehumanized, you are more likely to see not just antidemocratic forces, but extremism that leads to security challenges," both within the home country and for the world at large. It is clear that "societies with greater equality are more likely to be prosperous and sustain stable democratic institutions" (Htun and Weldon, 2010, p. 207).

Further gender differences continue at the most basic levels of human development, and it is easy to conclude that women remain victims of human rights abuse and discrimination nearly everywhere. More girls than boys die at a young age, and females' access to adequate health care is more restricted (WDI, 2018). "In the Middle East and South Asia, women deemed insufficiently conservative in their dress are attacked with acid. Across Africa, the use of mass rape as an instrument of war has jumped from one conflict to another" (Coleman, 2010a, p. 128). Women continue to be the primary victims of sex trafficking and sexual violence, and not until 2001 did the International Criminal Court confirm "sexual enslavement" as a war crime—a fact that feminists point out as an example of the traditional disregard for women's human rights.

Protecting women's rights is difficult because the issues touch deeply entrenched, as well as widely divergent, religious and cultural beliefs. In many Islamic countries, for example, women must hide their faces with veils in public, and women and men are often completely separated in social and religious activities. As American sociologist Herbert Spencer (1970, p. 186) says, "A people's condition may be judged by the treatment which women receive under it." For many in liberal Western countries that focus on social, political, and economic equality of the sexes, these traditions are difficult to understand.

"Gender empowerment" is based on the conviction that only through realizing the full potential of *all* human beings can true human development occur, and that this includes women's human rights. Social constructivism points to the critical role of women being able to shape ideas and values as well as the freedom to make choices and participate equally in social,

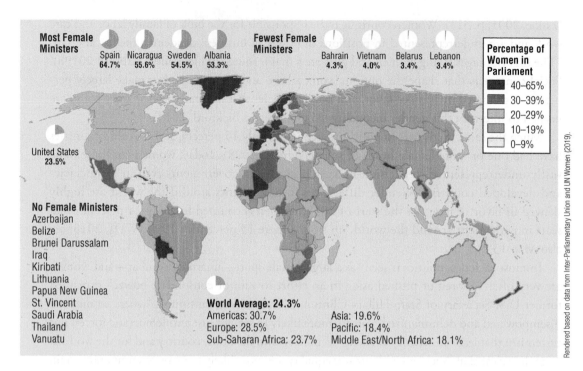

Rendered based on data from Inter-Parliamentary Union and UN Women (2019).

MAP 13.3 Gender Politics There are now more women in government than ever before. The proportion of women in national parliaments grew by only 1 percent between 1975 and 1995, compared to 8 percent between 1998 and 2008. Nonetheless, gender parity remains scarce in democratic governance. There is only one woman for every three males in legislatures around the world, and at the beginning of 2019, only twenty heads of state were female. According to the United Nations, "countries with 'first past the post' electoral systems without any type of quota arrangements will not reach the 40 percent threshold of women in public office until near to the end of this century" (UNIFEM, 2013).

 Think it Through What regional patterns in female leadership do you see? What factors do you think contribute to these differences across regions?

political, and economic life. "This participation is not only a matter of participating in creating specific policy options … but also of participating in creating the social contexts—material, ideological, and discursive—that shape us" (Markovits and Bickford, 2014, p. 85).

Once the concept of empowerment gained acceptance as a lens through which to construct a view of the core issues on the global agenda, gender issues became a central concern. Though grave threats to the rights and security of women and girls remain, there are signs that a transformation is under way. In many countries, significant efforts are being made to promote gender equality:

Greater economic empowerment for women has been achieved through progressive legislation that has prohibited discriminatory practices, guaranteed equal pay, provided for maternity and paternity leave, and put in place protection against sexual harassment in the workplace. Governments have turned their back on the idea that violence against women is a private affair,

IMAGES 13.4A AND 13.4B How to Transcend the Gender Gap?
Shown here are examples of how the empowerment of women is changing. Shown left is Michelle Bachelet, the UN High Commissioner for Human Rights. A physician by training, before taking the UN position she served two terms as the President of Chile and was the first Executive Director of UN-Women. Pictured right is U.S. Major General Maggie Woodward, who, in 2011, became the first woman in U.S. history to command a military air campaign when the United States participated in attacks against Libya. When asked about her thoughts on being a role model, she responded "We're not going to get into the first woman thing, are we? . . . I hope I'm an inspiring figure to lots of little boys and girls" (Thompson, 2011, p. 38).

with laws in every region now outlawing this scourge in its many manifestations. Legislation prohibiting discrimination based on sex with respect to inheritance and citizenship, laws that guarantee equality within the family and policies to ensure that women and girls can access services including health and education have also contributed to significant advances in women's standard of living (UNIFEM, 2011, p. 8).

Feminist theory, a departure from classical realist theory, seeks to rectify the ways conventional but distorted images of world politics are, as constructivism informs us, socially constructed (see Chapter 2). The objective is to show the world its neglect of gender and of women in global society and to offer an alternative theoretical vision that empowers women, secures their basic human rights, and challenges realist theories that honor the state and military power (Tickner, 2010; Enloe, 2007).

Gendercide, Slavery, and Human Trafficking

Under normal circumstances, females live longer than males, and so there are more women than men in much of the world, even in poor regions such as much of Latin America and Africa. "Yet in places where girls have a deeply unequal status, they *vanish*" (Kristof and WuDunn 2009, p. xv). In northern India and China, more than 117 boys continue to be born for every 100 girls due to a cultural partiality for sons, a modern preference for small families, and the availability of technology that enables couples to determine the gender of their unborn child. A growing number of countries, especially in Asia, are experiencing the effects of a generation of **gendercide**; Indian economist Amartya Sen estimates that well over 107 million females are "missing" due to abortion, murder, and death due to severe neglect. Over the last fifty years, more girls were killed precisely because of their gender than men killed in all the wars of the twentieth century (Coleman, 2010a; Kristof and WuDunn, 2009).

gendercide
Systematic killing of members of a specific gender.

Another human rights horror to which women, as well as children, are particularly vulnerable is human trafficking (see Brysk and Choi-Fitzpatrick, 2013). Although many people assume that slavery is an obsolete practice, the reality is that trade in human beings is enormous (see Maps 13.4A and 13.4B). The growing modern-day slave trade crisscrosses the entire globe and, "despite more than a dozen international conventions banning slavery in the past 150 years, there are more slaves today than at any point in human history" (Skinner, 2010, p. 56).

Roughly 80,000 Africans were brought to the New World each year during the peak of the slave trade in the 1780s. By way of comparison, today, according to the U.S. State Department, between 600,000 and 800,000 people are trafficked across borders each year to suffer the fate of being bought and sold as sex slaves or bonded laborers (Coleman, 2010a). Some estimates put the total number of people enslaved today around 40.3 million (MAF, 2018):

> Modern slavery is a hidden crime that affects every country in the world… found in many industries including garment manufacturing, mining, and agriculture, and in many contexts, from private homes to settlements for internally displaced people and refugees. Instances have been identified in Thai fishing, coal mining in North Korea, in the homes of diplomats in Australia, car-wash stations in the United Kingdom, cocoa agriculture in Côte d'Ivoire, and cattle ranching in Brazil, just to name a few examples. Modern slavery impacts all of us, from the food we consume to the goods we purchase. It is everyone's responsibility to address and eliminate this crime everywhere it occurs (Global Slavery Index, 2019).

Adult women comprise the greatest proportion of victims (49 percent), with children (30 percent: 23 percent female and 7 percent male) making up the next largest group. Adult males account for 21 percent of victims. The United Nations has found that the leading form of human trafficking is sexual exploitation, which accounts for 83 percent of the trafficking of women and 59 percent of the slave trade overall. The second leading form of human trafficking is forced labor. This form of human trafficking is on the rise and accounts for 82 percent of male trafficking victims and 34 percent of the slave trade as a whole. Among children, 72 percent of girls and 27 percent of boys are trafficked for sexual exploitation. About half of all trafficked boys and 21 percent of girls are subject to forced labor (UNODC, 2018b). "Children's nimble fingers are exploited to untangle fishing nets, sew luxury goods or pick cocoa," reports the United Nations (UNODC, 2009). "Their innocence is abused for begging, or exploited for sex as prostitutes, pedophilia or child pornography. Others are sold as child brides or camel jockeys."

Although many victims of human trafficking are moved across continents, intraregional and domestic trafficking is far more common. Human trafficking is a lucrative criminal activity. According to U.S. Ambassador Luis C. deBaca, who directed the U.S. State Department's

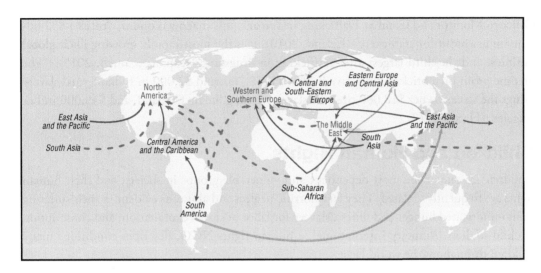

——— Transregional flows: detected victims in destination countries

– – – Transregional flows: less than 5% of detected victims in destination countries

——— Transregional flows: victims repatriated from destination countries

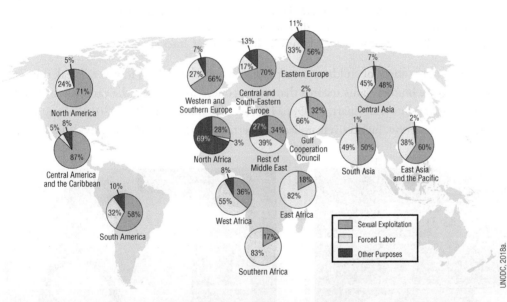

UNODC, 2018a.

MAPS 13.4A AND 13.4B Global Human Trafficking Flows Almost every country is affected by the slave trade; in 2016, trafficking victims from 97 different countries were identified (UNODC, 2018b). Map 13.4A shows the major trafficking flows between global regions, which are just a handful of the estimated 510 flows currently traversing the globe. While victims are exploited in multiple ways, the two most common forms of exploitation are sexual and forced labor/servitude. As shown in Map 13.4B, the prevalence of each varies across different regions. Sexual exploitation is the most common form in Europe as well as Central and North America, while forced labor predominates in Africa and the Middle East.

Think it Through What do the flows of human trafficking suggest about dynamics between the Global North and South? What do they suggest about the relationship between trafficking and regular migration?

Office to Monitor and Combat Trafficking in Persons, this shadow economy "turns a $32 billion annual profit for traffickers" (Ireland, 2010). It is the most rapidly growing illicit global business, and the third largest after trafficking in drugs and weapons (Couch, 2015). "The lifetime profit on a brickmaking slave in Brazil is $8,700, and $2,000 in India. Sexual slavery brings the slave's owner $18,000 over the slave's working life in Thailand, and $49,000 in Los Angeles" (Hardy, 2013).

Children and Human Rights

Children are one of the most dependent and vulnerable groups in society, and their human rights are frequently violated. They face horrific neglect and abuse, as evident in their suffering from unmitigated hunger and illness, slavery for labor or sexual exploitation, and conscription as child soldiers. Amnesty International, a human rights NGO, describes conditions many children throughout the world face:

> Children are tortured and mistreated by state officials; they are arbitrarily or lawfully detained, often in appalling conditions; in some countries they are subjected to the death penalty. Countless thousands are killed or maimed in armed conflicts, many more have fled their homes to become refugees. Children forced by poverty or abuse to live on the streets are sometimes detained, attacked and even killed in the name of social cleansing. Many millions of children work at exploitative or hazardous jobs, or are the victims of child trafficking and forced prostitution. Because children are "easy targets," they are sometimes threatened, beaten or raped in order to punish family members who are not so accessible (Amnesty International, 2009).

Human rights abuse of children takes place all across the globe. However, "weak states typically have worse human rights records than strong ones," as they lack the capacity to effectively protect human rights (Englehart, 2009, p. 163; see also Borzel and Risse, 2013). They are often plagued by corruption, ineffectively police their territory, and are unable to provide basic services.

IMAGES 13.5A AND 13.5B Modern-Day Slavery "More must be done to reduce the vulnerability of victims, increase the risks to traffickers, and lower demand for the goods and services of modern-day slaves," says Antonio Maria Costa, former executive director of the UN Office on Drugs and Crime. Shown on the left is a seventeen-year-old sex worker in Bangladesh after her service with a customer. She ran away from home to escape marriage at the age of fifteen, and sought work at a factory where she was deceived and sold to a brothel. Shown right, a starving farmer in Afghanistan, Akhtar Mohammed, watches his ten-year-old son, Sher, whom he traded to a wealthy farmer in exchange for a monthly supply of wheat. "What else could I do?" he asked. "I will miss my son, but there was nothing to eat."

To bring about a transformation in the human condition, UNICEF (2009) contends that "improvements in public health services are essential, including safe water and better sanitation. Education, especially for girls and mothers, will also save children's lives. Raising income can help, but little will be achieved unless a greater effort is made to ensure that services reach those who need them most." Though child mortality has declined in every region of the world since 1960, almost 7 million children every year still do not live to see their fifth birthday. "Of these, the vast majority dies from causes that are preventable through a combination of good care, nutrition, and simple medical treatment" (World Bank, 2009, p. 44).

Most of the children who die every year live in the Global South, where death claims almost 7 in every 100 children under the age of five in low-income countries, as compared to the Global North, where less than 1 in 100 children die (WDI, 2017a). Malnutrition lies at the root of nearly half of the deaths of children worldwide; it weakens children's immune systems and leaves them vulnerable to illness and disease, such as malaria, pneumonia, diarrhea, measles, and AIDS (see Chapter 12). Progress is being made toward improving conditions for children, and the under-five mortality rate is declining faster than at any other time during the past two decades, with many regions halving the number of children that die young. However, the pace and scale of regional progress varies, with under-five deaths increasingly concentrated in South Asia and sub-Saharan Africa (UNICEF, 2015a).

Poor human rights conditions are exacerbated in countries where there is armed conflict. Not only are children often orphaned or separated from their families without food or care, but also many are direct participants in war. The United Nations (2018e) estimates that in 2017, 8,185 boys and girls between the ages of seven and eighteen were recruited and used as child soldiers in over fifteen countries in violation of international law. Because children are smaller than adults and more easily intimidated, they typically make obedient soldiers. Some are abducted from their homes, others fight under threat of death, and others join out of desperation or a desire to avenge the death of family members.

A 2019 United Nations report on humanitarian action for children further highlights the harmful consequences for children, expressing concern that:

> More countries are embroiled in internal and international fighting now than at any time in the past 30 years. And every conflict comes with terrible consequences for children, who are always among the most vulnerable. In the worst cases, children are at risk of immediate harm from targeted and indiscriminate attacks, as well as abuses such as sexual and gender-based violence, abduction and recruitment into armed forces and groups. If we fail to stop these violations—and if perpetuators are not held accountable for committing them—children will grow up seeing violence as normal, acceptable, even inevitable (UNICEF, 2019, p. 2).

To confront these consequences of armed conflict, it is essential that political leaders be committed to the welfare of children. On August 4, 2009, the UN Security Council unanimously adopted a resolution that expanded the secretary-general's annual report on grave violations of children by groups involved in armed conflict to include the names of groups that kill or maim children contrary to international law, or perpetrate grave sexual violence against children in wartime. "This is a major step forward in the fight against impunity for crimes against children and a recognition of the reality of conflict today, where girls and boys are increasingly targeted and victimized, killed and raped, as well as recruited into armed groups" said former UN Special Representative for Children and Armed Conflict Radhika Coomaraswamy (see UN, 2009b).

The treatment of children has traditionally been seen as a "private" issue of family life that is firmly rooted in cultural values and traditions. Nonetheless, as innocents in our global society, many believe that security and sustenance are basic human rights to which children are entitled, and that the international community must help to protect these rights (see "A Closer Look: Insecurity in Childhood"). The Convention on the Rights of the Child (CRC) embraced these sentiments, which the United Nations adopted on November 20, 1989. The basic human rights that the CRC establishes for children everywhere, spelled out in fifty-four articles and two optional protocols, include:

- The right to survival

- The right to develop to the fullest

- The right to protection from harmful influences, abuse, and exploitation

- The right to participate fully in family, cultural, and social life

Emphasizing entitlement to human dignity and harmonious development, and ratified by all of the UN member states except the United States and Somalia, this treaty is widely seen as a major victory for human rights. As the human rights NGO Amnesty International (2015) enthusiastically proclaimed, "Here for the first time was a treaty that sought to address the particular human rights of children and to set minimum standards for the protection of their rights. It is the only international treaty to guarantee civil and political rights as well as economic, social, and cultural rights."

Responding to Human Rights

LO 13-4 Appraise the methods through which human rights may be promoted, and evaluate the challenges faced in enforcing these rights.

There are at least three arguments against making the promotion and enforcement of human rights a responsibility of the global community. Realists reject promoting human rights because, as former Executive Director of Amnesty International William Shulz (2001, p. 13) explains, they "regard the pursuit of rights as an unnecessary, sometimes even a dangerous extravagance, often at odds with the national interest." Statists or legalists reject protecting human rights in other states because it represents an unwarranted intrusion into the domestic affairs of others and an infringement upon state sovereignty. Relativists or pluralists view human rights promotion as a form of moral imperialism (Blanton and Cingranelli, 2010).

Nonetheless, by 2005, there was widespread agreement among states "on the abstract notion of an international responsibility to protect (R2P): that if a sovereign state failed to exercise its primary responsibility to prevent gross violations of human rights, being unable or unwilling to do so, outside states inherited a responsibility to act" (Forsythe, 2012, p. 26). As constructivists tell us, the evolution of global values can have a powerful impact on international behavior. "Virtually any explanation of the rise of human rights must take into account the political

A Closer Look

INSECURITY IN CHILDHOOD

In August 2017, Myanmar launched a brutal campaign of violence against the Rohingya minority group, including widespread rape and torture as well as the destruction of hundreds of villages. Within a few months, more than 700,000 people fled into neighboring countries, primarily neighboring Bangladesh. Though the military-led crackdown was ostensibly in response to an attack on army and police facilities by a small militant group, the Arakan Rohingya Salvation Army (ARSA), the brutality marked a decades-long process of disenfranchising and repressing the Rohingya, an impoverished Muslim group indigenous to the southwestern part of Myanmar.

Children make up an estimated 60 percent of Rohingya refugees. Currently an estimated 500,000 children are in Bangladesh alone; several thousand of these children are unaccompanied due to either separation from their parents or the deaths of their parents. Child refugees have very limited options. For the most part, they live in overcrowded refugee camps with poor living conditions, rampant illness, and little access to education or healthcare. They are often vulnerable to kidnapping, rape, or being trafficked, and many live in a constant state of fear; as one report noted, "for an adult, this place is tough. For a child, it is a waking nightmare" (Pierce and Murphy, 2018).

Tragically, this story is one that is repeated frequently in other countries throughout the world, as a majority of refugees and displaced people are children. Yet to what extent does the global community have a responsibility to protect children around the world? Advocates for intervention by the global community argue that "principled foreign policy defies the realist prediction of untrammeled pursuit of national interest" (Brysk, 2009, p. 4). Instead, it is necessary for state and nonstate actors to serve as a "global Good Samaritan" who, in the spirit of a fundamental Christian belief, "loves thy neighbor as thyself."

A 2018 report by the United Nations lambasted the military's "contempt for human life," recommending that Myanmar's military leaders be investigated for genocide and crimes against humanity, and arguing that "(m)ilitary

necessity would never justify killing indiscriminately, gang raping women, assaulting children, and burning entire villages" (UN Office of the High Commissioner on Human Rights, 2018). Nikki Haley, U.S. Ambassador to the UN at the time, declared that Myanmar had carried out a "brutal, sustained campaign to cleanse the country of an ethnic minority" (Albert and Chatzky, 2018) and urged the Security Council to impose sanctions. However, virtually no concrete actions were taken against Myanmar, due largely to resistance from Russia and China.

Shorter-term humanitarian aid has provided for basic needs such as protection, food, and healthcare. Yet in the long term, education is widely seen as vital to ensuring the future well-being of these children. Since Bangladesh refuses to provide education for the refugees, the UN and multiple NGOs are making efforts to provide some modicum of instruction, generally through informal learning centers aimed at younger children (Reuters, 2018). While laudable, such efforts are ultimately not adequate, particularly for older children. However, as argued by UNICEF Representative Edouard Beigbeder, "if we don't make the investment in education now, we face the very real danger of seeing a lost generation of Rohingya children," who "lack the skills they need to deal with their current situation, and who will be incapable of contributing to their society whenever they are able to return to Myanmar" (UN, 2018f).

Watch the Carnegie Council Video:
"Am I My Brothers' Keeper?"

You Decide:
1. What are the consequences of serious violations of children's human rights and neglect of their human development for national development and global security?

2. What role should other states, IGOs, and NGOs play in addressing the condition of children throughout the world?

Note: Prepared with the advice and assistance of Robert G. Blanton, Ph.D.

power of norms and ideas and the increasingly transnational way in which those ideas are carried and diffused" (Sikkink, 2008, p. 172).

The most common manifestations of this phenomenon are the expanding laws that regulate the practices that sovereign states may use. The human rights revolution has advanced moral progress by breaking states' monopoly on international affairs and over citizens. In this sense, liberalism triumphed and realism was repudiated, for the human rights movement has rejected the harsh realist vision expressed by Thomas Hobbes, who argued in the seventeenth century in his classic work *Leviathan* (1651) that because world politics is in essence a "war of every man against every man… nothing can be unjust. The notions of right and wrong, justice and injustice have there no place."

Moreover, international law has fundamentally revised the traditional realist conception of the state by redefining the relationship of states to humans. As former UN Secretary-General Kofi Annan (1999) notes, "States are now widely understood to be instruments at the service of their people, and not *vice versa*. When we read the Charter today, we are more than ever conscious that its aim is to protect individual human beings, not to protect those who abuse them."

The Human Rights Legal Framework

The global community has expanded its legal protection of human rights significantly over the past sixty years. Multilateral treaties have proliferated as part of a global effort to construct a consensus on the rights of all humanity and put an end to human rights violations. Numerous conventions have been enacted that have increasingly recognized individual rights—asserting that people must be treated as worthy of the freedom and dignity traditionally granted by international law to states and rulers. Moreover, from the perspective of international law, a state is obligated to respect the human rights of its own citizens as well as those of another country, and the international community has the prerogative to challenge any state that does

IMAGES 13.6A AND 13.6B Human Rights Violations "Women between the ages of 15 and 44 are more likely to be maimed or killed by male violence than by war, cancer, malaria, and traffic incidents combined" (Coleman, 2010a, p. 127). Pictured on the left is Bibi Aisha, an Afghan woman whose husband cut off her nose and ears as punishment for running away from her abusive in-laws. Pictured on the right is actress Emma Watson, appointed by the United Nations as a Goodwill Ambassador in July 2014. She launched the *HeForShe* gender equality campaign and called on men to help support the fight for women's human rights.

TABLE 13.2 Core Conventions of the International Human Rights Legal Framework

Year	Instrument
1948	Universal Declaration of Human Rights
1965	International Convention on the Elimination of All Forms of Racial Discrimination (ICERD)
1966	International Covenant on Civil and Political Rights (ICCPR)
1966	International Covenant on Economic, Social, and Cultural Rights (ICESCR)
1979	Convention on the Elimination of All Forms of Discrimination against Women (CEDAW)
1984	Convention against Torture and Other Cruel, Inhumane or Degrading Treatment or Punishment (CAT)
1989	Convention on the Rights of the Child (CRC)
1990	International Convention on the Protection of the Rights of All Migrant Workers and Members of Their Families (ICRMW)
2006	Convention on the Rights of Persons with Disabilities (CRPD)

not respect these rights. Table 13.2 highlights eight international agreements, in addition to the Universal Declaration of Human Rights, that provide a foundation for the legal framework of international human rights.

Among these treaties and instruments of international law, the Universal Declaration of Human Rights; the International Covenant on Economic, Social, and Cultural Rights; and the International Covenant on Civil and Political Rights together form the "International Bill of Human Rights." Additionally, there are hundreds of widely accepted legal instruments and political declarations across a broad array of human rights issues. They provide specific standards for the human rights protection of vulnerable groups such as women, children, migrant workers, and disabled persons and for the collective rights of minorities and indigenous groups. The United Nations and its members have been a driving force behind the development of a global human rights legal system. The International Labor Organization (ILO) and regional organizations, such as the African Union, the Inter-American Commission on Human Rights, and the European Court of Human Rights, also have established human rights protections.

> *Every human life is precious . . . it is not just about our criminal justice system, which we also want to be proportionate and restorative; it is about the type of society that we want to build—a society that values every person, and one that doesn't give up on its people.*
>
> **—LAURENCE LIEN, MEMBER OF PARLIAMENT OF SINGAPORE**

The Challenge of Enforcement

Once the content of human rights obligations was enumerated in multilateral treaties, international attention shifted to monitoring their implementation and addressing violations. Unfortunately, "the deepening international human rights regime creates opportunities for rights-violating governments to display low-cost legitimating commitments to world norms, leading them to ratify human rights treaties without the capacity or willingness to comply with the provisions" (Hafner-Burton et al., 2008, p. 115; see also Powell and Staton, 2009).

In addition, some countries endorse human rights treaties merely as a superficial symbolic commitment and continue to repress human rights.

Moreover, full agreement has yet to be reached on the extent to which the international community has a responsibility to intervene in order to enforce human rights. As the International Commission on Intervention and State Sovereignty (2001) noted in its report, *The Responsibility to Protect*, "If intervention for human protection purposes is to be accepted, including the possibility of military action, it remains imperative that the international community develop consistent, credible, and enforceable standards to guide state and intergovernmental practice." Although expanding global norms that elevate human security do much to advance human rights, critical policy questions remain about what steps can and should be taken to safeguard these rights and prevent violations (Ramcharan, 2010).

humanitarian intervention
The use of peacekeeping troops by foreign states or international organizations to protect endangered people from gross violations of their human rights and from mass murder.

Humanitarian intervention encompasses the international community's actions to assist the population of a state that is experiencing severe human suffering caused by political collapse, deliberate government policy, or natural disaster (see Chapters 6 and 7). The principles that guide humanitarian intervention continue to be a matter of heated debate. The issue is not whether there exists a compelling need and moral obligation to express concerns about populations at risk of slaughter, starvation, or persecution; the issue is about how to craft a just response, when any response will comprise interference in the domestic affairs of a sovereign state. Humanitarian intervention is controversial because it pits the legal principle of territorial sovereignty against what some see as a moral responsibility to protect vulnerable populations from egregious violations of human rights.

Although the construction of global human rights norms has made great strides over the past sixty years, the enforcement of these laws has lagged. Within the United Nations, the Office of the High Commissioner for Human Rights (OHCHR) is responsible for implementing international human rights agreements, overseeing major human rights programs, and providing global leadership in promoting and protecting human rights. It also supervises the Human Rights Council (UNHRC).

Created by the UN General Assembly on March 15, 2006, the Human Rights Council is an intergovernmental organization designed to evaluate allegations of human rights abuse and make recommendations about the best course of action. The 47 members of the council are elected for a three-year term based on geographic region. There is concern that the UNHRC does not have the ability to prevent states with poor human rights records from membership on the council, and the United States has consistently objected to the inclusion of countries that lack representative government, violate human rights, and are highly critical of its ally, Israel. In 2018, for instance, Human Rights Council members included Venezuela where free speech and political opposition were restricted, Saudi Arabia where widespread abuses and arbitrary arrests persist, and Egypt where any criticism of the government is banned (Calamur, 2018).

Though the United States had shifted from rejecting the Human Rights Council to attempting to influence the organization from within, in June 2018 the United States withdrew from the organization, with the Trump Administration citing as reason the lack of institutional reform. Others, however, questioned whether U.S. withdrawal was influenced by the UN High Commissioner for Human Rights' criticism of its policy of separating immigrant children from their families at the U.S. southern border. Amidst reports that the U.S. government detained hundreds of children in harsh and dangerous conditions, the UN High Commissioner said the practice "amounts to arbitrary and unlawful interference in family life, and is a serious violation of the rights of the child" (UN OHCHR, 2018b).

Studies have shown that international organizations such as the United Nations "play an important role" in punishing human rights violators and "that seemingly symbolic resolutions of a politically motivated IO [international organization] can carry tangible consequences" (Lebovic and Voeten, 2009, p. 79; see also Greenhill, 2010; Mertus, 2009b). Nonetheless, despite the significant efforts to monitor human rights and enforce norms and agreements, the effectiveness of the United Nations and other intergovernmental organizations is constrained as they can exercise only the authority that member states delegate to them.

In response to these limitations, NGOs have assumed an important role in promoting human rights. They have developed an array of transnational advocacy networks and strategies designed to pressure governments to modify their behavior and conform to prevailing human rights norms and laws (Keck and Sikkink, 2008). As Ellen Lutz, executive director of Cultural Survival (an NGO that protects the human rights of indigenous peoples) explains:

> These organizations investigate human rights abuses wherever they occur, including in places enduring armed conflict. Because of their reputation for accuracy, their findings are relied on by the news media, many governments, and most intergovernmental institutions. While these NGOs hope their reports will bring about a change in the behavior of the government or other entity whose abuses they spotlight, their main targets are the policymakers who are in a more powerful position to put pressure on human rights violators. They lobby other governments to take human rights into account in their foreign aid and press the United Nations and other intergovernmental organizations to put pressure on rights abusers (Lutz, 2006, p. 25).

With greater openness to institutional activism in the post–Cold War era, human rights activists have pressed to strengthen enforcement mechanisms. Their efforts account, in part, for the establishment of UN tribunals that review gross human rights abuse, as in the cases of the former Yugoslavia and Rwanda, and the creation of the *International Criminal Court*. Activists are also credited with monitoring human rights situations and targeting a publicity "spotlight" on abusive practices to shame those who violate human rights into changing their behavior (Barry, Clay, and Flynn, 2012; Blanton and Blanton, 2012a; Murdie and Davis, 2012). "When citizens, even those who are relatively powerless by themselves, partner with non-governmental organizations (NGOs) and intergovernmental organizations (IGOs), they have promoted positive changes in human rights" (Smith-Cannoy, 2012, p. 3).

Although some individuals remain skeptical of claims that we all have transcendent moral obligations to humanity as a whole, others believe that every person, by virtue of being human, has certain inherent and inalienable rights that warrant international protection. Decrying the realist premise that human rights are at odds with national interest, former Executive Director of Amnesty International William Schulz (2001, p. 13) laments that "What they seem rarely to garner is that in far more cases than they will allow, defending human rights is a prerequisite to protecting that interest." Human rights buttress political and economic freedom, "which in turn tends to bring international trade and prosperity. And governments that treat their own people with tolerance and respect tend to treat their neighbors in the same way."

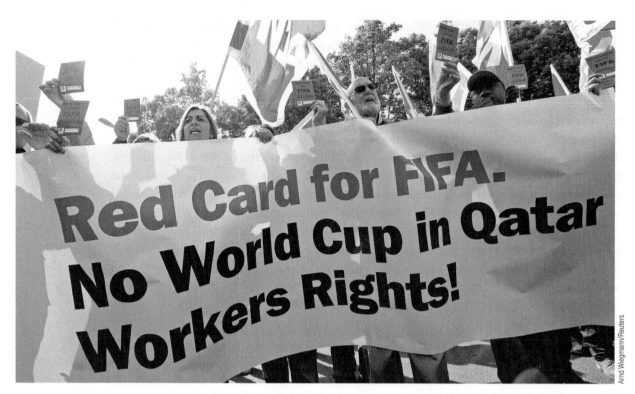

IMAGE 13.7 **For the People** Governments make choices about the priority placed on human development and human rights. The 2022 World Cup in Qatar has come under intense controversy due to human rights abuses. Amnesty International first documented severe problems in 2013, including inhumane and unsafe work conditions (over 1,200 workers died between 2009 and 2014) and squalid living quarters for workers (ITUC, 2014). Exacerbating the situation, almost the entire labor force is foreign and the worker visa system prevents them from changing jobs or even leaving the country without their employers' permission (Visser, 2015). Given this pattern of abuse, as well as the unwillingness of the Qatari state to make meaningful changes, many oppose Qatar's hosting of the world sporting event.

Promoting the rights and dignity of ordinary people around the world is a formidable challenge. Yet, as global security analyst David Rieff (1999, p. 37) observes, "The old assumption that national sovereignty trumps all other principles in international relations is under attack as never before." As political scientist Alison Brysk (2009, p. 4) notes, "Even in a world of security dilemmas, some societies will come to see the linkage between their long-term interest and the common good—at some times and places, states can overcome their bounded origins as sovereign security managers to act as 'global citizens.'" Because concerns for human rights have gained stature under international law and are being monitored more closely than ever before by IGOs and NGOs, we can expect human rights to receive continuing attention, as long as people are caught in emergency situations such as genocide or the threat of famine. Eleanor Roosevelt championed the *cosmopolitan* ideal, and her energetic leadership was largely responsible for global acceptance in 1948 of the Universal Declaration of Human Rights. When thinking about the human condition in the early twenty-first century, we can profit by the inspiration of her nightly prayer: "Save us from ourselves and show us a vision of a world made new."

John D. Rockefeller Jr., once said, "I believe that every right implies a responsibility; every opportunity, an obligation; every possession, a duty." In the next chapter of *World Politics*, you have an opportunity to look at another major issue that entails rights and responsibility to humanity. As the cascading globalization of our world accelerates, the human choices about our natural environment have consequences for the entire planet and affect the Earth's capability to sustain human life and security.

Study. Apply. Analyze.

Chapter Summary

13-1 Describe the role of individual rights in the global system. Over time, the belief in the fundamental value of the individual has gained popularity and shaped our approach to international relations. Encouraging human development and human security, as well as protecting human rights, are increasingly important in global politics.

13-2 Explain the concepts of human security and human development. Human security and human development describe the extent that a country protects its citizenry and ensures that personal needs are met. These multidimensional concepts are measured through multiple indicators, including poverty, income inequality, maternal mortality rates, life expectancy, and educational attainment. Increased globalization has implications for both human security and human development.

13-3 Describe the globally recognized facets of human rights, and examine ways in which these rights are threatened. Human rights are the individual rights and protections applicable to all people. They include five categories: individual rights, right to equal legal recognition and protection, political rights, economic and social rights, and community rights. Several groups are particularly vulnerable to the repression of human rights, including indigenous peoples, women, and children.

13-4 Appraise the methods through which human rights may be promoted, and evaluate the challenges faced in enforcing these rights. A well-developed body of international law delineates different aspects of human rights. IGOs, particularly the UN, and NGOs can take measures to hold states accountable for human rights violations. However, human rights laws are difficult to enforce, particularly if governments see them as conflicting with state sovereignty.

Key Terms

devolution	Gender Inequality Index (GII)	human needs	Inequality-adjusted Human
ethnocentrism	gendercide	human rights	Development Index (IHDI)
gender inequality	Human Development Index (HDI)	humanitarian intervention	

Suggested Readings and Resources

Ackerly, Brooke A. *Just Responsibility: A Human Rights Theory of Global Justice.* (New York: Oxford University Press, 2009).

Blanton, Shannon Lindsey, and David L. Cingranelli. "Human Rights and Foreign Policy Analysis," in *The International Studies Compendium Project*, Robert

Denemark et al., (eds.). (Oxford: Wiley-Blackwell, 2010), 3478–3494.

Brysk, Alison, and Austin Choi-Fitzpatrick, eds. *From Human Trafficking to Human Rights: Reframing Contemporary Slavery.* (Philadelphia, PA: University of Pennsylvania Press, 2012).

Human Rights Now Blog: blog.amnestyusa.org. A blog sponsored by Amnesty International documenting global human rights issues.

Kristof, Nicholas D., and Sheryl WuDunn. *Half the Sky: Turning Oppression into Opportunity for Women Worldwide* (New York: Random House, 2009).

Mertus, Julie. *Human Rights Matters: Local Politics and National Human Rights Institutions* (Stanford, CA: Stanford University Press, 2009).

Politics of Poverty: politicsofpoverty.oxfamamerica.org/. A website with articles about international and national poverty specifically dealing with politics.

Smith-Cannoy, Heather. *Insincere Commitments: Human Rights Treaties, Abusive States, and Citizen Activism.* (Washington, DC: Georgetown University Press, 2012).

UNDP. *Human Development Report 2019* (New York: United Nations, 2019).

UNICEF Connect: blogs.unicef.org. A blog by UNICEF consisting of articles regarding international human rights.

World Bank Blogs: Human Development: blogs.worldbank.org/developmenttalk. A collection of blog posts by the World Bank regarding poverty and human development.

Carnegie Council Videos

Key Term Videos

- Human Rights
- Human Development Index (HDI)
- Gender Inequality
- Humanitarian Intervention

Additional Videos

- Goldhagen, Daniel Jonah. "Worse Than War: Genocide, Eliminationism, and the Ongoing Assault on Humanity."
- Moossy, Robert, Roger Plant, and Maria Suarez. "Forced to Labor: The Cost of Coercion."
- Rodin, David. "How Rights Move: Losing and Acquiring Rights in the International Domain."
- Vocke, William. "Your Income, Your Liberty, and Your Equality?"

Chapter 14

Global Responsibility for the Preservation of the Environment

IMAGE 14.1 Preserving Our Planet Many of the world's waterways face serious pollution threats—from sources such as industrial wastewater, raw sewage, garbage, and oil spills—that pose great risk to human health and environmental sustainability. Shown here, two children scavenge from the floating garbage on the increasingly polluted River Buriganga, one of the filthiest in Bangladesh. The water is so contaminated that all fish have died and human waste has turned the river to a black gel.

Learning Objectives

LO 14-1 Articulate key concepts underlying global ecological controversies.

LO 14-2 Investigate three major areas of ecopolitical contention: climate change, biodiversity, and energy supply.

LO 14-3 Assess the interrelationship between environmental preservation and two aspects of human rights: economic and food security.

LO 14-4 Examine efforts of international actors, including IGOs and multinational corporations, to enhance environmental protections.

> *To waste, to destroy our natural resources, to skin and exhaust the land instead of using it so as to increase its usefulness, will result in undermining in the days of our children the very prosperity which we ought by right to hand down to them amplified and developed."*
>
> **—THEODORE ROOSEVELT, FORMER U.S. PRESIDENT**

"Where you stand depends on where you sit" is an aphorism used to describe the determinants of people's decisions. Where do you stand on one of the more "hotly" debated issues created by a warming globe and deteriorating environment? You may already have strong feelings about this controversy. Many others do. On whichever side of the environmental debate you fall, there is at least one scholar and several politicians who share your opinion.

Some politicians, corporations, and scientists reject the idea that the planet is really in danger; they claim that there is not a real problem because technological innovation can reverse global warming (which they argue may not even be "real" because the long-term cyclical pattern of the Earth's evolution suggests that our present period of rising temperatures is temporary). These people claim that environmental deterioration and resource depletion have many people needlessly alarmed.

Most scientists are pessimistic and are now certain that the threat of global warming is real. They are themselves alarmed by optimists who fail to face the "clear and present danger" of environmental threats and undertake the reforms necessary to stem the tide of global change. The ecological threats that rivet the worried scientific community have led many to advocate immediate and sweeping changes by governments, before it is too late to save the human race from doom.

In this chapter, you have the opportunity to sharpen your own thinking by weighing the available evidence about prevailing global trends that affect the environment that we all share. So look at various dimensions of the planet's ecology now in transformation and base your stand on these global issues on information that can better ground your existing opinions. Consider also the extent to which humanity is responsible for preserving our global environment.

> *Earth provides enough to satisfy every man's needs, but not every man's greed.*
>
> **—MOHANDAS GANDHI, INDIAN PEACE ACTIVIST**

Framing the Ecological Debate

LO 14-1 Articulate key concepts underlying global ecological controversies.

environmental security
A concept recognizing that environmental threats to global life systems are as dangerous as the threat of armed conflicts.

The environment is linked to other priorities, such as security, economic prosperity, and social well-being. "Security" means freedom from fear, risk, and danger. Because fears of a nuclear holocaust and other forms of violence have long haunted the world, security has been conventionally equated with *national security*, the struggle for state power central to *realist theory* and its emphasis on armed conflict.

Environmental security broadens the idea of national security by focusing on the transnational nature of the perils that the global environment faces, such as global warming, ozone depletion, and the loss of tropical forests and marine habitats. These problems are just as much a threat to humanity as to the environment. Because environmental degradation undercuts economic well-being and quality of life, *liberalism* informs current thinking about cooperation between states, *international organizations (IGOs)*, and *nongovernmental organizations (NGOs)* to preserve the global environment. The liberal **epistemic community** has redefined "security" in order to move beyond realism's conventional state-centric and militaristic portrayal of international politics.

Today, many experts urge people and governments to construct a broader definition of what really constitutes security, much like what the U.S. Department of Defense did in April 2007 when it warned that global warming should be regarded as a threat to American national security. This shift is compatible with liberal theory, which emphasizes that we should define security as the capacity to protect quality of life. Out of conditions of global poverty and want emerge the so-called **politics of scarcity**, which anticipates that future international conflict will likely be caused by resource scarcities—restricted access to food, oil, and water, for example—rather than by overt military challenges. Moreover, insufficient or polluted resources will depress the living conditions of all of the people on the Earth, but particularly those in the Global South, where the ability and political will to address environmental challenges are limited.

epistemic community
Scientific experts on a subject of inquiry such as global warming that are organized internationally as NGOs to communicate with one another and use their constructed understanding of "knowledge" to lobby for global transformations.

politics of scarcity
The view that the unavailability of resources required to sustain life, such as food, energy, or water, can undermine security in degrees similar to military aggression.

IMAGE 14.2 The Toll of Disaster On April 25, 2015, a massive earthquake measuring 7.8 on the Richter scale hit Nepal. Just three weeks later, on May 12, the country suffered a second earthquake measuring 7.3. More than 8500 lives were lost, and despair and frustration wracked the country as it became apparent "how powerless the Nepali government is to care for its own people when faced with calamity" (Iyengar, 2015, p. 2). Members of the international community including India, China, the United States, and Israel provided relief-and-rescue assistance. Estimates put the total cost of repairs at more than $6 billion, which is equal to about 30 percent of Nepal's annual economic output (Riley, 2015).

cornucopians
Optimists who
question limits-to-
growth perspectives
and contend that
markets effectively
maintain a balance
between population,
resources, and the
environment.

neo-Malthusians
Pessimists who
warn of the global
ecopolitical dangers
of uncontrolled
population growth.

global commons
The physical
and organic
characteristics
and resources
of the entire
planet—the air in
the atmosphere and
conditions on land
and sea—on which
human life depends
and which is the
common heritage of
all humanity.

**carrying
capacity**
The maximum
number of humans
and living species
that can be
supported by a given
territory.

**tragedy of the
commons**
A metaphor, widely
used to explain
the impact of
human behavior on
ecological systems,
which explains
how rational self-
interested behavior
by individuals may
have a destructive,
undesirable
collective impact.

These global environmental issues engage the competing perspectives of optimistic **cornucopians** and pessimistic **neo-Malthusians**. Cornucopians adhere to the belief that if free markets and free trade prevail, ecological imbalances that threaten humanity will eventually be corrected. For them, prices are the key adjustment mechanism that ultimately produces the greatest good for the greatest number of people. Neo-Malthusians, on the other hand, have a lot in common with economic *mercantilism*, which argues that free markets fail to prevent excessive resource exploitation and that, accordingly, intervention by governing institutions is necessary. This latter perspective rejects the belief that the free market will always maximize social welfare.

The neo-Malthusian pessimists sounding the alarm about the signs of ecological deterioration, and the cornucopian optimists confidently extolling the virtues of free markets and technological innovation in saving the planet, portray very different visions of the global future. How we frame our understanding of environmental challenges will affect our policy prescriptions. It will also influence the extent to which the world community has the political will and capacity to cope with ecological problems and expand the possibilities for *human security*.

Ecologists—those who study the interrelationships of living organisms and the Earth's physical environment—use the term the **global commons** to highlight our growing interdependence, because they see the Earth as a common environment outside the political control of any single state or group. In a world where everything affects everything else, the fate of the global commons is the fate of all humanity. The planet's **carrying capacity**—the Earth's ability to support and sustain life—is at the center of this discussion. Lester R. Brown, a renowned environmental analyst, has voiced serious concerns:

> Tonight there will be 219,000 people at the dinner table who were not there last night, many of them with empty plates. Tomorrow night there will be another 219,000 people. Relentless population growth is putting excessive pressure on local land and water resources in many countries, making it difficult if not impossible for farmers to keep pace (Brown, 2012, p. 9).

Humanity faces enormous challenges of unprecedented scope and danger: arresting global climate change, preserving biodiversity, providing clean water, and restoring forests, fisheries, and other overly exploited renewable resources. No single cause is by itself responsible for the alarming trends in the global environment. Rather, many causes interact with each other to produce the dangers that are damaging the world's life systems upon which human existence depends. But among the ecologists who scientifically study the origins of planetary predicaments and problems, one explanation has become very popular—environmental degradation is seen, in part, as a product of the individual pursuit of private gain.

The **tragedy of the commons** is a popular term constructed to capture the human roots of the growing threats to the planet's resources and its delicately balanced ecological system. First articulated in 1833 by English political economist William Foster Lloyd, the concept was later popularized and extended to contemporary global environmental problems by human ecologist Garrett Hardin, in his famous 1968 article published in the journal *Science*. This approach emphasizes the impact of human behavior driven by the search for personal self-advantage. Although it stresses the importance of individual action and personal motivations, it also ascribes those motives to collectivities or groups such as corporations and entire countries.

The central question asked through the "commons" analogy is, what is the probable approach to resources held in common in an unregulated environment? If individuals (and corporations and countries) are interested primarily in advancing their own personal welfare, what consequences should be anticipated for the finite resources held in common for all?

Lloyd, and later Hardin, asked observers to consider what happened in medieval English villages, where the village green was typically considered common property on which all villagers could let their cattle graze. Freedom of access to the commons was a cherished village value. Sharing the common grazing area worked well as long as individuals (and their cattle) did not reduce the land's usefulness to everyone else.

However, assuming that the villagers were driven by the profit motive and that no laws existed to restrain their greed, herders had incentive to increase their stock as much as possible. If pushed, individual herders might concede that the collective interest of all would be served if each contained the size of his herd rather than increasing it, so that the commons could be preserved. But self-restraint—voluntary reduction of the number of one's own cattle to relieve the pressure on the village commons—was not popular. This is especially true because there was no guarantee that others would do the same. By contrast, adding more animals to the village green would produce a personal gain whose costs would have to be borne by everyone.

Therefore, in accordance with economic *rational choice*, the individual pursuit of wealth encouraged all to increase indiscriminately the size of their herds, and it discouraged self-sacrifice

for the common welfare. Ultimately, the collective impact of each effort to maximize individual gain was to place more cattle on the village green than it could sustain. In the long run, the overgrazed green was destroyed. The lesson? "Ruin is the destination toward which all men rush," Hardin (1968) concluded, "each pursuing his own best interest."

The tragedy of the commons has become a standard concept in ecological analysis because it aptly illuminates the sources of environmental degradation as well as many other global problems and predicaments. It is particularly applicable to the debate today about pressures on the global environment because the English common green is comparable to planetary "common property," such as the oceans and the atmosphere from which individual profit is maximized on the basis of a first-come, first-served principle. Overuse of common property is also highlighted, as when the oceans and atmosphere are used by some as a sink for environmental pollutants whose costs are borne by all.

© 2019 NPR

IMAGE 14.3 **On the Precipice of Extinction?** In 2019 the International Union for Conservation of Nature (IUCN) published its "Red List" of endangered species, finding that an unprecedented 28,338 of the over 105,000 plant and animal species that they assessed are at risk of extinction. As one IUCN scientist notes, "nature is declining at rates unprecedented in human history" (quoted in Aguilera, 2019). The primary cause for these extinctions is human activity. Pictured above is a massive "dead zone"—an area in which water no longer has sufficient oxygen to support life—in the Niger Delta in Nigeria. This once-thriving ecosystem was destroyed by the practice of "oil bunkering" in which oil is illegally siphoned off from pipelines to sell on the black market (Lambert and Ellis, 2019).

Are the dynamics underlying the tragedy of the commons responsible for global ecological dangers? Many people think so. However, you have probably already noted that experts disagree about the moral and ethical implications of Hardin's interpretation. Note that the logical conclusion is that reforms are necessary if we are to save planet Earth. The needed changes will require both self-restraint on people's freedom of choice as well as a modicum of regulation to control the ruinous consequences of the tragedy of an unmanaged global commons.

Theorists adhering to realism and free-market mercantilism resolutely defend freedom of economic choice without regulation as the best path to realizing the greatest good for the greatest number. Theorists from these traditions believe that pursuing self-interest and personal profit will benefit all in the long run, producing more income and technological innovation than would otherwise occur under supervisory regulation of corporations, entrepreneurs, and investors. They also feel that minimal interference in the pursuit of personal gain is helpful to the preservation of the Earth's environment. According to their reasoning, the pursuit of private gain with little restraint is a virtue, not a vice.

Almost all religious moral traditions question this realist and mercantilist conclusion. Christianity, for example, follows ancient Hebrew ethics in defining greed as one of the seven deadly sins. As Timothy 6:10 in the Bible warns, "For the love of money is the root of all evil." The predictable outcome of selfishness and blind dedication to personal financial gain over other values such as altruistic love and compassion for humankind is a path to certain ruin and sin. In this sense, religious traditions join some of the thinking underlying radical Marxist theorizing (see Chapter 2). These lines of thought argue that concern for the welfare of all provides happiness and benefits because only if community interests are protected can individuals realize their most precious personal interest in advancing such common values as the opportunity for maintaining a clean and sustainable environment.

Global Ecopolitical Challenges

LO 14-2 Investigate three major areas of ecopolitical contention: climate change, biodiversity, and energy supply.

Ecopolitics forces you to weigh rival perspectives and to evaluate competing values. Do you want income and prosperity? Of course—but at what cost? Countries and companies all seek wealth. Does this mean that their quest for profits justifies dumping toxic wastes into lakes, rivers, and oceans, and letting others bear the burden of these actions?

These and other ethical questions bear directly on the debate about what is causing the degradation of the planetary commons and what, if anything, should be done to counter it, and at what cost. The next step is for you to characterize and estimate the nature and magnitude of environmental threats and challenges. Consider three interrelated clusters of problems on the global ecopolitical agenda: (1) climate change and ozone depletion; (2) biodiversity, deforestation, and water shortages; and (3) energy supply and demand. The clusters illustrate some of the obstacles to the preservation of common properties and renewable resources.

The Ecopolitics of the Atmosphere

The scores of government negotiators and nongovernmental representatives who converged in Rio de Janeiro in 1992 came in the wake of the hottest decade on record. For years, scientists had warned that global warming—the gradual rise in world temperature—would cause destructive changes in world climate patterns and that rising sea levels, melting glaciers, and freak storms would provoke widespread changes in global political and economic relationships. Perhaps because they had been burned by the chronic heat wave throughout the 1980s, negotiators agreed at Rio to a *Framework Convention on Climate Change*. Since then, fears have spread with the continuing rise in planetary temperatures and extreme weather events, and attention to the pollutants blamed for global warming has also risen.

Most climate scientists are now convinced that the gradual rise in the Earth's temperature, especially evident since the late eighteenth century when the invention of power-driven machinery produced the Industrial Revolution, is caused by an increase in human-made gases that alter the insulating effects of the atmosphere. The gas molecules, primarily carbon dioxide (CO_2) and chlorofluorocarbons (CFCs), form the equivalent of a greenhouse roof by trapping heat emitted from Earth that would otherwise escape into outer space. Over the past fifty years, the emission of carbon dioxide has increased by almost 90 percent, with about 78 percent of the total greenhouse gas emissions resulting from fossil fuel combustion and industrial processes (EPA, 2019). Additionally, "tropical forest loss currently accounts for 8 percent of the world's annual carbon dioxide emissions… if tropical deforestation were regarded as a country, it would be the third-biggest emitter globally—ranking just below the United States and significantly above the European Union" (Fritts, 2018).

As these gases are released into the atmosphere, they create a **greenhouse effect**, which has caused global temperatures to rise (see Figure 14.1). The average global temperature on the Earth's surface since the late 1800s has increased between 0.7 and 1.4 degrees Fahrenheit (0.4 to 0.8 degrees Celsius). The changing temperatures are expected to have a profound effect on animal and plant life across the world. Furthermore, "there is wide consensus that the 2 degrees Fahrenheit of global warming of the last century is behind the rise in sea levels, more intense hurricanes, more heat waves, and more droughts and deluges" (Begley, 2011b, p. 43).

The globe's temperature is now projected to increase even more dramatically by 2100 if aggressive preventive action is not taken (see Map 14.1). France's National Center for Scientific Research (CNRS), the atomic energy commission (CEA), and weather office Meteo-France anticipate that "average global temperatures could rise between 6 and 7 degrees Celsius (10.8 degrees to 12.6 degrees Fahrenheit) above pre-industrial levels" by the end of the century (Mortiz-Rabson, 2019). The Intergovernmental Panel on Climate Change (IPCC), an international body established in 1988 to assess the scientific basis of climate change and provide options for adaptation and mitigation to policymakers, makes a similar forecast, predicting that global temperatures will probably rise about 2 to 12 degrees Fahrenheit by 2100, with longer and more intense heat waves along the way. In 2019, the IPCC (2019) stated that global temperatures could rise by 2.7 degrees Fahrenheit in as little as 11 years—and almost certainly within 20 years—unless there are major reductions in carbon dioxide emissions.

greenhouse effect
The phenomenon producing planetary warming when gases released by burning fossil fuels act as a blanket in the atmosphere, thereby increasing temperatures.

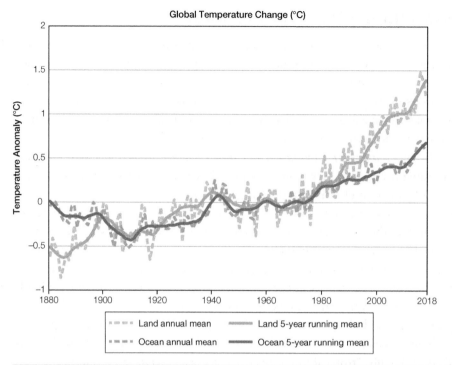

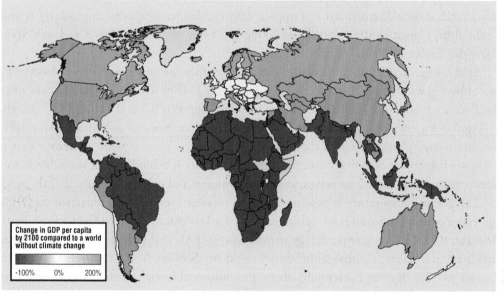

FIGURE 14.1 AND MAP 14.1 Rising Average Global Temperatures The NASA Goddard Institute for Space Studies monitors average global surface temperatures around the world. Its records indicate historically unprecedented temperature increases, as shown by the graph. With greenhouse gas emissions and atmospheric carbon dioxide levels on the rise, scientists predict that long-term temperatures will continue to increase. As the map shows, the economic cost of these changes will be considerable, as rising temperatures result in damage to property and infrastructure, increased health risks, and lost productivity. Overall, it is estimated that—if current trends hold—climate change will lower average GDP per capita by 25 percent by 2100 (Burke, Hsiang, and Miguel, 2015).

Think It Through Given these predictions, what do you think will be the impact of climate change for the global distribution of power and wealth?

Although CO_2 is the principal greenhouse gas, concentrations of methane in the atmosphere are growing even more rapidly. Methane gas emissions arise from livestock populations, rice cultivation, and the production and transportation of natural gas. To the alarm of many scientists, the largest concentrations of methane are not in the atmosphere but are locked in ice, permafrost, and coastal marine sediments. This means that as the global temperature increases, more methane will be released into the atmosphere, which would then increase global temperatures because of methane's strong warming potential.

The effects of continued rising temperatures around the globe will be both dramatic and devastating:

- Sea levels will rise, mostly because of melting glaciers and the expansion of water as it warms up. This will produce massive flooding in vast areas of low-lying coastal lands, especially in Asia and the U.S. Atlantic coast. New York City could be submerged. Millions of people are likely to be displaced by major floods each year.

- Winters will get warmer and heat waves will become increasingly frequent and severe, producing avalanches from melting glaciers in high altitudes.

- Rainfall will increase worldwide and deadly storms, such as the devastating Cyclone Idai in 2019, the worst on record to affect Africa and the Southern Hemisphere, will become more common. As ocean temperatures continue to rise, hurricanes, which draw their energy from warm oceans, will become stronger and more frequent.

- Because water evaporates more easily in a warmer climate, drought-prone regions will become even drier.

- One in six living species will face an increasing risk of extinction as entire ecosystems vanish from the planet. For those that avoid extinction, climate change will lead to substantial changes in their number and where they are located (Vaughan, 2015). A hotter Earth will drive some plant life to higher (or lower) latitudes and greater elevations.

- The combination of flooding and droughts will cause tropical diseases such as malaria and dengue fever to flourish in previously temperate regions that were formerly too cold for their insect carriers; "a warmer CO_2-rich world will be very, very good for plants, insects, and microbes that make us sick" (Begley, 2007).

- The world will face increased hunger and water shortages, especially in the poorest countries. Africa, where the United Nations predicts that the population will almost double to 2.5 billion by 2050, is already suffering from water shortages (Dontoh and Cohen, 2019).

Some scientists insist the rise in global temperature is only part of a cyclical change the world has experienced for thousands of years. They are able to cite evidence of "sudden and dramatic temperature swings over the past 400,000 years, from warm climates to ice ages. [These] global warming skeptics say the climate changes we're seeing today reflect these natural variations" (Knickerbocker, 2007), and that cold water needs to be poured on all the "hot air" because global warming is a climate myth.

IMAGES 14.4A AND 14.4B **Global Warming, Climatic Catastrophes, and Mass Suffering** "Global warming is expected to make the climate warmer, wetter, and wilder. It is predicted that such climate change will increase the severity and frequency of climate-related disasters like flash floods, surges, cyclones, and severe storms" (Bergholt and Lujala, 2012, p. 147). Experiencing the worst snow storm in twenty years, Jerusalem was temporarily brought to a standstill in January 2013 (left). In June 2015, severe flooding in Tbilisi, Georgia, caused widespread chaos with hillsides collapsing, roads washed out, and enclosures in the zoo destroyed (right). Many see the increase in extreme weather events such as these as evidence of global climate change.

But "most climate scientists say human-induced greenhouse gases are at work—and note that these temperature changes correlate with levels of carbon dioxide" (Knickerbocker, 2007). The IPCC first stated in 1995 its belief that global climate trends are "unlikely to be entirely due to natural causes," that humans are to blame for at least part of the problem, and that the consequences are likely to be very harmful and costly. Speaking of his fellow climatologists, glaciologist Lonnie Thompson declared that "virtually all of us are now convinced that global warming poses a clear and present danger to civilization" (McKibben, 2011, p. 62). Gavin Schmidt, director of NASA's Goddard Institute of Space Studies, supports this contention saying, "We expect that heat records will continue and get broken—not everywhere and not every year—but increasingly and that does not bode well for a civilization that is continuing to add greenhouse gases to the atmosphere at an increasing rate" (Goldenberg, 2015).

Not all countries are contributing to global warming at the same rate. The high-income Global North states contribute more than half of global carbon emissions, in large measure because of their big buildings, millions of cars, and relatively inefficient industries. However, Asian dynamos China and India have rapidly increased their emissions as their economies have grown and generated increasing demands for fossil-fuel energy. In 2008, China surpassed the United States as the world's top emitter of greenhouse gases. A decade later, it was responsible for 27.2 percent of all emissions as compared to 14.6 percent by the United States (Fleming, 2019). The International Energy Agency forecasts that the increase of greenhouse gas emissions from 2000 to 2030 from China alone will nearly equal the increase from the entire industrialized world. India, though behind its Asian rival, already accounts for 6.8 percent of all greenhouse gas emissions (Fleming, 2019).

Compare the existing and new industrial giants' consumption of energy and production of greenhouse gases with those of the low-income Global South countries (see Figures 14.2A and 14.2B). They, too, are growing rapidly and their appetite for fossil fuel energy sources is on the rise (see Chapter 5). The Global South produces more than 60.8 percent of global energy and is responsible for 57.3 percent of the world's energy use (WDI, 2017). Thus, countries in all

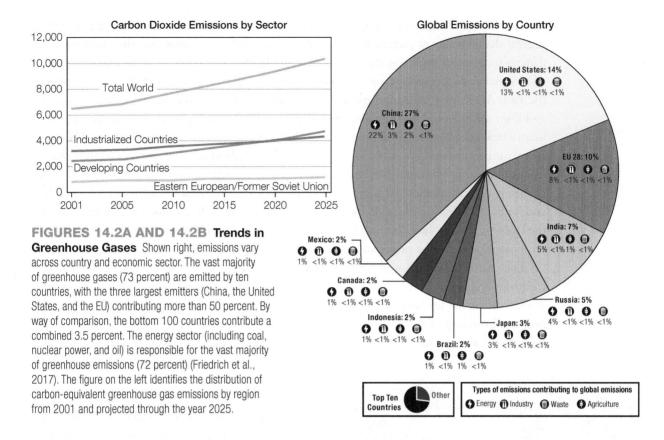

FIGURES 14.2A AND 14.2B Trends in Greenhouse Gases Shown right, emissions vary across country and economic sector. The vast majority of greenhouse gases (73 percent) are emitted by ten countries, with the three largest emitters (China, the United States, and the EU) contributing more than 50 percent. By way of comparison, the bottom 100 countries contribute a combined 3.5 percent. The energy sector (including coal, nuclear power, and oil) is responsible for the vast majority of greenhouse emissions (72 percent) (Friedrich et al., 2017). The figure on the left identifies the distribution of carbon-equivalent greenhouse gas emissions by region from 2001 and projected through the year 2025.

regions are contributing, at different rates, to the global trend in the growing level of carbon added to the atmosphere.

Total emissions by country provides one view of the problem, while per capita emissions suggest another. When taking into account population size, the countries with the highest carbon dioxide emissions are Qatar, Trinidad and Tobago, Kuwait, and United Arab Emirates. The United States is ranked eighth and China is not even in the top twenty (Fleming, 2019). Yet even then, as suggested by the *Proceedings of the National Academy of Sciences*, it may be "rich people, rather than rich countries, who need to change the most. The authors suggest setting a cap on total emissions, and then converting that cap into a global per-person limit. . . . So the high-living, carbon guzzling rich minority in India and China would not be able to hide behind their poor and carbon-thrifty compatriots" (*The Economist*, 2009c, p. 62). Although far too difficult to implement, the proposal highlights how the lower level of carbon emissions in the Global South masks the variation within states where the wealthy contribute at a far higher rate to environmental degradation than the poor. It also underscores how global warming contributes to the tragedy of the commons and that every individual has a role to play in protecting our planet:

> Looking at per capita figures rather than national-level totals could help bring the reality of the climate crisis closer to individuals. For example, a person may feel their decision to use less-polluting forms of transport is pointless in comparison to the colossal Chinese and American CO_2 figures. But seeing how population size alters the rankings, and where their country appears, may encourage people to see a connection between their actions and the results they can help bring about (Fleming, 2019).

These trends in greenhouse gas emissions, as well as the changing percentage by sector, suggest that the energy picture will change but that global warming and the environmental damage it causes are problems that are not likely to disappear any time soon. In a historic pact to address global climate change, on December 12, 2015, representatives from 196 parties adopted the Paris Agreement to "adopt green energy sources, cut down on climate change emissions and limit the rise of global temperatures—while also cooperating to cope with the impact of unavoidable climate change" (Domonoske, 2017). Having legal force under the United Nations' Framework Convention on Climate Change, it acknowledged that the threat of climate change is urgent, potentially irreversible, and necessitates deep reductions in global emissions. "Climate change is a global problem with grave implications: environmental, social, economic, political and for the distribution of goods," warns Pope Francis (2015). In an echo of the sensibilities of the Paris Agreement, he calls for swift, responsible, and moral action on climate change, saying, "It represents one of the principal challenges facing humanity in our day."

The politics of global warming are dramatically illustrated by the tensions between the countries trying to carve up the Arctic in order to reap economic payoffs from exploiting the resources that lie beneath the polar ice cap. Climate change affects the Arctic intensely, because the average temperature there has risen about twice as fast as that of the rest of the planet, with the melting of Arctic sea ice occurring more rapidly than projected by the IPCC, "largely because emissions of carbon dioxide have topped what the panel" expected (Begley, 2009, p. 30). This trend is paving the way for a geopolitical struggle over eco-politics among the five countries already laying claim to the resource-rich central zone (Russia, Norway, Canada, the United States, and Denmark).

The primary motive: possession of the mineral wealth of the Arctic. A "frozen conflict" is being waged in the melting north for what, according to the U.S. Geological Survey, amounts to one-eighth of the globe's untapped oil and perhaps as much as 25 percent of its gas reserves. The disappearing ice also offers new sea routes, at least for part of the year, which significantly reduces the time it takes for ships to travel from Europe to Asia. Between 1990 and 2015, ship traffic in the Arctic almost tripled. "Cargo ships as well as government vessels, including icebreakers, account for the largest share of traffic while pleasure craft, primarily private yachts, represent the fastest growing type of craft increasing more than 20-fold over the

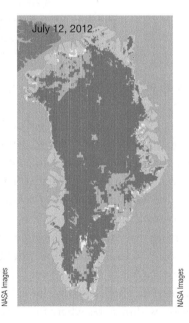

■ Melted ice

IMAGES 14.5A AND 14.5B **Feeling the Heat** The IPCC has concluded that evidence of the Earth's rising temperatures is "unequivocal" and that global warming is more than 90 percent likely to be the product of human activity. Shown here is one possible consequence: dramatic melting of Greenland's surface ice sheet. Satellite maps show that on July 8, 2012 (shown left), about 40 percent of the ice sheet's surface had melted, and that by July 12 (shown right) a shocking 97 percent of the ice sheet had turned to slush. "Scientists estimate that if all of Greenland's ice sheet were to melt, the global sea level would rise by 23 feet" (Than, 2012).

25-year period" (Humpert, 2018). As global warming melts the Arctic ice, countries are laying claims to portions of the territory. Canada plans to claim sovereign rights to part of the Arctic continental shelf, and both Russia and Denmark have staked a claim to the North Pole under the UN Convention on the Law of the Sea (UNCLOS). One-tenth of Russia's economic investments are in the Arctic region, it has reequipped seven military bases and, in the summer of 2019, engaged in extensive combat exercises (Astrasheuskaya and Foy, 2019). None of this international friction would have materialized had global warming not made competition for control of this geostrategic arena possible.

The Ecopolitics of Biodiversity, Deforestation, and Water Shortages

Forests and water resources are critical in preserving the Earth's **biodiversity** and protecting the atmosphere and land resources. For these reasons, they have become a rising ecological issue on the global agenda. Some rules have emerged to guide international behavior in the preservation of biodiversity, but issues concerning the preservation of forests and the supply of water resources have proven much more difficult to address.

biodiversity
The variety of plant and animal species living in the Earth's diverse ecosystems.

Threats to Global Biodiversity　Biodiversity, or biological diversity, is an umbrella term that refers to the Earth's variety of life. Technically, it encompasses three basic levels of organization in living systems: genetic diversity, species diversity, and ecosystem diversity. Until recently, public attention has focused almost exclusively on preserving species diversity by protecting ecosystems, including old forests, tall-grass prairies, wetlands, coastal habitats, and coral reefs.

Forests, especially tropical forests, are important to preserving biodiversity because they are home to countless species of animals and plants, many of them still unknown. Scientists believe that the global habitat contains between 8 and 10 million species. Of these, only about 1.5 million have been named, and most of them are in the temperate regions of North America, Europe, Russia, and Australia. Destruction of tropical forests, where two-thirds to three-fourths of all species are believed to live, threatens to destroy much of the world's undiscovered biological diversity and genetic heritage.

Many experts worry that the globe is relentlessly heading toward major species extinction. In addition to global warming, pressures from deforestation, pollution, and overfishing "have already seen the world lose half its animals in the past forty years" (Vaughan, 2015, p. 1). Of the nearly 300,000 plant species surveyed by the World Conservation Union, more than 8000 are threatened with extinction, mainly as a result of clearing land for housing, roads, and industries. Extinction risks will accelerate with a rise in future global temperatures and are expected to threaten one in six species. Arctic animals such as the polar bear are highly at risk, as are species in South America, Australia, and New Zealand (Urban, 2015).

Others doubt the imminence of a massive die-out, estimating that only a small fraction of the Earth's species have actually disappeared over the past several centuries. Indeed, optimistic cornucopians argue that species extinction may not be bad news, as new species may evolve that will prove even more beneficial to humanity (McKibben, 2006).

enclosure movement
The claiming of common properties by states or private interests.

Because much of the Earth's biological heritage is concentrated in the tropics, the Global South also has a growing concern about protecting its interests in the face of efforts by MNCs to reap profits from the sale of biological products. MNCs in the Global North are major players in the so-called **enclosure movement**, which is geared to privatize and commercialize the products derived from plant and animal genes that are the genetic bases for sustained life. Pharmaceutical companies, in particular, have laid claim to Global South resources. They actively explore plants, microbes, and other living organisms in tropical forests for possible use in prescription drugs. Concern in the Global South is centered on the idea that the genetic character of the many species of plants and animals should be considered a part of the global commons and therefore available for commercial use by all, for their medical benefit.

biodiversity hot spot
A region that has a high percentage of plant species found nowhere else in the world and is threatened by loss of at least 30 percent of its original natural vegetation.

Biogenetic engineering threatens to escalate the erosion of global diversity. Biological resources—animal and plant species—are distributed unevenly in the world. Map 14.2 shows the major "biodiversity bastions," where more than half of the Earth's species are found. They are located in primarily tropical wilderness territories laden with plant and animal species. It also shows the location of **biodiversity hot spots**, where human activity threatens to disturb and potentially destroy many species that international law defines as collective goods, resources for all humanity from which everyone benefits. According to the UN, about 50,000 plant and animal species become extinct each year as the global community wrestles with the ethics of biodiversity preservation and management policies. In 2019, there were 36 biodiversity hot spots covering only

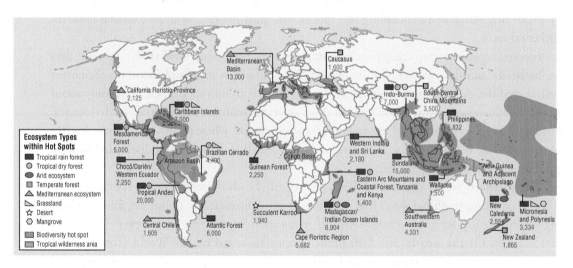

MAP 14.2 Locating Biodiversity Bastions and Endangered Hot Spots This map provides a picture of global "danger zones," identifying the estimated number of plant and animal species that are endangered in these biodiversity hot spots. According to a 2019 report from the United Nations, the average abundance of native species has declined by at least 20 percent, mostly since 1900. More than 40 percent of amphibian species and more than a third of all marine mammals are threatened (IPBES, 2019).

 Think It Through To what extent do you think demographic shifts, such as urbanization and increased population growth in the Global South, will affect these areas?

2.4 percent of the land, but supporting almost 43 percent of mammal, bird, reptile, and amphibian species and more than half of plant species (Conservation International, 2019).

With 193 country signatories, the goal of the UN Convention on Biological Diversity aims to conserve biodiversity, establish its sustainable use, and ensure the fair and equitable sharing of benefits derived from genetic resources. Such global efforts are critical to the environmental security of our world. According to a landmark report from the Intergovernmental Science-Policy Platform on Biodiversity and Ecosystem Services, a million plant and animal species are threatened with extinction, more than at any other point in human history (IPBES, 2019). Yet despite the alarming trend, "it is not too late to make a difference, but only if we start now at every level from local to global," says the report chair Sir Robert Watson. "Through 'transformative change', nature can still be conserved, restored and used sustainably" (UN, 2019e).

Shrinking Forests and Dust Bowls   Trends since the 1970s show considerable deforestation throughout much of the world. Almost half (46 percent) of the forests once covering the Earth have been converted for ranching, farmland, pastures, and other uses (Crowther et al., 2015), and deforestation has been on the rise in recent years. Between 1990 and 2016, 502,000 square miles (1.3 million square kilometers) of forest loss occurred (WDI, 2017), with 17 percent of the Amazonian rainforest destroyed over the past fifty years (Nunez, 2019a). "Deforestation is occurring most rapidly in the remaining tropical moist forests of the Amazon, West Africa, and parts of Southeast Asia" (WDR, 2008, p. 191).

More than 50 percent of deforestation is due to a combination of farming, cattle ranching, mining, and drilling. In Southeast Asia, forests are burned or cut for large-scale planting of palm to obtain the oil that is used in a wide array of products, including cosmetics and food processing. In Africa, individuals hack out small plots for farming (Harris, 2008). South American forests, most notably the Amazon, are generally burned for industrial-scale soybean farming or cattle grazing. Destruction of tropical rain forests in such places as Brazil, Indonesia, and Malaysia is a matter of special concern because they are home to much of the world's biodiversity. Removing trees alters the forest canopy, which causes a disruption that can be harmful to the 80 percent of the world's land animals and plants that live there. It also affects regional weather patterns and the local water supply (Nunez, 2019a).

Trees also play an important role in countering climate change—forests serve as a carbon sink that absorbs the carbon dioxide that humans exhale and the greenhouse gases generated by human activity. If tropical deforestation were a country, it would rank third in carbon dioxide-equivalent emissions, ahead of the European Union and behind only China and the United States (Gibbs et al., 2018). Tropical forests can provide 23 percent of the climate mitigation needed to meet the goal of the Paris Agreement to limit the rise in global temperatures by 2030. "This potential comes from the avoided emissions through stopping deforestation and degradation as well as the removal of atmospheric carbon that takes places through forest growth and restoration" (Gibbs et al., 2018). In other words, green plants remove carbon dioxide from the atmosphere during photosynthesis. Therefore, the natural processes that remove greenhouse gases are also being destroyed when forests

deforestation
The process of clearing and destroying forests.

are cut down and as the forests decay or are burned, the amount of carbon dioxide released into the atmosphere further increases.

Nonetheless, the Global South objects vigorously to the socially constructed view that the world's forests are a common property resource, the "common heritage of mankind." The developing countries fear that legally accepting this view would enable the Global North to interfere with the local management of their tropical forest resources. As Ogar Assam Effa, a tree plantation director in Nigeria, observes, "The developed countries want us to keep the forests, since the air we breathe is for all of us, rich countries and poor countries. But we breathe the air, and our bellies are empty." He asks, "Can air give you protein? Can air give you carbohydrates? It would be easy to convince people to stop clearing the forest if there was an alternative" (Harris, 2008, p. A2).

In the Global North, reforestation has begun to alleviate some of the danger. This is not the case, however, in many cash-starved Global South countries where the reasons for rapid destruction vary. Deforestation in the Amazon continues at an alarming pace amid heated national debate over whether to ease Brazil's Forest Code, which has required 80 percent of a landholding in the Amazon to remain forest. Supporters of the national law fear that change will lead to greater destruction of the Amazon rain forest, whereas those who seek to reduce the restrictions argue that the law presently inhibits economic development. As John Carter, founder of a nonprofit that promotes sustainable ranching in the Amazonian region, lamented, "You can't protect it. There's too much money to be made tearing it down" (as quoted in Grunwald, 2008). Such concerns appear to be well founded; since Brazilian President Jair Bolsonaro took office in January 2019, his emphasis has shifted from conservation to development and there has been "a dramatic fall in confiscations of timber and convictions for environmental crimes" (BBC, 2019b).

Meanwhile, as global temperatures rise and population growth continues, the world is vulnerable to **desertification**, which turns an increasing portion of the Earth's landmass into deserts that are useless for agricultural productivity or wildlife habitats (see Map 14.3). Additionally, soil degradation has stripped billions of acres of the Earth's surface from productive farming. Soil erosion and pollution are problems both in densely populated developing countries and in the more highly developed regions of mechanized industrial agriculture. "Global demand for food is projected to double in the next fifty years as urbanization proceeds and income rises. But arable land per capita is shrinking" (WDI, 2007, p. 124). Between 2000 and 2016, arable land declined from 0.23 to 0.19 hectares per person (WDI, 2017a).

The threat will surely increase because desertification spans more than 100 countries and the United Nations estimates that today the pace of arable land degradation is thirty to thirty-five times the historical rate (Nunez, 2019b; UN, 2019f). For example, in Uzbekistan and Kazakhstan, excessive water use for agricultural irrigation is causing the Aral Sea to shrink and leave behind a saline desert. In the Sahel region in Africa, bordered by the Sahara Desert and savannas, land degradation occurs as "population growth has caused an increase in wood harvesting, illegal farming, and land-clearing for housing, among other changes. The prospect of climate change and warmer average temperatures could amplify these effects" (Nunez, 2019b).

Adopted in 1994, 122 countries support the United Nations Convention to Combat Desertification (UNCCD) as the "sole legally binding international agreement linking

desertification
The creation of deserts due to soil erosion, overfarming, and deforestation, which converts cropland to nonproductive, arid sand.

MAP 14.3 Human-Induced Deserts Desertification affects roughly 25 percent of the world's landmass. Shown here are future trends in the aridity, or dryness, of land through 2040. Areas in red are expected to become increasingly arid, while the areas in green are predicted to become more humid. Increased aridity is one of the primary impacts of climate change; while some areas of the world are increasingly "wet," the overall prediction is towards an increasingly dry planet (Cherlet et al., 2018).

Think It Through What are some of the key ways in which increased aridity can affect societies?

environment and development to sustainable land management. Parties to the Convention work together to maintain and restore land and soil productivity, and to mitigate the effects of drought in drylands—the arid, semi-arid, and dry sub-humid areas where some of the most vulnerable ecosystems and peoples can be found" (UN, 2019f). Desertification poses an enormous threat to sustainable development and the environmental security of our planet, and collaborative efforts such as this are necessary to safeguard arable land and repair the degradation.

A Burgeoning Water Crisis   Water quality and supply is another critical issue affecting not only biodiversity but also the health and welfare of the globe's human population. Most of the population growth over the next twenty-five years—an additional 1.7 billion people—are expected to live in water-stressed areas. Water demand and water use in many areas is far greater than the rate of natural replenishment, and this trend will likely continue since demand seems destined to exceed supply (see "A Closer Look: Global Water Shortages"). Since 1950, the renewable supply of water per capita has declined by 58 percent (Galgano, 2018).

In arid and semiarid regions, major aquifers are dangerously over pumped, and poor irrigation practices are depleting limited groundwater reservoirs. Almost 2 billion people use water that is critically polluted with human waste. In India, for example, the Yamuna River—one of the most polluted rivers in the world—is the primary source of

European Commission Joint Research Centre, World Atlas of Desertification, wad.jrc.ec.europa.eu

IMAGE 14.6 From Farmland to Dust Bowl Desertification has hit many areas hard, and "man-made climate change is also causing more droughts on top of those that occur naturally" (Begley, 2008, p. 53). The UN Food and Agriculture Organization warned that drought in Central America has reduced maize output by around 9 percent, resulting in 400,000 families in El Salvador, Guatemala, and Honduras needing food assistance. Problems with food insecurity persisted, particularly in the so-called "dry corridor" hot spot that spans these three countries and can see up to 40 percent fluctuation in rainfall from year to year (Gustin and Henninger, 2019).

water for people in the capital territory of Delhi, which has a metropolitan population of around 16.3 million. Infrastructure is also lacking for many people around the world, where inequitable development of public utilities has benefited the elite while leaving the poor to fend for themselves (Sethi, 2015). "Each day, 44 percent of the world's people rely on water that must be carried back to their homes—mostly by women and girls who end up trapped in a kind of slavery, unable to get good educations or jobs, in part, because they must devote so much time to fetching water" (Fishman, 2015, p. 73).

Increasingly, water is seen as an urgent global priority. At the 2019 World Economic Forum held in Davos, Switzerland, business and political leaders identified climate change and natural resource security—such as threats posed by water crises—as having enormous potential impact as a source of risk facing the world. This was a dramatic change from ten years prior, when water ranked low on the list of global concerns. Yet despite the increased awareness of the interconnection between environmental stressors, conflict, inhibited economic growth, and human security, there is pessimism about the potential to solve water problems. This is because, in part, water problems are not so much about water as they are about politics, economics, culture, and habit:

> Due to long-standing policy and practice, for instance, farmers from Pakistan to Kansas pump groundwater for their crops not only without paying for it, but often without limit or even keeping track of how much they use. It's seen almost as an entitlement; charging farmers for water or insisting on better irrigation technology inspires outrage and resistance. Similarly, leisurely daily showers and lush lawns explain how Americans end up using twice the amount of water per person as Europeans do. Changing attitudes about water's value, in other words, is just as important as creating the correct mix of dams, treatment plants, and sustainable agriculture policies (Fishman, 2015, p. 75).

Water scarcity and impurity—and the conflict that it can cause—is a daunting threat to many of the world's almost 8 billion people. It "already affects every continent. Water use has been growing globally at more than twice the rate of population increase in the last century, and an increasing number of regions are reaching the limit at which water services can be sustainably delivered, especially in arid regions" (UN, 2018g). Will water issues continue to escalate, as anticipated by the tragedy of the commons? Or will people take action to become better stewards of the globe's resources? Jean Chrétien, former Canadian prime minister and co-chair of the InterAction Council, warns that the "future political impact of water scarcity may be devastating. Using water the way we have in the past simply will not sustain humanity in future."

A Closer Look

GLOBAL WATER SHORTAGES

March 22 marks World Water Day. Adopted by the United Nations in 1993, this annual observation draws global attention to the critical role of water in sustaining human life and well-being. Yet the "proportion of people living in countries chronically short of water, which stood at 8 percent (500 million) at the turn of the 21st century, is set to rise to 45 percent (four billion) by 2050" (Grimond, 2010, p. 3). In São Paulo, Brazil—a city of 20 million people that was once known as the City of Drizzle—residents drilled through basements and car parks to try to reach groundwater during a severe drought in 2015 (McKie, 2015). That same year, in the United States, California suffered from the worst drought in 1200 years, with farmers abandoning crops and selling their herds, and some cities rationing water (Specter, 2015). Moreover, nearly one out of every five people in the world lacks access to safe drinking water. The World Health Organization estimates that millions of people die every year from diseases caused by poor water quality, inadequate sanitation, or poor hygiene. A report by the UN World Water Assessment Programme concluded, "It is clear that urgent action is needed if we are to avoid a global water crisis" (UNESCO, 2009, p. vii).

Part of the problem is demographic. As the world's population has risen, the demand for water has also increased. With the simultaneous growth in urbanization, demand has exceeded the capacity of the already insufficient water supply and sanitation infrastructure in many cities throughout the Global South. By some estimates, "global water consumption

is doubling every twenty years, and the United Nations expects demand to outstrip supply by more than 30 percent come 2040" (Interlandi, 2010, p. 42). Furthermore, as countries across the world become wealthier, their populations tend to shift from vegetarian to meaty diets, which include foods that require more water to produce. Additionally, "there is growing evidence that global warming is speeding up the hydrologic cycle— that is, the rate at which water evaporates and falls again as rain or snow . . . . It brings longer droughts between more intense periods of rain" (*The Economist*, 2009a, p. 60). With rising population and consumption, in the absence of serious water conservation measures and cooperation among mutual water users for watershed preservation, water availability will become an ever-growing resource issue.

Watch the Carnegie Council Video:
"Has Water Become a Right?"

You Decide:

1. Is access to consumable water a basic human right?

2. What obligation, if any, do countries have to ensure the sustainability of freshwater resources for the world's 7 billion people?

3. What insights does the "tragedy of the commons" provide regarding this challenge?

The Ecopolitics of Energy Supply and Demand

According to naturalist Loren Eiseley, human history can be thought of as our ascent up "the heat ladder," where "coal bested firewood as an amplifier of productivity, and oil and natural gas bested coal" (Owen, 2009, p. 21). Throughout the twentieth century, the demand for and consumption of oil—the primary fossil fuel supplying energy—spiraled upward. An abundant supply of cheap oil facilitated the recovery of Western Europe and Japan after World War II and encouraged consumers to use energy-intensive technologies, such as the private automobile.

An enormous growth in the worldwide demand for and consumption of energy followed. The International Energy Agency predicts that, even taking into account gains in efficiency (the United States has doubled its energy efficiency since the 1970s), the world will be using 50 percent more oil in 2030 than it did in 2010. Although the Global North remains a major consumer of oil, this century has witnessed a globalization of demand, with 85 percent of the surge in oil demand occurring in emerging markets such as China, India, and the Middle East (Yergin, 2009).

The suppliers of oil have also changed over the past two decades. Following the severe deflation of oil prices in the 1990s, mergers took place between many of the large oil companies in an effort to improve the scale of production. There are now six "supermajors" in the oil industry—Chevron, ExxonMobil, BP, Royal Dutch Shell, Total, and Eni—also collectively called "Big Oil" in reference to their substantial economic power and political influence. Other dominant players in the oil industry include large state-owned oil companies such as Pemex in Mexico, Saudi Aramco, Petróleos de Venezuela, and China National Petroleum. State ownership of oil companies enables governments to maintain control over energy reserves and production sites, and retain the revenue generated by the production process within the national economy. The Organization of Petroleum Exporting Countries (OPEC), an intergovernmental organization of twelve oil-exporting developing countries that coordinates the petroleum policies of its members, remains important as well. Although its influence has decreased in recent years, historically OPEC has set production targets for its members in order to manage the price of oil on the global market for both economic and political purposes.

The global oil industry has experienced periods of boom and bust, as seen just within the past decade. On July 11, 2008, the price of a barrel of oil hit a high of $147.27. It was believed that the days of affordable oil were over. This may still be the case, but what we have now witnessed is that the price of oil as a commodity is extremely volatile. In December 2008, the price of oil had fallen to $32.40 per barrel; on July 11, 2009, exactly a year after the peak oil price, the price of oil was as low as $59.87 per barrel. By the middle of June 2013, the cost of a barrel of crude oil had risen again to just under $99 but fell to $52 per barrel by July 2015. These dramatic price swings can be even more threatening than an end to cheap prices, because it introduces a great deal of instability into our global economic and political systems, affects an array of industries and the individual consumer, and makes it very difficult to plan future energy investments (see Figure 14.3).

Despite our quest for stability, "the changing balance of supply and demand—shaped by economics, politics, technologies, consumer tastes, and accidents of all sorts—will continue to move prices" (Yergin, 2009, p. 95). Between 2009 and 2015, production in the United States almost doubled, due in large part to growth in American shale-oil firms. With wells that are small, inexpensive, and quickly drilled, these unconventional oil producers greatly increased the amount of oil on the global market that comes from **fracking** while simultaneously reducing the United States' dependence on foreign suppliers (*The Economist*, 2015d). At the same time, Iraqi and Canadian oil production and exports increased annually, and the Russians continued to be among the world's leading oil suppliers. Furthermore, in recent years

fracking
A drilling technique, also called hydraulic fracturing, that injects fluid at high pressure into shale beds to extract petroleum resources.

the members of OPEC have had difficulty agreeing to production quotas. Venezuela, Iran, and Algeria pressed the cartel to slow production in order to push prices up, but the United Arab Emirates and Saudi Arabia refused to do so. These factors all contributed to a decline in oil prices (Krauss, 2015). Despite the intensifying geopolitical tensions in the Middle East, particularly between Iran and the United Kingdom in the Strait of Hormuz, the crude oil price per barrel remained steady in July 2019 at $55.71. Assessing the potential impact of the conflict, global oil strategist Martijn Rats noted, "There is a difference in the oil market this time around because non-OPEC is simply growing so fast. That is the real game changer and that's why the price action is relatively benign" (Meredith, 2019).

Another challenge facing the world is how to balance the demand for oil against the environmental, economic, and health risks posed by drilling. This dilemma is starkly illustrated by the massive oil spill in the Gulf of Mexico in 2010. A U.S. presidential commission "concluded that a cascade of technical and managerial failures—including a faulty cement job—caused the disaster" (Burdeau and Weber, 2011). The controversy over fracking is another example, with critics lamenting the envi-

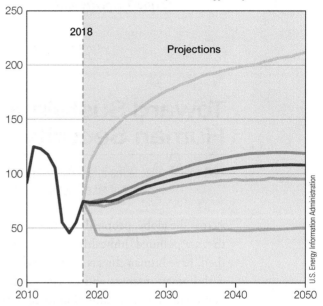

FIGURE 14.3 **The Ups and Downs of the Price for Oil**
Historically oil prices have fluctuated greatly, thus predicting future oil prices can be quite difficult. Shown here are multiple predictions for oil prices in 2050, which range from around $50 to over $200 per barrel. The supply and demand for oil—and thus oil prices—are driven by factors at multiple levels of analysis, including global economic growth, political conditions in oil-producing states, advances in oil-extraction technology, availability of additional oil reserves, and demand for alternative energy sources. These predictions are based on different scenarios for these variables; for example, the highest prediction assumes strong economic growth and limited success in increasing oil supply.

ronmental cost associated with the large amounts of water needed for the technique, the potentially dangerous chemicals that may escape and contaminate the groundwater at the fracking site, and the possibility that the fracking process can cause earth tremors (BBC, 2013b). Yet the public has used the ballot box to demonstrate their preference for cheap oil underwritten by risky drilling instead of a government committed to industry regulation. As political historian Sarah Elkind said, "This failure of government is government acting the way American people have said they want it to act" (as quoted in Walsh, 2010).

Do we have the capacity and will to make changes in our energy production and consumption? In response to the threat of future shortages and the risk of heavy dependence on oil, the Global North may be on the verge of a potentially historic juncture that would overturn the pivotal place of oil in the global political economy. In 2008, China and Japan ended a longtime dispute by agreeing to jointly develop two natural gas fields in the East China Sea; in August 2009, Russia reached an agreement with Turkey to build a gas pipeline from the Black Sea to the Mediterranean via the Anatolian Peninsula. There is also an array of efforts under way to develop alternative clean-energy fuel sources, such as wind and solar power, to break our dependence on fossil fuels.

> *Future prosperity and stability means rethinking how we exploit the planet's natural assets.*
>
> **—BAN KI-MOON, FORMER UN SECRETARY-GENERAL**

Toward Sustainability and Human Security

LO 14-3 Assess the interrelationship between environmental preservation and two aspects of human rights: economic and food security.

Across the globe, people desire to live in a clean and green environment and seek to avoid ones that are polluted, unhealthy, and prone to floods, hurricanes, tornadoes, and typhoons. Why, then, have human threats to the global ecology increased despite their conflictual relationship with human interests and values? Environmental activists argue that the Earth is at a critical point and even more attention to environmental preservation is needed.

The Quest for Sustainable Development

Environmental decay seems to recognize few borders; it is a worldwide problem, for both poor and rich countries. "The health of ecosystems on which we and all other species depend is deteriorating more rapidly than ever. We are eroding the very foundations of our economies, livelihoods, food security, health and quality of life worldwide," cautions a 2019 United Nations report (UN, 2019e). That transformation makes protection of the planetary environment a necessity, but the solutions are hard to find when many people put their personal advantage ahead of those of all humanity. Recommended changes to protect and preserve planet Earth's ecology may be expensive, but it is important to try.

sustainable development
Economic growth that does not deplete the resources needed to maintain life and prosperity.

    Sustainable development is now popularly perceived as an alternative to the quest for unrestrained growth. The movement began in earnest in 1972, when the UN General Assembly convened the first UN Conference of the Human Environment in Stockholm. Since then, conferences on a wide range of environmental topics have produced scores of treaties and created new international agencies to promote cooperation and monitor environmental developments.

    The concept of sustainable development is directly traceable to *Our Common Future*, the 1987 report of the World Commission on Environment and Development, popularly known as the "Brundtland Commission" after the Norwegian prime minister who chaired it. The commission concluded that the world cannot sustain the growth required to meet the needs and aspirations of the world's growing population unless it adopts radically different approaches to basic issues of economic expansion, equity, resource management, and energy efficiency, among other areas of concern. Rejecting the "limits to growth" maxim popular among neo-Malthusians, it emphasized instead "the growth of limits." The commission defined a "sustainable society" as one that "meets the needs of the present without compromising the ability of future generations to meet their own needs."

Another milestone in the challenge to the then-dominant cornucopian social paradigm occurred at the 1992 Earth Summit in Rio de Janeiro, Brazil, on the twentieth anniversary of the Stockholm conference. The meeting brought together more than 150 states, 1400 non-governmental organizations, and 8000 journalists. Before the Earth Summit, the environment and economic development had been treated separately—and often regarded as being at odds with each other because economic growth frequently imperils and degrades the environment. In Rio, the concept of sustainability galvanized a simultaneous treatment of environmental and development issues.

Other international conferences have since punctuated the strong consensus behind the proposition that all politics—even global politics—are local, as what happens any place ultimately affects conditions every place, and accordingly that protection of the Earth's environment is a primary international security issue. At the UN Climate Conference in Paris in December 2015, members gathered to discuss an agreement—now widely known as the Paris Agreement—that would reduce global emissions by at least 60 percent below 2010 levels by 2050. Says UN climate chief Christiana Figueres, "Whatever gets done over the next 10 to 15 years, whatever gets invested particularly in the energy system . . . is going to determine the energy matrix that we will have for at least 50 years. It is going to determine the quality of life of this century and beyond" (Ganley, 2015, p. 1).

Many scholars and policy makers are convinced that threats to the preservation of the global commons likewise threaten our basic welfare and security. Sustainable development is crucial to striking a responsible balance for preserving the global environment and providing the resources needed to sustain human life and prosperity. Yet sustainability cannot be realized without substantial changes. Is that possible? Are individuals willing to sacrifice personal consumption for the common good? Will they sacrifice now to enrich their heirs? What approaches are under way?

Although the goal of sustainable development remains distant and frustrations about lost opportunities are mounting, governmental and nonstate actors' acceptance of the concept continues to inspire creative, environmentally sensitive responses. In a political world in which growing population means growing demand for energy, food, and other resources, the politics of scarcity becomes central. This is the vulnerability created by interdependent globalization. Left unchecked, threats to environmental security will compromise human security. "Though governments have an enormous role to play . . . nongovernmental organizations, philanthropists, the private sector, social entrepreneurs, and technologists can help" to overcome the adverse effects of environmental degradation (Brainard et al., 2009, p. 1). Consider next some key global initiatives to counter environmental degradation.

Feeding the Masses

Progress in reducing global hunger has been made over the past several decades, with the share of the world's population that is undernourished declining 21.4 percent between 1990 and 2016. However, according to the UN's Food and Agricultural Organization, 820 million people around the world (more than one of every nine) remain undernourished and suffer from severe food insecurity. An additional 1.3 billion face moderate food insecurity, in that they do not have regular access to sufficient and nutritious food. The vast majority live in the Global South. Asia has the greatest number of food-insecure people, with roughly 354 million suffering from undernourishment. With a regional average of 19.9 percent and in some areas in excess of 30 percent, Africa has the greatest proportion of people without sufficient food to eat (FAO, 2019).

There are concerns that food insecurity is growing, and these fears are leading to political unrest (Hendrix and Haggard, 2015). Globally, increased food prices have created civil unrest and a wave of humanitarian crises in the developing world. Between 2007 and the start of 2009, nearly forty countries had food riots—such as the "tortilla riots" in Mexico and the "pasta riots" in Italy (Landau, 2010). "Oddly enough, almost none of the food riots had emerged from a lack of food. . . . The riots had been generated by the lack of money to buy food" (Kaufman, 2009, p. 51). In 2011, world food prices again escalated (see Figure 14.4), surpassing the peak that they had reached three years prior and causing hardship for many already impoverished people across the world (see Map 14.4). Persistently high and volatile food prices influence conditions of hunger and undernutrition, and contribute to health problems such as "obesity which may increase in the context of high prices as people opt for cheaper, less nutritious food to feed their families" (World Bank, 2013c). Currently, maternal and child undernutrition leads to "45 percent of deaths in children under five. Overweight and obesity are on the rise in almost all countries, contributing to 4 million deaths globally" (FAO, 2019).

Four ominous trends fuel fears about future food scarcity: the rate of increase in crop yields appears to be slowing, agricultural research expenditures have diminished (especially in Africa), global food supplies have begun to decline relative to demand, and economic slowdowns create greater difficulty in accessing food (FAO, 2019; Runge and Runge, 2010). Some of the reasons for the rise in food prices are environmental. Erosion and deforestation make farming difficult (Daniel, 2011). Extreme weather events—such as droughts in China, Russia, and Argentina and flooding in Canada, Pakistan, and the United States—destroy agricultural crops and lead to disruptions in the market. Former UN Secretary-General Ban Ki-moon (2010) noted, "Continued land degradation—whether from climate change, unsustainable agriculture or poor management of water resources—is a threat to food security, leading to starvation among the most acutely affected communities and robbing the world of productive land."

Other causes of global food insecurity are the result of structural changes that are quite averse to change in the short term (see "Controversy: Is There a Global Food Crisis?"). Growth in population and the explosion of megacities in the Global South have created changes in diet that occur due to increased wealth and urbanization. Slowing economies "often lead to a rise in unemployment and decline in wages and incomes," which makes it more challenging for the poor to purchase sufficient food (FAO, 2019). However, it is unlikely that big increases in food production can be achieved "because there is little unfarmed land to bring into production, no more water and, in some places, little to be gained by heaping on more fertilizer" (*The Economist*, 2011b, p. 12).

Food insecurity is garnering more attention and rising on the political agenda. How should we respond? Respect for human rights, strong political commitment, integration of development and humanitarian assistance, and inclusive economic growth are critical to successfully

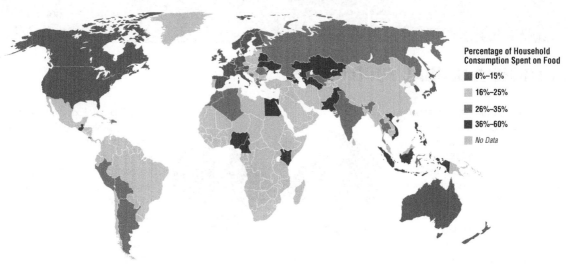

Share of Consumer Expenditure Spent on Food

Percentage of Household
Consumption Spent on Food

- 0%–15%
- 16%–25%
- 26%–35%
- 36%–60%
- No Data

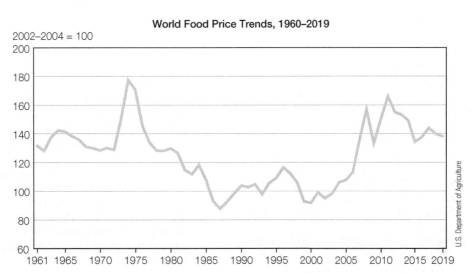

World Food Price Trends, 1960–2019

2002–2004 = 100

U.S. Department of Agriculture

MAP 14.4 AND FIGURE 14.4 A Hungry World The rising cost of agricultural commodities has led to food price inflation in many countries throughout the world. As shown in the map, the Global South is particularly vulnerable to food price inflation, as a greater portion of meager household incomes is required to purchase basic food necessities for a family. The graph shows that, despite a sharp drop in 2008, food prices have increased by over 40 percent since 2000.

Think It Through How does this map highlight the rising global wealth disparity?

addressing protracted food crises (FAO, 2019). Many international organizations have begun to articulate some type of response. In 2018, the World Bank allocated $6.8 billion to agriculture and related sectors, and provided an additional $1.6 billion in expedited emergency support to countries experiencing food emergencies (World Bank, 2018e). Calling for greater action by

Controversy

IS THERE A GLOBAL FOOD CRISIS?

There is more than enough food produced per capita to feed all of the people in the world today and, between 2005 and 2015, seventy-two countries in the Global South reduced the proportion of hungry people by 50 percent (167 million people). However, "more than 820 million people in the world are still hungry today, underscoring the immense challenge of achieving the Zero Hunger target by 2030" as called for by the United Nations' sustainable development goals (FAO, 2019, p. vii).

Those who live in poverty have the highest levels of food insecurity, and are hit the hardest by rising food prices. Since 2003, bread prices have gone up almost 75 percent, pork prices have more than doubled, and the price of bananas has gone up over 40 percent (Dykman, 2008, p. 35). According to the United Nations, it is likely that global food prices could nearly double by 2050. During the global food price spikes of 2007–2008 and 2010–2011, the world witnessed widespread rioting in developing countries as fears of food scarcity became pervasive (Hendrix and Haggard, 2015).

What factors have pushed us into this impoverished "danger zone"? Looking at some of the primary root causes of food insecurity provides insight into the interconnected nature of global threats, the trade-offs inherent in trying to provide for human needs, as well as the ways in which the policies of individual governments and international organizations can influence the international system as a whole:

- **Climate Shocks.** Climate-related disasters, such as tropical storms, floods, and droughts, play a key role in damaging agricultural production and causing food insecurity. "The scientists tell us that if the world warms by 2°C—warming that may be reached in 20 to 30 years—that will cause widespread food shortages, unprecedented heat waves, and more intense cyclones" warned former World Bank President Jim Yong Kim (World Bank,

2013f, p. xi). Extreme weather events have more than doubled since the early 1990s, and a warming climate hampers crop production and often reduces yields of staples such as rice, maize, and wheat. Small-scale farmers who rely on rain-fed agriculture and are more likely to experience extreme weather are particularly vulnerable (GRFC, 2019).

- **Government policies.** Governments have traditionally protected their agricultural markets through subsidies and tariffs, which have served to increase the price of many agricultural goods. Moreover, recent food shortages have resulted in a proliferation of another form of government intervention—limits on the export of agricultural products such as wheat and rice. Indeed, the UN World Food Programme found that forty countries were engaged in such export bans (Teslik, 2008). These bans serve to decrease the world supply of these goods, which raises prices. Government encouragement of biofuel production has also had an impact on food prices. "About 30 percent of the projected increases in global food prices over the next several decades can be attributed to increased biofuel production worldwide" (Runge and Runge, 2010, p. 14).

- **Prices.** The cost of agricultural inputs has risen greatly. Agriculture relies heavily on petroleum for many aspects of production as well as transport, and the sector has thus been hit hard by increases in energy prices. Moreover, fertilizer prices have also risen dramatically. For example, the price of nitrogen fertilizer has increased over 350 percent since 1999 (*Financial Times*, 2007).

- **Food consumption patterns.** In emerging markets, such as China, India, Russia, and Brazil, people have changed their eating habits as their countries have developed. In particular, these countries have greatly increased their consumption of meat and dairy products. Meat consumption in China, traditionally a vegetarian society, has more than doubled since

(Continues)

1980—and is now twice that of the United States—and dairy consumption has tripled (Larsen, 2012; Dymkan, 2008). This has contributed to increased demand for these products, as well as the inputs necessary for their production (such as cattle feed).

The dominant cornucopian social paradigm stressing the right to conspicuous consumption is under global attack, but many challenges remain to achieving sustainable development worldwide.

What Do You Think?

1. Of the causes of the food crisis mentioned here—environmental stress, government policies, prices of agricultural inputs, and food consumption patterns—which do you think is the most important to address in overcoming the crisis? Why?

2. As a policy maker, how would you balance the need for addressing domestic poverty with the need to contribute to assisting with the international humanitarian food crisis?

3. The food crisis raises a question fundamental to our existence: Is our world capable of supporting itself? What insights do realist, liberal, and constructivist theories provide regarding our future prospects?

the global community, former French President Nicolas Sarkozy warned of dire consequences of inaction: "If we don't do anything, we run the risk of food riots in the poorest countries and a very unfavorable effect on global economic growth."

However, maintaining the political will to enact fundamental changes is always difficult. Developed countries, for example, are very resistant to reducing agricultural subsidies. Moreover, some of the suggested solutions, such as **genetic engineering** and **transgenic crops** and livestock, are quite controversial and not supported by a variety of countries and NGOs.

Though many of the solutions to food insecurity center on increasing the amount and quality of food produced, it is important to note that the "most recent famines have been caused not because food wasn't available but because of bad governance—institutional failures that led to poor distribution of the available food, or even hoarding and storage in the face of starvation elsewhere" (Banerjee and Duflo, 2011, p. 71). As Amartya Sen observed, "no substantial famine has ever occurred in any independent and democratic country with a relatively free press" (1999, p. 7). Reform of national practices and policies is an intrinsic aspect of efforts to prevent and respond to food insecurity and promote sustainable development.

Converting to Renewable Sources of Energy

How countries meet their growing demand for energy directly influences the evolution and preservation of the global commons. A new and less destructive source of energy could soon emerge because of the advent of revolutionary new technologies that derive energy from the sun, wind, and other abundant and renewable sources of energy such as hydrogen. The impact of such a global transformation would be huge, overturning the past 125-year pattern in world energy development and consumption. Could the era of "big oil" really be ending? Together, widely fluctuating oil prices and public alarm about global warming are pushing the world, however haltingly, toward cleaner and cheaper energy systems.

The supply of fossil fuels will not run out anytime soon, but the *externalities* or consequences of environmental and health threats make burning fossil fuels excessively dangerous. The combustion of oil and coal is traced to lung cancer and many other health hazards. And, what is more, it leads to air pollution, urban smog, and **acid rain** that damage forests, water

genetic engineering The artificial modification of the DNA of an organism to change its characteristics.

transgenic crops New crops with improved characteristics created artificially through genetic engineering that combine genes from species that would not naturally interbreed.

acid rain Precipitation that has been made acidic through contact with sulfur dioxide and nitrogen oxides.

quality, and soil. There are powerful incentives to harness technology to shift to renewable sources of energy. Solar, tidal, and wind power, as well as geothermal energy and bioconversion, are among the alternatives to oil most likely to be technologically and economically viable, as Figures 14.5A and 14.5B show.

Among known technologies, nuclear energy, wherein sustained nuclear processes generate electricity and heat, often is championed as the leading alternative to fossil fuel dependence (see Figure 14.6). Currently, 98 nuclear plants provide 20 percent of the United States' electricity. Among clean energy sources, nuclear sources account for 56 percent of all carbon-free electricity in the United States (Hayunga, 2019). China is also increasing its nuclear energy, building 27 new reactors, and planning for almost 200 more to meet its demand for energy that is expected to triple by 2050 (Anderson, 2015).

However, safety and financial costs may limit the surge toward nuclear power; these problems have led some countries to reduce (or, like Germany, Sweden, and Spain, phase out) their nuclear programs. Well-publicized nuclear accidents in the United States at the Three Mile Island nuclear power plant in Pennsylvania in 1979 and at Chernobyl in Ukraine in 1986—and no less than five major accidents between 1995 and 1999 at Japan's fifty-two nuclear power

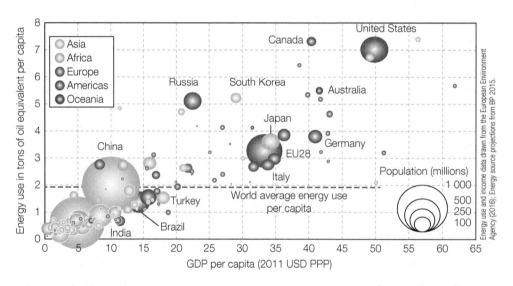

FIGURES 14.5A AND 14.5B Supplying the World's Growing Energy Needs by the Year 2035 Shown above, the relationship between energy usage and GDP per capita indicates that wealthy countries use much more energy than their developing counterparts do. In addition, much of the world's population—notably China, India, Brazil, and all of Africa—are close to or below the line demarcating the global average energy use. Thus, it is likely that global energy use will increase greatly as these countries develop; a report by the International Energy Agency (IEA) predicts that by 2040 demand for energy in the Middle East, Africa, and South Asia will grow by 67, 52, and 67 percent, respectively (Eule, 2018). Though the demand for energy from nonrenewable resources remains high, the development of renewable sources to meet the world's energy needs is on the rise (right).

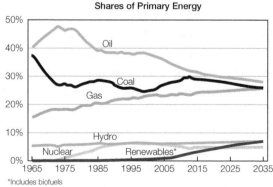

plants (which supply about a third of Japan's electricity)—dramatized the potential dangers of nuclear power.

Then, on March 11, 2011, a 9.0 earthquake and tsunami devastated Japan and caused extensive damage at its nuclear power stations. Some 70,000 people were forced to evacuate from a twelve-mile radius of the Fukushima Daiichi nuclear power plant due to leaking radio-

active materials. Since then, safety fears concerning nuclear power have spread around the world. Germany announced that it will close all of its nuclear power plants by 2022, Italy has abandoned plans to expand its nuclear industry, and France has indicated that it will reduce its dependence on nuclear energy (Anderson, 2015). Concerns about the risks of nuclear power extend beyond plant safety. How and where to dispose of highly radioactive nuclear waste that comes from the 449 nuclear power plants is an unresolved issue virtually everywhere (IAEA, 2019). There are no safe procedures for handling the 52,000 tons of toxic radioactive nuclear waste, some of which will remain dangerous for hundreds of thousands of years. "Not in my back yard" (NIMBY) is a divisive cry on the global ecopolitical agenda; the Global North prefers to dump waste outside its own territory, and the Global South would prefer not to be the dump—but often is (see Figure 14.6).

A related fear is that countries that do not currently possess nuclear know-how might develop nuclear weapons (see Chapter 8). Most nuclear energy generating facilities continue to produce weapons-grade material. Specifically, highly enriched uranium and plutonium present national security concerns because "with the underlying technical

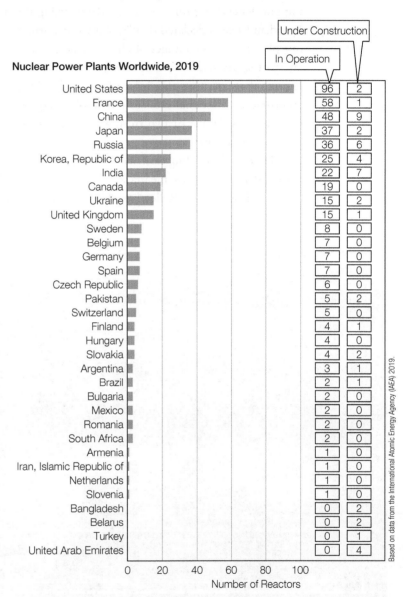

Nuclear Power Plants Worldwide, 2019

Based on data from the International Atomic Energy Agency (IAEA) 2019.

	In Operation	Under Construction
United States	96	2
France	58	1
China	48	9
Japan	37	2
Russia	36	6
Korea, Republic of	25	4
India	22	7
Canada	19	0
Ukraine	15	2
United Kingdom	15	1
Sweden	8	0
Belgium	7	0
Germany	7	0
Spain	7	0
Czech Republic	6	0
Pakistan	5	2
Switzerland	5	0
Finland	4	1
Hungary	4	0
Slovakia	4	2
Argentina	3	1
Brazil	2	1
Bulgaria	2	0
Mexico	2	0
Romania	2	0
South Africa	2	0
Armenia	1	0
Iran, Islamic Republic of	1	0
Netherlands	1	0
Slovenia	1	0
Bangladesh	0	2
Belarus	0	2
Turkey	0	1
United Arab Emirates	0	4

Number of Reactors

FIGURE 14.6 From Bombs to (Light) Bulbs On June 26, 1954, a nuclear power plant in Obninsk, Russia, became the first in the world to generate electricity for commercial use. By 2019, as the figure shows, the number of nuclear power plants had expanded to 449 in thirty countries, with an additional 54 reactors under construction in nineteen countries. The United States provided $8.3 billion in federal loan guarantees to construct two nuclear reactors slated to be operational in 2020, and issued permits for the construction of two additional reactors. (IAEA, 2017).

infrastructure able to support both weapons and electrons, there is no clear way to ensure nuclear energy can be developed without also building capabilities for weapons" (*Worldwatch Institute,* 2007, p. 34). This dilemma was highlighted as a significant concern with regard to North Korea's nuclear development program.

Other efforts to develop potential alternate fuel sources have also begun in hopes of breaking our dependence on fossil fuels. Recognizing the importance of such efforts, former U.S. President Obama declared that "to truly transform our economy, protect our security and save our planet from the ravages of climate change, we need to ultimately make clean, renewable energy the profitable kind of energy." Thomas L. Friedman (2008) echoed this sentiment, arguing that countries clinging to fossil fuels will see their security and prosperity decline as compared to those that pioneer renewable energy technologies. This emphasis reflects a shift over the past decade or two from a focus on conventional pollution issues to one on clean energy opportunities.

The cost of providing electricity from wind and solar power plants has declined dramatically since 2010, "so that in some markets renewable generation is now cheaper than coal or natural gas" (Cardwell, 2014). Reflective white roofs that reduce air-conditioning costs by 20 percent,

Yanin Arthus Bertrand/Terra/Corbis

IMAGE 14.7 The Unforgiving Cost of Nuclear Power Failure Shown here is the town of Pripyat, Ukraine, which was abandoned after the Chernobyl nuclear accident. Rather than learning from this lesson, and despite strong opposition from the public, Russia opened its borders to become the largest international repository for radioactive nuclear wastes, in the hope of earning billions of dollars over the next two decades.

and hence produce far fewer carbon dioxide emissions, are becoming more popular as a way to save energy and fight global warming (Barringer, 2009). Seaweed and algae fields are touted as a potential wave of the future, as "algal oil can be processed into biodiesel or nonpetroleum gasoline, the carbohydrates into ethanol, and the protein into animal feed or human nutritional supplements. The whole biomass can generate methane, which can be combusted to produce electricity" (Gies, 2008, p. 3). Indonesia and the Philippines, located within the "Pacific Ring of Fire," are looking to harness volcanic power as a source of geothermal power; in 2019, Kenya opened the largest wind farm in Africa. Although presently too expensive for most people, Honda Motor has begun producing the world's first hydrogen-powered fuel-cell car. "Unlike electric cars, which have a limited driving range and take hours to recharge, hydrogen vehicles run for up to 650 kilometers [404 miles] on a full tank and take just a few minutes to fill up. Their exhausts emit nothing but water vapor" (*The Economist*, 2015e, p. 1). Technological, economic, cultural, and environmental changes suggest that the early stage of a major energy transformation is under way, forced by supply scarcities and demand increases.

Conversion to renewable sources of energy represents a possible avenue away from global environmental degradation. Many believe this will not happen soon enough. They propose another path to reduce the dangers: forging international treaties among countries that provide for the protection of the environment and establish compliance mechanisms.

Global Efforts Toward Environmental Solutions

LO 14-4   Examine efforts of international actors, including IGOs and multinational corporations, to enhance environmental protections.

The 1992 Earth Summit in Stockholm was precedent setting. From it, a separate treaty, informally known as the Biodiversity Convention, set forth a comprehensive agreement for preserving biodiversity throughout the world. It committed state governments to devise national strategies for conserving habitats, protecting endangered species, expanding protected areas, and repairing damaged ones. Since then, the world has attempted to cooperate through increasingly concerted efforts to reach agreements and to back them with ratified treaties to protect the sustained global commons.

Success breeds success. Other international efforts followed the *Biodiversity Convention* to deal with environmental problems through global agreements. A big example was the Kyoto Protocol of 2005, in which 191 countries—55 of which accounted for at least 55 percent of global greenhouse emissions—pledged to cut emissions of gases linked to global warming below 1990 levels by the year 2012. More than 100 developing countries, including China and India, were exempt from the terms of the treaty. Only the United States refused to ratify the agreement, though Canada withdrew in 2011. In anticipation of the impending 2012 deadline for negotiating a successor to the Kyoto Protocol, the Global North committed to providing the Global South a total of $100 billion by 2020 to combat problems caused by climate change. In December 2012, the countries adopted the Doha Amendment agreeing to a second commitment period through 2020, though as of July 2019 only 130 of the required 144 signatories had ratified the agreement.

Yet the need to address environment challenges to the planet continues to be an issue of significant global concern. In December 2015, leaders from over 190 countries came together at the 2015 United Nations Climate Change Conference in Paris to discuss ways to keep global warming from reaching dangerous levels. Effectively replacing the Kyoto Protocol, under the 2015 Paris Agreement countries pledged to keep the rise in global temperatures well below 3.6 degrees Fahrenheit (2 degrees Celsius). Currently, however, country pledges to reduce carbon dioxide emissions will not halt global warming and will likely result in average temperatures rising to at least 5.4 degrees Fahrenheit (3 degrees Celsius) by 2100. At that level, the world is at risk of thawing large areas of permafrost—which could drive global temperatures even higher. "The challenge to stay below 3.6 degrees Fahrenheit is immense, requiring fossil fuel infrastructure to be phased out, non-fossil energy sources phased in, and large-scale removal of carbon from the atmosphere" (Leahy, 2018).

The number of international environmental treaties has grown exponentially in the last 130 years. However, many skeptics fear that these efforts are too little, too late, and not enough to save the global commons for future generations. Many question the ability of today's existing treaties to manage the environmental dangers they are meant to address. Some of them are weak and do not command the policy changes needed to remedy the various problems they identify. Of particular concern is the reluctant backing of the United States. Of the UN's thirty-one major global environmental agreements, the United States has ratified only one-third. Environmental protection activists worry that if the American hegemon refuses to lead, the prospects for strengthening the rules of the environmental preservation regime are dim.

Multinational corporations are also key players in the ecopolitics game that has the potential to determine the Earth's fate. Corporations rule globally, and they are strong advocates with powerful lobbyists of free trade. Are their power and quest supportive of, or detrimental to, sustainable development? The question is especially pertinent in a rapidly globalizing world in which trade increasingly links politics, economics, ecology, societies, and cultures in webs of ever-tightening interdependencies.

Beyond the issue of the gains from and the costs of trade, environmentalists and liberal economists differ in their assessments concerning the wisdom of using trade to promote environmental standards. Liberal economists see such efforts as market distortions, whereas environmentalists view them as useful instruments for correcting market failures, such as the market's inability to compensate for environmental exploitation (for example, atmospheric pollution by chemical companies). Some countries, however, particularly in the Global South, view the use of trade mechanisms to protect the environment as yet another way the rich states block entry into lucrative Global North markets and keep the Global South permanently disadvantaged.

Trade-offs must sometimes be made between goals that, in principle, all seem designed to increase human well-being and security. However, another interpretation holds that trade encourages states to live beyond their means. According to some ecologists, trade magnifies the damaging ecological effects of production and consumption by expanding the market for commodities beyond state borders. Countries that have depleted their resource bases or passed strict laws to protect them can easily look overseas for desired products, in ways that shift the environmental stress of high consumption to other states' backyards.

ITAR-TASS NEWS AGENCY/ALAMY STOCK PHOTO

IMAGE 14.8 **Playing in the "Poison Pond"** Children play in the shadow of the former Union Carbide factory in Bhopal, India, the site of one of the worst industrial accidents in history. The "pond" in which they are playing was a sludge pit containing chemical by-products from the former pesticide plant. Although the chemical leakage at Bhopal, which resulted in more than 3000 deaths, occurred in 1984, the area—which still contains more than 400 tons of toxic waste—has yet to be cleaned up. The picture is a stark reminder of how environmental crises can long outlive the political will necessary to resolve them.

The tragedy of the commons suggests a bleak future. Is ruin the destination toward which humanity must rush? Or is a more optimistic scenario possible?

A positive trend has emerged in global corporate culture that bodes well for the environment, as there is increasing recognition that profits can improve with development of "green" products, for which there is rising consumer demand worldwide. The environmental dimension of corporate social responsibility (CSR) (see Chapter 6) is increasing in importance, as industries are paying attention to the environmental impact of their production processes, including the effects on the communities in which they operate.

This is motivated, in part, by the increased scrutiny that corporations face regarding the environmental impact of their operations. Independent evaluations of how mindful corporations are of the environment—including multiple "green" and "sustainable corporation" rankings of good corporate citizenship as well as "Toxic 100" and "Worst Polluter" rankings for less responsible environmental behavior—are readily available to the public. This information can affect their bottom line, as surveys indicate that environmental concerns play a role in consumer purchasing decisions, particularly among younger buyers (Nielsen, 2014). As a result, "the environmental part of CSR is becoming increasingly important" as more corporations see the need for "taking a deeper hue of green" by making these responsibilities a key aspect of their strategic plans (Dans, 2018).

The possibility that the international political economy will provide economic incentives for producing products that can contribute to global environment sustainability has inspired hope that the environmental dangers may be contained. That hope is rising because some governments, corporations, and individuals are seeking local solutions to environmental sustainability.

A huge concern is that some very powerful states, advantageously positioned in the global hierarchy, are selfishly resisting painful and costly adjustments now. They are resisting reforms of their own existing environmental protection policies. Yet there are exceptions to this response to environmental degradation. Numerous countries have managed to balance the risk of short-term economic loss against the expectation of long-term economic growth by investing in costly renewable energy programs that can enable them to experience economic growth. Map 14.5 charts the rankings of countries according to the Environmental Performance Index. The score measures their investments in efforts to protect their future environments. Clearly, some countries more so than others see environmental sustainability as a priority that protects their interests.

The entire world stands at a critical juncture. The path humanity takes will affect human security far into the future. Evidence of serious ecological problems is getting harder and harder to ignore. Because the stakes are so high, all the pieces in the puzzle—population growth, natural resources, technology, and changing preferences in lifestyles—must be addressed simultaneously.

If necessity really is the mother of invention, there is hope. The planet *must* be saved, or all other opportunities will be closed, the global environment will face certain doom, and human

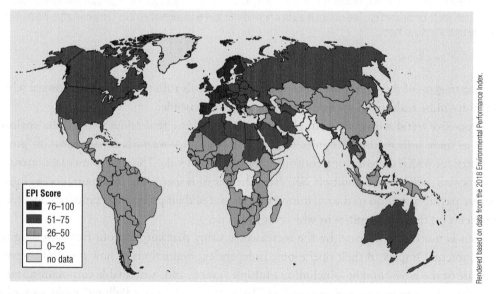

EPI Score
■ 76–100
■ 51–75
■ 26–50
□ 0–25
□ no data

Rendered based on data from the 2018 Environmental Performance Index.

MAP 14.5 Measuring National Commitments to Environmental Sustainability Measures of environmental protection performance suggest some countries are doing much more than many others to protect their environments. The Environmental Performance Index (EPI) gauges the relative performance of 180 countries across the categories of environmental health, air pollution, water resources, biodiversity and habitat, productive natural resources, and climate change. Pictured are the 2018 EPI ratings worldwide. Switzerland and France have the two best scores, while the United States ranks 27th, China 120th, and India 177th.

Think It Through Considering this map in comparison with Map 14.3 ("Human-Induced Deserts"), are there any areas of particular cause for hope or concern?

history will end. Therefore, the stakes are so high that perhaps solutions will be found. As the world struggles, the debate about solutions is likely to continue on two tracks: between those who think humankind's concentration should be geared toward trying to reverse environmental deterioration, and those who prefer to concentrate on creating new technologies to contain environmental damage. Both strategies are urgently needed.

> *Present generations have the responsibility to bequeath to future generations a planet that is not irreversibly damaged by human activity.*
>
> **— AUDREY AZOULAY, UNESCO DIRECTOR-GENERAL**

Study. Apply. Analyze.

Chapter Summary

14-1 Articulate key concepts underlying global ecological controversies. The concept of *environmental security* places issues such as climate change and deforestation under the broader purview of national security. Along these lines, scarcity of resources and other environmental threats may contribute to interstate and intrastate conflicts; these concerns exemplify the *politics of scarcity*. A common dilemma applied to issues related to the use, and overuse, of natural resources is the *tragedy of the commons*.

14-2 Investigate three major areas of ecopolitical contention: climate change, biodiversity, and energy supply. A scientific consensus exists that the average temperature of the planet is warming due in large part to human causes. This rise in global temperatures, and the broad array of problems that emerge from this, is known as climate change. A consequence of climate change is the reduction in biodiversity, which is marked by increases in extinctions among plant and animal species and damage to ecosystems such as coral reefs and forests. A key driver of climate change is the use of fossil fuels, thus a future challenge is to seek out sources of energy that are affordable, accessible, and not harmful to the environment.

14-3 Assess the interrelationship between environmental preservation and two aspects of human rights: economic and food security. A healthy environment provides a foundation for economic prosperity and food security. At the same time, there are ways in which economic growth as well as food production can be damaging to the environment and thus unsustainable over time. Given this dilemma, a key priority in economic development is how to pursue economic growth, as well as agricultural production, without undermining the longer-term viability of the environment.

14-4 Examine efforts of international actors, including IGOs and multinational corporations, to enhance environmental protections. As environmental challenges are a transnational threat, transnational actors such as IGOs have been a key force in responding to them. Several key treaties—such as the Kyoto Protocol and the Paris Agreement—exemplify international cooperation in this area as well as the limits to what such cooperation can accomplish. For good or bad, corporations can have a substantial impact on the environment. Traditionally, corporate concerns have focused purely on profitability, though many firms are paying increased attention to the impact of their activity on the environment.

Key Terms

acid rain
biodiversity
biodiversity hot spots
carrying capacity
cornucopian

deforestation
desertification
enclosure movement
environmental security
epistemic community

fracking
genetic engineering
greenhouse effect
neo-Malthusians
ozone layer

politics of scarcity
sustainable development
tragedy of the commons
transgenic crops

Suggested Readings and Resources

Bodansky, Daniel, Jutta Brunnée, and Lavanya Rajamani. (2017). *International Climate Change Law*. Oxford, UK: Oxford University Press.

Brown, Lester B. (2012). *Full Planet, Empty Plates: The New Geopolitics of Food Scarcity*. New York: W. W. Norton & Co.

Climate Progress: thinkprogress.org/climate/issue/. A website dedicated to global climate progress.

Dot Earth: dotearth.blogs.nytimes.com. A blog sponsored by *The New York Times* covering global environmental issues.

Environment Blog: Meet the World's Best New Environment Blogs: theguardian.com/environment/blog/2013/jun/07/meet-worlds-best-environment-bloggers. A collection of environment-related blogs put together by *The Guardian*.

Friedman, Thomas L. (2008). *Hot, Flat, and Crowded: Why We Need a Green Revolution, and How It Can Renew America*. New York: Farrar, Straus and Giroux.

Hannigan, John. (2012). *Disasters Without Borders: The International Politics of Natural Disasters*. Cambridge: Polity.

Coyle, Eugene D., and Melissa J. Dark, eds. (2014). *Understanding the Global Energy Crisis*. West Lafayette, IN: Purdue University Press.

Vanderheiden, Steve. (2011). "Globalizing Responsibility for Climate Change," *Ethics & International Affairs* 25, no 1: 65–84.

Watts Up With That? wattsupwiththat.com. "The world's most viewed site on global warming and climate change."

Carnegie Council Videos

Key Term Videos

- Epistemic Community
- Politics of Scarcity
- Greenhouse Effect
- Sustainable Development

Additional Videos

- Ahmed, Saraz, et al. "Sustainable Societies."
- Dorset, Steve. "Climate Change and the Precautionary Principle."
- Powers, Jonathan. "Security Threat of Climate Change."
- Stern, Nicholas. "Impact of Climate Change."

Part 5
Thinking About the Future of World Politics

People usually speculate about future prospects based on their understanding of prevailing trends. What makes prediction so difficult is the sheer complexity and uncertainty surrounding world politics. Some trends seem to move forward in the same direction, whereas others reverse course; some trends intersect, whereas others diverge; some trends act as catalysts, whereas others serve as barriers. Your challenge in deciphering their meaning is twofold: 1) to distinguish between those that are transient and those likely to have lasting impact, and 2) to project the interconnection of the most important trends rather than become preoccupied with any single one in isolation.

How will the combination of major trends unfolding in world politics today influence your global future? Will previous efforts to construct world order be found useful, or will past approaches be rejected as new issues arise on the global agenda?

Part 5 of *World Politics* does not posit answers or predictions, but instead offers some important, thought-provoking questions for you to contemplate about the prospects for the twenty-first century. When thinking about the issues raised by these questions, ask yourself how they might be addressed to create a more peaceful and just global future.

WANG ZHAO/Getty Images

Global Destiny: Which Priorities Will Triumph?
This photo shows a woman wearing a facial mask in Beijing, China to protect herself from the heavy smog caused by small particulate pollution. "Every year more than one million people die prematurely in China because of air pollution – but this could rise further as climate change increases heatwaves and instances of stagnant air, which have a detrimental impact on air quality" (Canter, 2019). In response to dangerous environmental conditions, the government has since converted around 4 million homes in the country's north to clean energy sources such as natural gas and, according to analysis of World Health Organization data, has likely helped prevent 400,000 premature deaths annually (Yu, 2018). Yet there remains tension between environmental protection and economic development—both conditions are products of prevailing trends in world politics. In which world are most people in the future likely to live?

Chapter 15

Looking Ahead at Global Trends and Transformations

IMAGE 15.1 Envisioning Our Global Destiny This satellite image of the world at night portrays an integrated world community in a globe without borders, but with variation in the degree of prosperity and development. Against a landscape of trend and transformation, humanity faces many dilemmas in a globalized world. As former U.S. first lady Eleanor Roosevelt once said, "It is today we must create the world of the future" (Roosevelt, 2012).

Learning Objectives

LO 15-1 Hypothesize which issues will dominate the future global agenda.

LO 15-2 Assess several vital questions concerning the future of politics.

LO 15-3 Integrate insights from throughout the text to speculate about global futures.

"
Change is the law of life. And those who look only to the past or present are certain to miss the future."

—JOHN F. KENNEDY, FORMER U.S. PRESIDENT

Many, sometimes conflicting, global trends are unfolding. Some point toward integration, others toward fragmentation; the world looks like it is coming together and at the same time it is coming apart. A new global system is on the horizon, but it is one whose characteristics have yet to develop definition. Uncertainty and unpredictability are today's prevailing mood. But one thing is certain: Seismic shifts that challenge the wisdom of old beliefs and traditions are under way. Because both turmoil and turbulence describe contemporary international affairs, they require us to ask unconventional questions about conventional ideas. They push us to think about the political, military, economic, demographic, and environmental pressures being brought to bear on the countries of the world, the people who reside in them, and their interactions.

Facing the future, you confront an awesome investigative challenge: anticipating and interpreting the probable future contours of world affairs and constructing compelling theoretical explanations of their causes and consequences. To do so, you must consider a number of unusual and controversial questions rising to the top of the global agenda throughout the world. Experts whose profession it is to help you may be somewhat informative. However, the rival conclusions boldly advanced by would-be prophets are not likely to be very definitive, and often diverge wildly.

> *Challenge and opportunity always come together—under certain conditions one could be transformed into the other.*
>
> —HU JINTAO, FORMER CHINESE PRESIDENT

Global Trends and Forecasts: Putting Yourself in the Picture

LO 15-1   Hypothesize which issues will dominate the future global agenda.

Many problems and challenges are expected to confront humanity in the twenty-first century. As recognized by former UN Secretary-General Kofi Annan (2006, p. 205), "We face a world of extraordinary challenges—and of extraordinary interconnectedness. We are all vulnerable to new security threats, and to old threats that are evolving in complex and unpredictable ways." Consider these six clusters of threats with which the world must be concerned now and in the decades ahead:

- Economic threats—including poverty, national debt, and trade wars

- Threats to health and well-being—from infectious disease, environmental degradation, and abuse of human rights

- Armed conflict—both between and within countries, including civil war, genocide, and other large-scale atrocities

- Proliferation of weapons of mass destruction—including nuclear, radiological, chemical, and biological weapons

- Terrorism

- Transnational organized crime

This inventory hints at what the world will be like in the years to come. To construct your own images of the future of world affairs, begin by thinking about the key questions that are likely to dominate international relations in the coming decades. The questions you identify will determine which scenarios and theories better inform your understanding of your global future.

Armed with an understanding of how ideas about international relations are formed and retained, rejected, or replaced, imagine yourself at the end of a semester preparing to take the final exam in your course about international relations. Your entire grade, your instructor tells you, will be determined by only one question. Sitting nervously, you open your blue book and are astonished at the instructions: "(1) state the question you wish had been asked in this exam for this course, and (2) then answer it; you will be graded on both the understanding you display in the kind of question you ask and the answers you provide." How would you respond?

Believe it or not, this kind of question is not fictional. It has been used to sort out candidates on exams for entry into the foreign service of several countries. There are really no right or wrong questions about international relations. Indeed, there is little agreement about the trends and issues that are the most important in international affairs, and no scholarly consensus exists about the questions that deserve the greatest attention today.

To stimulate your thinking, make a preliminary list, based on what you now know after reading *World Politics*, of what you believe will be the crucial questions about the future of the world. How would you go about interpreting your own questions? What rival theories (see Chapter 2) would you rely on to frame your analyses? This mental exercise will sharpen your critical thinking skills and tell you as much about yourself and your reasoned perspective as it does about your capacity to describe the present global condition, predict its future course, and explain *why* world politics is changing (or staying the same).

Rather than leave you in the lurch, *World Politics* puts itself to the same test. It concludes now by identifying a series of questions about the future that are high on the global agenda. As a further catalyst for framing your own thinking, look critically at these questions. How they are answered is widely expected to give shape to world politics throughout the remainder of the twenty-first century.

> *Those caught up in revolutionary change rarely understand its ultimate significance.*
>
> **—BOUTROS BOUTROS-GHALI, FORMER UN SECRETARY-GENERAL**

The Global Predicament: Key Questions about a Turbulent World

LO 15-2   Assess several vital questions concerning the future of politics.

World Politics has argued that international relations are subject to recurring patterns. Despite changes and chaos, behavior by transnational actors is not random. It is governed by regular propensities, and this makes it possible to uncover "laws" or generalized action-and-reaction patterns. As realist theorist Hans J. Morganthau argued in his classic text *Politics Among Nations*, the past historical record speaks with sufficient continuity to make the scientific study of international politics a meaningful intellectual endeavor. There are some lessons about how countries interact that are constant across time and place. It is the purpose of scholarship to uncover these patterns and influence sound policy decisions based on the lessons history provides.

Under certain conditions, we assume that certain types of transnational actors respond in similar ways to the same types of stimuli. Yet there are exceptions. Sometimes similar actors in similar situations make different decisions. Thus, despite regularities in world politics, social scientists cannot draw on a body of uniform, deterministic laws to predict precisely the global future. "Generalization and specification are different undertakings, but they are neither necessarily dichotomous nor separate on the path toward discovery" (Yetiv, 2011, p. 94).

Another factor that makes it difficult to predict the future is the role of happenstance in world politics. History is replete with what Greek philosopher Aristotle called accidental conjunctions—situations in which things come together by chance. Consider, for example, the outbreak of World War I. Recall from Chapter 4 that one of the proximate causes of the war was Austrian Archduke Franz Ferdinand's assassination in Sarajevo on June 28, 1914. Earlier that day, several would-be assassins had failed to find an opportunity to kill the archduke and had apparently given up in frustration. When Ferdinand's motorcade made a wrong turn enroute to visit patients in a city hospital, it stopped briefly in front of a café where Gavrilo Princip, one of the frustrated assassins, coincidentally had gone to get something to eat. Astonished to find the archduke's open-air car just five feet away, Princip fired two shots, killing the archduke and his wife. Given the political climate in Europe at the time, if Franz Ferdinand had not been assassinated, something else might have precipitated the war. But as political scientist Stuart Bremer (2000, p. 35) asks, "Who can say whether a different triggering event, a day, a month, or a year later, would have led to the same chain of events that produced World War I?"

Myriad possible futures lie ahead. Some are desirable; others, frightening. Although we cannot predict with certainty which will materialize, we can narrow the range of possibilities by forecasting how current trends will likely develop and what steps may be taken to channel the course of events toward a global future we prefer.

The following six questions are designed to help you think about the future of world politics. Each question is based on information presented in previous chapters. When pondering the long-term implications of these questions, you are encouraged to:

- Imagine what conceivable global futures are possible,
- Determine which are the most probable, and
- Identify what policies would be of the most help to bring about the global future you prefer.

Is Globalization a Cure or a Curse?

Why does it now appear that the world and the states within it are spinning out of control? One answer has to do with "globalization," a widely accepted socially constructed word understood as a transforming force that is creating sweeping governance crises in a new age of increasing interdependent complexity. *Globalization* captures the idea that everything on the planet is now more closely connected than ever before, but only within an unsteady institutional foundation that is largely unprepared for the future.

The integration of the globe in this transformed, interconnected, borderless world and common *cosmopolitan culture* has reduced old feelings of independence, identity, and autonomy, and driven many states to surrender some of their sovereignty in order to benefit from collaborative participation in a competitive global marketplace. "Globalization is deepening, becoming more inclusive and more balanced between different parts of the planet. And it is introducing us all to new ideas, products and arts" (Schuman, 2013). The message has been heard: borders and barriers are a nationalistic effort to isolate a country, and hamper progress on the many issues that transcend national boundaries. "Join the world or become irrelevant" is the way that Edouard Balladur, former French prime minister, described the trend toward globalization.

Optimists, who are aware of the common destiny of all and the declining ability of many sovereign states to cope with global problems through unilateral *self-help* approaches, will energize efforts to put aside interstate competition. According to this reasoning, conflict will recede as humanity begins to better recognize that national borders and oceans provide little protection against the multitude of challenges that arise from the global revolution in travel, communications, and trade. These shared problems can only be managed through collective, multilateral cooperation. Globalization is creating a strong web of constraints on the foreign policy behavior of those who are plugged into the network of global transactions. Consequently, because globalization makes cooperation crucial to the well-being of everyone, we should welcome the continued tightening of interstate linkages.

What is especially important about globalization is that when everyone depends on everyone else, all *must* work together. Former UN Secretary-General Kofi Annan once noted "it has been said that arguing against globalization is like arguing against the laws of gravity." Global interdependence makes it imperative for states to renounce aggressive competition because they increasingly have a shared interest in cooperation and fewer and fewer incentives to fight. Globalization, optimists argue, is an irreversible motor of unity and progress, and ought to be promoted because it will ultimately increase the wealth of everyone everywhere (Norberg, 2006).

Middle East/Alamy Stock Photo

IMAGE 15.2 Going Global In your reading of *World Politics*, you have considered many facets of globalization and the positive and negative implications of the increasing interconnectedness of the globe's states and peoples. Shown here in Egypt are horse-drawn carriages parked in front of a McDonald's, reflecting a blending of cultures and economies, traditionalism and modernity. Although globalization certainly presents many challenges, it also provides opportunities to learn, prosper, and enjoy a world of great diversity and possibility.

Pessimists, however, point out that globalization may be slowing down and identity politics, in part a resentful response to globalization, may be on the rise (Fukuyama, 2018; Abdelal and Segal, 2007). Even if the present period of globalization continues, pessimists fret about how to cope with our "flat, hot, and crowded" planet Earth (Friedman, 2008). Moreover, despite the successes of globalization, it is often difficult to maintain the necessary political will to support global initiatives—particularly regarding economic globalization—and international organizations only imperfectly fill this gap. As economist Dani Rodrik (2011, p. 88) argues, "[T]he reality is that we lack the domestic and global strategies needed to manage globalizations' disruptions." Regardless of how compelling the need or how rewarding the benefits, increased contact and the integration of a single society of states may breed enmity, not amity.

Another issue with globalization concerns the distribution of its benefits. Critics of globalization posit that it favors advantaged states but constrains the prospects of weak states, producing new inequalities as the gap between the wealthy and the poor widens. A similar pattern of inequality is apparent within states as well. "[Nobel Laureate Eric] Maskin theorizes that while average income has been rising as a result of more trade and global production, so has inequality within countries" (World Bank, 2014a).

Because its benefits may not be distributed equally, globalization may generate conflict between winners and losers. As neorealist theorist Kenneth Waltz (2000, p. 14) observed, "interdependence promotes war as well as peace." Intertwined economies will sour relations more than sweeten them. Under conditions of fierce competition, scarcity, and resurgent nationalism, the temptation to seek isolation from globalization's assault on national autonomy by creating barriers to trade and other transactions may be irresistible. The temptation to achieve political benefits by military force will also persist. Thus, the tightening web of globalization has the potential to lead to either danger or to opportunity.

Will Technological Innovation Solve Pressing Global Problems?

The surge in globalization that followed on the heels of late-twentieth-century discoveries in microelectronics and information processing has unleashed revolutionary changes. The consequences of the technological revolution, however, are not certain. Technological innovations solve some problems but cause others. "[F]or the most part the economy, and ultimately the society, must adapt to the conditions that technology creates," observes Nobel Laureate economist Wassily Leontief, "If it cannot adjust to the challenges of changing technology, it fails" (Carter, 1996). Technology can increase productivity and economic output, but it can also displace workers and trigger social unrest and environmental damage. "Some find that their skills are complementary to new technologies. Others find themselves out of work" (*The Economist*, 2014d).

Although acknowledging that there is often a significant time lag between the diffusion of new technology and the changes it causes in society, some people assert that technological innovation promises humanity a more secure and bountiful future (Fidler and Gostin, 2008). Indeed, the most optimistic members of this group believe that because of promising developments in such fields as biotechnology, artificial intelligence, and digital software, humanity is entering the most innovative period in history. From their perspective, with patience, technological solutions will eventually be found that will ease the most serious problems facing the world today.

Malnutrition and disease may still exist, but because of technological advances in agriculture and medicine, many people are alive today who might have perished otherwise. Agro-ecological innovation can enhance food production while also restoring rural economies and sustaining the natural resource base (Worldwatch Institute, 2013a). Others are hopeful about the potential role of technology in futuristic geo-engineering initiatives to curb global warming, such as "directly scrubbing the air with devices that resemble big cooling towers" (Victor et al., 2009, p. 68). As Internet pioneer Vinton Cerf explains, "when the world around us becomes plugged in and aware, it will drive efficiencies like never before" (as quoted in Basulto, 2012).

Technology is also profoundly important for the future of energy (see Chapter 14), both to identify alternative sources and to more efficiently use existing resources. For example, researchers at MIT and Harvard have created an artificial leaf that is capable of producing energy from sunlight and water and has self-healing capabilities (Quick, 2013). As advanced technology becomes cheaper and more accessible, it is likely to have a broader impact. Google, a multinational corporation specializing in internet-related products and services, is intentionally taking steps to expand its use of green energy because, even as traditional sources of power are becoming more expensive, green power is becoming more cost-effective (Kanellos, 2013). Perhaps such developments will reduce the need for states to compete over scarce energy resources, and thus lessen a potential source of global conflict.

In contrast to those who envision technological innovation as a way to increase economic growth and alleviate social welfare problems, some remain concerned that proposed technological solutions will only serve to compound current problems. Whereas genetically modified crops are seen by optimists as a way to reduce famine, pessimists worry about the public health consequences. Even the so-called green revolution had its drawbacks, they argue. Although fertilizers, pesticides, and herbicides initially increased crop yields in various Global South countries, they eventually spawned new problems such as contaminated water supplies. Without wise management, technological advances can have detrimental side effects.

Likewise, critics decry the manner in which technological advancements have enabled governments to engage in widespread surveillance and targeted killings from afar. From the proliferation of drones to clandestine electronic surveillance programs, an urgent need arises for greater transparency and global discussion about what constitutes the legitimate use of such technology, and what is an unacceptable infringement upon state sovereignty, individual rights, and due process. Reflecting upon the controversy surrounding the heavy use of drones, public policy expert Audrey Kurth Cronin (2013, p. 54) notes that while "there is nothing inherently wrong with replacing human pilots with remote-control operators . . . the problem is that the guidelines for how Washington uses drones has fallen well behind the ease with which the United States relies on them, allowing short-term advantages to overshadow long-term risks." Likewise, some fear that while technological advances have brought us closer to "a death of distance" in terms of increased access to information and improved ability to communicate with others around the world, these same technological advances and artificial intelligence enable audio and video manipulation and facilitate information warfare and disinformation campaigns (Polyakova and Freid, 2019).

What do you think? Is the customary way of seeing technological discoveries as the engines of progress really valid? Or is the tendency to overrate the positive impact of new technology based on wishful thinking? "Learning how to make new technology is one thing; learning how to use it is another" (Shapin, 2007, p. 146). Therefore, when you look at new technologies (stem cells, nanotechnology, human genomes, etc.), think counterfactually and imagine how things might turn out if new technologies had not been invented or how new ones might influence life on planet Earth for better or for worse.

What Types of Armed Conflict Will Become the Major Fault Line in the Geostrategic Landscape?

Prevalent practices tend to wither away when they cease to serve their intended purpose, as the examples of slavery, dueling, and colonialism illustrate. Trends point toward the possibility that this may also happen for interstate wars, which have almost disappeared in modern history. Even more impressively, the period since 1945 has been the longest span of great power peace since the sixteenth century. This achievement is raising expectations that large-scale warfare between countries will disappear and armed conflict between countries will become obsolete. Part of this confidence is based on the assumption that no sane national leader would dare to wage war against another state because any conceivable rewards would be greatly exceeded by the cost of mass destruction.

To be sure, most leaders are still preparing for traditional kinds of warfare against other states and are adhering to the abiding wisdom of the ancient Greek philosopher Aristotle: "A people without walls is a people without choice." That said, the usefulness of traditional weapons of warfare against the emergent threats that now haunt the globe is questionable. How can countries effectively combat the dangers presented by faceless and invisible nonstate terrorists willing to die in suicide bombings for their cause? Can these attacks be deterred when the adversary lacks any obvious vulnerability? How does a state destroy an enemy with preemptive strikes when those adversaries have neither a location nor things of value to attack?

The old forms of military power still used by states today may be becoming impotent, and no level of military might can guarantee a state's safety. When countries' primary security problem is no longer an attack by another country but instead the threat of internal armed conflict or an attack by a transnational terrorist network such as Al Qaeda, states face the challenging question of how to fight wars against the unconventional military threats in today's world.

The conduct of war has undergone several "generational" changes since the Thirty Years' War drew to a close and gave birth to the modern state system. Whereas "third-generation" military thinking has influenced most countries since World War II, the threat of being attacked today by the military forces of another country has diminished, particularly in the Global North. Instead, a "fourth generation" of warfare has emerged in which states are pitted against nonstate actors in hostilities that lack front lines and clear distinctions between soldiers and civilians (Lind and Thiele, 2015). Unable to defeat conventional armies on the field of battle, irregular forces using unconventional tactics focus on their adversary's will, using patience, ingenuity, and gruesome acts of violence to compel their opponent to face the mounting costs of continuing a long, drawn-out struggle.

Both state and nonstate actors are also turning to information technology and the internet as unconventional weapons of war. Across the globe, "military and intelligence organizations are preparing the cyber battlefield with things called 'logic bombs' and 'trapdoors,' placing virtual explosives in other countries in peacetime" (Clark and Knake, 2010, p. xi). The ability of high-tech weapons to rapidly attack and disable thousands of targets introduces the possibility of highly volatile crises. "We could face a cyber-attack that could be the equivalent of Pearl Harbor," warned former U.S. Secretary of Defense Leon Panetta, that could "take down our power grid system, take down our financial systems in this country, take down our government systems, take down our banking systems. They could virtually paralyze this country. We have to be prepared to deal with that." As a precursor to what may come, in December 2014 the U.S. government blamed North Korea for a cyberattack on Sony Pictures Entertainment in relation to a satiric movie about a plot to assassinate the North Korean dictator Kim Jong-un. The Sony hack is one of the few instances thus far of a country allegedly using cyberspace for explicitly coercive purposes, though it is consistent with the style of asymmetric conflict engaged in by North Korea vis-à-vis the United States and South Korea (Haggard and Lindsay, 2015).

Space is another dimension in which future conflict may emerge. It is particularly conducive to a security dilemma, as the dual-use nature of most space technology—it has value for both civilian and military purposes—means that competition for territory and influence is likely to increase tensions between major powers and generate concerns about security threats (Johnson-Freese, 2016). "Space war is inevitable because today's modern militaries use space for everything, from spy satellites to a soldier on a mountaintop using satnav to figure out exactly where he or she is. . . . And in any war, one side will seek to deprive the other of their ability to function. In this day and age, that means attacking the satellites" (Clark, 2018). U.S. President Donald Trump's plans to create a Space Force exemplifies the belief that it is critical to ensure that, in the words of his Vice President Michael Pence, "American national security is as dominant in space as it is on Earth."

Some political and military leaders, however, continue to think of warfare in third- generational terms, dismissing this new face of war as an annoyance that detracts from preparations for decisive, large-scale engagements (Woodward, 2006). Do the wars in Afghanistan and Iraq provide a glimpse into the future? Will most military clashes in the early twenty-first century follow their pattern?

Should the Global Community Intervene to Protect Human Rights?

Conflicts within countries are raging throughout the world. Many civilians are subject to widespread oppression and violence by governments presumably created to preserve law and order. Of great concern is whether the moral outrage of the global community will be sufficient to spur concerted peacekeeping and peacemaking interventions to end human rights abuses in those countries where acceptable standards of conduct in international law have been blatantly disregarded. Atrocities in many fragile states each year expel tens of millions of refugees and displaced people from their homes. The global community is being put to a test of its true ideals and its capacity to defend them, at potentially high costs. As UN Secretary-General Antonio Guterres remarked in 2016 upon taking his oath of office, "In the end, it comes down to values. . . We want the world our children inherit to be defined by the values enshrined in the UN Charter: peace, justice, respect, human rights, tolerance and solidarity" (United Nations, 2016). Will a humanitarian concern for the victims targeted for extermination crystallize into a response? Or will the victims perish in a sea of indifference?

In principle, human rights law now provides unprecedented protection for people everywhere to live in freedom without fear. The traditional legal rule of state sovereignty and its corollary, the *nonintervention norm* against external interference in the internal affairs of states, have been revised. There is growing support within the international community for a global *responsibility to protect* those who suffer from mass abuse at the hands of their state governments. Former UN Secretary-General Kofi Annan described well the redefinition when he noted, "the State is now widely understood to be instruments at the service of their people, and not vice versa."

Principle is one thing; the reality of preventing human suffering is another. Will the major powers and nonstate actors in the globalized community back their expressed convictions with action to free humanity from the oppression of mass murder? Can they agree on rules for humanitarian intervention that define when it is legitimate to militarily respond to gross violations of human rights? In the wake of a decade marred by ethnic cleansing, genocide, massacres, and atrocious human rights abuse in countries such as Bosnia and Herzegovina, Haiti, Rwanda,

IMAGE 15.3 The Tragedy of Human Rights Abuse The Islamic State and associated armed groups have violated international law and committed gross human rights abuses. These include "executions and other targeted killings of civilians, abductions, rape and other forms of sexual and physical violence perpetrated against women and children, forced recruitment of children, destruction or desecration of places of religious or cultural significance, wanton destruction and looting of property, and denial of fundamental freedoms" (UN, 2014, p. 10). Shown here, Islamic State militants appear to be carrying out an execution of Ethiopian Christians in Libya.

Somalia, and Serbia, Secretary-General Kofi Annan (1999) challenged the UN General Assembly, "[Can the world] reach consensus—not only on the principle that massive and systematic violations of human rights must be checked, wherever they take place, but also on ways of deciding what action is necessary, and when, and by whom." Contention over whether the international community should intervene to stop human suffering in Syria, which intensified following the alleged use of chemical weapons in 2013, shows that these questions remain unresolved.

The challenge is to transcend traditional notions of sovereignty and to construct a global consensus for intervention that, in the words of civil rights activist Dr. Martin Luther King Jr., is based on the belief that "injustice anywhere is a threat to justice everywhere." If the global community truly recognizes that all people have rights that transcend state borders and defines those human rights as the core of the community's "common global interests," then it will have to answer and act on essential unresolved questions: What is the common interest? Who shall define it? Who shall defend it? Under whose authority? And by what means of intervention?

Is the World Preparing for the Wrong War?

To preserve peace, one must prepare for war. That remains the classical realist formula for national security. However, would states not be wiser to prepare to fight the conditions that undermine prosperity, freedom, and welfare rather than each other?

Leaders have long been loath to fall prey to the single-mindedness of preparing to compete with other states. As former French President Francois Mitterand once urged, "together we must urgently find the solutions to the real problems at hand—especially unemployment and underdevelopment. This is the battlefield where the outlines of the [future] will be drawn." India's former Prime Minister Indira Gandhi warned that "either nuclear war will annihilate the human race and destroy the Earth, thus disposing of any future, or men and women all over must raise their voices for peace and for an urgent attempt to combine the insights of different civilizations with contemporary knowledge. We can survive in peace and goodwill only by viewing the human race as one, and by looking at global problems in their totality." These prescriptions adhere to a fundamental premise, as expressed by Martti Ahtisaari, then president of Finland: "To deal with the great security challenges of our time, including population growth, the spread of weapons of mass destruction, crime, environmental degradation, and ethnic conflicts, we must resolutely adopt new methods of managing change and building global security."

These rhetorical positions reflect the problems and self-interests leaders face at home and abroad. Nonetheless, they reveal only the view of a limited number of people. The war of people against people goes on. Human security remains precarious.

A large percentage of humanity faces famine, poverty, and a denial of basic human rights. Millions are threatened by genocide and terrorism sponsored by their own governments. "The increasingly widespread fear that environmental degradation threatens national and international security raises for some the specter of violent conflict, geopolitical maneuvering, and authoritarian responses" (Conca and Debelko, 2015, p. 23). Humankind may consequently self-destruct, not because it lacks opportunities, but because of its collective inability to see and to seize them. "Perhaps we will destroy ourselves. Perhaps the common enemy within us will be too strong for us to recognize and overcome," lamented eminent astronomer Carl Sagan (1988). "But," he continued, "I have hope. . . . Is it possible that we humans are at last coming to our senses and beginning to work together on behalf of the species and the planet?"

Is This the "End of History" or the End of Happy Endings?

To many observers, the history of world affairs is the struggle between tyranny and liberty. The contest has taken various forms since antiquity: between kings and mass publics, despotism and democracy, ideological principle and pragmatic politics. Labels are misleading and sometimes dangerous. However, they provide the vocabulary of diplomacy and inform theoretical discussion of governance and statecraft. History, in this image, is a battle for hearts and minds. It is an ideological contest for the allegiance of humanity to a particular form of political, social, and economic organization.

With the defeat of fascism in World War II and the collapse of the international communist movement a generation later, it has become fashionable to argue that the world had witnessed the end of a historic contest of epic proportions—and thus the triumph of liberalism and what Francis Fukuyama (1989, p. 3) called the "end of history":

> The twentieth century saw the developed world descend into a paroxysm of ideological violence, as liberalism contended first with the remnants of absolutism, then bolshevism and fascism, and finally an updated Marxism that threatened to lead to the ultimate apocalypse of nuclear war. But the [twentieth] century that began full of self-confidence in the ultimate triumph of Western liberal democracy [seemed] at its close to be returning full circle to where it started: . . . to the unabashed victory of economic and political liberalism.

The abrupt repudiation of communism raised expectations that history had indeed "ended," in the sense that liberal democratic capitalism had triumphed throughout most of the world. Free governments practicing free trade, liberalism contends, can best create a sound world order. As Woodrow Wilson argued, making the world "safe for democracy" would make the world itself safe. From this liberal perspective, the diffusion of democratic capitalism bodes well for the future of world politics.

A less reassuring possibility is that history has not "ended" and that the battle between totalitarian and democratic governance is not truly over. "The continued spread of democracy in the twenty-first century is no more inevitable than it is impossible" (Mandelbaum, 2007, p. 127). There are signals that the march of democracy's spread is stalling, and many countries are democracies in name only as they remain ruled by despots who, although elected, disregard constitutional limits on their power and deny their citizens basic political, religious, and economic freedoms. What is more, new democracies often lack the rule of law, political parties, or a free news media, and as a consequence are unstable and warlike (Mansfield and Snyder, 2005b). There is also compelling evidence that established democracies are under attack, as state and non-state actors are using sophisticated disinformation campaigns and cyber hacks to undermine electoral processes, the legitimacy of their targets, and public confidence in "facts" (Mueller, 2019). Identity and nationalist politics are also on the rise, sowing distrust and discord.

The recent global economic crisis also led to renewed speculation about the merits and shortcomings of global capitalism. "Marx would certainly relish pointing out how flaws inherent in capitalism led to the . . . crisis. He would see how modern developments in finance, such as securitization and derivatives, have allowed markets to spread the risks of global economic integration" (Panitch, 2009, p. 141). Although many countries have regained their financial footing, the consensus on the virtues of commercial liberalism has been shattered. The free market economies most exposed to the global economy bore the brunt of the financial damage, whereas the downturn had less effect on countries—ranging from India and China to Moldova—that were relatively less open. The persistence of leaders unaccountable to the electorate, the threat of economic crises, and the vulnerabilities that have emerged in our interconnected and globalized world, suggest that we may *not* be witnessing history's end.

> *The philosophies of one age have become the absurdities of the next, and the foolishness of yesterday has become the wisdom of tomorrow.*
>
> **—SIR WILLIAM OSLER, CANADIAN PHYSICIAN AND EDUCATOR**

A New World Order or New World Disorder?

LO 15-3   Integrate insights from throughout the text to speculate about global futures.

The paradox of contemporary world politics is that a world no longer haunted by the paralyzing fear of a looming all-out war between great powers now faces a series of challenges every bit as threatening and potentially unmanageable. Globalization has simultaneously enlarged the responsibilities and expanded the issues to be confronted. In a prosperous and stable period of history, when confidence in peace and economic growth was high, then–U.S. President Bill Clinton found it necessary to warn, "profound and powerful forces are shaking and remaking our world. And the urgent question of our time is whether we can make change our friend and not our enemy."

The changes in recent years have spawned transnational threats to world order, in addition to resurgent nationalism, ethnic conflict, fragile states, separatist revolts, and disinformation campaigns. These include contagious diseases, human and drug trafficking, climate change, gender inequality, energy and food scarcities, desertification and deforestation, youth bulges and aging populations, and financial crises and collapsing economies.

The potential impact of these additional threats is formidable, as emerging trends suggest that nonmilitary dangers will multiply alongside the continuing threat of arms and armed aggression in civil wars, as well as interstate wars in particular regions and terrorism in almost any place and at any time in the world. The distinction between geostrategic issues of security that pertain to matters of war and peace and global issues related to economic, social, demographic, and environmental aspects of relations between governments and people may disappear. How will humanity set priorities for action with so many interrelated issues and problems, all of which require attention if peace and prosperity with justice is to prevail?

This book has focused on global change. It has identified the most important changes under way that are leading to potential transformations in world politics. Change, as we have seen, can be abrupt or slow. It moves constantly, but at its own pace, and history reminds us that the evolutionary direction of global change is uncertain. Many trends are unfolding at the same time, and their combined impact can move the world along an unexpected trajectory. In addition, trends can reverse themselves, and each trend advances at its own rate. Some trends move very slowly in an evolutionary

Wang Jianmin/Xinhua/Photoshot/Newscom

IMAGE 15.4 The Next Frontier? India and China are joining the United States, Russia, Europe, and Japan as major players in space exploration. Will the quest for knowledge, territory, and power in space be characterized by similar opportunities, tensions, and interests that shape politics across the world? Pictured here is the first female Chinese astronaut, Liu Yang, during a departure ceremony on June 16, 2012. A famous Maoist maxim has it that women hold up half the sky. Her accomplishments show that they have now soared past it (Branigan, 2012).

process that can only result in dramatic transformations over many centuries, whereas others exhibit short bursts of rapid change, interrupted by long periods without much change.

To appreciate the diverse ways trends may combine to affect each other, it is helpful to construct your images both by using memories of the past and by being inspired by visions of the future. In 1775, American revolutionary Patrick Henry underscored the importance of history, stating that there was "but one lamp by which my feet are guided, and that is the lamp of experience. I know of no way of judging the future but by the past." Decades later, in 1848, another patriot, Italian political leader Giuseppe Mazzini, stressed the importance of forward thinking when he observed, "great things are achieved by guessing the direction of one's century." All of us need both perspectives, and a keen awareness that our images of history and the future must avoid the temptation to see ourselves and our own country as we wish to see them, without taking into account how differently others might view us and our state.

It now appears that the collective impact of the divergent trends under way is signaling a major transformation in world politics. Yet, juxtaposed against the revolutionary is the stable—the enduring rituals, existing rules, established institutions, and entrenched customs that resist the pull of the momentous recent changes in world politics. Persistence and change coexist uneasily, and it is this mixture that makes the future so uncertain.

The outcomes of two races will determine the difference between the world that is and the world that will be. The first is the race between knowledge and oblivion. Ignorance stands in the way of global progress and justice. Advances in science and technology far outpace the ability to resolve the social and political problems they generate. Building the knowledge to confront these problems may therefore present the ultimate challenge. "The splitting of the atom," Albert Einstein warned, has "changed everything save our modes of thinking, and thus we drift toward unparalleled catastrophe. Unless there is a fundamental change in [our] attitudes toward one another as well as [our] concept of the future, the world will face unprecedented disaster."

"Knowledge is our destiny," philosopher Jacob Bronowski declared. If the world is to forge a promising future, it must develop more sophisticated knowledge. Sophistication demands that we see the world as a whole, as well as its individual parts; it does not permit picturing others according to our self-images or projecting onto others our own values. We must discard belief in a simple formula for a better tomorrow and resist single-issue approaches to reform. A willingness to tolerate ambiguity is essential.

The future of world politics also rests on the outcome of a race between states' ability to cooperate and their historic tendency to compete and fight. Only concerted international cooperation stands in the way of slipping back into military conflicts and ruthless competition. To meet the global challenges of the future, and to make wise decisions to implement needed changes for bringing about a world that is more secure and just, vision is required.

The future is not fixed, and headlines are not trend lines. Therefore, we can overcome threatening present dangers by making wise and ethical choices. How, then, should we proceed?

"In times like these," futurologist David Pearce Snyder (2006, p. 17) counsels, "the best advice comes from ancient ideas that have withstood the test of time." As the Greek philosopher Heraclitus observed 2500 years ago, "Nothing about the future is inevitable except change." Two hundred years later, ancient Chinese general Sun Tzu advised, "the wise leader exploits the inevitable." Their combined message is clear: The wise leader exploits change.

Therefore, rather than fear the future, we should welcome its opportunities as we strive to build a more peaceful and just world. The moving words of former U.S. President John F. Kennedy describe a posture we might well assume: "However close we sometimes seem to that dark and final abyss, let no man of peace and freedom despair. For he does not stand alone. . . . Together we shall save our planet or together we shall perish in its flames. Save it we can, and save it we must, and then shall we earn the eternal thanks of mankind."

> *All of us are going to spend the rest of our lives in the future. Therefore, if we want to be practical, we must focus our attention on the trends and ideas that are shaping the future. What will these changes mean for you, your family, your career, your community and your investments?*
>
> **—TIM MACK, FUTURIST**

Study. Apply. Analyze.

Chapter Summary

15-1 Hypothesize which issues will dominate the future global agenda. Given the current state of international politics, as well as the various projected future challenges, many perspectives and predictions about future outcomes exist. To create a hypothesis, start with your own questions: by analyzing your own curiosity, therein lies the lens through which you can study the future. The answers to these questions will catalyze different approaches to future international affairs.

15-2 Assess several vital questions concerning the future of politics. In *World Politics*, we have argued that recurring patterns characterize international relations, even in the face of change and chaos. Myriad possible futures lie ahead, and we present several key questions to prompt you to draw on the material throughout this book to develop your own arguments and positions—from whether globalization is a force for good, to the impact of the revolution in technology, to the nature of war in the years to come.

15-3 Integrate insights from throughout the text to speculate about global futures. We have identified the most important changes under way that are leading to potential transformations in world politics. Change can be abrupt or slow, and history reminds us that future directions are uncertain. As you move on to the next stage in your academic journey—and prepare to effect great change in the world—it will continue to be important to expand your knowledge, embrace complexity, and make informed decisions to bring about a world that is more secure and just.

Suggested Readings and Resources

Cressey, Laura E., Barrett J. Helmer, and Jennifer E. Steffensen, eds. (2014). *Careers in International Affairs*. Washington, D.C.: Georgetown University Press.

Haigh, Stephen Paul. (2013). *Future States: From International to Global Order*. Burlington, VT: Ashgate Publishing Company.

Glenn, Jerome C., Elizabeth Florescu, and the Millennium Team. (2017). *State of the Future 19.0*. Washington, D.C.: The Millennium Project.

Global Matters Blog: global-matters.org. A blog by the Center for Global Politics at Freie Universität Berlin that focuses on an array of important global issues.

The Guardian: theguardian.com/world. A website providing news from around the world.

Mueller, Sherry Lee and Mark Overmann. (2014). *Working World: Careers in International Education, Exchange, and Development*. Washington, D.C.: Georgetown University Press.

Worldwatch Institute. (2015). *State of the World 2015: Confronting Hidden Threats to Sustainability*. New York: Norton.

Yetiv, Steve. (2011). "History, International Relations, and Integrated Approaches: Thinking about Greater Interdisciplinarity," *International Studies Perspectives* 12 (2): 94–118.

Carnegie Council Videos

- Ancram, Michael. "Emerging Challenges in a Network World."
- Bueno de Mesquita, Bruce. "The Predictioneer's Game: Using the Logic of Brazen Self-Interest to See and Shape the Future."
- Friedman, George. "The Next 100 Years: A Forecast for the 21st Century."
- Khanna, Parag. "How to Run the World: Charting a Course to the Next Renaissance."
- Nye, Joseph. "The Future of Power."

Glossary

A

absolute advantage The liberal economic concept that a state should specialize in the production of goods in which their costs of production are lowest compared with those of other countries (**Chapter 11**).

acid rain Precipitation that has been made acidic through contact with sulfur dioxide and nitrogen oxides (**Chapter 14**).

acquired immune deficiency syndrome (AIDS) An often fatal condition that can result from infection with the human immunodeficiency virus (HIV) (**Chapter 12**).

actor An individual, group, state, or organization that plays a major role in world politics (**Chapter 1**).

adjudication A conflict-resolution procedure in which a third party makes a binding decision about a dispute in an institutional tribunal (**Chapter 2**).

affective intelligence theory A theory of how emotions shape beliefs, attitudes, and decisions (**Chapter 3**).

agency The capacity of an actor to make choices and achieve objectives (**Chapter 2**).

agenda setting The thesis that by their ability to identify and publicize issues, the communications media determine the problems that receive attention from governments and international organizations (**Chapter 12**).

agent-oriented constructivism A variant of constructivism that sees ideas and identities as influenced in part by independent actors (**Chapter 2**).

alignments The acceptance by a neutral state threatened by foreign enemies of a special relationship short of formal alliance with a stronger power able to protect it from attack (**Chapter 8**).

alliances Coalitions of two or more states that combine their military capabilities and promise to coordinate their policies to increase mutual security (**Chapter 8**).

anarchy A condition in which the units in the global system are subjected to few, if any, overarching institutions to regulate their conduct (**Chapter 1**).

antidumping duties Taxes placed on another exporting state's alleged selling of a product at a price below the cost to produce it (**Chapter 11**).

antipersonnel landmines (APLs) Weapons buried below the surface of the soil that explode on contact with any person—soldier or citizen—stepping on them (**Chapter 9**).

appeasement A strategy of making concessions to another state in the hope that, satisfied, it will not make additional claims (**Chapter 4**).

arbitrage The selling of one currency (or product) and purchase of another to make a profit on changing exchange rates (**Chapter 10**).

arbitration A conflict-resolution procedure in which a third party makes a binding decision between disputants through a temporary ruling board created for that ruling (**Chapter 7**).

armed conflict Combat between the military forces of two or more states or groups (**Chapter 7**).

arms control Multilateral or bilateral agreements to contain arms races by setting limits on the number and types of weapons states are permitted (**Chapter 9**).

arms race The buildup of weapons and armed forces by two or more states that threaten each other, with the competition driven by the conviction that gaining a lead is necessary for security (**Chapter 9**).

asylum The provision of sanctuary to safeguard refugees escaping from the threat of persecution in the country where they hold citizenship (**Chapter 12**).

asymmetric warfare Armed conflict between belligerents of vastly unequal military strength, in which the weaker side is often a nonstate actor that relies on unconventional tactics (**Chapter 7**).

atrocities Brutal and savage acts against targeted citizen groups or prisoners of war, defined as illegal under international law (**Chapter 12**).

autocratic rule A system of authoritarian or totalitarian government in which unlimited power is concentrated in a single leader (**Chapter 3**).

B

balance of power The theory that peace and stability are most likely to be maintained when military power is distributed to prevent a single superpower hegemon or bloc from controlling the world (**Chapter 2**).

ballistic missile defense (BMD) A planned antiballistic missile system using space-based lasers that would destroy enemy nuclear missiles before they could enter Earth's atmosphere (**Chapter 8**).

bandwagoning The tendency for weak states to seek alliance with the strongest power, irrespective of that power's ideology or type of government, in order to increase their security (**Chapter 8**).

bargaining model of war An interpretation of war's onset as a choice by the initiator to bargain through aggression with an enemy in order to win on an issue or to obtain things of value, such as territory or oil (**Chapter 7**).

bilateral Interactions between two transnational actors, such as treaties they have accepted to govern their future relationship (**Chapter 5**).

bilateral agreements Exchanges between two states, such as arms control agreements, negotiated cooperatively to set ceilings on military force levels (**Chapter 9**).

biodiversity The variety of plant and animal species living in the Earth's diverse ecosystems (**Chapter 14**).

biodiversity hotspot A region that has a high percentage of plant species found nowhere else in the world and is threatened by loss of at least 30 percent of its original natural vegetation (**Chapter 14**).

bipolarity A condition in which power is concentrated in two competing centers so that the rest of the states define their allegiances in terms of their relationships with both rival great power superstates, or "poles" (**Chapter 4**).

blowback The propensity for actions undertaken for national security to have the unintended consequence of provoking retaliatory attacks by the target when relations later sour (**Chapter 8**).

bounded rationality The concept that a decision maker's capacity to choose the best option is often constrained by many human and organizational obstacles (**Chapter 3**).

brinkmanship The intentional, reckless taking of huge risks in bargaining with an enemy, such as threatening a nuclear attack, to compel its submission (**Chapter 8**).

bureaucracy The agencies and departments that conduct the functions of a central government or of a nonstate transnational actor (**Chapter 3**).

bureaucratic politics model A description of decision making that sees foreign policy choices as based on bargaining and compromises among competing government agencies (**Chapter 3**).

Bush Doctrine   The unilateral policies of the George W. Bush administration proclaiming that the United States will make decisions only to meet America's perceived national interests, not to concede to other countries' complaints or to gain their acceptance (**Chapter 3**).

C

capitalism   An economic system characterized by private ownership of the means of production and distribution (**Chapter 2**).

carrying capacity   The maximum number of humans and living species that can be supported by a given territory (**Chapter 14**).

cartel   A convergence of independent commercial enterprises or political groups that combine for collective action, such as limiting competition, setting prices for their services, or forming a coalition to advance their group's interests (**Chapter 12**).

caucuses   Informal groups that individuals in governments and other groups join to promote their common interests (**Chapter 3**).

civil society   A community that embraces shared norms and ethical standards to collectively manage problems without coercion and through peaceful and democratic procedures for decision making aimed at improving human welfare (**Chapter 6**).

civil war   Wars between opposing groups within the same country or by rebels against the government (**Chapter 7**).

classical liberal economic theory   A body of thought based on Adam Smith's ideas about the forces of supply and demand in the marketplace, emphasizing the social and economic benefits when individuals pursue their own self-interest (**Chapter 5**).

coercive diplomacy   The use of threats or limited armed force to persuade an adversary to alter its foreign and/or domestic policies (**Chapter 8**).

cognitive dissonance   The general psychological tendency to deny discrepancies between one's preexisting beliefs (cognitions) and new information (**Chapter 1**).

Cold War   The forty-four-year (1947–1991) rivalry between the United States and the Soviet Union, as well as their competing coalitions, which sought to contain each other's expansion and win worldwide predominance (**Chapter 4**).

collective action dilemma   Paradox regarding the provision of collective goods in which there is no accountability for paying the costs of maintaining or providing the goods (**Chapter 11**).

collective security   A security regime agreed to by the great powers that set rules for keeping the peace, guided by the principle that an act of aggression by any state will be met by a collective response from the rest (**Chapter 2**).

colonialism   The rule of a region by an external sovereign power (**Chapter 4**).

commercial liberalism   An economic theory advocating free markets and the removal of barriers to the flow of trade and capital as a locomotive for prosperity (**Chapter 7**).

communism   The Marxist ideology maintaining that, if society is organized so that every person produces according to his or her ability and consumes according to his or her needs, a community without class distinctions will emerge, sovereign states will no longer be needed, and imperial wars of colonial conquest will vanish from history (**Chapter 5**).

comparative advantage   The concept in liberal economics that every state will benefit if it specializes in the production of goods that it can produce at a lower opportunity cost relative to other goods (**Chapter 11**).

compellence   A method of coercive diplomacy usually involving an act of war or threat to force an adversary to make concessions against its will (**Chapter 8**).

complex interdependence   A model of world politics based on the assumptions that states are not the only important actors, security is not the dominant national goal, and military force is not the only significant instrument of foreign policy. This theory stresses cross-cutting ways in which the growing ties among transnational actors make them vulnerable to each other's actions and sensitive to each other's needs (**Chapter 2**).

concert   A cooperative agreement among great powers to jointly manage the global system (**Chapter 4**).

conciliation   A conflict-resolution procedure in which a third party assists both parties to a dispute but does not propose a solution (**Chapter 9**).

conflict   Discord, often arising in international relations over perceived incompatibilities of interest (**Chapter 7**).

consequentialism   An approach to evaluating moral choices on the basis of the results of the action taken (**Chapter 2**).

constitutional democracy   Government processes that allow people, through their elected representatives, to exercise power and influence the state's policies (**Chapter 3**).

constructivism   A paradigm based on the premise that world politics is a function of the ways that states construct and then accept images of reality and later respond to the meanings given to power politics; as consensual definitions change, it is possible for either conflictual or cooperative practices to evolve (**Chapter 2**).

containment   A strategy of confronting attempts of a power rival to expand its sphere of influence, with either force or the threat of force, thereby preventing it from altering the balance of power (**Chapter 4**).

cornucopians   Optimists who question limits-to-growth analyses and contend that markets effectively maintain a balance between population, resources, and the environment (**Chapter 14**).

cosmopolitan   An outlook that values viewing the cosmos or entire world as the best polity or unit for political governance and personal identity, as opposed to other polities such as one's local metropolis or city of residence (**Chapter 12**).

counterterrorism   Strategies and methods used to combat or prevent terrorism (**Chapter 7**).

countervailing duties   Government tariffs to offset suspected subsidies provided by foreign governments to their producers (**Chapter 11**).

covert operations   Secret activities undertaken by a state outside its borders through clandestine means to achieve specific political or military goals with respect to another state (**Chapter 8**).

crimes against humanity   A category of activities, made illegal at the Nuremberg war crime trials, condemning states that abuse human rights (**Chapter 9**).

crisis   A situation in which the threat of escalation to warfare is high and the time available for making decisions and reaching compromised solutions in negotiations is compressed (**Chapter 9**).

cyberspace   A metaphor used to describe the global electronic web of people, ideas, and interactions on the Internet, which is unencumbered by the borders of the geopolitical world (**Chapter 12**).

cycles   The periodic reemergence of conditions similar to those that existed previously (**Chapter 1**).

D

decolonization   The process by which sovereign independence was achieved by countries that were once colonies of the great powers (**Chapter 5**).

defensive realism   A variant of realist theory that emphasizes the preservation of power, as opposed to the expansion of power, as an actor's primary security objective (**Chapter 2**).

deforestation   The process of clearing and destroying forests (**Chapter 14**).

democratic peace   The theory that although democratic states sometimes wage wars against nondemocratic states, they do not fight one another (**Chapter 7**).

demography   The study of population changes, their sources, and their impact (**Chapter 12**).

dependency theory   A theory hypothesizing that less developed countries are exploited because global capitalism makes them dependent on the rich countries that create exploitative rules for trade and production (**Chapter 2**).

desertification The creation of deserts due to soil erosion, overfarming, and deforestation, which converts cropland to nonproductive, arid sand (**Chapter 14**).

détente In general, a strategy of seeking to relax tensions between adversaries to reduce the possibility of war (**Chapter 4**).

deterrence Preventive strategies designed to dissuade an adversary from doing what it would otherwise do (**Chapter 7**).

developed countries A category used by the World Bank to identify Global North countries with an annual GNI per capita of $12,055 or more (**Chapter 5**).

developing countries A category used to identify countries according to income, based on World Bank classification of low-income Global South countries with an annual GNI per capita at or below $995, lower-middle income countries with an annual GNI per capita of more than $995 but less than $3,895, and upper-middle income countries with an annual GNI per capita of more than $3,895 but less than $12,055 (**Chapter 5**).

development The processes, economic and political, through which a country develops to increase its capacity to meet its citizens' basic human needs and raise their standard of living (**Chapter 5**).

devolution States' granting of political power to minority ethnic groups and indigenous people in particular national regions under the expectation that greater autonomy will curtail the groups' quest for independence as a new state (**Chapter 13**).

digital divide The division between the Internet technology-rich Global North and the Global South in the proportion of Internet users and hosts (**Chapter 5**).

diplomacy Communication and negotiation between global actors that is not dependent upon the use of force and seeks a cooperative solution (**Chapter 2**).

disarmament Agreements to reduce or destroy weapons or other means of attack (**Chapter 9**).

disinformation False information that is intentionally disseminated to harm an individual, organization, or state (**Chapter 12**).

diversionary theory of war The hypothesis that leaders sometimes initiate conflict abroad as a way of increasing national cohesion at home by diverting national public attention away from controversial domestic issues and internal problems (**Chapter 3**).

dollar overhang Condition that precipitated the end of the Bretton Woods era, in which total holdings of dollars outside of the U.S. central bank exceeded the amount of dollars actually backed by gold (**Chapter 10**).

domino theory A metaphor popular during the Cold War that predicted that if one state fell to communism, its neighbors would also fall in a chain reaction, like a row of falling dominoes (**Chapter 4**).

dualism The separation of a country into two sectors, the first modern and prosperous and centered in major cities, and the second at the margin, neglected and poor (**Chapter 5**).

E

ecological fallacy The error of assuming that the attributes of an entire population—a culture, a country, or a civilization—are the same attributes and attitudes of each person within it (**Chapter 7**).

economic peace The premise that economic institutions associated with a contract-intensive economy are the source of peace between countries (**Chapter 7**).

economic sanctions Punitive economic actions, such as the cessation of trade or financial ties, by one global actor against another to retaliate for objectionable behavior (**Chapter 11**).

embedded liberalism Dominant economic approach during the Bretton Woods system, which combined open international markets with domestic state intervention to attain such goals as full employment and social welfare (**Chapter 10**).

emerging powers Countries with rising political and economic capabilities and influence that seek a more assertive role in international affairs (**Chapter 5**).

enclosure movement The claiming of common properties by states or private interests (**Chapter 14**).

enduring internal rivalry (EIR) Protracted violent conflicts between governments and insurgent groups within a state (**Chapter 7**).

enduring rivalries Prolonged competition fueled by deep-seated mutual hatred that leads opposed actors to feud and fight over a long period of time without resolution of their conflict (**Chapter 1**).

environmental security A concept recognizing that environmental threats to global life systems are as dangerous as the threat of armed conflicts (**Chapter 14**).

epistemic community Scientific experts on a subject of inquiry such as global warming who are organized internationally as NGOs to communicate with one another and use their constructed understanding of "knowledge" to lobby for global transformations (**Chapter 14**).

ethics Criteria for evaluating right and wrong behavior and the motives of individuals and groups (**Chapter 9**).

ethnic cleansing The extermination of an ethnic minority group by a state (**Chapter 12**).

ethnic groups People whose identity is primarily defined by their sense of sharing a common ancestral nationality, language, cultural heritage, and kinship (**Chapter 1**).

ethnic nationalism Devotion to a cultural, ethnic, or linguistic community (**Chapter 6**).

ethnicity Perceptions of likeness among members of a particular racial grouping leading them to prejudicially view other nationality groups as outsiders (**Chapter 6**).

ethnocentrism A propensity to see one's nationality or state as the center of the world and therefore special, with the result that the values and perspectives of other groups are misunderstood and ridiculed (**Chapter 13**).

European Commission The executive organ administratively responsible for the European Union (**Chapter 6**).

European Union (EU) A regional organization created by the merger of the European Coal and Steel Community, the European Atomic Energy Community, and the European Economic Community (called the European Community until 1993) that has since expanded geographically and in its authority (**Chapter 6**).

exchange rate The rate at which one state's currency is exchanged for another state's currency in the global marketplace (**Chapter 10**).

export quotas Barriers to free trade agreed to by two trading states to protect their domestic producers (**Chapter 11**).

export-led industrialization A growth strategy that concentrates on developing domestic export industries capable of competing in overseas markets (**Chapter 5**).

externalities The unintended side effects resulting from choices, such as inflation from runaway government spending, that are not taken into account at the time of the decision (**Chapter 3**).

F

fascism A far-right ideology that promotes extreme nationalism and the establishment of an authoritarian society built around a single party with dictatorial leadership (**Chapter 4**).

feminist theory Body of scholarship that emphasizes gender in the study of world politics (**Chapter 2**).

fertility rate The average number of children born to a woman (or group of women) during her lifetime (**Chapter 12**).

fixed exchange rates A system in which a government sets the value of its currency at a fixed rate for exchange in relation to another country's currency so that the exchange value is not free to fluctuate in the global money market (**Chapter 10**).

floating exchange rates An unmanaged process in which governments neither establish an official rate for their currencies nor intervene to affect the value of their currencies, and instead allow market forces and private investors to influence the relative rate of exchange for currencies between countries (**Chapter 10**).

foreign aid Economic assistance in the form of loans and grants provided by a donor country to a recipient country for a variety of purposes (**Chapter 5**).

foreign direct investment (FDI) A cross-border investment through which a person or corporation based in one country purchases or constructs an asset such as a factory or bank in another country so that a long-term relationship and control of an enterprise by nonresidents results (**Chapter 5**).

fracking A drilling technique, also called hydraulic fracturing, that injects fluid at high pressure into shale beds to extract petroleum resources (**Chapter 14**).

fragile cities Cities in a state of violent crisis, with the municipal government incapable or unwilling to govern and provide public services (**Chapter 12**).

fragile states Countries whose governments have so mismanaged policy that their citizens, in rebellion, threaten revolution to divide the country into separate independent states (**Chapter 7**).

G

game theory Mathematical model of strategic interaction in which outcomes are determined not only by a single actor's preferences, but also by the choices of all actors involved (**Chapter 3**).

gender inequality Differences between men and women in opportunity and reward that are determined by the values that guide states' foreign and domestic policies (**Chapter 13**).

Gender Inequality Index (GII) An index that uses female reproductive health, political and educational empowerment, and participation in the labor market to assess the extent to which gender inequality erodes a country's human development achievements (**Chapter 13**).

gendercide Systematic killing of members of a specific gender (**Chapter 13**).

genetic engineering The artificial modification of the DNA of an organism to change its characteristics (**Chapter 14**).

genocide The attempt to eliminate, in whole or in part, an ethnic, racial, religious, or national minority group (**Chapter 7**).

geo-economics The relationship between geography and the economic conditions and behavior of states that defines their levels of production, trade, and consumption of goods and services (**Chapter 10**).

geopolitics The relationship between geography and politics and its consequences for states' national interests and relative power (**Chapter 3**).

global commons The physical and organic characteristics and resources of the entire planet—the air in the atmosphere and conditions on land and sea—on which human life depends

and that is the common heritage of all humanity (**Chapter 14**).

Global North A term used to refer to the world's wealthy, industrialized countries located primarily in the Northern Hemisphere (**Chapter 5**).

Global South A term now often used instead of "Third World" to designate the less developed countries located primarily in the Southern Hemisphere (**Chapter 5**).

global system The predominant patterns of behaviors and beliefs that prevail internationally and define the major worldwide conditions that heavily influence human and state activities (**Chapter 1**).

global village A popular cosmopolitan perspective describing the growth of awareness that all people share a common fate because the world is becoming an integrated and interdependent whole (**Chapter 12**).

globalization The integration of states through increasing contact, communication, and trade, as well as increased global awareness of such integration (**Chapter 10**).

globalization of finance The increasing transnationalization of national markets through the worldwide integration of capital flows (**Chapter 10**).

globalization of labor Integration of labor markets, predicated by the global nature of production as well as the increased size and mobility of the global labor force (**Chapter 11**).

globalization of production Transnationalization of the productive process, in which finished goods rely on inputs from multiple countries outside of their final market (**Chapter 11**).

globally integrated enterprises MNCs organized horizontally with management and production located in plants in numerous states for the same products they market (**Chapter 6**).

good offices Provision by a third party to offer a place for negotiation among disputants, but the party does not serve as a mediator in the actual negotiations (**Chapter 7**).

great powers The most powerful countries, militarily and economically, in the global system (**Chapter 1**).

greenhouse effect The phenomenon producing planetary warming when gases released by burning fossil fuels act as a blanket in the atmosphere, thereby increasing temperatures (**Chapter 14**).

gross domestic product (GDP) Total value of all goods and services produced in a country within a year (**Chapter 10**).

gross national income (GNI) A measure of the production of goods and services within a given time period, which is used to delimit the geographic scope of production. GNI measures

production by a state's citizens or companies, regardless of where the production occurs (**Chapter 5**).

Group of 77 (G-77) The coalition of Third World countries that sponsored the 1963 Joint Declaration of Developing Countries calling for reform to allow greater equality in North–South trade (**Chapter 5**).

groupthink The propensity for members of a group to accept and agree with the group's prevailing attitudes rather than speak out for what they believe (**Chapter 3**).

gunboat diplomacy A show of military force, historically naval force, to intimidate an adversary (**Chapter 8**).

H

hegemon A preponderant state capable of dominating the conduct of international political and economic relations (**Chapter 4**).

hegemonic stability theory A body of theory that maintains that the establishment of hegemony for global dominance by a single great power is a necessary condition for global order in commercial transactions and international military security (**Chapter 7**).

history-making individuals model An interpretation of world politics that sees foreign policy decisions that affect the course of history as products of strong-willed leaders acting on their personal convictions (**Chapter 3**).

horizontal nuclear proliferation An increase in the number of states that possess nuclear weapons (**Chapter 8**).

Human Development Index (HDI) An index that uses life expectancy, literacy, average number of years of schooling, and income to assess a country's performance in providing for its people's welfare and security (**Chapter 13**).

human needs Those basic physical, social, and political needs, such as food and freedom, that are required for survival and security (**Chapter 13**).

human rights The political rights and civil liberties recognized by the international community as inalienable and valid for individuals in all countries by virtue of their humanity (**Chapter 13**).

human security A measure popular in liberal theory of the degree to which the welfare of individuals is protected and promoted, in contrast to realist theory's emphasis on putting the state's interests in military and national security ahead of all other goals (**Chapter 8**).

humanitarian intervention The use of peacekeeping troops by foreign states or international organizations to protect endangered people from gross violations of their human rights and from mass murder (**Chapter 13**).

I

identity politics   The politics of focusing on specific interests and issues based on one's particular ethnic, racial, religious, cultural, sexual or social identity rather than the concerns and interests of a broader political group (**Chapter 7**).

ideology   A set of core philosophical principles that leaders and citizens collectively construct about politics, the interests of political actors, and the ways people ought to behave (**Chapter 4**).

illicit financial flows   Money that is either illegally earned, used or moved across borders (**Chapter 10**).

imperial overstretch   The historic tendency for past hegemons to sap their own strength through costly imperial pursuits and military spending that weaken their economies in relation to the economies of their rivals (**Chapter 4**).

imperialism   The policy of expanding state power through the conquest and/or military domination of foreign territory (**Chapter 2**).

import quotas   Numerical limits on the quantity of particular products that can be imported (**Chapter 11**).

import-substitution industrialization   A strategy for economic development that centers on providing investors at home with incentives to produce goods so demand for previously imported products from abroad will decline (**Chapter 5**).

indigenous peoples   The native ethnic and cultural inhabitant populations within countries. (**Chapter 5**).

individual level of analysis   An analytical approach that emphasizes the psychological and perceptual variables motivating people, such as those who make foreign policy decisions on behalf of states and other global actors (**Chapter 1**).

individualistic fallacy   The logical error of assuming that an individual leader, who has legal authority to govern, represents the people and opinions of the population governed, so that all citizens are necessarily accountable for the vices and virtues (to be given blame or credit) of the leaders authorized to speak for them (**Chapter 7**).

Inequality-adjusted Human Development Index (IHDI)   To further assess human welfare, this index accounts for the effect of the inequality in the distribution of health, education, and income upon human development within a society (**Chapter 13**).

infant industry   Newly established industries ("infants") that are not yet strong enough to compete against mature foreign producers in the global marketplace until in time they develop and can then compete (**Chapter 11**).

information age   The era in which the rapid creation and global transfer of information through mass communication contributes to the globalization of knowledge (**Chapter 7**).

information and communications technology (ICT)   The technological means through which information and communications are transferred (**Chapter 5**).

information technology (IT)   The techniques for storing, retrieving, and disseminating recorded data and research knowledge through computerization and the Internet (**Chapter 5**).

information warfare   Attacks on an adversary's telecommunications and computer networks to degrade the technological systems vital to its defense and economic well-being (**Chapter 7**).

intergovernmental organizations (IGOs)   Institutions created and joined by states' governments, which give them authority to make collective decisions to manage particular problems on the global agenda (**Chapter 1**).

Intermediate-Range Nuclear Forces (INF) Treaty   The U.S.–Russian agreement to eliminate an entire class of nuclear weapons by removing all intermediate and short-range ground-based missiles and launchers with ranges between 300 and 3500 miles from Europe (**Chapter 9**).

internally displaced persons (IDPs)   People who have been forced to flee their homes, but remain within their country of origin (**Chapter 12**).

International Court of Justice (ICJ)   The primary court established by the United Nations for resolving legal disputes between states and providing advisory opinions to international agencies and the UN General Assembly (**Chapter 9**).

International Criminal Court (ICC)   A court established by the United Nations for indicting and administering justice to people committing war crimes (**Chapter 9**).

international criminal tribunals   Special tribunals established by the UN to prosecute those responsible for wartime atrocities and genocide, bring justice to victims, and deter such crimes in the future (**Chapter 9**).

international liquidity   Reserve assets used to settle international accounts (**Chapter 10**).

international monetary system   The financial procedures used to calculate the value of currencies and credits when capital is transferred across borders through trade, investment, foreign aid, and loans (**Chapter 10**).

international regime   Embodies the norms, principles, rules, and institutions around which global expectations unite regarding a specific international problem (**Chapter 2**).

Internet of Things (IoT)   The networked connectivity of objects or devices that have unique identifiers and the ability to transfer data without requiring human interaction (**Chapter 12**).

interspecific aggression   Killing others who are not members of one's own species (**Chapter 7**).

intra-firm trade   Cross-national trade of intermediate goods and services within the same firm (**Chapter 11**).

intraspecific aggression   Killing members of one's own species (**Chapter 7**).

irredentism   A movement by an ethnic national group to recover control of lost territory by force so that the new state boundaries will no longer divide the group (**Chapter 4**).

isolationism   A policy of withdrawing from active participation with other actors in world affairs and instead concentrating state efforts on managing internal affairs (**Chapter 4**).

J

jus ad bellum   A component of just war doctrine that establishes criteria under which a just war may be initiated (**Chapter 9**).

jus in bello   A component of just war doctrine that sets limits on the acceptable use of force (**Chapter 9**).

just war doctrine   The moral criteria identifying when a just war may be undertaken and how it should be fought once it begins (**Chapter 9**).

K

Kellogg-Briand Pact   A multilateral treaty negotiated in 1928 that outlawed war as a method for settling interstate conflicts (**Chapter 2**).

L

laissez-faire economics   The philosophical principle of free markets and free trade to give people free choices with little governmental regulation (**Chapter 5**).

least developed countries (LDCs)   The most impoverished countries of the Global South (**Chapter 5**).

levels of analysis   The different aspects of and agents in international affairs that may be stressed in interpreting and explaining global phenomena, depending on whether the analyst chooses to focus on "wholes" (the complete global system and large collectivities) or on "parts" (individual states or people) (**Chapter 1**).

Liberal International Economic Order (LIEO)   The set of regimes created after World War II designed to promote monetary stability and reduce barriers to the free flow of trade and capital (**Chapter 10**).

liberalism   A paradigm predicated on the hope that the application of reason and universal ethics to international relations can lead to a more orderly, just, and cooperative world; liberalism assumes that anarchy and war can be policed by institutional reforms that empower international organization and law (**Chapter 2**).

linkage strategy   A set of assertions claiming that leaders should take into account another country's overall behavior when deciding whether to reach agreement on any one specific issue so as to link cooperation to rewards (**Chapter 4**).

long-cycle theory   A theory that focuses on the rise and fall of the leading global power as the central political process of the modern world system (**Chapter 4**).

long peace   Long-lasting periods of peace between any of the militarily strongest great powers (**Chapter 7**).

M

Marxism   A theoretical critique of the capitalist status quo that views the ruling class as benefiting unfairly through the exploitation of the subordinate working class (**Chapter 2**).

massive retaliation   The Eisenhower administration's policy doctrine for containing Soviet communism by pledging to respond to any act of aggression with the most destructive capabilities available, including nuclear weapons (**Chapter 8**).

mediation   A conflict-resolution procedure in which a third party proposes a nonbinding solution to the disputants (**Chapter 7**).

megacities   Metropolitan areas where the population is more than 10 million people (**Chapter 12**).

mercantilism   Political economic perspective that views international trade in zero-sum terms and calls for active state intervention into domestic economies (**Chapter 5**).

middle powers   See emerging powers (**Chapter 5**).

militant religious movements   Politically active organizations based on strong religious convictions, whose members are fanatically devoted to the global promotion of their religious beliefs (**Chapter 6**).

military necessity   The legal principle that violation of the rules of warfare may be excused for defensive purposes during periods of extreme emergency (**Chapter 9**).

mirror images   The tendency of states and people in competitive interaction to perceive each other similarly—to see others the same hostile way others see them (**Chapter 1**).

modernization   A view of development popular in the Global North's liberal democracies that wealth is created through efficient production, free enterprise, and free trade, and that countries' relative wealth depends on technological innovation and education more than on natural endowments such as climate and resources (**Chapter 5**).

monetary policy   The decisions made by states' central banks to change the country's money supply to manage the national economy and control inflation, such as changing the amount of money in circulation and raising or lowering interest rates (**Chapter 10**).

money laundering   Financial and legal processing designed to hide the criminal origins of money (**Chapter 10**).

money supply   The total amount of currency in circulation, calculated to include demand deposits, such as checking accounts in commercial banks, and time deposits, such as savings accounts and bonds (**Chapter 10**).

morals   Principles clarifying the difference between good and evil and the situations in which they are opposed (**Chapter 9**).

most-favored-nation (MFN) principle   WTO rule requiring any advantage given by one WTO member also be extended to all other WTO members (**Chapter 11**).

multilateral agreements   Cooperative compacts among many states to ensure that a concerted policy is implemented toward alleviating a common problem, such as levels of future weapons capabilities (**Chapter 9**).

multilateralism   Cooperative approaches to managing shared problems through collective and coordinated action (**Chapter 4**).

multinational corporations (MNCs)   Business enterprises headquartered in one state that invest and operate extensively in many other states (**Chapter 5**).

multiple independently targetable reentry vehicles (MIRVs)   A technological innovation permitting many weapons to be delivered from a single missile (**Chapter 8**).

multiplex   A global system in which there are multiple consequential actors connected through complex interdependence, but no single power or idea has hegemonic domination (**Chapter 4**).

multipolarity   The distribution of global power into three or more great power centers, with most other states allied with one of the rivals (**Chapter 4**).

murky protectionism   Nontariff barriers to trade that may be "hidden" in government policies not directly related to trade, such as environmental initiatives and government spending (**Chapter 11**).

mutual assured destruction (MAD)   A condition of mutual deterrence in which both sides possess the ability to survive a first strike with weapons of mass destruction and launch a devastating retaliatory attack (**Chapter 8**).

N

nation   A collectivity whose people see themselves as members of the same group because they share the same ethnicity, culture, or language (**Chapter 1**).

national character   The collective characteristics ascribed to the people within a state (**Chapter 7**).

national interest   The goals that states pursue to maximize what they perceive to be selfishly best for their country (**Chapter 2**).

national security   A country's psychological freedom from fears that the state will be unable to resist threats to its survival and national values emanating from abroad or at home (**Chapter 8**).

nationalism   A mind-set glorifying a particular state and the nationality group living in it, which sees the state's interest as a supreme value (**Chapter 4**).

nature versus nurture   The controversy over whether human behavior is determined more by the biological basis of "human nature" than it is nurtured by the environmental conditions that humans experience (**Chapter 7**).

near-sourcing   Locating production or services closer to where the goods or services are sold, in order to increase efficiency (**Chapter 11**).

negotiation   Diplomatic dialogue and discussion between two or more parties with the goal of resolving through give-and-take bargaining perceived differences of interests and the conflicts they cause (**Chapter 9**).

neoclassical realism   A variant of realist theory that explains state behavior in terms of the constraints of binding systemic-level structure and the influence of domestic politics and perceptions of state policymakers (**Chapter 2**).

neoconservative   A political movement in the United States calling for the use of military and economic power in foreign policy to bring freedom and democracy to other countries (**Chapter 2**).

neoliberalism   The "new" liberal theoretical perspective that accounts for the way international institutions promote global change, cooperation, peace, and prosperity through collective programs for reforms (**Chapter 2**).

neo-Malthusians   Pessimists who warn of the global ecopolitical dangers of uncontrolled population growth (**Chapter 14**).

neorealism   A theoretical account of states' behavior that explains it as determined by differences in their relative power within the global hierarchy, defined primarily by the distribution of military power, instead of by other factors such as their values, types of government, or domestic circumstances (**Chapter 2**).

neutrality   The legal doctrine that provides rights for states to remain nonaligned with adversaries waging war against each other (**Chapter 9**).

New International Economic Order (NIEO)   The 1974 policy resolution in the United Nations that called for a North–South dialogue to open the way for the less developed countries of the Global South to participate more fully in making international economic policy (**Chapter 5**).

newly industrialized countries (NICs)   The most prosperous members of the Global South, which have become important exporters of manufactured goods as well as important markets for the major industrialized countries that export capital goods (**Chapter 5**).

nondiscrimination   Principle that goods produced by all member states should receive equal treatment, as embodied in the ideas of most-favored nation (MFN) and national treatment (**Chapter 11**).

nongovernmental organizations (NGOs)   Transnational organizations of private citizens maintaining consultative status with the United Nations; they include professional associations, foundations, multinational corporations, or simply internationally active groups in different states joined together to work toward common interests (**Chapter 1**).

nonintervention norm   A fundamental international legal principle, now being challenged, that traditionally has defined interference by one state in the domestic affairs of another as illegal (**Chapter 8**).

nonlethal weapons (NLWs)   The wide array of "soft kill," low-intensity methods of incapacitating an enemy's people, vehicles, communications systems, or entire cities without killing either combatants or noncombatants (**Chapter 8**).

nonproliferation regime   Rules to contain arms races so that weapons or technology do not spread to states that do not have them (**Chapter 8**).

nonstate nations   National or ethnic groups struggling to obtain power and/or statehood (**Chapter 6**).

nontariff barriers (NTBs)   Measures other than tariffs that discriminate against imports (**Chapter 11**).

norms   Generalized standards of behavior that, once accepted, shape collective expectations about appropriate conduct (**Chapter 2**).

North Atlantic Treaty Organization (NATO)   A military alliance created in 1949 to deter a Soviet attack on Western Europe that since has expanded and redefined its mission to emphasize not only the maintenance of peace but also the promotion of democracy (**Chapter 8**).

Nth country problem   The expansion of additional new nuclear weapon states (**Chapter 8**).

Nuclear Nonproliferation Treaty (NPT)   An international agreement that seeks to prevent horizontal proliferation by prohibiting further nuclear weapons sales, acquisitions, or production (**Chapter 8**).

nuclear winter   The expected freeze that would occur in the Earth's climate from the fallout of smoke and dust in the event nuclear weapons were used, blocking out sunlight and destroying the plant and animal life that survived the original blast (**Chapter 8**).

offensive realism   A variant of realist theory that stresses that, in an anarchical international system, states should always look for opportunities to gain more power (**Chapter 2**).

official development assistance (ODA)   Grants or loans to countries from donor countries, now usually channeled through multilateral aid institutions such as the World Bank, for the primary purpose of promoting economic development and welfare (**Chapter 5**).

opportunity costs   The sacrifices that sometimes result when the decision to select one option means that the opportunity to realize gains from other options is lost (**Chapter 8**).

orderly market arrangements (OMAs)   Voluntary export restrictions through government-to-government agreements to follow specific trading rules (**Chapter 11**).

outsourcing   The transfer of jobs by a corporation usually headquartered in a Global North country to a Global South country able to supply trained workers at lower wages (**Chapter 11**).

P

pacifism   The liberal idealist school of ethical thought that recognizes no conditions that justify the taking of another human's life, even when authorized by a head of state (**Chapter 7**).

paradigm   Derived from the Greek paradeigma, meaning an example, a model, or an essential pattern; a paradigm structures thought about an area of inquiry (**Chapter 2**).

peace building   Post-conflict actions, predominantly diplomatic and economic, that strengthen and rebuild governmental infrastructure and institutions in order to avoid renewed recourse to armed conflict (**Chapter 9**).

peace enforcement   The application of military force to warring parties, or the threat of its use, normally pursuant to international authorization, to compel compliance with resolutions or with sanctions designed to maintain or restore peace and order (**Chapter 9**).

peace operations   A general category encompassing both peacekeeping and peace enforcement operations undertaken to establish and maintain peace between disputants (**Chapter 9**).

peaceful coexistence   Soviet leader Nikita Khrushchev's 1956 doctrine that war between capitalist and communist states is not inevitable and that inter-bloc competition could be peaceful (**Chapter 4**).

peacekeeping   The efforts by third parties such as the United Nations to intervene in civil wars and/or interstate wars or to prevent hostilities between potential belligerents from escalating, so

that by acting as a buffer a negotiated settlement of the dispute can be reached (**Chapter 9**).

peacemaking   The process of diplomacy, mediation, negotiation, or other forms of peaceful settlement that arranges an end to a dispute and resolves the issues that led to conflict (**Chapter 9**).

plurilateral agreement   Treaties between a subset of WTO members that apply only to a specific issue (**Chapter 11**).

polarity   The degree to which military and economic capabilities are concentrated in the global system that determines the number of centers of power, or "poles" (**Chapter 3**).

polarization   The formation of competing coalitions or blocs composed of allies that align with one of the major competing poles, or centers, of power (**Chapter 3**).

policy agenda   The changing list of problems or issues to which governments pay special attention at any given moment (**Chapter 3**).

policy networks   Leaders and organized interests (such as lobbies) that form temporary alliances to influence a particular foreign policy decision (**Chapter 3**).

poliheuristic theory   A decision-making theory that accounts for process and outcome of decisions through a two-stage analytic model that incorporates cognitive approaches with rational choice expectations (**Chapter 3**).

political economy   A field of study that focuses on the intersection of politics and economics in international relations (**Chapter 4**).

political efficacy   The extent to which policy makers' self-confidence instills in them the belief that they can effectively make rational choices (**Chapter 3**).

political integration   The processes and activities by which the populations of many or all states transfer their loyalties to a merged political and economic unit (**Chapter 6**).

politics of scarcity   The view that the unavailability of resources required to sustain life, such as food, energy, or water, can undermine security in degrees similar to military aggression (**Chapter 14**).

pooled sovereignty   Legal authority granted to an IGO by its members to make collective decisions regarding specified aspects of public policy heretofore made exclusively by each sovereign government (**Chapter 6**).

population density   The number of people within each country, region, or city, measuring the geographical concentration of the population as a ratio of the average space available for each resident (**Chapter 12**).

population implosion   A rapid reduction of population that reverses a previous trend toward progressively larger populations; a severe reduction in the world's population (**Chapter 12**).

positivist legal theory   A theory that stresses states' customs and habitual ways of behaving as the most important source of law (**Chapter 9**).

postmodern terrorism   Terrorism practiced by an expanding set of diverse actors with new weapons "to sow panic in a society to weaken or even overthrow the incumbents and to bring about political change" (**Chapter 7**).

power   The factors that enable one actor to change another actor's behavior against its preferences (**Chapter 1**).

power potential   The capabilities or resources held by a state that are considered necessary to its asserting influence over others (**Chapter 8**).

power transition theory   The theory that war is likely when a dominant great power is threatened by the rapid growth of a rival's capabilities, which reduces the difference in their relative power (**Chapter 7**).

preemptive warfare   A quick first-strike attack that seeks to defeat an adversary before it can organize an initial attack or a retaliatory response (**Chapter 8**).

preventive diplomacy   Diplomatic actions taken in advance of a predictable crisis to prevent or limit violence (**Chapter 9**).

preventive warfare   Strictly outlawed by international law, a war undertaken by choice against an enemy to prevent it from suspected intentions to attack sometime in the distant future—if and when the enemy might acquire the necessary military capabilities (**Chapter 8**).

private military services   The outsourcing of activities of a military-specific nature to private companies, such as armed security, equipment maintenance, IT services, logistics, and intelligence services (**Chapter 8**).

proliferation   The spread of weapon capabilities from a few to many states in a chain reaction, so that an increasing number of states gain the ability to launch an attack on other states with devastating (e.g., nuclear) weapons (**Chapter 8**).

prospect theory   A social psychological theory explaining decision making under conditions of uncertainty and risk that looks at the relationship between individual risk propensity and the perceived prospects for avoiding losses and realizing big gains (**Chapter 3**).

protectionism   Barriers of foreign trade, such as tariffs and quotas, which protect local industries from competition for the purchase of products local manufacturers produce (**Chapter 11**).

public good   Collective goods, such as clean air or sunlight, whose use is nonexclusive and nonrival in nature; thus, if anyone can use the good, it is available to all (**Chapter 11**).

purchasing power parity (PPP)   An index that calculates the true rate of exchange among currencies when parity—when what can be purchased is the same—is achieved; the index determines what can be bought with a unit of each currency (**Chapter 4**).

R

rapprochement   In diplomacy, a policy seeking to reestablish normal cordial relations between enemies (**Chapter 4**).

rational choice   Decision-making procedures guided by careful definition of situations, weighing of goals, consideration of all alternatives, and selection of the options most likely to achieve the highest goals (**Chapter 3**).

realism   A paradigm based on the premise that world politics is essentially and unchangeably a struggle among self-interested states for power and position under anarchy, with each competing state pursuing its own national interests (**Chapter 2**).

realpolitik   The theoretical outlook prescribing that countries should increase their power and wealth in order to compete with and dominate other countries (**Chapter 5**).

reciprocity   Mutual or reciprocal lowering of trade barriers (**Chapter 11**).

refugees   People who flee for safety to another country because of a well-founded fear of political persecution, environmental degradation, or famine (**Chapter 12**).

regimes   Norms, rules, and procedures for interaction within a given issue or issue area agreed to by a set of states (**Chapter 6**).

regional trade agreements (RTAs)   Treaties that integrate the economies of members through the reduction of trade barriers (**Chapter 11**).

relative burden of military spending   Measure of the economic burden of military activities calculated by the share of each state's gross domestic product allocated to military expenditures (**Chapter 8**).

relative deprivation   Inequality between the wealth and status of individuals and groups, and the outrage of those at the bottom about their perceived exploitation by those at the top (**Chapter 7**).

relative gains   Conditions in which some participants in cooperative interactions benefit more than others (**Chapter 2**).

remittances   The money earned by immigrants working in rich countries (which almost always exceeds the income they could earn working in their home country) that they send to their families in their country (**Chapter 5**).

replacement-level fertility   One couple replacing themselves on average with two children so that a country's population will remain stable if this rate prevails (**Chapter 12**).

reserve currency   Currency held in large amounts by governments for the purpose of settling international debts and supporting the value of their national currency (**Chapter 10**).

responsibility to protect   Unanimously adopted in a resolution by the UN General Assembly in 2005, this principle holds that the international community must help protect populations from war crimes, ethnic cleansing, genocide, and crimes against humanity (**Chapter 2**).

responsible sovereignty   A principle that requires states to protect not only their own people but to cooperate across borders to protect global resources and address transnational threats (**Chapter 6**).

revolution in military technology (RMT)   The sophisticated new weapons technologies that make fighting war without mass armies possible (**Chapter 8**).

roles   The constraints written into law or custom that predispose decision makers in a particular governmental position to act in a manner and style that is consistent with expectations about how the role is normally performed (**Chapter 3**).

S

sanctuary   A place of refuge and protection (**Chapter 12**).

schematic reasoning   The process of reasoning by which new information is interpreted according to a memory structure, a schema, which contains a network of generic scripts, metaphors, and simplified characterizations of observed objects and phenomena (**Chapter 1**).

second-strike capability   A state's capacity to retaliate after absorbing an adversary's first-strike attack with weapons of mass destruction (**Chapter 8**).

security community   A group of states whose high level of institutionalized or customary collaboration results in the settlement of disputes by means other than military force (**Chapter 6**).

security dilemma   The tendency of states to view the defensive arming of adversaries as threatening, causing them to arm in response, so that all states' security declines (**Chapter 2**).

selective engagement   A great power grand strategy using economic and military power to influence only important particular situations, countries, or global issues by striking a balance between a highly interventionist "global policeman" and an uninvolved isolationist (**Chapter 4**).

self-determination   The liberal doctrine that people should be able to determine the government that will rule them (**Chapter 5**).

self-help   The principle that because in international anarchy all global actors are independent, they must rely on themselves to provide for their security and well-being (**Chapter 2**).

shadow banks   Financial entities outside of the formal banking structure that engage in lending and credit-issuing activities (**Chapter 10**).

small powers   Countries with limited political, military, or economic capabilities and influence (**Chapter 5**).

smart bombs Precision-guided military technology that enables a bomb to search for its target and detonate at the precise time it can do the most damage (**Chapter 8**).

social constructivism A variant of constructivism that emphasizes the role of social discourse in the development of ideas and identities (**Chapter 2**).

socialism Body of scholarship that emphasizes public ownership and control of property and resources (**Chapter 2**).

socialization The processes by which people learn to accept the beliefs, values, and behaviors that prevail in a given society's culture (**Chapter 7**).

soft power The capacity to co-opt through such intangible factors as the popularity of a state's values and institutions, as opposed to the "hard power" to coerce through military might (**Chapter 4**).

sovereign equality The principle that states are legally equal in protection under international law (**Chapter 9**).

speculative attacks Massive sales of a country's currency, caused by the anticipation of a future decline in its value (**Chapter 10**).

spiral model A metaphor used to describe the tendency of efforts to enhance defense to result in escalating arms races (**Chapter 9**).

standard operating procedures (SOPs) Rules for reaching decisions about particular types of situations (**Chapter 3**).

state An independent legal entity with a government exercising exclusive control over the territory and population it governs (**Chapter 1**).

state level of analysis An analytical approach that emphasizes how the internal attributes of states influence their foreign policy behaviors (**Chapter 1**).

state sovereignty A state's supreme authority to manage internal affairs and foreign relations (**Chapter 1**).

state-sponsored terrorism Formal assistance, training, and arming of foreign terrorists by a state in order to achieve foreign policy and/or domestic goals (**Chapter 7**).

state-owned enterprise A business directly owned or partially owned by the government (**Chapter 11**).

Strategic Arms Limitation Talks (SALT) Two sets of agreements reached during the 1970s between the United States and the Soviet Union that established limits on strategic nuclear delivery systems (**Chapter 9**).

Strategic Arms Reduction Treaty (START) The U.S.–Russian series of negotiations that began in 1993 and, with the 1997 START-III agreement by Russia in 2000, pledged to cut the nuclear arsenals of both sides by 80 percent of the Cold War peaks, in order to lower the risk of nuclear war (**Chapter 8**).

Strategic Offensive Reductions Treaty (SORT) The U.S.–Russian agreement to reduce the number of strategic warheads to between 1700 and 2200 for each country by 2012 (**Chapter 9**).

strategic trade policy Government subsidies for particular domestic industries to help them gain competitive advantages over foreign producers (**Chapter 11**).

structural realism See neorealism (**Chapter 2**).

structuralism The neorealist proposition that states' behavior is shaped primarily by changes in the properties of the global system, such as shifts in the balance of power, instead of by individual heads of states or by changes in states' internal characteristics (**Chapter 4**).

subsidies Government-directed financial support for a firm, usually intended to encourage increased exports and/or decreased imports (**Chapter 11**).

surplus value From a Marxist perspective, the difference between the value of the raw materials and the value of the final product as enhanced through workers' labor (**Chapter 2**).

survival of the attest A realist concept derived from Charles Darwin's theory of evolution advising that ruthless competition is ethically acceptable to survive, even if the actions violate moral commands not to kill (**Chapter 7**).

sustainable development Economic growth that does not deplete the resources needed to maintain life and prosperity (**Chapter 14**).

systemic level of analysis An analytical approach that emphasizes the impact of worldwide conditions on foreign policy behavior and human welfare (**Chapter 1**).

T

tariffs Tax assessed on goods as they are imported into a country (**Chapter 11**).

terrorism Premeditated violence perpetrated against noncombatant targets by sub national or transnational groups, or clandestine agents, usually intended to influence an audience (**Chapter 6**).

theocracy A country whose government is organized around a religious dogma (**Chapter 6**).

theory A set of hypotheses postulating the relationship between variables or conditions advanced to describe, explain, or predict phenomena and make prescriptions about how to pursue particular goals and follow ethical principles (**Chapter 2**).

tit-for-tat strategy A bargaining approach that consistently reciprocates in kind the offers or threats made by the other party in a negotiation, with equivalent rewards returned and equivalent punishing communications returned in retaliation (**Chapter 9**).

trade integration The difference between growth rates in trade and gross domestic product (**Chapter 11**).

tragedy of the commons A metaphor, widely used to explain the impact of human behavior on ecological systems, that explains how rational self-interested behavior by individuals may have a destructive and undesirable collective impact (**Chapter 14**).

transformation A change in the characteristic pattern of interaction among the most active participants in world politics of such magnitude that it appears that one "global system" has replaced another (**Chapter 1**).

transgenic crops New crops with improved characteristics created artificially through genetic engineering that combine genes from species that would not naturally interbreed (**Chapter 14**).

transnational relations Interactions across state boundaries that involve at least one actor that is not the agent of a government or intergovernmental organization (**Chapter 2**).

transnational religious movements A set of beliefs, practices, and ideas administered politically by religious organizations to promote the worship of their conception of a transcendent deity and its principles for conduct (**Chapter 6**).

transparency With regard to free trade, the principle that barriers to trade must be visible and thus easy to target (**Chapter 11**).

Truman Doctrine The declaration by President Harry S. Truman that U.S. foreign policy would use intervention to support peoples who allied with the United States against communist external subjugation (**Chapter 4**).

turbo-urbanization Refers to extremely rapid and unregulated urban growth (**Chapter 12**).

two-level games A concept referring to the growing need for national policy makers to make decisions that will meet both domestic and foreign goals (**Chapter 3**).

U

unilateralism An approach to foreign policy that relies on independent, self-help strategies in foreign policy (**Chapter 4**).

unipolarity A condition in which the global system has a single dominant power or hegemon (**Chapter 4**).

unitary actor A transnational actor (usually a sovereign state) assumed to be internally united, so that changes in its domestic opinion do not influence its foreign policy as much as do the decisions that actor's leaders make to cope with changes in its global environment (**Chapter 3**).

V

vertical nuclear proliferation The expansion of the capabilities of existing nuclear powers to inflict increasing destruction with their nuclear weapons (**Chapter 8**).

virtuality   Imagery created by computer technology of objects and phenomena that produces an imaginary picture of actual things, people, and experiences (**Chapter 12**).

voluntary export restrictions (VERs) A protectionist measure popular in the 1980s and early 1990s, in which exporting countries agree to restrict shipments of a particular product to a country to deter it from imposing an even more burdensome import quota (**Chapter 11**).

W

war   A condition arising within states (civil war) or between states (interstate war) when actors use violent means to destroy their opponents or coerce them into submission (**Chapter 7**).

war crimes   Acts performed during war that the international community defines as crimes against humanity, including atrocities committed against an enemy's prisoners of war, civilians, or the state's own minority population (**Chapter 9**).

world politics   The study of how global actors' activities entail the exercise of influence to achieve and defend their goals and ideals, and how it affects the world at large (**Chapter 1**).

world-system theory   A body of theory that treats the capitalistic world economy originating in the sixteenth century as an interconnected unit of analysis encompassing the entire globe, with an international division of labor and multiple political centers and cultures whose rules constrain and share the behavior of all transnational actors (**Chapter 2**).

X

xenophobia   Antipathy for members of a foreign nationality, ethnic, or linguistic group (**Chapter 12**).

Y

Yalta Conference   The 1945 summit meeting of the Allied victors to resolve postwar territorial issues and to establish voting procedures in the United Nations to collectively manage world order (**Chapter 4**).

youth bulge   A burgeoning youth population, thought to make countries more prone to civil conflicts (**Chapter 7**).

Z

zeitgeist   The "spirit of the times," or the dominant cultural norms assumed to influence the behavior of people living in particular periods (**Chapter 3**).

zero-sum   An exchange in a purely conflictual relationship in which what is gained by one competitor is lost by the other (**Chapter 2**).

References

Aaronson, Susan, and Rodwan Abouharb. (2011). "Unexpected Bedfellows: The GATT, the WTO and *Some* Democratic Rights." *International Studies Quarterly* 55 (2): 379–408.

Aaronson, Susan, and Jamie Zimmerman. (2007). *Trade Imbalance: The Struggle to Weigh Human Rights Concerns in Trade Policymaking*. Cambridge: Cambridge University Press.

Abbot, Sebastian. (2012). "Pakistan Tests Missile Days after India's Launch." *Associated Press* (April 25). news.yahoo.com/pakistan-tests-missile-days-indias-launch-074942245.html.

Abdelal, Rawi, and Adam Segal. (2007). "Has Globalization Passed Its Peak?" *Foreign Affairs* 86 (January/February): 103–114.

Abdi, Dekha Ibrahim, and Simon J. A. Mason. (2019). *Mediation and Governance in Fragile Contexts: Small Steps to Peace*. Retrieved from css.ethz.ch/en/think-tank/themes/mediation-support-and-peace-promotion/mediation-governance.html.

Abouharb, Rodwan, and David Cingranelli. (2007). *Human Rights and Structural Adjustment*. New York: Cambridge University Press.

Abramowitz, Morton. (2002). "The Bush Team Isn't Coping." *International Herald Tribune* (August 20): 6.

ACA (Arms Control Association). (2019). "U.S. Missile Defense Programs at a Glance." armscontrol.org/factsheets/usmissiledefense.

——— (2019). "Treaty on the Prohibition of Nuclear Weapons." *United Nations*. armscontrol.org/treaties/treaty-prohibition-nuclear-weapons.

——— (2019). "The Nuclear Testing Tally." armscontrol.org/factsheets/nucleartesttally.

Acemoglu, Daron, and James A. Robinson. (2012). *Why Nations Fail: The Origins of Power, Prosperity, and Poverty*. New York: Random House.

Acharya, Amitav. (2018). *Constructing Global Order: Agency and Change in World Politics*. Cambridge: Cambridge University Press.

——— (2017). "After Liberal Hegemony: The Advent of a Multiplex World Order." *Ethics and International Affairs (EIA)*. ethicsandinternationalaffairs.org/2017/multiplex-world-order/.

——— (2014). "Global International Relations and Regional Worlds." *International Studies Quarterly*, 58 (December): 647–659.

Ackerly, Brooke, and Jacqui True. (2008). "Reflexivity in Practice: Power and Ethics in Feminist Research on International Relations." *International Studies Review* 10: 693–707.

Adams, Gordon, and Matthew Leatherman. (2011). "A Leaner and Meaner Defense: How to Cut the Pentagon's Budget While Improving Its Performance." *Foreign Affairs* 90 (1): 139–152.

Adler, Emanuel. (2013). "Constructivism in International Relations: Sources, Contributions, and Debates." In *Handbook of International Relations*, edited by Walter Carlsnaes, Thomas Risse, and Beth A. Simmons. London, UK: Sage Publications Ltd.

AFP. (2012). "China Shuts Coke Plant after Chlorine Reports." *AFP* (April 29).

Aggarwal, Vinod, and Simon Evenett. (2013). "A Fragmented Global Economy: A Weakened WTO, Mega FTAs and Murky Protectionism." *Swiss Political Science Review* 19 (4): 550–557.

Aguilera, Jasmine. (2019). "'The Numbers Are Just Horrendous.' Almost 30,000 Species Face Extinction Because of Human Activity." *TIME* (July 18). time.com/5629548/almost-30000-species-face-extinction-new-report/.

Ahmed, Nafeez Mosaddeq. (2013). "Why Food Riots Are Likely to Become the New Normal." *The Guardian* (March 6). guardian.co.uk/environment/blog/2013/mar/06/food-riots-new-normal.

Alesina, Alberto, Carlo Favera, and Francesco Giavazzi. (2019). *Austerity: When It Works and When It Doesn't*. Princeton, New Jersey: Princeton University Press. Retrieved from press.princeton.edu/titles/13244.html.

Albert, Eleanor. (2019). "China-Taiwan Relations" *Council on Foreign Relations* (June 27). cfr.org/backgrounder/china-taiwan-relations.

——— (2017). "China in Africa." *Council on Foreign Affairs*. cfr.org/backgrounder/china-africa.

Albert, Eleanor, and Andrew Chatzky. (2018). "The Rohingya Crisis." *Council on Foreign Relations*. cfr.org/backgrounder/rohingya-crisis.

Albright, Madeleine, and Susana Malcorra. (2019). "This Year's G20 Summit Is a Major Test of International Cooperation in a Trying Time." *TIME*. time.com/5616978/g20-summit-osaka/.

Alden, Edward. (2018). "Trump, China, and Steel Tariffs: The Day the WTO Died." *Council on Foreign Relations*. cfr.org/blog/trump-china-and-steel-tariffs-day-wto-died.

Ali, Idrees. (2019). "North Korea Nuclear, Missile Activity 'Inconsistent' with Denuclearization: U.S. General." *Reuters*. reuters.com/article/us-usa-northkorea-military/north-korea-nuclear-missile-activity-inconsistent-with-denuclearization-us-general-idUSKCN1R81RJ.

Ali, Shimelse, Uri Dadush, and Rachel Esplin Odell. (2011). "Is Protectionism Dying?" *The Carnegie Papers* (May). Carnegie Endowment for International Peace. carnegieendowment.org/files/is_protectionism_dying.pdf.

Aljazeera. (2011). "Child Slaves." *Aljazeera*. aljazeera.com/programmes/slaverya21stcenturyevil/2011/10/20111010152040468529.html.

Allison, Graham T. (1971). *Essence of Decision: Explaining the Cuban Missile Crisis*. Boston: Little, Brown.

Allison, Graham T., and Philip Zelikow. (1999). *Essence of Decision: Explaining the Cuban Missile Crisis*, 2nd ed. New York: Longman.

Altman, Daniel. (2015). "You Don't Know Zhou." *Foreign Policy* (August 17). foreignpolicy.com/2015/08/17/you-dont-know-zhou-china-central-bank-renminbi-value/.

Altman, Roger. (2009). "Globalization in Retreat: Further Geopolitical Consequences of the Financial Crisis." *Foreign Affairs* 88 (4): 2–16.

Amadeo, Kimberly. (2019). "How the Yuan Could Become a Global Currency: China's Plan to Replace the U.S. Dollar." *The Balance*. thebalance.com/yuan-reserve-currency-to-global-currency-3970465.

——— (2019b). "Farm Subsidies with Pros, Cons, and Impact: How Farm Subsidies Affect You." *The Balance* (July 4). thebalance.com/farm-subsidies-4173885.

Amighini, A. A., R. Rabellotti, and M. Sanfilippo. (2013). "Do Chinese State-owned and Private Enterprises Differ in their Internationalization Strategies?" *China Economic Review* 27: 312–325.

Amnesty International. (2019). *Death Sentences and Executions 2018*. UK: Amnesty International. amnesty.org/download/Documents/ACT5098702019ENGLISH.PDF.

Amnesty International. (2017). "Was Shell Complicit in Murder?" amnesty.org/en/latest/news/2017/11/was-shell-complicit-in-murder/.

———— (2015). "Protect Children's Human Rights." amnestyusa.org/our-work/issues/children-s-rights/convention-on-the-rights-of-the-child.

———— (2009). "Children's Rights: The Future Starts Here." amnesty.org/en/library/info/ACT76/014/1999/en.

Anderlini, Sanam N. (2007). *Women Building Peace: What They Do, Why It Matters*. Boulder, CO: Lynne Rienner.

Anderson, Kym. (1996). "Social Policy Dimensions of Economic Integration: Environmental and Labour Standards." *NBER Working Paper No. 5702*. Cambridge, MA: National Bureau for Economic Research.

Anderson, Richard. (2015). "Nuclear Power: Energy for the Future or Relic of the Past?" *BBC* (February 27). bbc.com/news/business-30919045.

Andreas, P. (2011). "Illicit Globalization: Myths, Misconceptions, and Historical Lessons." *Political Science Quarterly* 126(3), 403–425.

Andreas, P., and Nadelmann, E. A. (2008). *"Policing the Globe: Criminalization and Crime Control in International Relations.* Oxford University Press.

Angell, Norman. (1910). *The Grand Illusion: A Study of the Relationship of Military Power in Nations to Their Economic and Social Advantage*. London: Weidenfeld & Nicholson.

Annan, Kofi. (2006). "Courage to Fulfill Our Responsibilities." In *World Politics 05/06*, edited by Helen E. Purkitt, 205–209. Dubuque, Iowa: McGraw-Hill/Dushkin.

———— (1999). "Two Concepts of Sovereignty." *Economist* (September 18): 49–50.

Appiah, Kwame Anthony. (2006). *Cosmopolitanism: Ethics in a World of Strangers*. New York: Norton.

Ariely, Dan. (2012). *The (Honest) Truth About Dishonesty: How We Lie to Everyone—Especially Ourselves*. New York: Harper.

———— (2008). *Predictably Irrational: The Hidden Forces That Shape Our Decisions*. New York: Harper.

Art, Robert J. (2005). "Coercive Diplomacy." In *International Politics*, 7th ed., edited by Robert J. Art and Robert Jervis. New York: Pearson Longman.

Asal, V., B. Nussbaum, and D.W. Harrington. (2007). "Terrorism as Transnational Advocacy: An Organizational and Tactical Examination." *Studies in Conflict & Terrorism* 30(1): 15–39.

ASEAN. (2018). *ASEAN Statistical Highlights 2018*. aseanstats.org/wp-content/uploads/2018/10/ASEAN-Statistical-Highlights-2018.pdf.

Astrasheuskaya, Nastassia, and Henry Foy. (2019). "Polar powers: Russia's bid for supremacy in the Arctic Ocean." *Financial Times*. ft.com/content/2fa82760-5c4a-11e9-939a-341f5ada9d40.

Auboin, Marc. (2009). "Restoring Trade Finance: What the G-20 Can Do." In *The Collapse of Global Trade, Murky Protectionism, and the Crisis: Recommendations for the G20*, edited by Richard Baldwin and Simon Evenett. London: VoxEU.org. voxeu.org/content/collapse-global-trade-murky-protectionism-and-crisis-recommendations-g20.

Avlon, John. (2011). "The 21st-Century Statesman." *Newsweek*. thedailybeast.com/newsweek/2011/02/20/a-21st-century-statesman.html.

Axelrod, Robert M. (1984). *The Evolution of Cooperation*. New York: Basic Books.

Aydin, Aysegul. (2010). "The Deterrent Effects of Economic Integration." *Journal of Peace Research* 47 (5): 523–533.

Aydin, Aysegul, and Patrick M. Regan. (2012). "Networks of Third-Party Interveners and Civil War Duration." *European Journal of International Relations* 18 (3): 573–597.

Azevêdo, Roberto. (2019). "Global Trade Growth Loses Momentum as Trade Tensions Persist." *World Trade Organization* (April 2). wto.org/english/news_e/pres19_e/pr837_e.htm.

Babcock, Linda, and Sara Laschever. (2003). *Women Don't Ask: Negotiation and the Gender Divide*. Princeton: Princeton University Press.

Bacchus, James. (2012). "A Way Forward for the WTO." In *The Future and the WTO: Confronting the Challenges*, edited by Ricardo Meléndez-Ortiz, Chistophe Bellmann, and Miguel Rodriguez Mendoza, 6–9. Geneva, Switzerland: International Centre for Trade and Sustainable Development.

Badwal, Karun. (2012). "Deforestation: A Major Threat to the Destruction of Our Planet." *Earth Reform* (April 21). earthreform.org/deforestation-a-major-threat-to-the-destruction-of-our-planet/.

Baker, Aryn, and Loi Kolay. (2009). "The Longest War." *Time* (April 20): 25–29.

Baker, Peter, and Dan Bilefsky. (2010). "Russia and U.S. Sign Nuclear Arms Reduction Act." *New York Times* (April 8): A8.

Baker, Scott, Nicholas Bloom, and Steven Davis. (2019). *Economic Policy Uncertainty Index*. policyuncertainty.com/index.html (accessed June 20, 2019).

Baldwin, David A. (1999/2000). "The Sanctions Debate and the Logic of Choice." *International Security* 24 (Winter): 80–107.

Baldwin, Richard, and Simon Evenett. (2009). "Introduction and Recommendations for the G-20." In *The Collapse of Global Trade, Murky Protectionism, and the Crisis: Recommendations for the G20*, edited by Richard Baldwin and Simon Evenett. London: VoxEU.org. voxeu.org/content/collapse-global-trade-murky-protectionism-and-crisis-recommendations-g20.

Baldwin, Richard, Masahiro Kawai, and Ganeshan Wignaraja (eds.). (2013). *The Future of the World Trading System: Asian Perspectives*. London: Centre for Economic Policy Research.

Balmer, Crispian. (2019). "Despite Falling Numbers, Immigration Remains Divisive EU Issue." *Reuters*. reuters.com/article/us-eu-election-migrants/despite-falling-numbers-immigration-remains-divisive-eu-issue-idUSKCN1SK1GD.

Ban, Ki-moon. (2010). "Secretary-General's Message to Second International Conference on Climate, Sustainability and Development in Semi-Arid Regions on the Launch of the UN Decade for Deserts and the Fight against Desertification." *United Nations* (August 16). un.org/sg/STATEMENTS/index.asp?nid=4727.

Banerjee, Abhijit, and Esther Duflo. (2011). "More Than 1 Billion People Are Hungry in the Word: But What If the Experts Are Wrong?" *Foreign Policy* (May/June): 66–72.

Bank for International Settlements (BIS). (2018). "OTC Derivatives Statistics at End-June 2018." bis.org/publ/otc_hy1810.htm.

———— (2016). *Tricentenical Central Bank Survey*. bis.org/publ/rpfx16.htm.

———— (2015). *Debt Securities Statistics*. bis.org/statistics/secstats.htm.

Bapat, Navin A. (2011). "Transnational Terrorism, US Military Aid, and the Incentive to Misrepresent." *Journal of Peace Research* 48 (3): 202–218.

Bapat, Navin A., Tobias Heinrich, Yoshiharu Kobayashi, and T. Clifton Morgan. (1995). *Jihad vs. McWorld*. New York: Random House.

Barber, Benjamin R. (1995). *Jihad vs McWorld*. New York: Random House.

Barkin, Samuel. (2003). "Realist Constructivism." *International Studies Review* 5 (September): 328–342.

Barnet, Richard J. (1977). *The Giants: Russia and America*. New York: Simon & Schuster.

Barnett, Michael. (2005). "Social Constructivism." In *The Globalization of World Politics*, 3rd ed., edited by John Baylis and Steve Smith, 251–270. New York: Oxford University Press.

Barratt, Bethany. (2007). *Human Rights and Foreign Aid: For Love or Money?* New York: Routledge.

Barringer, Felicity. (2009). "Cool Roofs Offer a Tool in Fight against Global Heat." *International Herald Tribune* (July 29): 1.

Barry, C. M., K. Chad Clay, and M. E. Flynn. (2013). "Avoiding the Spotlight: Human Rights Shaming and Foreign Direct Investment." *International Studies Quarterly* 57(3), 532–544.

——— (2012). "Avoiding the Spotlight: Human Rights Shaming and Foreign Direct Investment." *International Studies Quarterly*. DOI: 10.1111/isqu.12039.

Basham, Kevin. (2016). "Corporate Social Responsibility: Three Ps." *A Medium Corporation*. medium.com/@KevinBasham/corporate-social-responsibility-three-ps-ec8753027ad7.

Basulto, Dominic. (2012). "The Internet, IPv6 and a World of Abundance." *The Big Think*. bigthink.com/endless-innovation/the-internet-ipv6-and-a-world-of-abundance.

Bates, B. C., Z. W. Kundzewicz, S. Wu, and J. P. Palutikof. (eds.). (2008). *Climate Change and Water*. Technical Paper of the Intergovernmental Panel on Climate Change, IPCC Secretariat, Geneva.

Batmanghelidj, Esfandyar. (2018). "Tougher U.S. Sanctions Will Enrich Iran's Revolutionary Guards." *Foreign Policy*. foreignpolicy.com/2018/10/04/irans-revolutionary-guard-corps-wont-suffer-from-stronger-u-s-sanctions-theyll-benefit-irgc-trump-sanctions/.

Battelle and R&D Magazine. (2019). "2019 Global R & D Funding Forecast." Battelle and *R & D Magazine*. digital.rdmag.com/researchanddevelopment/2019_global_r_d_funding_forecast?pg=1#pg1.

——— (2013). "2014 Global R & D Funding Forecast." Battelle and *R & D Magazine*. battelle.org/docs/tpp/2014_global_rd_funding_forecast.pdf.

BBC. (2019). "Schengen: Controversial EU Free Movement Deal Explained." bbc.com/news/world-europe-13194723.

——— (2019b). "Amazon Deforestation: Brazil's Bolsonaro Dismisses Data as 'Lies'." bbc.com/news/world-latin-america-49052360.

——— (2018). "Migration to Europe in Charts." bbc.com/news/world-europe-44660699.

——— (2013). "Who, What, Why: Why Do Criminals Smuggle Garlic?" (12 January). Available at: bbc.com/news/magazine-20976887.

——— (2013). "What Is Fracking and Why Is It Controversial?" bbc.com/news/uk-14432401.

BEA (Bureau of Economic Analysis). (2019). "U.S. International Trade in Goods and Services, April 2019." bea.gov/news/2019/us-international-trade-goods-and-services-april-2019.

Beardsley, Kyle. (2011). jstor.org/stable/10.1017/s0022381611000764?seq=1#metadata_info_tab_contents.

Beardsley, Kyle, and Kristian Skrede Gleditsch. (2015). "Peacekeeping as Conflict Containment." *International Studies Review* 17 (March): 67–89.

Beattie, Alan. (2011). "Watchdog Says IMF Missed Crisis Risks."*Financial Times* (February 9). ft.com/intl/cms/s/0/59421568-344e-11e0-993f-00144feabdc0.html#axzz1V7p2MKKP.

Bechtol, Bruce E. (2018). "North Korean Illicit Activities and Sanctions: A National Security Dilemma." *Cornell Law School*. lawschool.cornell.edu/research/ILJ/upload/Bechtol-final.pdf.

Becker, Elizabeth. (2003). "WTO. Rules against U.S. on Steel Tariff." *New York Times* (March 27).

Begley, Sharon. (2011a). "I Can't Think!: The Twitterization of Our Culture Has Revolutionized Our Lives, but with an Unintended Consequence—Our Overloaded Brains Freeze When We Have to Make Decisions." *Newsweek* (March 7): 28–33.

Begley, Shannon. (2011b). "The Reality of Global Climate Change Is Upon Us." *Newsweek*. newsweek.com/reality-global-climate-change-upon-us-67757.

——— (2009). "Climate-Change Calculus: Why It's Even Sores than We Feared." *Newsweek* (August 3): 30.

——— (2008). "Global Warming Is a Cause of This Year's Extreme Weather." *Newsweek* (July 7/14): 53.

——— (2007). "Get Out Your Handkerchiefs." *Newsweek* (June 4): 62.

Behsudi, Adam. (2018). "What the U.S. and China Want from Trade Talks." *Politico*. politico.com/story/2018/11/27/us-china-trade-talks-990766.

Beitz, Charles R. (2009). *The Idea of Human Rights*. New York: Oxford University Press.

——— (2001). "Human Rights as a Common Concern." *American Political Science Review* 95 (June): 269–282.

Benson, Michelle. (2007). "Extending the Bounds of Power Transition Theory." *International Interactions* 33 (July/September): 211–215.

Bergesen, Albert, and Ronald Schoenberg. (1980). "Long Waves of Colonial Expansion and Contraction, 1415–1969." In *Studies of the Modern World-System*, edited by Albert Bergesen. New York: Academic Press.

Bergholt, Drago, and Paivi Lujala. (2012). "Climate-Related Natural Disasters, Economic Growth, and Armed Civil Conflict." *Journal of Peace Research* (49): 147–162.

Berliner, Daniel, and Aseem Prakash. (2014). "Bluewashing" the Firm? Voluntary Regulations, Program Design, and Member Compliance with the United Nations Global Compact" *Policy Studies Journal*. 43(1). doi.org/10.1111/psj.12085.

Bernier, A., J. Schlandt, and K. Wu. (2018). "Literature Review: WTO Accession and Economic Growth. " USAID Economic Analysis and Data Services.

Beyer, Peter. (2013). *Religion in the Context of Globalization: Essays on Concept, Form, and Political Implication*. New York: Routledge.

Bhagwati, Jagdish. (2008a). *Termites in the Trading System: How Preferential Agreements Undermine Free Trade*. New York: Oxford University Press.

——— (2008b). *In Defense of Globalization*. New York: Oxford University Press.

——— (2004). *In Defense of Globalization*. New York: Oxford University Press.

Bianchi, Daniel. (2019). "Five Reasons Bitcoin Could Enter a More Extreme Death Spiral." *The Conversation* (Jan 2). theconversation.com/five-reasons-bitcoin-could-enter-a-more-extreme-death-spiral-108766 (accessed June 15, 2019).

BIJ (The Bureau of Investigative Journalism) (2019). "Drone Warfare." thebureauinvestigates.com/projects/drone-war.

Birmbaum, Michael. (2015). "A Year Into a Conflict with Russia, Are Sanctions Working?" *Washington Post* (March 27). washingtonpost.com/world/europe/a-year-into-a-conflict-with-russia-are-sanctions-working/2015/03/26/45ec04b2-c73c-11e4-bea5-b893e7ac3fb3_story.html.

Blackmon, Pamela. (2008). "Rethinking Poverty through the Eyes of the International Monetary Fund and the World Bank." *International Studies Review* 10 (2): 179–202.

Blanchard, Olivier. (2016). "Slow Growth Is a Fact of Life in the Post-crisis World." *Financial Times*. ft.com/content/c84e2bfe-0171-11e6-99cb-83242733f755.

——— (2015). "Greece: A Credible Deal Will Require Difficult Decisions By All Sides." *IMF Direct* (June 14). blog-imfdirect.imf.org/2015/06/14/greece-a-credible-deal-will- require-difficult-decisions-by-all-sides/.

Blanton, Robert G. (2012). "Zombies and International Relations: A Simple Guide for Bringing the Undead into Your Classroom." *International Studies Perspectives* (14): 1–13.

Blanton, Robert G., and Shannon Lindsey Blanton. (2012a). "Rights, Institutions, and Foreign Direct Investment: An Empirical Assessment." *Foreign Policy Analysis* 8(4): 431–452.

——— (2012b). "Labor Rights and Foreign Direct Investment: Is There a Race to the Bottom?" *International Interactions* 38 (3): 267–294.

——— (2008). "Virtuous or Vicious Cycle? Human Rights, Trade, and Development." In *North and South in the World Political Economy*, edited by Rafael Reuveny and William R. Thompson, 91–103. Malden, MA: Blackwell.

——— (2007). "Human Rights and Trade." *International Interactions* 33 (April/June): 97–117.

Blanton, Robert G., Shannon Lindsey Blanton, and Dursun Peksen. (2015). "Financial Crises and Labor: Does Tight Money loosen Labor Rights?" *World Development* 76: 1–12.

Blanton, Shannon Lindsey. (2005). "Foreign Policy in Transition? Human Rights, Democracy, and U.S. Arms Exports." *International Studies Quarterly* 49 (December): 647–667.

Blanton, Shannon Lindsey, and David L. Cingranelli. (2010). "Human Rights and Foreign Policy Analysis." In *The International Studies Compendium Project*, edited by Robert Denmark et al. Oxford: Wiley-Blackwell.

Blanton, Shannon Lindsey, and Katharine Andersen Nelson. (2012). "Arms Transfers." In *Encyclopedia of Globalization*, edited by George Ritzer. Oxford: Wiley-Blackwell.

Blanton, Shannon Lindsey, and Robert G. Blanton (2009). "A Sectoral Analysis of Human Rights and FDI: Does Industry Type Matter?" *International Studies Quarterly* 53 (2): 473–498.

Blasetti, Robert. (2017). "Is Bitcoin Real Money? Some Things You Need To Know." *Block Geeks*. blockgeeks.com/is-bitcoin-real-money/.

Blockchain.com. (2019). "Market Price." blockchain.com/charts/market-price?timespan=all (accessed June 14, 2019).

Bloom, Mia. (2017). *Women and Terrorism*. Oxford University Press. DOI: 10.1093/acrefore/9780190228637.013.124.

Bloom, Mia. (2005). *Dying to Kill: The Allure of Suicide Terror*. New York: Columbia University Press.

Bloomberg News. (2011). "Vietnam Cheaper-than-China Appeal Diminishes as Labor Strikes." bloomberg.com/news/2011-06-15/vietnam-cheaper-than-china-appeal-diminshes-as-labor-strikes.html (June 15).

Blyth, Mark. (2015). *Austerity: The History of a Dangerous Idea*. New York: Oxford University Press.

Boehmer, Charles, and Timothy Nordstrom. (2008). "Intergovernmental Organization Memberships: Examining Political Community and the Attributes of International Organizations." *International Interactions* 34: 282–309.

Bokhari, Farhan. (2018). "India's Nuclear Submarine Provokes Pakistan to Renew Arms Race." *Nikkei Asian Review*. asia.nikkei.com/Politics/International-relations/India-s-nuclear-submarine-provokes-Pakistan-to-renew-arms-race.

Boli, John, Michael A. Elliott, and Franziska Bieri. (2004). "Globalization." In *Handbook of Social Problems*, edited by George Ritzer, 389–415. London: Sage.

Bollyky, Thomas. (2012). "Reinventing the World Health Organization." *Council on Foreign Relations* (March 23). cfr.org/global-health/reinventing-world-health-organization/p28346.

Bolzendahl, Catherine. (2009). "Making the Implicit Explicit: Gender Influences on Social Spending in Twelve Industrialized Democracies, 1980–1999." *Social Politics* 16: 40–81.

Boon, Hoo Tiang (2018). *China's Global Identity: Considering the Responsibilities of Great Power*. Washington, DC: Georgetown University Press.

Boot, Max. (2013). "The Evolution of Irregular War: Insurgents and Guerrillas from Akkadia to Afghanistan." *Foreign Affairs* (March/April). foreignaffairs.com/articles/138824/max-boot-the-evolution-of-irregular-war#.

Borenstein, Seth. (2006). "Pentagon Accused of Wasteful Spending." *The Idaho Statesman* (January 24): Main 3.

Börzel, Tanja A., and Thomas Risse. (2013). "Human Rights in Areas of Limited Statehood: The New Agenda." In *The Persistent Power of Human Rights: From Commitment to Compliance*, edited by Thomas Risse, Stephen C. Ropp, and Kathryn Sikkink. Cambridge: Cambridge University Press.

Bosco, David. (2011). "Dreaming of SDRs." *Foreign Policy*. foreignpolicy.com/articles/2011/09/07/dreaming_of_sdrs?page=0,0 (September 7).

Boyer, Mark A., Brian Urlacher, Natalie Florea Hudson, Anat Niv-Solomon, Laura L. Janik, Michael Butler, and Andri Ioannou. (2009). "Gender and Negotiation: Some Experimental Findings from an International Negotiation Simulation." *International Studies Quarterly* 53 (1): 23–47.

Brainard, Lael, Abigail Jones, and Nigel Purvis. (eds.). (2009). *Climate Change and Global Poverty*. Washington, DC: Brookings Institution Press.

Braithwaite, Alex. (2010). "Resisting Infection: How State Capacity Conditions Conflict Contagion." *Journal of Peace Research* 47(3): 311–319.

Branigan, Tania. (2012). "China's First Female Astronaut Shows How 'Women Hold Up Half the Sky.'" *The Guardian* (16 June). guardian.co.uk/world/2012/jun/17/china-woman-space-liu-yang.

Braudel, Fernand. (1973). *The Mediterranean and the Mediterranean World at the Age of Philip II*. New York: Harper.

Breen, C. (2003). "The Role of NGOs in the Formulation of and Compliance with the Optional Protocol to the Convention on the Rights of the Child on Involvement of Children in Armed Conflict." *Human Rights Quarterly* 25: 453.

Bremer, Stuart A. (2000). "Who Fights Whom, When, Where, and Why?" In John A. Vasquez (ed.), *What Do We Know About War?* Lanham, MD: Rowman & Littlefield.

British Broadcasting Corporation (BBC). (2013b). "What Is Fracking and Why Is It Controversial?" bbc.com/news/uk-14432401.

Bromley, Daniel, and Glen Anderson. (2013). *Vulnerable People, Vulnerable States: Redefining the Development Challenge*. London, UK: Routledge.

Bronfenbrenner, Urie. (1961). "The Mirror Image in Soviet-American Relations." *Journal of Social Issues* 17 (3): 45–56.

——— (2005a). "Hunch Power." *New York Times Book Review* (January 16): 1, 12–13.

——— (2005b). "Our Better Understanding of Who the Terrorists Are." *Columbia, S.C., The State* (August 6): A11.

Brook, Tom Vanden, and Michael Collins. (2019). "Mueller Report: 5 Things to Know about Russian Interference in U.S. Elections." *USA Today*. usatoday.com/story/news/politics/2019/04/22/mueller-report-what-know-russian-election-interference/3538877002/.

Brooks, David. (2005). "Hunch Power." *New York Times Book Review* (January 16): 1, 12–13.

Brown, Lester R. (2012). *Full Planet, Empty Plates: The New Geopolitics of Food Scarcity*. New York: W. W. Norton & Company.

Brummer, Klaus, and Valerie M. Hudson (eds.). (2015). *Foreign Policy Analysis: Beyond North America*. Boulder, CO: Lynne Rienner.

Brunk, Darren C. (2008). "Curing the Somalia Syndrome: Analogy, Foreign Policy Decision Making, and the Rwandan Genocide." *Foreign Policy Analysis* 4 (July): 301–320.

Brysk, Alison. (2009). *Global Good Samaritans: Human Rights as Foreign Policy*. Oxford: Oxford University Press.

Brysk, Alison, and Austin Choi-Fitzpatrick, eds. (2012). *From Human Trafficking to Human Rights: Reframing Contemporary Slavery*. Philadelphia, PA: University of Pennsylvania Press.

Brzezinski, Zbigniew. (2010). "From Hope to Audacity: Appraising Obama's Foreign Policy." *Foreign Affairs* 89 (1): 16–30.

——— (2004). *The Choice: Global Domination or Global Leadership*. New York: Basic Books/Perseus.

Burke, M., S. M. Hsiang, and E. Miguel. (2015). "Global Non-linear Effect of Temperature on Economic Production." *Nature* 527 (7577): 235.

Buruma, Ian. (2005). "The Indiscreet Charm of Tyranny." *New York Review of Books* 52 (May 12): 35–37.

Butcher, Charity, and Maia Hallward. (2018). "Religious vs. Secular Human Rights Organizations: Discourse, Framing, and Action." *Journal of Human Rights* 17(4): 502–523. doi: 10.1080/14754835.2018.1486701.

Buzan, Barry. (2004). *From International to World Society?: English School Theory and the Social Structure of Globalization*. Cambridge, UK: Cambridge University Press.

——— (2004b). "A Reductionist, Idealistic Notion that Adds Little Analytical Value." *Security Dialogue* 35(3): 369–370.

Byrne, Andrew. (2013). "Conflicting Visions: Liberal and Realist Conceptualisations of Transatlantic Alignment." *Transworld* (March). iai.it/pdf/Transworld/TW_WP_12.pdf.

Cain, Geoffrey. (2019). "Ukraine's War on Russian Disinformation Is a Lesson for America." *The New Republic* (March 29). newrepublic.com/article/153415/ukraines-war-russian-disinformation-lesson-america.

Calamur, Krishnadev. (2018). "The UN Human Rights Council Is a Deeply Flawed Body." *The Atlantic*. theatlantic.com/international/archive/2018/06/us-un-human-rights/563276/.

Calhoun, Craig. (2011). "Civil Society and the Public Sphere." *LSE Research Online*. eprints.lse.ac.uk/42621/1/__lse.ac.uk_storage_LIBRARY_Secondary_libfile_shared_repository_Content_Calhoun,C_Civil%20society_Calhoun_Civil%20Society_2014.pdf.

Call, Charles T. (2012). *Why Peace Fails: The Causes and Prevention of Civil War Recurrence*. Washington D.C.: Georgetown University Press. Retrieved from books.google.com/books?hl=en&lr=&id=n0t2ihrzM9gC&oi=fnd&pg=PP2&dq=civil+war+recurrence&ots=q6KVXWffLI&sig=RyPC2JOxY8buFk3p3u7OYY6GeT0#v=onepage&q&f=false.

Calvocoressi, Peter, Guy Wint, and John Pritchard. (1989). *Total War: The Causes and Courses of the Second World War*, 2nd ed. New York: Pantheon.

Campbell, Charlie. (2017). "Ports, Pipelines, and Geopolitics: China's New Silk Road Is a Challenge for Washington." *Time*. time.com/4992103/china-silk-road-belt-xi-jinping-khorgos-kazakhstan-infrastructure/.

Canetti-Nisim, Daphna, Eran Halperin, Keren Sharvit, and Stevan E. Hobfoll. (2009). "A New Stress-Based Model of Political Extremism: Personal Exposure to Terrorism, Psychological Distress, and Exclusionist Political Attitudes." *Journal of Conflict Resolution* 53 (3): 363–389.

Canter, Lilly. (2019). "How Air Pollution Makes People Unhappy and Irrational, and Why in China it Is Likely to Keep Getting Worse." *South China Morning Post* (September 23). scmp.com/lifestyle/health-wellness/article/3029918/how-air-pollution-makes-people-unhappy-and-irrational-and.

Capaccio, Tony. (2013). "China's Anti-Carrier Missile Now Opposite Taiwan, Flynn Says." *Bloomberg* (April 18). bloomberg.com/news/2013-04-18/china-s-anti-carrier-missile-now-opposite-taiwan-flynn-says.html.

Caprioli, Mary. (2005). "Primed for Violence: The Role of Gender Inequality in Predicting International Conflict." *International Studies Quarterly* 49 (June): 161–178.

Cardwell, Diane. (2014). "Solar and Wind Energy Start to Win on Price vs. Conventional Fuels." *New York Times* (November 23). nytimes.com/2014/11/24/business/energy-environment/solar-and-wind-energy-start-to-win-on-price-vs-conventional-fuels.html.

Carey, Glen. (2019). "U.S. Warns Syrian Forces Against Chemical Weapons in Idlib Fight." *Bloomberg*. bloomberg.com/news/articles/2019-06-07/u-s-warns-syrian-forces-against-chemical-weapons-in-idlib-fight?utm_source=google&utm_medium=bd&cmpId=google.

Carns, Katie. (2009, November 25). "Globalization and Opportunity." Carnegie Council.

Carpenter, Charli. (2009). "Orphaned Again: Children Born of Wartime Rape as a Non-Issue for the Human Rights Network." In *The International Struggle for New Human Rights*, edited by Clifford Bob, 14–29. Philadelphia: University of Pennsylvania.

Carpenter, R. C. (2011). "Vetting the Advocacy Agenda: Network Centrality and the Paradox of Weapons Norms." *International Organization* 65(1): 69–102.

Carr, E. H. (1939). *The Twenty-Years' Crisis, 1919–1939*. London: Macmillan.

Carty, Anthony. (2008). "Marxist International Law Theory as Hegelianism." *International Studies Review* 10 (March): 122–125.

Caselli, Francesco, Massimo Morelli, and Dominic Rohner. (2015). "The Geography of Interstate Resource Wars." *Quarterly Journal of Economics* 130 (1): 267–315.

Cashman, Greg. (2014). *What Causes War?: An Introduction to Theories of International Conflict*. Lanham, MD: Rowman & Littlefield.

Cashman, Greg, and Leonard C. Robinson. (2007). *An Introduction to the Causes of War*. Lanham, MD: Rowman & Littlefield.

Caspary (1993).

CDC (Centers for Disease Control and Prevention). (2019). "2014–2016 Ebola Outbreak in West Africa." cdc.gov/vhf/ebola/history/2014-2016-outbreak/index.html.

Cederman, Lars-Erik, Kristian Skrede Gleditsch, and Simon Hug. (2012). "Elections and Ethnic Civil War." *Comparative Political Studies* 46 (3): 387–417.

Chapman, P. (2014). *Bananas: How the United Fruit Company Shaped the World*. Open Road+ Grove/Atlantic.

Charlesworth, Hilary. 1995. "Human Rights as Men's Rights." In *Women's Rights, Human Rights: International Feminist Perspectives*, edited by J. Peters and A. Wolper, 103–113. New York: Routledge.

Chase-Dunn, Christopher, and E. N. Anderson (eds.). (2005). *The Historical Evolution of World-Systems*. London: Palgrave.

Chatterjee, Deen K. (ed.). (2013). *The Ethics of Preventive War*. Cambridge, UK: Cambridge University Press.

Chatzky, Andrew. (2019). "What Would a No-Deal Brexit Look Like?" Council on Foreign Relations. cfr.org/article/what-would-no-deal-brexit-look. Accessed 18 Feb. 2019.

Chauffour, Jean-Pierre, and Mariem Malouch. (2011). *Trade Finance during the Great Trade Collapse*. Washington, DC: World Bank.

Cherlet, M., C. Hutchinson, J. Reynolds, J. Hill, S. Sommer, and G. von Malitz. (eds.). (2018). *World Atlas of Desertification*. Luxembourg: Publication Office of the European Union.

Chernoff, Fred. (2008). *Theory and Metatheory in International Relations*. London: Palgrave Macmillan.

Chipman, Kim. (2015). "Jamie Dimon Says He's Unsure if Elizabeth Warren Understands Global Banking System." *Bloomberg* (June 10). bloomberg.com/news/articles/2015-06-10/dimon-says-unsure-if-warren-understands-global-banking-system.

Christensen, Jen, and Jessie Yeung. (2019). "Scientists Are One Step Closer to an Ebola Cure in the Congo." *CNN.com* (August 13). cnn.com/2019/08/12/health/ebola-breakthrough-congo/index.html.

Choucri, Nazli. (2012). *Cyberpolitics in International Relations*. Cambridge, MA: MIT Press.

Cimino-Isaacs, Cathleen D. (2019). *World Trade Organization: Overview and Future Direction*. Washington D.C.: Congressional Research Service. Retrieved from fas.org/sgp/crs/row/R45417.pdf.

Cincotta, Richard P., and Robert Engelman. (2004). "Conflict Thrives Where Young Men Are Many." *International Herald Tribune* (March): 18.

Cirincione, Joseph. (2008). "The Incredible Shrinking Missile Threat." *Foreign Policy* (May/June): 68–70.

Clapham, Andrew. (2001). "Human Rights." *The Oxford Companion to Politics of the World*, 2nd ed., edited by Joel Krieger, 368–370. New York: Oxford University Press.

Clark, Gregory. (2008). *A Farewell to Alms: A Brief Economic History of the World*. Princeton, NJ: Princeton University Press.

Clark, Stuart. (2018). "'It's Going to Happen': Is the World Ready for War in Space?" *The Guardian*. theguardian.com/science/2018/apr/15/its-going-to-happen-is-world-ready-for-war-in-space.

Clarke, Michael. (2013). "Pakistan and Nuclear Terrorism: How Real Is the Threat?" *Comparative Strategy* 32 (2): 98–114.

Clarke, Richard A., and Robert Knake. (2010). *Cyber War: The Next Threat to National Security and What to Do About It*. New York: HarperCollins.

Claude, Inis L., Jr. (1989). "The Balance of Power Revisited." *Review of International Studies* 15 (January): 77–85.

——— (1967). *The Changing United Nations*. New York: Random House.

Clinch, Matt. (2015). "Russia Peace Talks in Doubt as Ruble Falls." *CNBC* (January 12). cnbc.com/id/102328502.

Cloward, K. (2016). *When Norms Collide: Local Responses to Activism Against Female Genital Mutilation and Early Marriage*. Oxford University Press.

Cohen, Benjamin J. (ed.). (2005). *International Political Economy*. Burlington, VT: Ashgate.

——— (1973). *The Question of Imperialism*. New York: Basic Books.

Cohen, Roger. (2005). "Next Step: Putting Europe Back Together." *New York Times International* (June 5): Section 4, 3.

Cohn, Carol, and Sara Ruddick. (2008). "A Feminist Ethical Perspective on Weapons of Mass Destruction." In *Essential Readings in World Politics*, 3rd ed., edited by Karen A. Mingst and Jack L. Snyder, 458–477. New York: W. W. Norton & Company.

Coker, Christopher. (2012). *Warrior Geeks: How 21st Century Technology Is Changing the Way We Fight and Think About War*. New York: Columbia University Press.

Cole, Juan. (2015). "5,000 Hanging Skirts: How Women Remember War Rape in Kosova." *Informed Comment* (June 15). juancole.com/2015/06/hanging-remember-kosova.html.

——— (2006). "9/11." *Foreign Policy* 156 (September/October): 26–32.

Coleman, Isobel. (2010a). "The Better Half: Helping Woman Help the World." *Foreign Affairs* 89 (1): 126–130.

——— (2010b). "The Global Glass Ceiling: Why Empowering Women Is Good for Business." *Foreign Affairs* 89 (3): 13–20.

Coll, Steve. (2009). "Comment: No Nukes." *The New Yorker* (April 20): 31–32.

Collier, Paul. (2009). "The Dictator's Handbook." *Foreign Policy* (May/June): 146–149.

——— (2005). "The Market for Civil War." In *World Politics 04/05*, edited by Helen E. Punkitt, 28–32. Dubuque, IA: McGraw-Hill/Dushkin.

——— (2003). "The Market for Civil War." *Foreign Policy* 136 (May/June): 38–45.

Coltart, C. E., Lindsey, B., Ghinai, I., Johnson, A. M., and Heymann, D. L. (2017). "The Ebola Outbreak, 2013–2016: Old Lessons for New Epidemics." *Philosophical Transactions of the Royal Society B: Biological Sciences* 372(1721), 20160297.

Combs, Cynthia C. (2013). *Terrorism in the Twenty-First Century*, 7th ed. Boston, MA: Pearson.

Comisky, Mike, and Pawan Madhogarhia. (2009). "Unraveling the Financial Crisis of 2008." *PS: Political Science & Politics* 42: 270–275.

Conca, Ken, and Geoffrey Dabelko. (2015). *Green Planet Blues: Critical Perspectives on Global Environmental Politics*. Boulder, CO: Westview Press.

Conservation International. (2019). "Biodiversity Hotspots: Targeted Investment in Nature's Most Important Places." conservation.org/priorities/biodiversity-hotspots.

Constante, Jonathan. (2015). "Islamic State Poured Acid on Women's Faces for not Wearing a Niqab in Public." *Opposing Views* (February 20). opposingviews.com/i/world/isis-poured-acid-womens-faces-not-wearing-niqab-public.

Conteh-Morgan, Earl. (2005). "Peacebuilding and Human Security: A Constructivist Perspective." *International Journal of Peace Studies* 10 (Spring/Summer): 69–86.

Cook, John, and Paul Nyhan. (2004). "Outsourcing's Long-Term Effects on U.S. Jobs an Issue." *Seattle Post-Intelligencer*. March 10.

Cooper, Richard N. (2004). "A False Alarm: Overcoming Globalization's Discontents." *Foreign Affairs* 83 (January/February): 152–155.

Copeland, Dale C. (2014). *Economic Interdependence and War*. Princeton, NJ: Princeton University Press.

Coplin, William. (1965). "International Law and Assumptions about the State System." *World Politics* 17 (July): 615–634.

Correlates of War Project (COW). (2017). "State System Membership List, v2016." correlatesofwar.org.

——— (2015). "News and Notes." correlatesofwar.org/.

Cortright, David, and George A. Lopez (eds.). (2008). *Uniting against Terror*. Cambridge, MA: MIT Press.

Couch, Robbie. (2015). "Human Trafficking Is Still Globe's Fastest-Growing Crime Despite Increased Awareness." *The Huffington Post* (January 7). huffingtonpost.com/2015/01/07/human-trafficking-increasing_n_6425864.html.

Council on Foreign Relations. (2019). *Global Conflict Tracker*. cfr.org/interactive/global-conflict-tracker/conflict/civil-war-syria.

Coyle, Eugene D., and Melissa J. Dark (eds.). (2014). *Understanding the Global Energy Crisis*. West Lafayette, IN: Purdue University Press.

Cressey, Laura E., Barrett J. Helmer, and Jennifer E. Steffensen. (eds.). (2014). *Careers in International Affairs*. Washington, DC: Georgetown University Press.

Cronin, Audrey Kurth. (2013). "Why Drones Fail." *Foreign Affairs* (July/August). foreignaffairs.com/articles/139454/audrey-kurth-cronin/why-drones-fail.

Crook, Clive. (2003). "A Cruel Sea of Capital." *Economist* (May 3): 3–5.

Crowther, T. W., H. B. Glick, K. R. Covey, C. Bettigole, D. S. Maynard, S. M. Thomas, et al. (2015). "Mapping Tree Density at a Global Scale." *Nature*. DOI: 10.1038/nature14967.

Cukierman, Alex. (2015). "The Crisis and the Renminbi's International Role." *VOX* (January 7). voxeu.org/article/global-crisis-and- global-renminbi.

Da Costa, Ana Nicolaci. (2018). "How the World Is Grappling with China's Rising Power." *BBC News*. bbc.com/news/business-45948692.

Da Porto, Luigi. (1509). "Letter of 7 March." In *War and Society in the Seventh Century*, edited by Sir George Clark, 26. London: Cambridge University Press.

Daadler, Ivo H., and James M. Lindsay. (2004). "An Alliance of Democracies." *Washington Post* (May 24): B.07.

Daase, Christopher, and Cornelius Friesendorf. (2010). *Rethinking Security Governance: The Problem of Unintended Consequences*. Retrieved from books.google.com/books?hl=en&lr=&id=X5haBwAAQBAJ&oi=fnd&pg=PP1&dq=blowback+consequences&ots=DP-OfzaF0u&sig=UpIiMn4HrvBxt6FyPn4ejQbfy1s#v=onepage&q&f=false.

Dafoe, Allan, John R. Oneal, and Bruce Russett. (2013). "The Democratic Peace: Weighing the Evidence and Cautious Inference." *International Studies Quarterly* 57 (1): 201–214.

Daniel, Trenton. (2011). "Haiti Again Feels Pinch of Rising Food Prices." *Associated Press* (May 2). usatoday.com/news/world/2011-05-01-haiti-food-prices_n.htm.

Dans, Enrique. (2018). "Corporate Social Responsibility Is Turning Green, And That's A Good Thing." *Forbes*. forbes.com/sites/enriquedans/2018/09/14/corporate-social-responsibility-is-turning-green-and-thats-a-good-thing/#39fc66a4dca8.

Davenport, Andrew. (2013). "Marxism in IR: Condemned to a Realist Fate?" *European Journal of International Relations* 19 (1): 27–48.

Davis, Julie Hirschfield, Laura Lilvan, and Greg Stohr. (2013). "Obama Faces Bipartisan Pressure on Drone Big Brother Fear." *Bloomberg* (March 7). bloomberg.com/news/2013-03-08/obama-faces-bipartisan-pressure-on-drone-big-brother-fear.html.

DeBardeleben, Joan. (2012). "Applying Constructivism to Understanding EU-Russian Relations." *International Politics* 49 (4): 418–433.

Debusman, Bernd. (2012). "America's Decline—Myth or Reality?" reuters.com/article/2012/04/20/column-debusmann-idUSL2E8FK5IH20120420.

Deets, Stephen. (2009). "Constituting Interests and Identities in a Two-Level Game: Understanding the Gabcikovo-Nagymaros Dam Conflict." *Foreign Policy Analysis* 5 (January): 37–56.

Department of Defense (DOD). (2019). "United States Department of Defense Fiscal Year 2020 Budget Request." comptroller.defense.gov/Portals/45/Documents/defbudget/fy2020/fy2020_Budget_Request.pdf.

Department of the Treasury (DOT). (2019). "Major Foreign Holders of Treasury Securities." ticdata.treasury.gov/Publish/mfh.txt.

DeRouen, Karl R., Jr., and Jacob Bercovitch. (2008). "Enduring Internal Rivalries: A New Framework for the Study of Civil War." *Journal of Peace Research* 45 (January): 55–74.

DeRouen, Karl, and C. Sprecher. (2006). "Arab Behaviour Towards Israel: Strategic Avoidance or Exploiting Opportunities?" *British Journal of Political Science*, 36(3): 549–560.

DeRouen, Karl R., Jr., Jacob Bercovitch, and Christopher Sprecher. (2006). "Arab Behaviour towards Israel: Strategic Avoidance or Exploiting Opportunities?" *British Journal of Political Science* 36 (3): 549–560.

Desai, Raj M., and James Raymond Vreeland. (2014). "What the New Bank of BRICS Is All About." *Washington Post* (July 17). washingtonpost.com/blogs/monkey-cage/wp/2014/07/17/what-the-new-bank-of-brics-is-all-about/.

——— (2011). "Global Governance in a Multipolar World: The Case for Regional Monetary Funds." *International Studies Review* 13 (1): 109–121.

De Soysa, Indra, Thomas Jackson, and Christin Ormhaug. (2009). "Does Globalization Profit the Small Arms Bazaar?" *International Interactions* 35: 86–105.

Destler, I. M. (2005). *American Trade Politics*, 4th ed. Washington, DC: Institute of International Economics.

Deutsch, Karl W. (1957). *Political Community and the North Atlantic Area*. Princeton, NJ: Princeton University Press.

Larry Diamond. (2015). "Facing Up to the Democratic Recession." *Journal of Democracy* 26, no. 1: 141–155.

Diehl, Paul F., and J. Michael Greig. (2012). *International Mediation*. Cambridge: Polity Press.

Dietz, Mary G. (2003). "Current Controversies in Feminist Theory." *Annual Review of Political Science* 6: 399–431.

Dilanian, Ken, and Courtney Kube. (2017). "Trump Administration Wants to Increase CIA Drone Strikes." *NBC News*. nbcnews.com/news/military/trump-admin-wants-increase-cia-drone-strikes-n802311.

Dimerel-Pegg, Tijen, and James Moskowitz. (2009). "US Aid Allocation: The Nexus of Human Rights, Democracy, and Development." *Journal of Peace Research* 46 (2): 181–198.

Dingwerth, Klaus. (2014). "Global Democracy and the Democratic Minimum: Why a Procedural Account Alone is Insufficient." *European Journal of International Relations* 20 (4): 1124–1147.

Dittmer, Lowell. (2013). "Asia in 2012: The Best of a Bad Year?" *Asian Survey* 53 (1): 1–11.

Dobson, William J. (2006). "The Day Nothing Much Changed." *Foreign Policy* 156 (September/October): 22–25.

Doctor, Rina Marie. (2016). "FAA Predicts Drones Will Number 7 Million By 2020." *Tech Times*. techtimes.com/articles/144405/20160326/faa-predicts-drones-will-number-7-million-by-2020.htm.

Doctors Without Borders. (2019). "Ebola Outbreak in DRC: Crisis Update May 2019." doctorswithoutborders.org/what-we-do/news-stories/news/ebola-outbreak-drc-crisis-update-may-2019.

Dolan, Thomas M. (2016). "Emotion and Strategic Learning in War." *Foreign Policy Analysis* 12: 571–590.

Dombrowski, Peter, and Eugene Gholz. (2007). *Buying Military Transformation*. New York: Columbia University Press.

Domonoske, Camila. (2017). "So What Exactly Is In The Paris Climate Accord?" *NPR*. npr.org/sections/thetwo-way/2017/06/01/531048986/so-what-exactly-is-in-the-paris-climate-accord.

Donadio, Rachel. (2011). "Greece Approves Tough Measures on the Economy." *New York Times* (June 29).

Donadio, Rachel, and Scott Sayare. (2011). "Violent Clashes in the Streets of Athens." *New York Times* (June 29): A8.

Donnelly, Jack. (2013). *Universal Human Rights Theory and Practice*. New York: Cornell University Press.

Dontoh, Ekow, and Michael Cohen. (2019). "Africa's Booming Cities Are Running Out of Water." *Bloomberg* (March 19). bloomberg.com/news/articles/2019-03-18/africa-is-running-out-of-water-as-cities-see-populations-boom.

Doran, Charles F. (2012). "Power Cycle Theory and the Ascendance of China: Peaceful or Stormy?" *SAIS Review* 32 (1): 73–87.

Dos Santos, Theotonio. (1971). "The Structure of Dependence." In *Readings in U.S. Imperialism*, edited by K.T. Fann and Donald C. Hodges. Boston: Porter Sargent.

Doyle, Michael W. (2012). In *Foreign Policy: Theories, Actors, Cases* edited by Steve Smith, Amelia Hadfield, and Tim Dunne (Oxford, UK: Oxford University Press).

——— (2011). "International Ethics and the Responsibility to Protect." *International Studies Review* 13: 72–84.

Draper, Robert. (2008). *Dead Certain: The Presidency of George W. Bush*. New York: Free Press.

Dreier, S. K. (2018). "Resisting Rights to Renounce Imperialism: East African Churches' Strategic Symbolic Resistance to LGBTQ Inclusion." *International Studies Quarterly*, 62(2), 423–436.

Drezner, Daniel. (2014). *The System Worked; How the World Stopped Another Great Depression*. New York: Oxford University Press.

——— (2011). "Sanctions Sometimes Smart: Targeted Sanctions in Theory and Practice." *International Studies Review* 13 (1): 96–108.

——— (2011a). *Theories of International Politics and Zombies*. Princeton, NJ: Princeton University Press.

——— (2010). "Night of the Living Wonks." *Foreign Policy* (July/August): 34–38.

——— (2009). "Backdoor Protectionism." *The National Interest Online*. nationalinterest.org/Article.aspx?id521192.

——— (2007). *All Politics Is Global*. Princeton, NJ: Princeton University Press.

——— (2000). "Bottom Feeders." *Foreign Policy* (November/December): 64–70.

Drost, Nadja. (2009). "Postcard: Medellin." *Time* (May 4): 8.

Duffin, Erin. (2019). "Manufacturing Labor Costs per Hour for China, Vietnam, Mexico from 2016 to 2020 (in U.S. Dollars)." *Statista*. statista.com/statistics/744071/manufacturing-labor-costs-per-hour-china-vietnam-mexico/.

Dur, Andreas. (2010). *Protectionism for Exporters: Power and Discrimination in Transatlantic Trade Relations 1930–2010*. Ithaca, NY: Cornell University Press.

Dworkin, Ronald. (2001). *Sovereign Virtue*. Cambridge, MA: Harvard University Press.

Dykman, Jackson. (2008). "Why the World Can't Afford Food." *Time* (May 19): 34–35.

Dyson, Stephen Benedict. (2006). "Personality and Foreign Policy: Tony Blair's Iraq Decisions." *Foreign Policy Analysis* 2: 289–306.

Easterbrook, Gregg. (2002). "Safe Deposit: The Case for Foreign Aid." *New Republic* (July 29): 16–20.

Easton, Stewart C. (1964). *The Rise and Fall of Western Colonialism*. New York: Praeger.

Eberstadt, Nicholas. (2010). "The Demographic Future: What Population Growth—and Decline—Means for the Global Economy." *Foreign Affairs* (November/December): 54–64.

Eckhardt, William. (1984). "Global Imperialism and Global Inequality." *International Interactions* 11(3–4): 299–332. doi: 10.1080/0305062840 8434638.

The Economist. (2018). "Is the Greek Financial Crisis Over at Last?" *The Economist*. economist.com/the-economist-explains/2018/08/21/is-the-greek-financial-crisis-over-at-last.

——— (2015a). "The IMF Changes Its Tune on China's Currency." *The Economist* (May 30). economist.com/news/finance-and-economics/21652321-imf-changes-its-tune-chinas-currency-feeling-valued.

——— (2015b). "Getting Around Uncle Sam." *The Economist* (January 29). economist.com/news/finance-and-economics/21641260-how-reform-imf-without-congresss-help-getting-around-uncle-sam.

——— (2015c). "Why Everyone Is So Keen to Agree New Trade Deals." *The Economist* (June 24). economist.com/blogs/graphicdetail/2015/06/global-trade-graphics.

——— (2015d). "After OPEC." *The Economist* (May 16). economist.com/news/business/21651267-american-shale-firms-are-now-oil-markets-swing-producers-after-opec.

——— (2015e). "Betting on Hot Air." *The Economist* (May 9). economist.com/news/asia/21650914-government-pushes-what-it-hopes-will-be-clean-fuel-future-betting-hot-air.

——— (2014a). "From the Graveyard." *The Economist* (December 20): 59.

——— (2014b). "Internet Companies and Their Abuse of Power." *The Economist* (December 20): 11.

——— (2014d). "The Onrushing Wave." *The Economist* (January 18). economist.com/news/briefing/21594264-previous-technological-innovation-has-always-delivered-more-long-run-employment-not-less.

——— (2012b). "Big Mac Index." *The Economist* (January 12). economist.com/blogs/graphicde-tail/2012/01/daily-chart-3.

——— (2012c). "Speaking in Tongues." *The Economist*. economist.com/blogs/graphicdetail/2012/02/daily-chart-9.

——— (2011a). "Another Project in Trouble: First the Euro, Now Schengen. Europe's Grandest Integration Projects Seem to be Suffering." *The Economist* (April 30): 57.

——— (2011b). "Crisis Prevention: What Is Causing Food Prices to Soar and What Can be Done about It?" *The Economist* (February 26): 12.

——— (2011c). "A Prospect of Plenty: For the First Time in History, the Whole of Mankind May Get Enough to Eat." *The Economist* (February 26): 16.

——— (2011d). "A Tale of Many Cities." *The Economist* (February 12): 91–92.

——— (2011e). "Ali Baba Gone, but What about the 40 Thieves?" *The Economist* (January 22): 31–33.

——— (2010a). "Climbing Mount Publishable." *The Economist* (November 14): 95–96.

——— (2010b). "Fewer Dragons, More Snakes." *The Economist* (November 13): 27–29.

——— (2010c). "Old Worry, New Ideas." *The Economist* (April 17): 67.

——— (2010e). "Economic and Financial Indicators." *The Economist* (May 1): 97–98.

——— (2009a). "Sin aqua non." *The Economist* (April 11): 59–61.

——— (2009b). "Coca-Cola and China: Hard to Swallow." *The Economist* (March 21): 68–69.

——— (2009c). "Wanted: Fresh Air." *The Economist* (July 11): 60–62.

——— (2009d). "Coca-Cola and China: Hard to Swallow." economist.com/business/2009/03/19/hard-to-swallow.

——— (2009i). "Coca-Cola and China: Hard to Swallow." *The Economist* (February 21): 68–69.

——— (2007). "Finance and Economics: Smaller Shares, Bigger Slices." *The Economist* (April 7): 84.

Economy, Elizabeth C. (2018). *The Third Revolution: Xi Jinping and the New Chinese State*. Oxford University Press.

——— (2015). "The AIIB Debacle: What Washington Should Do Now." *Council on Foreign Relations* (March 16). blogs.cfr.org/asi a/2015/03/16/the-aiib-debacle-what-washington-should-do-now/.

Eder, Franz. (2019). "Making Concurrence-Seeking Visible: Groupthink, Discourse Networks, and the 2003 Iraq War." *Foreign Policy Analysis* 15: 21–42.

Ehrlich, Sean. (2011). "The Fair Trade Challenge to Embedded Liberalism." *International Studies Quarterly* 54 (1): 1013–1033.

Eichengreen, Barry. (2014). "The Dollar and the Damage Done." *Project Syndicate* (February 13). project-syndicate.org/commentary/barry-eichengreen-blames-us-policymakers-for-torpedoing-imf-reform–leaving-no-global-lender-of-last-resort.

——— (2009). "The Dollar Dilemma: The World's Top Currency Faces Competition." *Foreign Affairs* 88 (5): 53–68.

Eichengreen, Barry, and Kevin O'Rourke. (2009). "A Tale of Two Depressions." VoxEU.org, June 4. voxeu.org/index.php?q5node/3421.

Eichengreen, Barry, Arnaud Mehl, and Livia Chiṭu. (2018). "Mars or Mercury? The Geopolitics of International Currency Choice." *Vox EU*. voxeu.org/article/geopolitics-international-currency-choice.

——— (2017). *How Global Currencies Work: Past, Present, and Future*. Princeton, New Jersey: Princeton University Press.

Ekhoragbon, Vincent. (2008). "Nigeria: Influx of Illegal Immigrants Worries Immigration Service." allafrica.com/stories/200808080481.html.

Ellis, David C. (2009). "On the Possibility of 'International Community'" *The International Studies Review* 11 (March): 1–26.

Elman, Colin, and Michael Jensen. (eds.). (2014). *Realism Reader*. New York: Routledge.

Elms, Deborah Kay. (2008). "New Directions for IPE: Drawing from Behavioral Economics." *International Studies Review* 10 (June): 239–265.

Elshtain, Jean Bethke. (2003). *Just War against Terror: The Burden of American Power in a Violent World*. New York: Basic Books.

Emporis. (2012). "Press Release: World's 10 Biggest Shopping Malls." *Emporis*. emporis.com/pdf/Pressrelease_20120207_ENG.pdf.

Engardio, Pete, Michael Arndt, and Dean Foust. (2006). "The Future of Outsourcing: How Its Transforming Whole Industries and Changing the Way We Work." *Businessweek* (January 30).

Engen, Lars, and Annalisa Prizzon. (2018). *A Guide to Multilateral Development Banks*. London, UK: Overseas Development Institute. odi.org/sites/odi.org.uk/files/resource-documents/12274.pdf.

Englehart, Neil A. (2009). "State Capacity, State Failure, and Human Rights." *Journal of Peace Research* 46 (2): 163–180.

Enloe, Cynthia H. (2007). "The Personal Is International." In *Essential Readings in World Politics*, 3rd ed., edited by Karen A. Mingst and Jack L. Snyder, 202–206, New York: W. W. Norton & Company.

——— (2004). *The Curious Feminist*. Berkeley: University of California Press.

——— (2001). "Gender and Politics." In *The Oxford Companion to Politics of the World*, 2nd ed., edited. by Joel Krieger. New York: Oxford University Press, 3.

——— (1989). *Bananas, Beaches and Bases: Making Feminist Sense of International Politics*. London: Pandora.

EPA (United States Environmental Protection Agency). (2019). *Global Greenhouse Gas Emissions Data*. epa.gov/ghgemissions/global-greenhouse-gas-emissions-data#Trends.

——— (2013). "Causes of Climate Change." *Environmental Protection Agency*. epa.gov/climatechange/science/causes.html.

Epatko, Larisa. (2012). "In Syria, Aid Groups Look for Break in Fighting to Deliver Supplies." *PBS NewsHour*. pbs.org/news-hour/rundown/2.012/03/syria-aid.html.

Erästö, Tytti. (2019). "Fifty Years of the NPT—Cause for Celebration or Commemoration?" *SIPRI*. sipri.org/commentary/blog/2019/fifty-years-npt-cause-celebration-or-commemoration.

Erästö, Tytti, and Tarja Cronberg. (2018). "Opposing Trends: The Renewed Salience of Nuclear Weapons and Nuclear Abolitionism." *SIPRI*. sipri.org/publications/2018/sipri-insights-peace-and-security/opposing-trends-renewed-salience-nuclear-weapons-and-nuclear-abolitionism.

Eriksson, Johan. (2014). "On the Policy Relevance of Grand Theory." *International Studies Perspectives* 15 (1): 94–108.

Erlanger, Steven, and Megan Specia. (2019). "European Parliament Elections: 5 Biggest Takeaways." *New York Times*. nytimes.com/2019/05/27/world/europe/eu-election-takeaways.html.

Ermer, John. "Why President Trump's Hard-line Approach to Cuba Is a Mistake." *The Washington Post*. washingtonpost.com/outlook/2019/04/17/why-president-trumps-hard-line-approach-cuba-is-mistake/?utm_term=.c1dcd012ac58.

Eshbaugh-Soha, Matthew, and Christopher Linebarger. (2014). "Presidential and Media Leadership of Public Opinion on Iraq." *Foreign Policy Analysis* 10 (4): 351–369.

Esty, Daniel. (2002). "The World Trade Organization's Legitimacy Crisis." *World Trade Review* 1 (1): 7–22.

Eule, Stephen. (2018). "A Look at IEA's New Global Energy Forecast." *Global Energy Institute*. globalenergyinstitute.org/look-iea%E2%80%99s-new-global-energy-forecast.

Eurobarometer. (2019). "Eurobarometer Spring 2019 Report: EU Support Highest Since 1983." *Government Europa*. governmenteuropa.eu/eurobarometer-spring-2019-report/93072/.

——— (2014). "Public Opinion in the European Union." *European Commission* (Autumn). ec.europa.eu/public_opinion/archives/eb/eb82/eb82_first_en.pdf.

European Commission. (2012). *The 2012 Ageing Report: Economic and Budgetary Projections for the 27 EU Member States (2010–2060)*. Brussels, Belgium: European Commission.

European Environment Agency. (2016). eea.europa.eu/data-and-maps/figures/correlation-of-per-capita-energy.

Evans, Gareth. (2008). *The Responsibility to Protect: Ending Mass Atrocity Crimes Once and for All*. Washington, DC: Brookings Institution Press.

Evenett, Simon J. (2019). "Protectionism, State Discrimination, and International Business Since the Onset of the Global Financial Crisis." *Journal of International Business Policy*, 1–28.

Fackler, Martin. (2009). "North Korea Vows to Produce Nuclear Weapons." *New York Times* (June 14): A12.

Fahrenthold, David A., and Paul Kane. (2011). "Lawmakers Urging Speedy Pullout in Afghanistan Unlikely to Make Headway." *Washington Post* (May 5). washingtonpost.com/politics/lawmakers_urging_speedy_pullout_in_afghanistan_unlikely_to_make_headaway/2011/05/05/AFgvJf1F_story.html?nav5emailpage.

Fahs, Ramsey. (2019). "How Coca-Cola Came to China, 40 Years Ago." *China Channel* (February 6). chinachannel.org/2019/02/06/coke-in-china/.

——— (1993). "How the World Works." *The Atlantic* (December).

Fallows, James. (1993). "How the World Works." *The Atlantic* (December).

FAO. (2019). "The State of Food Insecurity in the World." *World Food Programme*. Rome: FAO.

Farrell, Henry. (2015). "The U.S.-led Global Economic Order Is Dying." *Washington Post* (Jan 7). washingtonpost.com/news/monkey-cage/wp/2015/01/07/the-u-s-led-global-economic-order-is-dying/ (accessed June 16, 2019).

Farrell, Theo. (2002). "Constructivist Security Studies: Portrait of a Research Program." *International Studies Review* 4 (Spring): 49–72.

FAS (Federation of American Scientists). (2019). (May, prepared by Hans M. Kristensen and Matt Korda). "Status of World Nuclear Forces." *FAS*. fas.org/issues/nuclear-weapons/status-world-nuclear-forces/.

Federation of German Industries. (2019). *China – Partner and Systemic Competitor: How Do We Deal with China's State-Controlled Economy?* Berlin: BDI. Retrieved from english.bdi.eu/publication/news/china-partner-and-systemic-competitor/.

Feinstein, Lee, and Anne-Marie Slaughter. (2004). "A Duty to Prevent." *Foreign Affairs* 83 (January/February): 136–150.

Feldman, Noah. (2013). *Cool War: The Future of Global Competition*. New York: Random House.

Felter, Claire, and Danielle Renwick. (2018). "Mercosur: South America's Fractious Trade Bloc." *Council on Foreign Relations*. cfr.org/backgrounder/mercosur-south-americas-fractious-trade-bloc.

Ferchen, Matt. (2013). "Whose China Model Is It Anyway? The Contentious Search for Consensus." *Review of International Political Economy (RIPE)* 20 (2): 390–420.

Ferguson, Niall. (2011). "The Mash of Civilizations: Social Networks Might Promote Democracy, but They Also Empower the Enemies of Freedom." *Newsweek* (April 18): 9.

——— (2010). "Complexity and Collapse: Empires on the Edge of Chaos." *Foreign Affairs* 89 (2): 18–32.

——— (2009). "The Axis of Upheaval." *Foreign Policy* (March/April): 56–58.

——— (2008). *The Ascent of Money*. New York: Penguin Press.

——— (2004). *Colossus: The Price of America's Empire*. New York: Penguin.

——— (2001). *The Cash Nexus*. New York: Basic Books.

Ferris, Elizabeth. (2005). "Faith-based and Secular Humanitarian Organizations." *International Review of the Red Cross* 87(858): 311–325. doi:10.1017/S1816383100181366.

Fidler, David P., and Lawrence O. Gostin. (2008). *Biosecurity in the Global Age*. Palo Alto, CA: Stanford University Press.

Fieldhouse, D. K. (1973). *Economics and Empire, 1830–1914*. Ithaca, NY: Cornell University Press.

Financial Action Task Force (FATF). (2019). "What is Money Laundering?" fatf-gafi.org/faq/moneylaundering/.

Financial Times. (2007). "Why Are Food Prices Rising?" media.ft.com/cms/s/2/f5bd920c-975b-11dc-9e08-0000779fd2ac.html?from5 textlinkindepth.

Finnemore, Martha. (2013). "Constructing Norms of Humanitarian Intervention." In *Conflict After the Cold War: Arguments on Causes of War and Peace*, 4th ed., edited by Richard K. Betts. Boston, MA: Pearson.

——— (2009). "Legitimacy, Hypocrisy, and the Social Structure of Unipolarity: Why Being a Unipole Isn't All It's Cracked Up to Be." *World Politics* 61: 58–85.

——— (2003). *The Purpose of Intervention: Changing Beliefs about the Use of Force*. Ithaca, N.Y.: Cornell University Press.

Fisher, Max. (2014). "40 More Maps that Explain the World." *The Washington Post*. washingtonpost.com/news/worldviews/wp/2014/01/13/40-more-maps-that-explain-the-world/?noredirect=on&utm_term=.d29be8556453.

Fishman, Charles. (2015). "Don't Let Water Be the Problem: If Iran and the United States Can Cooperate on Water Issues, Anyone Can." *Foreign Policy* (July/August): 72–75. foreignpolicy.com/2015/07/20/starving-for-answers-food-water-united-nations/.

Fleming, Sean. (2019). "Chart of the Day: These Countries Create Most of the World's CO2 Emissions." *World Economic Forum* (June 7). weforum.org/agenda/2019/06/chart-of-the-day-these-countries-create-most-of-the-world-s-co2-emissions/.

Fletcher, Dan. (2010). "Friends without Borders." *Time* (May 31): 32–38.

Flückiger, Matthias, and Markus Ludwig. (2018). "Youth Bulges and Civil Conflict: Casual Evidence from Sub-Saharan Africa." *Journal of Conflict Resolution*. doi: 10.1177/0022002717707303.

Føllesdal, Andreas, Johan Karlsson Schaffer, and Geir Ulfstein. (eds.). (2013). *The Legitimacy of International Human Rights Regimes: Legal, Political and Philosophical Perspectives*. Cambridge, UK: Cambridge University Press.

Forbes. (2013; various years). "The World's Biggest Public Companies." *Forbes*. forbes.com/global2000/.

Fordham, Benjamin. (2010). "Trade and Asymmetric Alliances." *Journal of Peace Research* 47 (6): 685–696.

Foreign Policy/A.T. Kerney Inc. (2014). "The Fragile States Index." library.fundforpeace.org/library/cfsir1423-fragilestatesindex2014-06d.pdf.

Forero, Juan. (2005). "Bolivia Regrets IMF Experiment." *International Herald Tribune*, (December 14).

Forsberg, Erika. (2014). "Diffusion in the Study of Civil Wars: A Cautionary Tale." *International Studies Review* 16 (June): 188–198.

Forsythe, David P. (2012). *Human Rights in International Studies*. Cambridge, UK: Cambridge University Press.

Foster, Dennis, M., and Johnathan W. Keller. (2014). "Leaders' Cognitive Complexity, Distrust, and the Diversionary Use of Force." *Foreign Policy Analysis* 10, no. 3: 205–223, doi.org/10.1111/fpa.12019.

Foulon, Michiel. (2015). "Neoclassical Realism: Challengers and Bridging Identities." *International Studies Review* 17: 635–661.

Foust, Joshua, and Ashley S. Boyle. (2012). "The Strategic Context of Lethal Drones: A Framework for Discussion." *American Security Project*. scribd.com/doc/102744195/The-Strategic-Context- of-Lethal-Drones.

Frank, Andre Gunder. (1969). *Latin America: Underdevelopment or Revolution*. New York: Monthly Review Press.

Frasquieri, Manuel Hevia. (2011). *The Seven-League Giant*. Havana, Cuba: Editorial Capitan San Luis.

Fravel, M. Taylor. (2010). "International Relations Theory and China's Rise: Assessing China's Potential for Territorial Expansion." *International Studies Review* 12 (December): 505–532.

Frederking, Brian, and Paul F. Diehl. (eds.). (2015). *The Politics of Global Governance: International Organizations in an Interdependent World*, 5th ed. Boulder, CO: Lynne Reinner.

Free the Slaves. (2015). *Free the Slaves*. freetheslaves.net/.

Freedman, Lawrence. (2010). "Frostbitten: Decoding the Cold War, 20 Years Later." *Foreign Affairs* (March/April).

Freedom House. (2019). *Freedom in the World 2019*. freedomhouse.org/sites/default/files/Feb2019_FH_FITW_2019_Report_ForWeb-compressed.pdf.

——— (2015). *Freedom in the World 2015*. freedomhouse.org/sites/default/files/01152015_FIW_2015_final.pdf.

Freeland, Chrystia. (2012). "The Cost of Modern Revolution." *The Atlantic Magazine* (July/August). theatlantic.com/magazine/archive/2012/07/the-cost-of-modern-revolution/9035/.

Freeman, Charles. (2010). "President Obama to Meet the Dalai Lama." *Center for Strategic and International Studies* (February 17). csis.org/publication/president-obama-meet-dalai-lama.

French, George. (2009). "A Year in Bank Supervision: 2008 and a Few of Its Lessons." *Supervisory Insights* 6 (1): 3–18.

Friedman, Alan. (1997). "Soros Calls Mahathir A 'Menace' to Malaysia." *New York Times* (September 22). nytimes.com/1997/09/22/news/22iht-soros.t.html.

Friedman, George. (2011). *The Next Decade: Where We've Been . . . and Where We're Going*. New York: Doubleday, Random House.

Friedman, Milton. (1970). "The Social Responsibility of Business is to Increase its Profits." *The New York Times Magazine*. Retrieved from umich.edu/~thecore/doc/Friedman.pdf.

Friedman, Thomas L. (2008). *Hot, Flat, and Crowded: Why We Need a Green Revolution, and How It Can Renew America*. New York: Farrar, Straus and Giroux.

——— (2007a). "It's a Flat World, After All." In *Global Issues 06/07*, edited by Robert M. Jackson. Dubuque, IA: McGraw-Hill Contemporary Learning Series.

——— (2007b). *The World Is Flat 3.0: A Brief History of the 21st Century*. New York: Farrar, Straus, and Giroux.

Friedman, Uri. (2018). "Syria's War Has Never Been More International." *The Atlantic*. theatlantic.com/international/archive/2018/02/syria-civil-war-next/553232/.

——— (2014). "The Other 9/11: A CIA Agent Remembers Chile's Coup." *The Atlantic*. theatlantic.com/international/archive/2014/09/chile-coup-salvador-allende-cia/380082/.

Friedrich, Johannes, Mengpin Ge, and Andrew Pickens. (2017). "This Interactive Chart Explains World's Top 10 Emitters, and How They've Changed." World Resources Institute. wri.org/blog/2017/04/interactive-chart-explains-worlds-top-10-emitters-and-how-theyve-changed.

Fritts, Rachel. (2018). "Tropical Deforestation is the Third-Biggest Carbon Emitter in the World." *Pacific Standard* (Oct 19). psmag.com/environment/tropical-deforestation-leads-to-more-carbon-emissions.

Fukuyama, Francis. (2018). *Identity: The Demand for Dignity and the Politics of Resentment*. New York: Farrar, Straus and Giroux.

——— (2018b). "Can Liberal Democracies Survive Identity Politics?" *The Economist*. economist.com/open-future/2018/09/30/can-liberal-democracies-survive-identity-politics.

——— (2011). *The Origins of Political Order: From Prehuman Times to the French Revolution*. New York: Farar, Straus and Giroux.

——— (ed.). (2008). *Blindside: How to Anticipate Future Events and Wild Cards in Global Politics*. Washington, DC: Brookings Institution.

——— (1999a). *The Great Disruption: Human Nature and the Reconstitution of Social Order*. New York: Free Press.

——— (1992). "The Beginning of Foreign Policy." *New Republic* (August 17 and 24): 24–32.

——— (1989). "The End of History?" *The National Interest* 16: 3–18.

Futurist. (2007). "Forecasts from the Futurist Magazine." wfs.org/book/export/html/68.

Gaddis, John L. (2006). *The Cold War: A New History*. Penguin.

Gaetan, Victor. (2013). "The Church Undivided: Benedict's Quest to Bring Christians Back Together." *Foreign Affairs* 92 (May/June): 117–128.

Galgano, Frank. (2018). "The Challenges of Global Water Supply and Demand." *GreenBiz*. greenbiz.com/article/challenges-global-water-supply-and-demand.

Gallagher, Maryann E., and Susan H. Allen. (2013). "Presidential Personality: Not Just a Nuisance." *Foreign Policy Analysis* (February): 1–21.

Ganley, Elaine. (2015). "AP Interview: UN Climate Chief: Paris to Set 50-Year Agenda." *Beaumont Enterprise* (July 22). beaumontenterprise.com/business/energy/article/AP-Interview-UN-climate-chief-says-Paris-talks-6399103.php.

Garamone, Jim. (2010). "Gates Calls for Significant Cuts in Defense Overhead." *U.S. Department of Defense*. archive.defense.gov/news/newsarticle.aspx?id=59082.

Garfield, Richard. (1999). "Morbidity and Mortality among Iraqi Children from 1990 through 1998." cam.ac.uk/societies/casi/info/garfield/drgarfield.html.

Garrett, Geoffrey. (2004). "Globalization's Missing Middle." *Foreign Affairs* 83 (November/December): 84–96.

Garrett, Laurie. (2007). "The Challenge of Global Health." *The New York Times* (January 2). nytimes.com/cfr/world/20070101faessay_v86n1_garrett.html?pagewanted=all&_r=3&.

Gartzke, Erik, and Matthew Kroenig. (2009). "A Strategic Approach to Nuclear Proliferation." *Journal of Conflict Resolution* 53: 151–160.

Gartzke, Erik, and Quan Li. (2003). "How Globalization Can Reduce International Conflict." In *Globalization and Armed Conflict*, edited by Nils Petter Gleditsch, Gerald Schneider, and Katherine Barbieri, 123–140. New York: Rowman & Littlefield.

Gartzke, Erik, and Alex Weisiger. (2013). "Permanent Friends? Dynamic Difference and the Democratic Peace." *International Studies Quarterly* 57 (1): 171–185.

Gayle, Damien. (2013). "The Incredible U.S. Military Spy Drone That's So Powerful It Can See What Type of Phone You're Carrying from 17,500 ft." *Daily Mail* (January 28). dailymail.co.uk/sciencetech/article-2269563/The-U-S-militarys-real-time-Google-Street-View-Airborne-spy-camera-track-entire-city-1-800MP.html.

Gebrekidan, Fikru. (2010). "Ethiopia and Congo: A Tale of Two Medieval Kingdoms." *Callaloo* 33 (1): 223–238.

Gelb, Leslie H. (2009). *Power Rules: How Common Sense Can Rescue American Foreign Policy*. New York: HarperCollins.

Gershenfeld, Neil, and J. P. Vasseur. (2014). "As Objects Go Online." *Foreign Affairs* (March/April): 60–67.

Gibbs, David, Nancy Harris, and Frances Seymour. (2018). "By the Numbers: The Value of Tropical Forests in the Climate Change Equation." *World Resources Institute*. wri.org/blog/2018/10/numbers-value-tropical-forests-climate-change-equation.

Gibbs, Nancy. (2011). "The Best Investments: If You Really Want to Fight Poverty, Fuel Growth and Combat Extremism, Try Girl Power." *Time* (February 14): 64.

Gibler, Douglas M. (2007). "Bordering on Peace." *International Studies Quarterly* 51 (September): 509–532.

Gideon, Jasmine. (2006). "Accessing Economic and Social Rights under Neoliberalism: Gender and Rights in Chile." *Third World Quarterly* 27, no. 7: 1269–1283. amherst.edu/media/view/92441/original/Gideon.gender%2Brights%2BChile.pdf.

Gies, Erica. (2008). "New Wave in Energy: Turning Algae to Oil." *International Herald Tribune* (June 30): 3.

Gilens, Naomi. (2013). "New Documents Reveal U.S. Marshals' Drones Experiment, Underscoring Need for Government Transparency." *ACLU* (February 27). aclu.org/blog/national-security/secrecy/new-documents-reveal-us-marshals-drones-experiment-underscoring-need.

Giles, Martin. (2010). "A World of Connections." *The Economist* (January 30): 3–4.

Gilley, Bruce, and Andrew O'Neil. (eds.). (2014). *Middle Powers and the Rise of China*. Washington, DC: Georgetown University Press.

Gilligan, Michael, and Stephen John Stedman. (2003). "Where Do the Peacekeepers Go?" *International Studies Review* 5 (4): 37–54.

Gilpin, Robert. (2001). "Three Ideologies of Political Economy." In *The Global Agenda*, 6th ed., edited by Charles W. Kegley and Eugene R. Wittkopf, 269–286. Boston: McGraw-Hill.

Gladstone, Rick. (2014). "U.S. Lays Groundwork to Reduce Land Mines and Join Global Treaty." *New York Times*. nytimes.com/2014/06/28/us/us-to-cut-its-land-mine-stockpile.html.

Glaeser, Edward. (2011). *Triumph of the City: How Our Greatest Invention Makes Us Richer, Smarter, Greener, Healthier and Happier*. New York: Penguin.

Glaser, Charles L. (2011). "Security Dilemma in Structural International Relations Theory." *The Encyclopedia of Peace Psychology* (November). doi: 10.1002/9780470672532.wbepp245.

Glass, Ira, and Adam Davidson. (2008, May 9). *This American Life: The Giant Pool of Money*. National Public Radio. thisamerican-life.org/extras/radio/355_transcript.pdf.

Glenn, Jerome C., Theodore J. Gordon, and Elizabeth Florescu. (2017). *State of the Future 19.0*. Washington, DC: The Millennium Project.

Glenny, M. (2008). *McMafia: A Journey through the Global Underworld*. Knopf.

Global Edge. (2015). "Mercosur: Statistics." Michigan State University. globaledge.msu.edu/trade-blocs/mercosur/statistics.

Globalfirepower.com. (2019). "Taiwan Military Strength." globalfirepower.com/country-military-strength-detail.asp?country_id=taiwan.

——— (2013). *World Military Strength Ranking 2013*. globalfirepower.com.

Global Financial Integrity. (2019). "Illicit Financial Flows are Significant and Persistent Drag on Developing Country Economies." gfintegrity.org/press-release/2019-iff-update-press-release/.

Global Slavery Index. (2019). "About the Index." *The Minderoo Foundation*. globalslaveryindex.org/about/the-index/.

Gluck, Caroline, and Iffath Yeasmine. (2019). "Rohingya Refugees Fret for their Children's Futures." *UNHCR Canada*. unhcr.ca/news/rohingya-refigees-fret-childrens-futures/.

Gogel, Robert. (2014). "LPO Fastest Growing Segment in India." *Value Notes* (March 12). sourcingnotes.com/content/view/913/1/.

Goldenberg, Suzanne. (2015). "2014 Officially the Hottest Year on Record." *The Guardian* (January 16). theguardian.com/environment/2015/jan/16/2014-hottest-year-on-record-scientists-noaa-nasa.

Goldin, Ian, and Mike Mariathasan. (2015). *The Butterfly Defect: How Globalization Creates Systemic Risks, and What to Do About It*. Princeton, NJ: Princeton University Press.

Goldsmith, Jack. (2008). *The Terror Presidency: Law and Judgment Inside the Bush Administration*. New York: Norton.

Goldsmith, Jack I., and Eric A. Posner. (2005). *The Limits of International Law*. New York: Oxford University Press.

Goldstein, Jacob. (2016). "The Last Bank Bailout." *National Public Radio (NPR)*. npr.org/templates/transcript/transcript.php?storyId=507125309.

Goldstein, J. S. (2012). *Winning the War on War: The Decline of Armed Conflict Worldwide*. Plume Books.

Goldstone, Jack. (2010). "The New Population Bomb: The Four Megatrends That Will Change the World." *Foreign Affairs* 89 (1): 31–43.

Golubski, Christina. (2017). "Figure of the Week: Growing Illicit Financial Flows in the Developing World." *Brookings Institution: Africa in Focus* (May 18), brookings.edu/blog/africa-in-focus/2017/05/18/figure-of-the-week-growing-illicit-financial-flows-in-the-developing-world/ (accessed June 10, 2019).

Gomis, B., and N.C. Botero. (2016). "Sneaking a Smoke: Paraguay's Tobacco Business Fuels Latin America's Black Market." *Foreign Affairs* (February 5). foreignaffairs.com/articles/paraguay/2016-02-05/sneaking-smoke.

González, Anabel. (2014). "Introduction." In *Global Agenda Council on Trade & Foreign Direct Investment, Mega-regional Trade Agreements: Game-Changers or Costly Distractions for the World Trading System?* Geneva: World Economic Forum. weforum.org/docs/GAC/2014/WEF_GAC_TradeFDI_MegaRegionalTradeAgreements_Report_2014.pdf.

Goodman, Peter. (2019). "The Dollar is Still King." *New York Times* (Feb. 22). nytimes.com/2019/02/22/business/dollar-currency-value.html (accessed June 18, 2019).

Gore, Al. (2006). *An Inconvenient Truth: The Planetary Emergency and What We Can Do About It*. Emmaus, PA: Rodale.

Goudreau, Jenna. (2013). "Eight Leadership Lessons from the World's Most Powerful Women." *Forbes* (March 21). forbes.com/sites/jennagoudreau/2013/03/21/eight-leadership-les-sons-from-the-worlds-most-powerful-women/.

Government Accounting Office (2009). "Financial Markets Regulation: Financial Crisis Highlights the Need to Improve Oversight of Leverage at Financial Institutions and Across Systems." Washington, DC: Government Accounting Office.

Graeber, Daniel. (2018). "The Populist Appeal of American Decline."

Graham, Edward Montgomery. (2000). *Fighting the Wrong Enemy: Antiglobal Activists and Multinational Enterprises*. Peterson Institute.

Graham, Sarah Ellen. (2014). "Emotion and Public Diplomacy: Dispositions in International Communications, Dialogue, and Persuasion." *International Studies Review* 16 (4): 522–539.

Gramer, Robbie, and Lara Seligman. (2019). "The INF Treaty is Dead. Is New START Next?" *Foreign Policy*. foreignpolicy.com/2019/02/01/the-inf-treaty-is-dead-is-new-start-next-russia-arms/#.

Granville, Kevin. (2015). "The Trans-Pacific Partnership Trade Deal: What It Would Mean." *New York Times* (May 11). nytimes.com/2015/05/12/business/unpacking-the-trans-pacific-partnership-trade-deal.html?_r=0.

Gray, Eliza. (2015). "Japan's Population Falls to 15-Year Low." *Time* (April 18). time.com/3827440/japans-population-falls/.

Gray, John. (2010). "World Wide Web: The Myth and Reality of the United Nations." *Harper's Magazine* (June): 78–82.

Green, Jessica. (2013). *Rethinking Private Authority: Agents and Entrepreneurs in Global Environmental Governance*. Princeton: University Press.

Greenhill, Brian. (2010). "The Company You Keep: International Socialization and the Diffusion of Human Rights Norms." *International Studies Quarterly* 54: 127–145.

Greenhill, B., L. Mosley, and A. Prakash (2009). "Trade-based Diffusion of Labor Rights: A Panel Study, 1986–2002." *American Political Science Review* 103(4): 669–690.

Greene, Toby. (2019). "When Conviction Trumps Domestic Politics: Tony Blair and the Second Lebanon War." *Foreign Policy Analysis* 15: 43–64.

Gregorio, José De, Barry Eichengreen, Takatoshi Ito, and Charles Wyplosz. (2018). *IMF Reform: The Unfinished Agenda*. Geneva, Switzerland: International Center for Monetary and Banking Studies (ICMB). cepr.org/sites/default/files/events/Geneva20.pdf.

GRFC. (2019). "Global Report on Food Crises: Joint Analysis for Better Decisions." *Food Security Information Network*. fsinplatform.org/sites/default/files/resources/files/GRFC_2019-Full_Report.pdf.

Grieco, Joseph M. (1995). "Anarchy and the Limits of Cooperation: A Realist Critique of the Newest Liberal Institutionalism." In *Controversies in International Relations Theory*, edited by Charles W. Kegley, 1. New York: St. Martin's.

Griffin, Penny. (2013). "Gendering Global Finance: Crisis, Masculinity, and Responsibility." *Men and Masculinities* 16 (1): 9–34.

Grimond, John. (2010). "For Want of a Drink." *The Economist* (May 20): 3.

Grunwald, Michael. (2009). "How Obama Is Using the Science of Change." *Time* (April 13): 28–32.

Grusky, Sara. (2001). "Privatization Tidal Wave: IMF/World Bank Water Policies and the Price Paid by the Poor." *The Multinational Monitor* 22 (September). multinationalmonitor.org/mm2001/01september/sep-01corp2.htm.

Guanglie, Liang. (2011). "A Better Future through Security Cooperation." *2011 Shangri-la Dialogue*. newspaper-vietblues.blogspot.com/2011/06/fourth-plenary-session-general-liang.html.

Gustin, Georgina, and Mariana Henninger. (2019). "Central America's Choice: Pray for Rain or Migrate." *NBC News*. nbcnews.com/news/latino/central-america-drying-farmers-face-choice-pray-rain-or-leave-n1027346.

Gutner, Tamar. (2018). "AIIB: Is the Chinese-led Development Bank a Role Model?" *Council on Foreign Relations*. cfr.org/blog/aiib-chinese-led-development-bank-role-model.

Gwartney, James, Robert Lawson, and Joshua Hall. (2014). *Economic Freedom of the World: 2014 Annual Report*. Vancouver, Canada: Fraser Institute.

Gygli, Savina, Florian Haelg, Niklas Potrafke, and Jan-Egbert Sturm. (2019). "The KOF Globalisation Index: Revisited." *Review of International Organizations*. doi.org/10.1007/s11558-019-09344-2.

Gvosdev, Nikolas K. (2005). "The Value(s) of Realism." *SAIS Review of International Affairs* 25 (Winter/Spring): 17–25.

Habermas, Jürgen. (1984). *The Theory of Communicative Action*, 2 vols. Boston: Beacon Press.

Haddad, H. N. (2013). "After the Norm Cascade: NGO Mission Expansion and the Coalition for the International Criminal Court." *Global Governance*, 187–206.

Hafner-Burton, E. M., and H.M. McNamara. (2019). "United States Human Rights Policy: The Corporate Lobby." *Human Rights Quarterly* 41(1): 115–142.

Hafner-Burton, Emilie M., Kiyoteru Tsutsui, and John W. Meyer. (2008). "International Human Rights Law and the Politics of Legitimation: Repressive States and Human Rights Treaties." *International Sociology* 23 (January): 115–141.

Hagan, Shelly. (2019). "Global Uncertainty Gauge Enters 2019 at Record High Level." *Bloomberg*. bloomberg.com/news/articles/2019-02-04/global-uncertainty-gauge-enters-2019-at-record-high-level.

Haggard, Stephan, and Jon R. Lindsay. (2015). "North Korea and the Sony Hack: Exporting Instability through Cyberspace." *East-West Center*. eastwestcenter.org/system/tdf/private/api117.pdf?file=1&type=node&id=35164.

Haigh, Stephen Paul. (2013). *Future States: From International to Global Order*. Burlington, VT: Ashgate.

Halder, Ben. (2019). "The Monopolies of the Future Will Be Chinese — and State-Owned." *Microsoft News*. msn.com/en-us/money/companies/the-monopolies-of-the-future-will-be-chinese-%E2%80%94-and-state-owned/ar-AACYWa0.

Hales, Mike, and Andres Pena. (2012). "2012 Global Cities Index and Emerging Cities Outlook." *ATKearny*. atkearney.com/documents/10192/dfedfc4c-8a62-4162-90e5-2a3f14f0da3a.

Hall, Anthony J. (2004). *The America Empire and the Fourth World*. Montreal: McGill-Queen's University Press.

Halperin, Sandra. (2013). *Re-Envisioning Global Development: A Horizontal Perspective*. New York: Taylor and Francis.

Halsey, Ashley. (2011). "Terrorism Threat Remains, Experts Say." *Washington Post* (May 2), washingtonpost.com/local/terrorism-threat-to-us-remains-despite-bin-ladens-killing-experts-say/2011/05/02/AF9dPcaF_story.html?utm_term=.ff8c7d683371.

Hamilton, Alexander. (1913, 1791). *Report on Manufactures*. Washington, DC: U.S. Government. books.google.com.

Hamilton, G. (2013). "The Maple Syrup Cartel." *National Post*. Available at news.nationalpost.com/news/canada/the-maple-syrup-cartel-quebecs-syrup-monopoly-helped-spawn-smuggling-prohibition-style.

Hannah, Mark. (2019). "Afghanistan May Be a Mess if US Troops Leave; They Should Leave Anyway. Trump is Right." *USA Today*. usatoday.com/story/opinion/2019/01/23/trump-pull-us-troops-end-unwinnable-war-afghanistan-taliban-column/2645055002/.

——— (2009). "Issue Advocacy on the Internet, Part 1." *Mediashift* (May 7). pbs.org/mediashift/2009/05/issue-advocacy-on-the-internet-part-1127.html.

Hannigan, John. (2012). *Disasters without Borders: The International Politics of Natural Disasters*. Cambridge: Polity.

Hardin, Garrett. (1968). "The Tragedy of the Commons." *Science* 162 (December): 1243–1248.

Hardy, Quentin. (2013). "Global Slavery, by the Numbers." *New York Times*. bits.blogs.nytimes.com/2013/03/06/global-slavery-by-the-numbers/?r=0.

Harknett, Richard J., and Hasan B. Yalcin. (2012). "The Structure for Autonomy: A Realist Structural Theory of International Relations." *International Studies Review* 14 (4): 499–521.

Harper's (2008). "Harper's Index." *Harper's Magazine* (January): 15.

Harris, Bill. (2018). "Bitcoin is the Greatest Scam in History." *Vox*. vox.com/2018/4/24/17275202/bitcoin-scam-cryptocurrency-mining-pump-dump-fraud-ico-value.

Harris, Edward. (2008). "World Chopping Down Trees at Pace That Affects Climate." *The Cincinnati Enquirer* (February 3): A2.

Harrison, Neil E. (2006). "Thinking About the World We Make." In *Complexity in World Politics: Concepts and Methods of a New Paradigm*, 17–18. Albany: State University of New York.

Hartzell, Caroline, and Matthew Hoddie. (2007). *Crafting Peace: Power-Sharing Institutions and the Negotiated Settlement of Civil Wars*. University Park, PA: Pennsylvania State University Press.

Haskin, Jeanne. (2005). *The Tragic Congo: From Decolonization to Dictatorship*. New York: Algora.

Hathaway, Oona A. (2007). "Why We Need International Law." *The Nation* (November 19): 35–39.

Haynes, Jeffrey (2004). "Religion and International Relations." *International Politics* 41 (September): 451–462.

Hayunga, Robbie. (2019). "Congress Searches for Answers to Climate Change, Experts Say We Need Nuclear." *NEI*. nei.org/news/2019/congress-answers-climate-change-experts-nuclear.

Hecht, Jeff. (2007). "Military Wins Ig Nobel Peace Prize for 'Gay Bomb.'" *New Scientist*. newscientist.com/article/dn12721.

Hegre, Håvard, John R. Oneal, and Bruce M. Russett. (2010). "Trade Does Promote Peace: New Simultaneous Estimates of the Reciprocal Efforts of Trade and Conflict." *Journal of Peace Research* 47 (6): 763–774.

Helleiner, Eric. (2014). *The Status Quo Crisis: Global Financial Governance after the 2008 Meltdown*. New York: Oxford University Press.

Hellion, Christophe. (2010). "The Creeping Nationalism of the EU Enlargement Policy." *Swedish Institute for European Policy Studies* 6 (November).

Hendrix, Cullen S., and Stephan Haggard. (2015). "Global Food Prices, Regime Type, and Urban Unrest in the Developing World." *Journal of Peace Research* (March): 143–157.

Hensel, Howard M. (ed.). (2007). *The Law of Armed Conflict*. Burlington, VT: Ashgate.

Heredia, Blanca. (1999). "Prosper or Perish? Development in the Age of Global Capital." In *Global Issues 1999/00*, 15th ed., edited by Robert M. Jackson. Guilford, CT: Dushkin/McGraw-Hill.

Hermann, Charles F. (1988). "New Foreign Policy Problems and Old Bureaucratic Organizations." In *The Domestic Sources of American Foreign Policy*, edited by Charles W. Kegley and Eugene R. Wittkopf, 2. New York: St. Martin's.

Hermann, Margaret G. (2007). *Comparative Foreign Policy Analysis: Theories and Methods*. Upper Saddle River, NJ: Prentice Hall.

——— (1988) "The Role of Leaders and Leadership in the Making of American Foreign Policy." In *The Domestic Sources of American Foreign Policy*, edited by Charles W. Kegley and Eugene R. Wittkopf, 266–284. New York: St. Martin's.

——— (1976). "When Leader Personality Will Affect Foreign Policy." In *In Search of Global Patterns*, edited by James N. Rosenau, 3. New York: Free Press.

Herz, John H. (1951). *Political Realism and Political Idealism*. Chicago: University of Chicago Press.

Higgins, Michelle. (2011). "New Ways to Visit Cuba—Legally." *New York Times* (June 30): TR3.

Hindle, Tim. (2004). "The Third Age of Globalization." In *The Economist: The World in 2004*, 97–98. London: The Economist.

Hironaka, Ann. (2005). *Neverending Wars*. Cambridge, MA: Harvard University Press.

Hirschman, Albert. (1945). *National Power and the Structure of Foreign Trade*. Berkeley: University of California Press.

Hittner, Jeffrey. (2010, September 23). "Sustainability: An Engine for Growth." carnegiecouncil.org/resources/ethics_online/0049.html.

Hobson, John A. (1965; 1902). *Imperialism*. Ann Arbor: University of Michigan Press.

Hoekman, Bernard M., and Petros C. Mavroidis. (2015). "Embracing Diversity: Plurilateral Agreements and the Trading System." *World Trade Review* 14 (1): 101–116.

Hoffman, David E. (2011). "The New Virology: The Future of War by Other Means." *Foreign Policy* (March/April): 77–80.

Hoffmann, Matthew. (2009). "Is Constructivist Ethics an Oxymoron?" *International Studies Review* 11 (2): 231–252.

Hoffmann, Stanley. (1961). "International Systems and International Law." In *The International System*, edited by Klaus Knorr and Sidney Verba, 2. Princeton, NJ: Princeton University Press.

Holstein, William J. (2005). "One Global Game, Two Sets of Rules." *New York Times* (August 14): BU9.

Holsti, Kalevi J. (2004). *Taming the Sovereigns: Institutional Changes in International Politics*. Cambridge: Cambridge University Press.

——— (1991). *Peace and War*. Cambridge: Cambridge University Press.

Holton, Kate. (2017). "Russian Twitter Accounts Promoted Brexit Ahead of EU Referendum: Times Newspaper." *Reuters*. reuters.com/article/us-britain-eu-russia/russian-twitter-accounts-promoted-brexit-ahead-of-eu-referendum-times-newspaper-idUSKBN1DF0ZR.

Hook, Stephen. (2012). "The Post-Cold War Era." In *Routledge Handbook of American Foreign Policy*, edited by Stephen Hook and Christopher Jones, 46–58. New York: Routledge.

Hooper, Charlotte. (2001). *Manly States*. New York: Columbia University Press.

Horkheimer, Max. (1947). *Eclipse of Reason*. New York: Oxford University Press.

Horn, Laura, Olivier Rubin, and Laust Schouenborg. (2015). "Undead Pedagogy: How a Zombie Simulation Can Contribute to Teaching International Relations." *International Studies Perspectives*: 1–15.

Horowitz, Michael. (2009). "The Spread of Nuclear Weapons and International Conflict: Does Experience Matter?" *Journal of Conflict Resolution* 53 (2): 234–257.

Hotten, Russel. (2015). "Volkswagen: The Scandal Explained." *BBC News*. bbc.com/news/business-34324772.

Houry, Nadim. (2019). "Bringing ISIS to Justice: Running Out of Time?" *Human Rights Watch*. hrw.org/news/2019/02/05/bringing-isis-justice-running-out-time.

Htun, Mala, and S. Laurel Weldon. (2010). "When Do Governments Promote Women's Rights? A Framework for the Comparative Analysis of Sex Equality Policy." *Perspectives on Politics* 8 (1): 207–216.

Hudson, Kimberly A. (2009). *Justice, Intervention, and Force in International Relations: Reassessing Just War Theory in the 21st Century*. New York: Routledge.

Hudson, Natalie F. (2005). "En-Gendering UN Peacekeeping Operations." *International Journal* 60 (3): 785–807.

Hudson, Valerie M. (2012). *Sex and World Peace*. New York: Columbia University Press.

Hufbauer, Gary Clyde. (2014). "A Good Deal Settles the Brazil Cotton Dispute." *Peterson Institute for International Economics*. piie.com/blogs/trade-investment-policy-watch/good-deal-settles-brazil-cotton-dispute.

Hufbauer, Gary Clyde, Jeffrey J. Schott, and Kimberly Ann Elliott. (1990). *Economic Sanctions Reconsidered*, 2nd ed. Washington, DC: Institute for International Economics.

Hufbauer, Gary Clyde, Jeffrey J. Schott, Kimberly Ann Elliott, and B. Oegg. (2007). *Economic Sanctions Reconsidered*, 3rd ed. Washington, DC: Institute for International Economics.

Hughes, Emmet John. (1972). *The Living Presidency*. New York: Coward, McCann and Geoghegan.

Human Rights Watch. (2019). "Saudi Arabia: 10 Reasons Why Women Flee." hrw.org/news/2019/01/30/saudi-arabia-10-reasons-why-women-flee.

——— (2019b). "Cuba, Events of 2018." *World Report 2019*. hrw.org/world-report/2019/country-chapters/cuba.

Human Security Centre. (2006). *Human Security Brief 2006*. Vancouver, Canada: University of British Columbia.

Hume, David. (1817). *Philosophical Essays on Morals, Literature, and Politics*, Vol. 1. Washington, DC: Duffy.

Humpert, Malte. (2018). "Shipping Traffic in Canadian Arctic Nearly Triples." *High North News*. highnorthnews.com/en/shipping-traffic-canadian-arctic-nearly-triples.

Hunt, Swanee, and Cristina Posa. (2005). "Women Making Peace." In *Developing World 05/06*, edited by Robert J. Griffiths, 2. Dubuque, IA: McGraw-Hill/Dushkin.

Huntington, Samuel P. (2005). "The Lonely Superpower." In *American Foreign Policy: Theoretical Essays*, edited by G. John Ikenberry, 540–550. New York: Pearson/Longman.

——— (2001a). "The Coming Clash of Civilizations, or the West against the Rest." In *The Global Agenda*, 6th ed., edited by Charles W. Kegley and Eugene R. Wittkopf. Boston: McGraw-Hill.

——— (1996). *The Clash of Civilizations and the Remaking of World Order*. New York: Simon & Schuster.

——— (1993). "The Clash of Civilizations." *Foreign Affairs*. foreignaffairs.com/articles/united-states/1993-06-01/clash-civilizations.

——— (1991a). *The Third Wave: Democratization in the Late Twentieth Century*. Norman: University of Oklahoma Press.

——— (1991b). "America's Changing Strategic Interests." *Survival* (January/February): 5–6.

Hutchings, Kimberly. (2008). "1988 to 1998: Contrast and Continuity in Feminist International Relations." *Millennium—Journal of International Studies* (37): 97–105.

Hutchins, Reynolds. (2015). "High-tech Shippers Moving Operations Closer to Buyers." *Journal of Commerce* (May 20). joc.com/international-logistics/high-tech-shippers-increasingly-seen-moving-operations-closer-buyers_20150520.html?destination=node/3193636.

(IAEA) International Atomic Energy Agency. (2019). Nuclear Power Reactors in the World, (2). Vienna, IAEA.

——— (2017). *Country Nuclear Power Profiles*. pub.iaea.org/MTCD/Publications/PDF/cnpp2017/countryprofiles/UnitedStatesofAmerica/UnitedStatesofAmerica.htm.

Ibrahim, Abadir M. (2013). "International Trade and Human Rights: An Unfinished Debate." *German Law Journal* 14: 321.

Ikenberry, G. John. (2014). "The Illusion of Geopolitics: The Enduring Power of the Liberal Order." *Foreign Affairs* (May/June): 2.

——— (2011b). "The Future of the Liberal World Order: Internationalism after America." *Foreign Affairs* (May/June): 56–68.

Inglehart, Ronald, and Christian Welzel. (2009). "How Development Leads to Democracy." *Foreign Affairs* 88 (March/April): 33–48.

Insight on Conflict. (2015). "Sudan: Conflict Profile." *Insight on Conflict* (April). insightonconflict.org/conflicts/sudan/conflict-profile/?gclid=CPjw2tPJjbICFYqR7QodbV0AqQ.

Institute for Economics & Peace. (2018). *Global Peace Index 2018: Measuring Peace in a Complex World*. Sydney. Retrieved from visionofhumanity.org/reports.

——— (2014). *Global Terrorism Index 2014: Measuring and Understanding the Impact of Terrorism*. Sydney: Institute for Economics and Peace.

Institute for International Finance (IIF). (2018). "Global Debt Monitor." iif.com/Research/Capital-Flows-and-Debt/Global-Debt-Monitor/lapg-908/2.

Interlandi, Janeen. (2010). "The Race to Buy Up the World's Water." *Newsweek* (October 18): 39–46.

International Commission on Intervention and State Sovereignty. (2001) *Responsibility to Protect*. International Development Research Centre, Ottawa, Canada. responsibilitytoprotect.org/ICISS%20Report.pdf.

International Labour Organization (ILO). (2015). "Global Wage Report 2014/15." ilo.org/global/research/global-reports/global-wage-report/2014/lang--en/index.htm.

International Monetary Fund (IMF). (2019). "General Government Gross Debt: Percent of GDP." imf.org/external/datamapper/GGXWDG_NGDP@WEO/WEOWORLD/ADVEC/MAE.

——— (2019b). "Real GDP Growth: Annual Percent Change." imf.org/external/datamapper/NGDP_RPCH@WEO/OEMDC/ADVEC/WEOWORLD.

——— (2019c). "Currency Composition of Official Foreign Exchange Reserves (COFER)." data.imf.org/?sk=E6A5F467-C14B-4AA8-9F6D-5A09EC4E62A4.

International Monetary Fund (2019d). *World Economic Outlook (April 2019)*. imf.org/external/datamapper/datasets/WEO (accessed June 15, 2019).

International Monetary Fund (2019e). *IMF Data Mapper.*

International Monetary Fund. (2019f). "How the IMF Makes Decisions." (March 8) imf.org/en/About/Factsheets/Sheets/2016/07/27/15/24/How-the-IMF-Makes-Decisions (accessed June 17, 2019).

——— (2018). "World Economic Outlook Database." imf.org/external/pubs/ft/weo/2018/02/weodata/index.aspx.

——— (2015a). "World Economic Outlook Database." imf.org/external/pubs/ft/weo/2015/01/weodata/index.aspx.

——— (2015b). *World Economic Outlook: Hopes, Realities, Risks.* Washington, DC: International Monetary Fund Publication Services.

——— (2014). "Annual Report on Exchange Arrangements and Exchange Restrictions." imf.org/external/pubs/nft/2014/areaers/ar2014.pdf.

——— (2011, September 18). "Global Financial Stability Report." imf.org/external/pubs/ft/gfsr.

——— (2009). "Global Economy Contracts." *IMF Survey Online.* imf.org/external/pubs/ft/survey/so/2009/RES042209A.htm.

——— (2005). *World Economic Outlook, April 2005.* New York: International Monetary Fund.

International Organization for Migration. "Migration Data in Europe." *Migration data portal.* migrationdataportal.org/regional-data-overview/europe#past-and-present-trends.

International Union for the Conservation of Nature (IUCN). (2015). "IUCN Red List Status." iucnredlist.org/initiatives/mammals/analysis/red-list-status.

International Work Group for Indigenous Affairs. (2019a). "The Indigenous World." iwgia.org/regions.

Inter-Parliamentary Union. (2019). "Percentage of Women in National Parliaments." data.ipu.org/women-ranking?month=6&year=2019.

Inter-Parliamentary Union and UN Women. (2019). "Women in Politics 2019 Map." *UN Women.* unwomen.org/en/digital-library/publications/2019/03/women-in-politics-2019-map.

IPBES. (2019). *Global Assessment Report on Biodiversity and Ecosystem Services.* Retrieved from ipbes.net/global-assessment-report-biodiversity-ecosystem-services.

IPCC. (2019). *Special Report: Global Warming of 1.5 ºC.* ipcc.ch/sr15/chapter/summary-for-policy-makers/.

——— (2014). "Food Security and Food Production Systems." In *IPCC Climate Change 2014: Impacts, Adaptation, and Vulnerability. Part A: Global and Sectoral Aspects. Contribution of Working Group II to the Fifth Assessment Report of the Intergovernmental Panel on Climate Change.* Cambridge: Cambridge University Press.

Ireland, Corydon. (2010). "Slavery in 2010." *The Harvard Gazette.* news.harvard.edu/gazette/story/2010/02/slavery-in-2010/.

Irwin, Douglas. (2009). *Free Trade under Fire*, 3rd ed. Princeton, NJ: Princeton University Press.

ITU (International Telecommunications Union). (2017). *ICT Facts and Figures 2017*, Geneva: ITU. Retrieved from itu.int/en/ITUD/Statistics/Documents/facts/IC TFactsFigures2017.pdf

ITUC. (2014). *Case Against Qatar: Host of the FIFA 2022 World Cup.* Brussels, Belgium: ITUC. Retrieved from ituc-csi.org/IMG/pdf/the_case_against_qatar_en_web170314.pdf.

Iyengar, Rishi. (2015). "Why Nepal Wasn't Ready for the Earthquake." *Time* (April 28). time.com/3837805/nepal-earthquake-government-resources/?xid=newsletter-brief.

Jackson, Richard. (2013). "Balancing Adequacy and Sustainability: Lessons from the Global Aging Preparedness Index." *Over 65* (May 3). over65.thehastingscenter.org/balancing-adequacy-and-sustainability-lessons-from-the-global-aging-preparedness-index/.

Janis, Irving. (1982). *Groupthink: Psychological Studies of Policy Decisions and Fiascoes*, 2nd ed. Boston: Houghton Mifflin.

Jennings, Ralph. (2019). "Taiwan is Finally Luring Companies Back from China After More than 15 years of Trying." *South China Morning Post* (March 21).

Jensen, Lloyd. (1982). *Explaining Foreign Policy.* Englewood Cliffs, NJ: Prentice Hall.

Jentleson, Bruce, and Ely Ratner. (2011). "Bridging the Beltway-Ivory Tower Gap." *International Studies* 13 (1): 6–11.

Jervis, Robert. (2008). "Unipolarity: A Structural Perspective." *World Politics* 61: 188–213.

——— (2005). *American Foreign Policy in a New Era.* New York: Routledge.

Jing, Shi. (2018). "Coca-Cola Embarks on 'Healthy' Growth Route." *China Daily* (August 30). chinadaily.com.cn/a/201808/30/WS5b87454ea310add14f388906.html.

Joffe-Walt, Chana. (2013). "The Cotton Wars." *NPR* (May 3). npr.org/blogs/money/2013/05/03/180912847/episode-224-the-cotton-wars.

Johnson, Keith. (2018). "Is the Trade War About to Become a Currency War?" *Foreign Policy.* foreignpolicy.com/2018/10/03/us-china-trade-war-about-to-become-currency-war-yuan-renminbi/.

Johnson, James Turner. (2005). "Just War, as It Was and Is." *First Things* 149 (January): 14–24.

Johnson-Freese, Joan. (2016). *Space Warfare in the 21st Century: Arming the Heavens.* Abingdon, United Kingdom. Routledge.

Jones, Bruce, Carlos Pascual, and Stephen John Stedman. (2009). *Power & Responsibility: Building International Order in an Era of Transnational Threats.* Washington DC: Brookings Institute.

Jones, Terril Yue. (2013). "China Has 'Mountains of Data' about U.S. Cyber Attacks: Official." *Reuters* (June 5). news.yahoo.com/china-mountains-data-u-cyber-attacks-official-042422920.html.

Jordan, Jamie. (2015). "Life Under Austerity Shows Why Syriza Is Fighting It So Hard." *The Conversation* (June 9). theconversation.com/life-under-austerity-shows-why-syriza-is-fighting-it-so-hard-42953.

Joyner, Christopher C. (2005). *International Law in the 21st Century.* Lanham, MD: Rowman & Littlefield.

Joyner, James. (2011). "Back in the Saddle: How Libya Helped NATO Get Its Groove Back." *Foreign Policy* (April 15). foreignpolicy.com/articles/2011/04/15/back_in_the_saddle.

Jubilee Debt Campaign. (2019). "Crisis Deepens as Global South Debt Payments Increase by 85%." *Jubilee Debt Campaign.* jubileedebt.org.uk/press-release/crisis-deepens-as-global-south-debt-payments-increase-by-85.

Juris, Jeffrey S., and Alex Khasnabish (eds.). (2013). *Insurgent Encounters: Transnational Activism, Ethnography, and the Political.* Durham, NC: Duke University Press.

Justino, Patricia. (2009). "Poverty and Violent Conflict: A Micro-Level Perspective on the Causes and Duration of Warfare." *Journal of Peace Research* 46 (3): 315–333.

Kaarbo, Juliet. (2015). "A Foreign Policy Analysis Perspective on the Domestic Politics Turn in IR Theory." *International Studies Review* (June): 189–216.

Kabbani. (2019). brookings.edu/research/youth-employment-in-the-middle-east-and-north-africa-revisiting-and-reframing-the-challenge/.

Kagame, Paul. (2009). "Africa Has to Find its Own Road to Prosperity." *Financial Times* (May 7). ft.com/content/0d1218c8-3b35-11de-ba91-00144feabdc0.

Kahn, Robert. (2015). "A Bank Too Far?" *Council on Foreign Relations* (March 17). cfr.org/global-governance/bank-too-far/p36290.

Kahneman, Daniel. (2011). *Thinking, Fast and Slow*. New York: Farrar, Straus, and Giroux.

Kaiser, David. (1990). *Politics and War*. Cambridge, MA: Harvard University Press.

Kam, Cindy D., and Elizabeth N. Simas. (2010). "Risk Orientations and Policy Frames." *Journal of Politics* 72 (2): 381–396.

Kanellos, Michael. (2013). "Google Explains Why the Future of Energy Is Green." *Forbes* (March 20). forbes.com/sites/michaelkanellos/2013/03/20/google-explains-why-the-future-of-energy-is- green/.

Kant, Immanuel. (1964; 1798). *Anthropologie in Pragmatischer Hinsicht*. Darmstadt, Germany: Werke.

——— (1903; 1795). *Perpetual Peace: A Philosophical Essay*. London, UK: Swan Sonnenschein and Co.

Kapadia, Shefali. (2018). "Moving Parts: How the Automotive Industry is Transforming." *Supply Chain Dive* (February 20). supplychaindive.com/news/moving-parts-how-the-automotive-industry-is-transforming/516459/.

Kaplan, Morton A. (1957). *System and Process in International Politics*. New York: Wiley.

Kaplan, Robert D. (2012). "John J. Mearsheimer Is Right (About Some Things)." *Center for a New American Security* (January 11). cnas.org/media-and-events/cnas-in-the-news/op-eds/why-john-j-mearsheimer-is-right-about-some-things#.VaXazc4UpFI.

Kapstein, Ethan B. (2006). "The New Global Slave Trade." *Foreign Affairs* 85 (November/December): 103–115.

Kar, Dev, and Joseph Spanjers. (2014). "Illicit Financial Flows from Developing Countries: 2003–2012." *Global Financial Literacy*. Retrieved from gfintegrity.org/wp-content/uploads/2014/12/Illicit-Financial-Flows-from-Developing-Countries-2003-2012.pdf.

Karp, Aaron. (2018). "Estimating Global Civilian-Held Firearms Numbers." *Small Arms Survey*. smallarmssurvey.org/fileadmin/docs/T-Briefing-Papers/SAS-BP-Civilian-Firearms-Numbers.pdf.

Kassimeris, Christos. (2009). "The Foreign Policy of Small Powers." *International Politics* 46 (1): 84–101.

Kastner, Scott L. (2010). "The Security Consequences of China-Taiwan Economic Integration." *Testimony before the U.S.-China Economic and Security Review Commission* (March 18).

Kastner, Scott L., and Phillip C. Saunders. (2012). "Is China a Status Quo or Revisionist State? Leadership Travel as an Empirical Indicator of Foreign Policy Priorities." *International Studies Quarterly* 56 (1): 163–177.

Kathman, Jacob D. (2010). "Civil War Contagion and Neighboring Interventions." *International Studies Quarterly* 54: 989–1012.

Katz, Mark N. (2017). "What Exactly Is 'The War on Terror?': War on Terror In Perspective." *Middle East Policy Council*. mepc.org/commentary/what-exactly-war-terror.

Kaufman, Frederick. (2009). "Let Them Eat Cash." *Harper's* (June): 51–59.

Kaufman, Joyce P., and Kristen P. Williams. (2007). *Women, the State, and War: A Comparative Perspective on Citizenship and Nationalism*. Lanham, MD: Lexington Books.

Kavanagh, Jennifer. (2011). "Selection, Availability, and Opportunity: The Conditional Effect of Poverty on Terrorist Group Participation." *Journal of Conflict Resolution* 55 (1): 106–132.

Kay, Katty, and Claire Shipman. (2009). "Fixing the Economy Is Women's Work." *Washington Post* (July 12). washingtonpost.com/wp-dyn/content/article/2009/07/10/AR2009071002358.html.

Kearney, A. T. (2011). "How Do You Hire Mercenaries?: It Helps to Have Connections in Post-Conflict Countries." *Foreign Policy* (February 23). foreignpolicy.com/articles/2011/02/23/how_do_you_hire_mercenaries

——— (2009a). "The Longest Shadow." *Foreign Policy* (May/June): 28.

——— (2009b). "The New Coups." *Foreign Policy* (May/June): 28.

Keating, Joshua. (2011). "How Do You Hire Mercenaries?: It Helps to Have Connections in Post-Conflict Countries." *Foreign Policy* (February 23). foreignpolicy.com/articles/2011/02/23/how_do_you_hire_mercenaries.

——— (2009). "The Longest Shadow." *Foreign Policy* (May/June): 28.

Keck, M. E., and K. Sikkink (2014). *Activists Beyond Borders: Advocacy Networks in International Politics*. Cornell University Press.

——— (2008). "Transnational Advocacy Networks in International Politics." In *Essential Readings in World Politics*, 3rd ed., edited by Karen A. Mingst and Jack L. Snyder, 2. New York: Norton.

——— (1999). "Transnational Advocacy Networks in International and Regional Politics." *International Social Science Journal* 51(159): 89–101.

——— (1998). *Activists Beyond Borders: Advocacy Networks in International Politics*. Ithaca, New York: Cornell University Press.

Keegan, John. (1999). *The First World War*. New York: Knopf.

——— (1993). *A History of Warfare*. New York: Knopf.

Kegley, Charles W. (ed.). (2003). *The New Global Terrorism: Characteristics, Causes, Controls*. Upper Saddle River, NJ: Prentice Hall.

——— (1993). "The Neoidealist Moment in International Studies? Realist Myths and the New International Realities." *International Studies Quarterly* 37 (June): 131–146.

——— (1992). "The New Global Order: The Power of Principle in a Pluralistic World." *Ethics & International Affairs* 6: 21–42.

Kegley, Charles W., and Gregory Raymond. (2020). *The Great Powers and World Order: Patterns and Prospects*. Thousand Oaks, CA: Sage Publishing/CQ Press.

——— (2002). *Exorcising the Ghost of Westphalia: Building World Order in the New Millennium*. Upper Saddle River, NJ: Prentice Hall.

Kegley, Charles W., Jr., and Margaret G. Hermann. (2004). "Global Terrorism and Military Preemption: Policy Problems and Normative Perils." *International Politics* 41 (January): 37–49.

Kegley, Charles W., Jr., with Eugene R. Wittkopf. (1982). *American Foreign Policy*, 2nd ed. New York: St. Martin's.

Kelsen, Hans. (2009). *General Theory of Law and State*. Cambridge, MA: Harvard University Press.

Kennan, George F. (1985). "Morality and Foreign Policy." *Foreign Affairs* 64 (Winter): 205–218.

——— (1984). *The Fateful Alliance*. New York: Pantheon.

——— ["X"]. (1947). "The Sources of Soviet Conduct." *Foreign Affairs* 25 (July): 566–582.

Kennedy, John F. (1963). "American University Speech." usa.usembassy.de/etexts/speeches/rhetoric/jfkuniv.htm

Kennedy, Paul. (1987). *The Rise and Fall of the Great Powers*. New York: Random House.

Kentikelenis, Alexander, Thomas Stubbs, and Lawrence King. (2016). "Did the IMF Actually Ease Up on Structural Adjustment? Here's What the Data Say." *The Washington Post*. washingtonpost.com/news/monkey-cage/wp/2016/06/02/did-the-imf-actually-ease-up-on-demanding-structural-adjustments-heres-what-the-data-say/?noredirect=on&utm_term=.6fb924e3b732.

Keohane, Daniel. (2016). *European Defense and Brexit: A Tale of Three Cities*. Carnegie Europe, March 1, 2016. carnegieeurope.eu/strategiceurope/?fa=62922. Accessed 18 Feb. 2019.

Keohane, Robert O. (1998). "Beyond Dichotomy: Conversations between International Relations and Feminist Theory." *International Studies Quarterly* 42 (1): 193–197.

Keohane, Robert O., and Joseph S. Nye. (2013). "Power and Interdependence." In *Conflict after the Cold War: Arguments on Causes of War and Peace*, 4th ed. Boston, MA: Pearson.

Kerry, John. 1997. *The New War: The Web of Crime that Threatens America*. New York: Touchstone.

Keynes, John. (1936). *The General Theory of Employment, Interest, and Money*. London: Macmillan.

Khanna, Parag. (2010). "Beyond City Limits: The Age of Nations Is Over. The New Urban Era Has Begun." *Foreign Policy* (September/October): 120–123.

Kifner, John. (2005). "A Tide of Islamic Fury, and How It Rose." *New York Times* (January 30): Section 4, 4–5.

Kile, Shannon N., and Tytti Erästö. (2018). "Nuclear Dsarmament, Arms Control and Non-proliferation." *SIPRI Yearbook 2018* (New York: Oxford University Press). sipri.org/yearbook/2018/07.

Kim, Dongwook. (2013). "International Nongovernmental Organizations and the Global Diffusion of National Human Rights Institutions." *The IO Foundation*. 67(3), 505–539. doi.org/10.1017/S0020818313000131.

Kim, Min-hyung. (2019). "A Real Driver of US-China Trade Conflict." *ITPD* 3(1). emerald.com/insight/content/doi/10.1108/ITPD-02-2019-003/full/pdf?title=a-real-driver-of-uschina-trade-conflict-the-sinous-competition-for-global-hegemony-and-its-implications-for-the-future.

Kim, Samuel S. (1991). "The United Nations, Lawmaking and World Order." In *The United Nations and a Just World Order*, edited by Richard A. Falk, Samuel S. Kim, and Saul H. Mendlovitz, 1. Boulder, CO: Westview.

Kim, Sung-han. (2013). "Global Governance and Middle Powers: South Korea's Role in the G20." *Council of Foreign Relations*. cfr.org/report/global-governance-and-middle-powers-south-koreas-role-g20.

Kindleberger, Charles. (2001). *Manics, Panics, and Crashes: A History of Financial Crises*, 5th ed. Hoboken, NJ: John Wiley and Sons.

——— (2000). *Manics, Panics, and Crashes: A History of Financial Crises*, 4th ed. New York: John Wiley and Sons.

Kindleberger, Charles, Robert Ailber, and Robert Solow. (2005). *Manics, Panics, and Crashes: A History of Financial Crises*, 5th ed. Hoboken, NJ: Wiley.

Kinzer, S. (2007). *Overthrow: America's Century of Regime Change from Hawaii to Iraq*. Macmillan.

Kirsch, Philippe. (2006). "Applying the Principles of Nuremberg in the ICC: Keynote Address at the Conference 'Judgment at Nuremberg' held on the 60th Anniversary of the Nuremberg Judgment." Speech, Washington University, St. Louis, Mo. (September 30). icc-cpi.int/NR/rdonlyres/ED2F5177-9F9B-4D66-9386-5C5BF45D052C/146323/PK_20060930_English.pdf.

Kirshner, Jonathan. (2015). "American Power and the Global Financial Crisis: How About Now?" *Forbes* (March 12). forbes.com/sites/jonathankirshner/2015/03/12/american-power-and-the-global-financial-crisis-how-about-now/.

——— (2014). *American Power after the Financial Crisis*. Ithaca, NY: Cornell University Press.

Kissinger, Henry A. (2014). *World Order*. New York: Penguin Press.

——— (2012a). *On China*, 2nd ed. New York: Penguin Press.

——— (2012b). "The Future of U.S.-Chinese Relations: Conflict Is a Choice Not a Necessity." *Foreign Affairs* (March/April). foreignaffairs.com/articles/137245/henry-a-kissinger/the-future-of-us-chinese- relations.

——— (2001). *Does America Need a Foreign Policy? Toward a Diplomacy for the 21st Century*. New York, NY: Simon & Schuster.

——— (1991). "What Kind of New World Order?" *Washington Post* (December 3). washingtonpost.com/archive/opinions/1991/12/03/what-kind-of-new-world-order/978316f5-9c4a-4ad2-9fbe-89c8488cbd14/.

——— (1979). *White House Years*. Boston: Little, Brown.

——— (1973). "Moral Purposes and Policy Choices." *Department of State Bulletin* 69: 525–531.

Klare, Michael. (1994). *World Security: Challenges for A New Century*, 2nd ed. New York: St. Martin's Press.

——— (1990). "An Arms Control Agenda for the Third World." *Arms Control Today* 20 (3): 8–12.

Klein, Naomi. (2008). "China's All-Seeing Eye." *Rolling Stone* (May 29): 59–66.

Kluger, Jeffrey. (2007). "What Makes Us Moral." *Time* (December 3): 54–60.

——— (2006). "The Big Crunch." In *Global Issues 05/06*, edited by Robert M. Jackson. Dubuque, IA: McGraw-Hill/Dushkin.

Knickerbocker, Brad. (2007). "Might Warming Be 'Normal,'" *Christian Science Monitor* (September 20): 14, 16.

Kolb, Deborah M. (1996). "Her Place at the Table: Gender and Negotiation." In *Women, Men, and Gender: Ongoing Debates*, edited by Mary Roth Walsh. New York: Hamilton.

Kolbert, Elizabeth. (2008). "What Was I Thinking? The Latest Reasoning about Our Irrational Ways." *New Yorker* (February 25): 77–79.

——— (2005). "The Climate of Man-II." *New Yorker* (May 2): 64–73.

Kolodziej, Edward. (2005). *Security and International Relations*. Cambridge: Cambridge University Press.

Konrad, Kai, and Tim Stolper. (2016). "Buckling Under Pressure: Coordination and the Fight Against Tax Havens." *Vox EU*. voxeu.org/article/coordination-and-fight-against-tax-havens.

Koser, Khalid. (2010). "The Impact of the Global Financial Crisis on International Migration." *Whitehead Journal of Diplomacy and International Relations* 11(1): 13–20.

Kottasová, Ivana. (2018). "What is GDPR? Everything You Need to Know about Europe's New Data Law." *CNN Business*. money.cnn.com/2018/05/21/technology/gdpr-explained-europe-privacy/index.html.

Kotz, David M. (2013). "The Current Economic Crisis in the United States: A Crisis of Over-Investment." *Review of Radical Political Economics* (June 6). DOI: 10.1177/0486613413487160.

Kralev, Nicholas. (2018). "The U.S. Foreign Service and the Importance of Professional Diplomacy, with Nicholas Kralev." *Carnegie Council for Ethics in International Affairs*. carnegiecouncil.org/studio/multimedia/20180306-us-foreign-service-professional-diplomacy-nicholas-kralev.

Krauss, Clifford. (2015). "Iran Deal May Be Slow to Affect Oil Sector." *New York Times* (April 2). nytimes.com/2015/04/03/business/international/iran-deal-may-be-slow-to-affect-oil.html?_r=0.

Kreps, Sarah, and Micah Zenko. (2014). "The Next Drone Wars: Preparing for Proliferation." *Foreign Affairs* 93 (March/April): 68–79.

Kristensen, Hans M., and Matt Korda. (2019). "Status of World Nuclear Forces." *Federation of American Scientists*. fas.org/issues/nuclear-weapons/status-world-nuclear-forces/.

Kristof, Nicholas D., and Sheryl WuDunn. (2009). *Half the Sky: Turning Oppression into Opportunity For Women Worldwide*. New York: Vintage Books.

Kroenig, Matthew. (2009). "Exporting the Bomb: Why States Provide Sensitive Nuclear Assistance." *American Political Science Review* 103: 113–133.

Krogstad, Jens Manuel, and Ana Gonzalez-Barrera. (2019). "Key Facts about U.S. Immigration Policies and Proposed Changes." *Pew Research Center*. pewresearch.org/fact-tank/2019/05/17/key-facts-about-u-s-immigration-policies-and-proposed-changes/.

Krueger, Alan B. (2007). *What Makes a Terrorist*. Princeton, NJ: Princeton University Press.

Krugman, Paul. (2015). "Nobody Understands." *New York Times* (February 9). nytimes.com/2015/02/09/opinion/paul-krugman-nobody-understands-debt.html?_r=0.

——— (1987). "Is Free Trade Passé?" *Journal of Economic Perspectives* 1 (Autumn): 131–144.

Kshetri, Nir. (2019). "How Cryptocurrency Scams Work." *The Conversation.* theconversation.com/how-cryptocurrency-scams-work-114706.

Kugler, Jacek. (2006). "China: Satisfied or Dissatisfied, the Strategic Equation." Paper presented at the Annual Meeting of the International Studies Association, March 22–25, San Diego.

Kugler, Jacek, Ali Fisunoglu, and Birol Yesilada. (2015). "Consequences of Reversing the European Union Integration." *Foreign Policy Analysis* 11 (January): 45–67.

Kugler, Jacek, Ronald L. Tammen, and Brian Efird. (2004). "Integrating Theory and Policy." *International Studies Review* 6 (December): 163–179.

Kuhn, Patrick M., and Nils B. Weidman. (2013). "Unequal We Fight: The Impact of Economic Inequality within Ethnic Groups on Conflict Initiation." Draft at Princeton University. princeton.edu/politics/about/file-repository/public/KuhnWeidmann_PrincetonIRTalk.pdf.

Kurlantzick, Joshua. (2015). "The Great Deglobalizing." *Boston Globe* (February 1). bostonglobe.com/ideas/2015/02/01/the-great-deglobalizing/a8TNmTd7pZNNtjhcK5hBZP/story.html.

Kuttner, Robert. (2018). "The Crash that Failed." *The New York Review of Books* (November 22).

Laeven, Luc and Fabien Valencia. (2012). "Systemic Banking Crises Database; An Update." *International Monetary Fund*, 12/163. Retrieved from ideas.repec.org/p/imf/imfwpa/12-163.html.

Lagarde, Christine. (2015). "What's Next for the Global Economy: A Look Ahead at 2015." *Council on Foreign Relations* (January 15). cfr.org/economics/next-global-economy-look-ahead-2015/p35962.

Lake, Anthony. (2015). "What Future for the Children of Syria?" *UNICEF* (March 12). unicef.org/ceecis/media_27506.html.

Lambert, Jonathan, and Rebecca Ellis. (2019). "Oh Dear: Photos Show What Humans Have Done To The Planet." *NPR* (June 15). npr.org/sections/goatsandsoda/2019/06/15/727583729/the-anthropocene-project-captures-humanitys-indelible-mark-on-the-planet.

Lamy, Pascal. (2013). "A Trade Facilitation Deal Could Give a $1 Trillion Boost to World Economy—Lamy." WTO (February 1). wto.org/english/news_e/sppl_e/sppl265_e.htm.

——— (2011). "Time for a System Upgrade." foreignpolicy.com/articles/2011/04/18/system_upgrade.

Lamy, Pascal. (2010). Speech in Shanghai. wto.org/english/news_e/sppl_e/sppl163_e.htm (accessed June 14, 2019).

Landau, Julia. (2010). "Food Riots or Food Rebellions? Eric Holt-Giménez Looks at the World Food Crisis." Common-Dreams.org (March 25). common-dreams.org/view/2010/03/25–11.

Lanz, R., and S. Miroudot (2011). "Intra-Firm Trade: Patterns, Determinants and Policy Implications." *OECD Trade Policy Working Papers*, No. 114. dx.doi.org/10.1787/5kg9p39Irwnn-en.

Laqueur, Walter. (1996). "Postmodern Terrorism: New Rules for an Old Game." *Foreign Affairs* (September/October). foreignaffairs.com/articles/1996-09-01/postmodern-terrorism-new-rules-old-game.

Larsen, Janet. (2012). "Plan B Updates." *Earth Policy Institute* (April 24). earth-policy.org/plan_b_updates/2012/update102.

Larsen, Jeffrey A., and Kerry M. Kartchner (eds.). (2014). *On Limited Nuclear War in the 21st Century.* Stanford, CA: Stanford University Press.

Lauricella, Tom, Christopher S. Stewart, and Shira Ovide. (2013). "Twitter Hoax Sparks Swift Stock Swoon." *Wall Street Journal* (April 23). online.wsj.com/article/SB10001424127887323735604578441201605193488.html.

Lawson, Marian L., and Emily M. Morgenstern. (2019). *Foreign Aid: An Introduction to U.S. Programs and Policy.* Washington D.C.: Congressional Research Service. Retrieved from everycrsreport.com/files/20190416_R40213_e1b7c668965b89cbe29ef287c0572fe640992afc.pdf.

Leahy, Stephen. (2018). "Climate Change Impacts Worse than Expected, Global Report Warns." *National Geographic.* nationalgeographic.com/environment/2018/10/ipcc-report-climate-change-impacts-forests-emissions/.

Leander, Anna. (2005). "The Market for Force and Public Security: The Destabilizing Consequences of Private Military Companies." *Journal of Peace Research* 42 (5): 605–622.

Lebada, Ana Maria. (2019). "'New Year, New United Nations: Structural Reforms Begin." *SDG Knowledge Hub.* sdg.iisd.org/commentary/policy-briefs/new-year-new-united-nations-structural-reforms-begin/.

LeBeau, Philip. (2013). "U.S. Manufacturing No More Expensive Than Outsourcing to China by 2015: Study." *Huffington Post* (April 19). huffingtonpost.com/2013/04/19/china-manufacturing-costs_n_3116638.html.

Lebovic, James H., and Erik Voeten. (2009). "The Cost of Shame: International Organizations and Foreign Aid in the Punishing of Human Rights Violators." *Journal of Peace Research* 46 (1): 79–97.

Lee, Amanda. (2019). "China's State-Owned Companies Enjoy Record Profits, Even as Private Sector Flounders." *South China Morning Post.* scmp.com/economy/china-economy/article/2182552/chinas-state-owned-companies-enjoy-record-profits-even-private.

Leffler, Melvyn, and Odd Arne Westad (ed.). (2009). *The Cambridge History of the Cold War.* Cambridge, UK: Cambridge University Press.

Lehrer, Jonah. (2012). "Groupthink: The Brainstorming Myth." *New Yorker* (January 30).

Lektzian, David, and Mark Souva. (2009). "A Comparative Theory Test of Democratic Peace Arguments, 1946–2000." *Journal of Peace Research* 46 (1): 17–37.

Lemke, Douglas. (2003). "Development and War." *International Studies Review* 5 (December): 55–63.

Lemmon, Gayle Tzemach. (2011). "The Hillary Doctrine." *Newsweek.* newsweek.com/hillary-doctrine-66105.

Leopard, Brian D. (2010). *Customary International Law: A New Theory with Practical Applications.* New York: Cambridge University Press.

Levy, Jack S. (2001). "War and Its Causes." In *The Global Agenda*, 6th ed. Boston: McGraw-Hill.

——— (1998). "Towards a New Millennium." In *The Global Agenda*, 5th ed., edited by Charles W. Kegley and Eugene Wittkopf, 47–57. New York: McGraw-Hill.

——— (1998). "The Causes of War and the Conditions of Peace." fas-polisci.rutgers.edu/levy/articles/1998%20causes%20of%20war%20&%20conditions%20of%20peace.pdf.

——— (1989). "The Causes of War: A Review of Theories and Evidence." In *Behavior, Society, and Nuclear War*, edited by Philip E. Tetlock, Jo L. Husbands, Robert Jervis, Paul C. Stern, and Charles Tilly. New York: Oxford University Press.

Levy, Jack, and William R. Thompson. (2010). *Causes of War.* Malden, MA: Wiley-Blackwell.

Lewis, Michael. (2014). *Flash Boys: A Wall Street Revolt.* New York: W.W. Norton & Company, Inc.

Lieberman, Joseph. (2008). hsgac.senate.gov/media/majority-media/lieberman-calls-on-google-to-take-down-terrorist-content.

Lifsher, Marc. (2005). "Unocal Settles Human Rights Lawsuit Over Alleged Abuses at Myanmar Pipeline." *Los Angeles Times.* latimes.com/archives/la-xpm-2005-mar-22-fi-unocal22-story.html.

Lin, Liza, and Stephen Engle. (2013). "Coca-Cola to Invest More Than $4 Billion in China From 2015–2017." *Bloomberg* (November 7). bloomberg.com/news/articles/2013-11-07/coca-cola-to-invest-more-than-4-billion-in-china-from-2015-2017.

Lind, William S., and Gregory A. Thiel. (2015). *4th Generation Warfare Handbook*. Kouvola, Finland. Castalia House.

Lindberg, Staffan I. (2018). "The Nature of Democratic Backsliding in Europe." *Carnegie Europe*. carnegieeurope.eu/2018/07/24/nature-of-democratic-backsliding-in-europe-pub-76868.

Lipson, Charles. (1984). "International Cooperation in Economic and Security Affairs." *World Politics* 37 (October): 1–23.

List, Friedrich. (1841). *National System of Political Economy*. Available at: socserv2.socsci.mcmaster.ca/~econ/ugcm/3ll3/list/list.

Lobell, Steven E., Norrin M. Ripsman, and Jeffrey W. Taliaferro. (2009). *Neo-classical Realism, the State, and Foreign Policy*. New York: Cambridge University Press.

Londoño, Ernesto. (2019). "Jair Bolsonaro, on Day 1, Undermines Indigenous Brazilians' Rights." *New York Times*. nytimes.com/2019/01/02/world/americas/brazil-bolsonaro-president-indigenous-lands.html.

Loescher, Gil. (2005). "Blaming the Victim: Refugees and Global Security." In *Developing World 05/06*, edited by Robert J. Griffiths, 1. Dubuque, IA: McGraw-Hill/Dushkin.

Lombardi, M., E. Ragab, and V. Chin (eds.). (2015). *Countering Radicalisation and Violent Extremism among Youth to Prevent Terrorism*. Amsterdam, Netherlands: IOS Press BV.

Lopez, J. Humberto, et al. (2010). "Big Senders." *Foreign Policy* (January/February): 35.

Lowrey, Annie. (2012). "U.S. Candidate Is Chosen to Lead the World Bank." *New York Times* (April 16): B3.

Lupovici, Amir. (2009). "Constructivist Methods: A Plea and Manifesto for Pluralism." *Review of International Studies* 35: 195–218.

Lute, Douglas, and Nicholas Burns. (2019). "NATO at Seventy: An Alliance in Crisis." *President and Fellows of Harvard College*. Retrieved from belfercenter.org/sites/default/files/files/publication/NATOatSeventy.pdf.

Lutz, Ellen L. (2006). "Understanding Human Rights Violations in Armed Conflict." In *Human Rights and Conflict: Exploring the Links Between Rights, Law, and Peacebuilding*, edited by Julie Mertus and Jeffrey W. Helsing. Washington, DC: United States Institute of Peace Press.

Lyons, Daniel. (2010). "Short-Circuiting Malaria." *Newsweek* (April 19): 36–41.

Maasdorp, Leslie. (2015). "What Is 'New' about the New Development Bank?" *World Economic Forum*. weforum.org/agenda/2015/08/what-is-new-about-the-new-development-bank/.

Macalister, Terry. (2012). "Oil Demand in 2013 to Rise as World Economy Recovers, IEA Says." *The Guardian* (December 12). guardian.co.uk/business/2012/dec/12/oil-demand-rise-2013-iea.

MacAskill, Ewen, Nick Davies, Nick Hopkins, Julian Borger, and James Ball. (2013). "GCHQ Intercepted Foreign Politicians' Communications at G20 Summits." *The Guardian* (June 16). guardian.co.uk/uk/2013/jun/16/gchq-intercepted-communications-g20-summits.

MacDonald, James. (2015). *When Globalization Fails: The Rise and Fall of Pax Americana*. New York: Farrar, Straus and Giroux.

MacDuffie, John Paul, and David Zaring. (2019). "Exhausted by Scandal: 'Dieselgate' Continues to Haunt Volkswagen." *Wharton School*. knowledge.wharton.upenn.edu/article/volkswagen-diesel-scandal/.

Machiavelli, Niccolò. (1972; 1532). *The Prince*. Paris: Seghers.

Mackinder, Sir Halford. (1919). *Democratic Ideals and Reality*. New York: Holt.

MAF. (2018). "Foreword." *The Minderoo Foundation*. globalslaveryindex.org/2019/findings/foreword/.

Magee, Christopher, and Tansa George Massoud. (2011). "Openness and Internal Conflict." *Journal of Peace Research* 48 (1): 59–72.

Mahan, Alfred Thayer. (1890). *The Influence of Sea Power in History*. Boston: Little, Brown.

Mahbulbani, Kishore. (2009). *The New Asian Hemisphere: The Irresistible Shift of Global Power to the East*. New York: Basic Civitas Books.

Malcomson, Scott. (2008). "Humanitarianism and Its Politicization." *International Herald Tribune* (December 13–14): 9.

Malena, Carmen. (1995). "Working with NGOs : A Practical Guide to Operational Collaboration between the World Bank and Nongovernmental Organizations." Washington, DC: The World Bank.

Mallaby, Sebastian. (2011). "The Wrong Choice to Head the IMF." *Council on Foreign Relations* (June 1). cfr.org/economics/wrong-choice-head-imf/p25166.

Malmgren, Harald, and Mark Stys. (2011). "Computerized Global Trading 24/6: A Roller Coaster Ride Ahead?" *The International Economy* (Spring): 30–32.

Malone, David M., Sebastian von Einsiedel, and Bruno Stagno Ugarte (eds.). (2015). *The UN Security Council in the 21st Century*. Boulder, CO: Lynne Reiner.

Malpass, David. (2019). "Achieving Good Development Outcomes From Country Level Programs." *World Bank*. worldbank.org/en/news/immersive-story/2019/06/07/achieving-good-development-outcomes-from-country-level-programs.

Mandelbaum, Michael. (2007). "Democracy without America." *Foreign Affairs* 86 (September/October): 119–130.———

——— (2006a). "David's Friend Goliath." *Foreign Policy* (January/February): 49–56.

Mankoff, Jeffrey. (2009). *Russian Foreign Policy: The Return of Great Power Politics*. New York: Rowman & Littlefield.

Mansfield, Edward D., and Jack Snyder. (2005a). *Electing to Fight*. Cambridge, MA.: MIT Press.

——— (2005b). "When Ballots Bring on Bullets." *International Herald Tribune* (November 29–30): 6.

Manuel, Claire. (2018). "Coca-Cola's 5by20 Recipe to Empower 5 Million Women by 2020." *Ethical Corporation*. ethicalcorp.com/coca-colas-5by20-recipe-empower-5-million-women-2020.

Maoz, Zeev, and Errol A. Henderson. (2013). "The World Religion Dataset, 1945–2010: Logic, Estimates, and Trends." *International Interactions* 39 (3): 265–291.

Mapel, David R. (2007). "The Right of National Defense." *International Studies Perspectives* 8 (February): 1–15.

Markoe, Lauren, and Seth Borenstein. (2005). "We Overpay by 20% for Military Goods." *Columbia, S.C., The State* (October 23): A1, A8.

Markoff, John. (2009). "A Map of the World, in 4 Billion Pockets." *International Herald Tribune* (February 188): 1, 11.

Markovits, Elizabeth K., and Susan Bickford. (2014). "Constructing Freedom: Institutional Pathways to Changing the Gender Division of Labor." *Perspectives on Politics* 12 (1): 81–99.

Markusen, Ann R. (2003). "The Case against Privatizing National Security." *Governance* 16 (4): 471–501.

Martin, Susan F. (2014). *International Migration: Evolving Trends from the Early Twentieth Century to the Present*. New York: Cambridge University Press.

Martínez-Zarzoso, I. (2018), "Assessing the Effectiveness of Environmental Provisions in Regional Trade Agreements: An Empirical Analysis." *OECD Trade and Environment Working Papers*, No. 2018/02, Paris: OECD Publishing. doi.org/10.1787/5ffc615c-en.

Marx, Anthony W. (2003). *Faith in Nation: Exclusionary Origins of Nationalism*. New York: Oxford University Press.

Mattes, Michaela, and Burcu Savun. (2010). "Information, Agreement Design, and the Durability of Civil War Settlements." *American Journal of Political Science* 54 (2): 511–524.

Mattis, Jim. (2018). *Nuclear Posture Review*. media.defense.gov/2018/Feb/02/2001872886/-1/-1/1/2018-NUCLEAR-POSTURE-REVIEW-FINAL-REPORT.PDF.

Maull, Hanns W. (2015). "Sifting Through American Foreign Policy." *International Studies Review 17* (March): 147–149.

Maves, Jessica, and Alex Braithwaite. (2013). "Autocratic Institutions and Civil Conflict Contagion." *Journal of Politics* 75(2): 478–490.

Maza, Cristina. (2018). "China Involved in 90 Percent of Espionage and Industrial Secrets Theft, Department of Justice Reveals." *Newsweek*. newsweek.com/china-involved-90-percent-economic-espionage-and-industrial-secrets-theft-1255908.

Mazarr, Michael J. (1999). *Global Trends 2005*. London: Palgrave.

Mazower, Mark. (2009). *No Enchanted Palace: The End of Empire and the Ideological Origins of the United Nations*. Princeton, NJ: Princeton University Press.

McBride, James. (2019). *What Brexit Means*. Council on Foreign Relations, 16 Jan. 2019. cfr.org/backgrounder/what-brexit-means. Accessed 18 Feb. 2019.

McBride, James, and Andrew Chatzky. (2019). "What Is the Trans-Pacific Partnership (TPP)?" *Council on Foreign Relations*. cfr.org/backgrounder/what-trans-pacific-partnership-tpp.

McCrae, R. R., and Paul T. Costa. (2003). *Personality in Adulthood: A Five-Factor Theory Perspective*, 2nd ed. New York: Guilford Press.

McDermott, Rose. (2013). "The Biological Bases for Aggressiveness and Nonaggressiveness in Presidents." *Foreign Policy Analysis*: 1–15.

McDermott, Rose, James H. Fowler, and Oleg Smirnov. (2008). "On the Evolutionary Origin of Prospect Theory Preferences." *The Journal of Politics* 70 (April): 335–350.

McDonnell, Tim (2019). "New HIV Map Offers Most Detailed Look Yet at the Epidemic." *NPR* (May 15). npr.org/sections/goatsand-soda/2019/05/15/723564110/new-hiv-map-offers-most-detailed-look-yet-at-the-epidemic.

McGrew, Anthony. (2008). "The Logics of Globalization." In *Global Political Economy*, edited by John Ravenhill, 277–310. New York: Oxford University Press 277–310.

McGurn, William. (2002). "Pulpit Economics." *First Things*. firstthings.com/article/2002/04/pulpit-economics.

McKibben, Bill. (2011). "Resisting Climate Reality." *The New York Review* (April 7): 60–64.

McKibben, Bill. (2006). "A Special Moment in History." In *Global Issues 05/06*, edited by Robert M. Jackson, 3–7. Dubuque, Iowa: McGraw-Hill/Dushkin.

McKie, Robin. (2015). "Why Fresh Water Shortages Will Cause the Next Great Global Crisis." *The Guardian* (March 7). theguardian.com/environment/2015/mar/08/how-water-shortages-lead-food-crises- conflicts.

McKinnon, Ronald I. (2013). *The Unloved Dollar Standard: From Bretton Woods to the Rise of China*. Oxford and New York: Oxford University Press.

Mead, Walter Russell. (2014). "The Return of Geopolitics: The Revenge of Revisionist Powers." *Foreign Affairs* (May/June): 4.

——— (2010). "The Carter Syndrome." *Foreign Policy* 177 (January/February): 58–64.

Mearsheimer, John. (2014). nationalinterest.org/commentary/can-china-rise-peacefully-10204.

Mearsheimer, John J. (2001). *The Tragedy of Great Power Politics*. New York: Norton.

Mearsheimer, John J., and Stephen W. Walt. (2003). "An Unnecessary War." *Foreign Policy* (January/February): 50–58.

Meltzer, Joshua. (2011). "The Future of World Trade." foreignpolicy.com/articles/2011/04/18/the_future_of_trade.

Menon, Rajan. (2007). *The End of Alliances*. New York: Oxford University Press.

Mentan, Tatah. (2004). *Dilemmas of Weak States: Africa and Transnational Terrorism in the Twenty-First Century*. Burlington, VT: Ashgate.

Meredith, Sam. (2019). "Oil Prices Will Stay 'Relatively Benign' Despite Escalating Iran Tensions, Morgan Stanley Says." *CNBC*. cnbc.com/2019/07/22/oil-iran-tensions-unlikely-to-lead-to-a-price-spike-morgan-stanley-says.html.

Merle, Renae. (2018). "A Guide to the Financial Crisis—10 Years Later." *The Washington Post*. washingtonpost.com/business/economy/a-guide-to-the-financial-crisis--10-years-later/2018/09/10/114b76ba-af10-11e8-a20b-5f4f84429666_story.html?utm_term=.11c68092b0de.

Mertus, Julie. (2009a). *Human Rights Matters: Local Politics and National Human Rights Institutions*. Stanford, CA: Stanford University Press.

——— (2009b). *The United Nations and Human Rights: A Guide for a New Era*, 2nd ed. New York: Routledge.

Midlarsky, Manus L. (2006). *The Killing Trap: Genocide in the Twentieth Century*. New York: Cambridge University Press.

Milewicz, K., J. Hollway, C. Peacock, and D. Snidal. (2018). "Beyond Trade: The Expanding Scope of the Nontrade Agenda in Trade Agreements." *Journal of Conflict Resolution* 62(4): 743–773.

Miller, Mark Crispin. (2006). "What's Wrong with This Picture?" In *Global Issues 05/06*, edited by Robert M. Jackson, 1. Dubuque, IA: McGraw-Hill/Dushkin.

Miller, Terry, Anthony Kim, and James Roberts. (2019). *2019 Index of Economic Freedom*. Washington, DC: The Heritage Foundation.

Milner, Helen V., and Andrew Moravcsik. (2009). *Power, Interdependence, and Nonstate Actors in World Politics*. Princeton, NJ: Princeton University Press.

Minorities at Risk Project. (2009). "Minorities at Risk Dataset." College Park, MD: Center for International Development and Conflict Management. cidcm.umd.edu/mar/.

Mintz, Alex. (2007). "Why Behavioral IR?" *International Studies Review* 9 (June): 157–172.

Mintz, Alex, and Karl DeRouen. (2010). *Understanding Foreign Policy Decision Making*. New York: Cambridge University Press.

Missile Defense Agency (MDA). (2015). "Elements." *Missile Defense Agency*. mda.mil/system/aegis_status.html.

Missile Defense Project, "Missiles of Taiwan." Missile Threat, Center for Strategic and International Studies. Last modified June 15, 2018. missilethreat.csis.org/country/taiwan/.

Mitchell, Sara McLaughlin, Kelly M. Kadera, and Mark J. C. Crescenzi. (2008). "Practicing Democratic Community Norms: Third Party Conflict Management and Successful Settlements." In *International Conflict Mediation*, edited by Jacob Bercovitch and Scott Sigmund Gartner, 2. New York: Routledge.

Mo, Lavinia. (2013). "New Bird Flu May Be Capable of Human to Human Spread-Study." *Reuters* (May 24).

Modelski, George. (1964). "The International Relations of Internal War." In *International Aspects of Civil Strife*, edited by James N. Rosenau, 14–44. Princeton, NJ: Princeton University Press.

Mohanty, Chandra Talpade. (1988). "Under Western Eyes: Feminist Scholarship and Colonial Discourse." *Feminist Review* 30 (Autumn): 61–88.

Monaco, Lisa, and Vin Gupta. (2018). "The Next Pandemic Will Be Arriving Shortly." *Foreign Policy* (September 28). foreignpolicy.com/2018/09/28/the-next-pandemic-will-be-arriving-shortly-global-health-infectious-avian-flu-ebola-zoonotic-diseases-trump/.

Mondack, Jeffrey J., and Karen D. Halperin. (2013). "A Framework for the Study of Personality and Political Behavior." *British Journal of Political Science* 38: 335–362.

Morgan, Nicky. (2018). "Ten Years After the Crash: Have the Lessons of Lehman Been Learned?" *The Guardian*. theguardian.com/commentisfree/2018/sep/14/the-panel-lehman-brothers-ten-year-anniversary-financial-crash.

Morgenthau, Hans J. (1985; 1948). *Politics Among Nations*, 6th ed. Revised by Kenneth W. Thompson. New York: Knopf.

Morrow, James D. (2014). *Order within Anarchy: The Laws of War as an International Institution*. New York: Cambridge University Press.

Mortiz-Rabson, Daniel. (2019). "Temperatures Could Rise Up to 7 Degrees Celsius Above Pre-Industrial Levels, Startling Study Shows." *Newsweek* (September 17). newsweek.com/climate-change-temperature-rise-seven-degrees-new-un-report-1459666.

Mosley, Layna. (2011). *Labor Rights and Multinational Production*. Cambridge, UK: Cambridge University Press.

Moyes, Richard, and Thomas Nash. (2011). *Global Coalitions: An Introduction to Working in International Civil Society Partnerships*. London, UK: Action on Armed Violence (AOAV). globalcoalitions.org.

Mueller, John. (2004). *The Remnants of War*. Ithaca, NY: Cornell University Press.

Mueller, John, and Karl Mueller. (1999). "Sanctions of Mass Destruction." *Foreign Affairs* 78 (3): 43–52.

Mueller, Robert S, III. (2019). "Report On The Investigation into Russian Interference in the 2016 Presidential Election." *U.S. Department of Justice*, 1:1. cdn.cnn.com/cnn/2019/images/04/18/mueller-report-searchable.pdf.

Mueller, Sherry Lee, and Mark Overmann. (2014). *Working World: Careers in International Education, Exchange, and Development*. Washington, D.C.: Georgetown University Press.

Muggah, Robert. (2015). "Fixing Fragile Cities." *Foreign Affairs* (January 15). foreignaffairs.com/articles/africa/2015-01-15/fixing-fragile- cities.

Muller, Jerry Z. (2013). "Capitalism and Inequality: What the Right and the Left Get Wrong." *Foreign Affairs* (March/April). foreignaffairs.com/articles/138844/jerry-z-muller/capitalism-and-inequality.

Murdie, Amanda M., and David Davis. (2012). "Shaming and Blaming: Using Events Data to Assess the Impact of Human Rights INGOs." *International Studies Quarterly* 56 (1): 1–16.

Murdie, Amanda. (2014). *Help or Harm: The Human Security Effects of International NGOs*. Stanford: Stanford University Press.

Murdie, A., and D. Peksen. (2013). "The Impact of Human Rights INGO Activities on Economic Sanctions." *The Review of International Organizations* 8(1): 33–53.

Murithi, Timothy. (2004). "The Myth of Violent Human Nature." *Peace & Policy* 8: 28–32.

Murphy, Andrea, Jonathan Ponciano, Sarah Hansen, and Halah Touryalai. (2019). "GLOBAL 2000: The World's Largest Public Companies." *Forbes*. forbes.com/global2000/#2394fbc8335d.

Naím, Moisés. (2007). "The Free-Trade Paradox." *Foreign Policy* (September/October): 96–97.

Nakatomi, Michitaka. (2013). "Plurilateral Agreements: A Viable Alternative to the WTO?" In *The Future of the World Trading System: Asian Perspectives* edited by Richard Baldwin, *Masahiro Kawai, and Ganeshan Wignaraja,*. London, UK: Centre for Economic Policy Research.

Nasdaq. (2018). "U.S. Stock Market Is Biggest & Most Expensive in World, But U.S. Economy Is not the Most Productive." nasdaq.com/article/us-stock-market-is-biggest-most-expensive-in-world-but-us-economy-is-not-the-most-productive-cm942558.

National Institute of Justice. (2012). "Transnational Organized Crime." nij.gov/topics/crime/trans-national-organized-crime/welcome.htm.

Nelson, Rebecca, Paul Belkin, and Derek Mix. (2010). *Greece's Debt Crisis: Overview, Policy Responses and Implications*. Washington, DC: Congressional Research Service.

Neumayer, Eric, and Indra de Soysa. (2005). "Trade Openness, Foreign Direct Investment, and Child Labor." *World Development* 33 (1): 43–63.

Newlin, Cyrus, and Jeffery Mankoff. (2018). "U.S. Sanctions against Russia: What You Need to Know." *Center for Strategic & International Studies* (October 31). csis.org/analysis/us-sanctions-against-russia-what-you-need-know.

Nicholls, Natsuko H., Paul K. Huth, and Benjamin J. Appel. (2010). "When Is Domestic Political Unrest Related to International Conflict? Diversionary Theory and Japanese Foreign Policy, 1890–1941." *International Studies Quarterly* 54: 915–937.

Nichols, John. (2002). "Enron's Global Crusade." *The Nation* (March 4). thenation.com/doc/20020304/nichols.

Nichols, Michelle. (2019). "U.N. Members Owe $2 Billion in Debt to Peacekeeping, U.S. Owes a Third." *Reuters*. reuters.com/article/us-un-peacekeepers-usa/u-n-members-owe-2-billion-in-debt-to-peacekeeping-u-s-owes-a-third-idUSKCN1PB2OD.

Niebuhr, Reinhold. (1947). *Moral Man and Immoral Society*. New York: Scribner's.

Nielsen. (2014). "Global Consumers are Willing to Put their Money Where their Heart Is when it Comes to Goods and Services from Companies Committed to Social Responsibility." *Nielsen*. nielsen.com/us/en/press-releases/2014/global-consumers-are-willing-to-put-their-money-where-their-heart-is/.

9/11 Commission. (2004). *Final Report of the National Commission on Terrorist Attacks upon the United States: The 9/11 Commission Report*. New York: Norton.

Nike. (2012). "Nike Foundation Launches New Girleffect.org." news.nike.com/news/nike-foundation-launches-new-girleffectorg.

Nimubona, Desire. (2018). "Burundi President Pierre Nkurunziza Pledges to Step Down In 2020." *Bloomberg*. bloomberg.com/news/articles/2018-06-07/burundi-president-pierre-nkurunziza-pledges-to-step-down-in-2020.

Norberg, Johan. (2006). "Three Cheers for Global Capitalism." In *Global Issues 05/06*, edited by Robert M.Jackson. Dubuque, IA: McGraw-Hill/Dushkin.

Nordas, Ragnhild, and Christian Davenport. (2013). "Fight the Youth: Youth Bulges and State Repression." *American Journal of Political Scientists* 57 (October): 926–940.

Norton-Taylor, Richard. (2013). "UK Approves 12bn of Arms Exports to Countries with Poor Human Rights." *The Guardian*. theguardian.com/world/20 13/jul/17/uk-approves-arms-exports-human-rights.

NPR (National Public Radio). (2019), "U.S. National Debt Hits Record $22 Trillion." npr.org/2019/02/13/694199256/u-s-national-debt-hits-22-trillion-a-new-record-thats-predicted-to-fall.

Nunez, Christina. (2019a). "Climate 101: Deforestation." *National Geographic*. nationalgeographic.com/environment/global-warming/deforestation/.

——— (2019b). "Desertification, Explained." *National Geographic*. nationalgeographic.com/environment/habitats/desertification/.

Nunn, Nathan. (2007). "Historical Legacies: A Model Linking Africa's Past to its Current Underdevelopment." *Journal of Development Economics* 83(1): 157–175. Retrieved from scholar.harvard.edu/nunn/publications/historical-legacies-model-linking-africas-past-its-current-underdevelopment.

Nye, Joseph S., Jr. (2015). *Is the American Century Over?* Cambridge, UK: Polity.

——— (2013). "Do Presidents Matter?" *The Atlantic* (June).

——— (2008). "Soft Power and American Foreign Policy." In *The Domestic Sources of American Foreign Policy*, edited by Eugene R. Wittkopf and James M. McCormick. Lanham, MD: Rowman & Littlefield.

——— (2007). *Understanding International Conflicts*, 6th ed. New York: Pearson Longman.

Nygren, Bertil. (2012). "Using the Neo-classical Realism Paradigm to Predict Russian Foreign Policy Behaviour as a Complement to Using Resources." *International Politics* 49 (July): 517–529.

Oatley, Thomas. (2012). *International Political Economy*, 5th ed. New York: Norton.

Ocampo, José Antonio. (2019). "Time for a True Global Currency." *Project Syndicate*. project-syndicate.org/commentary/imf-special-drawing-right-global-currency-by-jose-antonio-ocampo-2019-04.

O'Driscoll, Cian. (2015). "Rewriting the Just War Tradition: Just War in Classical Greek Political Thought and Practice." *International Studies Quarterly* 59 (March): 1–10.

OECD (Organisation for Economic Co-operation and Development). (2019). "Development Aid Drops in 2018, Especially to Neediest Countries." *OECD*. oecd.org/development/development-aid-drops-in-2018-especially-to-neediest-countries.htm.

——— (2019b). "Global Value Chains and Trade." oecd.org/trade/topics/global-value-chains-and-trade/.

——— (2017). *Size and Sectoral Distribution of State-owned Enterprises: Main Findings of the Latest Review. Review.* Retrieved from oecd.org/industry/ind/Item_6_3_OECD_Korin_Kane.pdf

——— (2015). "Official Development Assistance (ODA)." *OECDiLibrary*. oecd-ilibrary.org/development/official-development- assistance-oda/indicator-group/english_5136f9ba-en.

——— (2013). "FDI in Figures." *OECD* (April). oecd.org/daf/inv/FDI%20in%20figures.pdf.

Office of the President. (2019). "President Tsai Issues Statement on China's President Xi's 'Message to Compatriots in Taiwan.'" english.president.gov.tw/News/5621.

Ogden, Chris. (2013). *Handbook of China's Governance and Domestic Politics*. New York: Routledge.

Oneal, John R., and Bruce Russett (2001). *Triangulating Peace: Democracy, Interdependence, and International Organizations*. New York, NY: Norton, 146.

Oppermann, Kai. (2014). "Delineating the Scope Conditions of the Poliheuristic Theory of Foreign Policy Decision Making: The Noncompensatory Principle and the Domestic Salience of Foreign Policy." *Foreign Policy Analysis* 10 (1): 23–41.

O'Reilly, Kelly. (2013). "A Rogue Doctrine? The Role of Strategic Culture on US Foreign Policy Behavior." *Foreign Policy Analysis* 9: 57–77.

Owen, David. (2009). "Comment: Economy vs. Environment." *New Yorker* (March 30): 21–22.

Owen, John M., IV. (2005). "When Do Ideologies Produce Alliances?" *International Studies Quarterly* 49 (March): 73–99.

Oxford Business Group. (2019). *The Report: Kuwait 2018*. oxfordbusinessgroup.com/kuwait-2018.

Pakpahan, Beginda. (2013). "Can the WTO Deliver on Its Promise to Find a Breakthrough for Doha Round Talks in Bali?" *Global Policy Journal* (March 21). globalpolicyjournal.com/blog/21/03/2013/can-wto-deliver-its-promise-find-break-through-doha-round-talks-bali.

Palan, Ronen. (2000). "A World of Their Making: An Evaluation of the Constructivist Critique in International Relations." *Review of International Studies* 26 (4): 575–598.

Panagariya, Arvind. (2003). "Think Again: International Trade." *Foreign Policy* (November/December): 20–28.

Panda, Ankit. (2018). "Cryptocurrencies and National Security." *Council on Foreign Relations*. cfr.org/backgrounder/cryptocurrencies-and-national-security.

Pandya, Jayshree. (2019). "The Weaponization of Artificial Intelligence." *Forbes*. forbes.com/sites/cognitiveworld/2019/01/14/the-weaponization-of-artificial-intelligence/#328d59333686.

Panitch, Leo. (2009). "Thoroughly Modern Marx." *Foreign Policy* (May/June): 140–143.

Pankhurst, Donna. (ed.). (2008). *Gendered Peace: Women's Struggles for Post-War Justice and Reconciliation*. New York: Routledge.

Pape, Robert A. (2003). "The Strategic Logic of Suicide Terrorism." *American Political Science Review* 97(3): 343–361.

Parker, Clifton B. (2018). "Armed Drones Changing Conflict Faster than Anticipated, Stanford Scholar Finds." *Stanford University*. news.stanford.edu/press-releases/2018/03/05/armed-drones-chaster-anticipated/.

Parker, John. (2010). "Another Year, Another Billion." *The Economist: The World in 2011* (December): 28.

Patrick, Stewart. (2011). "The Brutal Truth." *Foreign Policy* (July/August). foreignpolicy.com/articles/2011/06/20/the_brutal_truth.

——— (2010). "Irresponsilbe Stakeholders? The Difficulty of Integrating Rising Powers." *Foreign Affairs* (November/December): 44–53.

Patterson, Eric. (2005). "Just War in the 21st Century: Reconceptualizing Just War Theory after September 11." *International Politics* 42 (March): 116–134.

Paust, Jordan J. (2007). *Beyond the Law: The Bush Administration's Unlawful Responses in the War on Terror*. New York: Cambridge University Press.

Payosova, Tetyana, Gary Clyde Hufbauer, and Jeffrey J. Schott. (2018). "EU Proposals to Resolve the WTO Appellate Body Crisis Represent Partial Progress." *Peterson Institute for International Economics*. piie.com/blogs/trade-investment-policy-watch/eu-proposals-resolve-wto-appellate-body-crisis-represent-partial.

Payseno, Kaya. (2018). "Top 20 Corporate Social Responsibility Initiatives of 2018." *Smart Recruiters*. smartrecruiters.com/blog/top-20-corporate-social-responsibility-initiatives-of-2018/.

Peet, John. (2017). "The Future of the European Union." *The Economist*. economist.com/special-report/2017/03/23/the-future-of-the-european-union?FEATURE_ARTICLES_V1=0.

Peksen, Dursun. (2012). "Does Foreign Military Intervention Help Human Rights?" *Political Research Quarterly* 65 (3): 558–571.

Permanyer, Iñaki, and Jeroen Smits. (2018). "The Subnational Human Development Index: Moving beyond country-level averages." *UNDP*. hdr.undp.org/en/content/subnational-human-development-index-moving-beyond-country-level-averages.

Peterson, T. M., A. Murdie, and V. Asal. (2018). "Human Rights, NGO Shaming and the Exports of Abusive States." *British Journal of Political Science* 48(3): 767–786.

Peterson, V. Spike, and Anne Sisson Runyan. (2010). *Global Gender Issues in the New Millennium*, 3rd ed. Boulder, CO: Westview Press.

Petras, James, and Henry Veltmeyer. (2004). *A System in Crisis: The Dynamics of Free Market Capitalism*. London: Palgrave.

Pettersson, Therese, Stina Högbladh, and Magnus Öberg. (2019). "Organized Violence, 1989–2018 and Peace Agreements." *Journal of Peace Research* 56(4): 589–603.

Pew Research Center. (2019). "The Future of World Religions: Population Growth Projections, 2010–2050." *Pew Research Center* (April 2). pewforum.org/2015/04/02/religious-projections-2010-2050/pf_15-04-02_projectionstables8/.

Piasecki, Bruce. (2007). "A Social Responsibility Revolution in the Global Marketplace." *Christian Science Monitor* (August 9): 9.

Piazza, James. (2008). "Incubators of Terror: Do Failed and Failing States Promote Transnational Terrorism?" *International Studies Quarterly* 52 (3).

Pierce, Mark, and Orla Murphy. (2018). "Rohingya Crisis: A Children's Emergency of the Highest Order." *Al Jazeera Media Network*.aljazeera .com/indepth/opinion/rohingya-crisis-children-emergency-highest-order-180225091834385.html.

Pincin, Jared, and Brian Brenberg. (2013). "Foreign Aid More About Helping Friends at Home: Column." *USA Today* (May 4). usatoday.com/story/ opinion/2013/05/04/foreign-food-aid-column/2122089/.

Pine, Richard. (2018). "Austerity has Left Greeks so Poor that Recovery is a Distant Dream." *The Irish Times*. irishtimes.com/news/world/europe/aus-terity-has-left-greeks-so-poor-that-recovery-is-a-distant-dream-1.3687211.

Pinstrup-Andersen, Per, and Peter Sandøe (eds.). (2007). *Ethics, Hunger and Globalization: In Search of Appropriate Policies*. The Netherlands: Springer.

Pisani-Ferry, Jean. (2014). *The Euro Crisis and Its Aftermath*. New York: Oxford University Press.

Pogge, Thomas. (2005). "World Poverty and Human Rights." *Ethics & International Affairs* 19 (1): 1–7.

Politi, James, and Jonathan Wheatley. (2010). "Tariff Move by Brazil Risks US Trade War." *Financial Times* (March 9). ft.com/intl/cms/s/0/c5da3202-2b1a-11df-93d8-00144feabdc0.html#axzz2aN0Zfze8.

Polsky, Andrew. (2010). "Staying the Course: Presidential Leadership, Military Stalemate, and Strategic Inertia." *Perspectives on Politics* 8 (1): 127–139.

Polyakova, Alina, and Daniel Fried. (2019). *Democratic Defense Against Disinformation 2.0*. Washington, D.C.: Atlantic Council. Retrieved from brookings.edu/wp-content/uploads/2019/06/Democratic-Defense-Against-Disinformation-2.0.pdf.

Pope Francis. (2015). *Encyclical Letter Laudato Si' of the Holy Father Francis on Care for Our Common Home* (May 24). Liberia Editrice Vaticana. w2.vatican.va/ content/francesco/en/encyclicals/documents/papa-francesco_20150524_ enciclica-laudato-si.html.

Porter, Jon. (2019). "Ex-VW CEO Charged Over Dieselgate, Faces Millions in Fines and 10 Years in Prison." *The Verge*. theverge .com/2019/4/16/18369528/vw-ceo-martin-winterkorn-dieselgate-ger-many-volkswagen-emissions-scandal.

Potts, Malcom, and Martha Campbell. (2009). "Sex Matters."*Foreign Policy* (July/August): 30–31.

Powell, Emilia Justyna, and Jeffrey K. Staton. (2009). "Domestic Judicial Institutions and Human Rights Treaty Violation." *International Studies Quarterly*. 53: 149–174.

Powell, Jonathan. (2012). "Determinants of the Attempting and Outcome of Coups D'etat." *Journal of Conflict Resolution* 56 (December): 1017–1040.

Powell, Jonathan, and Clayton Thyne. (2011). "Global Instances of Coups from 1950–Present." *Journal of Peace Research* 48 (2): 249–259.

Powers, Matthew, Bryce W. Reeder, and Ashly Adam Townsend. (2015). "Hot Spot Peacekeeping." *International Studies Review* 17 (March): 46–66.

Prakash, Aseem, and Matthew Potoski. (2007). "Investing Up." *International Studies Quarterly* 51 (September): 723–744.

Prasad, Eswar. (2014). "The Dollar Reigns Supreme, by Default." *International Monetary Fund* (March). imf.org/external/pubs/ft/fandd/2014/03/prasad. htm.

Prasad, Eswar. (2014a). *The Dollar Trap: How the US Dollar Tightened Its Grip on Global Finance*. Princeton, NJ: Princeton University Press.

Prashad, Vijay. (2013). *The Poorer Nations: A Possible History of the Global South*. London, UK: Verso.

Press, Eyal. (2018). "The Wounds of the Drone Warrior." *The New York Times Magazine* (June13). nytimes.com/2018/06/13/magazine/veterans-ptsd-drone-warrior-wounds.html.

Price, Richard. (2003). "Transnational Civil Society and Advocacy in World Politics." *World Politics* 55 (July): 519–606.

Price Waterhouse. (2017). "The World in 2050." pwc.com/gx/en/issues/economy/ the-world-in-2050.html.

Prunckun, H., and T. Whitford. (2019). *Terrorism and Counterterrorism: A Comprehensive Introduction to Actors and Actions*. Lynne Rienner Publishers.

Puchala, Donald J. (2003). *Theory and History in International Relations*. New York: Routledge.

——— (1994). "The History of the Future of International Relations." *Ethics & International Affairs* 8: 177–202.

Puchala, Donald, Katie Verlin Laatikainen, and Roger A. Coate. (2007). *United Nations Politics*. Upper Saddle River, NJ: Prentice Hall.

Putnam, Robert D. (1988). "Diplomacy and Domestic Politics: The Logic of Two-Level Games." *International Organization* 42 (Summer): 427–460.

PWC. (2017). "The World in 2050." (February). pwc.com/gx/en/world-2050/ assets/pwc-the-world-in-2050-full-report-feb-2017.pdf

——— (2015). "The World in 2050." (February). pwc.com/gx/en/iss ues/the-economy/assets/world-in-2050-february-2015.pdf.

"Pyeongchang 2018 Welcomes the World With a Message of Peace and Hope." olympic.org/news/pyeongchang-2018-welcomes-the-world-with-a-message-of-peace-and-hope.

Quester, George H. (1992). "Conventional Deterrence." In *Conventional Forces and the Future of Deterrence*, edited by Gary L. Guertner, Robert Haffa Jr., and George Quester. Carlisle Barracks, PA: U.S. Army War College.

Quick, Darren. (2013). "Self-Healing 'Artificial Leaf' Produces Energy from Dirty Water." *Gizmag* (April 10). gizmag.com/artificial-leaf-self-healing/ 27004/.

Rachman, Gideon. (2012). "Think Again: American Decline." In *The Domestic Sources of American Foreign Policy: Insights and Evidence*, edited by James M.McCormick. Langham, MD: Rowman & Littlefield.

Ram, Uri. (2008). *The Globalization of Israel: McWorld in Tel Aviv, Jihad in Jerusalem*. New York: Routledge.

Ramcharan, Bertrand. (2010). *Preventive Human Rights Strategies*. New York: Routledge.

Rames, Victoria S. (2013). "Healing the Spirit: Reparations for Survivors of Sexual Violence Related to the Armed Conflict in Kosovo." *United Nations Human Rights*. ohchr.org/Documents/Issues/Women/WRGS/ PeaceAndSecurity/StudyHealingTheSpirit.pdf.

Ranasinghe, Dhara. (2013). "Consumer Spending Playing a Greater Role in China's Economy." *NBC News* (March 12). nbcnews.com/ business/consumer-spending-playing-greater-role-chi-nas-economy-1C8827106.

Rapoza, Kenneth. (2019). "Tariffs 101: Understanding Trump's Trade War." *Forbes*. forbes.com/sites/kenrapoza/2019/06/07/tariffs-101-understanding-trumps-trade-war/#27ad4cc95f20.

Rasler, Karen A., and William R. Thompson. (2006). "Contested Territory, Strategic Rivalries, and Conflict Escalation." *International Studies Quarterly* 50 (March): 145–167.

——— (2005). *Puzzles of the Democratic Peace: Theory, Geopolitics, and the Transformation of World Politics*. London: Palgrave Macmillan.

Rathbun, Brian. (2012). "Politics and Paradigm Preferences: The Implicit Ideology of International Relations Scholars." *International Studies Quarterly* 56: 607–622.

Ravenhill, John. (2008). *Global Political Economy*. New York: Oxford University Press.

Rayman, Noah. (2015a). "Yemen's Chaotic Civil War Sucks In Regional Rivals." *Time* (March 26): 16.

——— (2015b). "What to Know about the Paris Terrorist Attack." *Time* (January 7). time.com/3658966/charlie-hebdo-paris-shooting- terror-attack/.

Raymond, Gregory A. (1999). "Necessity in Foreign Policy." *Political Science Quarterly* 113 (Winter): 673–688.

Redfield, Robert. (1962). *Human Nature and the Study of Society*, vol. 1. Chicago: University of Illinois Press.

Rediker, Douglas A. (2018). "Why US Multilateral Leadership Was Key to the Global Financial Crisis Response." *Brookings*. brookings.edu/blog/future-development/2018/09/12/why-us-multilateral-leadership-was-key-to-the-global-financial-crisis-response/.

Rehak, Melanie. (1999). "The Unselfish Gene." *The New York Times Magazine*. archive.nytimes.com/www.nytimes.com/library/magazine/home/19990502mag-rehak.html.

Reich, Robert B. (2010). "The Job Picture Still Looks Bleak." *Wall Street Journal* (April 12). online.wsj.com/article/SB100014240527023042225045751737806710115468.html.

Reilhac, Gilbert. (2019). "EU Parliament Calls for Freeze on Turkey's Membership Talks." *Reuters*. reuters.com/article/us-eu-turkey/eu-parliament-calls-for-freeze-on-turkeys-membership-talks-idUSKCN1QU2LD.

Reiter, Dan. (2009). *How Wars End*. Princeton, NJ: Princeton University Press.

——— (2003). "Exploring the Bargaining Model of War." *Perspectives on Politics* 1 (March): 27–43.

Renshon, Jonathan, and Stanley A. Renshon. (2008). "The Theory and Practice of Foreign Policy Decision Making." *Political Psychology* 29: 509–536.

Reus-Smit, Christian. (2019). "International Relations Theory Doesn't Understand Culture." *Foreign Policy*. foreignpolicy.com/2019/03/21/international-relations-theory-doesnt-understand-culture/.

Reuters. (2019). "Global Legal Process Outsourcing (LPO) Market 2019: Analysis by Major Players Size, Share, Growth, Trends and Forecast to 2024." reuters.com/brandfeatures/venture-capital/article?id=88026.

Reuters. (2018). "'Lost Generation': Unicef Warns on Fate of Rohingya Children." *The Guardian*. theguardian.com/world/2018/aug/23/lost-generation-unicef-warns-on-fate-of-rohingya-children.

Reuveny, Rafael, and William R. Thompson. (2008). "Observations on the North-South Divide." In *North and South in the World Political Economy*, edited by Rafael Reuveny and William R. Thompson. Malden, MA: Blackwell.

Ridley, Matt. (2003). *Nature vs. Nurture: Genes, Experiences and What Makes Us Human*. New York: HarperCollins.

Rieff, David. (1999) "The Precarious Triumph of Human Rights." *New York Times Magazine* (August 8): 36–41.

Riley, Charles. (2015). "Nepal's Second Quake Piles on the Pain." *CNN* (May 12). money.cnn.com/2015/05/12/news/nepal-second-earthquake-damages/index.html.

Riley-Smith, Jonathan. (1995). "Religious Warriors." *The Economist* (December 23/January 1): 63–67.

Rischard, Jean-François. (1998). "A Crisis of Complexity and Global Governance." *The New York Times* (Oct 2). nytimes.com/1998/10/02/opinion/IHT-a-crisis-of-complexity-and-global-governance.html.

Rivoli. Pietra. (2014). *The Travels of a T-Shirt in the Global Economy: An Economist Examines the Markets, Power, and Politics of World Trade*. New York: Wiley.

Roberts, Kari. (2014). "*Détente 2.0?* The Meaning of Russia's 'Reset' with the United States." *International Studies Perspectives* 15: 1–18.

Robinson, Mary. (2002). "Tell Leaders That Human Rights Aren't Optional." *The New York Times* (February 7). nytimes.com/2002/02/07/opinion/07iht-edmary_ed3_.html.

Rodrik, Dani. (2019). "Globalization's Wrong Turn and How it Hurt America." *Foreign Affairs*. foreignaffairs.com/articles/united-states/2019-06-11/globalizations-wrong-turn.

——— (2011). *The Globalization Paradox: Democracy and the Future of the World Economy*. New York: W.W. Norton.

——— (2008). *One Economics, Many Recipes: Globalization, Institutions, and Economic Growth*. Princeton, NJ: Princeton University Press.

Rodrigues, M. G. M. (2005). "Global Environmentalism and Local Politics: Transnational Advocacy Networks in Brazil, Ecuador, and India." *Journal of Sociology & Social Welfare* 32(2).

Rogoff, Kenneth. (2003). "The IMF Strikes Back." *Foreign Policy* 134 (January/February): 38–46.

Rohwer-Kahlmann, Malte. (2017). "UN Global Compact: Is Big Business Saving the World?" *The DW*. dw.com/en/un-global-compact-is-big-business-saving-the-world/a-40614516.

Roosevelt, Eleanor. (2012). *Tomorrow Is Now: It Is Today That We Must Create the World of the Future*. London: Penguin Books.

Rosenau, James N. (1980). *The Scientific Study of Foreign Policy*. New York: Nichols.

Rosecrance, Richard. (1997). "Economics and National Security." In *Security Studies for the Twenty-First Century*, edited by Richard Shultz, Roy Godson, and George Quester, 209–238. New York: Brassey's.

Rosecrance, R. (1996). *The Clash of Civilizations and the Remaking of World Order*. By Samuel P. Huntington. New York: Simon and Schuster.

Rosen, Steven. (1970). "A Model of War and Alliance." In *Alliance in International Relations*, edited by Julian R. Friedman, Christopher Bladen, and Steven Rosen. Boston, MA: Allyn and Bacon Publishers.

Rosenberg, Elizabeth, and Edoardo Saravalle. (2018). "China and the EU Are Growing Sick of U.S. Financial Power." *Foreign Policy*. foreignpolicy.com/2018/11/16/us-eu-china-trump-sanctions/.

Rostow, W. W. (1960). *The Stages of Economic Growth*. Cambridge: Cambridge University Press.

Rothkopf, David. (2012). *Power, Inc: The Epic Rivalry between Big Business and Government—and the Reckoning That Lies Ahead*. New York: Farrar, Straus, and Giroux.

Rowe, David M. (2010). "Economic Sanctions and International Security." In *The International Studies Encyclopedia*, edited by Robert A. Denemark. Hoboken, NJ: Blackwell.

Ruggie, John. (2017). "The Theory and Practice of Learning Networks: Corporate Social Responsibility and the Global Compact." In *Learning to Talk: Corporate Citizenship and the Development of the UN Global Compact*, edited by M. McIntosh, S. Waddock, and G.Kell, 32–42. Routledge.

——— (2013). *Just Business: Multinational Corporations and Human Rights*. New York: W.W. Norton.

——— (1982). "International Regimes, Transaction, and Change: Embedded Liberalism in the Postwar Economic Order." *International Organization* 36 (2).

Ruiz, Tricia. (2003). "Feminist Theory and International Relations: The Feminist Challenge to Realism and Liberalism." *Soundings Journal*.

Rundell, Sarah. (2019). "Digital Currencies: The Pros and Cons." *Raconteur*. raconteur.net/finance/digital-currencies-cbdcs.

Runge, Carlisle Ford, and Carlisle Piehl Runge. (2010). "Against the Grain: Why Failing to Complete the Green Revolution Could Bring the Next Famine." *Foreign Affairs* 89 (1): 8–14.

Russett, Bruce. (2005). "Bushwhacking the Democratic Peace." *International Studies Perspectives* 6 (November): 395–408.

——— (2001a). "How Democracy, Interdependence, and International Organizations Create a System for Peace." In *The Global Agenda*, 6th ed., edited by Charles W. Kegley Jr., and Eugene Wittkopf, 2. Boston: McGraw-Hill.

Rynning, Sten, and Jens Ringsmose. (2008). "Why Are Revisionist States Revisionist? Reviving Classical Realism as an Approach to Understanding International Change." *International Politics* 45 (January): 19–39.

Sachs, Jeffrey. (2005). *The End of Poverty*. New York: Penguin Press.

Sagan, Carl. (1989). "Understanding Growth Rates: The Secret of the Persian Chessboard." *Parade* (February 14): 14.

——— (1988). "The Common Enemy." *Parade* (February 7): 4–7.

Sageman, Marc. (2008). *Leaderless Jihad: Terror Networks in the Twenty-First Century*. Philadelphia: University of Pennsylvania Press.

——— (2004). *Understanding Terror Networks*. Philadelphia: University of Pennsylvania Press.

Saginor, Jeff. (2012). "US Tech Companies Outsourcing Fewer Jobs." *Digital Trends* (February 15). digitaltrends.com/home/us-tech-companies-outsourcing-fewer-jobs/.

Saint Augustine. (2018). *The City of God: A treaty of Christian philosophy by St Augustine of Hippo*. Norderstedt, Germany: Books on Demand Gmbh.

Saiya, Nilay, and Anthony Scime. (2014). "Explaining Religious Terrorism: A Data-mined Analysis." *Conflict Management and Peace Science* (December 22): 1–26.

Salami, Iwa. (2019). "Cryptocurrencies are Finally Going Mainstream—the Battle Is on to Bring Them Under Global Control." *The Conversation*. theconversation.com/cryptocurrencies-are-finally-going-mainstream-the-battle-is-on-to-bring-them-under-global-control-117112.

Salas, Rafael M. (1985). *Reflections on Population*. New York: Pergamon Press.

Samin, Amir. (1976). *Unequal Development*. New York: Monthly Review Press.

Samuelson, Paul (1969). "The Way of an Economist." In *International Economic Relations: Proceedings of the Third Congress of the International Economic Association*, edited by Paul Samuelson, 1–11. London: Macmillan.

Sánchez, Oscar Arias. (1996). In *A Scourge of Guns: The Diffusion of Small Arms and Light Weapons in Latin America*, edited by Michael Klare and David Anderson, i–ii. Washington, D.C.: Federation of American Scientists fas.org/asmp/library/scourge/Titlepg.pdf.

Sanders, David. (2018). "Biggest Banks in The World 2018: The World's Biggest Banks Are Even Bigger than Last Year. China Has the Biggest; Europe Has the Most." *Global Finance*. gfmag.com/magazine/november-2018/biggest-banks-world-2018.

Sandler, Todd. (2011). "New Frontiers of Terrorism Research: An Introduction." *Journal of Peace Research* 48: 279–286.

——— (2010). "Terrorism and Policy: Introduction." *Journal of Conflict Resolution* 54 (2): 203–213.

Saner, Raymond. (2012). "Plurilateral Agreements: Key to Solving Impasse of WTO/Doha Round and Basis for Future Trade Agreements within the WTO Context." *CSEND Policy Brief Nr. 7*. csend.org/site-1.5/images/files/CSEND_Policy_Brief_Nr_7_Plurilaterals_April_2012_1.pdf.

Sanger, David E. (2009). "Obama's Worst Pakistan Nightmare." *New York Times Magazine* (January 11).

——— (2005). "The New Global Dance Card." *New York Times* (September 18): Section 4, 3.

Sassen, Saskia. (2008). *Territory, Authority, Rights: From Medieval to Global Assemblages*. Princeton, NJ: Princeton University Press.

Satariano, Adam. (2018). "Will There Be a Ban on Killer Robots?" *Forbes*. nytimes.com/2018/10/19/technology/artificial-intelligence-weapons.html.

Saurin, Julian. (2000). "Globalization, Poverty, and the Promises of Modernity." In *Poverty in World Politics*, edited by Sarah Owen Vandersluis and Paris Yeros, 2. New York: St. Martin's.

Savage, Charlie. (2011). "Attack Renews Debate over Congressional Consent." *New York Times* (March 21): A14.

Savage, Luiza Ch., and John F. Harris. (2019). "Trump's Nethod to the Madness on Trade." *Politico*. politico.com/story/2019/06/06/donald-trump-trade-policy-global-translations-1355868.

Saviano, R. (2016). *ZeroZeroZero: Look at Cocaine and All You See Is Powder. Look Through Cocaine and You See the World*. New York: Penguin Press.

Scherer, Michael. (2010). "The New Sheriffs of Wall Street." *Time* (May 13). time.com/time/magazine/article/0,9171,1989144,00.html.

——— (1986). *The Cycles of American History*. Boston: Houghton Mifflin.

Scheve, Kenneth F., and Matthew J. Slaughter. (2018). "How to Save Globalization: Rebuilding America's Ladder of Opportunity." *Foreign Affairs*. foreignaffairs.com/articles/united-states/2018-10-15/how-save-globalization.

Schlesinger, Arthur. (1967). "Origins of the Cold War." *Foreign Affairs* 46(1): 22–52.

Schmidt, Blake, and Elisabeth Malkin. (2009). "Leftist Wins Salvadoran Election for President." *International Herald Tribune* (March 19): 5.

Schmidt, Eric, and Jared Cohen. (2010). "The Digital Disruption: Connectivity and the Diffusion of Power." *Foreign Affairs* (November/December): 75–85.

Schneider, C. J. (2017). "The Political Economy of Regional Integration." *Annual Review of Political Science* 20: 229–248.

Schnepf, Randy. (2011). "Brazil's WTO Case against the U.S. Cotton Program." *Congressional Research Service* (June 21). fas.org/sgp/crs/row/RL32571.pdf.

Schui, Florian. (2014). *Austerity: The Great Failure*. New Haven, CT: Yale University Press.

Schultz, Michael, Kristin Dziczek, Yen Chen, and Bernard Swiecki. (2019). *U.S. Consumer & Economic Impacts of U.S. Automotive Trade Policies*. Ann Arbor, Michigan: Center for Automotive Research. Retrieved from cargroup.org/wp-content/uploads/2019/02/US-Consumer-Economic-Impacts-of-US-Automotive-Trade-Policies-.pdf.

Schulz, William F. (2001). *In Our Own Best Interest: How Defending Human Rights Benefits Us All*. Boston: Beacon Press.

Schulzinger, Robert. (2012). "America in the Cold War." In *Routledge Handbook of American Foreign Policy*, edited by Stephen Hook and Christopher Jones, 33–45. New York: Routledge.

Schuman, Michael. (2019). "Trump's Trade War With China Is Already Changing the World." *The Atlantic*. theatlantic.com/international/archive/2019/06/trumps-trade-war-with-china-is-changing-the-world/592411/.

Schuman, Michael. (2013). "Globalization Isn't Dead, It's Only Just Beginning." *Time* (November 19). world.time.com/2013/11/19/globalization-isnt-dead-its-only-just-beginning/.

Seligson, Mitchell A., and John T. Passé-Smith (eds.). (2014). *Development and Underdevelopment: The Political Economy of Global Inequality*. 5th ed. Boulder, CO: Lynne Rienner.

Sen, Amartya. (2006). *Identity and Violence: The Illusion of Destiny*. New York: Norton.

——— (1999). "Democracy as a Universal Value." *Journal of Democracy* 3: 3–17.

Sethi, Aman. (2015). "At the Mercy of the Water Mafia." *Foreign Policy* (July/August). newyorker.com/news/daily-comment/coming-water-wars.

Shah, Timothy Samuel. (2004). "The Bible and the Ballot Box: Evangelicals and Democracy in the 'Global South'." *SAIS Review of International Affairs* 24 (Fall): 117–132.

Shannon, Megan. (2009). "Preventing War and Providing the Peace? International Organizations and the Management of Territorial Disputes." *Conflict Management and Peace-Science* 26 (2): 144–163.

Shannon, Thomas Richard. (1989). *An Introduction to the World-System Perspective.* Boulder, CO: Westview.

Shapin, Steven. (2007). "What Else Is New?" *New Yorker* (May 14): 144–148.

Shapiro, Ian. (2008). *Futurecast: How Superpowers, Populations, and Globalization Will Change the Way You Live and Work.* New York: St. Martin's Press.

Shearman, Peter. (2013). *Power Transition and International Order in Asia: Issues and Challenges.* New York: Routledge.

Shelley, Louise I. (2018). *Dark Commerce: How a New Illicit Economy Is Threatening Our Future.* Princeton, New Jersey: Princeton University Press. Retrieved from amazon.com/dp/B07D5293NX/ref=dp-kindle-redirect?_encoding=UTF8&btkr=1.

Shifrinson, Joshua R. Itzkowitz, and Michael Beckley. (2012/2013). "Debating China's Rise and U.S. Decline." *International Security,* 37 (3): 172–181.

Shultz, George P., William J. Perry, and Sam Nunn. (2019). "The Threat of Nuclear War Is Still With Us." *Wall Street Journal.* wsj.com/articles/the-threat-of-nuclear-war-is-still-with-us-11554936842.

Shultz, Richard, and William Olson. (1994). *Ethnic and Religious Conflict.* Washington, DC: National Strategy Information Center.

Shultz, Richard H., Roy Godson, and George H. Quester. (1997). *Security Studies for the 21st Century.* 1st ed. London: Brassey's Military Books.

Shulz, William F. (2001). *In Our Own Best Interest: How Defending Human Rights Benefits Us All.* Boston, MA: Beacon Press.

Shwayder, Maya, and Lisa Mahapatra. (2013). "Drone: Which Countries Have Them for Surveillance and Military Operations?" *International Business Times* (May 18). ibtimes.com/drones-which-countries-have-them-surveillance-military-opera-tions-map-1264271.

Sikkink, Kathryn. (2008). "Transnational Politics, International Relations Theory and Human Rights." In *Essential Readings in World Politics,* 3rd ed., edited by Karen A. Mingst and Jack L. Snyder, 1. New York: Norton.

Silk Road Briefing. (2019). "BRICS New Development Bank on Course to Lend US$40 Billion in Green Infrastructure Projects." silkroadbriefing.com/news/2019/03/08/brics-new-development-bank-course-lend-40-billion-green-infrastructure-projects/.

Simmons, Beth. (2009). *Mobilizing for Human Rights: International Law in Domestic Politics.* New York: Cambridge University Press.

Simmons, Beth A., and Allison Danner. (2010). "Credible Commitments and the International Criminal Court." *International Organization* 64 (2): 225–256.

Simmons, Beth A., Frank Dobbin, and Geoffrey Garrett. (2006). "Introduction: The International Diffusion of Liberalism." *International Organization* 60 (4): 781–810.

Simon, Eszter. (2019). "When David Fights Goliath: A Two-Level Explanation of Small-State Role-Taking." *Foreign Policy Analysis* 15: 118–135.

Simon, Herbert A. (1997). *Models of Bounded Rationality.* Cambridge, MA: MIT Press.

Singer, J. David. (1991). "Peace in the Global System." In *The Long Postwar Peace,* edited by Charles W. Kegley Jr. New York: HarperCollins.

Singer, P. W. (2013). "The Global Swarm." *Foreign Policy* (March 11) foreignpolicy.com/articles/2013/03/11/the_global_swarm.

——— (2010). "We, Robot: Is It Dangerous to Let Drones Fight Our Wars for Us?" *Slate* (May). slate.com/id/2253692.

——— (2009a). "Robots at War: The New Battlefield." *The Wilson Quarterly* (Winter).

——— (2009b). *Wired for War: The Robotics Revolution and Conflict in the 21st Century.* New York: Penguin Press.

Singer, Peter. (2004). *One World: The Ethics of Globalization,* 2nd ed. New Haven, CT: Yale University Press.

SIPRI (Stockholm International Peace Research Institute). (2019a). *SIPRI Yearbook.* New York: Oxford University Press.

——— (2019b). "Trends in International Arms Transfers in 2011." *SIPRI Yearbook.* (March, prepared by Pieter D. Wezeman, Aude Fleurant, Alexandra Kuimova, Nan Tian, and Siemon T. Wezeman). New York: Oxford University Press.

——— (2019c). "World Military Expenditure Grows to $1.8 Trillion in 2018." sipri.org/media/press-release/2019/world-military-expenditure-grows-18-trillion-2018.

——— (2018). "Global Arms Industry: US Companies Dominate the Top 100; Russian Arms Industry Moves to Second Place." *SIPRI Yearbook.* New York: Oxford University Press.

———(2015). *SIPRI Yearbook.* New York: Oxford University Press.

——— (2012b). "Trends in International Arms Transfers in 2011." *SIPRI Yearbook.* (March, prepared by Paul Holtom, Mark Bromley, Pieter D. Wezeman, and Siemon T. Wezeman). New York: Oxford University Press.

——— (2012c). "The SIPRI Top 100 Arms-Producing and Military Services Companies, 2012." *SIPRI Yearbook.* New York: Oxford University Press.

——— (2009). *SIPRI Yearbook.* New York: Oxford University Press.

Sivard, Ruth Leger. (1991). *World Military and Social Expenditures* 1991. Washington, DC: World Priorities.

Sjoberg, Laura. (2013). *Gendering Global Conflict: Toward a Feminist Theory of War.* New York: Columbia University Press.

Skeldon, Ronald. (2010). "Managing Migration for Development Is Circular Migration the Answer?" *Whitehead Journal of Diplomacy and International Relations* 11 (1): 21–33.

Skidelsky, Robert. (2019). "Has Austerity Been Vindicated?" *Project Syndicate.* project-syndicate.org/commentary/budget-deficits-austerity-growth-alesina-keynes-by-robert-skidelsky-2019-05.

Skinner, E. Benjamin. (2010). "The New Slave Trade." *Time* (January 18): 54–57.

Sklair, Leslie. (1991). *Sociology of the Global System.* Baltimore: Johns Hopkins University Press.

Sly, Liz. (2019). "The Kidnapped Yazidi Children Who Don't Want to Be Rescued from ISIS." *The Washington Post.* washingtonpost.com/world/the-kidnapped-yazidi-children-who-dont-want-to-be-rescued-from-isis/2019/06/13/ef051578-87a1-11e9-9d73-e2ba6bbf1b9b_story.html.

Smits, J., and I. Permanyer. (2019). "The Subnational Human Development Database." *Scientific Data* 6, 190038.

Smith, Adam. (1902 [1776]). *The Wealth of Nations (Part 2)* New York: P.F. Collier and Son.

——— (1776). *An Inquiry into the Nature and Causes of the Wealth of Nations.* London: W. Strahan and T. Cadell.

Smith, Roger W. (2010). "Review of *Genocide: A Normative Account* by Larry May." *Ethics & International Affairs* 24 (4): 433–435.

Smith-Cannoy, Heather. (2012). *Insincere Commitments: Human Rights Treaties, Abusive States, and Citizen Activism.* Washington, DC: Georgetown University Press.

Snyder, David Pearce. (2006). "Five Meta-Trends Changing the World." In *Global Issues 05/06*, edited by Robert M. Jackson. Dubuque, IA: McGraw-Hill/ Dushkin.

Snyder, Glenn H. (1991). "Alliance Threats: A Neorealist First Cut." In *The Evolution of Theory in International Relations*, edited by Robert L. Rothstein. Columbia: University of South Carolina Press.

Snyder, Jack. (2019). "The Broken Bargain: How Nationalism Came Back." *Foreign Affairs* 98(2): 54–60.

——— (2004). "One World, Rival Theories." *Foreign Policy* (November/ December): 53–62.

Sofaer, Abraham. (2010). "The Best Defense? Preventive Force and International Security." *Foreign Affairs* 89 (1): 109–118.

Solana, Javier. (2006). *The Sound of Euurope Conference*. Salzburg: European Union (EU).

Solomon, Ty. (2012a). "Human Nature and the Limits of the Self: Hans Morgenthau on Love and Power." *International Studies Review* 14 (2): 201–224.

——— (2012b). "The Turn to Psychology in Constructivism." *International Studies Review* 14 (4): 637–639.

Somavia, Juan. (2004). "For Too Many, Globalization Isn't Working." *International Herald Tribune* (February 27): 6.

Sorensen, Theodore C. (1963). *Decision Making in the White House*. New York: Columbia University Press.

Spar, Debora. (1999). "Foreign Investment and Human Rights." *Challenge* 42 (1): 55–80.

Specter, Michael. (2015). "A Thirsy, Violent World." *New Yorker* (February 24). newyorker.com/news/daily-comment/coming-water-wars.

Spencer, Herbert. (1970). *Social Statistics*. New York: Robert Schalkenbach Foundation.

Spiegel, Peter. (2013). "Hostility to the EU Deepens." *Financial Times* (January 16). ft.com/intl/cms/s/0/d585cdaa-5fca-11e2-8d8d-00144feab49a.html#axzz2VB01jBjR.

Sprout, Harold, and Margaret Sprout. (1965). *The Ecological Perspective on Human Affairs*. Princeton, NJ: Princeton University Press.

Spykman, Nicholas. (1944). *The Geography of Peace*. New York: Harcourt Brace.

Standish, Reid. (2015a). "Kazakh Child Soldier Executes 'Russian Spies' in Islamic State Video." *Foreign Policy* (January 13). foreignpolicy.com/2015/01/13/ kazakh-child-soldier-executes-russian-spies- in-islamic-state-video/.

——— (2015b). "China and Russia Lay Foundation for Massive Economic Cooperation." *Foreign Policy* (July 10). foreignpolicy.com/2015/07/10/ china-russia-sco-ufa-summit-putin-xi-jinping-eurasian-union-silk-road/.

Stark, Sam. (2007). "Flaming Bitumen: Romancing the Algerian War." *Harper's* (February): 92–98.

Starr, Harvey. (2006). "International Borders." *SAIS Review* 26 (Winter/ Spring): 3–10.

Starr, Harvey, and Benjamin Most. (1978). "A Return Journey: Richardson, 'Frontiers,' and Wars in the 1945–1965 Era." *Journal of Conflict Resolution* 22 (September): 441–467.

START (National Consortium for the Study of Terrorism and Responses to Terrorism). (2018). *Global Terrorism 2017*. Maryland: University of Maryland. Retrieved from start.umd.edu/pubs/START_GTD_Overview 2017_July2018.pdf.

Steans, Jill. (2006). *Gender and International Relations*. Cambridge, UK: Polity.

Steinberg, Paul F., and Stacy D. VanDeveer. (2012). *Comparative Environmental Politics: Theory, Practice, and Prospects*. Cambridge, MA: MIT Press.

Steinberg, Richard. (2009). "The Future of the WTO." *University of Chicago Law School Faculty* (February 23). uchicagolaw.typepad.com/faculty/ 2009/02/future-of-the-wtorelevance.html.

Stephenson, Max, and Laura Zanotti. (2012). *Peacebuilding Through Community-Based NGOs: Paradoxes and Possibilities*. Boulder, CO: Kumarian Press.

Sterling-Folker, Jennifer. (2015). "All Hail to the Chief: Liberal IR Theory in the New World Order." *International Studies Perspectives* 16 (1): 40–49.

Stewart, Devin T., Nikolas K. Gvosdev, and David A. Andelman. (2008). "Roundtable: The Nation-State." *Carnegie Council* (August 29). www .carnegiecoun-cil.org/resources/ethics_online/0024.html/:pf_printable.

Stiglitz, Joseph. (2011). "The IMF Cannot Afford to Make a Mistake with Strauss-Kahn's Successor." *The Telegraph (UK)* (May 21).

Stiles, Kendall. (2005). "The Ambivalent Hegemon: Explaining the 'Lost Decade' in Multilateral Trade Talks, 1948–1958." *Review of International Political Economy* 2 (1): 1–26.

Story, Louise, Landon Thomas, Jr., and Nelson Schwartz. (2010). "Wall St. Helped to Mask Debt Fueling Europe's Crisis." *New York Times* (February 13). nytimes.com/2010/02/14/business/global/14debt. ntml?pagewanted5all.

Strand, Håvard, Siri Aas Rustad, Henrik Urdal, and Håvard Mokleiv Nygård. (2019). "Trends in Armed Conflict, 1946–2018." *Conflict Trends* 3 (Oslo: PRIO). prio.org/Publications/Publication/?x=11349.

Strang, David. (1991). "Global Patterns of Decolonization, 1500–1987." *International Studies Quarterly* 35 (December): 429–545.

Streeten, Paul. (2001). "Human Development Index." In *The Oxford Companion to Politics of the World*, 2nd ed., edited by Joel Krieger, 3. New York: Oxford University Press.

Stroup, S. S., and W.H. Wong (2016). "The Agency and Authority of International NGOs." *Perspectives on Politics* 14(1): 138–144.

Struett, Michael J. (2012). "Why the International Criminal Court Must *Pretend* to Ignore Politics." *Ethics and International Affairs* 26 (1): 83–92.

Stokes, Bruce. (2014). "Most of the World Supports Globalization in Theory, but Many Question it in Practice." *Pew Research Center*. pewresearch.org/ fact-tank/2014/09/16/most-of-the-world-supports-globalization-in-the-ory-but-many-question-it-in-practice/.

Stuckler, David, and Sanjay Basu. (2013). "How Austerity Kills." *New York Times* (May 12). nytimes.com/2013/05/13/opinion/how-austerity-kills. html?pagewanted=all&_r=0.

Stuenkel, Oliver. (2019). "After Correa, Ecuador's Moreno Is Struggling to Offer His Own Vision." *America's Quarterly* (February 27). americasquarterly.org/ content/ecuadors-moreno-overcoming-correas-legacy-struggles-articulate-his-own-vision.

Sturesson, Jan, Scott McIntyre, and Nick C. Jones. (2015). *State-Owned Enterprises: Catalysts for public value creation?* London: PwC. Retrieved from pwc.com/gx/en/psrc/publications/assets/pwc-state-owned-enterprise-psrc. pdf.

Subacchi, Paola. (2015). "Make Way for the RMB." *Foreign Policy* (June 16). foreignpolicy.com/2015/06/16/make-way-for-the-rmb-china- reserve-currency-imf-sdr-dollar/.

Suddath, Claire. (2009). "U.S.-Cuba Relations." *Time*. content.time.com/time/ nation/article/0,8599,1891359,00.html.

Suganami, Hidemi. (1983). "A Normative Enquiry in International Relations." *Review of International Studies* 9: 35–54.

Suominen, Kati. (2013). "RTA Exchange: Resuming WTO's Leadership in a World of Regional Trade Agreements." *International Development Bank* (June). e15initiative.org/wp-content/uploads/2013/06/E15_RTA_ Suominen.pdf.

Sutherland, Peter. (2008). "Transforming Nations: How the WTO Boosts Economies and Opens Societies." *Foreign Affairs* 87 (March): 125–136.

Sylvester, Christine. (2002). *Feminist International Relations*. New York: Cambridge University Press.

Taliaferro, Jeffrey, S. E. Lobell, and N. M. Ripsman. (2009). *Neo-Classical Realism, the State, and Foreign Policy.* Cambridge, UK: Cambridge University Press.

Tarrow, Sidney. (2006). *The New Transnational Activism.* New York: Cambridge University Press.

Tayler, Jeffrey. (2014). "Amid Record Waves of Refugees, Italy Finding Limits to Its Compassion." *National Geographic* (October 30). news.nationalgeographic.com/news/special-features/2014/10/141031-italy-immigration-crisis-human-trafficking/.

——— (2009). "'What Crisis?' Why Europe's Poorest Country Is a Paragon of Financial Stability." *The Atlantic* 304 (1): 28–30.

Taylor, Alan. (2014). "Bhopal: The World's Worst Industrial Disaster, 30 Years Later." *The Atlantic.* theatlantic.com/photo/2014/12/bhopal-the-worlds-worst-industrial-disaster-30-years-later/100864/.

Teitelbaum, Michael S., and Jay M. Winter. (2014). "Bye-Bye, Baby." *New York Times* (April 4). nytimes.com/2014/04/05/opinion/sunday/bye-bye-baby.html?_r=0.

Teslik, Lee Hudson. (2008). "Council for Foreign Relations Backgrounder: Food Prices." cfr.org/publication/16662/price_of_food.html?breadcrumb5%2Findex.

Thakur, Ramesh, and Thomas G. Weiss. (2009). "United Nations 'Policy': An Argument with Three Illustrations." *International Studies Perspectives* 10: 18–35.

Than, Ker. (2012). "'Shocking' Greenland Ice Melt: Global Warming or Just Heat Wave?" *National Geographic* (July 25). news.national-geographic.com/news/2012/07/120725-greenland-ice-sheet-melt-satellites-nasa-space-science/.

Thant, U. (1971). "In This I Believe." *New York Times* (September 21), A37.

The Balance. (2019). "Greek Debt Crisis Explained." thebalance.com/what-is-the-greece-debt-crisis-3305525.

The Economist. (2019). "The Big Mac Index Shows Currencies Are Very Cheap Against the Dollar." *The Economist* (Jan 19). economist.com/graphic-detail/2019/01/12/the-big-mac-index-shows-currencies-are-very-cheap-against-the-dollar (accessed June 13, 2019).

The Economist. (2010a) "Harmony—for now." (November 25). economist.com/international/2010/11/25/harmony-for-now.

The Guardian. (2018). "Argentina Agrees to $50bn Loan from IMF Amid National Protests." *The Guardian.* theguardian.com/business/2018/jun/08/argentina-loan-imf-protests-peso.

Themnér, Lotta, and Peter Wallensteen. (2014). "Armed Conflicts, 1946–2013." *Journal of Peace Research* 51 (4): 541–554.

——— (2013). "Armed Conflicts, 1946–2012." *Journal of Peace Research* 50: 509–521.

Thiagarajan, Kamala. (2019). "Millions of Women in India Join Hands to Form a 385-Mile Wall of Protest." *NPR.* npr.org/sections/goatsandsoda/2019/01/04/681988452/millions-of-women-in-india-join-hands-to-form-a-385-mile-wall-of-protest.

Thompson, Mark. (2011). "Air Boss: From Her Base in Germany, Major General Maggie Woodward Ruled the Skies over Libya. It Was Another First for Women in Combat." *Time* (April 18): 37–39.

Thomson, James W. (2011). "How the Mighty Are Falling." *USA Today* (March): 14–18.

Thorington, Kanzanira. (2019). "Europe's Elections: The Fight Against Disinformation." *Council on Foreign Relations.* cfr.org/blog/europes-elections-fight-against-disinformation.

Thyne, Clayton L. (2006). "Cheap Signals with Costly Consequences: The Effect of Interstate Relations on Civil War." *Journal of Conflict Resolution* 50 (December): 937–961.

Tickner, J. Ann. (2019). "Gender Research in International Relations." In *Gender Innovation in Political Science: New Norms, New Knowledge,* edited by M. Sawer and K. Baker. Cham, Switzerland: Palgrave Macmillan.

——— (2013). "Men, Women, and War." In *Conflict After the Cold War: Arguments on Causes of War and Peace,* 4th ed., edited by Richard K. Betts, 280–293. Boston, MA: Pearson.

——— (2010). "Searching for the Princess?" In *Readings on How the World Works,* edited by Russell Bova. New York: Pearson.

Tickner, J. Ann, and Laura Sjoberg. (2006). "Feminism." In *Theories of International Relations: Discipline and Diversity,* edited by Tim Dunne, Milya Kurki, and Steve Smith, 185–202. Oxford: Oxford University Press.

Tiessen, Rebecca. (2010). "Global Actors in Transnational and Virtual Spaces." *International Studies Review* 12: 301–304.

Timsit, Annabelle, and Jackie Bischof. (2019). "The Extreme Choices Before Europe Drew the Biggest Voter Turnout in 20 Years." *Quartz.* qz.com/1626267/european-elections-2019-see-highest-voter-turnout-in-two-decades/.

TMT (The Moscow Times). (2018). "Birth Rate Hits 10-Year Low in Russia." themoscowtimes.com/2018/01/29/birth-rate-hits-10-year-low-russia-a60321.

Tocqueville, Alexis de. (1969; 1835). *Democracy in America.* New York: Doubleday.

Toft, Monica Duffy. (2007). "Population Shifts and Civil War: A Test of Power Transition Theory." *International Interactions* 33 (July/September): 243–269.

Toner, Robin. (2002). "FBI Agent Gives Her Blunt Assessment." Columbia, S.C., *The State* (June 7): A5.

Tonkiss, Fran. (2012). "Economic Globalization." In *Wiley-Blackwell Encyclopedia of Globalization* (February 29). doi:10.1002/9780470670590.wbeog163

Tooze, A. (2018). *Crashed: How a Decade of Financial Crises Changed the World.* New York: Penguin.

Toynbee, Arnold J. (1954). *A Study of History.* London: Oxford University Press.

Trading Economics. (2019). "Greece Government Budget Value." tradingeconomics.com/greece/government-budget-value (accessed June 15, 2019).

——— (2015). "Greece External Debt." tradingeconomics.com/greece/external-debt.

——— (2013). "Greece Government Spending." tradingeconomics.com/greece/government-spending.

Transparency International. (2019). "Corruptions Perceptions Index 2018." *Transparency International.* transparency.org/news/feature/cpi_2018_global_analysis.

——— (2017). "A Year After Panama Papers, Is Enough Being Done to Stop Illicit Finance?" transparency.org/news/feature/a_year_after_panama_papers_is_enough_being_done_to_stop_illicit_finance.

Traynor, Ian, and John Hooper. (2011). "France and Italy in Call to Close UE Borders in Wake of Arab Protests: Sarkozy and Berlusconi Want Passport-Free Travel within the EU Suspended as North African Migrants Flee North." *The Guardian* (April 27). guardian.co.uk/world/2011/apr/26/eu-borders-arab-protests.

Tsygankov, Andrei P. (2014). "Contested Identity and Foreign Policy: Interpreting Russia's International Choices." *International Studies Perspectives* 15: 19–35.

Tuchman, Barbara. (1962). *The Guns of August.* New York: Dell.

Tzu-ti, Huang. (2018). "China Has 2,000 Ballistic Missiles Threatening Taiwan and US: US Military Report." *Taiwan News.* taiwannews.com.tw/en/news/3508977.

UNAIDS. (2018). *UNAIDS Data 2018*. unaids.org/sites/default/files/media_asset/unaids-data-2018_en.pdf.

UNCTAD. (2019). *Trade and Development Report 2018*. New York: United Nations. Retrieved from unctad.org/en /PublicationsLibrary/tdr2018_en.pdf.

———— (2019b). "Global Foreign Investment Flows Dip to Lowest Levels in a Decade." unctad.org/en/pages/newsdetails.aspx?OriginalVersionID=1980.

———— (2019c). Global Investment Trends and Prospects. *World Investment Report 2019: Special Economic Zones*. New York: United Nations. Retrieved from unctad.org/en/PublicationChapters/WIR2019_CH1.pdf.

———— (2015). *World Investment Report 2015: Reforming International Investment Governance*. Geneva: United Nations.

UNDESA. (2019). "World Population Prospects 2019." UNDESA Population Division. population.un.org/wpp/Download/Standard/Population/.

———— (2019b). "Indigenous Languages matter for development, peace building, and reconciliation." en.iyil2019.org/.

UNDESA (2018). population.un.org/wup/Download/.

UNDP (United Nations Development Programme). (2019). *Human Development Report 2015*. New York: United Nations.

———— (2019b). *Gender Inequality Index (GII)*. New York: United Nations. hdr.undp.org/en/content/gender-inequality-index-gii.

———— (2018). *Human Development Indices and Indicators*. New York: United Nations. Retrieved from hdr.undp.org/sites/default/files/2018_human_development_statistical_update.pdf.

———— (2014). *Human Development Report 2014*. New York: United Nations. hdr.undp.org/sites/default/files/hdr14-report-en-1.pdf.

———— (2011). *Human Development Report 2011*. New York: United Nations.

UNESCO (United Nations Educational, Scientific, and Cultural Organization). (2009). *Water in a Changing World: The United Nations World Water Development Report 3*. Retrieved from unesdoc.unesco.org/ark:/48223/pf0000181993.

Ungerer, Jameson Lee. (2012). "Assessing the Progress of the Democratic Peace Research Program." *International Studies Review* 14 (March): 1–31.

UNHCR. (2019). "Refugee Crisis in Europe." unrefugees.org/emergencies/refugee-crisis-in-europe/.

———— (2015). *Global Trends: Forced Displacement 2014*. Geneva: UN High Commissioner for Refugees.

———— (2014). *UNHCR Global Trends*. Geneva: UN High Commissioner for Refugees.

UNICEF. (2019). *UNICEF Humanitarian Action for Children 2019: Overview*. New York: United Nations. Retrieved from unicef.org/media/48796/file/Humanitarian-action-overview-cover-eng.pdf.

———— (2015a). "Levels and Trends in Child Mortality." data.unicef.org/corecode/uploads/document6/uploaded_pdfs/corecode/Child_Mortality_Report_2014_195.pdf.

———— (2009). "Statistics by Area: Child Survival and Health." childinfo.org/mortality_challenge.html.

UNIFEM (UN Women). (2013). "Democratic Governance." unifem.org/gender_issues/democratic_governance/.

———— (2011). "Democratic Governance." unifem.org/gender_issues/democratic_governance/, 33.

Union of International Associations. (2019). *Yearbook of International Organizations 2018–2019*. Brussels: Union of International Associations.

United Nations (UN). (2019a). "World Population Prospects 2019." population.un.org/wpp/Download/Probabilistic/Population/.

———— (2019b). *United Nations Global Compact*. unglobalcompact.org/about.

———— (2019c). "UN Peacekeeping: 70 Years of Service & Sacrifice." *United Nations Peacekeeping*. peacekeeping.un.org/en/un-peacekeeping-70-years-of-service-sacrifice.

———— (2019d). *World Economic Situation Prospects*. un.org/development/desa/dpad/wp-content/uploads/sites/45/WESP2019_BOOK-web.pdf.

———— (2019e). "UN Report: Nature's Dangerous Decline 'Unprecedented'; Species Extinction Rates 'Accelerating'." un.org/sustainabledevelopment/blog/2019/05/nature-decline-unprecedented-report/.

———— (2019f). "World Day to Combat Desertification and Drought 17 June." un.org/en/events/desertificationday/desertification.shtml.

———— (2018). "World Migration Report 2018." *IOM UN Migration*. iom.int/wmr/world-migration-report-2018.

———— (2018b). "Migration and Migrants: A Global Overview." In *World Migration Reports*. Grand-Saconnex, Switzerland: International Organization of Migration. Retrieved from iom.int/wmr/chapter-2.

———— (2018c). "Data Bulletin: Informing a Global Compact for Migration." International Organization for Migration. publications.iom.int/system/files/pdf/global_migration_trends_data_bulletin_issue_1.pdf.

———— (2018d). *2018 Revision of World Urbanization Prospects*. un.org/development/desa/publications/2018-revision-of-world-urbanization-prospects.html.

———— (2018e). *Children and Armed Conflict*. undocs.org/s/2018/465.

———— (2018f). "UNICEF Warns of 'Lost Generation' of Rohingya Youth, One Year after Myanmar Exodus." news.un.org/en/story/2018/08/1017632.

———— (2018g). "Water Scarcity." *UN Water*. unwater.org/app/uploads/2018/10/WaterFacts_water-scarcity_sep2018.pdf.

———— (2018h). "Human Development Indices and Indicators: 2018 Statistical Update." United Nations Development Programme. hdr.undp.org/sites/default/files/2018_human_development_statistical_update.pdf.

———— (2015a). "History of the UN." un.org/un70/en/content/history.

———— (2015b). "Human Security For All." un.org/humansecurity/about-human-security/human-security-all.

———— (2015c). "Integrating Population Issues into Sustainable Development, Including the Post-2015 Development Agenda." un.org/en/development/desa/population/commission/pdf/48/CPD48Concise Report.pdf.

———— (2014). "International Migrant Stock: Total." un.org/en/development/desa/population/migration/data/estimates2/estimatestotal.shtml.

———— (2013a). "Scale of Assessments to the Apportionment of the Expenses of the United Nations." un.org/ga/search/view_doc.asp?symbol=A/67/693.

———— (2013b). *Annual Report of the Secretary-General on Children and Armed Conflict*. childrenandarmedconflict.un.org/annual-report-of-the-secretary-general-on-children-and-armed-conflict/.

———— (2010). "Dialogue and Cooperation Vital to Tackling Shared Concerns, Ban Tells Asian Forum." (June 7). news.un.org/en/story/2010/06/341062-dialogue-and-cooperation-vital-tackling-shared-concerns-ban-tells-asian-forum.

———— (2009b). "UN Security Council Breaks New Ground to Protect Children in War." childrenandarmedconflict.un.org/4aug09/.

———— (2004). United Nations Foundation. un.org/secureworld/report2.pdf.

———— (1997). "Secretary-General Stresses Need for Partnership, Building Consensus for UN Reform to Succeed, in Address to National Press Club." un.org/press/en/1997/19970124.sgsm6149.html.

———— (1945). Chapter IV: The General Assembly. In *Charter of the United Nations*. New York: United Nations. Retrieved from un.org/en/sections/un-charter/chapter-iv/index.html.

———— (2019g) "Where We Work." un.org/en/sections/where-we-work/index.html.

United Nations Office of the High Commissioner on Human Rights. (2018). "Myanmar: Tatmadaw Leaders Must Be Investigated for Genocide, Crimes Against Humanity, War Crimes – UN Report." ohchr.org/EN/NewsEvents/Pages/DisplayNews.aspx?NewsID=23475&LangID=E.

———— (2018b). "Press briefing note on Egypt, United States and Ethiopia." ohchr.org/EN/NewsEvents/Pages/DisplayNews.aspx?NewsID=23174&LangID=E.

UN Office on Drugs and Crime (UNODC). (2019). "Law Enforcement." unodc.org/unodc/en/organized-crime/law-enforcement.html.

———— (2018). "Global Report on Trafficking in Persons 2018." unodc.org/documents/data-and-analysis/glotip/2018/GLOTiP_2018_BOOK_web_small.pdf.

———— (2018b). *Global Report on Trafficking in Persons 2018*. Vienna: UN Office on Drugs and Crime. Retrieved from unodc.org/documents/data-and-analysis/glotip/2018/GLOTiP_2018_BOOK_web_small.pdf.

———— (2015). "Global Report on Trafficking in Persons 2014." unodc.org/documents/data-and-analysis/glotip/GLOTIP_2014_full_report.pdf.

———— (2010). *The Globalization of Crime: A Transnational Organized Crime Threat Assessment*. Vienna: UN Office on Drugs and Crime.

———— (2010a). "Executive Summary." unodc.org/documents/data-and-analysis/tocta/Executive_summary.pdf.

———— (2009). "Denial and Neglect Undermine the Fight against Human Trafficking." unodc.org/unodc/en/press/releases/2009/February/2009-02.12.html.

Urban, Mark C. (2015). "Accelerating Extinction Risk from Climate Change." *Science* (May 1). sciencemag.org/content/348/6234/571.

Urdal, Henrik. (2011). "A Clash of Generations? Youth Bulges and Political Violence." *United Nations Expert Group Meeting on Adolescents, Youth and Development*. un.org/esa/population/meet-ings/egm-adolescents/p10_urdal.pdf.

Urquhart, Brian. (2010). "Finding the Hidden UN." *New York Review* (May 27): 26–28.

U.S. Arms Control and Disarmament Agency (ACDA). (1997). *World Military Expenditures and Arms Transfers*. Washington, D.C.: U.S. Government Printing Office.

U.S. Department of Commerce. (2015). "Trends in Atmospheric Carbon Dioxide." *National Oceanic and Atmospheric Administration* (July 8). esrl.noaa.gov/gmd/ccgg/trends/global.html.

U.S. Department of State. (2019). Treaty on the Prohibition of Nuclear Weapons. armscontrol.org/treaties/treaty-prohibition-nuclear-weapons.

U.S. Department of Treasury. (2019). "Major Foreign Holders of Treasury Securities." ticdata.treasury.gov/Publish/mfh.txt.

U.S. National Security Strategy. (2010). obamawhitehouse.archives.gov/sites/default/files/rss_viewer/national_security_strategy.pdf.

———— (2002). georgewbush-whitehouse.archives.gov/nsc/nss/2002/.

U.S. Trade Representative. (2018). *2017 Report to Congress On China's WTO Compliance*. Retrieved from ustr.gov/sites/default/files/files/Press/Reports/China%202017%20WTO%20Report.pdf.

Van der Ploeg, Frederick, and Dominic Rohner. (2012). "War and Natural Resource Exploitation." *European Economic Review* 56 (8): 1714–1729.

Van Evera, Stephen. (1990–1991). "Primed for Peace." *International Security* 15 (Winter): 6–56.

Vasquez, John A. (2009). *War Puzzle Revisited*. Cambridge, UK: Cambridge University Press.

Vasquez, John A., and Colin Elman (eds.). (2003) *Realism and the Balancing of Power: A New Debate*. Upper Saddle River, NJ: Prentice Hall.

Vanderheiden, Steve. (2011). "Globalizing Responsibility for Climate Change." *Ethics & International Affairs* 25 (1): 65–84.

Vaughan, Adam. (2015). "One in Six of World's Species Faces Extinction Due to Climate Change-Study." *The Guardian* (April 30). theguardian.com/environment/2015/apr/30/one-in-six-of-worlds-species-faces-extinction-due-to-climate-change-study.

Vela, Hatzel. (2019). "Senior Cuban Official Describes U.S. Relations as 'Seriously Deteriorated.'" *Local 10 News*. local10.com/news/cuba/high-ranking-cuban-official-describes-us-relations-as-seriously-deteriorated.

Verba, Sidney. (1969). "Assumptions of Rationality and Nonrationality in Models of the International System." In *International Politics and Foreign Policy*, edited by James N. Rosenau, 2. New York: Free Press.

Verwimp, Philip, Patricia Justino, and Tilman Bruck. (2009). "The Analysis of Conflict: A Micro-Level Perspective." *Journal of Peace Research* 46 (3): 307–314.

Victor, David G., M. Granger Morgan, Fay Apt, John Steinbruner, and Katharine Ricke. (2009). "The Geoengineering Option: A Last Resort against Global Warming." *Foreign Affairs* 88 (March/April): 64–76.

Visser, Nick. (2015). "Illustrators Protest Qatar's Alleged World Cup Labor Abuses with Redesigned Logos." *Huffington Post* (May 27). huffingtonpost.com/2015/05/27/qatar-world-cup-abuse_n_7452540.html.

Vital Signs. (2006–2007). New York: Norton, for the Worldwatch Institute.

Vogel, David. (1995). *Trading Up: Consumer and Environment Regulation in a Global Economy*. Cambridge, MA: Harvard University Press.

Vogelstein, Rachel B., and Jamille Bigio. (2019). "Women and Terrorism: Hidden Threats, Forgotten Partners." *Council on Foreign Relations*. cfr.org/blog/women-and-terrorism-hidden-threats-forgotten-partners.

Vreeland, James Raymond. (2003). *The IMF and Economic Development*. Cambridge: Cambridge University Press.

Waddock, S., and G. Kell (eds.). *Learning To Talk: Corporate Citizenship and the Development of The Un Global Compact*. Routledge.

Walker, Paul F. (2014). "Syrian Chemical Weapons Destruction: Taking Stock and Looking Ahead." *Arms Control Association*. armscontrol.org/ACT/2014_12/Features/Syrian-Chemical-Weapons-Destruction-Taking-Stock-And-Looking-Ahead#note1.

Walker, Stephen, Akan Malici, and Mark Schafer. (2011). *Rethinking Foreign Policy Analysis: States, Leaders, and the Microfoundations of Behavioral International Relations*. New York: Routledge.

Walker, Thomas C., and Jeffrey S. Morton. (2005). "Re-Assessing the 'Power of Power Politics' Thesis: Is Realism Dominant?" *International Studies Perspectives* 16 (1): 40–49.

Wallensteen, Peter. (2011). *Understanding Conflict Resolution: War, Peace, and the Global System*. London: Sage.

Wallerstein, Immanuel. (2005). *World-Systems Analysis*. Durham, NC: Duke University Press.

———— (2002). "The Eagle Has Crash Landed." *Foreign Policy* (July/August): 60–68.

———— (1988). *The Modern World-System III*. San Diego: Academic Press.

Walsh, Bryan. (2016). "Why the Zika Outbreak Marks a New Normal for Infectious Disease." *TIME*. time.com/4197777/why-the-zika-outbreak-marks-a-new-normal-for-infectious-disease/.

———— (2010). "The Spreading Stain." *Time* (June 21): 51–59.

———— (2010). "The Gulf Disaster: Whose Asses Need Kicking?" *Time* (June 10): content.time.com/time/magazine/article/0,9171,1995843-2,00.html.

Walsh, Declan, and Jason Horowitz. (2019). "Why Pope Francis' Historic Visit to the Gulf Matters." *New York Times*. nytimes.com/2019/02/03/world/middleeast/pope-gulf-christians.html.

Walt, Stephen M. (2009). "Alliances in a Unipolar World." *World Politics* 61: 86–120.

Walter, Barbara F. (2004). "Does Conflict Beget Conflict?" *Journal of Peace Research* 41 (May): 371–388.

Waltz, Kenneth N. (2013). "The Origins of War in Neorealist Theory." In *Conflict after the Cold War: Arguments on Causes of War and Peace*, 4th ed., edited by Richard K. Betts. Boston, MA: Pearson.

——— (2001/1959). *Man, the State, and War*. Rev. ed. New York: Columbia University Press.

——— (2000). "Structural Realism after the Cold War." *International Security* 25 (Summer): 5–41.

——— (1979). *Theory of International Politics*. Reading, MA: Addison-Wesley.

Ward, Andrew. (2011). "Finnish Poll Turns on Anti-Euro Feeling." *Financial Times* (16 April). ft.com/intl/cms/s/0/aeed63d4-68d6-11e0-9040-00144fe-ab49a.html#axzz1dvjxCoHr.

Watts, Jonathan. (2017). "Operation Car Wash: Is this the Biggest Corruption Scandal in History?" *The Guardian*. theguardian.com/world/2017/jun/01/brazil-operation-car-wash-is-this-the-biggest-corruption-scandal-in-history.

WDI. (2019). *World Development Indicators 2019*. Washington, DC: World Bank.

——— (2018). *World Development Indicators 2018*. Washington, DC: World Bank.

——— (2017). *World Development Indicators 2017*. Washington, DC: World Bank.

——— (2017b). "Poverty." *World Bank*. worldbank.org/en/topic/poverty.

——— (2013). *World Development Indicators 2013*. Washington, DC: World Bank.

——— (2011). *World Development Indicators 2011*. Washington, DC: World Bank.

WDR. (2015). *World Development Report 2015*. Washington, DC: World Bank.

Weber, Cynthia. (2005). *International Relations Theory*, 2nd ed. New York: Routledge.

Weinberg, Joe, and Ryan Bakker. (2014). "Let Them Eat Cake: Food Prices, Domestic Policy and Social Unrest." *Conflict Management and Peace Science* 32 (3): 309–326.

Weir, Kimberly A. (2007). "The State Sovereignty Battle in Seattle." *International Politics* 44 (September): 596–622.

Weiss, Thomas, Richard Jolly, and Louis Emmerij. (2009). *UN Ideas That Changed the World*. Bloomington, IN: Indiana University Press.

Wendt, Alexander. (2013). "Anarchy Is What States Make of It." In *Conflict after the Cold War: Arguments on Causes of War and Peace*, 4th ed., Boston, edited by Richard K. Betts. MA: Pearson.

——— (1999). *Social Theory of International Politics*. Cambridge, UK: Cambridge University Press.

Westing, Arthur H. (2013). "Nuclear War: Its Environmental Impact." *Springer Briefs of Pioneers in Science and Practice* 1: 89–113.

Wharf, Benjamin L. (1929). "The Status of Linguistics as a Science." *Language* 5: 207–214.

Wheaton, Henry. (1846). *Elements of International Law*. Philadelphia: Lea and Blanchard.

White, Micah. (2018). "Ten Years After the Crash: Have the Lessons of Lehman Been Learned?" *The Guardian*. theguardian.com/commentisfree/2018/sep/14/the-panel-lehman-brothers-ten-year-anniversary-financial-crash.

White, Ralph K. (1990). "Why Aggressors Lose." *Political Psychology* 11 (June): 227–242.

White, William. (2015). "System Malfunction." *Finance and Development* 52 (1): 44–47.

WHO (World Health Organization). (2018). *Global Tuberculosis Report: Executive Summary*. who.int/tb/publications/global_report/tb18_ExecSum_web_4Oct18.pdf?ua=1.

——— (2018b). *World Malaria Report 2018*. who.int/malaria/publications/world-malaria-report-2018/en/.

——— (2015). "Report of the Ebola Interim Assessment Panel - July 2015." who.int/csr/resources/publications/ebola/ebola-panel-report/en/.

Widmaier, Wesley W., and Susan Park. (2012). "Differences Beyond Theory: Structural, Strategic, and Sentimental Approaches to Normative Change." *International Studies Perspectives* 13(2): 123–134.

Wiegand, Krista E. (2018). "Territorial Dispute Strategies as Domestic Diversions." *Journal of Territorial and Maritime Disputes* 5(1) (Winter/Spring): 42–63.

Wight, Martin. (2002). *Power Politics*. Continuum International Publishing Group.

Wilkenfeld, Jonathan, Kathleen J. Young, David M. Quinn, and Victor Asal. (2005). *Mediating International Crises*. London: Routledge.

Wilkinson, Paul. (2011). *Terrorism versus Democracy: The Liberal State Response*, 3rd ed. New York: Routledge.

Williams, Brock R., Cathleen D. Cimino-Isaacs, Rachel F. Fefer, Keigh E. Hammond, Vivian C. Jones, Wayne M. Morrison, and Andres B. Schwarzenberg. (2019). *Trump Administration Tariff Actions: Frequently Asked Questions*. Washington, D.C.: Congressional Research Service. Retrieved from fas.org/sgp/crs/row/R45529.pdf.

Williams, Laron K. (2013). "Flexible Election Timing and International Conflict." *International Studies Quarterly* (April 30). doi: 10.1111/isqu.12054.

Wills, Garry. (2004). "What Is a Just War?" *New York Review of Books* 51, no. 18: 32.

Williams, Greg, (2019). "Inside Bill Browder's Blood Money Battle with Vladimir Putin." *Wired*. wired.co.uk/article/bill-browder-russia-red-notice.

Wilmer, Franke. (2000). "Women, the State and War: Feminist Incursions into World Politics." In *Global Politics in a Changing World*, edited by Richard W. Mansbach and Edward Rhodes. Boston: Houghton Mifflin.

Wilson, James Q. (1993). *The Moral Sense*. New York: Free Press.

Wimmer, Andreas. (2013). *Waves of War: Nationalism, State Formation, and Ethnic Exclusion in the Modern World*. Cambridge, UK: Cambridge University Press.

Wise, Michael Z. (1993). "Reparations." *Atlantic Monthly* 272 (October): 32–35.

Withnall, Adam. (2015). "ISIS's Dirty Bomb: Jihadists Have Seized 'Enough Radioactive Material to Build Their First WMD'." *The Independent*. independent.co.uk/news/world/middle-east/isiss-dirty-bomb-jihadists-have-seized-enough-radioactive-material-to-build-their-first-wmd-10309220.html.

Wittkopf, Eugene R., Christopher M. Jones, and Charles W. Kegley Jr. (2008). *American Foreign Policy*, 7th ed. Belmont, CA: Thomson Wadsworth.

Wolf, M. (2004). *Why Globalization Works*. New Haven, CT: Yale University Press.

Wolf, Martin. (2014). *The Shifts and the Shocks: What We've Learned—and Still Have to Learn—From the Financial Crisis*. New York: Penguin.

——— (2013). "How Austerity Has Failed." *New York Review of Books* (July 11). nybooks.com/articles/archives/2013/jul/11/how-austerity-has-failed/.

Wolfe, Tom. (2005). "The Doctrine That Never Died." *New York Times* (January 30): Section 4, 17.

Wolfers, Arnold. (1962). *Discord and Collaboration*. Baltimore: Johns Hopkins University Press.

Wolff, Alan Wm. (2018). "The Future of the WTO and the Multilateral Trading System." Peterson Institute for International Economics. Washington D.C. piie.com/system/files/documents/2018-12-17prepared-remarks.pdf.

Woods, Ngaire. (2008). "Whose Aid? Whose Influence? China, Emerging Donors and the Silent Revolution in Development Assistance." *International Affairs* 84: 1205–1221.

Woodward, Bob. (2006). *State of Denial*. New York: Simon & Schuster.

Woodward, Susan L. (2009). "Shifts in Global Security Policies: Why They Matter for the South." *IDS Bulletin* 40: 121–128.

Woodwell, Douglas. (2008). *Nationalism in International Relations*. London: Palgrave Macmillan.

World Bank. (2019). "What We Do." worldbank.org/en/about/what-we-do.

——— (2019b). *Migration and Remittances: Recent Developments and Outlook*. Washington, DC: World Bank.

——— (2019c). "GDP (current US$)." data.worldbank.org/indicator/ny.gdp.mktp.cd.

——— (2019d). "Total Greenhouse Gas Emissions (kt of CO2 equivalent)." data.worldbank.org/indicator/EN.ATM.GHGT.KT.CE.

——— (2019e) "Tariff Rate, Applied, Weighted Mean, All Products (%)." data.worldbank.org/indicator/tm.tax.mrch.wm.ar.zs.

——— (2018). "Exports of Goods and Services (% of GDP)." data.worldbank.org/indicator/NE.EXP.GNFS.ZS.

——— (2018b). *Transforming Karachi into a Livable and Competitive Megacity: A City Diagnostic and Transformation Study*. Washington, D.C.: International Bank for Reconstruction and Development. Retrieved from documents.worldbank.org/curated/en/503701519291571040/pdf/123628-PUB-PUBLIC-date-02-20-2018.pdf.

——— (2018c). *Poverty and Shared Prosperity 2018: Piecing Together Poverty Puzzle*. Washington, D.C. Retrieved from openknowledge.worldbank.org/bitstream/handle/10986/30418/9781464813306.pdf.

——— (2018d). "Decline of Global Extreme Poverty Continues but Has Slowed: World Bank." worldbank.org/en/news/press-release/2018/09/19/decline-of-global-extreme-poverty-continues-but-has-slowed-world-bank.

——— (2018e). "Food Security." worldbank.org/en/topic/food-security.

——— (2017). *Special Focus 2: Global Economic Prospects*. Washington, D.C. Retrieved from pubdocs.worldbank.org/en/222281493655511173/Global-Economic-Prospects-June-2017-Topical-Issue-Arms-length-trade.pdf.

——— (2015b). *International Debt Statistics*. Washington, DC: World Bank.

——— (2015d). "Financing the End of Poverty." worldbank.org/en/news/feature/2015/07/10/financing-the-end-of-poverty.

——— (2014a). "Theorist Eric Maskin: Globalization Is Increasing Inequality." worldbank.org/en/news/feature/2014/06/23/theorist-eric-maskin-globalization-is-increasing-inequality.

——— (2013a). "People: Population Growth and Transition." app.collinsindicate.com/worldbankatlas-global/en-us.

——— (2013b). *Atlas of Global Development*, 4th ed. Washington, DC: World Bank.

——— (2013c). "Food Crisis." worldbank.org/foodcrisis/bankinitiatives.htm.

——— (2013d). *International Debt Statistics*. Washington, DC: World Bank.

——— (2013e). *Atlas of Global Development*, 3rd ed. Washington, DC: World Bank.

——— (2013f). *Turn Down the Heat: Climate Extremes, Regional Impacts, and the Case for Resilience*. Washington, D.C. documents.worldbank.org/curated/en/975911468163736818/pdf/784240WP0Full00D0CONF0to0June19090L.pdf.

——— (2009). *World Development Report 2009: Reshaping Economic Geography*. Washington, DC: World Bank.

——— (2007). *World Development Indicators 2007*. Washington, DC: World Bank.

World Federation of Exchanges (WFE). (2019). *Statistics*. world-exchanges.org/our-work/statistics.

World Population Review (WPR). (2019). "Theocracy Countries 2019." world-populationreview.com/countries/theocracy-countries/.

World Resources Institute (WRI). (2009). "What Is the State of EcoSystems Today?" archive.wri.org/newsroom/-wrifeatures_text.cfm?ContentID5288.

World Trade Organization (WTO). (2019). "Regional Trade Agreements." wto.org/english/tratop_e/region_e/region_e.htm.

——— (2019b). Introduction. *World Trade Statistical Review 2018*. Geneva, Switzerland, 4–7. Retrieved from wto.org/english/res_e/statis_e/wts2018_e/wts2018chapter01_e.pdf.

——— (2019c). "Dispute Settlement." wto.org/english/tratop_e/dispu_e/dispu_e.htm.

——— (2019d). "The Multilateral Trading System and Climate Change: Introduction." wto.org/english/tratop_e/envir_e/climate_intro_e.htm.

——— (2019f). "Regional Trade Agreements." rtais.wto.org/UI/PublicMaintainRTAHome.aspx.

——— (2019g). *World Trade Report 2018*. Geneva: WTO.

——— (2018). *World Trade Statistical Review 2018*. World Trade Organization. Retrieved from wto.org/english/res_e/statis_e/wts2018_e/wts2018_e.pdf.

——— (2015a). "Regional Trade Agreements." wto.org/english/trat op_e/region_e/region_e.htm.

——— (2015e). "Report on G-20 Trade Measures." wto.org/english/news_e/news15_e/g20_wto_report_june15_e.pdf.

——— (2015f). "Facts and Figures: How Many Regional Trade Agreements Have Been Notified to the WTO?" wto.org/english/tratop_e/region_e/regfac_e.htm.

——— (2014b). *The World Economy and Trade in 2013 and Early 2014*. Geneva: World Trade Organization.

——— (2014e). *World Trade Report 2014: Trade and Development: Recent Trends and the Role of the WTO*. Geneva: WTO.

——— (2010). *World Trade Report 2010: Trade in Natural Resources*. Geneva: World Trade Organization.

Worldwatch Institute. (2015). *State of the World 2015: Confronting Hidden Threats to Sustainability*. New York: Norton.

——— (2013a). "Food and Agriculture." worldwatch.org/food-agriculture.

Wright, Quincy. (1942). *A Study of War*. Chicago: University of Chicago Press.

Xinhuanet.org. (2013). "Coca-Cola to Invest Further in China." *Xinhua News Online*. news.xinhuanet.com/english/china/2013-05/09/c_132371245.htm.

Yao, Yang. (2011). *Beijing Consensus or Washington Consensus: What Explains China's Economic Success?* Washington, DC: World Bank.

Yellin, Jessica, and Tom Cohen. (2013). "Obama, Netanyahu Agree on Preventing Nuclear-Armed Iran." *CNN*. cnn.com/2013/03/20/politics/israel-obama-visit.

"Yemen Conflict Explained in 400 Words." *BBC News*. (2018). bbc.com/news/world-middle-east-44466574.

Yergin, Daniel. (2009). "It's Still the One." *Foreign Policy* (September/October): 88–95.

Yermack, David. (2015). *Handbook of Digital Currency: Bitcoin, Innovation, Financial Instruments, and Big Data*. Academic Press, 31–43. doi.org/10.1016/B978-0-12-802117-0.00002-3.

Yetiv, Steve. (2011). "History, International Relations, and Integrated Approaches: Thinking about Greater Interdisciplinarity." *International Studies Perspectives* 12 (2): 94–118.

Yu, Katrina. (2018). "The Good News (And Not So Good News) About China's Smoggy Air." *NPR*. npr.org/sections/goatsandsoda/

2018/12/18/669757478/the-good-news-and-not-so-good-news-about-chinas-smoggy-air.

Zakaria, Fareed. (2009). *The Post-American World*. New York: W. W. Norton.

Zalewska, Ania. (2018). "The Future of Cryptocurrencies is Bright." *Raconteur*. raconteur.net/finance/cryptocurrencies-future-bright.

Zarocostas, John. (2015). "WTO to Review European Claims of Illegal Tax Breaks for Boeing 777X." *Seattle Times* (February 23). seattletimes. com/business/boeing-aerospace/wto-panel-to-review-european-claims-of-illegal-tax-breaks-for-boeing-777x/.

Zartner, Dana. (2010). "The Rise of Transnational Crime: International Cooperation, State Contributions, and the Role of the Global Political Economy." *International Studies Review* 12 (2): 316–319.

Zeigler, Sean, Jan H. Pierskalla, and Sandeep Mazumder. (2013). "War and the Reelection Motive: Examining the Effects of Term Limits." *Journal of Conflict Resolution* (March 13). doi 10.1177/0022002713478561.

Zenko, Micah. (2013). "How Does the Recent Shift in U.S. Drone Policy Impact 'Signature Strikes'?" *Council on Foreign Relations* (June 11). cfr.org/united-states/does-recent-shift-us-drone-policy-impact- signature-strikes/p30885.

Zhang, Ketian Vivian. (2019). "China is Pushing Back Against Taiwan for these Three Reasons." *The Washington Post* (April 8). washingtonpost.com/politics/2019/04/08/china-is-pushing-back-against-taiwan-these-reasons/?noredirect=on&utm_term=.3cd0632262e3.

Ziegler, Charles. (2012). "Conceptualizing Sovereignty in Russian Foreign Policy: Realist and Constructivist Perspectives." *International Politics* 49: 400–417.

Zoellick, Robert B. (2012). "Why We Still Need the World Bank: Looking Beyond Aid." *Foreign Affairs* 91 (2): 66–78.

Zurayk, Rami. (2011). *Food, Farming, and Freedom: Sowing the Arab Spring*. Charlottesville, VA: Just World Books.

Name Index

A

Aaronson, Susan, 380
Abbot, Sebastian, 281
Abdelal, Rawi, 601
Abdi, Dekha Ibrahim, 313
Abouharb, Rodwan, 165, 380
Abramowitz, Morton, 73
Acemoglu, Daron, 216
Acharya, Amitav, 110, 111
Ackerly, Brooke, 42
Adams, John Quincy, 58
Adler, Emanuel, 275
Aggarwal, Vinod, 384
Aguilera, Jasmine, 463
Ahmadinejad, Mahmoud, 419
Ahtisaari, Martti, 506
Aisha, Bibi, 452
al-Assad, Bashar, 161
Al-Saud, Sultan bin Salman, 1
Albert, Eleanor, 451
Albright, Madeleine, 318
Alden, Edward, 387
Ali, Idrees, 287
Aliber, Robert, 341
Allen, Susan H., 67, 68, 70, 75
Allison, Graham, 71, 72, 248, 282
Altman, Roger, 344, 346
Amadeo, Kimberly, 344, 345, 378
Amighini, A. A., 386
Amin, Idi, 222
Andelman, David A, 13
Anderlini, Sanam N, 310
Andreas, P., 190
Andropov, Yuri, 102
Angell, Norman, 31
Annan, Kofi, 19, 158, 162, 183, 290,
    319, 355, 452, 497, 500, 505, 506
Appel, Benjamin J., 221
Arbatov, Georgi, 104, 105
Ariely, Dan, 8, 66
Aristotle, 304, 499, 504
Asal, V., 185
Auboin, Marc, 383
Augustine, Saint, 27, 304
Aydin, Aysegul, 220, 389
Azevêdo, Roberto, 387

B

Babcock, Linda, 311
Bachelet, Michelle, 445

Baker, James, 106
Baker, Scott, 351
Bakker, Ryan, 202
Baldwin, Richard, 357, 374, 383, 384
Ball, George W., 59
Balmer, Crispian, 406
Ban Ki-moon, 158, 225, 416,
    480, 482
Banerjee, Abhijit, 485
Bapat, Navin A., 228
Barber, Benjamin R., 419
Barkin, Samuel, 40, 41
Barrett, Bethany, 137, 306
Barringer, Felicity, 489
Barry, Colin, 185, 353
Basham, Kevin, 182
Basu, Sanjay, 339
Basulto, Dominic, 502
Batmanghelidj, Esfandyar, 190
Battelle, 132, 133, 241
Beardsley, Kyle, 220, 290
Bechtol, Bruce E., 190
Becker, Elizabeth, 379
Beckley, Michael, 370
Begley, Sharon, 465, 467, 470, 476
Behusdi, Adam, 386
Beitz, Charles, 437
Belkin, Paul, 340
Benson, Michelle, 210
Bercovitch, Jacob, 217
Bergesen, Albert, 123
Bergholt, Drago, 468
Bergsten, Fred, 111
Berliner, Daniel, 183
Berlusconi, Silvio, 406
Bevan, Aneurin, 250
Bhagwati, Jagdish, 365, 370, 390, 422
Bianchi, Daniel, 336
Bickford, Susan, 443, 444
Bieri, Franziska, 436
Bigio, Jamille, 188
bin Laden, Osama, 61, 186, 224
bin Mohamad, Mahathir, 324
Bischof, Jackie, 170
Bishop, Julie, 257
Blair, Tony, 35, 64, 65, 68
Blanton, Robert G., 109, 242, 296
Blanton, Shannon Lindsey, 47, 162,
    288, 312
Blasetti, Robert, 336
Bloom, Mia, 188
Bloom, Nicholas, 351

Bloom, Richard, 224
Blyth, Mark, 346
Bokhari, Farhan, 281
Boli, John, 435
Bollyky, Thomas, 414
Bolzendahl, Catherine, 311
Bonaparte, Napoleon, 70, 274
Boot, Max, 185, 223
Borzel, Tanja, 448
Bosco, David, 345
Botero, N. C., 188
Bouman, Katie, 4
Boutros-Ghali, Boutros, 158, 212, 498
Boyer, Mark A., 69, 311
Brahimi, Lakhdar, 394
Brainard, Lael, 481
Braithwaite, Alex, 217
Branigan, Tania, 509
Braudel, Fernand, 426
Breen, C., 185
Bremer, Stuart, 499
Bremmer, Ian, 353
Brenberg, Brian, 378
Brennan, John, 226, 255
Breuning, Marijke, 68
Brezhnev, Leonid, 104, 309
Bronfenbrenner, Urie, 9
Bronowski, Jacob, 510
Brooks, David, 63
Brown, Lester R., 462, 494
Bruck, Tilman, 198
Brysk, Alison, 446, 451, 456, 458
Brzezinski, Zbigniew, 72
Buffett, Warren, 274
Bunche, Ralph, 199
Bunn, Matthew, 251
Burdeau, Cain, 479
Burke, M., 466
Burns, Nicholas, 296
Bush, George H. W., 310
Bush, George W., 67, 108, 219, 228, 240,
    260
Bussmann, Margit, 202
Butcher, Charity, 175
Buzan, Barry, 38

C

Cain, Geoffrey, 419
Calamur, Krishnadev, 454
Calhoun, Craig, 427
Califano, Joseph A., 57

Subject Index

A

absolute advantage, 365
acid rain, 485
acquired immune deficiency syndrome (AIDS), 411, 412
action-and-reaction patterns, 499
actor(s). *See also* nonstate actors
  in constructivism, 37
  decision making by, models of, 60–75
  decision processes and, 56
  definition of, 12
  in liberalism, 37
  predicting actions of, 499
  primary transnational, 12–14
  in realism, 37
  unitary, 60
adjudication, 206, 312
Afghanistan, 13, 61, 102, 169, 217, 244, 254, 428
Africa, 447, 473, 486
AFRIPOL, 190
agency, 28, 427
agenda setting, 419
agent-oriented constructivism, 38
aggression, 198. *See also* armed conflict
aging populations, 397–402
agriculture, 502
AIDS (acquired immune deficiency syndrome), 411, 412
air quality, 495. *See also* environment
Al Qaeda, 106, 108, 178, 186, 187, 253, 269. *See also* September 11 attacks
algal oil, 489
Algeria, 126, 181, 241
alignments, 265
alliances
  changing European, 267
  definition of, 263
  flaws of, 265
  in liberalism, 263
  map of, 264
  in realism, 263–265
Almaz-Antey, 245
alternatives, identification of, 61
Alzheimer disease, 411
Amazon, 473, 474
Amsterdam, 408
anarchy, 18, 36, 208
Angola, 103, 220, 225, 256
Antarctic Treaty, 279

Anti-Ballistic Missile (ABM) Treaty, 285
antidumping duties, 376
antipersonnel landmines (APLs), 283
Antipersonnel Landmines Treaty (APLT), 279
ANZUS pact (Australia, New Zealand, and United States), 294
APEC (Asia Pacific Economic Cooperation), 171
appeasement, 95
Apple, 181
Arab Interior Minister's Council (AIMC), 190
Arab Spring, 161, 197, 419
Arakan Rohingya Salvation Army (ARSA), 451
arbitrage, 322, 329
arbitration, 206, 220, 312
Argentina, 134, 180, 248, 249, 330, 487
armed conflict. *See also* civil war; war
  causes of, 198–212
  children and, 218, 220, 449–450
  culture and, 201–202
  cyclical theories of, 211–212
  definition of, 197
  democracy and, 206–207
  demographic stress and, 202–204
  economic system and, 204–206
  in feminist theory, 201
  "fourth generation," 504
  frequency of, 212–215
  future and, 229–231, 503–505
  geopolitical factors in, 200–201
  global system and, 208–212
  globalization and, 211, 222, 503–505
  hegemonic stability theory and, 212
  human nature and, 198–200
  imperialism and, 205
  independence and, 200–201
  internal characteristics and, 200–208
  just war doctrine and, 304–306
  in liberalism, 306
  in long-cycle theory, 211
  militarization and, 204
  military necessity and, 306
  nationalism and, 201–202
  poverty and, 202–204
  power transitions and, 209–211
  regime type and, 206–208
  rules for, 307
  within states, 215–223
  terrorism and, 223–229

types of, 212–215
unmanned aerial vehicles in, 234, 253, 254, 503
armed forces, size of, 239. *See also* military capabilities
Armenia, 487
arms control
  bilateral, 277–278
  definition of, 276
  disarmament vs., 276
  future of, 282–287
  multilateral, 278–282
  in realism, 276
  treaties, 277
arms race, 275, 281
arms sales. *See also* weapons
  blowback and, 247
  companies in, 245
  in Global South, 244
  strategic consequences of, 245–248
  terrorism and, 244
  value of, 243
Arms Trade Treaty, 280
artificial intelligence (AI), 418
  and autonomous weapons systems, 253–255
ASEAN (Association of Southeast Asian Nations), 171
ASEANPOL, 190
Asia Infrastructure Investment Bank (AIIB), 349
Asia-Pacific Economic Cooperation (APEC), 139–141
Association of Southeast Asian Nations (ASEAN), 139, 294, 389
asylum, 47
asymmetric warfare, 223, 255
atmosphere, 465
atomic energy commission (CEA), 465
atrocities, 405. *See also* crimes against humanity; violence; war crimes
austerity, 340, 342, 346–347
Australia, 134, 180, 330, 359, 433, 471, 486
Australian Securities Exchange, 324
Austria, 134, 181
Austria-Hungary, 88, 91, 92, 125
autocratic rule, 77
autonomous weapons systems
  and artificial intelligence, 253–255
avian flu, 412